Critical Acclaim for *Above Top Secret*

"*Above Top Secret* tells a shocking, frightening, and deeply moving story. It reveals secrets that have desperately needed revealing for forty years, and in doing so proves that there has been extensive official suppression of evidence that UFOs are real. Timothy Good builds his case until it is overwhelmingly clear that visitors from some other world are not only here, but deeply involved in our lives, and that our governments know far more about this than they have told us.

"Citing interviews with officials and extraordinary documentary evidence—much of it authentic beyond controversy—Timothy Good shows that the cover-up has been designed—in the stunning words of a former CIA Director who has admitted its existence—around a program of 'denial and ridicule.' UFOs are indeed the ultimate official secret.

"The effect of this secrecy has been to leave the average American to face our visitors alone and in total ignorance—and to risk ridicule and the ruin of his career if he seeks help or even dares to tell his story.

"Whether the cover-up is something that governments have created for their own ends or that has been forced on them by the visitors themselves I do not know. But I do know one thing: the visitors can appear in anybody's life, at any time. For all of our sakes, it is time for government to admit what it knows. Indeed, it is urgently necessary that the truth be admitted—and fast. Thousands and thousands of people are coming face-to-face with the visitors. It is essential that they not continue to do so in ignorance and terror.

"*Above Top Secret* is absolutely stunning. This is because the weight of evidence presented is too powerful to deny: Mr. Good has proven his case. The amazing story he tells is true."

—Whitley Strieber
Author of the
best-selling *Communion*
and *Transformation*

BARRY GOLDWATER
ARIZONA

COMMITTEES:
AERONAUTICAL AND SPACE SCIENCES
ARMED SERVICES
  PREPAREDNESS INVESTIGATING SUBCOMMITTEE
  TACTICAL AIR POWER SUBCOMMITTEE
  NATIONAL STOCKPILE AND NAVAL PETROLEUM
    RESERVES SUBCOMMITTEE

United States Senate
WASHINGTON, D.C. 20510

March 28, 1975

Mr. Shlomo Arnon
U.C.L.A. Experimental College
308 Westwood Plaza
Los Angeles, California 90024

Dear Mr. Arnon:

The subject of UFOs is one that has interested me
for some long time. About ten or twelve years ago
I made an effort to find out what was in the building
at Wright Patterson Air Force Base where the information
is stored that has been collected by the Air Force, and
I was understandably denied this request. It is
still classified above Top Secret. I have, however,
heard that there is a plan under way to release some,
if not all, of this material in the near future. I'm
just as anxious to see this material as you are, and I
hope we will not have to wait too much longer.

Sincerely,

Barry Goldwater

(Shlomo Arnon)

THE WORLDWIDE U.F.O. COVER-UP

ABOVE TOP SECRET

TIMOTHY GOOD

With a foreword by
the former Chief of Defense Staff,
Lord Hill-Norton, G.C.B.

QUILL
WILLIAM MORROW
NEW YORK

To Donald Keyhoe

Library of Congress Cataloging-in-Publication Data

Good, Timothy.
    Above top secret: the worldwide UFO cover-up / Timothy Good; with a foreword by Lord Hill-Norton.
        p. cm.
    ISBN 0-688-09202-0
    Bibliography: p.
    Includes index.
    1. Unidentified flying objects.   I. Title.
    TL789.G64   1989
    001.9'42—dc20   89-10230
                                                                          CIP

Printed in the United States of America

First Quill Edition

1 2 3 4 5 6 7 8 9 10

BOOK DESIGN BY MARK STEIN

CONTENTS

FOREWORD

Tim Good has made a major contribution in this book to the UFO literature. He is one of the most thorough and best-informed researchers
into this arcane subject and, as those who know him and his work would
expect, he has based his book soundly upon fact and a great deal of most
convincing evidence which I have not seen in print before.

It is fashionable, almost mandatory, for any serious attempt such as
this to discuss UFOs to be rubbished by the media and dismissed by most
of the public as science fiction at one extreme, or the work of a nut case
at the other. I do not think what follows could possibly be so easily
ignored by any reader trained to weigh evidence—certainly I cannot do so.

I have frequently been asked why I am so keenly interested in UFOs;
people seem to think it odd that someone who has been so closely involved
with Defense for many years should be so simple. I am interested for
several reasons. First, I have the sort of inquiring mind that likes to have
things satisfactorily explained, and the one aspect of this whole matter
which is starkly clear to me is that UFOs have *not* been explained, to
my satisfaction. Indeed, so far as I am concerned the U stands more for
un*explained* than un*identified*. Second, there is a very wide range of other
unexplained phenomena which may or may not be related to UFOs but
which have come to my notice in the UFO connection. Third, I am
convinced that there is an official cover-up of the investigations which
governments have made into UFOs, certainly in the United States, probably in our own country, though not in France, and for all I know in
Russia and other countries as far apart as Argentina, Spain, Australia and
China to name just a few.

The evidence that there are objects which have been seen in our atmosphere, and even on terra firma, that cannot be accounted for either
as man-made objects or as any physical force or effect known to our
scientists seems to me to be overwhelming. I have read two or three
dozen respectable books, and many more less so, and I have listened to
addresses by a dozen or more eminent speakers, in which a very large
number of sightings have been vouched for by persons whose credentials
seem to me unimpeachable. It is striking that so many have been trained
observers, such as police officers and airline or military pilots. Their

observations have in many instances—though by no means a majority
—been supported either by technical means such as radar or, even more
convincingly, by visible evidence of the condition of the observers or—
and this is common to many events—interference with electrical apparatus of one sort or another. Tim Good gives chapter and verse for many
telling examples of all these matters, and some disquieting evidence from
witnesses of sightings, both in our own country and the USA, who claim
to have been silenced by unidentified "government" officials. It is difficult to credit that they have all been either lying or hallucinating.

From the earliest days of the modern outbreak of sightings some forty
years ago, there is a quite remarkable similarity between the descriptions
given by observers of the flying vehicles. It is the more remarkable that
there have been tens of thousands of these reports, from observers who
range from illiterate peasants in Argentina and Spain to people with
Ph.D.s in other countries and they have all been given spontaneously—
which has led to the generic term "flying saucer." It must be more than
a coincidence.

As for what I have called bizarre phenomena, I need only refer to the
astounding geometrical effects in the Alti Plano in South America of what
seem like gigantic airfields laid out in the days of prehistory by means
which would tax today's technology to the limit. And to the pyramid
effects, and to the so-called navigational beacons, which could only be
of use to a craft approaching earth from outside the atmosphere. These
are physical phenomena which exist, and can be touched and measured;
and no one knows how they were made, nor by whom, nor for what
purpose.

Let me turn to some views on what I and many others believe to be
the cover-up. There is no dispute that there have been at least two major
investigations into UFOs in the United States in the last forty years, and
there has been an acknowledged French government investigation since
1954, but there has been no public acknowledgment of anything similar
in Britain or elsewhere. Nothing of substance has ever been disclosed
about the US investigations, and though in France the government does
seem to be more ready to take the public into its confidence, quite the
reverse is true in both the United States and Russia, as many other official
pronouncements have emphasized. While I cannot prove that there is a
cover-up, I believe that Tim Good's book does so, certainly to my satisfaction. He shows beyond doubt that under the recent Freedom of
Information Act in the USA, there are secret, even top secret, files on
the subject which have not been released, and that what has fairly recently

been released there, as the result of a court decision against the Government, is telling enough.

There seem to me to be at least five possible explanations for a cover-up in the first rank, though there may well be others. The first possibility is that the UFOs are man-made, by one or both of the superpowers, and that their evident potential as weapons demands a degree of secrecy which makes Top Secret look like *Beano*. I must say that I simply do not believe this. If it were so, then I am sure that during my time as Chief of the Defense Staff I could not have failed to be let in on the secret, but I was not, and if I had been I should not be writing these words. Moreover, the enormous and very consistent weight of evidence from sightings, and even optical and radar measurements, make it clear enough to me that the technology of construction and propulsion of these devices is far in advance of even that of our space probes, never mind our manned space flights. I am certain that were such technology in actual use anywhere on earth it would have surfaced, either in war or, perhaps more likely, in industry. My final reason for rejecting this hypothesis is that I see no possible reason why, should these devices be man-made, the superpowers should not just say so. The man in the street could hardly be more frightened than he is already of nuclear weapons.

Second, it has been put about that all the major powers are seeking to capture a UFO, to learn its secrets, and that if they admit or disclose the results of their investigations the general public will get into the act and muddle up their plans. Third, is a variant of that notion which holds that one or more powers actually have captured a UFO (Tim Good asserts plainly in Chapter 16 that this has been done in the USA) and fear that public interest will force them to disclose the fact before they have got their answers. Certainly if either of these unlikely explanations were true, and the results of the undoubted investigations were to be made public, it might just be possible for informed students of the subject to discover more than was thought to be good for them. For my part I reject out of hand either of these explanations, partly because, as with the first possibility, I think I should have known (and not be allowed to say so) but more practically because I just cannot believe that the secret would not have got out. Practically every other secret, of a physical rather than a conceptual nature, is already widely known—though governments hate to admit it.

The two further possibilities on my list are both based on fear: fear by governments of public reaction. The first possibility is that official investigations have disclosed or revealed quite a lot about UFOs, even including their origin, method of construction and propulsion, and just possibly their purpose. If this is so, and if the enormous literature is to be believed, plainly there exists no human defense against them, should they be hostile. It is suggested that governments believe this would cause such public "alarm and despondency" (as we used to say in the Second World War) as to have even farther reaching social and political effects than the current opposition to nuclear weapons. This, I must concede, is just possible, though I do not myself believe it. On the contrary I think that were it true, the public would be relatively unmoved. Either they would not believe it or, through apathy or fatalism, they would instead shrug their shoulders and get on with what in 1987 is the difficult business of just living, winning the pools, planning holidays or going on strike— or all four.

The second of these last two possibilities is that investigations have disclosed that UFOs are not physical phenomena but paranormal, and they defy explanation. The reason for not disclosing these findings could then be reluctance to admit publicly that something very odd is going on, and that governments do not know what it is. If so, the same line of argument about public fear applies, and I would use the same counter-arguments as before.

However these five possibilities may strike you, what seems to be common ground is that there have been thousands, perhaps tens of thousands, of sightings and encounters, physical results and of the latter, by people all over the world whose evidence on any other subject would be accepted without question. There have been major investigations lasting thirty or forty years by the governments of the USA, Russia and France, for certain, and probably Britain and other countries. At the end of it all—today—we have no hard official information to weigh against some hundreds of books on the subject by private individuals or groups of individuals. I claim that the charge that there is a cover-up is thereby proved. What I admit defeats me is a plausible reason for it.

This excellent book adds a great deal of evidence to the whole dossier, and I warmly commend it to all who are interested in what, to me at any rate, remains a fascinating enigma.

Admiral of the Fleet, Lord Hill-Norton, G.C.B.

INTRODUCTION

Are governments of the world withholding dramatic evidence—or even proof—that UFOs exist as a serious reality? This question has been asked repeatedly since "flying saucers" made headline news throughout the world in 1947. The official denials have given rise to the suspicion that we are being told less than the truth, and that a wide-scale cover-up is in operation.

In October 1981, in response to an inquiry about the involvement of the intelligence community in the study of UFOs, I received the following reply from that well-known authority on the British security and secret services, Chapman Pincher:

> There is no way I can help you with UFOs because I am convinced that they are entirely mythical. I can assure you that the "world's secret services" are not wasting the smallest resource on keeping tabs on them. For many years I have had access to the highest levels of Defense Intelligence both in Britain and the US. There is not the slightest evidence there to support the existence of UFOs other than those explicable by normal means—meteorites, satellites, aircraft, etc. . . .[1]

Much as I respect Mr. Chapman Pincher, he has clearly been misinformed in this case, since documentary evidence made available in the US under, for example, provisions of the Freedom of Information Act—much of which is presented in this book—proves conclusively that UFOs have continued to be the subject of intensive secret research by intelligence agencies in the US since World War II.

Few governments deny the existence of unidentified flying objects *per se*. Lord Strabolgi, representing Her Majesty's Government in the historic House of Lords debate on the subject in January 1979, acknowledged this point: "There are undoubtedly many strange phenomena in the skies, and it can be readily accepted that most UFO reports are made by calm and responsible people. However, there are generally straightforward explanations to account for the phenomena."

Lord Strabolgi then went on to enumerate the many "straightforward explanations" that account for the majority of reports. Few would disagree with him on this point. UFO researchers concur that seventy to ninety percent of all sightings can be attributed to misidentifications, hallucinations, delusions and hoaxes. On the question of unexplainable sightings, which form the crux of the matter, Lord Strabolgi argued that in such cases "the description is too vague or the evidence too remote, coupled perhaps with a coincidence of different phenomena and with exceptional conditions." In some cases few would disagree, yet Lord Strabolgi conveniently overlooked the fact that hundreds, and possibly thousands, of sightings have been made by highly qualified observers whose descriptions are anything but vague, and the evidence compelling.

As to the suggestion of a cover-up, His Lordship was adamant:

> It has been suggested that our Government are involved in an alleged conspiracy of silence. I can assure your Lordships that the Government are not engaged in any such conspiracy . . . There is nothing to have a conspiracy of silence about. . . . There is no cover-up and no security ban. . . . There is nothing to suggest to Her Majesty's Government that such phenomena are alien spacecraft.[2]

A bona fide UFO, however, does not necessarily imply an extraterrestrial spacecraft. A wide range of hypotheses has been proposed to account for the unexplainable reports, of which the extraterrestrial hypothesis is but one. So the question should really be: Are there any unexplainable reports which represent something beyond our present knowledge, and are governments concealing what they have learned? And if the answer is positive, what exactly has been learned and why is there need for concealment? This book attempts to answer these and other questions relating to the ubiquitous UFO phenomenon—a phenomenon that has caused grave concern at high levels of many of the world's governments, despite their statements to the contrary.

PROLOGUE

GHOST AIRCRAFT, 1933–34

Official investigations into unidentified flying objects in comparatively recent times began in 1933 when, according to contemporary newspaper reports, mysterious unmarked aircraft appeared over Scandinavia and, to a lesser extent, the US and Britain. Often seen flying in hazardous weather conditions which would have grounded conventional aircraft of the period, the "ghost aircraft" (as they were called) frequently circled low, projecting powerful searchlights on to the ground. Another puzzling feature was that although engine noises accompanied the sightings, the aircraft sometimes described low-level maneuvers in complete silence.

On 28 December 1933 the 4th Swedish Flying Corps began an investigation, and on 30 April 1934 Major General Reuterswaerd, Commanding General of Upper Norrland, issued the following statement to the press:

> Comparisons of these reports show that there can be no doubt about illegal air traffic over our secret military areas. There are many reports from reliable people which describe close observation of the enigmatic flier. And in every case the same remark can be noted: No insignias or identifying marks were visible on the machines. . . . The question is: Who or whom are they, and why have they been invading our air territory?[1]

These questions remain unanswered to this day, to the best of my knowledge, although it is possible that some of the sightings could be explained in terms of secret German or Russian reconnaissance flights. There is no evidence of concealment in the major general's statement: rather, it was a frank admission by an official who was prepared to share his bewilderment with the press. Yet journalists did encounter official reluctance to discuss the matter, probably for the simple reason that the authorities were at a loss to explain how their airspace could be invaded by aircraft of unknown origin. One suggestion was that a Japanese aircraft was initially responsible for the sightings, as witness this report from Helsingfors, Finland, in February 1934:

> Continued night flights over North Finland, Sweden and Norway, by so called "ghost aviators" which have caused much apprehension already as to prompt the General Staff to organize reconnoitering on a wide scale by Army planes, all over Northern Finland, still remains a deep mystery. . . . As the authorities are extremely reticent, the newspapers have interviewed aviation experts, who state the mystery fliers show exceptional skill, undoubtedly superior to that of Northern European aviators. According to one expert's theory, the first of the ghost aviators was a Japanese, scouting the Arctic region, whose activities caused the Soviets to dispatch airplanes to watch the Japanese. The Soviet authorities, however, refute this theory.[2]

Researcher John Keel has catalogued the "ghost aircraft" sightings of this period, and believes that no nation on earth had the resources to mount such an operation at that time—least of all Japan. He also points out the similarity between the sightings in Scandinavia and those reported from the US and Britain at the time. Keel cites some reports from London, one of which refers to an unidentified aircraft seen flying over central London on 1 February 1934 for a period of two hours. *The Times* reported the following day that from the sound of the engines the plane was a large one, and that its altitude was sufficiently low for its course to be traced by its lights. The Air Ministry knew nothing about the aircraft, and inquiries at a number of civil airfields around London drew a blank. The sighting led to a question being asked in the House of Commons four days later, to which the Under-Secretary of State for Air, Sir Philip Sassoon, replied: "The aircraft to which my hon. friend evidently refers was a Royal Air Force aircraft carrying out a training exercise in cooperation with ground forces. Such training flights are arranged in the Royal Air Force without reference to the Air Ministry."

Four months later two unidentified aircraft were seen and heard circling low over London late on the night of 11 June. According to *The Times* the following day, the Air Ministry stated that "although night flying was frequently practiced by RAF machines, and several were up last night, service pilots were forbidden by regulations to fly over London at less than 5,000 ft. The identity of the machines in question was not officially known."

It is tempting to dismiss the ghost aircraft reports as conventional planes on illegal or secret flights but, as John Keel emphasizes, approximately thirty-five percent of the Scandinavian sightings took place during severe weather conditions, including blizzards and fog, and the mystery planes often flew dangerously low over hazardous terrain. It is also a fact that the governments of Sweden, Norway and Finland took the hundreds of reports very seriously and launched massive investigations which never led to a satisfactory explanation.[3]

WORLD WAR II

The Los Angeles Air Raid, 1942

On 25 February 1942, less than three months after the Japanese invasion of Pearl Harbor, unidentified aircraft appeared over the city of Los Angeles, causing widespread alarm, and 1,430 rounds of antiaircraft shells were fired in an attempt to bring down what were considered to be Japanese planes. On that day at least a million southern California residents awoke to the wail of air raid sirens as Los Angeles County cities blacked out at 2:25 a.m. Twelve thousand air raid wardens reported dutifully to their posts, most expecting nothing more than a dress rehearsal. At 3:16 a.m., however, the 37th Coast Artillery Brigade's antiaircraft batteries began firing 12.8-pound shells at the targets as searchlight beams studded the sky. The shelling continued intermittently until 4:14 a.m. Three people were killed and three died of heart attacks directly attributable to the barrage, and several homes and public buildings were severely damaged by unexploded shells. At 7:21 a.m. the blackout was lifted and the sirens sounded the all-clear. But what about the Japanese invaders?

Aircraft of the 4th Interceptor Command had been warming up waiting for orders to intercept and engage the intruders, yet no such orders were given during the fifty-one-minute period between the first air raid alert and the first military barrage. Clearly no enemy aircraft were involved in the "invasion." According to thousands of witnesses a large unidentified flying object remained stationary while the antiaircraft shells burst around it and against it. A *Herald Express* staff writer said he was certain that many shells burst directly in the middle of the object and he could not believe that it had not been shot down. The object eventually proceeded at a leisurely pace over the coastal cities between Santa Monica and Long Beach, taking about twenty minutes of actual "flight time" to move twenty miles, then disappeared from view.

An interesting eyewitness account of the phantom raid has been provided by Paul T. Collins, who had been working late at the Long Beach plant of the Douglas Aircraft Company and was returning home when he was stopped by an air raid warden in Pasadena who told him to turn out the lights of his car and stay parked beside the road until the all-clear sounded. Pacing back and forth across the street trying to keep warm, Collins suddenly saw bright red spots of light low on the horizon to the south which were moving in a strange manner:

> They seemed to be "functioning" or navigating mostly on a level plane at that moment—that is, not rising up from the ground in an arc, or trajectory, or in a straight line and then falling back to earth, but appearing from nowhere and then zigzagging from side to side. Some disappeared, not diminishing in brilliance at all, but just vanishing into the night. Others remained pretty much on the same level and we could only guess their elevation to be about ten thousand feet.

In less than five minutes at least half a dozen red flashes rent the sky among the strange spots of red light, followed in about 100 seconds by the dull, cushioned thuds of the bursting shells. One of the antiaircraft batteries around the Douglas Aircraft plant, Dougherty Field, or the Signal Hill Oil Field had fired a salvo into the moving spots of red light, according to Collins, whose position was about twenty miles from the aircraft factory:

> Taking into account our distance from Long Beach, the extensive pattern of firing from widely separated antiaircraft batteries, and the movement of the unidentified red objects among *and around* the bursting shells in wide orbits, we estimated their top speed conservatively to be five miles per second. . . . We did not see the enormous UFO seen by thousands of observers closer to the coast. Very likely it was below our horizon and a few miles farther up the coast at that time.

The military were thoroughly embarrassed and confused by the incident, but were obliged to come up with an explanation. In Washington, US Navy Secretary Knox announced that there had in fact been no planes over the city and that the barrage of antiaircraft fire had been triggered by a false alarm and jittery war nerves. This statement incensed the press, who called attention to the loss of life and implied that the raid was a propaganda exercise by government officials who wanted to move vital industries inland. Commented the *Long Beach Independent*: "There is a mysterious reticence about the whole affair and it appears some form of censorship is trying to halt discussion of the matter."[4]

This story, as with so many other UFO reports, reads like something straight out of science fiction. Yet it happened. A hitherto secret memorandum released in 1974 under provisions of the US Freedom of Information Act leaves little room for doubt that something extraordinary occurred that night. The memorandum was written by General George C. Marshall, Chief of Staff, and sent to President Franklin Roosevelt on 26 February 1942:

> The following is the information we have from GHQ at this moment regarding the air alarm over Los Angeles of yesterday morning:
> From details available at this hour:
>
> 1. Unidentified airplanes, other than American Army or Navy planes, were probably over Los Angeles, and were fired on by elements of the 37th CA Brigade (AA) between 3:12 and 4:15 a.m. These units expended 1430 rounds of ammunition.
> 2. As many as fifteen airplanes may have been involved, flying at various speeds from what is officially reported as being "very slow" to as much as 200 mph and at elevations from 9000 to 18000 feet.
> 3. No bombs were dropped.
> 4. No casualties among our troops.
> 5. No planes were shot down.
> 6. No American Army or Navy planes were in action.
>
> Investigation continuing. It seems reasonable to conclude that if unidentified airplanes were involved they may have been from commercial sources, operated by enemy agents for purposes of spreading alarm, disclosing locations of antiaircraft positions, and slowing production through blackout. Such conclusion is supported by varying speed of operation and the fact that no bombs were dropped.

Although General Marshall concluded that conventional aircraft were involved, he must have been baffled by the fact that none was shot down, despite the intensive barrage of shells.

The "officially reported" speeds of up to 200 mph come nowhere near Paul Collins' estimate of up to "five miles per second." Either Collins was way off the mark, or the official estimates were. There is also the possibility that none of the military observers was in a position to make an accurate assessment, or that they simply could not bring themselves to report such fantastic speeds and maneuvers.

Prior to the release of the Marshall memorandum, the Department of Defense stated that they had no record of the event.[5] Combined with the contradictory news releases at the time, the evidence points to a cover-up by those in the military who were in a position to know what really happened, even if they were at a loss to explain the incident.

Formations of Unidentified Aircraft, 1942

On the morning of 12 August 1942 formations of unidentified aircraft were seen by Sergeant Stephen J. Brickner of the 1st Paratroop Brigade, 1st Marine Division of the US Marine Corps, above the island of Tulagi in the Solomon Islands. The following is extracted from his personal account:

> . . . suddenly the air raid warning sounded. There had been no "Condition Red" . . . I heard the formation before I saw it. Even then, I was puzzled by the sound. It was a mighty roar that seemed to echo in the heavens. It didn't sound at all like the high-pitched "sewing-machine" drone of the Jap formations . . . the formation was huge; I would say over 150 objects were in it. Instead of the usual tight "V" of 25 planes, this formation was in straight lines of 10 or 12 objects, one behind the other. The speed was a little faster than Jap planes, and they were soon out of sight.
>
> A few other things puzzled me: I couldn't seem to make out any wings or tails. They seemed to wobble slightly, and every time they wobbled they would shimmer brightly from the sun. Their color was like highly polished silver. No bombs were dropped, of course. All in all, it was the most awe inspiring and yet frightening spectacle I have seen in my life.[6]

The skeptic would argue that Sergeant Brickner was suffering from combat fatigue, and that the aircraft were conventional. Yet the reference to the "wobbling" motion of the objects is typical of many postwar reports of unidentified flying objects, and the incident seems to have left the witness profoundly impressed.

The Foo-Fighters, 1943–44

According to the late journalist Frank Edwards, the British allegedly set up a small organization in 1943, headed by a Lieutenant General Massey, to investigate sightings of small, apparently remote-controlled devices which were being reported by Allied aircrews.[7] Rumors had spread that the Germans or Japanese had introduced a new weapon designed to interfere with the ignition systems of bombers, but since the "foo-fighters" (as they were nicknamed) never engaged in hostile action many flight crews became convinced that the objects were some type of psychological warfare device. Officially terminated the following year, the "Massey Project" (as it was allegedly code-named) determined that the foo-fighters were not German, and that the Germans had themselves set up a similar organization to investigate sightings then being reported by Luftwaffe pilots. Called "Sonder Büro [Special Bureau] No. 13," with the code-name "Operation Uranus," it was said by Henry Durrant to have been directed by Professor Georg Kamper, assisted by a team of flying officers, aeronautical engineers and scientific advisers.[8]

The US 8th Army also ordered a thorough investigation into the sightings but was apparently unable to arrive at a satisfactory solution. Explanations have been proposed, of course, including St. Elmo's fire, ball lightning, and combat fatigue, but it is improbable that these account for *all* the reports, especially those involving scores of objects observed simultaneously by different aircrews.

Reports of foo-fighters were not restricted to the European theater of operations. An interesting sighting took place in Sumatra on 10 August 1944, for example, witnessed by the crew of an American B-29 bomber commanded by Captain Alvah M. Reida of the 486th Bomb Group, 792nd Squadron, 20th Bomber Command, based at Kharagapur, India:

> I was on a mission from Ceylon, bombing Palembang, Sumatra . . . shortly before midnight. There were 50 planes on the strike going in on the target at about 2 or 3 minute intervals. My plane was last in on the target and the arrangement was for us to bomb, then drop photo flash bombs, attached to parachutes; make a few runs over the target area, photographing damage from preceding planes. . . . Our altitude was 14000 feet and indicated airspeed about 210 mph. While in the general target area we were exposed to sporadic flak fire, but immediately after leaving this area it ceased.
>
> At about 20 or 30 minutes later the right gunner and copilot reported a strange object pacing us about 500 yards off our starboard wing. At that distance it appeared as a spherical object, probably 5 or 6 feet in diameter, of a very bright and intense red or orange in color. . . . My gunner reported it coming in from about 5 o'clock position at our level. It seemed to throb or vibrate constantly. Assuming it was some kind of radio controlled object sent to pace us, I went into evasive action, changing direction constantly as much as 90° and altitude at about 2000 feet. It followed our every maneuver for about 8 minutes, always holding a position 500 yards out and about 2 o'clock in relation to the plane. When it left, it made an abrupt 90° turn, and accelerated rapidly, disappearing in the overcast . . . during the strike evaluation and interrogation following the mission, I made a detailed report to Intelligence thinking it was some new type of radio-controlled missile or weapon.[9]

THE GHOST ROCKETS, 1946

In 1946 over 2,000 sightings of "ghost rockets" and other unidentified flying objects were reported by witnesses in Finland, Norway, Sweden and Denmark, followed by reports from Portugal, Tangier, Italy, Greece, and India. The ghost rockets—so called because they often looked like rocket-shaped objects with fiery trails—sometimes performed fantastic maneuvers, crossing the sky at tremendous velocity, diving and climbing, and at other times moving in a leisurely manner.[10] There were also reports of landings and crashes.

An overwhelming majority of the reports came from Sweden, causing consternation not only in official circles in that country but also at the US Embassy in Stockholm. A hitherto secret Department of State telegram from the Embassy, dated 11 July 1946, provides a dramatic example of the situation at that time:

> For some weeks there have been numerous reports of strange rocket-like missiles being seen in Swedish and Finnish skies. During past few days reports of such objects being seen have greatly increased. Member of Legation saw one Tuesday afternoon. One landed on beach near Stockholm same afternoon without causing any damage and according to press fragments are now being studied by military authorities. Local scientist on first inspection stated it contained organic substance resembling carbide. Defense staff last night issued communique listing various places where missiles had been observed and urging public report all mysterious sound and light phenomena. Press this afternoon announces one such missile fell in Stockholm suburb 2:30 this afternoon. Missile observed by member Legation made no sound and seemed to be falling rapidly to earth when observed. No sound of explosion followed however.
>
> Military Attache is investigating through Swedish channels and has been promised results Swedish observations. Swedes profess ignorance as to origin, character or purpose of missiles but state definitely they are not launched by Swedes. Eyewitness reports state missiles came in from southerly direction proceeding to northwest. Six units Atlantic Fleet under Admiral Hewitt arrived Stockholm this morning. If missiles are of Soviet origin as generally believed (some reports say they are launched from Estonia), purpose might be political to intimidate Swedes in connection with Soviet pressure on Sweden being built up in connection with current loan negotiations or to offset supposed increase in our military prestige in Sweden resulting from the naval visit and recent Bikini tests or both.

On 13 August 1946 the *New York Times* reported that "the Swedish General Staff today described the situation as 'extremely dangerous,' and it is obvious that Sweden no longer is going to tolerate such violations." The violations continued, however, and it is revealing that Sweden chose not to retaliate against the Soviet Union.

Speculation centered on the theory that the Russians were testing V-2–type rockets with the aid of captured German scientists and engineers, and the Swedish General Staff summoned urgent assistance from the United States and Great Britain. Lieutenant General James Doolittle, a US Army Air Force intelligence expert with specialized knowledge of long distance bombing techniques, arrived in Stockholm together with General David Sarnoff, an intelligence expert in aerial warfare, and the two men were consulted by Colonel C. R. Kempf, the Chief of Swedish Defense. Sarnoff was later quoted as saying that the objects reported were neither mythological nor meteorological but were "real missiles."[11]

But then came the cover-up. On 22 August 1946 the *Daily Telegraph* stated:

> The discussion of the flight of rockets over Scandinavia has been dropped in the Norwegian newspapers since Wednesday. On that day the Norwegian General Staff issued a memorandum to the press asking it not to make any mention of the appearance of rockets over Norwegian territory but to pass on all reports to the Intelligence Department of the High Command. . . . In Sweden the ban is limited to any mention of where the rockets have been seen to land or explode.

The reasons for press censorship being introduced at this time are perfectly understandable. Firstly, it was an established practice during the V-1 and V-2 bombardments in World War II not to reveal where the rocket-bombs had fallen, so that the enemy would remain in ignorance of the degree of accuracy of his targeting. Secondly, the ghost rockets were undoubtedly causing considerable public concern, if not panic, and since the authorities had been unable to come up with an explanation for the sightings, they wanted to play down the situation.

On 23 August 1946 the British Foreign Office stated that English radar experts, having returned from Sweden, had "submitted secret reports to the British government on the origin of the rockets."[12] One of the scientists to examine the reports was R. V. Jones, Director of Intelligence on Britain's Air Staff at the time, as well as scientific adviser to Section IV of MI6, the Secret Intelligence Service. Professor Jones remains unimpressed by the reports he examined, attributing them to initial sightings of "two unusually bright meteors, which were clearly visible in daylight. One of these led to many reports almost simultaneously, from a wide area of Sweden." The subsequent wave of sightings was caused simply by overenthusiastic observers in the prevalent cold war climate, he believes. He totally dismisses the possibility that the sightings could have had anything to do with Soviet missiles:

> The Russians were supposedly cruising their flying bombs at more than twice the range that the Germans had achieved, and it was unlikely that

they were so advanced technologically as to achieve a substantially greater reliability at 200 miles than the Germans had reached at 100 miles. Even, therefore, if they were only trying to frighten the Swedes, they could hardly help it if some of their missiles crashed on Swedish territory. The alleged sightings over Sweden were now so many that, even giving the Russians the greatest possible credit for reliability, there ought to be at least 10 missiles crashed in Sweden. I would therefore only believe the story if someone brought me in a piece of a missile.

Although no crashed missiles were ever found, one observer claimed to have seen objects fall from one of the ghost rockets and had collected the pieces. These were passed by the Swedish General Staff to the other Director of Intelligence on the Air Staff, and were eventually analyzed at the Royal Aircraft Establishment, Farnborough. In great excitement, the scientists reported that one of the fragments contained over ninety-eight percent of an unknown element. Jones asked the head of the chemical department at the RAE if they had tested for carbon. "There was something of an explosion at the other end of the telephone," said Jones. "Carbon would not have shown up in any of the standard tests, but one had only to look at the material, as Charles Frank and I had done, to see that it was a lump of coke."[13]

Professor Jones may have been justified in his skepticism about the sample as well as the purported origin of the missiles, but he was evidently mistaken in his outright rejection of the reports, which continued to cause grave concern. The US State Department had upgraded their communications with the Embassy in Stockholm to Top Secret, and the following is the text of a telegram from the Embassy dated 29 August 1946:

> While over 800 reports have been received and new reports come daily, Swedes still have no tangible evidence. Full details of reports thus far received have been forwarded to Washington by our Military and Naval Attaches. My own source personally convinced some foreign power is actually experimenting over Sweden and he guesses it is Russia.

The *Daily Telegraph* published a photograph of one of the missiles in its issue of 6 September 1946, taken near Stockholm by Erik Reuter-swaerd, who reported it to the Swedish General Staff. Together with Allied experts the Swedish authorities came to the conclusion that the "projectile" was within the "flame" or trail, rather than ahead of it. "This supports the theory that a new method of propulsion is being used in these weapons," stated the *Telegraph*.

Something unprecedented had been haunting the airspace of Scandinavia, and in October 1946 the Swedish government announced the results of its official inquiry:

> Swedish military authorities said today that they had been unable to discover after four months of investigation the origin or nature of the ghost rockets that have been flying over Sweden since May.
>
> A special communique declared that 80 percent of 1,000 reports on the rockets could be attributed to "celestial phenomena" but that radar had detected some [200] objects "which cannot be the phenomena of nature or products of the imagination, nor can be referred to as Swedish airplanes."
>
> The report added, however, that the objects were not the V-type bombs used by the Germans in the closing days of the war.[14]

In an interview in London on 5 September 1946 the Greek Prime Minister, M. Tsaldaris, said that on 1 September a number of projectiles had been seen over Macedonia and Salonika.[15] The following year Greece's leading scientist, Professor Paul Santorini, was supplied by the Greek Army with a team of engineers to investigate what were believed to be Russian missiles flying over Greece. Santorini's credentials include the proximity fuse for the Hiroshima atomic bomb, two patents for the guidance system used in US Nike missiles, and a centimetric radar system. Educated at Zurich, where his physics professor was Albert Einstein (with whom he used to play violin duets!), Santorini retired as Director of the Experimental Physical Laboratory of Athens Polytechnic in 1964. On 24 February 1967 he gave a lecture to the Greek Astronautical Society, broadcast on Athens Radio, during which he revealed the results of the Greek investigation into the ghost rockets: "We soon established that they were not missiles. But, before we could do any more, the Army, after conferring with foreign officials, ordered the investigation stopped. Foreign scientists flew to Greece for secret talks with me."[16]

This statement was personally verified by the respected American researcher Raymond Fowler, who had written to Santorini to check on the accuracy of the newspaper quotes attributed to him following the broadcast. The professor confirmed that a "world blanket of secrecy" surrounded the UFO question because, among other reasons, the authorities were unwilling to admit the existence of a force against which we had "no possibility of defense."[17]

PART ONE

GREAT BRITAIN

1

1943–54

If the late American journalist Frank Edwards is to be believed, British government research into mysterious flying objects began as early as 1943 with Lieutenant General Massey's small organization in the War Office to investigate foo-fighters. Edwards claimed that this information was given to him by a Ministry of Defense source in 1966, but it has been disputed by Air Marshal Sir Victor Goddard, who was appointed first Deputy Director of Air Intelligence to the Air Ministry in 1935. "To the best of my knowledge," he states, "there has never been any official study made." As for the "Massey Project," the air marshal is categorical:

> This implies Treasury sanction; it suggests that in the middle of the War against Germany when we had our hands full and it was far from certain that we could survive, the Air Ministry was concerned that a UFO menace existed: it most certainly was not. . . . [General Massey] is not included in my earliest *Who's Who* of 1955. So, unless he died meanwhile, he did not exist in the British Army.[1]

I have no doubt that Sir Victor was telling the truth and that he was unaware of any clandestine research at that time, but it is possible that the War Office failed to inform the Air Ministry about the small research group, however unlikely that may seem. As to "Massey," there is certainly no one listed under that name and rank in *The Army List* or *Who's Who* of the relevant period (1943–45), and it is unlikely that as Deputy Director of Intelligence in the Air Ministry Sir Victor would not have heard of him, since a lieutenant general is the third highest rank in the British Army, equivalent to Goddard's rank of air marshal in the Royal Air Force. But interestingly there *is* a Lieutenant General Hugh R. S. *Massy* listed in the 1945 *Who's Who*. Born in 1884, he was appointed Director of Military Training at the War Office 1938–39 and then Deputy Chief of the Imperial General Staff 1939–40, retiring in 1942. Is it possible that this was the man Edwards was told about? My research has failed so far to throw any more light on the matter. If Edwards was not lying, did he get the spelling wrong? Or was he misinformed by the Ministry of Defense?

Edwards claimed that the "Massey Project" had been instigated to some extent by the reports of a spy who was in reality a double agent, working under the direction of the Mayor of Cologne. Edwards was told by his source that the research project was terminated in 1944. "Perhaps it is only coincidence," he wrote, "that the double agent was exposed and executed in the spring of 1944."[2]

If Edwards was misinformed, his misinformation was highly detailed, for he cites a signed report by "Major E.R.T. Holmes, FLO, 1st Bombardment Squadron, to the Minister of Information 15, War Office, Whitehall, London, under date of October 24, 1943. (Mission No. 115 in the British records)" detailing a sighting of "scores" of small, silvery disks which approached B-17 bombers of the 384th Group without causing any damage during a bombing run on the industrial complex at Schweinfurt on 14 October 1943.[3]

In order to get a proper perspective on the official attitude in Britain, it is essential to examine some reports made by qualified observers in the early fifties—a period when there was less secrecy about the subject. Where possible I have used the original sources as well as official documentation which has not been available hitherto.

The Ministry of Defense has consistently maintained that *all* UFO reports held by the prior to 1962 have been destroyed. I was told in 1980, for instance: "The earliest UFO records held by the MoD date from 1962. All the records held before that date were destroyed some years ago. If there had been any evidence or important papers the records would have been retained."[4] It came as a pleasant surprise therefore to discover that a number of UFO reports prior to 1962 have been retained at the Public Record Office in Kew, London, and I am indebted to John Berry for locating two reports for me from the Air Ministry Air 20 file. The first was classified secret at the time, and is a report of a sighting on 10 December 1950 by Group Captain Cartmel of the Deputy Directorate of Equipment, which he sent to the Deputy Director of Intelligence:

Unidentified "Aircraft"

Although there may possibly be some good explanation for it, I wish to report an unusual occurrence which I witnessed at 19.30 hours last night Sunday, 10th December. I tabulate details below:—

(a) *Place*
Wildernesse Country Club. 1½ miles N.E. of Sevenoaks, Kent.

(b) *Object Seen*
Bright light in sky moving in West-East direction which did not alter in size or intensity of light during movement. No flame or navigation lights were visible.

(c) *Weather*
Raining. Sky 10/10ths overcast. Cloud base estimated 3–4000 ft. Wind negligible.

(d) *Height and Speed*
Although weather conditions made assessment difficult, I estimate the object maintained a steady height of about 3000 ft at approximately 130–150 mph. It was visible for about *five minutes* until it passed out of sight behind the Club buildings.

2. The matter which really drew my attention to it was the *complete absence of sound*. Two friends who were with me witnessed the entire occurrence.

3. Although I am an Equipment Officer, I have done nearly 1400 hours flying in 81 different types of aircraft and I held a pilot's "A" license before, therefore, I feel you may regard the assessments I have made as reasonably accurate. I would be interested to know if this information is of any value and whether or not there is an explanation to the phenomena of straight-and-level flight, without sound.

Opinions from the Deputy Directorate of Operations were unenthusiastic. Wing Commander H. Russell said he thought the group captain had merely observed the moon, although Mr. H. L. Beards argued that "the moon theory is not very good because the passage of cloud before the moon only gives the illusion of speed. The actual movement of the moon in 5 minutes is about 1 degree and this could not make it disappear behind the clubhouse no matter how fast it *appeared* to be going. . . . I don't rule out the possibility of quite an ordinary aircraft with the white navigation light or even some special light fitted . . . the sound could have been bent upward sufficiently to have passed over his head. . . . I doubt whether any further action is necessary beyond saving these papers for future reference." Group Captain E. Douglas Jones agreed with Beards about preserving the account: "I suppose reports of this sort if kept and added to other reports of similar phenomena might one day be useful for analysis. I can't think of anything else we could do with this one."

SIR WINSTON CHURCHILL, 1952

Clearly the Air Ministry did not seem to be taking the subject of flying saucers very seriously in 1950. But two years later, presumably following the worldwide coverage of dramatic sightings over Washington, DC, in July 1952, Prime Minister Winston Churchill felt sufficiently concerned to write the following personal minute to the Secretary of State for Air, and Lord Cherwell, on 28 July 1952: "What does all this stuff about flying saucers amount to? What can it mean? What is the truth? Let me have a report at your convenience."

Back came the reply from the Air Ministry on 9 August 1952:

The various reports about unidentified flying objects, described by the Press as "flying saucers," were the subject of a full Intelligence study in 1951. The conclusions reached (based upon William of Occam's Razor) were that all the incidents reported could be explained by one or other of the following causes:—
    (a) Known astronomical or meteorological phenomena.
    (b) Mistaken identification of conventional aircraft, balloons, birds, etc.
    (c) Optical illusions and psychological delusions.
    (d) Deliberate hoaxes.

2. The Americans, who carried out a similar investigation in 1948/9, reached a similar conclusion.

3. Nothing has happened since 1951 to make the Air Staff change their mind, and, to judge from recent Press statements, the same is true in America. . . .

A copy of this minute was sent to Lord Cherwell, who wrote to the Prime Minister on 14 August 1952, stating that "I have seen the Secretary of State's minute to you on flying saucers and agree entirely with his conclusions."

Sir Winston Churchill was either deliberately or inadvertently misinformed. Firstly, the Air Staff were *not* able to explain all the incidents. The Deputy Director of Intelligence at the Air Ministry from 1950 to 1953 has confirmed that ten percent of reports came from well qualified witnesses, where there was corroboration, and where no explanation could be found (see p. 34). Secondly, the Americans had *not* "reached a similar conclusion" that all the incidents could be explained. An American top secret Air Intelligence Report concluded in 1948: "The frequency of reported sightings, the similarity in many of the characteristics attributed to the observed objects and the quality of observers considered as a whole, support the contention that some type of flying object has been observed. . . . The origin of the devices is not ascertainable."[5]

Even as early as 1947 the US Air Matériel Command had secretly concluded that "the phenomenon reported is something real and not visionary or fictitious. . . . There are objects probably approximating the shape of a disc, of such appreciable size as to appear to be as large as man-made aircraft.''[6] By the end of July 1952—the time of Churchill's minute—US authorities were in a state of near panic, and a CIA memorandum confirms that ''since 1947, ATIC [Air Technical Intelligence Center] has received approximately 1500 *official* reports of sightings. . . . During 1952 alone, *official* reports totaled 250. Of the 1500 reports, Air Force carries 20 percent as *unexplained* and of those received from January through July 1952 it carries 28 percent *unexplained*.''[7] [Emphasis in original]

We must therefore assume that either the Air Staff had not been given these facts by their American colleagues or that they chose to withhold the information from the Prime Minister.

RAF TOPCLIFFE, 1952

On 19 September 1952, during the NATO ''Exercise Mainbrace,'' two RAF officers and three aircrew at RAF Topcliffe observed a UFO apparently following a Meteor jet as it was coming into land at RAF Dishforth, Yorkshire, five miles away. The sighting took place at 10:53 a.m. as the Meteor was descending in a clear sky, reported Flight Lieutenant John Kilburn:

The Meteor was crossing from east to west when I noticed the white object in the sky. This object was silver and circular in shape, about 10,000 ft up some five miles astern of the aircraft. It appeared to be traveling at a lower speed than the Meteor but was on the same course.

I said: ''What the hell's that?'' and the chaps looked to where I was pointing. Somebody shouted that it might be the engine cowling of the Meteor falling out of the sky. Then we thought it might be a parachute. But as we watched the disk maintained a slow forward speed for a few seconds before starting to descend. While descending it was swinging in a pendulum fashion from left to right.

As the Meteor turned to start its landing run the object appeared to be following it. But after a few seconds it stopped its descent and hung in the air rotating as if on its own axis. Then it accelerated at an incredible speed to the west, turned southeast and then disappeared.

It is difficult to estimate the object's speed. The incident happened within a matter of 15 to 20 seconds. During the few seconds that it rotated we could see it flashing in the sunshine. It appeared to be about the size of a Vampire jet aircraft at a similar height.

We are all convinced that it was some solid object. We realized very quickly that it could not be a broken cowling or parachute. There was not the slightest possibility that the object we saw was a smoke ring, or was caused by vapor trail from the Meteor or from any jet aircraft. We have, of course, seen this, and we are all quite certain that what we saw was not caused by vapor or smoke.

We are also quite certain that it was not a weather observation balloon. The speed at which it moved away discounts this altogether. It was not a small object which appeared bigger in the conditions of light. Our combined opinion is that . . . it was something we had never seen before in a long experience of air observation.

The other witnesses were Flight Lieutenant Marian Cybulski, Master Signaller Albert Thomson, Sergeant Flight Engineer Thomas Deweys, Flight Lieutenant R. Paris, and Leading Aircraftsman George Grime.[8]

In spite of the Ministry of Defense's claim that all reports prior to 1962 had been destroyed, the official report on the Topcliffe incident was located at the Public Record Office. Copies were sent at the time to the Commander-in-Chief, Air/East Atlantic (a NATO command post), the Secretary of State for Air, the Chief of the Air Staff, the Assistant Chief of the Air Staff (Intelligence), the Assistant Chief of the Air Staff (Operations), as well as to the Defense Ministry's Scientific Intelligence Branch. Clearly the report was taken seriously.

Captain Edward Ruppelt, former head of the US Air Force Air Technical Intelligence Center's "Project Blue Book," relates that an RAF intelligence officer at the Pentagon told him that the Topcliffe incident was one of a number in 1952—including another report by RAF pilots during "Operation Mainbrace"—"that caused the RAF to officially recognize the UFO."[9] Ruppelt also relates that during his tenure as head of Blue Book at ATIC, based at Wright-Patterson Air Force Base, "two RAF intelligence officers who were in the US on a classified mission brought six single-spaced typed pages of questions they and their friends wanted answered."[10]

THE DEPUTY DIRECTORATE OF INTELLIGENCE

A week after the Topcliffe story was published, the *Sunday Dispatch* ran an article which claimed that the RAF had been secretly investigating flying saucer reports since 1947:

A staff of technical experts—mostly commissioned officers under the direction of a wing commander—are analysing every report of a flying saucer over British territory. Though the exact location of the flying saucer investigation bureau—known as the DDI [Deputy Directorate of Intelligence]

(Technical) Branch—is secret, I can reveal it occupies rooms in a building, formerly an hotel, not five minutes' walk from the Air Ministry in Whitehall. The building is closely guarded.

The *Sunday Dispatch* reporter added that intelligence officers at RAF Topcliffe had interrogated the two officers and three aircrew who witnessed the sighting. "Till the experts have made a thorough investigation," an Air Ministry spokesman was quoted as saying, "it is impossible to do more than guess. Our experts will examine this report in the same way as they have been examining every similar report of objects seen in the sky which are not aircraft and which are generally referred to as flying saucers."[11] The Air Ministry eventually admitted that they were unable to explain the sighting, after eleven weeks of inquiry, and a spokesman added: "The special branch which has been dealing with this is keeping an open mind on the subject and all reports received are still being studied."[12]

Details of the secret investigation bureau are given in the following chapter, but it is worth noting at this stage that during a meeting with an official at DDI (Tech.) in 1954, investigator Ronald R. Russell was told that the directorate had 15,000 reports on file from 1947 to 1954, and that these were stored in three drawers with Yale-type locks, doubly secured by a hinged plate locked in turn with a large padlock.[13]

Having established that a few reports from this period were retained by the Air Ministry, and that the Ministry of Defense has consistently denied this for many years, I wrote to the MoD in order to obtain an official reaction and received the following reply:

I am sure you will appreciate that I cannot go into the detailed arrangements for the disposal of our files. Nevertheless given the length of time since these documents must have been passed to the Air Ministry archives (I assume before 1955), it is quite possible that some may have been retained prior to the setting up of the Ministry of Defense, even though we have no record of this.[14]

Perhaps we should give the Ministry the benefit of the doubt. Certainly very few documents on the subject are available at the Public Record Office, and these may well have been overlooked by the MoD, but are we to believe that the vast majority of unexplainable reports have been arbitrarily destroyed? If the figure of 15,000 reports from 1947 to 1954 cited by Ronald Russell is accurate, and ten percent were unexplainable, I find it difficult to accept that these have been disposed of. While it is true that at least ninety-five percent of documents are periodically "weeded" by the MoD "reviewers," some are withheld for 100 years if it is felt that national security would be compromised, or the government embarrassed by their release.

The ten percent figure has been misrepresented by the MoD in misleading statements to Parliament and the general public since 1955, by attributing this category to "unexplained due to insufficient information." In fact, the opposite is true.

The Deputy Director of Intelligence at the Air Ministry during 1950–53 was Group Captain Harold B. Collins, and in a letter to former Ministry of Defense official Ralph Noyes, he summarizes the results of Air Ministry findings at that time:

> We found that there had been similar reports way back into the middle ages, though they took the form of "galleons in the sky" etc.
>
> If my memory serves, we prepared a paper which divided the more recent reports into four classifications:
>
> (1) Some 35% that could be immediately discounted.
> (2) Some 25% for which we were able to find a definite or probable explanation.
> (3) Some 30% where there was no corroboration or there were doubts about the reporter and for which we could find no explanation.
> (4) *Some 10% where the reporter was well qualified, i.e. Farnborough test pilot, etc. where there was corroboration and where the report itself carried conviction: but where we could find no explanation.*[15]
> [Emphasis added]

It is unfortunate that Group Captain Collins does not elaborate on the fourth category, but it is as well to emphasize that ten percent of 15,000 reports—or even 1,500—represents a significant number of sightings by well-qualified witnesses for which there was no explanation. This is completely at variance with official statements over the past thirty years or so.

Although not connected to DDI (Tech.), Ralph Noyes was private secretary to the late Air Chief Marshal Sir Ralph Cochrane, Vice Chief of the Air Staff from 1950 to 1952, and he recalls an occasion at the Air Ministry in 1952 when Cochrane chatted about the subject with Sir Robert Cockburn, Chief Scientific Advisor to the Air Ministry. Cochrane referred to the alarming wave of sightings over Washington, DC, in July that year, and mentioned that the US Chief of Staff, General Hoyt Vandenberg (whom Cochrane knew well), "didn't think there was much in it." Cockburn was asked to look into the flying saucer question, since the Washington sightings had caused alarm at the Air Ministry. Cochrane himself was very much inclined to take Vandenberg's view, Ralph Noyes told me.

Although General Vandenberg had dismissed a top secret *Estimate of the Situation* which concluded that the UFOs were interplanetary in origin—a report delivered to him by Air Technical Intelligence Center at the US Air Force headquarters on 5 August 1948—Vandenberg nevertheless ordered that the copy should be destroyed, because he feared that it might cause panic, and also because he felt there was insufficient proof to support its conclusions.[16]

THE WEST MALLING INCIDENT, 1953

On 3 November 1953, at 10:00 a.m., Royal Air Force Flying Officer T. S. Johnson and his navigator, Flying Officer G. Smythe, were flying a two-seat Vampire jet night fighter on a sector reconnaissance at 20,000 feet near their base at RAF West Malling in Kent, when they saw an object which at first appeared to be a star-like stationary light. Although unable to estimate its altitude, both officers said the object was much higher than their position. Suddenly it moved toward them at tremendous speed. It was perfectly circular in shape and appeared to be emitting a very bright light around the periphery. The sighting lasted thirty seconds in all.

Expecting derision when they reported the incident on landing to their Station Commander, Group Captain P. H. Hamley, the airmen were surprised when their report was immediately forwarded to Fighter Command Headquarters. Later, two RAF intelligence officers interrogated the men for an hour and a half.

On 11 November the War Office announced that at 2:30 p.m. on 3 November an Army radar set being tested at the Anti-Aircraft Command barracks at Lee Green, Kent, picked up a large echo on a southeast bearing at an angle of 42° and a sound range of seventeen miles. It was tracked on radar from 2:45 to 3:10 p.m. by a number of Army technicians, including Sergeant H. Waller, who commented that the object could not possibly have been a balloon. To obtain the sort of signal received the object must have been metallic, he said, and the signal was much stronger than those obtained from conventional aircraft—"three or four times larger than the largest airliner."

But on 12 November the War Office, which controlled inland radar at that time, claimed that the object was merely a meteorological balloon

released from Crawley, Sussex, at 2:00 p.m., and added that the object
seen by the Vampire crew was another balloon that had been released
that morning. A radio-sonde balloon of that period, however, was only
75 feet across, and according to Sergeant Waller the object he tracked
was about 350–450 feet in diameter.[17]

QUESTIONS IN THE HOUSE OF COMMONS, 1953

The West Malling and Lee Green incidents led to questions being asked
in the House of Commons. On 24 November 1953 Nigel Birch, Parliamentary Secretary, Ministry of Defense, replying to Lieutenant Colonel
Schofield, MP, and Mr. Bellenger, MP, who asked about the sightings,
replied: "Two experimental meteorological balloons were observed at
different times on November 3rd, one by officers of an RAF aircraft, and
another by a member of Anti-Aircraft Command. There was nothing
peculiar about either of the occurrences." (Laughter)

Birch added in answer to further questions that the balloons were fitted
with a special device to produce as large an echo on a radar screen as
an aircraft, and that they had been released at unusual times. He hoped
there would not be any more trouble. Mr. Isaacs, MP, then asked: "Will
the Minister agree that this story of flying saucers is all ballooney?" (loud
laughter), to which Mr. Birch responded that Mr. Isaacs' appreciation
was "very nearly correct." (Laughter)[18]

RAF PILOT'S CLOSE ENCOUNTER OVER SOUTHEND, 1954

Nearly a year later another sighting was reported by an RAF pilot which
has never been satisfactorily explained, and like the West Malling incident
is not available in the Air Ministry files at the Public Record Office.
Although the story is well known I am including it here because according
to the witness the original account, as it appeared in *Flying Saucer Review*[19]
contained some inaccuracies that have not been corrected until now.
I also believe that it is one of the most important sightings to have
been reported by an RAF pilot, and I was therefore delighted to interview Flight Lieutenant James R. Salandin in 1985 and check the details
with him.

On 14 October 1954 Flight Lieutenant Salandin, of No. 604, County
of Middlesex Squadron, Royal Auxiliary Air Force, took off at 4:15 p.m.

from his base at RAF North Weald in Essex, in a Meteor Mk 8. The weather was perfect:

> When I was at about 16,000 feet I saw a whole lot of contrails—possibly at 30–40,000 feet—over the North Foreland. Through the middle of the trails I saw three objects which I thought were airplanes, but they weren't trailing. They came down through the middle of that toward Southend and then headed toward me.
>
> When they got to within a certain distance two of them went off to my port side—one gold and one silver—and the third object came straight toward me and closed to within a few hundred yards, almost filling the windscreen, then it went off toward my port side. I tried to turn round to follow, but it had gone.
>
> It was saucer-shaped with a bun on top and a bun underneath, and was silvery and metallic. There were no portholes, flames, or anything.

The third object could not have been far away because it nearly overlapped the windscreen (the original story claimed that it actually overlapped the windscreen). A Meteor's 37-feet wingspan just fills the windscreen at 150 yards.

Salandin immediately reported the sighting by radio to North Weald. After landing he related further details to Derek Dempster, 604 Squadron's intelligence officer, who was fortuitously to become the first editor of *Flying Saucer Review* in 1955. The report was sent to the Air Ministry but nothing further was heard about it. Had it not been for Derek Dempster the story might never have come to light.

Derek has told me that he is absolutely convinced of Salandin's sincerity, having known him well as a fellow pilot in 604 Squadron. Prior to flying Meteors and Vampires, "Jimmy" Salandin told me that he gained experience in a number of other aircraft, including 100 hours in a Spitfire Mk XVI (this aircraft is still flying). Salandin only regrets that there was not sufficient time to trigger the gun-camera button. But his memory of the sighting remains vivid. "I haven't found a satisfactory explanation for what I saw," he told me, "*but I know what I saw.*"[20]

The current editor of *Flying Saucer Review* is the former diplomat and intelligence officer Gordon Creighton, who relates an intriguing sequel to the affair. Following a talk that Gordon had given to the House of Lords All-Party UFO Study Group in November 1983, he happened to broach the subject with a complete stranger whom he met on the train journey home. The Salandin case was brought up in the course of conversation, and the stranger turned out to be a former member of 604 Squadron. Gordon told him that *FSR* had investigated and published the case in its first issue, and asked if by chance he had ever heard of the magazine. "Oh, yes!" he replied. "We knew all about *Flying Saucer Review*. You were the people that we were always warned that we must keep away from!"[21]

MYSTERY FORMATIONS OF UFOS BAFFLE THE WAR OFFICE, 1954

Three weeks after Flight Lieutenant Salandin's sighting, the War Office admitted that it was completely baffled by strange formations of "blips" tracked on radar, moving from east to west. A thorough check revealed that they could not have been caused by aircraft. From late October to early November 1954 there were six sightings of the unidentified targets, which appeared from nowhere, usually at midday, flying at a height of 12,000 feet. First seen by a civilian radar scientist, they were subsequently plotted by all the radar sets in the area, on both fine and cloudy mornings. A War Office spokesman described the formations as follows:

> We cannot say what they are. They first appear in a "U," or badly shaped hairpin, formation. After a time they converge into two parallel lines and then take up a "Z" formation before disappearing. They are invisible to the human eye, but on the radar screen they appear as lots and lots of dots formed by between 40 and 50 echoes. They cover an area in the sky miles long and miles wide.
>
> Every time they have been seen they followed the same pattern. It was always around midday. We have checked and found that our sets are not faulty. We are still maintaining a watch. All our sets in the area have picked them up.

The location of the radar trackings was not identified, and one witness said that he had been given very high-level orders to maintain the utmost secrecy. "And even if I did know what they are," he added, "I am too worried myself to say anything."

The Air Ministry seemed anxious to play down the incidents, pointing out that there are many objects such as meteorological balloons, experimental aircraft, carrier pigeons with metal rings on their legs, and even toy kites, which could generate an image on radar. But the trained radar specialists said that none of these would produce such regular and repeated patterns.[22]

By 1954 defense chiefs in Britain were convinced that a problem existed, even if they were not prepared to admit as much in public. The following statement, for example, was made by the Defense Minister of the time, Earl Alexander of Tunis: "This problem has intrigued me for a long time. . . . There are of course many phenomena in this world which are not explained and it is possible to say that the orthodox scientist is the last person to accept that something new (or old) may exist which cannot be explained in accordance with his understanding of natural laws."[23]

HRH PRINCE PHILIP, DUKE OF EDINBURGH

In February 1954 young Stephen Darbishire, together with his cousin Adrian Myers, took two photographs of a flying saucer near Coniston, Lancashire. The object was identical to those photographed by the famous UFO contactee George Adamski, and the Duke of Edinburgh was sufficiently impressed to invite Stephen to Buckingham Palace just over a month later, so that the full details could be related to one of his aides. A full report of the interview was then sent to the Duke, who was in Australia at the time.[24] The Duke of Edinburgh has confirmed this story to me, via Major the Honorable Andrew Wigram, and has graciously allowed me to use the following comment, with regard to George Adamski's first book, co-authored with Desmond Leslie, which he referred to at a dinner party in 1962: "There are many reasons to believe that they [UFOs] do exist: there is so much evidence from reliable witnesses. The book *Flying Saucers Have Landed* has a lot of interesting stuff in it."

His Royal Highness points out that a story published at the time claiming that he had asked the Air Ministry to forward UFO reports to him "is a case of gossip columnist inaccuracy."[25] But the Duke's interest in the subject has remained with him since the early 1950s, and he continues to receive *Flying Saucer Review,* one of the world's leading publications on this controversial subject. In 1983 I was honored when he ordered a copy of *George Adamski—The Untold Story,* which I co-authored with Lou Zinsstag.[26]

LORD LOUIS MOUNTBATTEN

Admiral of the Fleet, Earl Mountbatten of Burma, Supreme Allied Commander in Southeast Asia during World War II and Chief of the Defense Staff from 1958 to 1965, showed an enormous interest in UFOs for a number of years. His biographer Philip Ziegler writes that Mountbatten once tried to persuade the *Sunday Dispatch* to put a team onto the more promising cases, and in a private letter to the editor he also propounded his hypothesis that the UFOs were themselves the inhabitants of other planets, rather than actual machines. "I know this sounds ridiculous," he wrote, "and I am relying on you . . . not to make capital out of the fact that I have put forward such a far-fetched explanation."[27]

The Landing at Broadlands, 1955

One wonders if Lord Mountbatten felt inclined to modify his hypothesis when in February 1955 a flying saucer complete with occupant was alleged to have landed on his estate at Broadlands, near Romsey, Hampshire. The story was related to me many years ago by Desmond Leslie who had investigated it personally and later published an account in *Flying Saucer Review*[28] following Mountbatten's tragic murder in 1979. Thanks to Philip Ziegler, Mollie Travis and the Trustees of the Broadlands Archives, photocopies of the original statements made immediately after the incident are published here for the first time. The first statement is by the witness, Frederick Briggs, with an appended drawing, and the second is by Mountbatten himself, with an endorsement by Ronald Heath, the electrician. Briggs' statement is as follows:

I am at present employed at Broadlands as a bricklayer and was cycling to my work from Romsey on the morning of Wednesday, the 23rd February 1955. When I was about half way between the Palmerston or Romsey Lodge and the house, just by where the drive forks off to the Middlebridge Lodge, I suddenly saw an object hovering stationary over the field between the end of the gardens and Middlebridge Drive, and just on the house side of the little stream.

The object was shaped like a child's huge humming-top and half way between 20 ft or 30 ft in diameter.

Its color was like dull aluminum, rather like a kitchen saucepan. It was shaped like the sketch which I have endeavored to make, and had portholes all round the middle, rather like a steamer has.

The time was just after 8:30 a.m. with an overcast sky and light snow on the ground.

I turned off the drive at the fork and rode over the grass for rather less than 100 yards. I then dismounted, and holding my bicycle in my right hand, watched.

While I was watching a column, about the thickness of a man, descended from the center of the Saucer and I suddenly noticed on it, what appeared to be a man, presumably standing on a small platform on the end. He did not appear to be holding on to anything. He seemed to be dressed in a dark suit of overalls, and was wearing a close fitting hat or helmet.

At the time the Saucer was certainly less than 100 yards from me, and not more than 60 ft over the level where I was standing, although the meadow has a steep bank at this point, so that the Saucer would have been about 80 ft over the lower level of the meadow.

As I stood there watching, I suddenly saw a curious light come on in one of the portholes. It was a bluish light, rather like a mercury vapor light. Although it was quite bright, it did not appear to be directed straight at me, nor did it dazzle me, but simultaneously with the light coming on I suddenly seemed to be pushed over, and I fell down in the snow with my bicycle on top of me. What is more, I could not get up again. Although the bicycle only weighs a few lbs it seemed as if an unknown force was holding me down.

Whilst lying on the ground I could see the tube withdrawn quickly into the Saucer, which then rose vertically, quite as fast as the fastest jet aircraft I have seen, or faster.

There had been no noise whatever until the Saucer started to move, and even then the noise was no louder than that of an ordinary small rocket let off by a child on Guy Fawkes Night.

It disappeared out of sight into the clouds almost instantaneously, and as it went, I found myself able to get up. Although I seemed to be lying a long time on the ground I do not suppose, in reality, it was more than a few seconds.

I felt rather dizzy, as though I had received a near knockout blow on the chin, but of course there was no physical hurt of any sort, merely a feeling of dizziness.

I picked up my bicycle, mounted it and rode straight on to Broadlands where I met Heath standing by the garage.

I was feeling very shaky and felt I must regain my confidence by discussing what I had seen. I said to him: "Look, Ron, have you known me long enough to know that I am sane and sober at this hour of the morning?" He laughed and made some remark like, "Well, of course." Then I told him what I had seen.

Heath and I went back along the road where I showed him the tracks of my bicycle. I then went back to work, where I saw my foreman, Mr. Hudson, and told him what I had seen.

Lord Mountbatten's statement reads:

The attached statement was dictated by Mr. Briggs to Mrs. Travis on the morning of the 23rd February 1955 at my request.

My own electrician, Heath, reported his conversation and I subsequently interviewed Mr. Briggs, with my wife and younger daughter, and as a result of his account, Heath and I accompanied him to the place from which he saw the Flying Saucer.

We followed the marks of his bicycle in the snow very easily, and exactly at the spot which he described the tracks came to an end, and foot marks appeared beside it. Next to the foot marks there were the marks of a body having fallen in the snow, and then the marks of a bicycle having been picked up again, there being a clear gap of 3 ft between where the front wheel marks originally ended and then started again. The rear wheel marks were continuous but blurred. From then on the bicycle tracks led back to the drive.

The bicycle tracks absolutely confirm Mr. Briggs' story, so far as his own movements are concerned.

He, Heath and I searched the area over the spot where the Flying Saucer was estimated to have been, but candidly we could see no unusual signs.

The snow at the bottom of the meadow had melted much more than that at the top, and it would have been difficult to see any marks.

This statement has been dictated in the presence of Heath and Mr. Briggs, and Heath and I have carefully read Mr. Briggs' statement, and we both attest that this is the exact story which he told us.

Mr. Briggs was still dazed when I first saw him, and was worried that no one would believe his story. Indeed, he made a point of saying that he had never believed in Flying Saucer stories before, and had been absolutely amazed at what he had seen.

He did not give me the impression of being the sort of man who would be subject to hallucinations, or would in any way invent such a story. I am sure from the sincere way he gave his account that he, himself, is completely convinced of the truth of his own statement.

He has offered to swear to the truth of this statement on oath on the Bible if needed, but I saw no point in asking him to do this.

At the bottom of Mountbatten's statement is an endorsement by Ronald Heath: "I confirm that I have read and agree with the above statement."[29]

Philip Ziegler makes short shrift of this episode, and comments that by 1957 Mountbatten had become disillusioned with the amount of rubbish published on the subject. "I must be honest and confess that I no longer take the same interest," he wrote to a more ardent student of the subject. Ziegler adds that Mountbatten never rejected the possibility that such objects existed, but insisted that they must be susceptible to rational explanation. "Few senior naval officers would have been ready to confront the paranormal with such equanimity," Ziegler commented, and quotes an interesting observation made by Lord Mountbatten, before his enthusiasm waned, in 1950: "The fact that they can hover and accelerate away from the earth's gravity again and even revolve around a V2 in America (as reported by their head scientist) shows they are far ahead of us. If they really come over in a big way that may settle the capitalist–communist war. If the human race wishes to survive they may have to band together."[30]

2

ROOM 801—TOP SECRET
(1955–59)

In April 1955 the Air Ministry announced that the results of a five-year investigation into flying saucers by the Royal Air Force had been submitted to high-ranking officers but that *it was never to be revealed to the public for security reasons*. In view of the Ministry's oft-repeated statement that UFOs do not constitute a threat to the nation's security, this was a curious announcement, and it provoked Major Patrick Wall, MP, to ask the Under-Secretary of State for Air, George Ward, to confirm whether he proposed to publish a report. Ward's reply failed to address the question: "Reports of flying saucers, as well as other abnormal objects in the sky, are investigated as they come in, but there has been no formal inquiry. About 90% of the reports have been found to relate to meteors, balloons, flares and many other objects. The fact that the other 10% are unexplained need be attributed to nothing more sinister than lack of data."[1]

The reference to ten percent of cases that might have been explained if it had not been for "lack of data" is without foundation, as is clear from the Air Ministry findings summarized by Group Captain Collins, which have been quoted in Chapter 1. George Ward eventually admitted to a friend of mine that he was obliged to cover up the facts about UFOs, a revelation discussed later in this chapter.

THE KILGALLEN STORY, 1955

On 22 May an International News Service syndicated report from London by the American journalist Dorothy Kilgallen stated:

British scientists and airmen, after examining the wreckage of one mysterious flying ship, are convinced these strange aerial objects are not optical illusions or Soviet inventions, but are flying saucers which originate on another planet.

The source of my information is a British official of Cabinet rank who prefers to remain unidentified. "We believe, on the basis of our inquiry thus far, that the saucers were staffed by small men—probably under four

feet tall. It's frightening, but there is no denying the flying saucers come
from another planet.''

This official quoted scientists as saying a flying ship of this type could
not possibly have been constructed on earth. The British government, I
learned, is withholding an official report on the ''flying saucer'' examination at this time, possibly because it does not wish to frighten the public.[2]

The story has been discounted as a hoax, and investigators in a number
of countries have never been able to authenticate it. The London news
editor of the International News Service, for example, told *Flying Saucer
Review* that he had tried hard to get to the bottom of the story but had
drawn a blank.[3] According to the present editor of *FSR*, Gordon Creighton, the crash was alleged to have taken place during World War II, and
the story related to Dorothy Kilgallen during a cocktail party given by
Lord Mountbatten in May, but I have been unable to substantiate this
with Mollie Travis, Mountbatten's private secretary at the time.

Gordon Creighton was unsuccessful in obtaining a reply to a letter he
addressed to Kilgallen, as was the Swedish researcher K. Gösta Rehn
who, like many others, reasoned that the story was simply a newspaper
gimmick and the journalist had been reprimanded for it. British authorities
are said to have issued a sharp denial of Kilgallen's report. ''Had Dorothy
Kilgallen been at a smart cocktail party at which a senior member of the
government passed her the 'sensation' as a joke?'' Gösta Rehn asks.
''This suggestion does not accord with the objective tone of the report.
Why should the Englishman have told her about it if he were not deeply
interested in the secret, relied on her confidence and his own anonymity?
And why should Dorothy Kilgallen risk her reputation as one of the
USA's star journalists by propagating an untrue story?''[4] Why indeed?
To the best of my knowledge Dorothy Kilgallen never denied the story.
Furthermore, a number of similar stories from reliable sources have sur-
faced over the years, not all of which can be discounted, however absurd
they may sound.

RAF BENTWATERS/LAKENHEATH, 1956

An impressive sighting by RAF and US Air Force personnel took place
on the night of 13/14 August 1956 when at least one UFO was simultaneously tracked by three different ground-based radars at RAF/USAF
Bentwaters and Lakenheath, Suffolk, as well as on airborne radar, and
the objects were also seen from the ground and in the air. This is the

little-known but definitive account by F.H.C. Wimbledon, RAF Fighter Controller on duty at RAF Neatishead, Norfolk, at the time:

> I was Chief Controller on duty at the main RAF Radar Station in East Anglia on the night in question. My duties were to monitor the Radar picture and to scramble the Battle Flight, who were on duty 24 hours a day, to intercept any intruder of British airspace not positively identified in my sector of responsibility. . . .
>
> I remember Lakenheath USAF base telephoning to say there was something "buzzing" their airfield circuit. I scrambled a Venom night fighter from the Battle Flight through Sector and my controller in the Interception Cabin took over control of it. The Interception Control team would consist of one Fighter Controller (an Officer), a Corporal, a tracker and a height reader. That is, four highly trained personnel in addition to myself could now clearly see the object on our radarscopes. . . .
>
> After being vectored onto the trail of the object by my Interception Controller, the pilot called out, "Contact," then a short time later, "Judy," which meant the Navigator had the target fairly and squarely on his own radar screen and needed no further help from the ground. He continued to close on the target but after a few seconds, and in the space of one or two sweeps of our scopes, the object appeared behind our fighter. Our pilot called out, "Lost Contact, more help," and he was told the target was now behind him and he was given fresh instructions.
>
> I then scrambled a second Venom which was vectored toward the area but before it arrived on the scene the target had disappeared from our scopes and although we continued to keep a careful watch was not seen by us.
>
> . . . the fact remains that at least nine RAF ground personnel and two RAF aircrew were conscious of an object sufficiently "solid" to give returns on radar. Naturally, all this was reported and a Senior Officer from the Air Ministry came down and interrogated us.[5]

In a letter to the *Sunday Times* Mr. Wimbledon revealed that the headquarters of Fighter Command were fully informed, *and that the strictest secrecy was imposed.*[6] The case was taken off the secret list in January 1969 when the USAF-sponsored scientific study of UFOs, headed by the late Dr. Edward Condon, published its findings. The investigative team concluded that "this is the most puzzling and unusual case in the radar-visual files. The apparently rational, intelligent behavior of the UFO suggests a mechanical device of unknown origin as the most probable explanation."[7]

During a televised public meeting at Banbury Town Hall on 26 January 1972, a member of the audience asked Ministry of Defense spokesman Anthony Davies what the Ministry had to say about the Bentwaters/

Lakenheath case. Mr. Davies replied that he could say nothing because the papers had been destroyed. The BBC "Horizon" team chose to exclude this exchange from the subsequent broadcast.[8] I asked Ralph Noyes if he was aware that the papers had been destroyed. He pointed out that as head of Defense Secretariat 8 (1969–72) he saw only a small proportion of the UFO material since the bulk of reports was handled by S4, another MoD department, but went on to say:

> I think it is *very* surprising if those papers were destroyed. There is every indication that at the time of the incident the Air Ministry, as it then was, was exceedingly interested, if not positively uneasy. If the papers have been destroyed this does look like a thoroughly improper step to have taken. There is no doubt that something important took place at Bentwaters/ Lakenheath, even if it was only a very extraordinary misperception by radar operators and pilots, and that should surely have remained on record.

Ralph Noyes, who retired from the Ministry of Defense in the grade of Under-Secretary of State in 1977, revealed to me that gun-camera film had been taken by one of the Venom pilots, and that he was shown this at Whitehall, together with a number of other film clips taken by RAF aircrew. The films were shown at a briefing arranged by the head of S4, attended by the Director of Air Defense, some Air Staff personnel, and a representative from the Meteorological Office. "The briefing was intended to inform those few of us who had a concern with these matters what the phenomena might be about," he told me. "The flavor of the discussion was that it *might* be something obscure meteorologically. The film clips were very brief, rather fuzzy and not particularly spectacular. But they existed!"[9]

THE WARDLE MYSTERY, 1957

On 15 February 1957 a large circular object was seen by independent witnesses at Wardle in Lancashire, which prompted J. A. Leavey, MP, to table a House of Commons question to the Secretary of State for Air, requesting an explanation. Shortly afterward a commercial-type aircraft was seen flying over Wardle, broadly following the course taken by the UFO, and displaying unusually powerful lights. Then a small radio transmitter (Air Ministry issue) was discovered, of the type normally suspended from meteorological balloons. Shortly after this, another piece of meteorological equipment was found attached to a parachute, also near a point on the UFO's flight path. It had been snowing shortly *after* the sighting, yet none of these objects was at all affected by snow, leading to the suspicion that they had been deliberately planted with the object of debunking the sighting.

Mr. Leavey's question was answered in the House of Commons on 20 March by Charles Orr-Ewing, Under-Secretary of State for Air, who replied that the object seen at Wardle was nothing more sinister than two hydrogen-filled toy balloons, illuminated with a flashlight bulb, which had been released by a laundry mechanic from Rochdale. All the investigators were unanimous in their rejection of this explanation, however, and the Air Ministry was evidently less than convinced itself, for on 17 April they sent an investigator to interview the witnesses, *who were told to keep his visit quiet*.[10] And when the man who was supposed to have released the balloon was interviewed by the local press, he said that he had no idea how to fill a balloon with hydrogen nor how to fit lights to it: in fact, he had nothing at all to do with the incident. As Geoffrey Norris, writing in the *Royal Air Force Flying Review,* concluded: "After officially debunking this sighting, the Air Ministry have confirmed that an investigator has been sent up to Wardle. After his researches the Air Ministry still maintain it was a balloon. It is small wonder that the public are both bemused and amused at such complicated events."[11]

AIR CHIEF MARSHAL LORD DOWDING

Air Chief Marshal Lord Dowding, Commander-in-Chief of RAF Fighter Command during the Battle of Britain in 1940, was greatly interested in the subject of UFOs and on a number of occasions made some courageous statements, such as the following:

> More than 10,000 sightings have been reported, the majority of which cannot be accounted for by any "scientific" explanation, e.g. that they are hallucinations, the effects of light refraction, meteors, wheels falling from airplanes, and the like. . . . They have been tracked on radar screens . . . and the observed speeds have been as great as 9,000 miles an hour. . . . *I am convinced that these objects do exist and that they are not manufactured by any nation on earth*. I can therefore see no alternative to accepting the theory that they come from some extraterrestrial source. . . .
>
> I think that we must resist the tendency to assume that they all come from the same planet, or that they are actuated by similar motives. It might be that the visitors from one planet wished to help us in our evolution from the basis of a higher level to which they had attained.
>
> Another planet might send an expedition to ascertain what have been these terrible explosions which they have observed, and to prevent us from

discommoding other people besides ourselves by the new toys with which we are so light-heartedly playing.

Other visitors might have come bent solely on scientific discovery and might regard us with the dispassionate aloofness with which we might regard insects found beneath an upturned stone.[12] [Emphasis added]

I have no hesitation in endorsing these sentiments, based on my own personal studies since 1955, although the subject is infinitely more complex than this.

In February 1957 Lord Dowding wrote to the Italian diplomat Alberto Perego, stressing that his interest went beyond the mere sightings of flying saucers. "What I am interested in," he wrote, "is accounts of *intelligible contacts* between human beings and the occupants of interplanetary ships."[13]

RAF WEST FREUGH, 1957

On 4 April 1957 an unidentified target was tracked at RAF West Freugh on the west coast of Scotland, and radar stations throughout Britain were ordered by RAF Intelligence to keep a twenty-four-hour watch for the object. Wing Commander Walter Whitworth, Commanding Officer at West Freugh, was quoted as saying:

I have been ordered by the Air Ministry to say nothing about the object. I am not allowed to reveal its position, course and speed. From the moment of picking it up, it was well within our area. It was an object of some substance—quite definitely not a freak. No mistake could have been made by the [Ministry of Supply] civilians operating the sets. They are fully qualified and experienced officers.[14]

Wing Commander Whitworth said later that the matter had been taken extremely seriously by the Air Ministry, where a spokesman said that until their experts had a full report, no detailed statement would be issued. *Flying Saucer Review* pressed inquiries at the Ministry and was informed that no final explanation for the radar tracking had been arrived at, although a meteorological balloon had been released from RAF Aldergrove, Northern Ireland, at a time which would have enabled it to have reached the west coast of Scotland at the time of the radar sighting. The spokesman was unable to say definitely that the balloon was responsible for the radar signal, however, which was perhaps just as well since the original report stated that the object, tracked at an estimated altitude of 60,000 feet, was too fast, too large and too maneuverable to have been a plane—much less a balloon.[15]

ROOM 801—TOP SECRET

Nine weeks after the West Freugh report, the *Reynolds News* claimed that the Air Ministry conducted top secret research into the UFO phenomenon at one of its offices in Northumberland Avenue, London. The report stated that on the ninth floor of what was formerly the Hotel Metropole, a top secret room existed—No. 801—where all reports of UFOs were collected and studied by experts.

In the ten years during which the Air Ministry had been analyzing the reports (1947–57), a Ministry spokesman was quoted as saying, they had "something like 10,000 sightings" on file and that although many reports had been "cleared up" there were some which could not be explained. "Nobody in the know," he admitted, "is prepared to say that all reports about these mystery objects are nonsense."

The interior of Room 801 was never seen by unauthorized persons. A large map of the British Isles hung on one wall, the report continued, and on it were literally thousands of colored pins, with the heaviest concentration appearing to be over the Norwich area. At airfields all over Britain fighter planes were kept ready to intercept, and if necessary to engage any UFO within combat range.[16]

Gordon Creighton, the indefatigable editor of *Flying Saucer Review,* had been an intelligence officer at Northumberland Avenue during the period in question, so I asked him if he could substantiate the story in any way, although he was not involved with the Air Ministry. "I was on the next floor to the department that dealt with UFOs," he told me. "There was only one floor above us: that floor was DDI (Tech.), so everybody that went up in the lift above us was from that department. There weren't any other departments on that floor. But I and one or two other people in my department used to have fun when we were going up or down in the lift with a bunch of these chaps, talking about UFOs!"

Creighton learned that the Deputy Directorate of Intelligence (Technical) employed full-time researchers into the UFO subject—a fact consistently denied by the MoD—and that there was close liaison with the Americans. "What I thought was fascinating," he told me in 1984, "was that in those early days I met quite a number of US Air Force Intelligence people, *and* CIA, who of course were deeply interested—always pretended they weren't—and we had *long* discussions about it."

AIRLINER COMMUNICATIONS INTERFERENCE, 1957

On 31 May 1957 at 7:17 a.m. a British airliner was flying over Kent, just south of Rochester, when both the captain and first officer sighted a UFO, which simultaneously cut out all radio communications. The following is a personal account by the captain, whose name has been withheld by request:

I was in command of a scheduled airline service from Croydon Airport to Holland. As we got to a position two nautical miles south of Rochester my First Officer and myself became aware of a brilliant object bearing 110° (T) from north and elevated about 10° above the haze level. We were flying at 5,000 feet above sea level, heading 082° magnetic 074° (T). The UFO was about two-thirds the size of a sixpence in the windscreen at first. It then appeared to come toward us. When it was about the size of a sixpence the object became oval in shape and turned away. Then it became as before and reduced in size to about half the size of a sixpence. Then to our astonishment the UFO disappeared completely as we watched it. We did not see the UFO go, but became aware that we were looking at an empty sky.

We were unable to contact "London Radar" due to a complete radio failure in the aircraft, nor were we able to report to "London Airways," nor to "London Flight Information." Radio failure, especially complete radio failure, is rare these days, and in our case was due to our circuit breakers not keeping "In." A radio circuit breaker "breaks circuit" when the system is overloaded by an extra source of electrical or thermal energy. On this occasion we were not using all our equipment, so there was no cause for overloading. *However, our radio equipment became fully serviceable after the UFO had gone*, and all circuit breakers stayed "In."

Is it too much to ask if the UFO was able, through overloading our electrical system, to prevent our reporting it or asking for radar confirmation? When we returned to the UK a similar report to the account I have given you was made to both the Ministry of Transport and Civil Aviation, and to the Air Ministry.[17] [Emphasis added]

RAF GAYDON, 1957

On 21 October 1957 Flying Officer D. W. Sweeney, flying a Meteor jet on a training exercise from RAF North Luffenham, nearly collided with an unidentified flying object over RAF Gaydon, Warwickshire. The incident occurred at 9:18 p.m. at an altitude of 28,000 feet. After taking evasive action Sweeney tried to approach the object, whereupon its six lights went out and it disappeared. The pilot's report was confirmed by radar a few minutes earlier at RAF Langtoft, when the object was tracked over Gaydon at about 28,000 feet. A check on military and civilian aircraft movements showed that the Meteor was the only plane in the area at the time.[18]

QUESTIONS IN THE HOUSE OF COMMONS, 1958–59

A sighting at RAF Lakenheath on 19 April 1958, when aircraft were scrambled to intercept unidentified targets which had been plotted on radar within ten miles of the base (subsequently explained as freak weather conditions by the US Air Force) led to a question in the House of Commons on 10 June by George Chetwynd, MP: "How many instances of unidentified flying objects had been reported on by the defense services of the United Kingdom during the past twelve months, and what steps were taken to coordinate such observations?"

Charles Orr-Ewing, the Under-Secretary of State for Air, replied: "Reports of 54 unidentified flying objects have been received in the last 12 months. Such coordination as is necessary is undertaken by the Air Ministry. Most of the objects turn out to be meteors, balloons or aircraft. Satellites have also accounted for a number of recent reports."[19]

This was the last time the government released figures of specifically military reports, and even in this guarded reply there is careful avoidance of the words "by the defense services." With one exception (see Chapter 3) I have been unable to extract such figures from the Ministry of Defense. In 1984 I was told, "It is not possible to say how many 'UFO' reports have been made by military personnel since 1947."[20]

On 30 July 1958 George Chetwynd pressed further questions in the House of Commons. He began by asking the Secretary of State for Air, George Ward, what action was being taken to ascertain the identity of UFOs which had not been recognized as meteors, balloons, aircraft or satellites. Replied Ward: "We investigate all reports of UFOs as fully as the details allow, but I am afraid there will always be some which remain unexplained because the reports are not sufficiently precise."

Mr. Chetwynd then asked if the Right Honorable Gentleman was aware that a number of scientific societies were conducting research to establish the existence of flying saucers. Could he say whether his Department had any information which would back up this claim and, if so, whether he would be prepared to give it to these societies? George Ward repeated that the bulk of reports was explained, and only a very small proportion was not, adding, "We think that the reason why these are not explained, too, is that the data we have about them is not sufficient." Mr. Chetwynd persisted: "Is there any evidence to back up the claims that there are flying saucers?" The Minister did not reply.[21]

On 5 November 1958 Roy Mason, MP—who was later to become Minister of Defense—asked the Air Minister to what extent official records were kept of sightings; what departments within the Air Ministry existed solely to collate information on this question; and to what extent this information suggested that some of the unidentified phenomena may not originate on this planet. In a written reply Air Minister George Ward said: "If a report of an unidentified flying object has a bearing on the air defense of this country it is investigated and the results recorded. No staff are employed whole-time on the task. Although some of the objects have not been identified for lack of data, nothing suggests that they are other than mundane."[22]

This was clearly an unsatisfactory reply for Roy Mason, and on 21 January 1959 he asked the Air Minister another question in the Commons: What specific instructions have been sent to the commanders of Royal Air Force stations to collect reports from air crews having allegedly sighted unidentified flying objects; what inquiries have been held following such sightings; and to what extent is there collaboration between the Department and the respective departments in Canada and the United States on this problem? Ward replied that RAF units had standing instructions to report unusual flying objects when they could not be readily explained. Reports which may have a bearing on air defense were investigated, he added, and no special collaboration with Canada or the United States was required.[23]

A sighting by officials at London Airport one month later led to further questions in the Commons. *The Times* of 26 February 1959 reported that RAF Fighter Command Headquarters had described the object as "a bright yellow light varying in intensity some 200 feet from the ground. It stayed in one position for about 20 minutes, then climbed away at high speed." Police, air traffic controllers and others examined the UFO through binoculars. In a written reply on 11 March Air Minister Ward stated: "A pale yellow light was seen by officials at London Airport above one of the runways from 7:25 to 7:45 on the evening of February 25. There was no corresponding response on the airport radars or on air defense radars. The light was not identified. . . . There was insufficient evidence to determine what the cause of this light could have been."[24]

THE AIR MINISTER ADMITS TO A COVER-UP

Desmond Leslie, the co-author (with George Adamski) of *Flying Saucers Have Landed*, is a second cousin to the late Sir Winston Churchill. Dubbed the "Saucerer Royal" because he was well acquainted with British royalty and various VIPs in the government at the time, he had also served in the Royal Air Force as a fighter pilot during World War II. He was thus ideally placed to assess the true attitude of officialdom to the subject— and that of George Ward in particular.

Ward was Parliamentary Under-Secretary of State for Air when Leslie first met him in 1953 and presented him with a copy of his book. I quote from part of the letter that Ward subsequently wrote to Leslie, dated 18 January 1954:

> Dear Saucerer Royal,
>
> Thank you so much for sending me your book. . . . I was delighted to have it. I read every word during the weekend. It is even more fascinating than I expected.
>
> I can well understand why you got so absorbed in the subject. My head has been full of thoughts about it for two days. . . . I was lost in admiration at the immense amount of research you had done. . . .
>
> Let's meet again as soon as possible. There is a mass of things I want to ask you and I should love to see Adamski's papers. . . .
>
> I spent the morning with old Handley Page at his works. I couldn't escape from the horrible thought that all our efforts to fly higher and faster and further are simply brute force. God, I wish we knew how to build a vimana![25] Let's damn well find out. . . .

It is evident that George Ward had become very interested in the subject prior to his debunking statements in the House of Commons. When the Air Ministry "explained" the sighting in 1953 by Flight Lieutenants Johnson and Smythe near RAF West Malling as "balloons," Desmond Leslie telephoned the Air Minister and politely hinted that he was a fibber. Ward laughed and replied: "What am I to say? *I* know it wasn't a balloon. *You* know it wasn't a balloon. But until I've got a saucer on the ground in Hyde Park and can charge the public sixpence a go to enter, *it must be balloons, otherwise the government would fall and I'd lose my job.*"

Ward went on to explain the difficult position he found himself in, along with other members of Her Majesty's Government, and said that if he admitted the existence of flying saucers without evidence that the general public could actually touch, they would consider that the government had gone barmy and lose their faith in them.

Leslie also challenged George Ward about the sighting by Flight Lieutenant Salandin of a UFO over the Thames estuary in 1954 (see Chapter 1) when RAF North Weald had its switchboard jammed with inquiries. He asked why the Air Minister had issued an order forbidding pilots to report such sightings to the public or press.[26] Replied Ward: "Look, I'm trying to run an air force. When a story like this breaks, the poor C.O. is driven frantic. His telephone is jammed with calls and he is unable to get on with the business of running an efficient airfield."[27]

These statements are conclusive proof of a cover-up by Her Majesty's Government, but for what seem perfectly legitimate and understandable reasons. However, insofar as George Ward's reason citing the lack of tangible proof is concerned, there are grounds for sustaining the belief that such proof does exist, even if it has not always been made available to successive government ministers.

3

A MATTER OF NATIONAL SECURITY (1960–79)

Sightings in the United Kingdom over the next few years declined considerably, and newspaper reports became correspondingly less frequent, leading to a suspicion in some quarters that they were being censored by officialdom. Journalist Roger Muirfield, for example, wrote in 1960: "Although I cannot explain why the truth is being suppressed, I am certain it is merely a rearguard action that is being fought, consciously or subconsciously, by those who are responsible for the molding of public opinion. Somewhere, I am certain, the penny has dropped, but the public must not be told."[1]

But Waveney Girvan, editor of *Flying Saucer Review* at the time, was convinced that there was no press censorship as such; rather, the media had become bored with a subject which for many had become ridiculous and no longer newsworthy.[2] These sentiments were echoed in 1962 by Robert Chapman, science correspondent of the *Sunday Express* and author of *Unidentified Flying Objects*. He has assured me that he has found no evidence of a D-Notice being brought to bear on UFOs in the press, and other journalists and editors have confirmed this.

The D-Notice and Official Secrets Act

A D-Notice is a formal letter of request circulated confidentially to newspaper editors, warning them that an item of news, which may be protected under the Official Secrets Act, is regarded by the defense authorities as a secret affecting national security. It has no legal authority and can only be regarded as a letter of advice or request, but it warns that "whether or not any legal sanction would attach to the act of publication, publication is considered to be contrary to the national interest."[3]

The Official Secrets Act prohibits all forms of espionage and bars government officials from divulging secrets and unauthorized persons from receiving them. The Act is invariably linked to the D-Notice system and, since a D-Notice warns an editor that publication of a given news item may violate the Act, the effect is similar to censorship. Is there any evidence that some news items on UFOs have been subject to this procedure?

In 1980 I wrote to the editors of several leading national newspapers, but not one was able to confirm this. I then wrote to Chapman Pincher, the well-known author and journalist who has written a number of books on Britain's intelligence and security services. "I can assure you," he replied, "that UFOs are not classified under the OSA nor have D-Notices ever been applied to reports about them." Chapman Pincher has also stated that none of the world's intelligence services is involved in UFO research, which is completely at variance with the facts, but I think he is right about the lack of D-Notice application.[4] As to the Official Secrets Act, that is another matter altogether, and there *is* some evidence that it has been used to silence witnesses.

The absence of evidence for the application of a D-Notice does not rule out the possibility that official pressure has been brought to bear on the media where UFOs are concerned. Freelance journalist Tony Gray, for example, told me that a colleague of his was once warned off a story by "someone in the government." Although this is only one of several rumors that have reached me indicating that subtle pressure has been applied to editors and journalists, I have been unable to substantiate them. If such pressure had ever been *widely* applied, this would in itself constitute a sensational story that Fleet Street would have lost little time capitalizing on—a counterproductive move as far as the Ministry of Defense is concerned, since they are in my view anxious to avoid any suggestion of a cover-up. Debunking is a far more effective weapon.

It has to be said that remarkably few television and radio news items are broadcast on the subject, however. In view of the fact that the BBC World Service, for example, receives a regular flow of foreign intelligence material collated from MI5, MI6, and GCHQ (Government Communications Headquarters), which has led some BBC staff to suspect that the Foreign Office *could* distort coverage by being selective in the presentation of their own intelligence,[5] the possibility of UFO censorship in broadcasting cannot be overlooked.

RAF COSFORD, 1963

The Royal Air Force Technical Training Establishment at Cosford, near Wolverhampton, was the scene of an alleged UFO landing on the night of 10/11 December 1963. Between 11:30 p.m. and midnight two boy entrants reported that a bright dome-shaped object came out of the sky and went behind a hangar, emitting a green beam of light which swept the area. The two witnesses watched it for about two minutes and then ran to tell the duty officer. The boys were interrogated at length by the commanding officer and fellow officers, and the sighting was actually reported to the camp over its own closed circuit radio.

Flying Saucer Review contacted RAF Cosford, which promptly denied that any such incident had occurred. In reply to further questions the Air Ministry in London admitted that two young students, not altogether sober, had been up to a pre-Christmas prank. When pressed, the Air Ministry said there was to be an inquiry into the incident, since some sketches had been made. *FSR* editor Waveney Girvan asked if he could see the sketches. No, the RAF did not have them, was the reply. How then could they hold an inquiry? Girvan asked. The answer to this question apparently tailed off into incomprehensibility. A few days later Girvan telephoned the Air Ministry again. The "drunken students" had now become "sober apprentices" who had perpetrated a hoax. What sort of hoax? asked Girvan. The boys had constructed their own saucer, and this was the explanation for the incident, came the reply.

On 9 January 1964 investigator Wilfred Daniels interviewed Flight Lieutenant Henry, the chaplain at RAF Cosford, who confirmed that the boys had indeed witnessed a UFO landing which had terrified them. "They ran until they were in a building and could tell someone about it. They were told to 'sober up' but they were not drunk and are quite sane and sensible," the chaplain explained, adding that he believed there would be a security clamp-down on the incident.

Waveney Girvan contacted RAF Cosford once again and spoke to Flight Lieutenant Stevens, who admitted that an investigation had been carried out behind the hangar where the object had been seen. No scorch marks had been found, apparently. Girvan then phoned the Air Ministry and asked which of the several explanations of the affair was to be regarded as official. The spokesman, Mr. B. E. Robson, appeared to waver between "nothing at all" and something that did not really amount to a hoax.

The visit to RAF Cosford on 6 March 1964 by a deputation which included the Secretary of State for Air, Hugh Fraser, an assortment of air vice marshals, and an MP led Waveney Girvan to suspect that the visit was in some way connected with the incident in December. The spokesman denied this, but, wrote Girvan: "In view of the long series

of misrepresentations by the Air Ministry on the subject of UFOs, it was
pointed out to Mr. Robson that the public could not be blamed if the
explanation and denials were received with a great deal of reserve. It
certainly seems to be an extraordinary coincidence that so many of the
'top brass' should descend on what is only a training station at the very
moment that *Flying Saucer Review* and others were applying pressure to
arrive at the truth."[6]

I doubt that the visit was in any way related, since such an investigation
would not have been conducted by air vice-marshals, nor would the
Secretary of State for Air and a Member of Parliament have been present,
in view of the attention the visit attracted.

Another UFO landing in 1963 led to official inquiries at a high level.
A close friend of mine whom I have known since 1952 witnessed the
landing of an unidentified flying object in Derbyshire in September 1963,
and subsequently came into contact with its operators. Four years afterward two men with Home Office identification cards turned up at my
friend's flat and politely asked a number of questions which clearly indicated that they were familiar with aspects of the incident. When my
friend refused to answer certain questions the men seemed pleased and
eventually left. There were no threats; the men seemed perfectly normal
in every way, and there was no follow-up. As in most such cases, nothing
can be proven, but I am sure of my friend's integrity.

Asked at a public meeting in 1963 why the government was trying to
"hush up the sightings of flying saucers," the former Minister of Defense
(1959–62) Harold Watkinson, returned an intriguing reply, without actually answering the question: "Before I left the Ministry I had to sign
a large number of papers promising never to reveal certain facts I had
learned as Minister of Defense. The subject of flying saucers may be
included."[7]

THE NEW MINISTRY OF DEFENSE, 1964

In 1964 the Air Ministry, Admiralty and War Office were unified into
the new Ministry of Defense, largely at the instigation of Lord Mountbatten, who was Chief of the Defense Staff at the time. The Air Ministry
became the Air Force Department, within which was a secretariat called
S4 (Air) that had, among other jobs, the task of handling complaints from
the public about alleged low-flying infringements as well as dealing with
reports of UFO sightings by members of the public. Another department

within the Central Staffs—Defense Secretariat 8 (DS8)—handled similar tasks at this time.

The newly formed DS8 took over the responsibilities of Secretariat 6. "The significant change was that instead of belonging to the Air Force Department it now belonged to the Secretary of State," the former head of DS8, Ralph Noyes, explained to me:

> It gave it a certain authority, and was one of Denis Healey's means of trying to get all information about all three services collated at the Central Staffs. The old S6, the old S4, had had the same uneasy division between them about these reports from the public that the new DS8 and the new S4 (Air) had, and that persisted. It was very frustrating to me, and the head of that other division. We would sometimes say to each other in the corridor: "We've got something here. Is it yours? Is it mine?" And if it looked very clearly like a low-flying complaint—something that suddenly frightened a lot of sheep in a valley in Wales, and was pretty clearly a Lightning [interceptor jet] or something—then it was for S4 to deal with, and I used to sigh with relief and let S4 get on with it, and find out from the unit if a Lightning had been outside the designated low-flying area.
>
> But often enough stuff came to DS8 because S4—very often having received it at the main point of entry—said, "Nothing to do with us. This isn't low-flying. This wasn't an exercise. There's nothing here that we've got any responsibility to the public for. Over to you." So DS8 tended to get a lot of reports, quite often through S4, sometimes directly from the public.

The prime task of dealing with UFO reports and replying to the public, however, lay with S4 at that time, as Ralph Noyes has confirmed. "Does this mean," I asked him, "that you didn't necessarily see the best material?" "It certainly does," replied Noyes. "If by 'best' material you mean close encounters on the ground—I wouldn't."

QUESTIONS IN THE HOUSE OF COMMONS, 1964–66

In July 1964 Mr. A. Henderson, MP, asked the Secretary of State for Defense, Hugh Fraser: "To what extent is there cooperation between the Royal Air Force and the United States Air Force with a view to ascertaining the facts relating to flying saucers or other unidentified flying objects; and what information is now available to his department on this matter?" Replied Mr. Fraser: "We are generally aware of the experience of the United States Air Force. Some 90 percent of the sightings investigated by my Department have had a perfectly rational explanation. In the remaining 10 percent of cases, the information available was insufficient to support an adequate inquiry. We have discovered no evidence for the existence of so-called flying saucers.''[8] Once again, the House of Commons was deliberately or inadvertently misinformed about the true nature of the ten percent of sightings.

On 19 July 1966 Sir John Langford-Holt, MP, asked Prime Minister Harold Wilson in the House of Commons whether, since the Defense Secretary was responsible only for the air defense implications associated with reports of unidentified flying objects, he would allocate to a department the assessment of their wider implications. The Prime Minister replied that he would not. Sir John then added that an enormous number of reports were coming in to the government from people who were not all cranks. It would be proper, he said, for someone in the government to take a serious interest in them. The Prime Minister answered that they were taken seriously when there was adequate information. Many reports were of natural phenomena, and those that were not were balloons, and so on.[9]

In 1984 I wrote to former Prime Minister Harold Wilson (now Lord Wilson of Rievaulx) asking to what extent he was aware of secret studies being conducted on the subject in the UK and USA, citing certain documentary evidence in my possession that I was prepared to send him if necessary. I received the following reply: ''I am afraid I have no knowledge of the matters to which you refer, and I am sorry that I cannot therefore be of any help to you with regard to the queries you raise.''[10]

I wrote a letter in similar vein to former Prime Minister Edward Heath in 1982, and received much the same sort of response. ''As far as UFOs are concerned,'' he said, ''I am afraid I cannot comment as I have no knowledge of the subject.''[11] A letter I sent to Prime Minister Margaret Thatcher in 1985 was referred to the Ministry of Defense, who replied in traditional vein.

THE BRITISH WAVE OF SIGHTINGS, 1967

This was one of the busiest years for sightings ever recorded in the United Kingdom, and the Ministry of Defense was inundated with reports. One of the more impressive cases took place at 11:30 a.m. on 28 April when eight coast guards at Brixham, Devon, reported a huge cone-shaped object hovering at about 15,000 feet. The coast guards observed the object through 25-power binoculars mounted on a tripod, and noticed that it appeared to be revolving. Coast Guard Brian Jenkins reported:

> I could see that the thing was shaped like a cone with the sharp end pointing upward. It was white and shining brightly. It seemed as if it were made of glass or highly polished metal. Near the bottom there was a triangular-shaped opening or door with a white rim on the top that reflected a lot of sunlight. The bottom was crinkled, very white, and seemed to consist of strips of metal hanging down.

Jenkins phoned the RAF station at Mount Batten, Plymouth, who said they would contact the Ministry of Defense in London. He then returned to observe the object and make sketches on his notepad. The object drifted slowly in a northwest direction, rising to about 22,000 feet and about eight miles in distance. And then: "At 12:40 an aircraft with thick vapor trail approached object from NE, flew above it and passed it, then turned and dived and approached object from below, slowing down as it approached until its vapor trail faded, and aircraft was lost from sight. A few minutes later the object was lost in cloud."[12]

The plane was at such a height that it was impossible to make out any insignia, but Jenkins assumed it was from the RAF since he had phoned them not long beforehand. He thought the plane could have been a Lightning, and from the size of this compared to the object he estimated the cone's size to be 150 feet wide and 200 feet high.

Flight Lieutenant David Smith, senior RAF controller at Plymouth, confirmed that he had received the report from Jenkins and had sent it to the Ministry of Defense. Asked about the aircraft, Smith replied: "We would know about any aircraft in the area and don't know about one going up to see the cone. . . . There was no tracking of a UFO on our radar." A spokesman for the MoD suggested that the object may have been "something like the reflection of car headlights or some sort of meteorological phenomena. I don't know anything about the plane that flew near it. I can't comment further."

The Coast Guard Station Commander, Harry Johnson, was not impressed with these explanations. "It's silly to suggest that well-trained and experienced observers thought a reflection of car headlights was a UFO," he said. "Remember, this was about midday. *Our head office told us not to discuss this but did not tell us why.* I don't see the harm in it, and if there is any, our superior officers should have told us."[13]

Some months later investigator Ronald Caswell visited Brian Jenkins, who confirmed that the coast guards had been told not to comment further on the sighting. Jenkins had disagreed strongly with this policy. "As far as I am concerned," he said, "my job is with the coastline and sea. Whatever I might see in the air is not necessarily coast guard business and doesn't come under its regulations."

Caswell also managed to trace Flight Lieutenant Smith to his home, and asked about a statement attributed to him by the *Sunday Express* of 21 May 1967, which differed from the American report previously quoted. "We reported all details," he said. "I cannot tell you where the aircraft came from, *and you will have a job to get anyone to admit that one was sent up*. I understand the UFO was also tracked on radar." Smith then examined the *Sunday Express* article. "Ah, this is dated May 21st. I was on leave at that time." "Then who was the senior RAF controller at Plymouth who made this statement to the press?" asked Caswell. "I've no idea," replied Smith. "We've no idea who this senior controller could have been." Throughout the interview Ronald Caswell and his two colleagues noticed that the flight lieutenant's hands were trembling.[14]

There was another case in 1967 when RAF jets were involved with UFOs, which was investigated by Robert Chapman, science correspondent of the *Daily Express*. On the afternoon of 27 October, thirteen-year-old Timothy Robinson and his family were startled by the roar of jet aircraft overhead. Timothy—a keen aircraft spotter—dashed to the back garden of his home in Winchester, Hampshire. "I saw [two] Lightnings go over at about four times the height of the house," he told Chapman. Ahead of the aircraft he saw a black mushroom-shaped object streaking away in the sky. "It was hanging tail down, not spinning, but going at a tremendous speed," said Timothy. "It was going west, then abruptly changed direction to northwest and disappeared into a cloud, climbing steeply. It looked as if the aircraft were banking to follow it but were outmaneuvered." The Ministry of Defense denied that they had any Lightnings over Winchester at the time, and were unable to explain the presence of any other type of aircraft.[15]

In response to my inquiry as to how many sightings had been reported to the Ministry of Defense by RAF pilots in 1967, I was informed that there was only one.[16] Eventually the MoD revealed that the sighting was made by the pilot of an RAF Victor aircraft on 13 July, but were unwilling to provide me with further details.[17] It is clear, at any rate, that it does not relate to the reports cited here.

The Moigne Downs Incident, 1967

One of the most remarkable sightings of the 1967 wave was that of J.B.W. (Angus) Brooks, a former RAF intelligence officer and British Airways flight administration officer. While walking his dogs on the morning of 26 October and taking a brief respite from a Force 8 gale at Moigne Downs, near Ringstead Bay, Dorset, Angus Brooks noticed an object which descended at lightning speed and then decelerated abruptly, leveling out to a point about a quarter of a mile from his position at roughly 200–300 feet altitude. In his own highly detailed report, Brooks describes the shape of the craft prior to leveling out:

> . . . a central circular chamber with a leading fuselage in the front and three separate fuselages together at the rear. On slowing to "hover" position, the two outer fuselages at the rear moved to position at side of "craft" to form four fuselages at equidistant position around center chamber. There were no visible power units and no noise of applied power for reverse thrust, movement of fuselages, or for "hovering." On attaining "hover" the "craft" rotated 90° clockwise and then remained motionless, unaffected by very strong wind.

The object remained motionless for the next twenty-two minutes while Brooks noted further details. The craft appeared to be constructed of a translucent material, and the central chamber was about 25 feet in diameter and the "fuselages" or appendages about 75 feet in length, making a total length of 175 feet. "At 11:47 a.m.," he wrote, "two of the fuselages moved around to line up with a center third fuselage and the 'craft' climbed with speed increasing" and then disappeared.[18]

The object was hovering equidistant between Winfreth Atomic Power Station, the Admiralty Underwater Weapons Establishment at Portland, and the US Air Force Communications Unit at Ringstead Bay. Neither the USAF nor the Atomic Energy Authority were able to confirm any unusual activity at the time in question. One of Angus Brooks' dogs, an Alsatian, seemed very distraught throughout the encounter, frantically pawing at him and refusing to obey orders to "sit," although she remained beside him. Brooks speculatively attributed this to VHF sounds emanating from the object which may have disturbed her, but on subsequent visits to the area she also exhibited signs of nervousness. The other dog, a Dalmatian, was unaffected by the object, and wandered off to hunt game. Six weeks later the twelve-year-old Alsatian died of cystitis; a fact which may be quite coincidental.

In February 1968 Angus Brooks was interviewed by a team from the
Ministry of Defense, comprising Dr. John Dickison, a scientist from the
Royal Aircraft Establishment at Farnborough, Alec Cassie, an RAF psychologist, and Leslie Akhurst from the MoD's S4 unit. In a lengthy letter
to Mr. Brooks following their investigation, the team offered its opinion
that what had really been seen was a "vitreous floater" or dead cell in
the fluid of the eyeball, which assumed more dramatic proportions owing
to the probability that Brooks "fell asleep or entered a near sleep state"
and dreamed the rest.

While it is true that Brooks had undergone a corneal transplant some
years prior to the Moigne Downs sighting, which might have engendered
larger than normal floaters in the vitreous humor of the eyeball, he argued
in his answering letter that "muscae volantes [vitreous floaters] move
upward and downward and, as the craft entered the vision circle at 030
deg., moved across descending to center of vision, hovered for twenty-
two minutes, then exited vision circle at 320 deg., this hardly conforms. . . ." Brooks was equally unimpressed with the MoD's dream
theory, pointing out that the combination of a howling gale and his dog
painfully clawing him was hardly conducive to "dropping off."[19] It is
difficult to accept that the Ministry actually believed in these fatuous
theories, either.

UFO Traces Covered Up by the Authorities

In the small hours of 6 November 1967, on a section of the A338 (now
B3347) road between Avon and Sopley, Hampshire, driver Karl Farlow
found that the lights of his diesel truck had suddenly and unaccountably
failed. As he pulled up he observed a glowing, fifteen-feet-wide egg-
shaped UFO, which moved slowly across the road from the right, moved
slowly to the left, then accelerated and disappeared. The object made a
sound like a refrigerator and gave off a smell like a drill boring through
wood.

Before the object disappeared a Jaguar car came from the opposite
direction, and its lights and engine stalled. "Our vehicles were stationary
25 to 30 yards from each other," Farlow reported. "The object was in
between us. It glowed in the most beautiful green color I have ever seen.
It was like nothing on earth. . . . I sat in the cab petrified. I don't want
ever to experience anything like that again. This was no hallucination."

The engine of the truck was unaffected by the encounter, and remained
ticking over (perhaps because it was a diesel). After the object had gone

the driver of the Jaguar, a veterinary surgeon, suggested to Farlow that they phone the police from a nearby call box (also with its lights out). The police arrived shortly afterward. "Mr. Farlow was very frightened," said Constable Roy Nineham who was in the patrol car. "The most startling part of his report is that his lights failed and came on again when the object he saw disappeared." The witnesses noticed that there were marks on the ground beside the road, and that the road surface appeared to have melted. The police took Farlow and the vet to Bournemouth police station, where they were interviewed separately until 4:30 a.m. The vet's girl passenger was taken to hospital suffering from shock.

The following day both men were taken to Christchurch police station and were interviewed by a man from the Ministry of Defense. Later that day Farlow was driven back to the site by the police in order to collect his belongings from the truck, and noticed *a group of people investigating the site with instruments, a bulldozer leveling the ground, and a man repainting the telephone booth*. A week later Farlow observed that a 200-foot stretch of the road *had been completely resurfaced*, as if to cover all traces of evidence.[20]

As Hilary Evans, a leading authority, comments: "£400 of [electrical] damage had been done to the truck: nothing is known about the damage to the Jaguar. This detailed case is rich in unanswered questions. Much of it suggests a military device of some kind, but if so the authorities have successfully kept it secret for a further sixteen years! Whether man-made or extraterrestrial, the Avon UFO was clearly capable of exerting some very remarkable physical effects."[21]

QUESTIONS IN THE HOUSE OF COMMONS, 1967–68

The wave of sightings over Britain in 1967 culminated in October when hundreds of reports were made, including the famous sighting of a "flying cross" which was chased by two policemen in Devon on 24 October and led to questions in the House of Commons on 8 November. Peter Mills, MP for Torrington, Devon, asked first about sightings in his own county, and received assurances from Merlyn Rees, Under-Secretary of State for Defense:

> The objects . . . had been proved on investigation to be either aircraft or lights. Of the lights, the majority were the planet Venus, but the source of a few lights has not been positively identified. I can say, however, that none of these unidentified lights was an alien object. There are standing

arrangements for RAF stations to report unusual objects and for the investigation of such reports. I do not think that any further action is necessary.

Peter Mills pressed further questions, and asked Merlyn Rees if he could give assurance that the Ministry of Defense consulted scientists for advice about UFO sightings. Replied Rees: "I can give that assurance. This is not just an air defense matter. We have access to scientists of high repute—they have been consulted on all these matters—and also to psychologists."[22]

Two weeks later, on 22 November, Major Patrick Wall, MP, asked the Secretary of State for Defense what exchange of information or other cooperation was taking place between his department and the official American and Russian investigations into the problem of UFOs. Rees answered: "We are in touch with the Americans on this subject but not with the Russians. I understand the conclusions which the Americans have reached coincide with ours."[23]

While it is true that the British government was not in touch with the Russians on the subject at that time, only two weeks later the British Embassy in Moscow was directed by London *"to further investigate the subject with a view to cooperating with the Russians in observation teams for UFOs,"* according to a Defense Intelligence Agency document released in 1985 (see Chapter 10).

In early 1968 Edward Taylor, MP, asked the Secretary of State for Defense "how many reports of unidentified flying objects were received in 1967; how many of these reports were subsequently shown to have a natural explanation; and if he will make a statement." In a written reply on 22 January, Merlyn Rees stated:

> The total number of reports received in 1967 reflects a wave of public interest in UFOs, reaching a peak toward the end of the year. The analysis of the reports published below shows that, as in previous years, the vast majority were found to have mundane explanations; the remainder of the reports contained insufficient information for conclusive investigation but nothing to suggest that they related to incidents materially different in kind from those that were explained.[24]

The MoD had supplied Rees with a list of statistics from 1 January 1959 to 31 December 1967. Out of 362 reports for 1967 only 46 were categorized as "unexplained" owing to "insufficient information." This nonsense has been trotted out regularly in the House of Commons and has seldom been challenged. A glance at the reports I have cited will show that, far from lacking sufficient information, they are highly detailed and clearly anomalous, no matter what the definitive explanation may be. For the year 1963 only *two* reports out of a total of fifty-one reported to the MoD were listed in the unexplained/insufficient information category. Was there really insufficient information in the RAF Cosford, Brixham, Moigne Downs and Avon incidents, or was the Ministry baffled and alarmed by these reports, preferring to state that there was "nothing to suggest that they related to incidents materially different in kind from those that were explained?"

On 11 June 1968 Sir John Langford-Holt asked Prime Minister Harold Wilson "whether he is aware that under the present arrangements some reports of unidentified flying objects are made to the Ministry of Defense and police reports are made to the Board of Trade; and whether he will arrange that all such reports are made to one department." Replied the Prime Minister: "No, I am not so aware. Reports from any source, including any received by the Board of Trade, are passed on to the Ministry of Defense."[25] The Prime Minister was correctly informed. All reports on UFOs made by the police are directed to be sent to the Ministry of Defense in the first instance, but it is likely that some reports are sent to other government departments from time to time.

In May 1968 a wing commander from RAF Fylingdales early warning station stated that much time is wasted by the Royal Air Force in investigating so called UFO reports, all of which have proved absolutely fruitless.[26] Yet the Ministry of Defense—and the RAF in particular— has continued to take sighting reports seriously, and some of the questions they ask civilian witnesses indicate their awareness of certain patterns to the phenomenon. Among the standard questions on MoD report forms are queries about installations, power lines, and bodies of water in the vicinity of the sighting. (See Appendix, p. 458).

MINISTRY OF DEFENSE COLLABORATION

A number of UFO researchers have approached the Ministry of Defense directly with a view to establishing a degree of collaboration. On 29 September 1967 Antony Pace and Roger Stanway of the British UFO Research Association (BUFORA) visited the MoD main building in Whitehall, London, and contacted the relevant office by internal telephone. They were told at first that no useful purpose would be served by seeing anybody, as a Mr. W. F. Allen, who apparently devoted most of his time to the UFO problem, was away until the following Monday. After repeated requests, however, the BUFORA researchers were granted an interview with Mr. Allen's colleague, Mr. Cassells of S4. It later transpired that Cassells was in fact the immediate superior of W. F. Allen.

Stanway and Pace related details of sightings that they had personally investigated in the Staffordshire area during the preceding two months, which subsequently formed the basis for their book on the subject.[27] Cassells began by explaining the Ministry's position on the subject, assuring the researchers that all UFO reports were treated seriously by the MoD, but that its interest was limited solely to aspects relating to defense; consequently there was no department, scientist or other person in the MoD exclusively devoted to the UFO question. He added that *no person from the Ministry ever made on-the-spot inquiries or field investigations when UFOs were reported*, owing to lack of manpower and financial resources.[28]

Following publication of their book, which they had sent to Leslie Akhurst at S4, Stanway and Pace again visited Whitehall on 20 June 1968, this time by appointment. The interview took place in an office on the sixth floor, and Mr. Akhurst was joined by Dr. John Dickison and Mr. Alec Cassie. (This group comprised the same team which had investigated the Moigne Downs sighting in February. Evidently the MoD's manpower and financial resources had been extended in the interim.) Stanway and Pace asked if they could record the interview but permission was denied as the recorder might pick up certain sounds from other parts of the building which were of a classified nature, it was explained. The meeting lasted over an hour, and "all three gentlemen were without exception friendly, helpful and as frank as I think they could have possibly been under the circumstances." Roger Stanway was particularly struck by the fact that Alec Cassie was able to recall instantly the exact page number in the book at which a certain case report started.

Nothing particularly significant emerged from the meeting. The following month Leslie Akhurst summed up the Ministry's attitude in a letter to Roger Stanway, which reiterated its standard policy, praised the two researchers for their book, but added:

> So far we have found no evidence of air defense implications or of craft under extraterrestrial control. We have an open mind on the possibilities of new evidence and are interested to see results of serious studies such as yours. Your report has been examined carefully and although we have found much of interest, we are unable to find any new scientific evidence in it.[29]

Instances of the Ministry of Defense requesting collaboration from civilian researchers are rare, but in 1972 the MoD approached Derek Mansell, Director of data research for Contact (UK)—one of the leading UFO organizations in Britain—asking if he would be prepared to send his best cases to S4 (Air) at Whitehall. Mansell readily agreed, and was provided with 500 printed envelopes to mail the reports, which were not to be more than a month old, he was advised. The men from the Ministry, Anthony Davies and Leslie Akhurst, suggested that Contact's report forms should be modified in order to keep them more in line with their own pro formas. Derek Mansell told me that an informal "investigation" of Contact was carried out by the two men. "We never hid anything," he said. "I told them all our sources, including the Russians and the police." Mansell has continued to send his best cases to the MoD ever since that time.

OFFICIAL PRESSURE

There have been a number of cases where Ministry of Defense personnel are alleged to have warned witnesses and investigators not to publicize or pursue the matter, although the evidence is far from conclusive in the majority of cases that the MoD was actually responsible.

Following a UFO sighting that was reported in a local newspaper in the late summer of 1974, three of the four witnesses were visited one evening by "a man from the government" who asked them to sign a printed form agreeing not to discuss the incident with the national media. "The man just turned up at my house, showed his identification and asked to come in," the principal witness told me in 1986. "There were three of us that had the sighting, and my little girl. He was not interested in her—just myself, my ex-wife, and my friend, who sadly to say is dead." The interviews lasted a total of about two hours:

> We were interviewed at length separately. . . . We were shown different drawings of various types of UFOs; incidentally, they were printed—in fact all the paper work was printed and not typewritten . . . the papers certainly had codes which didn't mean anything to either of us. . . .
>
> We were then told we had seen a UFO, *but should not tell or inform the [national] media.* He then produced three documents and we each signed saying that we would not. He then put his papers into a black case. . . . I would prefer if my name was left out of it, as I fear reprisal after signing the document.[30] [Emphasis added]

On 23 November 1986 I interviewed the witness in his hometown together with Mark Birdsall, the Yorkshire UFO Society Director of research, one of Britain's leading investigators. We are both satisfied that the witness is telling the truth.

What does the Ministry of Defense have to say about the incident? "That's absolute nonsense," David Ross of the MoD's Secretariat AS2 told me. "To whom else did he report the sighting? It certainly wouldn't come from the MoD. . . . I mean, we do on occasion visit [witnesses] and ask if they can describe what they've seen. . . . On no account has *anyone* in the Ministry of Defense the authorization to say, 'Don't discuss it with anyone else.' "[31]

"Is it possible," I asked Mr. Ross a few months later, "that there are other departments involved that you wouldn't be aware of?" "I would say categorically to that, no," he answered, "because this is the focal point within the United Kingdom for UFO reports so therefore it would have to come through this office. That's why we've always been able to say there is no such thing as a cover-up because everything comes through this office and we know everything that goes on." "Even if the security services were involved?" I suggested. "The security services wouldn't be involved," Mr. Ross replied. "There's no reason for them to be involved."[32]

Despite David Ross' genuinely expressed assurances I am unable to accept that the MoD Secretariat knows everything that goes on. I very much doubt that AS2—the successor to DS8—receives military sighting reports of any significance; Ralph Noyes certainly did not when he headed the unit. Nor would AS2 necessarily be aware of clandestine investigations carried out by the police Special Branch (which liaises closely with MI5) or even the Defense Intelligence Staff: compartmentation of intelligence would take care of that. The now proven involvement of America's Central Intelligence, National Security and Defense Intelligence agencies as well as other official bodies in UFO investigations (all of whom liaise with their British counterparts) leads me to suspect that covert inquiries are carried out in Britain, with few being aware of the fact. If I am mistaken, the only alternative is that people are using false Government ID cards and documents to gain access to witnesses' homes, persuade them that they represent the government, and discourage further dissemination of their reports. This may well be true in some instances.

Joyce Bowles, who claims to have encountered (with another witness) a landed UFO and occupant near Winchester, Hampshire, on 14 November 1976, was telephoned a week later by someone who told her that "the government" was annoyed by the amount of publicity the story had generated, that an official would be paying her a visit and that she should not discuss the matter with anyone. The anonymous caller rang back a little later and warned her that next time "they might take her away and connect her up with wires." Mrs. Bowles said to the caller, in the presence of BUFORA investigator Frank Wood: "This is a free country and I shall talk to whom I please, and neither you nor the government will stop me."[33]

Joyce Bowles recounted this incident on a BBC television documentary, "Out of This World," and came across as a sincere and genuinely puzzled witness. It is difficult to reconcile this story with any serious attempt by the government to stop her talking. Moreover, she was never actually visited by anyone from the Ministry of Defense, nor any other government department, although she did notice strange interference on her telephone for some while following the anonymous calls.

Ex-policewoman Maureen Hall related to me an occasion in October 1978 when she was visited by a man from the MoD who politely advised her to drop an investigation she was carrying out for BUFORA at the time. The case involved the sighting of a hexagonal-shaped object over Chingford, Essex, on 20 September 1978. The man was middle-aged, wore glasses, and produced an ID card. He said that he lived in the Belvedere, southeast London area, but unfortunately Mrs. Hall, being new to UFO investigations at the time, misplaced the man's name and address.

Charles Bowen, ex-editor of *Flying Saucer Review,* once spoke to a senior captain of British Airways who informed him that UFO sightings by aircrews should only be reported to the Ministry of Defense, and that *there should be no communication of information to the public or media.* The captain confided his own encounter with an unknown flying object and added that many of his colleagues had also had sightings. An RAF test pilot—who was a neighbor of Bowen's in the mid 1960s—volunteered a similar revelation, admitting that his interest in the subject stemmed from his own experience.[34]

In 1981 I interviewed a man who claimed to have been working at Heathrow Air Traffic Control in September 1966 when a UFO was observed during the small hours. All personnel in the control tower saw the object hovering at low altitude above the airport, at a time when there were no aircraft movements. The UFO was tracked on radar and its speed at departure clocked at 3,000 mph. The Ministry of Defense was notified, and investigators allegedly arrived on the scene and told the witnesses

that they had "seen nothing," threatening them with charges under the
Official Secrets Act if they revealed the sighting publicly. In response to
an inquiry to the MoD, I received the following statement: "As you are
no doubt aware, the Official Secrets Act applies to the release of information obtained in the course of official duty. However, our records show
no occasions on which the Official Secrets Act has been specifically
applied to the handling of UFO reports."[35] Secrecy also surrounded the
sighting of an unidentified object by air traffic controllers at Gatwick
Airport on 16 August 1978. "The controllers definitely saw something,"
an airport spokesman was quoted as saying, "but they have clammed up
over exactly what it was."[36]

1978 was one of the busiest years for sightings ever recorded in the
UK, attributed by many to the film *Close Encounters of the Third Kind*,
which was first shown in March. Whether this is true or not remains
debatable, but certainly many witnesses must have felt encouraged to
come forward, whereas hitherto they might have been inhibited by fear
of ridicule. The Ministry of Defense received a total of 750 reports—
more than twice as many as 1967—and hints of an official cover-up
persisted. Questioned by a reporter about some sightings near Heathrow
Airport in September, a spokesman for the Civil Aviation Authority
denied that any UFOs had been tracked on Heathrow radar, but added,
*"It's in the interest of national security that not too much fuss is made
about this sort of thing."*[37]

Perhaps national security was involved in the report of a landed UFO
seen by two fourteen-year-old girls at Meanwood, a suburb of Leeds, on
22 February 1979. That evening, as the girls were tobogganing down the
slopes that surround their housing estate, they were startled by an aerial
object which made a loud whining sound as it began to descend. On
landing, the noise changed to a hum which then faded as it rested on the
snow. It was gray and egg-shaped, with two "fins" on either side, and
its size was equivalent to a small car. Frightened, the girls made their
way back up the slope and then ran, pausing near the top to take another
look at the object. It rested on the ground for about three minutes, then,
humming again, rose into the air and came in the girls' direction, landing
once again on a steeper part of the slopes about eighty feet away. After
a few minutes the object began to wobble and then took off.

The girls, Lynsey Tebbs and Susan Pearson, ran home and were immediately separated by the adults present and asked to draw the object.
Their sketches were practically identical. Leading investigators Graham
and Mark Birdsall of the Yorkshire UFO Society visited the landing site

three days later and found—in two places—strange indentations in the still settled snow which were apparently consistent with the witnesses' testimony. Soil samples revealed no signs of radiation.[38]

The same or similar UFO was seen in the early hours of the following morning by ambulance drivers Michael Duke and Leslie Evans at the South Kirkby ambulance station near Hemsworth, twenty miles from Meanwood.[39]

Shortly after the story appeared in the press two days later[40] the girls were visited by "an official from the government" who interviewed them separately in private for twenty minutes and investigated the landing site. The man produced an identity card, Lynsey's father told me, but he cannot recall the name or any details on it. "After he'd finished speaking to them he turned round to me and said, 'Well, do you believe it?' And I said, 'I don't know—I'm a bit skeptical.' And he said, '*I can assure you that they have seen something, that is definite, because the questions I asked them they would not be able to answer unless it happened.*' He wouldn't tell us what he asked them, and the girls couldn't remember when they came out—they were only young at the time," Mr. Tebbs told me in 1986. "My wife and I were not allowed in the room while the interview took place."

The official, who said that he was from a government department that "kept a record of everything" on the subject, advised the girls not to discuss the incident further.[41]

THE HOUSE OF LORDS DEBATE, 1979

On 18 January 1979 a historic debate on UFOs took place in the House of Lords, the first time in its 700-year history that this controversial subject had been considered there. The debate had been instigated by the Earl of Clancarty (the author Brinsley Le Poer Trench). Of the many peers who supported his charge of a government cover-up, the Earl of Kimberley, former Liberal spokesman on aerospace, was one of the most vociferous:

I think the general public should be encouraged to come forward with evidence. Many do not, for fear of being ridiculed. Let them be open; let them be honest; let them badger their Member of Parliament and the government to be open with them and to cease what I am convinced is a cover-up here. The people of Britain have a right to know all that the governments, not only of this country but others throughout the world, know about UFOs.

Also supporting the charge was Lord Rankeillour, who stressed that each year there were many sightings of UFOs, and that the effect on the witnesses was always one of concern; yet this very point was ignored and ridiculed by most governments around the world. As far as the United Kingdom was concerned, he added:

> . . . those who report seeing UFOs are taken to be misinformed, misguided and rather below par in intelligence. If this is so, why has some of my information on this subject been given to me by the Ministry of Technology? Why should this Ministry waste its time gathering false information? Of course, it is not false information: it is data reported by civil and Air Force pilots, policemen, sailors and members of the general public who have all had personal experience which has intrigued and/or frightened them. . . .
> I suspect that the British government do have a Department studying UFO sightings, for why else should they bother to publicly debunk reported ones if they are of no interest to them? Quite apart from the fact that the government have not admitted to the existence of UFOs, these machines are potentially dangerous. . . .

Lord Rankeillour's statement that he received some of his information on the subject from the Ministry of Technology is indeed interesting, and his suspicion that the government has a special department studying the phenomenon (apart from a publicly acknowledged secretariat in Whitehall) is not without foundation, as is discussed later in the book. For too many years Members of Parliament and the public have been led to believe that only a small office handles UFO reports, and that this office is merely located in a department which among other duties handles low-flying complaints, thus conveying the impression that the Ministry attaches a very low priority to the problem.

Lord Strabolgi, representing Her Majesty's Government, insisted at the conclusion of the debate that there had been nothing to convince the government that any UFO reports showed evidence of visits by alien spacecraft, and went on: "It has been suggested in this debate that our government are involved in an alleged conspiracy of silence. I can assure your Lordships that the government are not engaged in any such conspiracy. . . . There is nothing to have a conspiracy of silence about."[42] Was Lord Strabolgi covering up for the government, or was he expressing his own personal opinions? It is my contention that he was not given all the facts by those who briefed him in the Ministry of Defense, and that what information he was given tended to support his own convictions, thus his endorsement of the official line was coincidental.

Although the Earl of Clancarty's motion was defeated, enormous interest in the debate was shown by both peers and members of the public, and all copies of the relevant *Hansard* were sold out. The House of Lords All-Party UFO Study Group was formed by the Earl of Clancarty shortly afterward, comprising about thirty peers, and its first meeting was held in June 1979. Guest speakers at its monthly meetings since then have included prominent ufologists from all over the world, and I had the honor of addressing the group on 24 June 1980. Sadly, it no longer functions, due in part to the unfortunate ill-health of its founder and also, I suspect, to the general apathy that has afflicted UFO research in the absence of a significant wave of sightings since 1983. But Admiral of the Fleet, Lord Hill-Norton, a former Chief of the Defense Staff, has been steadfastly pressurizing the government into admitting that there has indeed been a cover-up, as we shall learn.

4

DECEMBER 1980

UFO OVER SOUTH-EAST LONDON

Walking back to my flat in southeast London on 15 December 1980, my attention was drawn to a bright star-like object in the cloudless sky, which appeared to be motionless at an elevation of about 65° to 75°. The time, I noted, was 4:07 p.m. Realizing that it was in the wrong position for Venus, I considered the possibility that it might have been a balloon or an aircraft reflecting the last rays of the Sun, but naturally wondered if it could have been a UFO. I dashed the remaining distance back home, where I intended observing the object through my refractor telescope and taking photographs and movie film if necessary. I opened all the windows and scanned the sky, but there was no sign of anything apart from a few distant airliners. The time was now about 4:15 p.m.

The following day I received a phone call from Russell Bowie, a *Kentish Times* reporter, asking if I had had any reports of an unusual object the previous day. I told him I had not, but volunteered my own brief sighting. Mr. Bowie then told me that about forty witnesses at the Orpington Hospital redevelopment site had watched a UFO for one and a quarter hours which alternately hovered, moved slowly, shot across the sky, then finally "divided" and disappeared vertically—at 4:15 p.m.

I contacted Peter McSherry, Clerk of Works for Lovell (Southern) Ltd., who was a principal witness, and asked for further details. The object was first seen at 3:00 p.m. directly above the site, he told me, and was apparently motionless. Shortly afterward an aircraft was seen passing below the object, and the UFO proceeded to move across the sky and stop. After a while a puff of vapor emitted from the object, which then began to move slowly across toward the east, where it again remained stationary. Mr. McSherry fetched his 20X binoculars and was then able to see that the object was of an elongated triangular shape, with a reddish-orange nose, silvery body, and diamond-blue rear section, with its "nose" pointing southeast. He estimated the object's altitude to be 50,000 feet, which can only be very approximate since its size was not known.

The UFO then turned over on its axis and pointed the nose toward the west. Another puff of vapor appeared and in seconds it had traversed the sky and returned to its original position directly above the site. At 3:20 p.m. it turned over on its axis again and moved slowly across the sky. By this time at least forty people, including hospital engineers as well as workmen from Lovell's, were observing the object, which remained stationary in the west.

At 3:35 p.m. it turned on its axis yet again and shot off toward the moon at fantastic speed. Eventually it returned to the east where it remained until 4:00 p.m., at which time it turned on its axis and, emitting a puff of vapor from its "tail" section, accelerated at "thousands of miles per hour" and returned to its original position above the site. At 4:15 p.m. the nose was pointing toward the west, but it then turned upward and seemed to divide into two distinct objects which took off vertically, leaving two vapor trails for a moment before disappearing.

Video Film Taken

On 17 December a short extract from a thirty-minute video film taken of the UFO was shown on Thames Television News. The film had been taken in the presence of witnesses at Seal Chart, near Sevenoaks, Kent, and although it shows only a point of light in a cloudless sky, it nevertheless corroborated the sighting. I visited the family who had taken the film, and they kindly provided me with a copy. Although the object is indistinct, the recorded comments of the witnesses as they describe its maneuvers are invaluable. The Sony video camera they used was only 4X power at full zoom, so no shape can be made out. The family told me that the object appeared to divide into approximately three sections shortly after they set up the camera at about 3:00 p.m., disappeared vertically, then presumably regrouped and reappeared as a single object soon afterward.

A few minutes before departure the object split up into at least three sections (Peter McSherry reported only two) which moved around each other, disappeared again, regrouped, then divided and disappeared vertically. This does not, unfortunately, show on the video film, and although there are discrepancies between the two accounts, there are enough consistencies to conclude that highly unusual flying objects were performing maneuvers in a large area of sky on the afternoon of 15 December 1980. Surely such objects must have been tracked on radar, or reported by aircraft flying in the zone?

The Sevenoaks witnesses phoned Biggin Hill Airport while they were filming the object, but they were uninterested. Peter McSherry contacted the Meteorological Office in London and was informed that no balloons were in the area at the time. It was not possible to disclose whether or not an object had been tracked on radar, he was told. A few days after the sighting I visited the London Weather Center, who told me that they had received no unusual reports. I also wrote to the Civil Aviation Authority at Heathrow Airport, and was informed that they checked the log entries for the period in question and were unable to find any mention of unusual sightings reported from any source.[1]

Air traffic controllers have instructions to telephone immediately details of UFO reports they receive to the Aeronautical Information Service (Military), based at the London Air Traffic Control Center, West Drayton, Middlesex. A written report, based on Ministry of Defense questions, is then sent by the originating air traffic service unit to the Air Force Operations Room at the MoD Main Building in Whitehall (see Appendix, p. 458). Although I have been unable to confirm that the MoD received a report on the 15 December sighting (other than the one I sent them), there is evidence that they were very interested in learning more about the incident.

MoD Cons

In late January 1981 Peter McSherry called me to say that a man had phoned him at work claiming to be from the Ministry of Defense at Fort Halstead, near Sevenoaks (the Royal Armament Research and Development Establishment), and wanting to interview him in connection with the sighting. The evening of 30 January was arranged, and Mr. McSherry asked if I would like to come along. We waited all evening but no one showed up, nor did anyone from the MoD contact Mr. McSherry at a later date.

A few days later I had a private meeting with my MP, Sir Philip Goodhart, who was Army Minister at the time, and related details of the December sighting as well as Mr. McSherry's phone call from the MoD. Sir Philip and I had corresponded occasionally over a lengthy period about the subject in general, and although he had never been able to find evidence that UFOs were treated seriously by the government, he liked to be kept informed about sightings in his own constituency. He showed considerable interest in the sighting and was puzzled by the failure of the MoD to turn up at Mr. McSherry's house.

In February I wrote to the MoD, giving complete details of the December sighting, and asked if they could throw any light on Mr. Mc-

Sherry's phone call from the Royal Armament Research and Development Establishment. A copy of my letter was sent to Sir Philip Goodhart. Two months later I received the following reply:

> . . . I have been unable to establish the identity of the man you refer to in your letter and can only conclude that this was a hoax of some kind because the MoD is not in the habit of sending investigators to interview people about UFOs. . . .
>
> As far as your enclosed report is concerned, whilst it is not normally Ministry of Defense policy to comment on the identity of UFOs, the diagram and description of the object are indicative of the temperature gradient associated with a meteorite or similar body entering the earth's atmosphere.[2]

In a follow-up letter I pointed out that a meteorite or similar body entering the earth's atmosphere is always a fast-moving object. The object I had seen for a few minutes was *stationary,* and other witnesses reported that it remained so for periods before moving to another part of the sky. The shape was not consistent with a meteorite, nor was the movement of the object about its axis. The Ministry sensibly refrained from commenting on these glaring inconsistencies in their reply two months later.

As far as I am concerned the sightings of 15 December 1980 remain unexplainable in terms of balloons, meteorites, satellites, rockets, flares, or even remotely piloted vehicles (RPVs). Both the Civil Aviation Authority and the MoD claim that there were no unusual sightings reported from any source, so we are asked to believe that while UFOs were maneuvering over southeast London for one and a quarter hours not a single report was made by civilian or military pilots flying in the area. The objects should have been tracked on radar, unless they were able to screen themselves; not an impossible feat in view of the advanced stage of "Stealth" technology in the United States (and probably Britain) where aircraft such as the top secret F-19 Stealth fighter—which has been flying since the late 1970s—are able to reflect a very low radar profile.[3]

RAF/USAF WOODBRIDGE

Only two weeks after the London sighting one of the most sensational UFO events ever reported by military personnel is alleged to have occurred in Rendlesham Forest, just outside the perimeter of RAF/USAF Woodbridge, near Ipswich, Suffolk. Leaving aside later inconsistencies, the most impressive evidence has been provided by Lieutenant Colonel (now

Colonel) Charles Halt, US Air Force Deputy Base Commander at Woodbridge at the time. His official report (see Appendix, p. 456) was sent
to the Ministry of Defense on 13 January 1981:

> Subject: Unexplained Lights
> To: RAF/CC
>
> 1. Early in the morning of 27 Dec 80 (approximately 0300L), two USAF
> security police patrolmen saw unusual lights outside the back gate at RAF
> Woodbridge. Thinking an aircraft might have crashed or been forced down,
> they called for permission to go outside the gate to investigate. The on
> duty flight chief responded and allowed three patrolmen to proceed on-
> foot. The individuals reported seeing a strange glowing object in the forest.
> The object was described as being metallic in appearance and triangular
> in shape, approximately two to three meters across the base and approx-
> imately two meters high. It illuminated the entire forest with a white light.
> The object itself had a pulsing red light on top and a bank(s) of blue lights
> underneath. The object was hovering or on legs. As the patrolmen ap-
> proached the object, it maneuvered through the trees and disappeared. At
> this time the animals on a nearby farm went into a frenzy. The object was
> briefly sighted approximately an hour later near the back gate.
>
> 2. The next day, three depressions 1½" deep and 7" in diameter were found
> where the object had been sighted on the ground. The following night (29
> Dec 80) the area was checked for radiation. Beta/Gamma readings of 0.1
> milliroentgens were recorded with peak readings in the three depressions
> and near the center of the triangle formed by the depressions. A nearby
> tree had moderate (.05–.07) readings on the side of the tree toward the
> depressions.
>
> 3. Later in the night a red sun-like light was seen through the trees. It
> moved about and pulsed. At one point it appeared to throw off glowing
> particles and then broke into five separate white objects and then disap-
> peared. Immediately thereafter, three star-like objects were noticed in the
> sky, two objects to the north and one to the south, all of which were about
> 10° off the horizon. The objects moved rapidly in sharp angular movements
> and displayed red, green and blue lights. The objects to the north appeared
> to be elliptical through an 8–12 power lens. They then turned to full circles.
> The objects to the north remained in the sky for an hour or more. The
> object to the south was visible for two or three hours and beamed down
> a stream of light from time to time. Numerous individuals, including the
> undersigned, witnessed the activities in paragraphs 2 and 3.

The document was released to Robert Todd of the Citizens Against
UFO Secrecy (CAUS) group in the United States, under provisions of
the Freedom of Information Act. According to the letter of release (June

1983): ". . . the Air Force file copy has been properly disposed of in accordance with Air Force regulations. Fortunately, through diligent inquiry and the gracious consent of Her Majesty's Government, the British Ministry of Defense and the Royal Air Force, the US Air Force has provided a copy for you."[4]

Squadron Leader Donald Moreland, British Commander at the adjoining RAF/USAF base at Bentwaters, had been responsible for securing the document from Colonel Halt, and sent it to the Ministry of Defense. Yet in February 1981 Dot Street and Brenda Butler (co-authors with Jenny Randles of *Sky Crash,* a book which deals with the case) were told during a private meeting with Moreland that he knew nothing about the alleged incident,[5] and the MoD refused to be drawn until two years later, when Mrs. Titchmarsh of DS8 wrote to Jenny Randles: ". . . turning now to your interest in the sighting at RAF Woodbridge in December 1980. I can now confirm that USAF personnel did see unusual lights outside the boundary fence early in the morning of 27 December 1980; no explanation for the occurrence was ever forthcoming."[6]

Curiously, every copy of this letter, made for investigators and journalists, vanished, Jenny reports,[7] including the original which in October 1983 she had left with Thames Television's "TV Eye" team for photocopying, witnessed by Detective Inspector Norman Collinson, a colleague of Jenny's. When Jenny tried to recover the letter, with Collinson's help, Thames Television insisted they did not have it, nor had they photocopied it. They agreed to send a courier to the MoD to collect a file copy.

Colonel Halt's report, it should be noted, mentions a good deal more than "unexplained lights" being seen outside the base, so Jenny subsequently wrote several more letters to the MoD requesting further information about the case, but these were never answered. Neither could Martin Bailey of the *Observer* elicit any more details from the MoD. He was told that they had not received permission to release their files on the case.

Squadron Leader Moreland eventually admitted that there had been a "minor incident" outside the Woodbridge base, but this only involved "a few lights flipping among the trees."[8] He was more forthcoming in an interview with journalist Keith Beabey in September 1983: "I put the events the colonel related to me down to an inexplicable phenomenon. Whatever it was, it was able to perform feats in the air which no known aircraft is capable of doing."[9] These feats included the ability of the object to split into five sections, as witnessed by Colonel Halt on 29 December. It is worth recalling that the UFO seen over London also divided into at least three separate parts on occasions.

News of the Woodbridge incident first leaked out in January 1981 when Brenda Butler was approached by a US Air Force security officer who had proven to be a reliable source of information in the past. Given the pseudonym of "Steve Roberts" by the authors of *Sky Crash,* he confided that a UFO had crash-landed in Rendlesham Forest on the night of 27 December, and that he had himself witnessed its three small silver suited occupants carrying out repairs while suspended in a shaft of light. The craft had remained on the ground for several hours, he claimed, during which time General Gordon Williams, overall Base Commander at the time, had communicated with the "aliens!" Many military personnel were present, and films and photos were taken which were immediately confiscated by senior officers when the craft had taken off.[10]

The story seems preposterous, and yet a few weeks later another in-vestigator, Paul Begg, was told quite independently by a radar operator at RAF Watton in Norfolk that an "uncorrelated target" was picked up on their radar sets on the night of 27 December, but had been lost about fifty miles south—in the vicinity of Rendlesham Forest. The Air Defense Radar Center at West Drayton, Middlesex, was advised of the incident and it was learned that the object had been tracked elsewhere, including RAF/USAF Bentwaters, which adjoins the Woodbridge base. A few days later USAF intelligence officers (probably from the Air Force Office of Special Investigations) turned up at Watton and told the radar men that it was possible they had tracked an unknown structured object that had crash-landed in a forest near Ipswich. Military personnel who went to investigate found the engine and lights of their jeep failing as they ap-proached the landing site, and had to proceed on foot. They allegedly encountered an unidentified object on the ground, and General Williams was said to have communicated with its occupants.[11]

Regardless of whether the latter part of the story is a fabrication, this was the reason given by the USAF intelligence officers for confiscating RAF Watton's radar tapes! The claim of aliens being present has been refuted by General Williams, but he does confirm that the details in Colonel Halt's memorandum are essentially correct. If this is so, then *something* must have landed at Woodbridge in the small hours of 27 December.

James Archer's Story

Both Brenda Butler and Dot Street later spoke with another security officer who claimed to have been present on the night of the landing, and although his account differs drastically from that of Steve Roberts it corroborates some of Halt's report. The informant, given the pseudonym of "James Archer," claims that at about 2:00 a.m. guards at the Woodbridge gate had seen lights apparently descending out of sight into Rendlesham Forest. The guards radioed for permission to investigate but were told to wait until relief guards could be sent to replace them. Thus Archer and another security officer, Airman John Burroughs (real name), were ordered to drive out to the area in a jeep, leaving their guns behind. Since the lane from the gate was full of ruts and potholes, the two men were obliged to proceed on foot. After a short while their radios suddenly went dead. Then they came across the object.

Archer described it as triangular in shape, with three landing legs. It was about ten to twelve feet in diameter and eight feet high, with a blue light on top, red lights and a white light in the middle, and a brighter white light emanating from the underside. With the exception of the configuration of lights, and the number of security policemen involved, Archer's description conforms in some respects with Halt's report. This is important, because Archer's story was given to Brenda and Dot in October 1981: Halt's memorandum was not released until June 1983.

Archer was emphatic that no alien occupants were involved, although he was sure that something was inside the object. "I don't know what," he told the girls, "but the shapes did not look human. Maybe they were like robots." The two men followed the object as it maneuvered soundlessly around the forest, and at one stage got to within a few feet of it. They followed the craft as it moved into a small field, where it caused panic among the cows. Finally, the object emitted an intense burst of white light, rose to about 200 feet, then shot off at high speed.[12]

Sergeant Warren's Story

Yet another USAF security officer later came forward with a story of having witnessed the landed UFO. Given the pseudonym "Art Wallace" in *Sky Crash,* he was subsequently revealed as Sergeant Larry Warren, who was stationed at Bentwaters at the time. Although initially expressing fears for his life, Warren began to give interviews to the media, including

BBC TV, Nippon TV, and Cable News Network of Washington, DC. Larry Warren's story differs in many respects from that of Archer, Roberts, and Halt, but since we do not as yet know what precisely *did* occur in Rendlesham Forest between 27 and 30 December we cannot dismiss his account out of hand. Colonel Halt's document, although written as an official memorandum to the Ministry of Defense, may not be definitive, but it seems sensible to regard it for the moment as being essentially true, if lacking in certain crucial details.

Warren claims that the date of the actual landing was the 30th, not the 27th December. He says that the jeep in which he and other security officers were riding in en route to the landing site kept failing. But the greatest discrepancies lie in his description of the landed craft and the events that subsequently unfolded. On arrival at a clearing in the forest he encountered other groups of military personnel, including RAF officers, and he could hear helicopters overhead. A movie camera was pointing toward something which looked like a "transparent aspirin tablet" hovering just above the ground, about fifty feet in diameter, surrounded by security officers. A bright red light approached from behind the trees, descended silently over the "aspirin" and then exploded in a multiple-colored burst of light. Both the "aspirin" and light vanished, leaving in their place a large domed disk with intricate patterns on its surface. Warren and a couple of colleagues approached it, but the next thing he recalls is being back in bed at the Bentwaters base.

Together with other witnesses he was ordered to see the Base Commander, who told them all that they must not discuss what had happened as it had a "high security level." Warren also claims that his clothes were checked for radioactivity. He learned from other witnesses that those who had been on the far side of the object (i.e. opposite his position) had seen small alien beings. He was also told that false trails had been laid in the forest and that stories of alien *contact* were invented in order to discredit the entire story.

Warren, nineteen years old at the time, later told his family about the incident, as a result of which, he claims, he was given an honorable discharge from the Air Force. In view of the fact that he had broken the "high security level," I find this hard to believe. Although the authors of *Sky Crash* contend that the basic details of his story have been consistent,[13] Warren seems to have elaborated on occasions, and Jenny and Dot have told me that they are far from satisfied with his version of events.

Sergeant Bustinza's Story

Since publication of the first edition of *Sky Crash,* further witnesses have come forward, the most important of whom is undoubtedly Sergeant Adrian Bustinza, the Security Police Acting Commander at Woodbridge. He related his version of events to the investigators Ray Boeche and Scott Colborn on 15 April 1984, and Ray has kindly provided me with a copy of the interview.

Ray began by reading Colonel Halt's memorandum to Bustinza, asking him if it was accurate: "That's about right, because I remember the animals very clearly, because I bumped into the animals myself. . . . For a while there we sort of tried to forget everything, and joked around about the animals . . . but I was kind of glad I bumped into the animals!''

When asked whether he had been picked up in a truck and later met a convoy, as claimed by Larry Warren, Bustinza denied it, but his valuable testimony provides some corroboration for Warren's story:

We were in the alert area, and I was on my way over to RAF Woodbridge base [at around] midnight [date not specified]. While we were over there one of my patrols sighted an object of some sort—he didn't describe it, he just said it was like a fire in the forest area. I notified my acting commander, which was Lieutenant Englund, and he went ahead and called the commander that night, which was Colonel Halt, and he told Lieutenant Englund to check out the situation. We proceeded to check out the situation; myself and Lt. Englund and Sergeant Ball.

What I remember clearly was that when we got there [Col. Halt] pointed to the individuals he wanted to go with him. So we went back to Bentwaters base, grabbed two light-alls and had a patrol refuel them, and once we refueled them we took them out there to see if we could light up the area to see if there was anything out there. In the process of trying to check the light-alls, everything was malfunctioning. When we got to Point A— the sighting of the object—we had trouble turning the light-alls on. Our truck wouldn't run, either. It was kind of like all the energy had been drained out of both light-all units. . . .

We started to search. . . . One individual had said he had spotted the object—like sitting on the ground. We proceeded to look and in the process found kind of like triangular tripods . . . burned into the [ground] at three different standpoints. . . . They were like it was a heavy object. They took radiation readings of the holes, and they got a radiation reading as I recall. Then I recall we were walking through the woods and we came upon the lights again. And that's when I first saw the object. . . .

We got—I think it was the flight chief [Sergeant Ball], and I believe another individual officer. We kept searching the area, kind of like trying to follow the object. And it was moving through the trees. And in the process we came upon a yellow mist, about two or three feet off the ground. It was like dew but it was yellow . . . like nothing I've ever seen before. . . . We kind of, like, ignored it. We were worried about the [other] object . . . to see if we could locate it again, or catch up to it again. . . .

We did see the object again. It was hovering low, like moving up and down anywhere from 10 to 20 feet, back up, back down, back up. There was a red light on top and there were several blue lights on the bottom, but there was also like [a prism] . . . rainbow lights on top [and] several other colors of light. . . . It was a tremendous size. It even surprised me that it was able to fit into the clearing—a tremendous size, and I use the word tremendous carefully. It was a round, circular shape; I hate to say like a plate, but it was thicker at the center than it was at the edge.

Bustinza and the other witnesses were ordered to form a perimeter around the object at about fifteen-foot intervals. After observing the object for about thirty minutes, Bustinza says it took off suddenly. "It was gone in a flash," he said, "almost like it just disappeared. When it left, we were hit by a cold blast of wind which blew toward us for 5 or 10 seconds. . . . It was a really scary feeling. . . . I was just frozen in place at first: my life actually passed in front of my eyes."

Bustinza neither denies nor confirms the alleged presence of alien beings. But he does confirm that at some stage Gordon Williams, Base Commander, arrived at the site. He also claims that photographs and film were taken by both American *and* British personnel:

There was two bobbies there. . . . Colonel Halt approached myself and Larry [Warren]. . . . Was it Larry? I'm trying to remember—I'm not too sure of the other guy's name. [Halt] told us to approach the individuals, who at that time were standing in the grass area . . . they had some very sophisticated camera equipment, which wasn't unusual for the British. . . . [Halt] told us to confiscate the material from the British nationals. Well, we confiscated the film and we turned it over to Colonel Halt and [he] put it into a plastic bag and Colonel Halt said it would be dealt with at a higher level of command. He didn't say exactly at what level or anything. I would assume it went to the photography department on base at the time. It could easily have been the intelligence department as well.

Bustinza claims that two American law-enforcement officers had also taken photographs, but he cannot recall their names. In support of this claim, Ray Boeche was told by a highly placed USAF records management official at the Pentagon in March 1985 that photos were taken "and that some of them, but not all, were fogged. However, our records here do not show the existence of any photographs at all." In addition, Colonel Halt has confirmed to Ray Boeche that a movie film was taken which was immediately flown to the USAF European Headquarters at Ramstein AFB, West Germany.

Official and Unofficial Denials

The Woodbridge or Rendlesham Forest story was first briefly publicized in *Flying Saucer Review* in 1981[14] and an expanded account appeared in the same journal the following year,[15] but negligible interest was shown by the media. Then in October 1983, following release of the Halt memorandum, the story made headline news in an article by Keith Beabey in the *News of the World*.[16] Partly because the story appeared in a newspaper with a reputation for publishing sensational (and salacious) items, the more serious papers, such as *The Times,* lost no time in debunking it. Adrian Berry, science correspondent of the *Daily Telegraph,* commented: "All that had happened was that a United States Air Force colonel at RAF Woodbridge had seen an unexplained light in the surrounding woods. That was all. The newspaper ran its ridiculous story, and two days later a ranger from the Forestry Commission showed how the strange light could only have been the rotating beam of the Orford Ness Lighthouse five miles away."[17] Adrian Berry had evidently decided that the story should be debunked at all costs, ignoring practically every statement contained in Halt's memorandum, in particular the description of a landed, metallic, triangular-shaped object. My letter to Berry pointing out this disgraceful misrepresentation went unacknowledged.

On 24 October 1983 Major Sir Patrick Wall, MP, addressed some questions on the incident to Defense Minister John Stanley in the House of Commons, asking "if he has seen the United States Air Force memo dated 13 January 1981 concerning unexplained lights near RAF Wood-bridge" and "whether in view of the fact that the [memo] on the incident . . . has been released under the Freedom of Information Act, he will now release reports and documents concerning similar unexplained incidents in the United Kingdom," and finally, "how many unexplained sightings or radar intercepts have taken place since 1980." Replied the Defense Minister:

I have seen the memorandum of 13 January 1981 to which my honorable friend refers. Since 1980 the Department has received 1400 reports of sightings of flying objects which the observers have been unable to identify.

There were no corresponding radar contacts. Subject to normal security restraints, I am ready to give information about any such reported sightings that are found to be a matter of concern from a defense standpoint, but there have been none to date.[18]

The Woodbridge case is thus dismissed in one sentence. It is regrettable that Sir Patrick failed to press further questions, but MPs are understandably loath to become too involved in such a controversial and ridicule-prone subject, especially without a mandate from the electorate. Only about one hundred people have ever written to their MP about UFOs. The subject is of little or no relevance to the vast majority of citizens, and until such time as those who are interested or have had sightings start lobbying their MPs, little progress will be made. And the UFO movement, lacking as it does any effectively coordinated lobby in Britain, has not helped matters.

Ralph Noyes, former head of Defense Secretariat 8, wrote in November 1983 to the then head of DS8, Brian Webster, requesting further information about the case. Nearly four months later, following several reminders, he received a reply that stated in part:

> The Department satisfied itself at the time that there was no reason to consider that the alleged sighting had any defense significance. That is not to say, however, that Colonel Halt and the other personnel mentioned in the report were, as you suggest, suffering from hallucinations. . . . What the true explanation is, I do not know. . . . I can assure you, however, that there is no evidence of anything having intruded into British airspace and "landing" near RAF Woodbridge.[19]

So what was Colonel Halt referring to when he wrote about an apparently landed, metallic, unidentified flying object, which had evidently intruded into British airspace? The Ministry simply avoid answering this question directly. In February 1985 Ralph Noyes wrote to Brian Webster again, asking seven specific questions relating to the incident, of which I quote three: "Is the MoD aware of the tape recording which Col. Halt claims to have made on 29 December 1980 (and of which alleged copies are now in the hands of several members of the public)? Is the MoD aware of the cine film allegedly made on site on 29 December? In the light of the answers to these questions does the MoD adhere to its view that nothing unknown or untoward ventured into British airspace?"

A reply was received nearly three months later from Mr. Peter M. Hucker, of the newly formed Defense Secretariat (Air Staff) 2a, which replaced DS8 in January 1985, pointing out that Brian Webster was no longer its head. The questions posed by Noyes were answered as follows: "I can assure you that no unidentified flying object was seen on any radar recordings during the period in question, and that the MoD has no knowledge of the tape recording or cine-film you mention . . . there has been nothing to alter the view that there was no defense significance to the incident."[20]

The Halt Tape

In spite of the Ministry's denial of knowledge regarding a tape recording made by Colonel Halt, an edited copy was released to solicitor Harry Harris in 1984 by Colonel Sam Morgan, former Base Commander at Woodbridge. The tape describes some of the events that occurred on the night of 29/30 December when Halt and others were investigating the landing area and taking radiation readings. A transcript has been made by science journalist Ian Ridpath and Harry Harris, from which I quote the relevant passages:

VOICE   . . . 1:48. We're hearing very strange sounds out of the farmer's barnyard animals. They're very, very active, making an awful lot of noise. . . . You just saw a light? [garbled] Slow down. Where?

VOICE   Right on this position. Here, straight ahead in between the trees —there it is again. Watch—straight ahead off my flashlight, sir. There it is.

HALT   I see it too. What is it?

VOICE   We don't know, sir.

HALT   It's a strange, small red light. Looks to be maybe a quarter to a half mile, maybe further out. I'm gonna switch off. The light is gone now. It was approximately 120 degrees from our site. Is it back again?

VOICE   Yes sir.

VOICE   Well douse flashlights then. Let's go back to the edge of the clearing so we can get a better look at it. See if you can get the starscope on it. The light's still there and all the barnyard animals have gone quiet now. We're heading about 110, 120 degrees from the site out through to the clearing now, still getting a reading on the meter. . . . We're about 150 or 200 yards from the site. Everywhere else is just deathly calm. There is no doubt about it—there's some type of strange flashing red light ahead.

VOICE   Sir, it's yellow.

HALT   I saw a yellow tinge in it too. Weird. It appears to be maybe moving a little bit this way? It's brighter than it has been. It's coming this way. It is definitely coming this way! Pieces of it are shooting off. There is no doubt about it! This is weird!

VOICE Two lights! One to the right and one light to the left!

HALT Keep your flashlights off. There's something very, very strange. Keep the headset on; see if it gets any. . . . Pieces are falling off it again!

VOICE It just moved to the right.

VOICE Yeah! . . . Strange! . . . Let's approach to the edge of the woods up there. . . . OK, we're looking at the thing. We're probably about two to three hundred yards away. It looks like an eye winking at you. Still moving from side to side. And when you put the starscope on it, it's like this thing has a hollow center, a dark center, like the pupil of an eye looking at you, winking. And it flashes so bright in the starscope that it almost burns your eye. . . . We've passed the farmer's house and across into the next field and now we have multiple sightings of up to five lights with a similar shape and all but they seem to be steady now rather than a pulsating or glow with a red flash. We've just crossed a creek and we're getting what kind of readings now? We're getting three good clicks on the meter and we're seeing strange lights in the sky.

HALT 2:44. We're at the far side of the second farmer's field and made sighting again about 110 degrees. This looks like it's clear off to the coast. It's right on the horizon. Moves about a bit and flashes from time to time. Still steady or red in color. Also after negative readings in the center of the field we're picking up slight readings—four or five clicks now, on the meter.

HALT 3:05. We see strange strobe-like flashes to the er . . . well, they're sporadic, but there's definitely some kind of phenomenon. 3:05. At about ten degrees, horizon, directly north, we've got two strange objects, er, half-moon shape, dancing about with colored lights on 'em. That, er, guess to be about five to ten miles out, maybe less. The half-moons are now turning to full circles, as though there was an eclipse or something there, for a minute or two . . . 0315. Now we've got an object about ten degrees directly south, ten degrees off the horizon. And the ones to the north are moving. One's moving away from us.

VOICE It's moving out fast!

VOICE This one on the right's heading away too!

VOICE They're both heading north. OK, here he comes from the south; he's coming toward us now. Now we're observing what appears to be a beam coming down to the ground. This is unreal!

HALT 0330. And the objects are still in the sky although the one to the south looks like it's losing a little bit of altitude. We're going around and heading back toward the house. The object to the south is still beaming down lights to the ground.

HALT 0400 hours. One object still hovering over Woodbridge base at

about five to ten degrees off the horizon. Still moving erratic, and
similar lights and beaming down as earlier. . . .[21]

The duration of the complete tape is nearly eighteen minutes, although
it is evident from the extracts quoted that over two hours had elapsed. I
have omitted the first half of the tape, which relates to the radiation
readings taken at the landing site. Several voices share the commentary,
including Lieutenant (now Captain) Bruce Englund, already mentioned
in connection with Sergeant Bustinza, Major Malcolm Zickler (or Ziegler), Chief of Base Security, and Sergeant Nevells, a noncommissioned
officer assigned to the Disaster Preparedness Operations, who was, according to Colonel Morgan, handling the Geiger counter.

But is the tape a fake? Journalist John Grant traced Colonel Morgan
to the Space Command Headquarters linked to Peterson USAF base in
Colorado, and asked him this question via telephone. The colonel replied:

I do not think it is a hoax. I think the men really were out there that night
and they saw something which frightened them. You can hear their excited
conversations and references to frightening strange lights. The only opinion
I have is that, based on the evidence available, those guys definitely saw
something which cannot be explained. As for them fabricating it all and
putting on an act, I do not think they could have pulled it off.[22]

The witness, James Archer, says that the Halt tape was an edited
version "designed to create a certain impression." Ian Ridpath has pointed
out that the reference to a flashing red light seen at a bearing of 110° on
the horizon would place it in the direction of the Orford Ness lighthouse.
So perhaps *this* was the intended impression, yet it is only *one* of many
other references to UFOs on the tape, and therefore hardly likely to
discredit the complete recording, even if the USAF officers did momentarily mistake the lighthouse for a UFO in their excitement.

Confusion of Dates

Not the least confusing aspect of the Woodbridge affair is the fact that
witnesses come out with different dates. To add to the confusion, Chuck
de Caro of Cable News Network was shown the logbook at Woodbridge
police station which shows that on the night of *25/26* December Airman
Armald from the Woodbridge base law-enforcement desk called the
Woodbridge police concerning "lights in the woods." On the morning
of 26 December the police apparently returned to the site and were shown

"landing marks" by Air Force personnel, who told them how an object had landed there. So was this the actual date of the main event? We simply do not know. The British police may have entered an incorrect date in their notebook, or the witnesses to what seem to have been at least two separate incidents may have become confused about the dates. There is also the distinct possibility that false dates may have been given in order to sow disinformation among the ranks of the investigators. It would be a mistake, in my view, to dismiss the entire episode on these grounds alone.

The Pentagon's Response

In 1984 Chuck de Caro presented the US Air Force at the Pentagon with a list of questions relating to the Woodbridge/Bentwaters incidents, from which I quote, together with the written answers:

Q   How many USAF personnel witnessed the sightings?
A   The number of people witnessing the alleged sightings is unknown.
Q   Did Security Police Major Zeigler [sic] witness the incident(s)?
A   Unknown.
Q   Did Sgt. Burroughs witness the incident(s)?
A   Unknown.
Q   Was there a Lt. England [sic] in the Security Police unit at Bentwaters? Did he witness the incident?
A   Unknown.
Q   What are the current units and duty stations of Williams, Halt, Burroughs, Zeigler, and England?
A   Williams is currently assigned with the Air Force Inspection and Safety Center at Norton AFB, California. Col. Halt is currently assigned with the Oklahoma City Air Logistics Center at Tinker AFB, Oklahoma. Sgt. Burroughs is currently assigned to Luke AFB [Arizona]. The location of the others is unknown.
Q   What unit or personnel took the radioactivity readings referred to in Col. Halt's report? What unit or personnel established the geometry of the indentations on the ground? Where are the official measurements and reports?
A   Unknown.
Q   Were USAF OSI [Office of Special Investigations][23] personnel dispatched to the incident site? Did OSI personnel interview Lt. Col. Halt, Sgt. Larry Warren, Airman Steven La Plume, Gen. Williams, Maj. Zeigler, Lt. England, or Sgt. Burroughs?
A   The British MoD would have jurisdiction for any such investigation. OSI was not informed of the alleged incident and did not investigate or compile a report.

Q   Will the USAF provide a list of USAF personnel who witnessed the
     incident(s)?
A   No, because it is unknown who witnessed the alleged incident.
Q   What are the reasons that Gen. Williams, Col. Halt, and Sgt. Bur-
     roughs gave for not granting official interviews?
A   The individuals have declined interviews for personal reasons.
Q   Are there any photographs, tape recordings, videotapes, drawings, or
     descriptions of any kind in USAF files? If not, to what agency or
     agencies have the files been transferred?
A   There was no audiovisual documentation done.

Cover-up

It is evident from the responses to Cable News Network's questions that
the US Air Force is guilty of prevarication regarding the Woodbridge
affair. In October 1985 I met with the American investigator Ray Boeche,
who has done more research into the case in the United States than anyone
else. He told me that he has had many discussions on the matter with
Senator Exon (Democrat, Nebraska), who is a member of the Senate
Armed Services Committee and who, according to Ray, has spent much
time looking into the Woodbridge case. The results suggest a cover-up.

Ray telephoned Colonel Halt to ask him if he would agree to discuss
the Rendlesham incidents with the senator and provide corroborative
evidence. Halt agreed, saying: *"I've got a soil sample right here, and I
can put my hands on plaster casts."* Halt also stated that he would be
prepared to confirm that a certain captain drove General Gordon Williams,
overall Base Commander at the time, from the Rendlesham landing site
to a fighter plane at Bentwaters with what Williams told the captain was
a motion picture canister of the UFO. The film was quickly flown to the
USAF European Headquarters at Ramstein AFB, West Germany, and
has not been heard of since. The Air Force specifically denies that any
photographs or films were taken of the event.

According to the senator's defense aide, Exon did speak with Halt,
but Ray has been unable to obtain any information whatsoever about the
meeting other than *no comment*, and when he eventually managed to
speak directly with the senator was given extremely evasive answers.
"Has he found out something that's disturbed him?" Ray said to me,
"or has he been told to back off?"

During the course of many conversations and letters about the Woodbridge case, ex-Ministry of Defense official Ralph Noyes has left me in
no doubt that there has been an official cover-up. In view of his long

career with the MoD, which he joined after his World War II service as a navigator on operational missions in Beaufighter aircraft in the Middle East and Southeast Asia, his opinion cannot be lightly dismissed. Since his retirement in 1977 he has pursued a career as a novelist, and in the afterword of his science fiction book on UFOs he sums up his feelings about the Woodbridge case:

> The Ministry of Defense may well have good reasons for withholding information about the Rendlesham incidents. As a former Defense official, I would not wish to press questions on any matter touching national security; and in those circumstances I would not be surprised if questions pressed by others were met with a refusal to reply. But I cannot help feeling that it is something of a lapse from the usual standards of a government department to issue a direct misstatement. Concealment is one thing (and is often justified), false denial is another.
>
> The RAF Woodbridge case of December 1980 strikes me as one of the most interesting and important of recent years, anyway in this country.[24]

Admiral of the Fleet, Lord Hill-Norton, former Chief of the Defense Staff from 1971 to 1973, has also personally affirmed to me that there has been a cover-up on this extraordinary case. In May 1985 he wrote to the Secretary of State for Defense (then Michael Heseltine), asking pertinent questions. Nearly two months went by before he received a reply from Lord Trefgarne, on behalf of the Minister of Defense:

> You wrote to Michael Heseltine on 1 May 1985 about the sighting of an unidentified flying object near RAF Woodbridge in December 1980. Michael has asked me to reply as UFO questions fall within my responsibilities.
>
> I do understand your concern and I am grateful to you for having taken the trouble to write. I do not believe, however, that there are any grounds for changing our view, formed at the time, that the events to which you refer were of no defense significance.[25]

Lord Trefgarne was Parliamentary Under-Secretary of State for the armed forces at the time, and Lord Hill-Norton responded to his letter as follows:

> . . . I am astounded that a serious letter to a Minister from a member of the House of Lords was allowed to remain unanswered for seven weeks.
>
> I am sorry that you take the view that the sort of uproar which occurred in Suffolk in December 1980 is of "no defense significance," because I have no doubt from my rather longer experience that you are mistaken.

Unless Lt. Col. Halt was out of his mind, there is clear evidence in his report that British airspace—and probably territory—were intruded upon by an unidentified vehicle in that month, and that no bar to such intrusion was effective. If Halt's report is not believed, there is equally clear evidence of a serious misjudgment of events by members of the USAF at an important base in the UK. Either way the events can hardly be without defense significance.[26]

Lord Trefgarne's reply was more conciliatory this time, assuring the Admiral that the Ministry "does take the subject seriously," and he invited Lord Hill-Norton to a private meeting. A date was arranged in September 1985, but in the meantime Lord Trefgarne was promoted to the position of Minister of State for Defense, and official duties necessitated a postponement of the meeting to 9 October.

Both Ralph Noyes and myself had briefed Lord Hill-Norton about the subject in general, and Woodbridge specifically. Trefgarne personally flew down to Hampshire for the meeting in his private plane, together with a representative from the Ministry's Defense Secretariat (Air Staff) 2. The Minister was helpful and courteous, Lord Hill-Norton told us, but did not give the impression of having been briefed in great depth about the Woodbridge case. He was aware, he said, that reports had been made of unidentified events in British airspace and that some had remained unexplained, but he was convinced that none of them had ever been shown to have defense significance, including two reports from defense establishments made that year. In response to further questions, Lord Trefgarne admitted that traces of unidentified events certainly occurred from time to time on radar and were recorded on radar tapes. None had ever been considered to be of defense importance after proper study, and none was retained for long: they were costly, and the practice was to recycle them for operational use after a short while. Similarly, Lord Trefgarne said that he saw no defense significance in the Woodbridge case, and only after sustained questioning by the Admiral did he agree that it might be of defense significance if responsible Americans had had serious misperceptions at an important NATO base on British territory.

Conclusion

I doubt if there will be any further progress toward establishing the truth about the Woodbridge incident until such time as all the principal witnesses testify in public, but military regulations have evidently intimidated the majority. Ray Boeche believes there should be a subpoena requiring the active US Air Force personnel, as well as those out of the service, to testify at an open Senate hearing, or failing that a civil suit against the Air Force. But under military law, Ray explains, they would not be required to respond to a subpoena unless Congress itself ordered them to testify. With little or no media interest at the time of writing, I see little chance of this taking place.

In October 1986 I spoke with Colonel Charles Halt, who is currently based with the 485th Tactical Missile Wing. My first question dealt with the authenticity and accuracy of his document to the Ministry of Defense. "As far as you're concerned, Colonel Halt, your memorandum is legitimate?" I asked. "*It certainly is*," he affirmed. He denied that any movie film was taken of the UFO, or that he had ordered Adrian Bustinza to confiscate photographs taken by British policemen. "That's not true," he said. "I suspect time has clouded his memory. I confiscated nothing from anyone—I had no authority to. We were guests in your country. I can tell you that your bobbies wouldn't have probably given them to me if I'd asked."

I then asked Colonel Halt if the radar tapes at RAF Watton had been confiscated by USAF intelligence officers. "Well, I don't know that they were confiscated," he answered. "I do know that they were used at a later date because I was questioned specifically on times and areas of the sky and so on. . . . It's your government's business, not mine!"

And the story of aliens? Had this been thrown in to confuse the issue? I wanted to know. "There's only one individual who talks about that, and I can't speak for him," said the colonel. "I can't disprove what he says, but I can't corroborate it either. . . . *There are a lot of things that are not in my memo*, but there was no response from the Ministry of Defense so I didn't go any further with them."[27]

5

PER ARDUA AD ASTRA*
1981 Onward

Massive power failures have long been associated with UFO activity, and although there is no proof for this alarming theory it is significant that many such failures have occurred when there has been a surge in UFO sightings. 1981 was such a year. The Ministry of Defense received a total of 600 reports, although the actual number of sightings was probably far higher since the MoD, on its own admission, does not receive all of them.

On 5 August the largest power failure for nearly twenty years caused severe disruption to most of southern England and Wales. Two power lines failed within minutes of each other in separate incidents, and senior electrical engineers from the Central Electricity Generating Board were totally baffled. As one official admitted: ''We have never known anything like it before. For one power line to go for apparently no reason would be strange in itself but for two to go separately is incredible. . . . We have no idea what caused the failure.''

The first line to go at 9:08 a.m. was the Feckenham line from the West Midlands to Bristol, at a time when it was working well below capacity, since many factories were closed for the summer holiday and domestic consumption was down owing to the warm weather. Two minutes later the Dungeness to Canterbury line failed and the failure of the two lines caused a third to go because of the sudden increase in demand. Nearly all of Kent, Surrey, Berkshire, Hampshire, part of Gloucestershire, the whole of the West Country and most of South Wales were left without power, and it was two hours before electricity was restored to most areas. On the previous night (4 August) two power lines failed in Holland, plunging a large part of the country into darkness.[1]

There is no evidence that UFOs were responsible for this mysterious blackout, but it may not be without significance that the only sightings reported between 2 and 9 August 1981 were in southern England, if my press cuttings for that period are anything to go by. The link may be

* Through Hardship to the Stars—the RAF motto

tenuous, but we should not ignore it. During congressional hearings on UFOs before the House Committee on Science and Astronautics in July 1968, Dr. James McDonald, the late atmospheric physicist, felt it his duty to report that the great northeast American blackout of 9 November 1965 may have been caused by UFO activity:

> There were reports all over New England in the midst of that blackout. . . . It is rather puzzling that the pulse of current that tripped the relay at the Ontario Hydro Commission Plant has never been identified. . . . Just how a UFO could trigger an outage on a large power network is however not clear. But this is a disturbing series of coincidences that I think warrant much more attention than they have so far received.[2]

THE CASE OF DENISE BISHOP, 1981

At 3:00 a.m. on 11 September 1981 Bob Boyd, Chairman of the Plymouth (Devon) UFO Research Group (PUFORG), received a phone call from John Greenwell, who had just finished work as a disk jockey at a local radio station and had gone to collect his girlfriend from her mother's house. On arrival he was told that his girlfriend's sister, Denise Bishop, had experienced a UFO encounter three and three-quarter hours earlier at Weston Mill, Plymouth. Greenwell had immediately telephoned the nearest police station and was told that they had no procedure for handling UFO reports, but was given local investigator Bob Boyd's phone number. Bob, who happened to live in the vicinity of the alleged encounter, decided to investigate there and then, despite the late hour.

Denise Bishop, a twenty-three-year-old accounts clerk at the time, had hitherto given no consideration to the UFO question, neither had she read any books on the subject. Obviously she must at some time have read and absorbed newspaper or magazine accounts, and this factor must be taken into consideration. This is her story, as related to Bob Boyd only hours after the encounter on 10 September 1981:

> I was coming into my house at approximately 11:15 p.m., and as I approached the corner of the bungalow I thought I saw some lights behind the house. As I got to the back door and could see up the hill behind our house, I saw an enormous UFO hovering above the houses on top of the hill.
> The object was unlit and a dark metallic gray, but coming from underneath the object and shining down on the rooftops beneath it were six or seven broad shafts of light. These were lovely pastel shades of pink and purple and also white. I saw all this in an instant and I was terrified.

I hurriedly reached for the door but as I put my hand on the handle, from the unlit side of the ship, a lime green pencil beam of light came down and hit the back of my hand. As soon as it hit my hand I couldn't move. I was stopped dead in my tracks. The beam stayed on my hand for at least thirty seconds, in which time I could only stand and watch the UFO. I was very frightened, although the UFO was a fantastic sight to see. It was huge and silent. In fact the whole area seemed very quiet. The green beam, which didn't give off any illumination and was rather like a rod of light, then switched off and I continued to open the door. It was as if a film had been stopped then started again. I had been stopped in mid-stride and when the beam went off continued the same movement. I opened the door and rushed in the house. As I did so the UFO lifted into the sky slightly and moved away and out of my sight.

Rubbing my hand I ran in and told my sister. We went back outside but there was nothing to be seen. Coming in again my sister examined my hand but there was nothing there. I went and sat down, and a few minutes later my sister's dog sniffed my hand making it sting. On looking at it I noticed spots of blood and after washing it saw it was a burn. At 2:30 a.m. my sister's boyfriend came in and said we must report it to the police. He phoned the police but they couldn't help except to give us Bob Boyd's number.

On arrival at Denise's house Bob took a couple of black and white photographs of the burn mark, which appeared as a patch of shiny skin with spots of blood and bruising. "It looked as if a patch of skin had been removed, exposing the shiny, new skin beneath," Bob reported. He tried to persuade Denise to go to the casualty ward at the local hospital but she refused. Since the wound was hurting Bob suggested that she immerse her hand in cold water, but that only made it worse. Antiseptic cream, however, afforded some relief.

On the following day Bob Boyd, accompanied by Des Weeks, Secretary of PUFORG, and a nurse, visited Denise, who now appeared to be in a state of shock. The burn mark was worse. The nurse examined it and tried unsuccessfully to persuade Denise to see a doctor.

RAF Mount Batten

On 14 September Bob Boyd phoned RAF Mount Batten to ensure that the Ministry of Defense was notified about the incident. Later that day Denise received a phone call at work from a man with an American accent who identified himself as Chris Bloomfield of CBS Radio. He had heard about the case, he said, and wanted to learn more about it. Denise was rather suspicious and told him only about the sighting, but not the burn.

Bob wondered if this may have been a covert probe by the RAF to check on the validity of the case, so the following day he phoned Mount Batten again to impress upon them the rarity and importance of the case. Wing Commander J. S. Fosh took further details and explained that although RAF Mount Batten did not investigate UFO sightings, he felt sure that when the report was passed on to the Ministry of Defense in London they would probably want to interview the witness. To date there has been no interview.

Who could have tipped off "Chris Bloomfield"? Since Westward Television had been informed about the incident on 11 September by John Greenwell, Bob considered the possibility that Bloomfield had been alerted by them, but a contact at Westward denied that they would do such a thing. So the call was put down to a hoax, perhaps by someone connected with PUFORG who knew where Denise worked. Bob felt it was unlikely that the RAF could have discovered where she worked in such a short space of time. Bloomfield never called again, and my inquiries with CBS in New York and the Canadian Broadcasting System drew a blank.

Convincing Witness

On 15 September Denise attended the Plymouth UFO Research Group's fortnightly meeting, during which she was questioned closely by its fifteen members. The group was impressed by Denise's calm, matter-of-fact attitude, as indeed I had been when I met her in July 1982. I found her completely convincing and level-headed, and can see no reason why she should have concocted such a story. She had shunned publicity, having turned down a Westward Television interview, although she did eventually concede to allowing local reporter Roger Malone to write up her story in October 1981.[3]

Derek Mansell of Contact UK became intrigued with the case and offered his assistance. In December 1981 he wrote to Bob Boyd enclosing a report from a consultant orthopedic surgeon at a leading London hospital (who unfortunately but understandably prefers to remain anonymous). The surgeon stated his opinion that the burn mark had the characteristics of a laser burn, and that there was normally "a 48 hour delay in the commencement of the healing process." This was confirmed by Bob and his group who noted the formation of a scab on 15 September. This eventually disappeared, leaving Denise with a scar which gradually faded, although it became prominent in cold weather.[4] Though faint, the scar was still visible when I visited Denise ten months after the incident.

The pencil-thin beam of light that causes temporary paralysis has been reported by other witnesses, and it is not beyond the realms of possibility that Denise could at some time have read about this in a newspaper or magazine article and then stored it in her subconscious memory. Denise appears to have no predisposed belief in either UFOs or the paranormal, a prerequisite if we are to suggest that a strong "wish-to-believe" psychosomatically induced the scar (a theory put forward to account for stigmata, for instance).

It is unfortunate that no one else saw the object, as far as we know, although the Plymouth group was able to locate people whose pets had behaved in a peculiar manner at the precise location it hovered over.

Does this incident constitute a threat to the defense of the United Kingdom? Or a potential threat? If so, was the Ministry of Defense avoiding its responsibilities by not investigating further? Or could it be, as Bob Boyd believes, that the MoD are convinced that UFOs are not hostile and therefore saw no point in pursuing the matter further?

HOUSE OF LORDS, 1982

On 4 March 1982 the Earl of Clancarty asked in the House of Lords: "How many reports have been received by the Ministry of Defense on unidentified flying objects in each of the last four years, and what action had been taken in each case." Viscount Long, representing the government, replied: "My Lords, in 1978 there were 750 sightings; in 1979 there were 550 sightings; in 1980, 350 sightings; and in 1981, 600 sightings. All UFO reports are passed to operations staff who examine them solely for possible defense implications."

The Earl of Clancarty was not satisfied with these figures and stated that he believed the number to be far higher, but Viscount Long explained that not all reports reached the MoD: "If the noble Earl is suspicious that the Ministry of Defense is covering up in any way, I can assure him that there is no reason why we should cover up the figures which he has mentioned if they are true," he said.

The Earl of Kimberley, former Liberal spokesman on aerospace and a member of the House of Lords UFO Study Group, then asked Viscount Long how many of the 600 sightings reported to the MoD in 1981 "still remain unidentified and were not subject to security, or were Russian airplanes, or anything like that." Long's reply was as amusing as it was unconvincing: "My Lords, I do not have those figures. They disappeared into the unknown before we got them."

Replying to a question from Lord Strabolgi, who had represented the government in the 1979 House of Lords debate, Viscount Long stressed that most sightings can be "accounted for in one way or another, but nobody has got a really constructive answer for all of them." Another member of the Lords UFO Group, Admiral of the Fleet, Lord Hill-Norton, then asked "whether it is true that all sighting reports received by the Ministry of Defense before 1962 were destroyed because they were deemed to be 'of no defense interest.' And if it is true, who was it decided that they were of no interest?"

Long responded: "My Lords, my reply to the noble and gallant Lord—I was wondering whether he was going to say that the Royal Navy had many times seen the Loch Ness monster—is that since 1967 all UFO reports have been preserved. Before that time they were generally destroyed."[5] The Admiral chose not to pick up the gauntlet, but he must have wondered why only part of his first question was answered and the second one ignored.

During an interview on BBC Television transmitted a week after the Lords debate, Lord Hill-Norton was asked: "As a former Chief of the Defense Staff [1971–73], wouldn't you have known if there was information available which hadn't been released to the public?" He replied:

I think I *ought* to have known, but I certainly didn't and, had I known, I would not of course be allowed on an interview like this to say so. So that in itself seems significant. What I *do* believe is that information has come to the Ministry of Defense—probably over a period of twenty years or even longer—which is not available to the public, and was not available to me while I was in office.[6]

On 7 April 1982 another question was raised in the House of Lords, and I had the honor of attending the debate. The Earl of Cork and Orrery asked: "How many of the 2,250 sightings of UFOs reported to the Ministry of Defense in the years 1978–1981 were, and still are, classified for reasons of security?" Viscount Long, again replying for the Government, jumped up and stated enthusiastically: "None, my Lords." The Earl then asked two supplementary questions, one of which inquired into the possibility of the Ministry of Defense releasing reports to interested individuals and organizations. Long said that there was "no reason why he should not come and see the reports. Not many of them come in because not many people actually report sightings. There is no cover-up in that respect.''

The Earl of Kimberley challenged Viscount Long on his reply to a supplementary question he had asked at the previous debate. ''Why,'' he inquired, ''had he said that the figures had got lost on the way to the Ministry, whereas today he says that they are there and available for anyone to see? Can he therefore place them in the Library for all of us to see?'' Long replied that he would look into the possibility, and added: ''I should like all of your Lordships to see them in the Library, if possible.'' (This has yet to happen.)

Lord Shinwell asked if it was possible ''that all the information is well known to the Ministry of Defense, but that for diplomatic and other reasons it is not prepared to make an announcement.'' Long replied that the Ministry was not prepared to do so ''because it has not got the facts to make an announcement with authority behind it.''

Lord Beswick pointed out that the question on the Order Paper referred to 2,250 sightings, yet ''the noble Viscount says that there are very few sightings reported to the Ministry of Defense. Does this mean that the figure in the Question is incorrect?'' Long explained that this was on the original assumption that there were probably many sightings that were not reported to the Ministry, but after another question by Lord Beswick he confirmed that the figure of 2,250 sightings was correct.

An amusing exchange followed:

Viscount St. Davids: My Lords, has anybody yet found an empty beer can marked, ''Made in Centaurus,'' or any similar object? Until they have, will the Ministry deal with these matters with very considerable skepticism, please?

Viscount Long: My Lords, I am not the Minister for conservation, if it is a question of beer cans.

Lord Morris: My Lords, if something is said to be unidentified, how can it possibly be said to exist?

Viscount Long: A very good question, my Lords.

Lord Leatherland: My Lords, can the Minister tell us whether any of the unidentified flying objects are Ministers who are fleeing from the Cabinet just now?

Viscount Long: No, my Lords.

Finally, the Earl of Clancarty asked about an alleged MoD document published in 1978 in which under the heading ''Contacts'' eighteen names are listed, and alongside each name is given the hometown of the witness, plus dates and times. The document had supposedly been distributed to other government departments, as well as to the North American Aerospace Defense Command (NORAD) and the CIA. Replied Viscount Long: "Yes, my Lords, I have the document here, and it has nothing to do with the Ministry of Defense. It is made up to look rather like a Christmas menu. Its existence in the Ministry of Defense has been denied on television. Someone else has made it up."[7]

And someone else *had* made it up, in my opinion: the document is a forgery designed to discredit the subject. Of the eighteen names listed in the document, three are stated to be from London. Of those three, two are not listed in the current telephone directory, and the third—D. M. Smith, London (SW)—has no less than twelve entries for SW London alone: a convenient choice of name indeed. Similarly, another very common name—S.D.D. Patel of Southall, Middlesex—has at least twelve entries under "S. D. Patel" alone.[8]

RAF/USAF UPPER HEYFORD, 1983

On 15 March 1983 an unidentified object, described as a "primary target" by a US Air Force air traffic controller at Upper Heyford, Oxfordshire, was tracked from about 5:00 p.m. to 9:15 p.m., and was seen by a number of civilians in Berkshire. The air traffic controller, Sergeant Byrd Cormier, was quoted as having said: "This is a primary target but we have not been able to identify it, and do not have radio contact with it." However, according to air traffic controller Corporal Candellin at RAF Brize Norton, RAF radar was unable to pick up the object. Squadron Leader Hayes of RAF Benson said they had no contact with it either.[9]

I thought the report was sufficiently interesting to warrant a follow-up, and I began by writing to the Civil Aviation Authority at Heathrow Airport and to the Ministry of Defense. My letter to the CAA was referred to the Airspace Utilization Section of the National Air Services (a joint CAA/MoD service) in Uxbridge, Middlesex, who informed me that the MoD would be dealing with my inquiry. In due course I received their reply:

I have been informed that the radar at Upper Heyford did not track an unidentified target on that date. The events of 15 March were as follows:
Just after dusk, a local reporter for the *Reading Evening Post* telephoned the tower at Upper Heyford and asked if they could see "lights" at the opposite side of the airfield. The controller's assistant, after checking, told the reporter that the duty crew could indeed see the "lights" and that they

did not know what they were but could have been some airfield lights, traffic within the airfield or traffic outside the airfield. The conversation then ended.[10]

I immediately contacted the *Reading Evening Post* reporter, Kevin Connolly, and told him what the MoD had said. He insisted that the story as it appeared in the paper was accurate, and was annoyed that the MoD had misrepresented his report.

Letters that I sent to Squadron Leader Hayes at RAF Benson and Corporal Candellin at RAF Brize Norton were ignored, despite reminders. Three letters I sent to Sergeant Cormier at Upper Heyford went unanswered, but the second one was returned to me from the head post office in Oxford, marked "Addressee Unknown—Return to Sender." A phone call to Air Traffic Control at USAF Upper Heyford soon established that Sergeant Cormier *was* employed there, but that he was off-duty at the time. I therefore sent the returned letter back to Oxford and asked that it be delivered as addressed. In July 1983 I finally received a reply from Upper Heyford, not from Sergeant Cormier but the Chief of Public Affairs:

> I have been asked to respond to your letter 2 May concerning the alleged sighting of an unidentified target on our radar.
> We have not taken any further steps in identifying the target to which you refer. Our air traffic controllers frequently receive radar returns (or targets) on vehicles on the ground and weather fronts. I hope this clarifies the situation.[11]

Needless to say, this did not clarify the situation. First of all, the MoD letter specifically states that Upper Heyford did not track an unidentified target, while the USAF concede that something was tracked but that it was not anomalous. Secondly, a UFO had been seen in Hungerford, described as a slow-moving brilliant white light by the witness, which dimmed and disappeared at about 9:15 p.m., and Upper Heyford had confirmed to the *Reading Evening Post* that they had tracked an unknown object over Berkshire from about 5:00 p.m. to 9:30 p.m. on their battle radar.

THE CLOSE ENCOUNTER CASE OF ALFRED BURTOO,

1983

The remarkable story of Alfred Burtoo's alleged close encounter beside the Basingstoke Canal in Aldershot, Hampshire, during the small hours of 12 August 1983, is a fisherman's tale with a difference: the one that got away was a flying saucer—complete with little "green" men. If the witness was not lying—and I for one am convinced he was not—we are presented with an important and highly detailed account which may teach us a great deal about the UFO phenomenon, irrespective of what interpretation we choose to place on it. We may also come to understand more of the reasons why the authorities are anxious to play down the subject.

Background

Because of its many military establishments Aldershot is known as "The Home of the British Army," and Alfred Burtoo himself had an Army background, having served in the Queen's Royal Regiment in 1924 and the Hampshire Regiment during World War II. Well known as a local historian, he had in his time worked as a farmer and gardener, and while living in the Canadian outback hunted bear and fought wolves. Mr. Burtoo told me that he was afraid of nothing, and regarding his encounter, which would have terrified most people, said: "What did I have to fear? I'm seventy-eight now and haven't got much to lose." Prior to his experience he had read no books or magazines on the subject of UFOs, which held no interest for him, yet much of what he claimed has been corroborated by other witnesses.

Alfred Burtoo was a keen and experienced fisherman, and since the weather report for 11/12 August predicted a warm, fine night, he set off from his home in North Town, Aldershot, at 12:15 a.m., accompanied by his dog Tiny. On reaching Government Road he encountered a Ministry of Defense policeman on his beat, and after a brief chat headed toward his selected fishing site, about 115 yards north of the Gasworks Bridge on Government Road. He undid his fishing rod holdall and took out the bottom joint of his fishing umbrella, pushed it into the soil, and tied the dog to it. While unpacking his tackle box he heard the gong at Buller Barracks strike one o'clock. He set up the rod rests, cast out his tackle and then sat down watching the water for fish movements.

The Encounter

"After about fifteen minutes," Mr. Burtoo told me, "I decided to have a cup of tea, which I poured from my thermos. I stood up to ease my legs and was putting the cup to my mouth when I saw a vivid light coming toward me from the south, which is over North Town. It wavered over the railway line and then came on again, then settled down. The vivid light went out, though I could still see a light through the boughs of the trees. I thought, well that can't be an airplane; it's too low, because it was at about 300 feet.

"During this time I had set the cup down on the tackle box and lit a cigarette, and while smoking it my dog began to growl. It was then that I saw two 'forms' coming toward me, and when they were within five feet of me they just stopped and looked at me, and I at them, for a good ten or fifteen seconds." Tiny, an obedient dog, had stopped growling by this time, on her master's command.

"They were about four feet high, dressed in pale green coveralls from head to foot, and they had helmets of the same color with a visor that was blacked out," Mr. Burtoo said. "Then the one on the right beckoned me with his right forearm and turned away, still waving its arm. I took it that he wished me to follow, which I did. He moved off and I fell in behind him, and the chap that was on the left fell in behind me. We walked along the towpath until we got to the railings by the canal bridge. The 'form' in front of me went through the railings, while I went over the top, and we crossed Government Road then went down on the footpath.

The Craft

"Going around a slight left-hand bend I saw a large object, about 40 to 45 feet across, standing on the towpath, with about 10 to 15 feet of it over the bank on the left of the path. And I thought, Christ, what the hell's that?—didn't think about UFOs at the time. When we got down there this 'form' in front of me went up the steps and I followed. The steps were off-line to the towpath and we had to step onto the grass to go up them." Portholes were set in the hull, and the object rested on two ski type runners.

"Going in the door, the corners weren't sharp, they were rounded off. We went into this octagonal room. The 'form' in front of me crossed over the room, and I heard a sound as if a sliding door was being opened and closed. I stood in the room to the right of the door, and the 'form'

that had walked behind me stood just inside, between me and the door.
I don't know whether it was to stop me going out or not. . . .

"I stood there a good ten minutes, taking in everything I could see.
The walls, the floor and the ceiling were all black, and looked to me like
unfinished metal, whereas the outside looked like burnished aluminum.
I did not see any sign of nuts or bolts, nor did I see any seams where
the object had been put together. What did interest me most of all was
a shaft that rose up from the floor to the ceiling.[12] The shaft was about
four feet in circumference, and on the right-hand side of it was a Z-
shaped handle. On either side of that stood two 'forms' similar to those
that walked along the towpath with me.

"All of a sudden a voice said to me, *'Come and stand under the amber
light.'* I could not see any amber light until I took a step to my right,
and there it was way up on the wall just under the ceiling. I stood there
for about five minutes, then a voice said, *'What is your age?'* I said, 'I
shall be seventy-eight next birthday.' And after a while I was asked to
turn around, which I did, facing the wall. After about five minutes he
said to me, *'You can go. You are too old and infirm for our purpose.'*

"I left the object, and while walking down the steps I used the handrail
and found it had two joints in it, so I came to the conclusion it was
telescopic. I walked along the towpath to about halfway between the
object and the canal bridge, stopped, and looked back and noticed that
the dome of the object looked very much like an oversized chimney cowl,
and that it was revolving anticlockwise.

"I then walked on to the spot where I had left my dog and fishing
tackle, and the first thing I did when I got there was to pick up my cold
cup of tea and drink it. And then I heard this whining noise, just as if
an electric generator was starting up, and this thing lifted off and the
bright light came on again. It was so bright that I could see my fishing
float in the water 6 feet away from the opposite bank of the canal, and
the thin iron bars on the canal bridge. The object took off at a very high
speed, out over the military cemetery in the west, and then a little later
I saw the light going over the Hog's Back and out of sight. This was
around 2:00 a.m."

Mr. Burtoo settled down to wait for dawn, which came at 3:30 a.m.,
and then, he told me, "I got into what I had come out for—the fishing!"
Incredible though it may seem, he did not feel inclined to report his
experience to anyone at the time. He sat there fishing until 10 o'clock in
the morning, at which time two Ministry of Defense mounted policemen
rode up to him. "Any luck, mate?" one of them asked. "Yes," replied

Mr. Burtoo. "I've had three roach, five rudd, a tench of 2½ pounds, and lost a big carp which took me into the weeds." He then started to tell them about the UFO that he had seen, and one of them said, "Yes, I dare say you did see that UFO. I expect they were checking on our military installations."

Was this a tongue-in-cheek comment to placate the old boy? At that moment, anyway, a man from the canal lock yard came along and told the MoD policemen that horses were not allowed on the towpath, and so the conversation was cut short. Mr. Burtoo continued fishing until 12:30 p.m., and returned home at 1:00 p.m. He told his wife and a friend of hers that he had seen a UFO, but refrained from telling them that he had been taken on board. "I knew the wife would say, 'No more fishing for you, old man!' "

No Witnesses

Alfred Burtoo did not return to the landing site until two days later, when he noticed that the foliage between the canal and the towpath was in disarray. Unfortunately, no photos or soil samples were taken. Mr. Burtoo feels that someone in the guard hut of the nearby Royal Electrical and Mechanical Engineers workshops must have seen or heard something, but checks by investigator Omar Fowler drew a blank. He was also unable to trace the two mounted policemen. And the occupants of a bungalow near the canal lock beside Gasworks Bridge were away at the time.

Throughout his experience Mr. Burtoo was hoping that a train would cross the railway bridge (Aldershot to Waterloo main line) which is about 100 yards to the south of the landing site, but there was none, at least, not while he was outside the craft. But even if a train had gone by it is doubtful if anyone would have noticed the object except at those times when it was at its most brilliant, i.e. during landing and takeoff. No cars were seen on either Government Road or Camp Farm Road, which runs beside the Basingstoke Canal at the spot where Mr. Burtoo was fishing, nor have any witnesses come forward.

Publicity

The story of Alfred Burtoo's encounter made headline news in the local paper two months later, as a result of his having written to the *Aldershot News* initially inquiring if anyone had reported an unusual light at the time of the incident.[13] The paper then notified Omar Fowler, Chairman and Investigations Coordinator of the Surrey Investigation Group on Aerial Phenomena (SIGAP), who subsequently interviewed Mr. Burtoo in October. My first interview with the witness took place the following month, in the presence of local reporter Debbie Collins. The *Aldershot News* published our positive findings, and this attracted the attention of America's largest-selling tabloid, the *National Enquirer*, which ran a story on the case in 1984.[14]

Details of the Craft

Mr. Burtoo told me that the shape of the central room was octagonal and the ceiling very low. The floor appeared to be covered with a soft material of some kind because he was unable to hear his footsteps. The internal lighting did not appear to emanate from any particular source, with the exception of the beam of amber light underneath which he was asked to stand. The lighting in general was rather dim. There were no dials, controls, seats, or other objects seen, apart from the central column with its Z-shaped handle.

Mr. Burtoo said that the temperature inside the craft was a little warmer than outside, which would make it about 65° F. He noticed a faint smell similar to that of "decaying meat." If there is any truth to some of the more outlandish hypotheses about the motives of UFO operators, it is perhaps just as well that Mr. Burtoo was found to be too old and infirm for their purpose!

The Beings

The occupants moved like human beings, although they walked with a rather stiff gait, Mr. Burtoo explained to me. No facial features could be detected since these were covered by the visors. The pale-green one-piece suits also covered the hands and feet, and appeared to be molded onto their thin bodies "like plastic." Mr. Burtoo did not notice if the gloves covered fingers. There were no belts, zippers, buttons or fasteners. All four beings were of the same size and unusually thin shape. Had any females been present, Mr. Burtoo felt sure he would not have failed to have noticed!

The beings spoke in a kind of "singsong" accent, similar to "a mixture of Chinese and Russian." Mr. Burtoo, in fact, was convinced that they originated here on earth. "I myself do not think they come from outer space,'' he said, ''for we are told by scientists that this planet is the only one with water. If that is the case, how can they survive?''

I asked Mr. Burtoo why on earth he refrained from asking any questions: surely that would be the first thing to do in such a situation? He explained that he simply did not feel it was the right thing to do, as he was anxious to avoid causing offense. As to his ''rejection,'' which he found mildly disappointing, he attributed this to his bronchial and arterial problems, and thought that the amber scanning device (if that is what it was) detected the plastic replacement(s) following an operation for arteriosclerosis.

Alfred Burtoo suffered none of the side effects sometimes reported by close encounter witnesses, such as temporary paralysis, nausea, diarrhea, skin disorders, eye irritation, and so on; nor is he aware of any amnesia or time lapse. But he told me that he did feel ''different'' after the experience. He ate little for a while, resulting in some loss of weight, and felt less inclined to go out. He also found difficulty getting to sleep, due to continually turning the events over in his mind. But he had few regrets about his extraordinary experience, which in my opinion ranks as one of the most convincing close encounter cases I have investigated.

''Until I had this encounter with the UFO,'' he told me, ''I always took the talk about them with a pinch of salt, but now I know they are a fact. During the time I was with them I felt no fear, only curiosity, nor were they hostile toward me nor I to them. My only regret about the whole affair is that I did not have another person along with me to see and experience something that I did not believe until it happened to me, and I think myself lucky that I am here today to speak about it, for I am sure that these men were out to abduct some person, and that person could have been me. But at the same time I will say that it was the greatest experience of my life.''

Alfred Burtoo died on 31 August 1986, aged eighty. Mindful of the possibility that he had finally confessed the story to be a hoax, I wrote to his wife Marjorie and asked if this was so. ''It was not a hoax,'' she replied. ''What Alf told you was the absolute truth. My friend who was with me when Alf came home can verify what he said. He looked absolutely shaken and he told both of us about his experience that he had with the UFO. . . . He was just like a man that had seen a miracle happen and we knew he was telling the truth because no one could believe otherwise if they had heard him and saw him that morning. . . . My husband was not a man who believed in fantasies or had hallucinations.

He was down to earth, and you can take it from me that Alf never changed his mind on the story of what he had seen and experienced.''

But the Ministry of Defense remains unmoved. ''I was interested to see the report of Mr. Burtoo's alleged encounter,'' wrote Peter Hucker of Secretariat (Air Staff) 2a. ''We have no record of corresponding reports which might support this story. There was certainly no report submitted to us by the MoD police concerning the incident. . . . MoD interest in the subject is limited to those sightings which are directly relevant to the air defense of the UK. . . . The majority of reports received here are . . . often weeks old, and we simply cannot devote public funds to the detailed investigation of such sightings when no threat to national defense has been demonstrated.''[15]

THE MoD RELEASES SOME UFO REPORTS

In 1984 the Ministry of Defense released sixteen of its reports on UFO sightings to the British UFO Research Association (BUFORA), due largely to the initiative of the now defunct House of Lords UFO Study Group. Although this was an encouraging step forward, the reports (all of sightings in Wales) lack crucial information and the final sections containing the results of the MoD's investigations have been excised. The MoD had previously refused to release such reports, even in truncated form: ''. . . publication would involve much editorial work both to preserve the anonymity and privacy of the people who have written to the Department and also to delete any references to classified subjects. . . . The Ministry of Defense has not the resources to undertake this editing at present and there is no guarantee that it will be undertaken in the future.''[16]

However, an MoD spokesman told Martin Bailey of the *Observer* that they were now willing to ''consider providing reports on specific incidents to serious inquirers.''[17] A few more innocuous reports have since been released, such as those obtained by one of Britain's leading groups, the Yorkshire UFO Society. There is little evidence that these (as well as the Welsh reports) were investigated thoroughly, beyond ensuring that no defense implications were involved. This, after all, is where the Ministry's primary responsibility lies, as they have repeatedly reminded me.

The Ministry's approach is curiously ambivalent. They seem to be saying that their main concern is with unidentified flying objects that are of a decidedly terrestrial origin, since anomalous UFOs have demonstrated no threat. A sighting of Soviet MiG-25 jets reported by civilian witnesses over Bognor, for example, would certainly be of considerable interest, not to say embarrassment, to the MoD. But is this why they continue to monitor the UFO phenomenon? Hardly. The defense of our country would be in a sorry state if we had to rely on civilians for sightings of potential enemy aircraft. It may have helped in the last war, but it would be of little use today. Our radar systems are now so sophisticated that they can track incoming aircraft from a distance of 600 miles over the horizon, a facility currently being improved to the extent that an aircraft taking off thousands of miles from our shores will immediately be detected. In addition, radar is linked all over the country by microwave to a large computer which can "clean up" unwanted signals such as "ground clutter" and weather, above or below a selected height band. We also have the Ballistic Missile Early Warning System (BMEWS), based at Fylingdales, Yorkshire, operated jointly by the RAF and a detachment of the US Strategic Air Command; airborne early warning radar (AWACS), and a host of American satellites to warn us of an impending invasion.

It therefore seems obvious that the MoD need to receive sighting reports of *anomalous* UFOs from the public which could be of defense significance. Yet how does one define a defense threat in this context? We already have a multitude of reports involving interference with communications and power systems, temporary paralysis and physical damage (such as the Denise Bishop case), and abductions (Alfred Burtoo, for instance). Do these not constitute a defense threat?

FURTHER QUESTIONS IN THE COMMONS

On 9 March 1984 Sir Patrick Wall, MP, asked the Secretary of State for Defense "how many alleged landings by unidentified flying objects have been made in 1980, 1981, 1982 and 1983, respectively; and how many have been investigated by his Department's personnel; how many unexplained sightings there have been in 1980, 1981, 1982 and 1983, respectively; and which of these had been traced by radar and with what result."[18] John Lee, Defense Under-Secretary for Procurement, replied five days later in the House of Commons:

> For the years in question, the Ministry of Defense received the following numbers of reports of sightings of flying objects which the observer could not identify: 350, 600, 250, and 390. Reports of alleged landings are not separately identified. The Department was satisfied that none of these reports was of any defense significance and, in such cases, does not maintain records of the extent of its investigations.[19]

John Lee completely ignored the question of radar traces, but six weeks later Sir Patrick Wall focused on this issue when he asked the Secretary of State for Defense whether there had been any unusual radar traces of airborne objects in the Rossendale Valley (Lancashire) area. *"No, sir,"* came the written reply. Junior Transport Minister David Mitchell was even more abrupt. He answered a mere *"No!"* to Sir Patrick's written request for information on "whether he has received any reports of un-authorized landings from the air in the area of the Rossendale Valley."[20]

MULTIPLE-WITNESS POLICE SIGHTING

When a UFO sighting occurred at Stanmore, Middlesex, on 26 April 1984, police lost no time in arriving at the scene, perhaps because the headquarters of No. 11 Group, Strike Command, was located at nearby RAF Bentley Priory.

Terri West was first to spot the object from her home in Belmont Lane at about 9:45 p.m. She went to join neighbors Ruth and Bruno Novelli half an hour later. "We went out and saw what looked like a star but then realized it was changing colors all the time—blue to green to pink—and it was moving back and forth. We looked through binoculars and it was definitely moving about as it hovered," said Mrs. Novelli.[21]

Stars are frequently misperceived as UFOs by the untrained observer, since atmospheric refraction can produce a sequence of colors—red, blue, and green being most often reported. Refraction can also give an illusion of movement, as can autokinesis: if you stare at a star without a frame of reference (e.g. a nearby building) it will appear to move around slightly, due to small involuntary movements of the eye.

In all respects the Stanmore object could so far be explained in these terms, but when it emitted a large ball of light which shot toward the ground, the by now alarmed witnesses (who had just been joined by another neighbor, Gerri Ashworth) telephoned the police at 10:22 p.m. Mrs. Novelli told me that a team of police officers then turned up at her house and together they watched the object for about two hours. "One of the officers drew a very explicit diagram of what he saw," she said.[22]

Police Constable Richard Milthorp reported that the object was initially observed at an elevation of about 45°, but after about fifteen minutes it moved to the right and slightly higher. It was he who drew the sketch of the object, which he described as circular in the middle with a dome on top and below. "The dome on top had blue and white flashing lights, while the dome underneath was blue, green, white and pink," he said.

"It was moving erratically up and down and to and fro." A total of eight policemen witnessed the mysterious object.[23]

A Scotland Yard press bureau spokesman confirmed to me that the sighting had been reported to the police at 10:22 p.m. and that "a circular object which glowed" was visible over the Elstree and Wealdstone area. "No aircraft were in the vicinity," he told me. A full report was sent to the Ministry of Defense and the Civil Aviation Authority.[24] Chief Superintendent Ronald Poole of Harrow police station stated that he was quite satisfied with the validity of the report filed by PCs Richard Milthorp and Paul Isles. "They are two normal sensible men who are confident they saw a UFO," he affirmed.[25]

One of the police officers took photographs, but these did not come out at all, according to Tim Mahoney, the police area press officer. Mr. Mahoney also told me that some of the police chased the UFO by car for a short distance, but the object was already fading from view by that time. I asked if a copy of PC Milthorp's sketch would be released. "It'll be submitted to the Ministry of Defense first," he said. "I don't think it's for us to release that sort of thing."[26]

I wrote to the MoD and asked for a copy of the sketch, reminding them that there could hardly be any objection since UFOs do not threaten national security. "Despite my initial optimism," wrote Peter Hucker of AS2, "I am unable to provide this for you. Whilst we in MoD would have no objection to its release, this is, essentially, a matter for the Metropolitan Police. I have therefore been in touch with the area press office who confirm their earlier advice to you that the sketch cannot be released. I understand that the constable responsible has been approached and has asked that no further publicity be given to this report."[27]

CLOSE ENCOUNTERS REPORTED BY POLICE

While the Stanmore sighting is impressive in terms of the number of witnesses, there will always be lingering doubts that the object was a conventional helicopter or aircraft seen in unusual circumstances. There can be no such doubts about those reports by police officers when strange objects are seen at close quarters. Either the witnesses are lying or they saw a genuine UFO. There have been dozens of cases reported over the years, and I am including a few which have impressed me particularly.

Patricia Grant, an independent and thorough researcher, has interviewed a woman police constable who claims to have seen a UFO in Isfield, near Lewes, Sussex, on a bright day in the early autumn of 1977.

The witness prefers to remain anonymous, partly due to official pressure. At about 5:20 p.m. on the day in question the policewoman noticed a curious, silent object, estimated to be as large as a four-inch plate held at arm's length, at no more than 300 feet altitude. A conventional plane was immediately ruled out by the witness, who had been fully trained in aircraft recognition in the Royal Observer Corps. She felt no fear and on impulse waved at the object, which then came closer. It seemed to be of a light greenish-gray metal with a moderately reflective surface. On top of the dome protruded a blue-green light, and underneath the object could be seen a very dense black circular section (see Appendix, p. 457). At its closest approach the object was estimated to be no further than fifty feet away.

The witness had been waiting at a bus stop during the encounter, and when the bus eventually arrived she experienced a numbness, stiffness, and lack of coordination in her limbs as she fumbled with change for the fare. Stumbling to the top deck, from which she hoped to obtain a better view, she discovered that the object was nowhere to be seen. Almost immediately after taking her seat she developed an acute headache that persisted until the following morning. Other symptoms developed, including thirst and conjunctivitis: her eyes burned and watered for a week afterward, and she suffered recurrent gastric disturbances. (A point worth mentioning here is that the witness is also a qualified nurse, holding a General Nursing Certificate.) Even more peculiar was the sense of "time-lessness" experienced by the policewoman during the encounter: as much as twenty minutes seem to have been unaccounted for while she waited at the bus stop.

Patricia Grant, with whom I have discussed the case at length, is totally convinced of the witness's sincerity. Regrettably, no one else saw the object, it seems, and like Alfred Burtoo, this was the most frustrating aspect of the incident for the witness. Perhaps the most positive development is the fact that she now seldom becomes upset or angry, having admitted to having a short temper prior to the incident.[28]

Structured UFO Encountered by Three Police Officers

On a January night in 1978 Sergeant Tony Dodd and Police Constable Alan Dale were driving in the vicinity of Cononley, near Skipton, Yorkshire, in their official line of duty, when a strange aerial machine came into view. "We were going down a country lane," Sergeant Dodd told me, "and you know what it's like up there—it was *dark*—and the only light you've got is your headlights. Suddenly the road in front of us lit up. Of course, the immediate reaction is, where's the light coming from? But it was coming from above. We stopped the car, looked up, and there was this thing coming from our right to our left."

The object was about 100 feet away, moving at less than 40 mph. "It was glowing; like a bright white incandescent glow, and it came right over our heads," the police sergeant recalled. "The whole unit was glowing. It was as if the metal of what this thing was made of was white hot. And there were these three great spheres underneath, like huge ball bearings—three of them equally placed around it. There was a hollow area underneath and like a skirting around the bottom, but these things protruded below that.

"It was absolutely awe-inspiring to see it. I don't know how to explain it to you—it was such a beautiful-looking thing. It seemed to have portholes round the dome—an elongated domed area. And what stood out more than anything else was the colored lights dancing round on the outside of the skirt at the bottom . . . which gave the visual impression that it was rotating. Now whether the thing *was* going round, or whether it was just the lights that were going round and giving that impression, I don't know. I would say it was the lights that were going round because, when you were looking at the portholes, they didn't seem to be going round in a circle as you would have expected." The object was completely soundless.

"When the thing had passed over our heads it sort of went into the distance then suddenly appeared to come down: there's a big wood to our left, right on a distant hillside, and it *appeared* to go down in that wood," said Sergeant Dodd, who added that a third police officer had seen the object.

"We carried on along this road and as we got toward the village we could see these lights coming toward us from the other direction—it was another police car. We stopped, and he said, 'I've just been watching this damn great UFO, and it seems to have come right down somewhere over here!' "[29]

The three spheres seen under the craft have been observed in a number of incidents, most notably by the much vilified George Adamski, whose photographs and film of this type of craft taken in 1952 and 1965 have been ridiculed and denounced as hoaxes (see Chapter 15). I have spent enough time with Tony Dodd to know that he is completely sincere, and the fact that a highly unusual and silent machine was seen by three police officers must surely count as compelling evidence in the search for proof of UFO reality.

Police Officer Abducted by UFO?

Another close encounter case which has impressed me favorably is that of PC Alan Godfrey, whom I met in September 1986 following a Central Television program on which we both appeared. Godfrey's experience occurred on 29 November 1980 shortly after 5:00 in the morning in the town of Todmorden, Yorkshire, and a number of other witnesses, including police officers, reported a UFO in the vicinity around the same time. This is how Godfrey described his encounter on television:

> I was driving a police car at the time, and in the early hours of the morning I came across what I thought at that time was a bus that had slid across the road sideways. And when I approached the object—I got within about twenty yards of it—and immediately I came across what I now would describe as a UFO.
>
> It was about twenty feet wide and fourteen feet high [and] was diamond shaped. It had a bank of windows in it and the bottom half was rotating. The police blue beacon was bouncing back off it, as were my headlights. It was hovering off the ground about five feet. And it was very frightening—very frightening.

Jenny Randles describes the encounter in great detail in *The Pennine UFO Mystery,* and reports that Godfrey noticed the bushes and trees beside the road shaking, which he presumed to be caused by the object. Attempts to contact base by radio, using both VHF and UHF, failed, so the policeman decided to sketch the object on his clipboard. Then a strange thing happened: the next minute he found himself 100 yards further down the road and there was no sign of the UFO.

PC Godfrey drove back to the center of town where he picked up a colleague, gave him some brief details, then took him to the site, where both policemen noticed that the road above which the object had hovered was dry in patches, although soaked with rain elsewhere. Returning to the police station, Godfrey saw that the time was 5:30 a.m. This he found puzzling, since it had seemed to him that less time had elapsed. Later it transpired that he had experienced a peculiar time lapse and during several hypnotic regression sessions he came out with a bizarre story of having been taken on board the craft.[30] I have seen the videotapes of these sessions, and while the story of his abduction may be woven with strands of fantasy from his subconscious mind (Alan himself told me that he remains uncertain as to what actually happened to him during the missing time period), there is no doubting the very real fear that he relived when regressed to the time of the encounter.

Alan Godfrey was asked on television what had happened in the police as a result of the story becoming known. "Nothing happened at all for about twelve months within the Force," he said. "And then, due to publicity at that time being aroused around the case, a lot of pressure was put on me not to say anything. I was made to sign documents, I had to visit certain places. . . . I had to dissociate myself from any person that was interested in UFOs."

"Did you feel that you were maybe the victim of some kind of a cover-up?" Godfrey was asked. "Well . . ." he began cautiously, "that's Catch-22!" "Well, yes or no?" insisted the interviewer. "Er . . . yes," the former policeman admitted reluctantly.[31]

HOME OFFICE DIRECTIVE ON UFOS

In 1982 I interviewed a retired police inspector, who has asked not to be identified, in an effort to find out what official instructions the police have for reporting sightings of UFOs. "What I can say to you," my informant volunteered, "is that the subject itself was the subject of a Home Office Directive. The Home Office sends out directives to chief constables, or they send a letter, laying down certain procedures to be followed in the event of UFOs being sighted."

These directives are then incorporated in the Force Policy Manual, he explained. "I saw one of these directives . . . there were certain specified telephone numbers . . . monitoring stations in relation to aircraft [the UK Warning and Monitoring Service, part of Britain's Civil Defense network]. . . . We had a set procedure, because there was a time factor as to when you could report, because it would be out of range of a tracking station . . . they were Air Force stations, which would also have been contacted in the event of, say, if you saw an aircraft in distress. So it was obviously radar that they were relying on there, and also somebody that they were relying on who had control of aircraft in the area."

BRITAIN'S INTELLIGENCE COMMUNITY

The British intelligence community consists primarily of the Secret Intelligence Service (SIS or MI6), the Security Service (MI5), the MoD Defense Intelligence Staff (DIS), and Government Communications Headquarters (GCHQ), which works hand in glove with America's National Security Agency. The three separate service intelligence branches (Army, Navy and Air Force) were replaced in 1964 by the Directorate of Service Intelligence, although each service maintains responsibility for its own intelligence gathering and security. The Defense Intelligence Staff, headed by the Director-General of Intelligence, has ninety departments, divided into four main branches: (1) Service Intelligence; (2) Management and Support of Intelligence; (3) Scientific and Technical Intelligence; and (4) Economic Intelligence.[32]

. Widely regarded in Whitehall as the main body for collating and analysing intelligence reports from all over the world, the Joint Intelligence Organisation, which briefs the Joint Intelligence Committee (JIC), receives intelligence from friendly foreign intelligence services as well as British agents. The JIC is served by Current Intelligence Groups (CIGS) for daily analysis and an Assessments Staff for long-term intelligence estimates. JIC members include the Chief of SIS; the Director-General of MI5; the Director of GCHQ; the Deputy Chief of the Defense Intelligence Staff, and the Coordinator of Intelligence and Security, who reports on the JIC's assessments to the Cabinet's most secret intelligence committee, the Overseas and Defense Committee, chaired by the Prime Minister.[33]

A former Director and Deputy Chief of the SIS has informed me that MI6—Britain's equivalent of the CIA, with whom it liaises closely— did not have any interest in the UFO subject while he was in office. "It simply wasn't what we call a 'target of opportunity,' " he explained, and suggested that "perhaps we leave it to the Americans." That MI6 is not involved in UFO matters has been corroborated for me by other intelligence experts, including Donald McCormick and Nigel West. I can find no evidence—thus far—for the involvement of MI5 or GCHQ, although it is difficult to disregard the probability that GCHQ has been involved in view of its inseparable link with America's NSA, an agency that has been keenly interested in UFOs since its inception in 1952, as we shall see.

GCHQ, based in two locations in Cheltenham, but with worldwide listening posts, has four directorates: (1) Organisation and Establishment,

(2) SIGINT (Signals Intelligence) Plans, and two operational directorates, the largest being (3) SIGINT Operations and Requirements (processing and analysis) and (4) Communications Security (COMSEC).[34] Like NSA, GCHQ specializes in intercepting and decoding communications on a worldwide basis, notably diplomatic traffic, military communications, radar intelligence (RADINT), and broadcasts. Commercial Telex as well as civilian telephone calls do not escape attention, either. According to James Rusbridger (ex-MI6), the Foreign Office, through the joint GCHQ/ NSA agreement, intercepts and monitors *every* telephone call entering or leaving Britain. These are automatically monitored, he claims, "because the computers that operate this system are programmed to search every international circuit for particularly sensitive names and numbers."[35]

But we must now turn our attention to the Royal Air Force and its intelligence branches, where I have discovered tenuous but intriguing evidence for clandestine research into unidentified flying objects.

PER ARDUA AD ASTRA

Rumors of secret Ministry of Defense research into UFOs have occasionally surfaced over the years, but nothing of substance has emerged since 1957, when it was reliably reported that top secret studies were being conducted by the Air Ministry in Northumberland Avenue, London (where the Defense Intelligence Staff still carry out intelligence evaluation). This was corroborated by Gordon Creighton, a former intelligence officer who served with the Joint Intelligence Bureau among others, who told me that RAF intelligence officers regularly liaised with their American counterparts as well as the CIA on the UFO problem.

In 1985 I learned that a Birmingham witness who had telephoned the MoD in Whitehall one night to report a UFO incident was referred to another telephone number. The witness, George Dyer, told me that he had phoned the MoD at about 8 p.m. in the summer of 1984 and was advised to phone another number "in the West Country" (which he has since forgotten). "Well, I won't ring tonight; there won't be anybody there," Mr. Dyer told the MoD. "On the contrary," came the response. "*It's manned all the time.*"[36]

I contacted the MoD and asked about this number. "The only twenty-four hour number is the number here [in Whitehall]," I was told, "although often people will report sightings to RAF stations or the po-

lice. . . . I'm not aware of any official research center."[37] So George
Dyer was misinformed. Or was he?

Shortly afterward I learned from two completely independent sources
that top secret research into UFOs was carried out by the RAF at a certain
establishment in Wiltshire. The name of that establishment is RAF Rudloe
Manor. Situated exactly 100 miles from London in pastoral Wiltshire,
Rudloe Manor is officially listed as a headquarters of RAF Support Command (the main headquarters is at RAF Brampton, Cambridgeshire), as
well as the headquarters of the Provost and Security Services (UK),
located in separate facilities. The Provost and Security Services is the
branch of the RAF that investigates breaches of security in addition to
regular policing duties. A less-known function of Rudloe Manor is the
Defense Communication Network (Defense Concepts Staff).[38]

Perhaps the most relevant function of Rudloe Manor in the UFO context
is the Flying Complaints Flight, formerly based in Whitehall as part of
the old S4 unit but now housed at the Provost and Security Service
Headquarters. As ex-MoD official Ralph Noyes has confirmed, S4 handled complaints about low-flying infringements, as well as dealing with
reports of UFO sightings by members of the public. I have therefore
deduced that the Flying Complaints Flight is used as a cover for the
"lodger unit" wherein secret research into UFOs is conducted. The distinction between low-flying complaints and UFO reports appears to be
academic.

The UFO research center comprises no more than thirty personnel, I
am told, and is manned permanently. One of my informants told me that
Rudloe Manor also serves (or did serve) as a tracking station for UFOs.
In about 1971, for instance, a radar expert employed there tracked an
unknown aerial object for two days, and there was general agreement
that nothing on earth could account for the fantastic maneuverability of
the object.

Finding further evidence for Rudloe Manor's secret research has been
frustrating, even risky. In April 1985 I was questioned by vigilant MoD
police while walking around the perimeter of the base. Evidently unsa-
tisfied with my less than truthful answers, to say nothing of the spurious
identity I showed, the two policemen came to the Rudloe Park Hotel
(where I was staying) several hours later while I was in the middle of a
meal. Afterward I accompanied the officers for further questioning at
Copenacre, one of the Royal Navy's two facilities in the area. Since by
this time it was clear that I was in deep trouble, I felt bound to give the
true reasons for my visit during the half-hour interrogation that ensued.

It was obvious that the MoD personnel were far from convinced about my quest for evidence of UFO research, however, and quite reasonably suspected me of being a member of the Campaign for Nuclear Disarmament (which I am not), or worse.

I was brought back to the hotel, and after spiritual consolation at the bar retired to my room. At around midnight there came a knock on the door. This time it was the civil police. Following further questioning and a thorough search of my belongings I was driven to Chippenham police station, where after a most enjoyable discussion about flying saucers with the bemused officers, I was interrogated by a detective constable who had come from Swindon. Computer checks having established that I had no police record, and having been assured that I had not actually committed an offense of any kind, I was let off with a friendly warning to exercise greater precaution when walking around military bases in future. I volunteered the films from my cameras and these were developed, printed and returned free of charge to my door by the police some months later, nothing of any sensitivity having been found. By the time I arrived back at the hotel it was 3:30 a.m. It was a salutary experience.

Ralph Noyes was totally skeptical when I first told him about Rudloe Manor and its alleged clandestine research into UFOs. It was the first time such a rumor had surfaced as far as he was concerned: not once while he was head of DS8 in Whitehall had he heard the place mentioned in connection with UFOs. But supposing the lodger unit was only installed in 1972, the year Ralph left the MoD? Or had he simply been kept in the dark? My informants had made it clear that very few people were in the know, after all. We decided to try and find out more.

Late one night in May 1985, in my presence, Ralph telephoned Rudloe Manor, giving his name and a few details of his background in the MoD to the duty officer. He then explained that he had a perplexing UFO sighting to report that had occurred earlier that night in Hertfordshire (in fact it had occurred weeks earlier in London), but that before proceeding he needed to be absolutely certain that he was phoning the right place. "Surely I should be phoning Whitehall?" he asked. "No, sir," replied the duty officer, *"you've reached the right place."* When Ralph had finished relating his sighting and put down the phone, his astonishment was palpable. Maybe UFO reports *were* studied at Rudloe Manor, after all, he wondered.

Lord Hill-Norton was equally baffled. Certainly no one had ever told him anything about secret research into UFOs at Rudloe Manor when he was Chief of the Defense Staff. He questioned Lord Trefgarne, Minister of State for Defense, on the matter, but was informed that the Flying Complaints Flight dealt only with public complaints about low flying and had nothing whatsoever to do with the study of unidentified aerial events, which AS2 alone were responsible for handling at Whitehall. The MoD has consistently denied that any other unit is involved in UFO investigations, although in late 1986 they admitted to me that DI55 (presumably a department of the Defense Intelligence Staff) cooperated with AS2. Details of DI55's functions are not available at the time of writing.[39]

Ralph Noyes has pointed out to me that *if* there is a secret lodger unit monitoring UFO reports at Rudloe Manor (or any other establishment), the personnel and equipment used would need to be virtually indistinguishable from those used at the parent establishment; would be parented for "housekeeping" by the larger establishment in order to assist in burying its costs; operationally controlled by its own local director, who would report to some higher authority; and commanded by this separate authority, which would be firmly screened from having to give any account of itself either to the parenting establishment or to its command channels. Although there are precedents for making this type of arrangement (the research into radar in the late 1930s being one example), Ralph Noyes points out:

> You can't just smuggle a lodger unit with special tasks on to an existing establishment without clear instructions being issued down the command channels. This means issuing a few documents (though they can be brief, cryptic and highly classified), and it also needs clear understandings among at least a few senior officers (e.g. at least the Chief of Air Staff, the Vice Chief of Air Staff and the C. in C. Strike Command or . . . Support Command) so that the inevitable administrative problems can be swiftly sorted out with minimum risk of breaching security.[40]

That Rudloe Manor is involved in UFO research to some extent seems borne out by the fact that it functions as a twenty-four-hour receiving station for reports from members of the public, although this is denied by the MoD. That the Flying Complaints Flight is the receiving point is partly proven to my satisfaction by the fact that Ralph Noyes was advised by the duty officer at Rudloe Manor to address a letter giving further details of his sighting to the Flying Complaints Flight. What I am unable to prove is that RAF Rudloe Manor functions as a twenty-four-hour top secret UFO monitoring and research station (along the lines of Wright-Patterson Air Force Base in Dayton, Ohio), as revealed by my informants.

The most Lord Hill-Norton has been able to uncover so far about the matter is that reports received by Whitehall are referred elsewhere.

The Manual of Air Traffic Services gives precise instructions to air traffic controllers in the United Kingdom for the reporting of UFOs (see Appendix, p. 458) and states: "The details are to be telephoned immediately to AIS [Air Information Service] (Military), LATCC [London Air Traffic Control Center]. The completed form is to be sent by the originating air traffic service unit to the Ministry of Defense" at Whitehall.[41] The AIS unit is based at RAF West Drayton, which receives the input of all military and civil radar, together with all military and civil flight plans (with a few exceptions), so that a continuous and complete picture of all activity in British airspace is maintained. It is also to West Drayton that the civil police are requested to send reports of UFOs. Whether some, or all, of these reports are then routed to Rudloe Manor, I do not know.

A unit that would serve as a useful receiving point for photographs and films of UFOs taken by the military would be the Joint Air Reconnaissance Intelligence Center (JARIC) at Huntingdon, a combined services unit which receives undeveloped film from military sources—the RAF in particular. There is no evidence for this, but it is worth mentioning that in the United States pilots who take gun-camera films of UFOs have reported that the undeveloped films are usually spirited away to a base such as Wright-Patterson AFB. It is reasonable to assume that similar arrangements exist in Britain, and that there is close collaboration with the US Air Force, CIA, Defense Intelligence Agency, and National Security Agency, all of which have a long history of involvement in UFO research. Unless, possibly, the Americans have not taken Britain into their confidence. My sources inform me otherwise, however, although how Lord Hill-Norton, as former Chief of the Defense Staff, remains unaware of this collaboration continues to puzzle both of us.

Dr. Robert Creegan, Professor of Philosophy at the State University of New York, has made a number of research trips to Britain and has discussed the question of an official cover-up with various involved parties on an informal basis. "I did get the impression," he told me, "that 'pressure' applied by officials in the United States was a cause (or one of the causes) for a British policy of giving so little information vis-à-vis the UFO problem."[42] Dr. Creegan has also stated: "It was made evident to me that the British at that time [1970s] desired to please the US establishment. *And it was strongly hinted that US officials seemed rather excitable about UFO problems and were making frantic efforts to suppress public interest* . . . it was indicated that a panicky US attitude was the reason for British silence . . . the Ministry had to appease the American military-industrial complex and so could not assist one in a search for truth.'' [Emphasis added] He concluded:

> UFOs alarm the establishment because, whatever theory is correct, a major loss of control is apprehended, associated with reports of objects which affect mechanisms of control and which deeply puzzle and confuse both the public and many of its would-be leaders. From London to Palo Alto, I have registered many signs appearing to indicate that the present is, indeed, the dawn of an age of panic. Free and universal access to even more puzzling truths is one thing needed, if people are ever again to live undismayed.[43]

PART TWO

AROUND THE WORLD

6

FRANCE, ITALY, PORTUGAL AND SPAIN

I must say that if your listeners could see for themselves the mass of reports coming in from the airborne gendarmerie, from the mobile gendarmerie, and from the gendarmerie charged with the job of conducting investigations, all of which reports are being forwarded by us to the CNES [National Center for Space Studies], then they would see that it is all pretty disturbing.

Thus spoke France's Minister of Defense, Monsieur Robert Galley, in an interview with Jean-Claude Bourret, broadcast on *France-Inter* on 21 February 1974, following a wave of sightings in the latter part of 1973 and early 1974.

France, with its independent defense policy, has pursued an equally independent policy on *Objets Volants Non Identifiés*—OVNI—since the early 1950s. In July 1952 a government research committee was set up, replaced by a General Staff committee in 1954. French Secretary of State for Air, M. M. Catroux, was asked by French MP M. Jean Nocher to set up a commission "to study this phenomenon objectively by extracting the truth from among the mistakes and possible hoaxes."[1]

Robert Galley stated in the 1974 broadcast that a department had been established in the Ministère des Armées (Ministry of Defense) for the purpose of collecting and studying the many reports that were flooding in during the great global wave of sightings in 1954. That department was based at the headquarters of the French Air Force's Department of Research. Galley confirmed that there were "sighting reports from pilots, from the commanding personnel of various Air Force centers, with quite a lot of details, all of which agree in quite a disturbing manner—all in the course of the year 1954."[2]

A curious sequel to the French Minister's interview was that tapes of interviews with eminent ufologists (including Gordon Creighton) which were to have been broadcast as part of the series were stolen from Jean-Claude Bourret's office. Had the Minister's positive statements gone too far?

POLICE AND SECURITY SERVICES ALERTED BY

LANDING, 1954

During the 1954 UFO wave there were many reports of landed craft complete with occupants, and one of the most impressive cases is that of Marius Dewilde, of which I shall give only brief details, as related by the great pioneer Aimé Michel. On 10 September at about 10:30 p.m. Dewilde was alerted by the sound of his dog howling and trying to get inside his house near Quarouble. He took his flashlight and saw outside:

> Two creatures such as I had never seen before were not more than three or four yards from me. . . . The one in front turned toward me. The beam of my light caught a reflection from glass or metal where his face should have been. I had the distinct impression that his head was enclosed in a diver's helmet. In fact, both creatures were dressed in one-piece outfits like the suits divers wear. They were very short, probably less than three and a half feet tall, but very wide in the shoulders, and the helmets protecting their ''heads'' looked enormous. I could see their legs, small in proportion to their height, it seemed to me, but on the other hand I couldn't see any arms. I don't know whether they had any.

Dewilde tried to get hold of the entities, but when he was six feet away he was blinded by an extremely powerful light emitting from a sort of square opening in a dark object resting on the nearby railway tracks. ''I closed my eyes and tried to yell, but I couldn't,'' he reported. ''It was just as if I had been paralyzed. I tried to move, but my legs wouldn't obey me.'' Finally the beam of light went out and Dewilde found himself able to move again and ran toward the railway track. The object was rising from the ground and hovering, and a ''thick dark steam was coming out of the bottom with a low whistling sound.'' The craft went up vertically and eventually disappeared.

Having woken up his wife and a neighbor, Dewilde then ran to the nearest police station, about a mile away. As Michel reports, the witness was in such a state of agitation that the police took him for a lunatic and dismissed him. He then ran to the police commissioner's office where his report was taken more seriously.[3]

The investigation which followed involved the airborne gendarmerie, the mobile gendarmerie, and the *Direction de la Surveillance du Territoire*—or DST—France's equivalent of the British MI5 or the American FBI. Many years later Aimé Michel revealed to Gordon Creighton that the DST had calculated that the indentations made by the object indicated that it must have weighed at least thirty-five tons.[4]

HUGE UFO OBSERVED AND TRACKED OVER PARIS,

1956

At 10:50 p.m. on 19 February 1956 air traffic controllers at Orly Airport, Paris, were astonished to see a "blip" appear on their radar screens that was twice the size of a conventional aircraft. It appeared to cruise around, hover, then accelerate at fantastic speeds, and was tracked for a total of four hours. Shortly after it first showed up on radar, the unknown object was directly over Gometz-le-Châtel (Seine et Oise), then thirty seconds later it was thirty kilometers away, having moved at a speed of 3,600 kph (nearly 2,500 mph).

A second but smaller blip then appeared, identified as an Air France DC-3 Dakota flying over the military base at Les Mureaux at 4,500 feet—800 feet lower than the UFO. Orly radioed the pilot immediately and advised him that unidentified traffic was on his approximate path. Radio Officer Beaupertuis caught sight of the object through a window. It was on the starboard side—enormous in size, rather indistinct in outline, and lit in some areas with a red glow. Reporting to the French Ministry of Civil Aviation later, Captain Desavoi confirmed the sighting and provided further details:

> For a full thirty seconds we watched the object without being able to decide exactly on its size or precise shape. In flight it is virtually impossible to estimate distances and dimensions. But of one thing we are certain. It was no civil airliner. For it carried none of the navigation lights regulations stipulate are a must. I was then warned by Orly that the object had moved to my port side, so I turned toward it. But they called to say it had left us and was speeding toward Le Bourget. About 10 minutes later control called again to say the object was several miles above us. But we couldn't see it, nor did we see it again.[5]

FRENCH AIR FORCE COMMANDING GENERAL

CONFIRMS UFO REALITY

Neither the DST nor the DGSE (*Direction Général de Sécurité Extérieur*) have released any documents on their UFO research, to the best of my knowledge, since France, like Britain and many other countries, has nothing to compare with America's Freedom of Information Act. But a few statements by concerned military officers have added weight to the growing body of testimony in favor of UFO reality.

General Lionel Max Chassin (1902–70), who rose to the rank of Commanding General of the French Air Forces and served as General Air Defense Co-ordinator, Allied Air Forces, Central Europe (NATO), first became interested in UFOs in 1949 when he began receiving reports from pilots. From 1964 until his death in 1970 he acted as president of the *Groupement d'Étude de Phénomènes Aériens* (GEPA). In 1958 he wrote an important preface to Aimé Michel's second book, *Flying Saucers and the Straight-Line Mystery,* which began by referring to the various types of human response to extraordinary phenomena. Of the skeptic, Chassin writes:

> Obsessed with the notion of his own omniscience, it enrages him to be confronted by phenomena that do not agree with this conviction. Finding in his limited armoury no explanation that satisfies him, he chooses to doubt rather than himself, and rejects the most obvious facts in order to avoid putting his faith to the test. The mistaken pride and anthropocentrism that supposedly went out with Copernicus and Galileo make him a peril to science, as history abundantly proves. . . . That strange things have been seen is now beyond question, and the "psychological" explanations seem to have misfired. The number of thoughtful, intelligent, educated people in full possession of their faculties who have "seen something" and described it grows every day. Doubting Thomases among astronomers, engineers, and officials who used to laugh at "saucers" have seen and repented. To reject out of hand testimony such as theirs becomes more and more presumptuous.

I have alluded elsewhere to the nightmare scenario of nuclear war breaking out as a result of UFOs being mistaken for enemy missiles, a point taken up by General Chassin: "If we persist in refusing to recognize the existence of these unidentified objects, we will end up, one fine day, by mistaking them for the guided missiles of an enemy; and the worst will be upon us."[6]

That the world's defense forces have taken measures to deal with this contingency since 1958 (and earlier, in some countries), when Chassin wrote these words, I am certain of. And in any case, aerial radar cover is based on automatic analysis of electromagnetic signals picked up by radar, each "blip" being processed through a central computer and relayed to several air defense organizations, thus effectively eliminating the danger of subjective interpretation.[7]

SECRET SERVICE OFFICER CONFIRMS WORLDWIDE

COLLABORATION

In 1965 George Langelaan, novelist, journalist, and ex-officer of the secret service who during World War II was parachuted into France after being given a new face with plastic surgery, gave a lecture at Mourenx, Landes, during which the subject of UFOs cropped up. Langelaan declared that the Russian and American secret services had collaborated on the problem, and had arrived at the conclusion: "The Flying Saucers exist, their source is extraterrestrial, and the future—relatively quite soon—should permit confirmation of this statement."[8] No such confirmation has been forthcoming at an official level, though in later chapters I shall cite tenuous evidence for international collaboration dating back to 1955.

THE VALENSOLE CASE, 1965

No résumé of the French scene, however brief (as mine must necessarily be), would be complete without mentioning one of the most thoroughly investigated close encounters on record—the famous Valensole case of 1965.

At about 5:45 a.m. on 1 July, farmer Maurice Masse was in his lavender field near Valensole, Basses Alpes, when he heard a strange whistling sound. Stepping out from behind a heap of stones he saw an object shaped like a rugby football with a cupola on top, about the size of a Renault Dauphine car. It was standing on six legs, with a central pivot. Through an open doorway he could see two seats, back to back.

Masse at first thought the object was a helicopter or experimental craft, but was then surprised to notice what he took to be two eight-year-old boys stealing his lavender plants (some of which had been missing). The "boys" were less than four feet tall, clad in fairly dark gray-green one-piece suits. On seeing Masse approaching them they straightened up, and one of them leveled a "tube" at the farmer which immobilized him.

Masse noticed that the two humanoids had large hairless heads, smooth white skin, high fleshy cheeks, large eyes that slanted away, pointed chins, and mouths without lips. They made a strange gurgling ("gargouillement") sound from deep within their throats as they communicated with each other. "They were looking at me, and must have been making fun of me," Masse said in an unofficial statement to Maître Chautard, a local magistrate. "Nevertheless their facial expressions were not ill-natured, but very much the reverse." Masse said that in fact he felt a great sense of peace exuding from the beings.

Shortly afterward the humanoids returned to their craft via a sliding door. The legs whirled and retracted, and the machine took off. It was quarter of an hour before Masse recovered his mobility. The ground where the craft had rested was soaked with moisture, although it had not been raining, and investigators found strange, geometrically spaced indentations. More remarkable was the fact that no lavender plants would grow at the landing site until ten years later.

Four days after the incident Masse suddenly collapsed, seized with an irresistible urge to sleep, and would have done so for twenty-four hours had not his wife and father woken him up. From his usual five to six hours' sleep, Masse found he needed at least ten or twelve, for a period of several months.

All those who investigated the case, including the gendarmerie headed by Lieutenant-Colonel Valnet, Maître Chautard, and the mayor and parish priest of Valensole, concluded unanimously that Maurice Masse was telling the truth.[9]

UFOS AND THE GENDARMERIE NATIONALE

As Dr. Jean Gilles points out, the French gendarmerie are part of the French armed forces and as such are accountable exclusively to the highly centralized executive powers: the Attorney General or (in some cases) the President.[10] In an internal journal, not generally available to members of the public, Gendarmerie Capitain Kervendal and the journalist/researcher Charles Garreau give a résumé of the phenomenon, including the following significant statement:

What can we of the gendarmerie do about this business? By virtue of the gendarmerie's presence throughout the whole national territory of France, by virtue of its knowledge of places and, above all, of people; by virtue of the integrity and the intellectual honesty that are characteristic of its personnel, and also by virtue of the rapidity with which the gendarmerie can be on the spot, they are well placed indeed to serve as a valuable auxiliary in the search for truth about the UFOs. . . . *Something is going on in the skies . . . something that we do not understand. If all the airline pilots and Air Force pilots who have seen UFOs—and sometimes chased them—have been the victims of hallucinations, then an awful lot of pilots should be taken off and forbidden to fly.* [Emphasis added]

In Section II of a questionnaire that indicates which aspects of the phenomenon the gendarmerie should concentrate on, the authors emphasize that close attention should be paid to the shape of UFOs, effects felt by the witnesses (such as tingling sensations), and the behavior of animals in the vicinity. In those cases where an animal has died in unusual circumstances following a sighting, an autopsy and blood analysis should be made, as well as tests for traces of radiation.

Landing cases are thoroughly dealt with in Section III: traces left by the craft should be closely examined, and samples of soil, vegetation, and roots should be submitted to the nearest agricultural research center. The level of radioactivity should be measured and recorded at the landing site and compared with readings 100 meters away. Great importance is attached to aerial photography of the site by helicopter, *using infra-red film*.[11]

Quite evidently, the Gendarmerie Nationale takes UFOs extremely seriously.

GEPAN

In 1977 the *Groupe d'Études Phénomènes Aerospatiaux Non Identifiés* (GEPAN) was established under the auspices of the *Centre Nationale d'Études Spatiales* (CNES)—France's equivalent of the American space agency NASA. GEPAN had a committee of seven scientists, headed by Dr. Claude Poher, Director of the Sounding Rockets Division of CNES. The group was to collaborate with the gendarmerie, and was given access to laboratories and scientific centers all over France, as well as other agencies around the world. President Giscard d'Estaing took a close personal interest in the project.

It all looked very promising at first. For example, in an analysis of eleven cases studied in 1978, GEPAN concluded that in as many as nine cases a physical phenomenon existed whose origin, propulsion, and modus operandi were beyond human knowledge.[12] But later that year Dr. Gilles, Chargé de Recherche at the Center for Scientific Research (CNRS), attended a GEPAN meeting for private investigation groups at the CNES headquarters in Toulouse. He was told during the seven-hour meeting that the scientific attachés at GEPAN could only devote 10 percent of their time to those cases that were given to them by the gendarmerie. More significantly, Dr. Gilles discovered that those cases that GEPAN did receive had been screened by the highest authority in the Gendarmerie Nationale.

"Those with the very highest 'strangeness/probability' index,'' he learned, "do not go to GEPAN at all, but go to certain other bodies which are, if we might so term it, of a far less 'obtrusive' nature than GEPAN.'' In short, Dr. Gilles believed that GEPAN was no more than a government monitored public relations agency. The real, fundamental research on UFOs was done elsewhere.

Dr. Gilles is convinced that the meeting presaged the demise of GEPAN as an effective group. Commented Gordon Creighton: "It seems that France's Socio-Communists have indeed just attempted to kill off GE-PAN, since, being sensible chaps, they all know that UFOs don't exist anyway, and they are indeed convinced that the whole idea of the Center was simply a silly private fad of Giscard d'Estaing's.'' Creighton believes that GEPAN "ran into the truth and were stopped.'' But by whom? "Who, in France, is more powerful than the present socialist government and the present socialist President?'' he asks. "Answer: The French Army and the French secret and security services! These, then, are the people who have secured the reprieve of GEPAN, because indeed they are the people for whom it was created in the first place.''[13]

GEPAN has on several occasions appeared to be on the brink of collapse: at the meeting attended by Dr. Gilles, for instance, Dr. Poher announced his resignation and took off on a long cruise around the world. His place was taken by Alain Esterle, however, and investigations continued into those cases passed on to GEPAN by the military.

THE MASTERS OF SILENCE

Monsieur Fernand Lagarde, one of France's finest researchers (and editor of *Lumières Dans la Nuit*), also expressed serious misgivings about the state of official research, believing that the "Open Door Policy" seemingly initiated with the establishment of GEPAN had come to an end. Lagarde found that his requests for information and documents from official sources were blocked at every stage, just as elsewhere in the world. "We have now to face the fact that a lid . . . marked *secret*, has come down on all official research,'' he wrote in 1981. "Sighting reports likely to be of interest to us no longer find their way to us.'' The "Masters of Silence''—as he called them—had taken over once more.[14]

Another distinguished French researcher who shares this view is the astrophysicist Dr. Pierre Guérin of the French Institute of Astrophysics and Senior Research Officer in the CNRS. In November 1984 I had the pleasure of meeting Dr. Guérin in Paris, and over lunch we discussed the cover-up. The demise—or apparent demise—of GEPAN was first on the agenda. "It's now limited to only *two* people," said Dr. Guérin, "Monsieur Velasco, the head—he's not even a scientist, he's an engineer—and his Secretary. That is all!" GEPAN, he confirmed, is under the aegis of the CNES, which itself is under the direction of a scientific committee which is not well disposed toward the subject.

One of the main problems, Dr. Guérin explained to me, is that the majority of scientists reject UFOs because they simply do not fit into a current scientific framework. "In science there is no proof of any phenomenon if no scientific model for it exists. The *observation* of the facts is not the actual fact! We have the testimonial proof, but not the scientific proof. Scientists are not only embarrassed by UFOs: they're furious because they don't understand them. There is no possibility of explaining them in three-dimensional space-time physics."

But what about the more reliable reports of actual recovered UFOs? I asked, knowing that Dr. Guérin had published some positive statements on this controversial aspect of the phenomenon. "Even if there are crashes," he replied carefully, "scientists wouldn't understand the propulsion system. The idea that a scientific secret exists is false, I'm certain. I don't believe that a small group has material *proof*, but they do have evidence. If they had proof, other countries would have learned about it. I am completely convinced that nobody has the fundamental explanation."

I then asked him what hypothesis for the origin of UFOs best explained the facts. He replied that the extraterrestrial hypothesis, although not proven, is the most economic explanation, considering that the evolution of life in the universe can lead to other advanced forms of life.

As Dr. Guérin tucked into his steak, I raised the question of the horrific animal mutilations that have proliferated in the United States and elsewhere (including France) since 1967. In these disturbing incidents—and there have been thousands—carcasses of animals, usually cattle, have been found in remote areas with vital organs missing: eyes, tongues, udders, sexual organs and rectal areas removed with surgical precision. In many cases blood is completely drained from the animal, with no traces on the surrounding ground. While satanic cults and natural predators have been responsible for some of the mutilations, there have been numerous occasions when mysterious helicopters, lights, and UFOs have been observed at the scene, whose source has never been identified. "The testimonial facts are always doubtful," Dr. Guérin answered, "but the material facts, independent of the witnesses—in the case of the 'mutes' —are of a superior degree than testimonial evidence."

Dr. Guérin was somewhat guarded in his answers to my questions. Scientists are mindful of their reputations, especially when the subject of UFOs crops up, and I am sure he was bothered about being misquoted. But in published articles he has been more forthcoming—courageously so.

"Unless you are in the know," he wrote in 1982, "and are privy at the very highest level to the secrets of the military intelligence services or to the secrets of the heads of state to whom those military intelligences report (?) . . . nobody is capable of knowing for certain whether, yes or no, there do exist material, concrete (and therefore irrefutable) proofs of UFOs *as such.*" Dr. Guérin went on to admit that the stories of recovered UFOs "have the ring of truth about them. . . . But the material proofs alleged to exist remain concealed by the authorities, who are the sole possessors of them."

As to material proof for UFOs, Dr. Guérin is certain that the mutilation cases provide such proof. Dismissing official explanations and pointing out the worldwide nature of the incidents, Dr. Guérin notes that the incisions and excisions of organs on the animals' carcasses prove the existence of an ultra-sophisticated surgical skill, surpassing present-day capabilities; a fact confirmed by those private veterinarians who have examined the carcasses. He concludes:

Rather than invoking I know not what imaginary and gratuitous "para-normal" manifestation to explain these facts (as certainly all too many ufologists of the "New Wave" will want to do or even I know not what secret world organization of initiates dwelling clandestinely amongst us), I prefer, for my part, to apply *Occam's Law* in the interpretation of what we observe, and, consequently, to conclude that the animal mutilations, associated as they are with the passage overhead of flights of silent machines coming from the skies and impossible as they are for us to perform in the present state of our surgical techniques, *cannot be anything else but a manifestation of the activities of extraterrestrial visitors.*

The astronomer, in referring to the official FBI report which attributes all the mutilations to natural predators (such as coyotes), is unequivocal in his indictment: "*Here we have . . . an indubitable proof of the wilful and conscious intention of the American authorities to deceive public opinion over UFO phenomena,*" he states. "The US government agents who are talking about coyote bites to account for the animal mutilations are lying and are lying knowingly, in obedience obviously to orders received from above."

In discussing the reasons for the cover-up, Dr. Guérin offers the following hypothesis:

> To the extent that the discovery of the presence of a hyper-sophisticated non-human technological activity within our Terrestrial Space could not possibly be regarded with indifference by those who have the task of governing the world, these latter will attempt to exploit, each party for themselves, any data that is in their possession, while at the same time publicly denying that they have such data, [and] publicly suffocating all ufological research in a haze of "psychological" interpretations! *That is not to say that the "Invaders" may not be engaged in a pretty bit of suffocation of the subject themselves.*[15] [Original emphasis]

GEPAN REVIVED?

Despite rumors of GEPAN's demise the organization continues, albeit on a limited scale. In 1983 the Minister of Defense, Monsieur Charles Hernu, decided that GEPAN's research should continue, under the direction of two engineers of the National Center for Space Studies. Some of the results have been highly significant, as Dr. Guérin concedes.

A sixty-six-page internal memorandum submitted by GEPAN to CNES in March 1983 deals with a landing case that occurred near Nice (on 8 January 1981). Various laboratories independently analyzed samples taken from the site and discovered anomalies in the soil; these anomalies decreased in direct proportions to the distance from the spot where the object had landed.[16]

Another case investigated by GEPAN yielded even more impressive results. A farmworker in the Department of Gard in southern France heard a slight whistling sound, looked up and saw "a strange machine coming down very fast. It was not spinning and there were no flames or smoke." The object was about thirteen feet in diameter, eight feet high and shaped like two inverted soup plates of unequal size, joined together by a projecting rim. After touching down briefly the craft took off at fantastic speed.

GEPAN found that plant life had mysteriously changed at the site. Although it was summer when the incident took place, it was as if autumn had arrived overnight. Analysis carried out by four separate laboratories produced surprising results: chlorophyll and other substances in the plants had been reduced by between thirty and fifty percent. Furthermore, analysis of soil samples indicated that an extremely heavy object had scraped along the ground, leaving evidence of both thermic and mechanical effects, as well as possible "combustion" residue.

Concluded GEPAN's Alain Esterle: "We are in the presence of traces for which there is no satisfactory explanation and we can find no reason to suspect that the eyewitness is deliberately lying. For the first time we found a combination of factors which leads us to accept that something similar to what the eyewitness described actually did happen."[17]

In spite of these encouraging developments, doubts have continued to be raised about GEPAN's true function. In 1983 Dr. Jean-Pierre Petit of the National Center for Scientific Research was told by the head of GEPAN, Jean-Jacques Velasco: "We are collecting UFO reports, but we don't know what to do with them. Once a case has been investigated, we publish a note on it, and that is that. We have no scientific structure behind GEPAN."

Dr. Petit goes on to say that during a meeting in Paris, organized by *France-Inter* on 12 June 1984, with GEPAN representatives as well as fifty-five journalists present, the CNES public relations officer Monsieur Metzle made a curious admission. "In 1977," he is reported to have said, "*it was necessary to tranquilize public opinion concerning the UFO phenomenon. And it was in that spirit that GEPAN was created.*"[18]

More recently, Jean-Jacques Velasco announced that GEPAN has collaborated closely with the gendarmerie to log about 1,600 UFO reports (up to 1985). While the majority have been explained as natural phenomena or aircraft, Velasco emphasized that as many as thirty-eight percent do not fall into this category[19]—a high percentage of unknowns by any standards.

What is France's official position on these unexplained sightings, and is there any evidence that some UFOs are extraterrestrial in origin? Answers to these questions were given to me in 1986 by the Air Attaché at the French Embassy in London. "Despite the [fact that] UFO flights are still forbidden over France," he explained, "the trespassers are generally reported to the gendarmerie. As mentioned by Mr. Galley, our previous Minister of Defense, all inquiries are then centralized in a department of the Centre Nationale d'Études Spatiales for study."[20]

But what about the unexplained sightings? I insisted. Does the Air Force believe—like the air forces of some smaller countries such as Zimbabwe—that these relate to extraterrestrial civilizations? The Air Attaché was unimpressed. "So far," he told me, "the French Air Force is not concerned by this problem and no Air Staff generals are named for quotations about it. Perhaps the French sky is more cloudy than Zimbabwe's."[21]

Evidently the Air Attaché was unaware that General Chassin, former Commanding General of the French Air Force, had made some positive statements on the subject back in the 1950s. And to those already cited I would like to conclude with the following, made in 1961:

> We must become dedicated, then, in our zeal that the conspiracy of silence may not suppress news of phenomena of the highest importance, with consequences which may be incalculable for the whole human race. . . . Undoubtedly the day will come, whatever we do, when the truth will break in upon us. But we risk being taken by surprise. . . . We should begin a great crusade of common sense in order to avoid what could be very dangerous. We invite all earthmen to join it who will not allow themselves to be blinded by orthodoxy and who desire above everything to see the truth triumphant.[22]

UFO FLEETS OVER ROME, 1954

Critics who wonder why UFOs never appear over large cities in full view of thousands of witnesses would do well to consider the events that took place over Rome in November 1954, following a wave of sightings in Italy. The Italian diplomat Dr. Alberto Perego was among a crowd of about a hundred people near the Church of Santa Maria Maggiore on 30 October who stood and gazed upward in astonishment as two "white dots" moved around the sky in complete silence at a height of about 2,000 meters. Was this some new kind of aircraft? Dr. Perego wondered.

The critic will not be impressed with this sighting—and with good reason—but the events of November 1954 are harder to explain in conventional terms. Once again, Dr. Perego was witness to a series of aerial displays that left him and thousands of others in no doubt that something quite extraordinary was taking place in the skies above Rome.

On 6 November Dr. Perego was in the Tuscolano district when the "white dots" appeared, but this time there were dozens of them. "Today, between 11:00 a.m. and 1:00 p.m.," he noted at the time, "the sky of Rome has been crossed by several dozens of flying machines traveling at a height of around 7,000 or 8,000 meters. They were moving at variable speeds, which at times seemed to be as high as 1,200 or 1,400 km per hour. The machines appeared like 'white dots,' sometimes with a short white trail.

"At first I calculated that there were about fifty of them, but later I realized that there were at least one hundred. Sometimes they were isolated, sometimes in pairs, or in threes or fours or sevens or twelves. Frequently they were in diamond or 'lozenge' formations of four, or in 'V' formations of seven."

At noon, Dr. Perego reported, a large formation of twenty objects appeared from the east, followed by another twenty coming from the opposite direction. "The two 'V' shaped squadrons converged rapidly until the vertices of the two 'V's' met, thus forming a perfect 'St. Andrew's Cross' of forty machines, with ten to each bar." The convergence seemed to occur at a height of about 7,000 or 8,000 meters over the Trastevere-Monte Mario district of Rome—right over the Vatican City. The entire "cross" then performed a three-quarter turn on its axis, becoming more of an "X" shape, then broke off into two separate curves which moved off in opposite directions. The performance had lasted about three minutes, Dr. Perego noted. But the show was not over.

"As I watched, I saw what appeared like a large bluish shadow forming in the sky ten minutes later and realized that it was a fresh concentration building up as, in formations and squadrons of four and seven and twelve, they began to reappear. This time I was able to make a better count, and could see that they totaled at least one hundred. This time the concentration was in another part of the sky, and not directly above the Vatican."

Dr. Perego then noticed what appeared to be a shining filament-type material coming out of the sky, the substance that has subsequently been nicknamed "angel hair," reported by witnesses throughout the world. "I was able to seize a handful of it," he said. "It looked like the fine twigs and filaments of a Christmas tree, but thinner, and very long. It was not like the filaments used in the last war by the US bombers to disturb the enemy radar [chaff]. It was not tinfoil, but rather a 'glassy' sort of substance, which evaporated completely in a few hours."

The following day, 7 November, not a word appeared in the newspapers. Dr. Perego's inquiries at the Ministry of Foreign Affairs drew a blank: they knew nothing about the sightings. At 11:30 a.m., returning to the Tuscolano district, Perego was astonished to see further formations of objects, totaling about fifty, which remained in the sky for two-and-a-half hours. "The squadrons would always arrive from different directions," he recalled, "and always in regular formations. . . . They would fly away over the country around Rome, and return in formation ten minutes later for the next 'concentration.' "

Yet again, the strange "angel hair" descended over Rome, which thousands of people must have witnessed. But there was still no word from the press, apart from a report in *Il Messagero* that in England *RAF radar had detected squadrons of mysterious objects on 6 November.* "At the British War Office, they are concerned," concluded the report. But not, it seems, in the Italian War Office.

The next day Dr. Perego called on Air Force General Pezzi, Chief of the Cabinet of the Ministry of Defense. "He received me very courteously," said Perego, "but he said he knew nothing whatever about the events I described. I read my notes to him, and asked him to report the matter to the Minister of Defense."

On 10 November Dr. Perego was received by the Principal Secretary of Foreign Affairs, but drew a blank once more. He knew nothing about the matter, and was surprised that the military authorities had made no report to him. The reason became apparent the following day when Perego visited General de Vincenti, Commander of the Italian Air Force, who explained that since radar operated over certain fixed zones, at certain times, and only up to 6–7,000 meters, nothing had been tracked.

When the mysterious objects made yet another appearance over Rome, on 12 November (again in the morning), Dr. Perego immediately contacted General de Vincenti at Air Defense Headquarters, who said that orders had been issued for observations to be made. Although no official confirmation from military sources was forthcoming, Perego paid a visit to the Vatican Observatory at Castel Gandolfo near Rome and learned that a Brazilian priest on duty at about 11:00 a.m. had seen some strange objects pass twice over the Observatory, very low and at terrific speed, in complete silence.

It was two years before Dr. Perego came to accept the fact that what he and thousands of others witnessed over Rome could only have been the manifestation of an extraterrestrial intelligence, a revelation that inspired him to become a leading champion of *Dischi Volanti* (Flying Saucers).[23]

LANDING AT ISTRANA AIR BASE?

Istrana Air Base, thirty kilometers northwest of Venice, was allegedly the scene of a UFO landing—complete with occupants—on an evening in mid-November 1973. According to a newspaper account, two sentries at a lookout post on the perimeter of the base saw two beings dressed in white, about 1.5 meters tall. A little further away could be seen an unidentified craft.

After the occupants disappeared in their craft, the sentries immediately reported the incident. Marks were found at the landing site, the *Veneto Notte* claimed, and commented: "The authorities in charge of the Istrana military air base have classified the matter as top secret, and nobody is at present prepared to admit that it occurred."[24]

The story is lacking in details, but I have included it because so many similar incidents have taken place at military bases throughout the world; incidents that are invariably shrouded in a cloak of secrecy immediately afterward.

UFO BLACKS OUT NATO BASE AT AVIANO, 1977

The important NATO base at Aviano, northeast Italy, was the scene of a dramatic UFO sighting in the small hours of 1 July 1977. At 3:00 a.m. an American soldier, James Blake, noticed a peculiar large bright light hovering at a height of about 100 meters in the "Victor Alert Zone," where two military aircraft were kept. According to Antonio Chiumiento, who learned of the incident from a number of sources, including an Italian Air Force NCO, the object was seen by many military personnel. About fifty meters in diameter it resembled a spinning top revolving on its own axis, with a dome on top, changing colors from white to green then red. A noise like a swarm of bees in flight could be heard. The object remained over the base for about an hour, causing a massive power blackout.

One of the independent witnesses was Signor Benito Manfré, a night watchman living at Castello d'Aviano, one and a half kilometers away. Alerted by the incessant barking of his dog in the middle of the night, he went out on to the veranda and noticed that the NATO base was in total darkness, something that he had never seen before. "What particularly aroused my attention," he said, "was the presence of a 'mass' of stationary light low down over a certain spot on the base itself."

Signor Manfré tried to persuade his wife to come and join him, but she was too tired, so he remained alone, transfixed by the object, which he described as a "glowing disk." After five minutes or so the object slowly moved away from the "Victor Alert Zone" and then noiselessly climbed away beyond the mountains near Aviano. "Ten seconds or so after the mysterious object had left the base," said the night watchman, "the base's lights came on again. I must add that my dog only stopped barking when the luminous 'disk' had left the area . . . about half an hour later I was able to note a certain amount of movement of vehicles of the American Military Police.''

Although nothing about the episode was made public, it was the subject of intense speculation in Aviano. Predictably, the story was debunked by the military, and the official explanation was that ''the phenomenon must be attributed to a reflection of the moon on some low clouds.''

Just how the moon could have descended to an altitude of 100 meters, appeared to have a diameter of 50 meters, and caused a major security alert (NATO's Brussels headquarters was informed) as it blacked out the entire base, was of course left unexplained. And as Antonio Chiumiento emphasizes, the minimum temperature in the particular area was too high in relation to the percentage of humidity to allow for cloud formation at that altitude—nor was the moon in the right place.[25]

MINISTRY OF DEFENSE RELEASES FILE

In March 1978 the Italian Ministry of Defense released a file containing details of six unclassified reports by military personnel in 1977. One of the cases involved the sighting by two pilots of a ''luminous circle'' on 27 October over the military airfield at Cagliari, Sardinia, which had been tracked by other witnesses, including personnel at the control tower at Elmas. A jet was sent up to investigate but was unable to intercept the object.

The principal witnesses were Major Francesco Zoppi, chief pilot of the *Orsa Maggiore* Squadron of the Italian Army Light Aircraft Corps (ALE) 21st Helicopter Group, together with his co-pilot Lieutenant Riccardelli. In a statement published before the Ministry released the file on the case, the pilots described their experience:

We had taken off in the helicopters for a normal training flight when, at a distance of about 300 meters, I saw, in front of me, an extremely bright orange-colored circle . . . we at once contacted the control tower [who] replied that nothing was visible from the ground. Meanwhile, the fiery circle continued to be there, right in front of us, and moving at a speed almost identical to our own. Then I asked the other two helicopters of our squadron whether they could see it. One said they could, and that they were seeing the same thing as we were, while the third helicopter, piloted by Captain Romolo Romani, replied that they saw nothing.

The luminous circle then vanished at a speed impossible for any aircraft of this world to equal. I called the control tower again, and was informed that in the meantime other people had seen it and had been following it with binoculars. But the radar had detected nothing.[26]

On 5 January 1978 the Ministry of Defense explained that what had been seen was nothing more than "an aircraft operating out of Sardinia in the course of an ordinary flight mission" which the pilots had failed to recognize "owing to particular weather conditions during twilight."

Another case released by the Ministry—which had not received any publicity beforehand—also occurred in the vicinity of the Elmas air base. On 2 November 1977 Italian Air Force pilots and the pilots of two German Air Force F-104G Starfighters, as well as the personnel at the Elmas control tower, observed a similar circular or elliptical "ball of fire" flying at tremendous speed. These reports were included in the file released to the Italian National UFO Research Center and another group, but inadvertently a copy was sent to a group consisting of two teenagers, who promptly and irresponsibly handed it over to the press, creating considerable embarrassment for the Ministry, who were obliged once again to discredit the Elmas sightings.[27]

CLOSE ENCOUNTER NEAR MOUNT ETNA, 1978

Close encounter cases involving reports of UFO occupants seen by a group of people rather than a single witness are comparatively rare, and although this does not automatically rule out hoax or mass delusion, such cases obviously carry more weight. On the night of 4 July 1978 at about 10:30 p.m., two Italian Air Force sergeants, Franco Padellero and Attilio di Salvatore, together with Maurizio Esposito, an Italian Navy officer, and Signora Antonina di Pietro, were off duty near Mount Etna, Sicily, when they noticed a triangle of three bright red lights in the sky which seemed to be pulsating. All of a sudden one of the lights detached itself, headed toward the group, then disappeared down a slope about 1,000 feet away.

The group decided to investigate and drove in di Salvatore's car to where the light seemed to have landed. As they rounded a bend they noticed a dazzling light coming from a dip at the side of the road. Stopping the car they went and looked over the edge.

Resting near a rocky precipice on the slope below was a saucer-shaped object about forty feet across, with a brilliant yellow (illuminated) dome. The rest of the object was of a reddish hue with blue and red lights on top. By the side of the craft were five or six very tall beings, according to the report, with black overall-type tight-fitting suits and blond hair. Their features were described as human and "beautiful."

Two of the beings began climbing up the slope toward the witnesses, who by now found themselves immobilized by an unknown force. The beings smiled as they came to within about fifteen feet of the group, then one of them nodded toward the saucer and they both climbed back down the slope.

The saucer now began to glow with multicolored tiny points of light; yellow, red and blue predominating, but when a car went by all the lights went out, only brightening again when the car had passed. The witnesses recovered their mobility shortly afterward, then drove away without waiting to see the object depart. All four felt drained of energy for some time after the incident.[28]

Such stories do not provide proof of extraterrestrial visitors, yet there are intriguing aspects of the case that have been corroborated elsewhere, and witnesses have little to gain by hoaxing—particularly if they are in the military.

PORTUGUESE AIR FORCE JETS IN FORTY-MINUTE UFO ENCOUNTER, 1957

On the night of 4 September 1957 a flight of four US-built F-84 Thunderjets took off from Ota Air Base, Portugal, on a routine practice navigation mission. It was a clear night with an almost full moon, and the air to ground visibility reported in flight was well over fifty statute miles. The pilots were Captain José Lemos Ferreira, the flight commander, Sergeant Alberto Gomes Covas, Sergeant Manuel Neves Marcelino and Sergeant Salvador Alberto Oliveira. Captain Ferreira takes up the story:

After we reached Granada, at 2006 hours, and started a port turn to change course to Portalegre I noticed on my left and above the horizon a very unusual source of light . . . after three or four minutes I decided to report it to the other pilots. At that time the pilot flying on my right wing told me he had already noticed it. The other two pilots flying on my left wing had not yet seen it. Together we started exchanging comments over the radio about our discovery and we tried several solutions but none seemed to be a reasonable explanation for the thing we were observing at the moment. The thing looked like a very bright star unusually big and scintillating, with a colored nucleus which changed color constantly, going from deep green to blue to passing through yellowish and reddish colorations.

The pilots dismissed the possibility that the object could have been either Venus or another planet or star, or a balloon or aircraft. Captain Ferreira continued:

> All of a sudden the thing grew very rapidly, assuming five or six times its initial volume, becoming quite a spectacle to see . . . [then] fast as it had grown, [it] decided to shrink, almost disappearing on the horizon, becoming a just visible, small, yellow point. These expansions and contractions happened several times, but without becoming periodic and always having a pause, longer or shorter, before modifying volume. The relative position between us and the thing was still the same, that is about 40° on our left, and we could not determine if the changing dimensions were due to very fast approaches and retreats on the same vector or if the modifying took place stationary. . . . After about seven or eight minutes of this the thing had been gradually getting down below the horizon and dislocated itself for a position about 90° to our left. . . . At 2038 hours I decided to abandon the mission and to make a port turn in the general direction of Coruche since nobody was paying any attention to the exercise. We turned about 50° to port but still the thing maintained its position of 90° to our left which could not be possible with a stationary object.
>
> By now the phenomenon was well below our level of 25,000 feet and apparently quite near, presenting a bright red and looking like a curved shell of beans at an arm's length. After several minutes on our new course we discovered a small circle of yellow light apparently coming out of the thing and before our surprise elapsed we detected three other identical circles on the right of the thing. The whole was moving with their relative positions changing constantly and sometimes very rapidly. Still we could not estimate the distance between us and them, although they were below us and apparently very near. In any case the big "thing" looked ten to fifteen times greater than the yellow circles and apparently was the director of operations since the others were moving around it.
>
> As we were near Coruche the "big thing" suddenly and very rapidly made what looked like a dive, followed up by a climb in our direction. Then everybody went wild and almost broke formation in the process of crossing over and ahead of the UFO. We were all very excited and I had a hard time to calm things down. As soon as we crossed over everything disappeared in a few seconds and later we landed without further incident. Since the first moment we detected the UFO to the final show a registered time of forty minutes had elapsed, and during it we had ample opportunity to verify every possible explanation for the phenomenon. We got no conclusions, except that after this *do not give us the old routine of Venus, balloons, aircraft and the like which has been given as a general panacea for almost every case of UFOs.* [Emphasis added]

At the same time that the pilots had their encounter, the Coimbra Meteorological Observatory registered extraordinary localized variations in the earth's magnetic field, as proven by charts at that establishment.[29]

SPANISH AIR FORCE JETS ENCOUNTER UFOS, 1967

On 9 June 1967 a Spanish Air Force Lockheed T-33 encountered an unidentified object over the province of Extremadura, while flying at an altitude of 1,200 meters. Attempts to contact the object failed; in fact, when directly above or below the object, the plane's radios ceased to function and emitted nothing but static.

The object alternately moved ahead of the jet, hovered as if waiting for it to catch up, then moved away again. The pilots notified their base at Talavera-Badajoz and two faster planes were sent up from the base at Torréjon. According to one of Europe's leading researchers, Antonio Ribera, these aircraft also experienced the same radio interference when in the vicinity of the object, which once again performed similar maneuvers before disappearing vertically at fantastic speed.[30]

UFO ELUDES AIR FORCE JET, 1968

My first sighting of a UFO took place on the evening of 1 August 1963, when together with other witnesses I observed a bright star-like object over Beckenham. Through binoculars the stationary object looked tetrahedral in shape, of a translucent or glass-like appearance. I learned that thousands of people in London and the home counties had seen the object; that a US Air Force F-100 Super Sabre from RAF/USAF Bentwaters and another plane from the De Havilland Aircraft Company had been sent up to investigate but were unable to get anywhere near, owing to its great altitude (at least 90,000 feet); and that an amateur astronomer from Bushey in Hertfordshire took a clear photo.

The official explanation that the object was a balloon has failed to satisfy me, not least because identical objects seen and photographed elsewhere in Europe in the 1960s have never been positively identified. One such "balloon" was seen by thousands over Madrid on 5 September 1968, as this dramatic report by Barry James the following day describes:

Madrid (UPI)—The Spanish Air Force said Friday an "unidentified flying object" eluded one of its supersonic jet fighter-bombers as a rash of flying saucer reports spread from Latin America to Europe.

The sighting of a bright object in the night sky Thursday over Madrid caused a monumental traffic jam and sent the US-built F-104 jet scrambling to find out what it was.

An official Air Force announcement said the pilot climbed to an altitude of more than 50,000 feet and reported the object was still above him when he had to return to base for fuel. The pilot of another plane flying at 36,000 feet reported seeing the same object.

Air Force radar screens tracked the UFO and said it was flying at 90,000 feet and moving slowly.

Thousands of Spaniards jammed the streets of Madrid to get a look at the object, and traffic backed up for miles.

One reporter, sent to the Madrid Astronomical Observatory for a look through its powerful telescope, said the object gave off "a blinding light." A photo taken through the telescope revealed a triangular object, apparently solid on one side and translucent in some sections.

The official Air Force announcement said it had no scientific explanation for the phenomenon but theorized that the object might have been a meteorological balloon.

The Madrid Weather Bureau said it had no lost balloons and offered the theory that the object was part of a space satellite returning to earth.

Could it have been a balloon? Philip Klass, former senior avionics editor of *Aviation Week & Space Technology* and America's leading UFO debunker, has told me that he believes the tetrahedral objects were of French rather than extraterrestrial origin, made in Toulouse for the National Center of Space Studies (CNES), although he has been unable to confirm this. Klass explained that these balloons could remain within a fifty-mile radius for days on end by radio-controlled ballast adjustments. Some could maintain "station" (like the objects seen over London and Madrid), he believes, but only "within a few tens of miles for a few hours."[31]

It sounds a plausible hypothesis, and may well account for the majority of these reports. But there are still question marks. For example, I have yet to see an official photo of this type of balloon that looks exactly like the tetrahedron "UFOs." I sent a print of the 1963 photo to the Max Planck Institute for Aeronomie in Germany, which had launched some of the balloons for cosmic ray research in the 1960s. "Our Institute launched some from near Göttingen," came the reply, "but I cannot confirm that the balloon you observed was indeed launched from here. . . . At that time many balloons were tetrahedral in shape. They were built by a French factory. The volume of these balloons amounted to about 4.000 to 10.000 m^3. Your photo . . . possibly shows a balloon, if you turn it by 180°. Then you can also recognize the tetrahedral shape with the flat side to the top. . . . These balloons drift with the high altitude wind (in August, 10–30 km/h)."[32]

The object I saw in 1963, however, did not have a flat side to the top.

Jan Willemstyn, the amateur astronomer and former pilot who took the best photograph of the object, told me that the base consisted of three triangles with a common apex, the bases of the triangles forming a triangular periphery roughly equilateral. At the top apex he observed a rod-like extension with several transverse members—a detail confirmed by the pianist John Bingham, living near me at the time, through his reflector telescope. Jan Willemstyn said that the object was stationary in the field of view of his four-inch refractor telescope for over two hours—an impossible feat for a balloon.

The 1968 Madrid "balloon" managed to climb to a great altitude when pursued by the F-104 Starfighter and then *disappeared at great speed,* according to the official Air Force report as well as the *Daily Telegraph* in London.[33] No balloon can do that. Neither would the Air Force scramble a jet to chase an unidentified object unless they were reasonably certain it was *not* a balloon, although there have been instances when air defense centers have mistaken balloons for UFOs.

UFOS AT AIR FORCE TARGET RANGE, 1975

On the night of 2 January 1975 six military personnel at the Air Force bombing and gunnery range at Las Bardenas Reales near the Zaragoza Air Base saw two unidentified objects, one of which apparently landed or hovered low over the ground for twenty-five minutes, between 11:00 and 11:25 p.m.

According to the official report (see Appendix, p. 459), the principal witness (name deleted) observed the second object through binoculars and described it as "shaped like an inverted cup" with white lights on the upper and lower parts and intermittent white and amber lights on the sides. He was unable to estimate the size precisely, but thought it was about that of a truck. When it took off a powerful light on its underside illuminated the entire area. No sound could be heard.[34]

Spanish military authorities of the Third Air Force Region appointed an investigating judge to inquire into the incident.[35] The official explanation given at the time was that the soldiers reporting the landing had experienced an optical illusion, but the following year the Air Ministry released some documents on the case which prove this explanation false. Concluded the Air Force: "All the witnesses were questioned one by one and separately; no contradictions were found; all coincided exactly in their descriptions. From their reports could be established the fact that

. . . unidentified flying objects flew . . . at a low altitude and low speed over the ground . . . [then] rapidly ascended and, gaining high speed, disappeared in a NW direction."

AIR FORCE GENERAL CONFIRMS UFO REALITY, 1976

In June 1976 General Castro, Divisional General commanding the air zone of the Canary Islands at the time, granted an interview with *La Gaceta del Norte* during which he announced that UFOs were taken extremely seriously at a high level. "As a general, my opinion is the same as the Air Ministry," he said, "but in my own personal capacity, as Carlos Castro Cavero, I have for some time held the view that UFOs are extraterrestrial craft."

The general said that he had personally witnessed a UFO for more than an hour over the town of Sadaba, near Zaragoza. "It was an extremely bright object," he recalled, "which remained there stationary for that length of time and then shot off toward Egea de los Caballeros, covering the distance of twenty kilometers in less than two seconds. No human device is capable of such a speed."

General Castro revealed that the Spanish Air Ministry possessed about twenty cases that had been thoroughly investigated by experts and found to be completely unexplainable in conventional terms. He added that pilots had flown alongside UFOs in aircraft, but when they tried to close in the objects moved off at speeds far higher than anything made by man. Many countries collaborated on research into the subject, he said, and when definite conclusions had been arrived at it might then be possible to inform the world.[36]

SPANISH AIR MINISTRY RELEASES UFO FILES

In October 1976 Señor Juan José Benitez, a reporter for *La Gaceta del Norte*, was invited to the Air Ministry in Madrid where, in the office of an Air Force lieutenant general and Chief of Staff, he was handed a file containing documentation by the Spanish government on twelve of their most outstanding cases. The documents were backed up with photographic evidence, including clips of gun-camera film taken by Air Force pilots.

Although it was made clear to Señor Benitez that release of the documents was not on an official basis, he was nevertheless given the go-ahead to publish the reports.[37] "The first twelve files were handed to me

in person on October 20 1976, in the old Air Ministry building in Madrid,''
said Benitez. ''The other two files came to me in the closing weeks of
1978 and also from the hands of a senior general.'' Benitez pointed out:
''When you read and analyze these files, which total almost 300 folio
pages, *it becomes definitely and categorically clear that the UFOs exist
and, quite evidently, are a matter of the deepest concern to the governments of the whole planet.*''[38] [Emphasis added]

One of the most unusual cases in the Air Ministry files is that of a
doctor and two other witnesses who encountered a UFO with beings
inside it on the Grand Canary Islands. The date was 22 June 1976, the
time 21:27. Dr. Padrón León was traveling by taxi with Santiago del
Pino, the son of a sick woman whom he was on his way to treat. It was
a clear, starry night. Suddenly, rounding a bend, the witnesses were
startled to see a perfect sphere about sixty meters ahead of them, hovering
a few meters off the ground.

''We experienced a terrible feeling of cold,'' Dr. León said in his
statement to the Air Ministry. ''The chauffeur even started trembling—
especially when the taxi's radio, which had been turned on, suddenly cut
out.'' The sphere was transparent ''like a gigantic soap bubble'' with a
diameter of a two-story house. Inside could be seen a platform, some
panels, and two large beings (see Appendix, p. 460).

''We were astonished at the great size of the beings; maybe 2 meters
80, or 3.00 meters,'' said Dr. León. ''They were wearing black 'divers'
helmets' and their clothing, which was very tight-fitting, was of a shade
of red that I have never seen in my life. . . . Their hands seemed to be
enclosed in by 'cones,' also black. . . . The two beings were facing each
other, moving their hands about, and operating levers. They were in
profile to us.'' What surprised the doctor in particular was the dispro-
portionate size of the back part of their heads (perhaps due to the helmet?)
and their relatively short legs.

When the taxi-driver switched on his headlights the sphere began to
rise. The witnesses then noticed that a bluish ''gas'' seemed to be coming
out of a transparent tube, ''expanding'' the sphere until it was the size
of a twenty-story building! The beings, panels and platform, however,
retained their original size.

''We were terrified,'' said Dr. León, ''and we turned the car round
and went to some nearby houses, and went inside one of them. The
people there told us that their television had just blacked out.'' Dr. León
and the others remained in the house and continued watching the object

through a window. When the sphere had ceased expanding, the "gas" or "fluid" that was moving around inside suddenly became motionless, there was a high pitched whistle and the object shot off toward Tenerife, appearing to change shape to that of a spindle surrounded by a large white halo.[39]

In commenting on this sighting—and others, including a report that night in the Canary Islands from a Spanish Navy vessel—the Air Force reporting judge stopped short of offering an extraterrestrial explanation, but concluded nonetheless: "If we study jointly the three reports issued up to now, Nos. 1/75, 1/76, and 2/76 we would have to face seriously the necessity of having to consider the possibility of accepting the hypothesis that *a craft of unknown origin and driven by an energy likewise unknown is operating freely in the skies above the Canary Islands.*"[40] [Emphasis added]

SIGHTINGS FROM AIRCRAFT, 1976–80

On 19 September 1976 a Portuguese TAP Boeing 707 nearly collided with an unidentified object shortly after takeoff from Lisbon, according to a newspaper report. The object, described as oval and bright, glowing blue with a horizontal row of red and white lights, was also seen by an air traffic controller, who said it did not show up on radar.[41]

Two months later the pilot of an Iberian Airlines Boeing 727 on a flight from Santiago de Compostela in northwest Spain to Madrid reported an unknown object that accompanied his plane for twenty minutes. The sighting was one of many on 19 November 1976, and in this case may have been due to a barium cloud experiment released into the upper atmosphere by rocket, although Comandante Parreno said the phenomenon was like nothing he had seen in his twenty-five years' flying experience.[42]

Portuguese Air Force Pilot's Alarming Encounter, 1977

On 17 June 1977 José Francisco Rodrigues, a twenty-three-year-old pilot of the Portuguese Air Force 31st Squadron, based at Tancos, had a disturbing encounter with a UFO in his Dornier 27 light aircraft. The original information on this important story was supplied by Joaquim Fernandes, a journalist with the *Journal de Noticias*, who in turn passed it to the Center for UFO Studies, to whom I am indebted for the following report.

On the day in question the weather was poor, with intermittent rain and a cloud ceiling of less than 3,000 feet. Visibility was about five miles. Sergeant Rodrigues was flying over the Castelo de Bode dam at around noon when suddenly, emerging from the clouds, he saw a dark object against a backdrop of white stratocumulus, slightly to the right of his plane. Thinking that the object was perhaps a cargo plane he banked to the left and immediately radioed to ask if there was any traffic in the vicinity. A reply came in the negative.

As the young pilot completed a turn to port, the unknown object suddenly appeared at his 11 o'clock position "no more than six meters away." It was definitely not a cargo plane. The upper section, partially concealed by cloud, was black, and on the lower section there appeared to be four or five "panels." The object was approximately thirteen to fifteen meters in diameter. Suddenly it accelerated and vanished from what the pilot believes was an initial stationary position.

The Dornier began to vibrate violently and went into an uncontrolled dive. Struggling to regain control, Sergeant Rodrigues pushed the control column forward. Airspeed increased to 140 knots, then 180 knots as the ground came nearer. Control was fortunately regained when almost "touching the tree tops" and the plane was landed in one piece—with a badly shaken pilot. During the encounter the directional electric gyroscope (connected to a magnetic compass) rotated wildly, and by the time the plane landed it had deviated by 180° relative to the magnetic compass.

Sergeant José Vicente Saldanha, the duty controller that day, confirmed Rodrigues' radio call and that about a minute later he heard a loud shout. The base is about five kilometers from the dam above which the incident occurred, but owing to hills and poor visibility nothing was seen from the tower. However, the pilot spoke with two witnesses (presumably from another area of the base) who saw the plane falling in a "dead-leaf" pattern, then disappearing from view. They also heard the engine roaring as the pilot regained control.

Such was Sergeant Rodrigues' state of shock when he landed that he had difficulty speaking. An examination by the base doctor revealed no untoward medical cause that might have accounted for his condition, and the duty controller felt certain that a simple engine problem would not have upset the pilot to such a degree. Nor could any fault be found with the engine.

The Portuguese Air Force Chief of Staff eventually (and reluctantly) allowed veteran researchers José Garrido and Vitor Santos to interview both the pilot and controller. Their conclusions were as follows:

> As Sergeant Rodrigues completed his 315° turn . . . with a large radius, the object reappeared to his left "at 11 o'clock" and very close. It is hard to decide . . . whether the object moved or not during the 40 seconds that the plane took to complete the turn, although the original [report] conveys that idea. At any rate, during his second glimpse Sergeant Rodrigues thought that the object was motionless, or practically so, and then accelerated and departed. In either case this implies a series of maneuvers by the object, including an anomalous acceleration which . . . rules out . . . a balloon or a conventional machine.

No official explanation for the incident was offered by the Air Force.[43]

Near Collision Over Spain, 1979

Spain's most dramatic airline encounter with UFOs happened on 11 November 1979, when Comandante Francisco Lerdo de Tejada, flying a Super Caravelle of the TAE company from Salzburg in Austria to Tenerife, was forced to take evasive action to avoid colliding with an unknown object. The airliner had 109 passengers on board, most of whom were German and Austrian tourists. Captain Tejada stated in an interview with Juan José Benitez:

> A few minutes before 11:00 p.m. we got a call from Air Control Barcelona. They asked us to switch over to 121.5 megacycles, which is an emergency frequency. . . . So we switched to that frequency, and imagined that there might perhaps be a ship or aircraft in difficulties. But then, when we made contact, all we got was the noise of a transmitter, though we were unable to identify what it was all about. It was at that moment, or a few seconds later, that we saw the red lights . . . Two very red, powerful lights.
> They were heading toward us at 9 o'clock of our position. . . . The two lights seemed to be set at the two extremities. All of the movements of the two lights were perfectly coordinated, just as if it were one single device we were dealing with. . . . The speed at which they came at us was staggering. I have never seen anything like that speed. . . . The two lights, in line, came up to us on a bearing of 250°. . . . When we saw them first, they were at about 10 miles. Then they made toward us, and then were literally "playing with us" at not much under half a mile or so. . . .
> The object was moving upward and downward at will, all round us, and performing movements that it would be quite impossible for any

conventional machine to execute. . . . What sort of aircraft flies at that sort of speed? What sort of aircraft takes up a position at less than half a mile from my jet liner and then sets about "playing games" with me?

Captain Tejada said that the object's size was "*approximately the same as a jumbo jet*," and that its approach speed was such that he was obliged to make a "break"—turning the aircraft sharply to avoid collision. According to one news report, an elderly male passenger collapsed when he saw the objects zigzagging across the night sky toward the plane. "The situation finally got so serious," said the airline pilot, "that we decided to call Manises and request permission to make an emergency landing."

The plane touched down at Valencia shortly before midnight, with the UFO still visible over the airport buildings, seen by the airport director, Señor Morlan, together with his air traffic controller and a number of ground personnel.

According to Señor Benitez, there was an immediate response by the Spanish Air Force Defense Command Center in Madrid. Radar had registered a number of echoes in precisely the area where the airliner was flying at the time, and Air Defense Command HQ ordered two Mirage F1 jets to take off on an intercept mission from Los Llanos Air Base, near Albacete, five minutes after the airliner had landed. Although Señor Benitez was unable to secure official confirmation, he learned that the Mirage pilots established visual contact with the UFO, and that one of the planes was subjected to a number of sudden close approaches by the unknown object—or objects.

Captain Tejada and his flight crew were interrogated by the Air Force shortly after landing. "As is usual in all cases of this sort," reported Benitez, "the Spanish Air Force . . . initiates an extensive investigation and appoints an official with the title of *Juez-Informador* to preside over it. He is generally a high-ranking Air Force officer."[44]

Anniversary Sightings?

Precisely one year after the TAE Super Caravelle sighting, at least six Spanish airliners reported sighting UFOs—or possibly the same object —in northeast Spain. Again, leading researcher and journalist Juan José Benitez has uncovered important details about these sightings, which all took place on the evening of 11 November 1980.

The airliners included Iberia Flights 350, 810, 1800, and 1831, Trans-

europa Flight 1474, and an air-taxi flight en route from the Balearic
Islands to Marseilles. In an interview with Señor Benitez, Comandante
Ramos—one of the Iberia pilots—described his sighting:

> It was 6:40 p.m. We were flying at about 10,000 meters, and I think, if
> my memory serves me right, that we were in the vicinity of Maella. The
> Second Pilot was at the controls at the time . . . when we were about 108
> miles from the Barcelona VOR [VHF Omnirange] "it" appeared. . . . At
> first, we took it for another plane. We saw a green light, and we thought
> it must be the green light carried by planes on the starboard wing. But this
> supposed plane was coming straight at us. . . . The Second Pilot said
> "Look!" It was coming toward us at an angle of 230° . . . almost on a
> collision course.
>   It was like a sphere. Or rather, like an enormous soap bubble. When I
> saw it, it was almost on a level with us and coming straight for our 727.
> I made an instant reflex movement. The Second Pilot had switched off the
> automatic pilot, and I pushed the controls forward and . . . did a dive of
> 300 or 400 feet. . . . The whole thing happened just in a minute or less.
> The sphere or "soap bubble," colored a very bright green on its surface,
> crossed our course and when we dived it made off toward the south. It
> was then that we saw it was emitting other lights. . . . When it passed
> close to us we also saw a second ball—or whatever—close to the big one,
> but much smaller in size. . . .
>   I asked Barcelona Flight Control if there was any other traffic in the
> area. They replied that there was only an English plane [Monarch Flight
> 148] bound for Alicante. Shortly after that another plane came in on the
> radio. I think, if my memory is not at fault, that it was a Transeuropa
> [Flight 1474]. And he also asked Barcelona if there was a "green traffic"
> on his flight route. Then I talked to the Transeuropa plane and told him
> what had just happened to me.

The crew of Iberia Flight 1831 sighted the UFO while their Boeing
727 was still on the ground, and when the captain signaled to it by flashing
his landing lights the object immediately "went out" and disappeared.
Other witnesses at Barcelona Airport said that the UFO "buzzed" the
runway and then shot up into the sky.

Is there a logical explanation for these multiple-witness sightings? As
the pilots interviewed by Señor Benitez commented: "It is totally impossible for a machine that comes along in a horizontal flight, then changes
course when one aircraft takes an evasive dive, then comes down and
'buzzes' the runways at Barcelona Airport and then turns off its light
when another plane flashes light signals at it—it is totally impossible for
a machine that does all these things to be anything else but controlled by
some type of intelligence."[45]

"I believe in the existence of UFOs," said Spanish Air Force General Castro in 1976, and went on to give his own carefully reasoned thoughts on why it was difficult for governments to come out in the open. "The position is that it is as difficult for official quarters to admit that something exists as it is for the Church to affirm that this or that is a miracle," he explained.

General Castro believes that the reason governments do not publicly acknowledge this reality is not due to fear on their part, but rather to a sense of misgiving in the face of an intangible fact on which they are being asked to venture an opinion.[46]

The general is being honest insofar as his own government is concerned, and one wonders if he was partly responsible for the Air Ministry releasing its files to Señor Benitez five months after he made these statements. UFOs—with their superior abilities—may well appear "miraculous" to us in comparison. But there is ample evidence that some unidentified flying objects are far from intangible; that a number of them have been recovered intact, and that yet another reason for the cover-up is because the superpowers are intent on duplicating their technology, as will be shown in Part III.

7

AUSTRALIA

Responsibility for monitoring Unidentified or Unusual Aerial Sightings (UAS), as they are officially designated in Australia, rests solely with the Royal Australian Air Force (RAAF), I was informed by the Department of Defense in 1982. At each RAAF base specific officers are appointed to investigate sightings, investigation being restricted to those instances formally reported to the RAAF. When required, assistance is sought from other government departments such as Aviation, Meteorology, Science and Technology (for satellite predictions), plus observatories. "No Australian Secret Service participates in the investigations," I was assured.[1]

The Air Force Office of the Department of Defense also sent me a copy of their *Summaries of Unusual Aerial Sightings 1976–1980*. The percentage breakdown of RAAF investigations, it was pointed out, closely matches those of the Royal Air Force and US Air Force investigations, and only about three percent of the reports are attributable to "unknown causes." In all its investigations to date, which average about 100 per year, the RAAF "have found no tangible evidence of life from other planets."[2]

EARLY OFFICIAL INVESTIGATIONS

Official Australian investigation into unidentified flying objects goes back as far as 1920, according to researcher Paul Norman, when the ship SS *Amelia J.* disappeared at a time when strange unexplained lights were being reported around the entrance to Bass Strait. A search aircraft sent to investigate the lights also disappeared and never returned.[3] The Bass Strait area has featured in a number of mysterious cases, most notably the disappearance of the young pilot Frederick Valentich in 1978 (discussed later in this chapter).

In 1930 the RAAF sent a squadron leader to Warrnambool, Victoria, on the north shore of Bass Strait, where witnesses had reported sightings of unidentified "aircraft." No evidence could be found that the aircraft were either Australian or foreign; nor could they even be positively identified as normal aircraft.

The squadron leader who conducted the investigation subsequently became Air Marshal Sir George Jones, Chief of the Air Staff 1942–52.[4] Sir George had his own sighting of a UFO from his home in Mentone, Melbourne, on 16 October 1957, when together with Lady Jones he observed a balloon-like object traveling at the speed of a Sabre jet at about 1,000–1,500 feet altitude.[5] He maintained a serious interest in the subject, and on retirement became a member of the Victorian UFO Research Society.[6]

Bill Chalker (of the Australian Center for UFO Studies) has unearthed two interesting RAAF reports dating back to World War II. The first took place during the summer of 1942, when an RAAF pilot was on flying patrol off the Tasman Peninsula late one afternoon, following reports by fishermen of strange lights on the sea at night in Bass Strait. At 5:50 p.m. an unidentified object came out of a cloud bank, which the pilot described as "a singular airfoil of glistening bronze color," about 150 feet in length and 50 feet in diameter, with a dome on top that reflected sunlight. The UFO flew alongside the plane for a few minutes, then suddenly turned away at "a hell of a pace." It made another turn then dived straight into the ocean, throwing up "a regular whirlpool of waves."

The second sighting took place one night in February 1944, when at around 2:30 a.m. a Beaufort bomber flying at 4,500 feet over Bass Strait was joined by an unidentified object, described as a "dark shadow" with a flickering light and flame coming out of the rear. The object appeared to be only 100–150 feet away, and stayed with the plane for 18–20 minutes, during which time both radio and direction-finding instruments failed. Eventually the object shot off at about three times the speed of the bomber (235 mph at that time).

Bill Chalker reports that no enemy action was ever confirmed in Bass Strait, although a total of seventeen aircraft went missing in that area during World War II.[7]

In 1952 officers of the Department of Civil Aviation sought to establish a special bureau to collate facts about UFOs. From the Cabinet itself, however, came instructions that the subject was *more properly a matter for the security services to investigate*, and accordingly a security spokesman confirmed shortly afterward that they had investigators working on reports with the aid of scientists from the radiophysics division of the Commonwealth Scientific and Industrial Research Organization (CSIRO).[8]

Although UFO files were initially classified secret, a sighting in 1954 was rated top secret, and details would never have been known for many years had the story not been leaked to the media five months after the incident. On 31 August 1954 a Navy Hawker Sea Fury aircraft was approached by two strange lights with vague shapes underneath, 5,000 meters above Goulburn, New South Wales. The pilot radioed Nowra Naval Air Station and was informed that the objects were tracked on radar. The lights shot past the Sea Fury "spinning at fantastic speed." So sensitive was the security ban on the incident that not even the Minister for Navy was advised about it at the time. That same year, the Minister for Air, William McMahon, contracted the RAAF formally to investigate UFO reports.[9]

MISSING FILMS

On 23 August 1953 the Deputy Director of Civil Aviation in New Guinea, Tom Drury, took an 8mm movie film (using a telephoto lens) of a UFO over Port Moresby. The object was elongated like a bullet and shot out of a cloud, traveling at a speed estimated to be at least five times faster than a jet flying at the speed of sound. "It never slackened speed or changed direction," said Drury, "but simply faded into the blue sky while its vapor trail faded after it. The vapor trail was very clear-cut. . . . This is visible in the remaining section of the film in my possession. . . . I was absolutely certain of its reality. It was filmed, my wife and children saw it. If anyone in the Territory had qualifications to identify an unknown aircraft, I had. It is my business to know what is in the air. I know all types of aircraft and have flown thirty-two of them."

Tom Drury refers to the "remaining section of the film in his possession." What became of the rest? He had sent the original film, consisting of ninety-four frames, to the Minister for Air (William McMahon), who in turn sent it to the US Air Force at the Pentagon. The film was returned about nine months later—minus the most important frames showing the actual object.[10]

Bill Chalker eventually discovered five negatives of photographs of some individual frames from the film in a 1973 Directorate of Air Force Intelligence file, but the actual film showing the UFO has never been returned to its owner. Chalker has confirmed that it was examined by the Naval Photographic Interpretation Center, Maryland, then apparently under the aegis of the CIA,[11] and a former employee of the National Security

Agency, Todd Zechel, charges that the film was retained by the CIA's Office of Scientific Intelligence.[12]

In the spring of 1954 some 200 photographs as well as cine-film were taken of an unidentified flying object that paced three young men who were driving through the Australian interior near the border between Western Australia and South Australia. Shortly afterward, while they were still driving, an RAAF light aircraft suddenly appeared and landed not far from them. The men were ordered to halt and a member of the crew asked them to hand over their films, saying they wanted to borrow them. The photographs and film have never been seen since.

The story was briefly recounted by Stan Seers and William Lasich in FSR,[13] and in a reprint fourteen years later Gordon Creighton added further details, including the fact that the account was given to him by Colin McCarthy, an Australian electronics engineer and UFO researcher.[14] My inquiries in Australia in 1987 revealed that the facts relating to this case have become distorted with time, and it is therefore difficult to draw any conclusions. I did learn from Bill Chalker, however, that the "light aircraft" was a helicopter, and that the witnesses had reported the incident prior to its arrival.

THE MARALINGA CASE, 1957

An extraordinary eyewitness account of a UFO seen hovering over the former British nuclear test site at Maralinga, South Australia, was given to the British researcher Jenny Randles by a Royal Air Force corporal stationed there at the time. Following nuclear detonations in September and October of 1957, an unidentified object was seen hovering over the airfield by the corporal and some colleagues. Described as a "magnificent sight," the craft was of a silver-blue color, with a metallic luster. The corporal said that the object had a line of "windows" or "portholes" along its edge, and that it was seen so distinctly that metallic plating could be made out on its surface.

An air traffic control officer is also alleged to have seen the object, and checks with Alice Springs and Edinburgh airfields revealed that there were no aircraft in the vicinity at the time. No photographs were taken, the RAF corporal said, because the top security status of the base area meant that all cameras had to be locked away. The UFO departed swiftly and silently after about fifteen minutes. "I swear to you as a practising Christian this was no dream, no illusion, no fairy story—but a solid craft of metallic construction," the witness told Jenny Randles.[15]

THE AUSTRALIAN SECURITY AND INTELLIGENCE

ORGANIZATION

The Australian Security and Intelligence Organization (ASIO), developed from the Allied Intelligence Bureau with the co-operation of the British in 1948, is divided into two main branches, one for intelligence gathering and the other responsible for counterespionage. The RAAF stated in their letter to me that there had been no participation by either the ASIO or the ASIS (Australian Secret Intelligence Service) in UFO investigations, yet there is some evidence for involvement of the former.

In 1959 Stan Seers, President of the Queensland Flying Saucer Research Bureau at the time (now UFO Research Queensland), received a phone call from a man requesting a meeting in a large car park in Brisbane, hinting that Seers might learn something to his advantage about UFOs. Suspecting a hoax, Seers let the man make two or three further calls before agreeing to a meeting. At no time did the caller identify himself or his business until Seers met him at the appointed meeting place, where he produced an identity card and introduced himself as D—— D—— of the Australian Security and Intelligence Organization. Mr. D insisted that the conversation should take place in his own car (probably because it was bugged), and since he seemed to be courteous and genuine, Seers agreed.

Mr. D began the conversation with a résumé, covering quite a number of years, of the background of not only Seers but also two close friends, the Secretary and the Public Relations Officer of the Queensland Flying Saucer Research Bureau. Mr. D then "dangled the Communist bogey, this being very much in the forefront in those days," Seers said. "I promptly reminded him that the QFSRB was strictly nonpolitical as well as nonreligious, and as its president I rigidly enforced the rules. He then changed his tack to 'national security' but quickly realized that I was fast becoming sick of hearing the 'reasons,' and finally got down to the 'nitty-gritty,' " which was as follows:

> He asked would I personally "play ball" (to use his expression) with his department; in return they would assist us in the field of UFO research wherever and whenever they could, all of which was to be strictly between him and me. The crux of the suggested agreement was the understanding that in the event of any really "hot" UFO information—landings, contacts, etc., he would if necessary put me into direct telephone communication with Prime Minister Bob Menzies.

Stan Seers understandably had difficulty in believing any of this, but nevertheless agreed to meet Mr. D at a later date. To test the man's authenticity and degree of authority, Seers asked him if he could obtain the return of a letter on loan to the RAAF from the QFSRB. *The letter was returned within forty-eight hours.* "Mr. D—— was obviously of some standing in his own department," relates Seers. "Further proof of this was the unlisted phone number he gave me for use in emergencies only: I recall how easy it was to remember—22222."

After conferring with other members of the QFSRB committee, Seers called the number and was promptly answered by a well-educated female voice who "having inquired my name and business (all without answering my query regarding the 'firm' she represented) swiftly put me through to friend D——." A further meeting was arranged, at which Seers informed Mr. D that the committee had decided unanimously to cooperate with the ASIO. This provoked an angry response from Mr. D, who was furious that the other committee members had been told, but, as Seers pointed out, at no time had he consented to the request for secrecy, having merely indicated that he required time to consider the proposal.

Seers informed Mr. D that all UFO information would be made available to his department on a reciprocal basis, and agreed to refrain from publicity. "Needless to say," said Seers, "we had never at any time considered it to be any other than a one-way arrangement—in their direction only."

During the weeks that followed, Mr. D personally interviewed all twelve members of the QFSRB committee, informing them that with regard to the first meeting, Stan Seers had "twisted the truth." Mr. D carefully cultivated the friendship of at least two committee members, and to all intents and purposes became an ardent UFO enthusiast himself. But Seers' misgivings about this ploy were realized when about a year later the close friendship that had always existed between the committee members began to deteriorate. "The cause for this was, in my opinion, never in doubt," he said, "but unfortunately I found that I could do nothing whatever about it and finally resigned in disgust."

Two years later Seers was persuaded to rejoin and assist with the reorganization of the by now practically defunct group, but still found himself unable to shake off the persistent Mr. D. "On two occasions he invited himself, with the connivance of a member, along to committee meetings, although he was not even an ordinary group member. On the second . . . the Secretary was informed in no uncertain terms that it was to be his last appearance. I am happy to relate that it was. However, he remained in close contact with the group for a total of eleven years before departing this life in 1970.''

Seers claims to have evidence from members of at least one other state UFO group that similar surveillance and attempts at destabilization by the ASIO have been carried out, although in a more covert manner.[16]

Some aspects of this story have been confirmed by Colin Phillips, a committee member of the QFSRB at the time, but he takes a less sinister view than Stan Seers. He told me, for instance, that although Mr. D attended the meetings in his professional capacity, ''it must be remembered that the Australian government in 1950–1960 was very sensitive about Communists, and people with new and different ideas who talked about peace etc. were suspect. It was therefore quite natural that ASIO should send someone along to our meetings to keep an eye on us—I would not be very impressed with the operation of ASIO if they had not.''[17] Quite so. But the ASIO would also have had an interest in monitoring those UFO reports that were not made available to it through official channels, just as the CIA evidently considered America's National Investigations Committee on Aerial Phenomena (NICAP) a target of opportunity in the 1950s and 1960s, to the extent of infiltrating the organization on a large scale (see Chapter 14).

ASIO is not the only Australian intelligence agency said to have been involved in studying the UFO problem. Bill Chalker—a thorough and reliable investigator—confirms that a scientist attached to the Directorate of Scientific and Technical Intelligence, which was part of the Joint Intelligence Bureau (now the Joint Intelligence Organization), cooperated with other defense intelligence scientists in 1968–69 in organizing a proposal for a ''rapid intervention team'' to investigate those UFO incidents involving ''physical evidence.'' However, as a result of criticizing the Air Force's handling of UFO reports, he was denied access to them, and plans for the ''rapid intervention team'' were shelved. The former JIB scientist affirms that although the Directorate of Air Force Intelligence files on UFOs are the most substantial, there are other files held by the Department of Defense that are unlikely to see the light of day. This owes more, however, to the sensitive methods by which the reports were received than the actual content.[18]

USAF PILOT'S SIGHTING, 1960

Bill Chalker has found many interesting reports among the files released by the RAAF Directorate of Air Force Intelligence. On 15 November

1960, about fifty kilometers from Cressy, Tasmania, a US Air Force RB-57 aircraft operating out of RAAF East Sale encountered a UFO, and the following is the pilot's official report:

> Approximately 1040 LCL while flying on a mission track 15 miles north of Launceston, my navigator called out an aircraft approaching to our left and slightly lower. Our altitude at this time was 40,000 feet, TAS of 350 knots, heading of 340 degrees.
>
> I spotted the object and immediately commented to [the navigator] that it was not an aircraft, but looked more like a balloon. We judged its altitude to be approximately 35,000 feet, heading 140 degrees and its speed extremely high.
>
> From a previous experience I would say its closing rate would have been in excess of 800 knots. We observed this object for five or seven seconds before it disappeared under the left wing.
>
> Since it was unusual in appearance, I immediately banked to the left for another look, but neither of us could locate it.
>
> The color of the object was nearly translucent somewhat like that of a "poached egg." There were no sharp edges but rather fuzzy and undefined. The size was approximately 70 feet in diameter and it did not appear to have any depth.[19]

OFFICIAL CONTROVERSY

In 1963 Senator J. L. Cavanagh asked that the federal government dossier on UFOs should be made public, but the Minister for Air refused, stating that no single dossier containing all the facts was available, and although three to four percent of sightings remained unexplained, the vast majority of reports could be explained in terms of balloons, aircraft, and astronomical objects.[20] But others were convinced that a cover-up was in operation, including Dr. Harry Messel, Professor of Physics at Sydney University, who stated in 1965: "The facts about saucers were long tracked down and results have long been known in top secret defense circles of more countries than one. Whatever the truth, it might be regarded as inadvisable to give people at large no clue about the true nature of these things."[21]

But is the cover-up due more to confusion in high places rather than a deliberate policy to withhold sensational information? Two minute papers dating back to 1966 provide evidence against a cover-up. The first was part of a submission by the Directorate of Public Relations in the Department of Air to the Directorate of Air Force Intelligence, and argues for a change in RAAF policy: ". . . by continuing with the old policy of playing our UFO cards close to the chest," the minute states, "we only foster the incorrect (but nevertheless widely held) belief that we have much vital information to hide." The other minute paper comments on the current RAAF files as follows: "It would . . . appear that there is some need for rationalization of our files on this subject. There are at least four different files which contain a confusion of policy, reported sightings and requests for information. Three of these files are classified, two of which are secret although there appears to be nothing in the files consistent with this classification."[22]

These minutes would seem to argue against a deliberate cover-up policy, yet we should bear in mind that those who wrote the submissions were probably not cleared for access to information about UFOs that had been classified as top secret *or above*. From my own investigations into the British Ministry of Defense's UFO investigations, I know that only relatively few people are cleared for access to the sort of information that is held in the highest security classification, so I see no reason for believing that the official position in Australia is any different.

An example of a report that probably never found its way into the RAAF files, but certainly ended up with the CIA (if not the ASIO), has been provided by Budd Hopkins. A US Air Force sergeant with a top secret clearance, known to Hopkins, states that in 1967 he was shown a movie film of a UFO at a CIA screening in Texas which had been taken from a converted RAAF aircraft during a photo-mapping flight over central Australia in about 1965. The short film extract showed "a huge, hovering, windowed craft" with three smaller UFOs attached to it "as a kind of tail." A door on the largest object opened—two vertical panels and two horizontally aligned ones sliding apart—and the three smaller UFOs flew inside. The panels closed, the large object canted at an angle, then disappeared in seconds. According to Budd Hopkins's informant, the filmed image of the UFOs was extraordinarily large and clear, filling the entire movie screen.[23] If the authorities have nothing to hide, why are we denied access to films such as these?

ANSETT-ANA SIGHTING, 1965

At about 3:25 a.m. on 28 May 1965 an Ansett-ANA DC-6b airliner (registration VH-INH) was paced by an unidentified flying object during a flight from Brisbane to Port Moresby, New Guinea. Captain John Barker described the object as oblate in shape with exhaust gases emanating from it, and related that it paced the airliner for ten to fifteen minutes, witnessed by the co-pilot and a stewardess.

The sighting took place in the vicinity of Bougainville Reef, off the Queensland coast, and Captain Barker radioed details to Townsville Ground Control, adding that he was taking photographs of the object. On landing at Port Moresby, Barker was informed that he was not to have the film processed in New Guinea but was to return with it to Australia. When he eventually arrived at Brisbane, Captain Barker was flown directly to Canberra, *where both the film and the flight recorder were confiscated.*

The source of this story is William Orr, Duty Officer of the Department of Civil Aviation at Townsville, who was in radio contact with Captain Barker when he relayed details of the sighting. Orr passed on the information to John Meskell, a detective with the Criminal Investigation Branch who had been on duty at the Townsville Control Tower at the time. Meskell stated that Orr had been forbidden to discuss the incident, but added: "This latter part is only hearsay and came from Orr [who] then told me that the Chief of DCA [Department of Civil Aviation] came to Townsville and took the twelve-hour tapes from the DCA Control Tower with the full conversation between Orr and the pilot, and Orr was told to 'shut his mouth' about the whole thing, under threat of his job."[24]

The Directorate of Air Force Intelligence in Canberra denied in a letter to Peter Norris that any such incident had taken place: "This is the first information we have received of the reported sighting and therefore have no record of the incident. Perhaps you may care to follow the matter up with the Department of Civil Aviation, but as it is normal practice for that Department to refer all sightings to the RAAF it seems most unlikely that they had it reported."[25]

Peter Norris accordingly wrote to the DCA and received the following reply:

> . . . we asked our Brisbane office to check whether Air Traffic Control personnel at Townsville had any knowledge of the reported sightings on 28th May. No persons on duty that day have any recollection of unusual communications and we have not received any formal incident report by any Airline Captain operating in the vicinity of Townsville that day. Unfortunately, our communications recording tapes are reused after a holding period of 90 days and we therefore cannot use this source to confirm belief that there were no unusual communications through Departmental facilities.[26]

But according to Stan Seers, the distinguished researcher Dr. J. Allen Hynek obtained a copy of Captain Barker's official statement to the

Australian authorities from the US Air Force, via the Australian Department of Air,[27] which states in part: *"I had always scoffed at these reports, but I saw it. We all saw it. It was under intelligent control, and it was certainly no known aircraft."*[28] There is no reference to this remarkable sighting in the RAAF Summary of Unidentified Aerial Sightings Reported to the Department of Air (1960–1965)—a revealing omission indeed.

ANOTHER MISSING FILM, 1968

In 1968 members of the Queensland Flying Saucer Research Bureau set up two magnetic monitoring devices attached to self-activating cine-cameras at sites where UFO activity had previously been reported. One site was at Horseshoe Lagoon, Tully, Queensland, where in January 1966 George Pedley claimed to have seen a saucer-shaped object take off, causing his tractor engine to stall and leaving a circular swirled imprint in the reeds where it had taken off from. Further sightings and saucer "nests" had subsequently been reported in the vicinity.

On 2 March the North Queensland radio station 4KZ broadcast a newsflash which announced that an airliner flying from Cairns to Iron Range had been paced at 6,000 feet for a short while by an unidentified flying object some 2,000 feet above them, which then shot off at an estimated 1,500 mph. Inspection of the monitoring device at Horseshoe Lagoon revealed that it had been triggered, and the Eumig 8mm cine-camera was found to be still running slowly; one side of its fifty feet of film having been expended. The batteries were renewed, the film spool turned over, and the camera was then set up to cover a wider area of the lagoon.

On 4 March a number of local witnesses reported a UFO sighting, and the camera was again found to have been activated. For some reason, unfortunately, only fifteen or sixteen frames had been exposed and the batteries were completely dead, Stan Seers reported. "The remainder of the film was wound through by hand, removed from the camera, sealed in the usual container and addressed to Kodak of Melbourne, all in the presence of two reliable witnesses," he reported. "It was next handed in at the Tully post office counter, weighed, a fourteen-cent stamp affixed and then placed directly into the mailbag by the post office official. I personally checked on this aspect of the affair and there is no doubt whatever that Vincent Mele, the owner of the film, did not handle it again after handing it across the counter for weighing.''

Fourteen days later Mele received a package from Kodak. Inside was an empty container complete with wrapping and the fourteen-cent stamp, plus a covering letter asking if Mele had forgotten to enclose the film. Had it really been intercepted or merely misplaced? Stan Seers learned later that the posting of the film had been discussed by several members of the QFSRB in the presence of Mr. D of the ASIO. Suspecting that the ASIO may have planted an agent in the Kodak processing department (which was later confirmed by two independent sources), Seers telephoned Mr. D and made a direct accusation, demanding the immediate return of the film to its owner:

> In the event of its nonreturn I made it quite clear that I would lodge a complaint through Parliament. He was too shrewd to make an immediate denial, merely saying that he would inquire and phone me back. One hour later he did so and said, ''You've got the wrong department, Stan.'' But from his manner I felt reasonably sure that he knew where it was. By this time I was thoroughly furious and phoned Colin Bennett, a well-known barrister and Member of Parliament, and lodged a complaint but refrained from mentioning ASIO as at that stage I had no acceptable proof. I have always considered the probability that the film contained nothing but a view of the lagoon. But the fact remained that it had been probably stolen by a government department.

After Colin Bennett had examined the available evidence, he agreed to take up the case on behalf of the QFSRB, but the outcome was not encouraging. Gordon Freeth, Minister for Air, denied all knowledge of the missing film in a letter to Bennett in August 1968: ''I can assure you that my Department has not in any way attempted to interfere with the processing or return of these films. In fact my Department has no knowledge of any such films having been sent to Kodak for processing.''

Vincent Mele lodged a complaint with his local police, but some weeks later he was taken aside by a plainclothes detective (a personal friend) who advised him to drop the matter. ''You haven't got a hope of getting it back,'' he said.[29]

On about 13 March 1968, shortly after the loss of the film, two RAAF helicopters were seen for some while over the Horseshoe Lagoon, witnessed by the owner of the land. Whether this was just coincidental, of course, is not known, but in view of the fact that circular ''nests'' had been formed in the vicinity where UFOs had been seen to take off from, there is a probability that the RAAF needed aerial photographs of the sites.

Stan Deyo, a former US Air Force pilot, claims that in 1972, during a meeting with Dr. Tom Keeble, Director of the Mechanical Engineering Division of the Department of Defense Aeronautical Research Laboratory in Melbourne, Keeble disclosed that the RAAF have extensive movie-film libraries of UFOs. Deyo claims that these films and other classified material on UFOs are kept at RAAF East Sale, Victoria.[30] I wrote to Dr. Keeble checking on the veracity of this story, but received no reply. Certainly, if such films exist in RAAF archives—and I am confident they do—East Sale would be the logical repository, since it is a center for military photographic interpretation.

AIRCRAFT COMMUNICATIONS INTERFERENCE
DURING MULTIPLE UFO SIGHTING, 1968

A sighting by Captains Walter Gardin and Gordon Smith during a flight from Adelaide to Perth on 22 August 1968, involving temporary loss of communications between their aircraft and ground control, contains some striking parallels with the famous observation by Captain James Howard and his crew over Labrador, Newfoundland, in 1954 (see Chapter 8). The following report was made by the co-pilot, Captain Gordon W. Smith of Murchison Air Services/Southern Airlines of Western Australia. The aircraft, an eight-seat Piper Navajo, registration VH-RTO, was returning empty from Adelaide and cruising at 8,000 feet, with an airspeed of 190–195 knots and tracking 270° magnetic, and Smith was asleep in the cabin when the sighting first occurred:

> At 0940 (1740 WST) Walter abruptly wakened me in great excitement and asked me to come into the cockpit quickly. I did so, and he asked me if I could see what he was looking at. At first I didn't, because I was still suffering from the effect of sleep. However, after about thirty seconds I could see what he was excited about.
>
> Some distance ahead at the same level, and about 50° to my right (I was in the right seat), I saw a formation of aircraft. In the middle was a large aircraft, and formated to the right and left and above were four or five smaller aircraft. We were on a track of 270° and these aircraft appeared to be maintaining station with us.
>
> As we had not been notified of this traffic, I radioed Kalgoorlie DCA [Department of Civil Aviation] communications center asking them what traffic they or RAAF had in our area. The answer was none. So I then

notified Kalgoorlie that we had this formation in sight and they, in turn, notified some east bound traffic of the danger of unidentified traffic 130 NM east of Kalgoorlie.

At about this time we lost communications with Kalgoorlie on all frequencies. We were receiving Kalgoorlie carrier wave with no voice propagation, only a hash and static. In the next ten minutes I transmitted about seven times and I believe Walter did about five times with no results.

Also at about this time we noticed that the main ship split into two sections still maintaining the same level, and the smaller aircraft then flew out left and right but staying in the same level and coming back to the two main halves of the bigger ship. At this time there appeared to be about six smaller aircraft taking turns of going out and coming back and formating on the two halves.

Sometimes the two halves joined and split, and the whole cycle continued for ten minutes. The shape of the main ship seemed to have the ability to change, not drastically, but from, say spheroid to a slightly elongated form with the color maintaining a constant dark gray to black.

However, the smaller craft had a constant cigar shape and were of a very dark color. Their travel out and back had a peculiarity not associated with normal aircraft in that they appeared to travel out and come back without actually turning like a normal airplane would have to do.

At 0950 GMT the whole formation joined together as if at a single command, then departed at a tremendous speed. It did not disappear as, say, gas would, but it departed in about three or four seconds diminishing in size till out of sight.

Captain Smith reported that radio communications were restored immediately following the departure of the UFOs. Distance of the objects was impossible to estimate, since their size was unknown, but for comparative size the main craft compared with a Boeing 707 as seen from ten miles away. Neither Gardin nor Smith "had the presence of mind to check if any deviation existed in our magnetic compass or Automatic Direction Finder whilst in the presence of the UFOs," they said. Explanations in terms of balloons, conventional aircraft, tricks of light, gases, etc., were ruled out by the pilots. "We conclude that the UFOs were in fact aircraft with the solidity of aircraft, except perhaps for the fact of the ability of the larger UFO to split and change shape slightly."[31]

When the distinguished American atmospheric physicist and UFO researcher Dr. James McDonald attempted to make further inquiries about the incident, the pilots refused to respond. Years later, a pilot member of the Victorian UFO Research Society who was personally acquainted with Gardin and Smith confirmed that the captains had been ordered not to discuss the encounter further.[32]

RAAF, 1969

On 31 August 1969 an RAAF Canberra bomber chased but failed to catch a UFO over northern New South Wales. The plane was sent from RAAF Amberley when hundreds of people in Kyogle and along the Darling Downs reported the object, which was shaped like an aluminum Zeppelin. Some witnesses observed the UFO for more than three hours as it hovered low over towns and farms. The object finally disappeared when the Canberra tried to close in on it.[33]

On 20 October 1969 the Minister for Air, the Honorable F. M. Osborne, made a statement in Parliament summarizing the Defense Department's analysis of Unusual Aerial Sightings to date. He concluded: "Nothing that has arisen from that 3 or 4 percent of unexplained cases gives any firm support for the belief that interlopers from other places in this world or outside it have been visiting us."[34]

Australia seems to have the lowest percentage of unexplained sightings in the world, if the Minister for Air and his department are to be taken at their word. But whatever the percentage, the highly detailed and convincing reports by qualified observers described in this chapter render official explanations totally invalid. It should be obvious to all but the most bone-headed skeptic that intelligently controlled objects are intruding into our airspace, even if their origin and purpose remain undetermined at this stage.

INCIDENT AT NORTH WEST CAPE, 1973

On 25 October 1973 two US Navy personnel observed a UFO hovering near the restricted Naval Communication Station at North West Cape, Western Australia, which is used by the National Security Agency (in conjunction with Australia's Defense Signals Directorate). The Department of Defense (RAAF) report relating to the incident was acquired a few years later by Bill Chalker, who was surprised that such a report was made available to a civilian researcher.

At about 19:15 hours that day, Lieutenant Commander M—— (USN) sighted a "large black, airborne object" approximately eight kilometers to the west at an estimated altitude of 600 meters. "After about 20–25 seconds the craft accelerated at unbelievable speed and disappeared to the north," he reported. There was no noise or exhaust. The second witness, Fire Captain (USN) Bill L——, described the sighting as follows:

At 1920 hours, I was called by the POW to close the Officers' club. I proceeded toward the club in the Fire Department pick-up 488, when my attention was drawn to a large black object, which at first I took to be a small cloud formation, due west of Area ''B'' [the location of the high frequency transmitter]. . . . On alighting from pick-up 488, I stood for several minutes and watched this black sphere hovering. The sky was clear and pale green-blue. No clouds were about whatsoever. The object was completely stationary except for a halo around the center, which appeared to be either revolving or pulsating. After I had stood watching it for approx. 4 minutes, it suddenly took off at tremendous speed and disappeared in a northerly direction, in a few seconds. I consider this object to have been approx. 10 meters in diameter, hovering at 300 meters over the hills due west of the Base. It was black, maybe due to my looking in the direction of the setting sun. No lights appeared on it at any time.

On the very same day that the UFO was seen, Bill Chalker reports, the North West Cape facility was communicating a full nuclear alert to the region, based on National Security Agency communications intelligence (COMINT) intercepts! The nuclear alert was originally due to an NSA misreading of a Syrian message to the USSR, which led the Americans to believe that Soviet troops might be sent to the Middle East (the Yom Kippur War had broken out on 11 October 1973).[35]

THE DISAPPEARANCE OF DELTA SIERRA JULIET, 1978

Of all sightings in Australia none has generated so much worldwide attention and concern than that of Frederick Valentich, a twenty-year-old flying instructor who disappeared in his Cessna 182 aircraft shortly after reporting a UFO sighting over the Bass Strait near Cape Otway, on a flight from Moorabin, Victoria, to King Island, Tasmania, on 21 October 1978.

Forty-seven minutes after taking off from Moorabin Airport, Melbourne, at 6:19 p.m., Valentich reported sighting an unidentified aircraft to the Melbourne Flight Service Unit Controller, Steve Robey. The official transcript of the recorded transmissions between the Cessna (registration VH-DSJ) and Melbourne Flight Service Unit (FSU) has been kindly provided for me by Bill Chalker. The following communications between the aircraft and Melbourne FSU were recorded from 19.06 hours. The word/words in brackets are open to other interpretations:

TIME	FROM	TEXT
1906:14	VH-DSJ	MELBOURNE this is DELTA SIERRA JULIET is there any known traffic below five thousand

:23	FSU	DELTA SIERRA JULIET no known traffic
:26	VH-DSJ	DELTA SIERRA JULIET I am seems (to) be a large aircraft below five thousand
:46	FSU	D D DELTA SIERRA JULIET what type of aircraft is it
:50	VH-DSJ	DELTA SIERRA JULIET I cannot affirm it is four bright it seems to me like landing lights
1907:04	FSU	DELTA SIERRA JULIET
:32	VH-DSJ	MELBOURNE this (is) DELTA SIERRA JULIET the aircraft has just passed over me at least a thousand feet above
:43	FSU	DELTA SIERRA JULIET roger and it is a large aircraft confirm
:47	VH-DSJ	er unknown due to the speed it's traveling is there any air force aircraft in the vicinity
:57	FSU	DELTA SIERRA JULIET no known aircraft in the vicinity
1908:18	VH-DSJ	MELBOURNE it's approaching now from due east towards me
:28	FSU	DELTA SIERRA JULIET
:42		// open microphone for two seconds //
:49	VH-DSJ	DELTA SIERRA JULIET it seems to me that he's playing some sort of game he's flying over me two to three times at a time at speeds I could not identify
1909:02	FSU	DELTA SIERRA JULIET roger what is your actual level
:06	VH-DSJ	my level is four and a half thousand four five zero zero
:11	FSU	DELTA SIERRA JULIET and confirm that you cannot identify the aircraft
:14	VH-DSJ	affirmative
:18	FSU	DELTA SIERRA JULIET roger standby
:28	VH-DSJ	MELBOURNE DELTA SIERRA JULIET it's not an aircraft it is // open microphone for two seconds //
:46	FSU	DELTA SIERRA JULIET can you describe the er aircraft
:52	VH-DSJ	DELTA SIERRA JULIET as it's flying past it's a long shape // open microphone for three seconds // (cannot) identify more than (that it has such speed) // open microphone for three seconds // before me right now Melbourne
1910:07	FSU	DELTA SIERRA JULIET roger and how large would the er object be
:20	VH-DSJ	DELTA SIERRA JULIET MELBOURNE it seems like it's stationary what I'm doing right now is orbiting and the thing is just orbiting on top of me also it's

		got a green light and sort of metallic (like) it's all shiny (on) the outside
:43	FSU	DELTA SIERRA JULIET
:48	VH-DSJ	DELTA SIERRA JULIET // open microphone for five seconds // it's just vanished
:57	FSU	DELTA SIERRA JULIET
1911:03	VH-DSJ	MELBOURNE would you know what kind of aircraft I've got is it (a type) military aircraft
:08	FSU	DELTA SIERRA JULIET confirm the er aircraft just vanished
:14	VH-DSJ	say again
:17	FSU	DELTA SIERRA JULIET is the aircraft still with you
:23	VH-DSJ	DELTA SIERRA JULIET (it's ah nor) // open microphone for two seconds // (now) approaching from the southwest
:37	FSU	DELTA SIERRA JULIET
:52	VH-DSJ	DELTA SIERRA JULIET the engine is rough idling I've got it set at twenty three twenty four and the thing is (coughing)
1912:04	FSU	DELTA SIERRA JULIET roger what are your intentions
:09	VH-DSJ	my intentions are ah to go to King Island ah Melbourne that strange aircraft is hovering on top of me again // two seconds open microphone // it is hovering and it's not an aircraft
:22	FSU	DELTA SIERRA JULIET
:28	VH-DSJ	DELTA SIERRA JULIET MELBOURNE // 17 seconds open microphone //
:49	FSU	DELTA SIERRA JULIET MELBOURNE

There is no record of any further transmissions from the aircraft. The weather in the Cape Otway area was clear with a trace of stratocumulus cloud at 5000 to 7000 feet, scattered cirrus cloud at 30,000 feet, excellent visibility and light winds. The end of daylight at Cape Otway was at 1918 hours.

The Alert Phase of SAR [Search and Rescue] procedures was declared at 1912 hours and, at 1933 hours when the aircraft did not arrive at King Island, the Distress Phase was declared and search action commenced. An intensive air, sea and land search was continued until 25 October 1978, but no trace of the aircraft was found.[36]

The search and rescue operation was headed by an RAAF Orion maritime reconnaissance aircraft assisted by some light aircraft. Although an oil slick was found about eighteen miles north of King Island on 22 October it was not established as having any connection with Valentich's plane. The Cessna was equipped with a radio survival beacon, but nothing was heard from it.[37]

Paul Norman learned that aircraft pilots were requested to report sightings of UFOs and lights in the sky, and those who were flying at the same time and using the same radio frequency were instructed not to divulge any details of their communications. Attempts were made to make it look as though Valentich's plane was not in the location he reported.[38]

One month later the outline of a submerged aircraft was allegedly sighted about forty-eight miles north of King Island by the pilot of a Cessna 337 from Hawk Flying Service, who was unable however to confirm the observation on a second pass over the area. Aviation officials apparently dismissed the sighting because the seas were too rough and the water too deep for anything to have been seen on the seabed from the air.

Steve Robey, the Melbourne Flight Service Unit Controller, was absolutely convinced that Valentich was not perpetrating a hoax. "Towards the end I think he was definitely concerned for his safety," he said. "I considered that he would have had to have been a good actor to have put it all together the way he did. . . . It was a kind of rushed communication . . . as if he was startled."[39]

The Tape

Frederick Valentich's father, Guido, told me that he was given a copy of the recorded communications of his son by the Department of Transport, with Robey's voice deleted.[40] But Bill Chalker has heard part of the complete tape which is in the possession of Dr. Richard Haines, a NASA research scientist.[41] Haines' preliminary findings concluded that a strange seventeen-second burst of metallic noise which followed Valentich's last transmission contained "36 separate bursts with fairly constant start and stop pulses bounding each one: there are no discernible patterns in time or frequency." The effect, Dr. Haines said, was similar to rapid keying of the microphone, but control tests were noticeably different from the original sound.[42]

As to the *original* tape, Bill Chalker told me that the Department of Aviation erased it, or so he was informed by the Assistant Secretary of

Air Safety Investigation, A. R. Woodward, who also claimed that no further copies existed.

The Official Verdict

In May 1982 the Bureau of Air Safety Investigation (Australian Department of Aviation) released its official findings "to parties having a bona fide interest in the occurrence." The Aircraft Accident Investigation Summary Report concludes:

Location of occurrence:	Not known
Time:	Not known
Degree of injury:	Presumed fatal
Opinion as to cause:	The reason for the disappearance of the aircraft has not been determined.

Bill Chalker was highly dissatisfied with this conclusion and tried to extract further information from G. V. Hughes, then Assistant Secretary of Air Safety Investigation. Chalker asked if there had been any further official investigation of a possible UFO connection with the disappearance. Hughes replied: "The RAAF is responsible for the investigation of reports concerning 'UFO' sightings, and liaison was established with the RAAF on these aspects of the investigation. The decision as to whether or not the 'UFO' report is to be investigated rests with the RAAF and not this Department."

In 1982 Bill Chalker was given officially sanctioned, direct access to the RAAF UFO files, held by the Directorate of Air Force Intelligence in Canberra, but the file on the Valentich case was conspicuous by its absence. "The Intelligence Liaison Officer explained to me that the RAAF did not investigate the affair because they were not asked to by the Department of Aviation!" said Chalker. The RAAF saw the report as more appropriately in the domain of an air accident/safety inquiry, he was told.

In November 1982 Chalker was finally given permission to examine the Department of Aviation UFO files in Melbourne, but was specifically denied access to the Valentich file on the grounds that they were Air Accident Investigation files and not UFO files. Mr. G. V. Hughes explained the reason for this:

The file concerning this occurrence is no more or less restricted than any other accident investigation file. As a signatory to the International Convention on Civil Aviation, we subscribe to the Standards and Recommended Practices contained in Annex 13 to the Convention, in respect of aircraft accident investigation specifically, when it is considered that the disclosure of records, for purposes other than accident prevention, might have an adverse effect on the availability of information in that or any future investigation, such records are considered privileged.[43]

The Cessna Found?

In December 1982 Ron Cameron, an independent film producer working on a documentary about the Valentich case, told Bill Chalker that two divers had told him they had located the missing Cessna on the seabed off Cape Otway. The divers claimed to have taken sixteen photographs of the plane, and offered them to Cameron (together with details of the plane's position) for $10,000. Cameron understandably refused the offer in the absence of verification, but the divers did show him five photographs purporting to show the Cessna—mostly intact, and with the correct registration marks. There was no body inside the aircraft, he was told.

A salvage operation was considered, involving the Department of Aviation, but the latter dropped the idea on the grounds that it would lead to unwelcome publicity. Cameron then lost track of the divers, one of whom supposedly joined the Coast Guard in California. In 1983 he was still considering the possibility of a salvage operation, but nothing further seems to have been done, and the story is widely regarded as a hoax.[44]

What Happened to Valentich?

Many theories have been advanced to account for the mysterious disappearance of Delta Sierra Juliet and its young pilot, some feasible, others bizarre. Had Valentich staged the whole incident, for example? There is no evidence at all for this, other than an unsubstantiated rumor that he was seen alive and well and working at a gas service station in Tasmania.[45] But Valentich had good reasons for completing the flight: to log up more night-flying experience, to pick up some crayfish in Tasmania for the officers of the Air Training Corps (of which he was an instructor), and to join his family and friends in a reunion back in Melbourne at 10:00 p.m. that night. Also we have the testimony of Steve Robey, the Flight Service Unit Controller, who was convinced by the tone of Valentich's voice that he was genuinely alarmed.

Guido Valentich told me that his son was a very keen student of the UFO subject from the age of fifteen. "As he grew older and joined the

Air Training Corps and going to various RAAF bases, he became more and more convinced of UFO existence and in other words he also convinced us, not in fear but in a friendly way to an expression that he would like perhaps to come to a close encounter.'' Guido added that his son had learned a lot about the subject from the RAAF. ''I learned that he met a few Air Force pilots, especially last time when he was at one base for fifteen days in August–September 1978, when he came home more positive than ever on UFO existence.'' Had the RAAF or the government given Guido any explanation as to what had actually happened to his son? I asked. ''No. The Department of Transport gave me a briefing on the search and how it was conducted for four days after my son went missing, and that was all,'' he said. ''I have asked for the result of the analysis of the tape (air to ground) but they have not been able to give me any satisfactory answer of any kind.''

Unofficially, the chief co-ordinator of the search and rescue team, Mr. Eddie, told Guido Valentich that he thought the Cessna had simply ditched in the water and disappeared within a minute, taking the pilot with it. But as Guido pointed out, the Cessna 182 is constructed of modular units which should float on impact. Secondly, VHF radio would not be able to transmit below 1,000 feet from the aircraft's position of ninety miles from Melbourne, and Valentich's communications with the Flight Service Unit were loud and clear to the last word, as was the seventeen-second burst of ''metallic'' noise which followed. This confirms that he was still above 1,000 feet, and Guido is convinced that his son was still at 4,500 feet when contact was lost.[46]

Sightings on the Same Day

Many people reported seeing UFOs on the same day and during the night of Valentich's disappearance, fifteen of which reports have survived rigorous investigation, according to Bill Chalker. These sightings all took place between midday and 9:00 p.m., six in Victoria, one on King Island, and the rest further afield. Roy Manifold, who was vacationing at Crayfish Bay, Cape Otway, inadvertently took two photographs of peculiar objects just twenty minutes before Valentich reported his sighting. Of Manifold's six photos of the sunset, the fourth shows a ''dense black lump'' apparently stirring up the sea, while the sixth shows a strange mass situated in the sky directly above the anomaly in the fourth picture, taken some forty seconds earlier, which appears to show an object accompanied by a trail of small, bright blue shapes.

Film faults and processing defects were ruled out by Kodak. The RAAF dismissed the sixth photo as showing nothing more than a cumulus cloud breaking up, but as Bill Chalker argues, this would require the cloud to have suddenly moved into view at over 200 mph, since it does not appear in any of the other frames.[47]

We may never know exactly what happened to Frederick Valentich, but the evidence strongly suggests that he encountered an unidentified aerial object which was in some way responsible for his disappearance. If so, the Australian government would have a good reason for playing down the incident—and the UFO subject in general.

On 2 May 1984 the RAAF curtailed its lengthy public association with the UFO controversy when the Minister of Defense, Gordon Scholes, stated: "The vast majority of reports submitted by the public have proved not to have a national security significance."[48] This is probably correct, but what about the small residue of unexplained sightings by the public, to say nothing of military reports? It is self-evident that these are of enormous significance, and clearly affect national security. Yet the public must not be told the truth.

8

CANADA

One of the most important documents on UFOs to be released in Canada is a hitherto top secret memorandum from Wilbert B. Smith, senior radio engineer with the Canadian government Department of Transport at the time and a highly respected scientist who held a master's degree in electrical engineering and several patents. The memo, dated 21 November 1950, was sent to the Controller of Telecommunications, and recommended that a research project be set up to study the subject.

"We believe that we are on the track of something which may well prove to be the introduction to a new technology," Smith wrote. "The existence of a different technology is borne out by the investigations which are being carried on at the present time in relation to flying saucers." Smith went on to state that through discreet inquiries made at the Canadian Embassy in Washington he had learned (from Dr. Robert Sarbacher) that:

a. The matter is the most highly classified subject in the United States government, rating higher even than the H-bomb.
b. Flying saucers exist.
c. Their modus operandi is unknown but concentrated effort is being made by a small group headed by Doctor Vannevar Bush.
d. The entire matter is considered by the United States authorities to be of tremendous significance.

Here we have incontrovertible evidence for the high security classification attached to the subject. The reference to the "small group" headed by Dr. Vannevar Bush is equally significant, since in 1947, following the retrieval of parts of a UFO near Roswell, New Mexico, a small, select group, code-named Majestic 12, was established to inform the President about UFO developments, and it was headed by Dr. Bush. (See Chapter 11.)

PROJECT MAGNET, 1950–54

The Department of Transport was not slow in accepting Smith's recommendation, and on 2 December 1950 Project Magnet was established by Commander C. P. Edwards, then Deputy Minister of Transport for

Air Services. Smith was appointed Engineer-in-Charge, with another two engineers and two technicians working part time. The broadcast and measurement section of the Telecommunications Division was given a directive to carry out the project with whatever assistance could be obtained from sources such as the Defense Research Board and National Research Council. Dr. O. M. Solandt, Chairman of the Defense Research Board, offered his full cooperation.[1]

The Canadian government has continually tried to play down the work of Wilbert Smith and Project Magnet. In 1964, for example, the Department of Transport informed an inquirer:

> . . . we would reiterate that at no time has this Department carried out research into the field of unidentified flying objects. As stated by Mr. Depuis in Hansard on December 4, 1963, a small program of investigation in the field of geomagnetics was carried out by the Telecommunications Division of this Department between 1950 and 1954. This minor investigation was for the purpose of studying magnetic phenomena, particularly those phenomena resulting from unusual boundary conditions in the basic electromagnetic theory. . . . This personal project was at no expense to the Department, nor did it have any Departmental sponsorship.[2]

That the government was lying has now been established with the release of official Project Magnet documents, obtained by Arthur Bray. One of these is the "Summary of Sightings Reported to and Analyzed by Department of Transport During 1952," containing twenty-five UFO reports, from which I would like to cite two sightings by qualified observers. The first took place at Halifax, Nova Scotia:

> On June 15 at 8:32 a.m., A.S.T., a meteorological assistant on reserve army maneuvers, noticed what seemed to be a large silver disk in the sky southeast of Halifax. It moved southwest for about 30 seconds at an estimated altitude of 5,000 to 8,000 feet and then ascended vertically and in 2 to 5 seconds merged in altocumulus clouds at 11,000 to 12,000 feet. If the altitude estimates are correct, from the bearing and elevation data obtained from this observer, the diameter of the disk works out at about 100 feet. A large standard aircraft was in the sky at the time and the object seemed to move much more rapidly than the plane. The object's speed was estimated to be at least 800 miles per hour.[3]

The second sighting occurred at MacDonald Airport, Manitoba, on 27 August 1952:

A disk-shaped object with shadows on it as if it had an irregular surface was seen by two meteorological officers at 4:45 a.m., C.S.T. at MacDonald Airport. The object made two turns about the field and when struck by the light from the rotating beacon made off toward the northeast and was out of sight within a second. There was no sound whatsoever. The object glinted like shiny aluminum when the beacon light struck it.[4]

In an interim report on Project Magnet dated 25 June 1952, Wilbert Smith stated:

If, as appears evident, the Flying Saucers are emissaries from some other civilization, and actually do operate on magnetic principles, we have before us the Fact that we have missed something in magnetic theory but have a good indication of the direction in which to look for the missing quantities. It is therefore strongly recommended that the work of Project Magnet be continued and expanded to include experts in each of the various fields involved in these studies.[5]

On 10 August 1953 Smith filed another report on Project Magnet, which contained some astonishing conclusions:

It appears then, that we are faced with a substantial probability of the real existence of extraterrestrial vehicles, regardless of whether they fit into our scheme of things. Such vehicles of necessity must use a technology considerably in advance of what we have. It is therefore submitted that the next step in this investigation should be a substantial effort toward the acquisition of as much as possible of this technology, which would without doubt be of great value to us.[6]

The Canadian government has denied that Smith's conclusions are in any way representative of "officialdom" and Smith himself disclaimed official status for the report, emphasizing that it simply represented his own views and those of his small research group. It was neither endorsed nor rejected by the government, yet Smith's credentials and integrity are beyond dispute, and for years afterward he continued to represent his department before the House of Commons Broadcasting Committee.[7]

In December 1953 Smith set up a UFO detecting station at Shirleys Bay, outside Ottawa, with registering devices including a gamma ray counter, a magnetometer, a radio receiver, and a recording gravimeter. But so intent were government scientists to avoid being associated with such a controversial project that even on the day the station went into operation Dr. Solandt was quoted as saying that reports of its establishment were completely untrue. In fact, the building housing the detecting equipment was loaned to Smith by the Defense Research Board, of which Dr. Solandt was Chairman!

A definitely anomalous disturbance was recorded on 8 August 1954, but heavy fog prevented Smith and his associates from seeing anything in the sky. Perhaps coincidentally, the Department of Transport announced two days later that it was closing down the station, although the actual decision to do so had been made in June that year. Smith explained that the reason for discontinuing Project Magnet was that it had become an embarrassment to the government due to unwelcome publicity. But Smith himself was given the go ahead to continue with the project on an unofficial basis in his own free time. As researcher Arthur Bray comments, a cover-up is indicated by the fact that the public was led to believe that the government was no longer interested in flying saucers.[8]

PROJECT SECOND STORY, 1952–54

In April 1952 another secret government committee, separate from Project Magnet, but also involving Wilbert Smith, was established by Dr. O. M. Solandt, Chairman of the Defense Research Board. With the code name of Project Second Story, the committee comprised the following members: Flight Lieutenant V. L. Bradley, Defense Research Board; Group Captain D. M. Edwards, Directorate of Air Intelligence; Dr. Peter Millman (Chairman), Dominion Observatory; H. C. Oatway (Secretary), Defense Research Board; Commander J. C. Pratt, Directorate of Naval Intelligence; Wilbert B. Smith, Department of Transport.

According to the minutes made available to Arthur Bray by the National Research Council, only five meetings took place, although it is known that there were more. The minutes of the first meeting on 21 April 1952 refer to a Royal Canadian Air Force report relating to the US Air Force Project Blue Book UFO investigation. This report was not made available, but Bray was eventually able to acquire a copy from a private source. Hitherto classified secret, the RCAF document noted that there were certain patterns of sightings over major US port areas and atomic energy establishments, and that five percent of the reports came from scientists at the White Sands (missile) Proving Grounds, New Mexico. The report concluded with hopes that an official exchange of data could take place between Canada and the United States.

At the fifth meeting, on 9 March 1953, it was pointed out that although the evidence to date did not warrant a full-scale investigation by the Canadian armed forces, reports should continue to be collected at a central point, namely, the Directorate of Scientific Intelligence, Defense Research Board. The minutes make it clear that Project Second Story should continue to hold meetings at the discretion of the Chairman, yet no further minutes have been made officially available since they are probably still classified. Among them are almost certainly the minutes of a meeting to discuss Wilbert Smith's extraordinary Project Magnet report, dated 10 August 1953, wherein he concluded that "we are faced with the substantial probability of the real existence of extraterrestrial vehicles." Arthur Bray was informed by a reliable source that this report went as high as Prime Minister Louis St. Laurent, who held it for three months.

Dr. Allen McNamara of the National Research Council admitted in a letter to Arthur Bray that the Project Magnet report *was* submitted to the Project Second Story Committee in 1953, but that "Mr. Smith's conclusions were not supported by his own Department or the Second Story Committee."[9] Why then are the minutes of this and other meetings still classified? A clue to the degree of sensitivity over the UFO projects is contained in a Canadian government memorandum in my possession, dated 15 September 1969, which states in part:

Dr. P. M. Millman, National Research council, has advised me that the documents reporting the results of the Second Story studies in project "Magnet" be declassified. . . . Since the question of flying saucers is still attracting public attention and since this file covers documents relating to the studies behind project "Magnet" and, indeed, records much of the discussion in the Department of Transport surrounding project "Magnet" *which is confidential in nature,* it is recommended that this file be down classified at least to the confidential level. *At no time should it be made available to the public.* [Emphasis added]

Eventually, as we have seen, certain Project Magnet and Second Story documents were released to bona fide researchers, but there is no doubt that some of the material is still classified. Arthur Bray subsequently acquired a copy of the minutes of another Project Second Story meeting from a private source. The government transmittal slip is dated 15 March 1954, and it is assumed that the meeting was held no earlier than a few weeks prior to that date. The minutes contain nothing really interesting, however, apart from some comments by Wilbert Smith on the experiments being conducted at the Shirleys Bay detecting station:

> Whether the phenomenae be due to natural magnetic causes, or alien vehicles, there would probably be associated with a sighting some magnetic or radio noise disturbance. Also, there is a possibility of gamma radiation being associated with such phenomenae. It has been suggested by some mathematicians that gravity waves may exist in reality. . . . While we know practically nothing of such waves in nature, nevertheless, if the possibility exists, flying saucer phenomenae, being largely an unknown field, might be a good place to look for such waves.[10]

Physical Evidence

During a recorded interview with C. W. Fitch and George Popovitch in November 1961, Wilbert Smith admitted that a number of fragments from UFOs had been recovered and analyzed by his research group, including one that had been shot from a UFO near Washington, DC, in July 1952. Said Smith:

> I was informed that the disk was glowing and was about two feet in diameter. A glowing chunk flew off and the pilot saw it glowing all the way to the ground. He radioed his report and a ground party hurried to the scene. The thing was still glowing when they found it an hour later. The entire piece weighed about a pound. The segment that was loaned to me was about one third of that. It had been sawed off. . . .
>
> There was iron rust—the thing was in reality a matrix of magnesium orthosilicate. The matrix had great numbers—thousands—of 15-micron spheres scattered through it.

Smith was asked if he had returned the piece to the US Air Force when he had completed his analysis. "Not the Air Force. *Much higher than that,*" he replied. "The Central Intelligence Agency?" asked the interviewers. "I'm sorry, gentlemen, but I don't care to go beyond that point," said Smith, but added, "I can say to you that it went to the hands of a highly classified group. You will have to solve that problem—their identity—for yourselves."[11] In my opinion, that group was Majestic 12, referred to earlier in this chapter and elsewhere.

Wilbert Smith also confirmed that a mass of unidentified metal was recovered by his group in July 1960 in Canada. "There is about three thousand pounds of it," he told Fitch and Popovitch during the same interview.

We have done a tremendous amount of detective work on this metal. . . . We have something that was not brought to this earth by plane nor by boat nor by any helicopter. We are speculating that what we have is a portion of a very large device which came into this solar system—we don't know when—but it had been in space a long time before it came to earth; we can tell that by the micrometeorites embedded in the surface. . . . We have it but we don't know what it is![12]

Naturally, all such documentation on these cases, which simply must have been discussed by the Project Second Story Committee, remains classified to this day. And how curious that in an interview in 1969, Dr. Peter Millman, former Chairman of the committee, should say that meteorites are the "only proven thing that comes from outer space that we can examine. After all, we've never had a piece of a flying saucer."[13]

UFOS FOLLOW BRITISH AIRLINER OVER LABRADOR,

1954

Although the following case has frequently been cited in the literature, I have included it here because the principal witness's own account is less well known and is more accurate than previous versions.

Captain James Howard was in command of a British Overseas Airways Corporation (now British Airways) Boeing Stratocruiser, G-ALSC, Flight 510-196 from New York to London via Goose Bay, on 29 June 1954, which left New York at 21:03 GMT. About thirty minutes later, nearing the boundary of New York Air Traffic Center, Boston informed Captain Howard to hold at a position somewhere near the coast of Rhode Island. No reason for the hold was given, but Howard assumed that there was conflicting traffic ahead. After about ten to twelve minutes he pointed out to Boston that his fuel reserves were not limitless, and requested onward clearance. Control then said he could proceed providing that he accepted a detour via Cape Cod, rejoining the original track well north of Boston.

About three hours later, crossing the St. Lawrence estuary near Seven Islands, Quebec, flying at 19,000 feet above broken cloud at about 14,000 feet, Captain Howard saw some strange objects:

They were moving at about the same speed as we were (230 knots approx) on a parallel course, maybe 3 or 4 miles to the north west of us (we were heading NE). They were below the cloud at this time, at a guess at 8,000 ft. Soon after crossing the coast into Labrador, the cloud layer was left behind and the objects were now clearly in view, seeming to have climbed more nearly to our altitude. At this time the sun was low to the northwest, sky clear, visibility unlimited.

Captain Howard and the crew had ample time to study and sketch the objects as they accompanied the airliner for twenty minutes. Some passengers had also seen the objects and were staring out of the windows on the port side. Howard reported:

There was one large object and six smaller globular things. The small ones were strung out in a line, sometimes 3 ahead and 3 behind the large one, sometimes 2 ahead and 4 behind, and so on, but always at the same level. The large object was continually, slowly, changing shape, in the way that a swarm of bees might alter its appearance. They appeared to be opaque and hard-edged, gray in color, no lights or flames visible.

After watching the UFOs for ten minutes or so, Captain Howard judged that he was now within VHF radio range of Goose Bay, Labrador, so he asked his co-pilot, Lee Boyd, to request information from control.

They asked us to describe what we were seeing, and told us that they had an F-94 on patrol and would vector him toward us. (The F-94 was a radar-equipped two-seat fighter.) A little later Goose Bay asked us to change frequency and talk direct to the fighter. On doing so we learned that he had us in radar contact—no mention of anything else visible. I gave him a bearing of the objects from us, and as I did so I noticed that the small objects had disappeared. (My navigator who was watching them closely at this time said that they appeared to converge on, and enter, the large one.)

As the F-94 approached, the large object dwindled in size, still on the same relative bearing as the Stratocruiser, and after a few seconds disappeared. Captain Howard then started his descent into Goose Bay for the refueling stop, and landed at 01:45 GMT. "We were questioned at length by USAF Intelligence at Goose Bay (who, incidentally, seemed totally unsurprised at the sighting—they told us there had been several others in the Labrador area recently)," said Howard. "We left Goose Bay at 03:14 GMT for London, arriving at 12:27 on the 30th."

Captain Howard subsequently learned that a doctor and his wife, who were on holiday in Massachusetts, had seen a number of objects flying overhead in a northeasterly direction at about the time the Stratocruiser was being held near the coast of Rhode Island. Unfortunately, Goose Bay had only short range airfield control radar at the time, and the F-94 did not report having tracked the objects on its radar equipment. Since the Stratocruiser left for London before the fighter returned, Captain Howard had no opportunity to question the crew. But if the hold *was* caused by unidentified traffic in the Boston control area, Howard surmised, the objects were presumably tracked on radar there.[14]

MORE OFFICIAL CONTRADICTIONS

In a classified Canadian government memorandum of December 1957, the contents of which were later forwarded by the Department of External Affairs to the High Commissioner's Office in London in response to an inquiry, it was stated that: "The RCAF has no official policy concerning the subject [of UFOs]. There is no office within the National Defense Headquarters commissioned to deal with the reports of these phenomena. . . . There has never been a serious investigation of any report on file at AFHQ [Air Force Headquarters]."[15]

That the Royal Canadian Air Force was seriously concerned with the UFO subject has been established with the release of the hitherto secret RCAF report, dating back to 1952, referred to earlier, in which the hope was expressed that there would be future cooperation between the RCAF and the US Air Force. Also, two of the committee members of the secret Project Second Story group were Flight Lieutenant Bradley (Defense Research Board) and Group Captain Edwards (Directorate of Air Intelligence), so the statement that "there has never been a serious investigation of any report on file at AFHQ" is nonsense.

In February 1959 the Department of National Defense instituted a series of *Communications Instructions for Reporting Vital Intelligence Sightings*[16], in line with the US Joint Chiefs of Staff JANAP 146 procedure orders of the same title. Later, cooperation between the United States and Canada in the reporting of UFOs was laid down, for example, in the *Canadian-United States Communications Instructions for Reporting Vital Intelligence Sightings* (CIRVIS) JANAP 146 (E), issued in March 1966 by the Joint Chiefs of Staff as well as the Canadian Defense Staff. This publication lists instructions for the reporting of "information of vital importance to the security of the United States of America and Canada and their forces, which in the opinion of the observer, requires very urgent defensive and/or investigative action by the US and/or Canadian armed forces.'' Sightings within the scope of JANAP 146 include ''Unidentified flying objects'' as distinct from ''Hostile or unidentified single aircraft or formations of aircraft,'' and there are lengthy and elaborate instructions for reporting UFOs.[17]

Further proof for the serious involvement of the Canadian armed forces, and the RCAF in particular, is contained in a memorandum dated 24 November 1967 from Wing Commander D. F. Robertson, together with other documents. In 1967 it was decided to transfer the RCAF UFO files to the National Research Council. ''If NRC accepts the responsibility of investigating UFOs and they work with the University of Toronto in cooperation with DND [Department of National Defense], in my opinion we are on the right track,'' wrote Robertson nine days after he had prepared a lengthy brief on UFOs in the hope that the NRC would undertake responsibility for continuing investigations. Robertson's file contained several reports which he had hoped would convince the NRC that *extraterrestrial activity was behind some of the sightings in Canada.*

So why was the RCAF apparently no longer interested in UFO research? An unsigned assessment of Wing Commander Robertson's brief stated: ''The marked increase in the air section administrative work load which is directed toward actioning UFO reports is reaching a stage which is considered detrimental to the primary operational responsibilities and duties of the section,'' and blamed high administrative costs during the previous year and ''overzealousness'' on the part of its research team. Another and more significant reason was given for the DND opting out of UFO research: ''The primary interest of UFOs lies in the field of science and, to a lesser degree, *to one that is associated with national security.*''[18] [Emphasis added]

In February 1968 the NRC agreed to become the government's official archive for all existing and subsequent UFO reports, and the files were kept in an office of the Council's Upper Atmosphere Section (Astrophysics Branch) in Ottawa. This was *apparently* only a custodial function, however, and the NRC neither solicited nor investigated UFO reports. ''We do not feel, in general, that there's any point in us spending any time and energy chasing all over after such vague reports. I think we have better things to do,'' said Dr. Allen G. McNamara, head of the Upper Atmosphere Section.[19] ''No scientific evidence indicates that any of these objects are of extraterrestrial origins.''[20] But there was one dissenting voice, at least. Professor Rupert Macneill, a geologist on the

Above: This damaged and retouched photograph by a *Los Angeles Times*
reporter shows searchlight beams converging on a mysterious aerial intruder over
the Culver City area of Los Angeles on the morning of 25 February 1942. The UFO
can just be made out. The small blobs of light are *not* UFOs, but bursts of antiaircraft shells. 1,430 rounds of ammunition were fired at the UFOs during the five-
hour alarm, as confirmed by General Marshall. (*Los Angeles Times*)

Below left: General George Marshall, US Army Chief of Staff in World War II and
Secretary of State for Foreign Affairs (1947–49). In 1951 General Marshall
informed Dr Rolf Alexander that the US authorities had established contact with
UFOs, and that some of the craft and occupants had actually been retrieved.
(*Imperial War Museum*)

Below right: An Associated Press story reporting on the 'foo-fighter' sightings,
13 December 1944. (*Gordon Creighton*)

Silver Balls Floating in Air
Nazis' Newest War Device

(The Associated Press) **1944**

Paris, Dec. 13.—As the Allied armies ground out
new gains on the western front today, the Germans
were disclosed to have thrown a new "device" into the
war—mysterious silvery balls which float in the air.

Pilots report seeing these objects, both individually and in clusters, during forays over the Reich.

(The purpose of the floaters was not immediately evident. It is possible that they represent a new
anti-aircraft defense instrument or weapon.)

(This dispatch was heavily censored at supreme
headquarters.)

Above: 'What does all this stuff about flying saucers amount to? What can it mean? What is the truth? Let me have a report at your convenience.' Prime Minister Winston Churchill, in a minute to the Secretary of State for Air, Lord Cherwell, 28 July 1952. (*Popperfoto*)

Below left: ' . . . More than 10,000 sightings have been reported, the majority of which cannot be accounted for by any 'scientific' explanation. . . . I am convinced that these objects do exist and that they are not manufactured by any nation on earth. . . .' Air Chief Marshal Lord Dowding, Commander-in-Chief of RAF Fighter Command during the Battle of Britain, 11 July 1954. (*Imperial War Museum*)

Below right: Ralph Noyes, former head of Defence Secretariat 8, a division in the central staffs of the Ministry of Defence which dealt with UFO reports from members of the public. While with DS8, Noyes was shown gun-camera film clips of UFOs taken by RAF pilots. (*Author*)

James Salandin, whose sketch of three UFOs he encountered while flying in a Meteor jet on 14 October 1954, is shown below. One of the objects nearly collided with his plane. (*Author*) *Bottom:* A Gloster Meteor 8, similar to the aircraft Salandin was flying when the incident occurred. (*Quadrant/Flight International*)

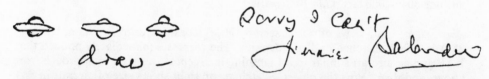

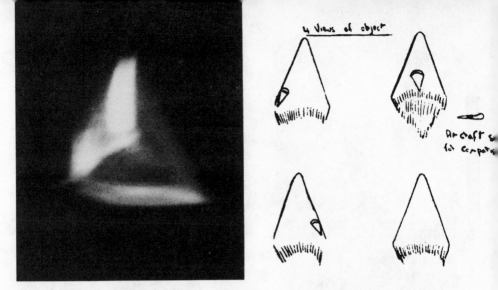

Above left: Balloon or UFO? This object was seen by thousands as it hovered over London and the home counties for several hours on 1 August 1963. While it is probable that it was a tetrahedral balloon released from Germany, its ability to remain stationary in the field of view of a telescope is still puzzling. This photograph was taken by an amateur astronomer through a 4-inch refractor telescope from Bushey in Hertfordshire. He estimated the span to be about 400 feet; altitude 80–90,000 feet. (*Jan Willemstyn*)

Above right: Four views of object seen by H.M. Coastguards at Brixham, Devon, on 28 April 1967, sketched by Brian Jenkins. The witnesses immediately phoned the RAF and an aircraft similar to a Lightning interceptor was seen to approach from above, and then below the object. Sketch at top right shows size of aircraft in comparison to the object which was therefore estimated to be about 200 feet high and 150 feet wide at the base. The MoD denied that an aircraft had been sent up and the coastguards were told not to discuss the incident. (*Brian Jenkins*)

Below left: Police Sergeant Tony Dodd, who together with PC Alan Dale, encountered this object (*right*) in the vicinity of Cononley, near Skipton, Yorkshire, in January 1978. (*Author*) The sketch, by Mark Birdsall of the Yorkshire UFO Society, has been approved by Sgt Dodd. (*Mark Birdsall/YUFOS*)

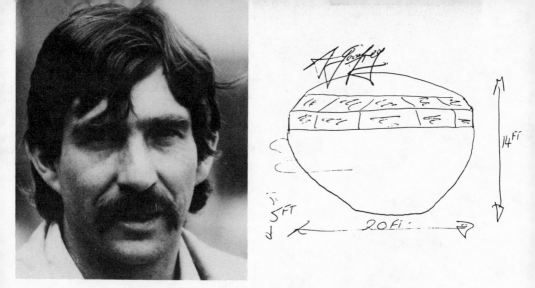

Above left: Former PC Alan Godfrey encountered this object (*right*) hovering five feet above a road in Todmorden, Yorkshire, in the early hours of 29 November 1980. Attempts to contact base by both VHF and UHF radio failed. A number of other witnesses, including police officers, reported sightings in the vicinity on the same morning. (*Photo: Author; Sketch: Alan Godfrey*)

Below left: Denise Bishop, who was struck by a thin beam of light from a UFO outside her home in Weston Mill, Plymouth, on 10 September 1981, which immobilized her for thirty seconds. (*Author*) The scar on Denise's hand as it appeared the following day. A doctor gave his opinion that the scar was similar to a burn from a laser beam. (*Bob Boyd*)

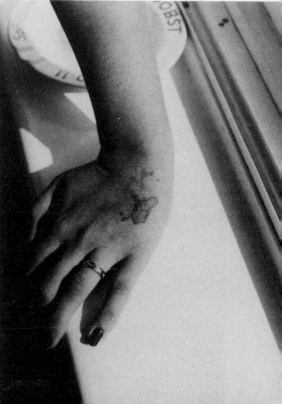

Above: Part of RAF Rudloe Manor in Wiltshire where, according to information received by the author, secret research into UFOs has been carried out for many years. This photograph shows the Headquarters, Provost and Security Services. (*Author*)

Below: Admiral of the Fleet The Lord Hill-Norton GCB, Chief of Defence Staff 1971–73.

Above: 'I must say that if listeners could see for themselves the mass of reports coming in from the airborne gendarmerie, from the mobile gendarmerie, and from the gendarmerie charged with the job of conducting investigations, all of which reports are forwarded by us to the National Centre for Space Studies, then they would see that it is all pretty disturbing.' M. Robert Galley, French Minister of Defence, interviewed by Jean-Claude Bourret, 21 February 1974. (*Jacques Vainstain*)

Below: Dr Pierre Guérin of the French Institute of Astrophysics, and a Senior Research Officer with the National Centre for Scientific Research. 'Unless you are in the know and are privy to the highest level of the secrets of the military intelligence services', he stated in 1982, 'nobody is capable of knowing for certain whether there do exist material, concrete (and therefore irrefutable) proofs of UFOs as such.' (*Author*)

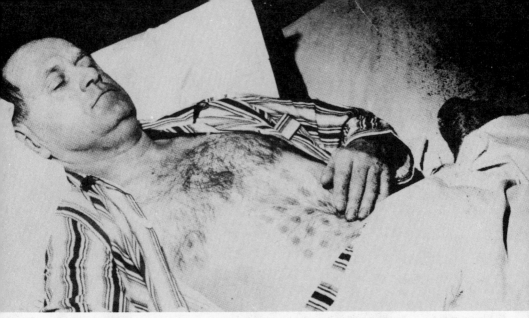

Above: Stephen Michalak, who encountered a landed UFO (*below*) near Falcon Lake, Canada, on 20 May 1967, is shown in hospital following the incident. When Michalak examined and touched the object a blast of hot air struck him, setting his clothes alight. He immediately became very ill, suffering initially from nausea and a pounding headache, followed by a host of alarming symptoms. Note the peculiar pattern of burn marks which matched the ventilation or exhaust grill from which the blast emitted. *(Photo: Mary Evans Picture Library; Sketch: Canadian UFO Report)*

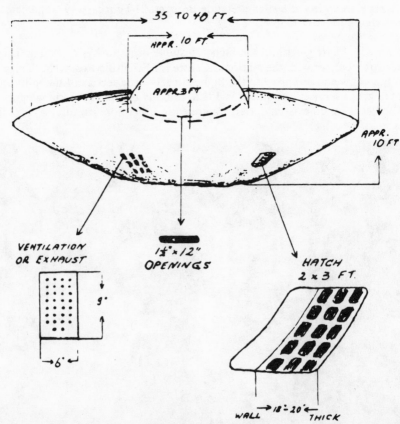

35 TO 40 FT

APPR. 10 FT

APPR 3 FT

APPR. 10 FT

VENTILATION
OR EXHAUST

9"

6"

1½" × 12"
OPENINGS

HATCH
2 × 3 FT.

WALL   18"-20"   THICK

NRC's Associate Committee on Meteorites, commented: "I may be wrong. . . . But my opinion is that there are definitely things that are being seen that we know nothing about, and as far as I'm concerned, they're definitely real. They've got to be! Now if we don't know what these things are, and if we can find out, we should do so."[21]

Although the NRC supposedly undertook only custodial duties regarding UFO reports, a letter from the Department of National Defense in my possession, dated 1972, states that since the beginning of 1968 "UFO reports received by the Canadian forces are passed to the National Research Council. The branch examines reports for scientific reasons warranting further investigation. The Department of National Defense and other federal goverment agencies may be called upon to carry out these investigations for NRC." So, the NRC was definitely involved in investigations, despite statements to the contrary.

The DND letter goes on to state its official position on the subject: "We neither agree with nor deny the existence of UFOs. Investigations to date indicate that there is no evidence to suggest that UFOs present a threat to the world, however, *certain reports suggest that they exhibit a unique scientific or advance technology that could possibly contribute to scientific or technical research.*" [Emphasis added]

The 1972 letter confirms that prior to 1968 all sightings of UFOs reported to Canadian Forces Headquarters were investigated by the Director of Operations, but that "it has not been the practice to allow the general public to study these files."[22]

Having written a letter to Prime Minister Pierre Trudeau in 1971, the former RCAF and Navy pilot Arthur Bray was referred to the Department of External Affairs, from whom he received the following interesting comment on the official attitude: "The Canadian government *does not underestimate the seriousness of the question of UFOs* and this matter is being kept under consideration and study in a number of departments and agencies."[23] [Emphasis added]

One of those departments was the Institute for Aerospace Studies at the University of Toronto, which commenced a study into UFOs in late 1967, headed by Dr. Gordon Patterson. In October 1968 the press reported that this study group was on the verge of collapse "owing to a lack of something to investigate."[24] Arthur Bray failed to obtain any information from the Institute, however, and neither was any report forthcoming from scientists at the IAS despite the fact that it is normal procedure for such reports to be made public.[25]

COVER-UP

In 1964 an enormous circular object, spewing flame-colored exhaust, passed slowly over a car occupied by Bert Gammie and his mother and daughter. After he telephoned the RCAF in Vancouver, Gammie was visited by a senior officer who carried a briefcase full of UFO photographs to make comparisons. The officer, whom Gammie knew, emphasized that despite their acquaintanceship he would deny having been there if the visit received any publicity.[26]

The Royal Canadian Mounted Police also takes UFO sightings very seriously, and has received hundreds of reports over the years. Former RCMP officer John Pushie confirms that he has spoken to people who have served in military radar stations, as well as other people, who had apparently seen something but had been afraid to say anything about it. "I realize that many government agencies take UFO sightings seriously, the RCMP being one," he admitted in 1980. "Policy in the past has been to report all investigations concerning sightings on 'Secret' letter-head. I can personally vouch for this as I served with the RCMP for five years."

On 3 December 1979 Pushie managed to take seven photographs of an unidentified object (four of which came out) from his home at Sydney, Nova Scotia, which he showed to the CFS Sydney Radar Base Commanding Officer, who said he would like to send the photographs and negatives to the National Research Council. One month later they were returned, with a memo stating that Pushie had probably photographed the star Vega. Needless to say, he was far from satisfied with this explanation, since at one point the object he saw "moved from its position so quickly after spending so long in one spot."

Pushie also relates a sighting that took place in Sydney in July of 1968. A man was driving his car around Blacketts Lake Road when he noticed a saucer-shaped object descending below the treeline near the lake. He parked his car and ran toward the object along a trail through the woods. When he was about seventy-five feet from the object, which was now hovering about six feet above the ground in a clearing adjacent to the lake, it suddenly took off. The RCMP were called and while carrying out their investigation blocked off both access roads to the lake. "The incident received very little media coverage," said Pushie. "No further facts were made available."[27]

Bill Toffan, a young RCMP constable, sighted a UFO on Highway 16 about sixty miles east of Prince Rupert, British Columbia, in April

1976. As he drew closer to it there was a blinding flash and he nearly lost control of his car. After a brief press report appeared, Toffan was ordered not to discuss the incident. But RCMP subdivision head Edward Trefry denied that there was a cover-up. "We're not trying to hide anything," he said. "It's simply policy which has been laid down throughout this subdivision that all press releases are made by senior personnel at each detachment instead of by the individual officer."[28]

Researcher Henry McKay has experienced difficulties in dealing with the National Research Council which have contributed to suspicions of a cover-up. In 1969 he submitted his field notes on a particular case to the NRC. A year later when he went back to determine the results of their investigation, they claimed they had no information on the case, but after McKay pointed out that he had submitted certain data to a specific individual and office, the file was suddenly discovered. Bureaucracy rather than secrecy, one wonders? On another occasion some substance from an alleged UFO landing site discovered by a farmer in southern Ontario was submitted to the NRC by the Ontario Provisional Police. "The substance was turned over to the Ontario government forensic lab and to this date they haven't released the results of their analysis," McKay reports. "The only official answer I got was that it was a police matter and didn't concern me."[29]

THE FALCON LAKE INCIDENT, 1967

By far the most evidential case ever to have been reported in Canada is that of Stephen Michalak, who encountered a landed UFO near Falcon Lake, on the boundary between Manitoba and Ontario, on 20 May 1967. For the following summary I am indebted to Chris Rutkowski's thorough analysis in *Flying Saucer Review,* which I have leaned heavily on.

At 12:15 p.m. that day Michalak, who was engaged in some amateur prospecting, was startled to see two cigar-shaped objects with "bumps" on them, glowing red, and descending. The objects appeared more oval and disk shaped as they came closer. Suddenly, the object furthest away stopped in midair as the other came nearer and then landed about 160 feet away. The object in the air hovered for a short period then departed silently, changing color from red to orange to gray, then back to orange as it disappeared behind clouds. The craft on the ground also changed color, from red to gray and finally "hot stainless steel," surrounded by a goldenish glow. It was about thirty-five feet in diameter and twelve feet high.

Michalak knelt on a rock as he observed the object through welding goggles that he normally wore to protect his eyes from chips of rock. A dazzling purple light flooded out of openings in the upper part of the object. The witness sat on the rock for the next half hour, sketching the object and noting as many details as possible. Waves of warm air and a smell of sulphur radiated from the craft, and there were noises like the whirring of an electric motor as well as a hissing sound.

A door then opened in the side of the craft, with lights coming from the inside. Michalak decided to approach closer, and when he was sixty feet away heard two human-like voices, one higher pitched than the other. Convinced by now that the device was a new experimental American aircraft, he asked the occupants if they were having trouble. There was no response, although the voices had subsided, so he asked in Russian, "Do you speak Russian?" There was still no response, even when he tried German, Italian, French, and Ukrainian, then English again.

Michalak approached even closer—so close that the light from it became unbearable, so he pushed down the tinted green lenses on his goggles and peered inside the opening. He saw a "maze" of lights on a panel, and beams of light in horizontal and diagonal patterns, as well as a group of lights flashing in a random sequence. He then stepped back and awaited a reaction.

Suddenly, three panels closed completely over the opening, so Michalak began to examine the side of the craft with his gloved hand. He could see no indications of welding or joints, and the surface was highly polished, appearing like colored glass reflecting light. When he pulled his hand back he found that the glove had burned and melted, as had his hat. The craft—or at least the rim—then seemed to change position, for he found himself facing a grid-type "exhaust vent," which he had noticed earlier to the left of the opening. A blast of hot air then struck his chest, setting his shirt and vest alight, causing severe pain. He ripped these off and looked up to see the craft taking off like the first object, and felt a rush of air.

A strong smell similar to burned electrical circuits combined with sulphur pervaded the air. Michalak's burning clothes set some moss on fire, so he stamped on the ground to extinguish the flames and then walked back to where he had left his things. He noticed that his compass was behaving erratically, but after a short while went back to normal. Returning to the landing site, which looked as though it had been swept clean apart from a fifteen-foot circle of pine needles, dirt, and leaves,

Michalak began to suffer from a pounding headache as well as nausea. He headed back to his motel, vomiting frequently on the way.

On reaching the highway, Michalak realized that he was now about a mile from where he had originally entered the woods, so set off in the correct direction. A passing RCMP officer stopped in his car, listened to Michalak's story, and then left, explaining that he had other duties to perform. The witness eventually made it back to the motel, but believing he was "contaminated," decided to remain outside. At 4:00 p.m., however, he went into the motel coffee shop and asked for a doctor, but as the nearest was forty-five miles away he decided to catch the next bus home to Winnipeg. While waiting, he telephoned the *Winnipeg Tribune*. "The pain was unbearable. . . . I was afraid that I had ruined my health and visualized the resulting hell should I become disabled," he said. "There had to be some way of getting medical help. . . . I thought of the press. . . . I did not want to alarm my wife, or cause a panic in the family. I phoned her as a last resort, telling her that I had been in an accident." When he arrived home his son took him to Misericordia Hospital, where he stayed overnight.

Physiological Effects

On arrival at the hospital Michalak refrained from telling the examining physician the full story, preferring to say only that he had been burned by "exhaust coming out of an airplane." He was treated for first-degree burns and released. Two days later he was examined by his family doctor, who prescribed pain-killers and seasickness tablets. Tests a week later by the Whiteshell Nuclear Research Establishment showed no radiation above the normal background level.

For several days after the incident Michalak was unable to keep his food down and lost twenty-two pounds. His blood lymphocyte count was down from twenty-five to sixteen percent, returning to normal after four weeks. Medical reports also showed that he had skin infections, "having hive-like areas with impetiginous centers." He suffered from diarrhea, "generalized urticaria" (hives), and periodically felt weak, dizzy, and nauseated. He also experienced numbness and chronic swelling of the joints. An "awful stench" seemed to come from inside his body at times.

A hematologist's report indicated that Michalak's blood had "some atypical lymphoid cells in the marrow plus a moderate increase in the number of plasma cells." The witness also complained of a burning sensation around his neck and chest, and occasions when his body "turned violet," his hands swelled "like a balloon," his vision failed and he lapsed into unconsciousness.

In August 1968 Michalak spent two weeks at the Mayo Clinic in Rochester, Minnesota, USA, at his own expense. He was found to be in good health, apart from neurological dermatitis, and simple syncope (fainting spells due to sudden cerebral blood pressure loss) attributed to hyperventilation or impaired cardiac input (Michalak had been suffering from heart problems for a number of years). Psychiatric tests showed no evidence of delusions, hallucinations or other emotional disorders.[30] A peculiar geometric pattern of burn marks which appeared on Michalak's chest and abdomen was diagnosed as being thermal in origin. The marks matched the "exhaust grill" of the UFO, which had about thirty small openings.

Altogether, Michalak was examined by a total of twenty-seven doctors, and none was able fully to explain the cause of his symptoms.[31] Investigations were carried out by the Departments of Health and Social Welfare, National Defense, the National Research Council, the University of Colorado, the Canadian Aerial Phenomena Research Organization, the RCMP, the RCAF, as well as at the Whiteshell Nuclear Research Establishment. Dr. Horace Dudley, former Chief of the Radioisotope Laboratory, US Naval Hospital, New York, believes that the symptoms of nausea and vomiting, followed by diarrhea, loss of weight, and the drop in the lymphocyte count, "is a classical picture of severe whole body [exposure to] radiation with X or gamma rays.

"I would guess," said Dr. Dudley, "that Mr. Michalak received in the order of 100–200 roentgens. It is very fortunate that this dose of radiation only lasted a very short time or he would certainly have received a lethal dose . . . ."[32]

Findings at the Landing Site

Stewart Hunt, an investigator for the Department of Health and Social Welfare, found a small contaminated area at the landing site, no larger than 100 square inches, that showed a "significant" level of radium 226, for which no satisfactory explanation could be found. Tests conducted by the Whiteshell Nuclear Research Establishment, however, apparently revealed nothing abnormal, and in June 1979 a reanalysis confirmed that all the energies detected could be adequately explained in terms of the decay of natural uranium. Despite these findings, the radiation found by

Hunt was of sufficient quantity for the Radiation Protection Division to consider restricting entry to the forest area in 1967.

A year after the encounter, Michalak returned to the landing site with a friend and, using a Geiger counter, discovered two "W-shaped" silver bars, four and a half inches in length, as well as some other chunks of the same material, under some lichen above which the UFO was alleged to have hovered. In spite of doubts raised by the University of Colorado UFO Project investigator Roy Craig, researcher Brian Cannon found that the silver concentration was "much higher than would normally be found in native silver such as sterling or coinage," though the amount of copper, at one or two percent, was consistent with commercial silver, if less than many specimens. The metal showed signs of heating, bending, *and* radioactivity, and was imbedded on the outside with fine quartz crystals as well as small crystals of a uranium silicate material and pitchblende, and feldspar and hematite. Yet why, asks Chris Rutkowski, was this silver missed earlier by other investigators?

Official Reactions

Squadron Leader P. Bissky, representing the Royal Canadian Air Force, concluded that the entire case was a hoax, yet a statement in the National Research Council's Non-Meteoritic (i.e. UFO) Sightings File (Department of National Defense, DND 222) reads: "Neither the DND, nor the RCMP investigation teams were able to provide evidence which could dispute Mr. Michalak's story." And the RCMP forensic analysis was "unable to reach any conclusion as to what may have caused the burn damage" to Michalak's clothing.

On 27 May 1967 MP Ed Schreyer asked in the House of Commons about UFO investigations, with the Michalak case in mind. The Speaker of the House *"cut off the subject without government reply."* On 6 November 1967 Defense Minister Leo Cadieux, replying to requests by several Cabinet members to obtain information on the Michalak case, stated that *"it is not the intention of the Department of National Defense to make public the report of the alleged sighting."* On 11 November 1967 Ed Schreyer (who subsequently became Governor-General) formally placed a written question on the Commons order paper seeking information on UFOs.

On 14 October 1968—seventeen months after the incident—House Leader Donald MacDonald refused MP Barry Mather access to reports on the Michalak case. But on 6 February 1969 Mather was given permission by a member of the Privy Council to examine their file on UFOs, "from which a few pages have simply been removed." Significantly, it was stated that outright release of the file *"would not be in the public's interest and* [would] *create a dangerous precedent that would not contribute to the good administration of the country's business."*[33]

Although most of the government report on the Michalak case was eventually made available to inquirers at the National Research Council, the complete file has never been released. In 1982, when the Canadian government passed the Freedom of Information Act, researcher Graham Conway filed a FOIA request for the Michalak file, which an authoritative document listed as being the most complete and extensive among the UFO reports, containing between 125 and 150 pages. He received only 113 pages.

Graham Conway has confirmed that the Canadian government clandestinely collects UFO material on a daily basis from all the various UFO groups that keep up to date with developments in the field.[34]

FURTHER SIGHTINGS BY PILOTS

Less than six weeks after the Falcon Lake incident, three air traffic controllers and two technicians monitoring an eastbound Air Canada flight suddenly noticed an unknown object on the radarscope, heading at high speed toward Kenora, Ontario. The date was 7 July 1967, and later that evening the same or a similar object was detected on the Kenora Airport radarscope, heading northeast. For a total of *three hours* the object described a series of maneuvers, executing 180° turns and chasing two Air Canada flights before resuming its original northeast heading and finally disappearing from the radarscope.[35]

On 15 November 1967 the crew of Quebec Air, Flight 650, sighted a very bright object at the end of the runway at Sept-Îles, Quebec. It was larger than a star, stationary, and at an unknown altitude.

In July 1974 a Scandinavian Airlines captain flying thirty-five to forty miles southeast of Quebec City reported a triangular-shaped object moving in a southwesterly direction. During the sighting, Bagotville [Airport] experienced radio frequency interference.[36]

On 10 October 1974 John Breen, a Canadian armed forces pilot, was paced by a UFO over Newfoundland, en route from Deer Lake to Gander. A passenger flying with him first noticed a strange light following the plane when they were about fifty miles from Gander. Every time Breen looked at the light it seemed to turn off, but finally he got a better view of it. "It seemed to be a sort of triangle—or delta-shaped, luminescent greenish light following us," Breen told investigator Gregory Kanon. "It was on for, say, two or three or four seconds and then off for a bit and on again. It was fairly regular. And then, as it carried on, it became pretty well a steady light."

About twenty-five to thirty miles from Gander, Breen radioed the airport and asked if they had any other traffic in the vicinity. They replied in the negative. "Then I said, well, we've definitely got an aircraft or something here with us," Breen reported. The object was not a reflection of his Cessna 150's lights, and about fourteen miles north of the airport, where the Gander River opens out into Gander Lake, the object could clearly be seen reflected in the water, but when flying over land the reflection could no longer be seen.

"I started a right turn and then cut hard left," Breen said. "Gander then picked up the object for two or three sweeps, which would have been about 10 to 12 seconds. When we turned around, I just saw it going off the other way and then I lost it because of the back of the airplane."[37]

Less than ten hours later, at approximately 4:15 a.m. on 11 October 1974, an unidentified object was sighted by the captain and crew of a Capital Airlines DC-8 airliner, en route to Gander Airport at 7,500 feet. The object drew alongside the plane, flashing red and white lights, maintaining a parallel course until finally disappearing in cloud cover about five miles from Gander. The airliner was flying at approximately 290 mph at the time, and the object maintained the same speed but occasionally accelerated a little ahead of the jet, then resumed its position alongside. Both the captain and first officer stated that the object was not an aircraft, and Air Traffic Control Gander confirmed that no other aircraft were in the vicinity.[38]

The following week, the pilot of a small private plane nearly collided with a gigantic, apparently metallic object which shot across a runway at Saint Anthony, Newfoundland.[39]

Researcher Arthur Bray contacted Transport Canada, the department responsible for civil air safety in Canada, and inquired about official studies and regulations regarding sightings of UFOs reported by pilots. "No studies on UFOs have been carried out by Transport Canada," a senior official informed him, "nor does Transport Canada have any regulations regarding UFOs."[40]

RADAR/VISUAL CASE AT FALCONBRIDGE, 1975

In October and November 1975 a spate of low-level UFO sightings over Strategic Air Command bases in Maine, Michigan, Montana, and North Dakota caused widespread official concern, particularly since some of the unknown objects exhibited a "clear intent" over nuclear missile sites. A log extract from the Alert Center Branch of the US Air Force Aerospace Intelligence Division, on 31 October, mentions sightings near the Canadian border: "CONTACTED CIA OPS CENTER AND INFORMED THEM OF U/I FLIGHT ACTIVITY OVER TWO SAC BASES NEAR CANADIAN BORDER. CIA INDICATED APPRECIATION AND REQUESTED THEY BE INFORMED OF ANY FOLLOW UP ACTIVITY."

Then, on 11 November, a UFO was reported visually and tracked on radar at the Canadian forces radar site at Falconbridge, Ontario. The following message from the Commander-in-Charge of North American Aerospace Defense Command (NORAD) was relayed to NORAD units in North America:

THIS MORNING, 11 NOV 75, CFS FALCONBRIDGE REPORTED SEARCH AND HEIGHT FINDER RADAR PAINTS ON AN OBJECT UP TO 30 NAUTICAL MILES SOUTH OF THE SITE RANGING IN ALTITUDE FROM 25,000 FT. TO 72,000 FT. THE SITE COMMANDER AND OTHER PERSONNEL SAY THE OBJECT APPEARED AS A BRIGHT STAR BUT MUCH CLOSER. WITH BINOCULARS THE OBJECT APPEARED AS A 100 FT DIAMETER SPHERE AND APPEARED TO HAVE CRATERS AROUND THE OUTSIDE.

On 13 November NORAD informed the media in Sudbury, Ontario, that the sighting had occurred at 4:05 a.m., and that two F-106 jets of the USAF Air National Guard's Fighter Interceptor Squadron at Selfridge Air Force Base, Michigan, were scrambled, but the pilots reported no contact with the object.

In the 11 November message, the NORAD Commander-in-Charge confirmed that "reliable military personnel" had reported the sightings in the US and at Falconbridge, and concluded:

BE ASSURED THAT THIS COMMAND IS DOING EVERYTHING POSSIBLE TO IDENTIFY AND PROVIDE SOLID FACTUAL INFORMATION ON THESE SIGHTINGS. I HAVE ALSO EXPRESSED MY CONCERN TO SAFOI [Secretary of the Air Force Office of Information] THAT WE COME UP SOONEST WITH A PROPOSED AN-SWER TO QUERIES FROM THE PRESS TO PREVENT OVER REACTION BY THE PUBLIC TO REPORTS IN THE MEDIA THAT MAY BE BLOWN OUT OF PROPORTION. TO DATE EFFORTS BY AIR GUARD HELICOPTERS,

SAC HELICOPTERS AND NORAD F-106s HAVE FAILED TO PRODUCE
POSITIVE ID.

The USAF was anxious to play down these disturbing incidents. An
Air Force document of the same date advised that "unless there is evidence which links sightings, queries can best be handled individually at
the source and as questions arise. Responses should be direct, forthright
and emphasize that the action taken was in response to an isolated or
specific incident. IOS should keep all levels and appropriate Majcoms
informed of questions asked, media affiliations and responses given."

OFFICIAL RETICENCE

Wilbert Smith, whose untimely death of cancer in 1962 robbed not only
Canada but the world of one of the most intelligent and original minds
in the field of UFO research, was well qualified to assess the various
reasons behind the official cover-up, having headed Canada's first secret
investigation into the subject. To most people, Smith pointed out, the
government is the final authority on all matters. Government, however,
is comprised of a large number of individuals who, although experts in
their own fields, are very much laymen in other areas. If a new
situation—such as UFOs—develops, and there is no suitable bureau for
it, he said, it was unfair to expect early answers from the government.
"The best that a government can do," he explained, "is to make use of
a 'back door' arrangement with which we are all familiar, namely, the
'classified project.' But even this is a gamble in that it is predicated on
the project yielding positive results with the answers all tied up in a neat
little bundle, otherwise the project flops and slips into oblivion."

Smith affirmed that the United States authorities *were well aware that
UFOs were of alien origin*, and that "it was soon apparent that these
objects did not constitute any particular menace to humanity and there
was practically nothing which we could do about it if they did." The
aliens were in complete control of the situation, while we were mere
observers.

Since the various classified US Air Force projects were largely aimed
at debunking UFO reports, Smith said, the Air Force had painted themselves into an awkward corner:

What solid information did come out of these projects was most disturbing
indeed, striking at the very roots of our conventional science. But there

wasn't enough of this information on which to base any substantial reform in scientific thinking: just enough to produce an uneasy feeling that all was not well. So naturally, the least said about this the better, until more was known. . . . Meanwhile, since they do not have enough answers for the questions that are now being raised, they most certainly are not going to invite a deluge of further questions by admitting anything.

Wilbert Smith reasoned that the reluctance of politicians to speak out on the subject was largely due to lack of public support. "Furthermore," he said, "because of the type of publicity from which the whole matter of flying saucers has suffered, politicians, who are naturally very sensitive to public reaction, are reluctant to stick their necks out."

Smith believed that we could not expect any significant statement on UFOs by any government agency, and the nearest we would come to any sort of official statement would be from those few researchers in the government service who (like Smith, although he did not say as much) were personally satisfied of their findings and who were willing to risk the censure of their colleagues and the prestige of their positions. "More often than not," he said, "these people must wait until they retire from government service before they feel free to make any statement at all."[41]

Wilbert Smith was right. However, the UFO situation has become increasingly more complex since he expressed these opinions in the late 1950s, and there is evidence that not all UFOs are harmless, as the Falcon Lake incident exemplifies. Even if outright hostility was unproven, there is no doubt in my mind that the Canadian government was reluctant to release its conclusions on the case for fear of arousing public overreaction. Indeed, as already mentioned, the government stated categorically that release of the Michalak file "would not be in the public's interest" and "would create a dangerous precedent." So this is one aspect of national security that undoubtedly heads the list of reasons for official reticence on the matter, and I fully sympathize with the government's dilemma in this respect.

Another aspect was cited by Smith himself in a 1953 secret Project Magnet report: that the UFOs exhibited a technology considerably in advance of ours, leading him to propose that the next stage in official investigations should be a "substantial effort toward the acquisition of as much as possible of this technology." If the military has now acquired new technology as a result of top secret research into UFOs—and I am inclined to support this hypothesis—it would be yet another perfectly understandable reason for withholding information on UFOs in the interests of national security.

Wilbert Smith made no secret of his unofficially expressed opinion that actual contact had been established with the occupants of UFOs, and that he had acquired a great deal of information as a result of investigating such contacts. "But it soon became apparent," he wrote in an article in 1958, "that there was a very real and quite large gap between this alien science and the science in which I had been trained. Certain crucial experiments were suggested and carried out, and in each case the results confirmed the validity of the alien science. Beyond this point the alien science just seemed to be incomprehensible."

Smith was convinced that earth had been colonized many times by the people from elsewhere (or "The Boys Topside," as he liked to call them). "To orthodox thinkers this may seem strange," he said, "but not nearly so strange as our orthodox ideas on evolution!"[42] But if Smith was personally convinced about such controversial matters, to what extent were the authorities aware that extraterrestrial contact had been established at this time? An illuminating answer is provided in a letter that Wilbert Smith wrote to a friend of mine in 1959: "For your information every nation on this planet has been officially informed of the existence of the space craft and their occupants from elsewhere, and as nations they must accept responsibility for any lack of action or for any official position which they may take."[43]

9

CHINA

Since the modern era of UFO sightings began in World War II, practically no information has been available from the country with the largest population in the world—the People's Republic of China. But in 1978, China's leading newspaper, the *People's Daily,* published the first article to appear on the subject, written by Sheng Heng Yen, of the Chinese Academy of Social Sciences.[1] Further articles were published in the *Guang Ming Daily* during the following two years. In 1980 a Chinese UFO researcher, Paul Dong (Moon Wai), a resident of California, wrote an article featuring reports by pilots, scientists and other reliable observers throughout the world.[2]

Tremendous interest in a hitherto forbidden subject was now aroused throughout China. *Aerospace Knowledge* journal, for example, received several hundred letters requesting the Chinese government to launch an investigation into the phenomenon. And in May 1980 the Chinese UFO Studies Association was established under the auspices of Wuhan University in central China, with branches in Peking (Beijing), Shanghai, and in the provinces of Guangdong, Sichuan, Shanxi, Hubei and Guangxi. The Association was headed by a twenty-five-year-old astrophysics student, Cha Leping. Subsequently the Association became incorporated into the China UFO Research Organization as an official branch of the Chinese Academy of Social Sciences.

Some measure of the degree of enthusiasm for UFOs in China is reflected in the fact that the China UFO Research Organization's first issue of the *Journal of UFO Research* sold 300,000 copies on the newsstands. Paul Dong—editor-in-chief of the journal—lectured on the subject all over China in 1981, creating something of a sensation, speaking to packed audiences at the Peking Ching Hua University Students Union, the Peking Planetarium, Canton (Guangchou) Science Museum, and Canton Jinan University, for example, and during his one-month tour collected hundreds of UFO cases from the period 1978–81. Since that time hundreds more cases—some dating back to 1940 and even earlier—have been gathered and published in the journal. Many of these reports have been compiled by Paul Dong and published privately in a valuable book, *UFOs over Modern China,* and I am indebted to Paul and his publisher,

Wendelle Stevens, for allowing me to cite some of these reports, which have been translated by the Foreign Language Bureau in Peking. I am also grateful to Paul for allowing me to use material from his Chinese-published book, *Questions and Answers on UFOs*.

Why did the Chinese wait so long to take the UFO problem seriously? According to Paul Dong, three specific factors prompted the Chinese government to recognize the phenomenon. On a summer evening in 1965 two bright, disk-shaped objects violated Peking's airspace. Two years later a similar incident occurred near the outskirts of Peking when a bright, globe-shaped object was observed by thousands of witnesses as it streaked across the night sky at fantastic speeds, stopped and hovered, then disappeared over the horizon. Speculation among the masses that Taiwan or another hostile country had developed a secret weapon that might threaten China's national security led to the sanctioning of the academic research group. The third factor leading to official recognition was the frequency of reports received by the authorities from the provinces in the late 1970s.[3]

Britain's *Flying Saucer Review* has been taken for many years by the Chinese Academy of Sciences, and *FSR* editor Charles Bowen and Gordon Creighton (the present editor) tried to obtain further information from the Chinese authorities in 1980. But when they visited the offices of the *Xinhua* news agency in London, the agency was unable to provide any information at all about the Chinese UFO Research Association.[4] My own efforts were also thwarted in February 1982 when the Scientific Attaché at the Chinese Embassy in London told me that no such organization had been set up at Wuhan University. Nevertheless, official recognition for the subject is now beyond dispute, and the Chinese government seems keen to educate its people about the mysterious phenomenon. In 1981, for example, the Chinese Television Service showed an American documentary, "UFOs Are Real," which has yet to be shown in Britain.[5]

The first sighting to be published in postwar China described an "enormous [flying] platter [which] emanated luminous rays in all directions . . . and dazzled all who saw it."[6] The date was July 1947, weeks after pilot Kenneth Arnold's famous sighting in the USA, and the report was released by the Chinese Palace of State; the only firsthand Chinese report to be made public before the victory of the Chinese Revolution isolated China from the West as far as UFO reports (and much else) was concerned. With the new People's Republic of China under Mao Tse Tung nothing was spoken or written about the subject until the period of the

Cultural Revolution, when UFO reports began to filter out through underground channels. But officially the subject was considered to be "counter-revolutionary."[7] Under China's new regime, however, hundreds of reports from this period—and beyond—have now been published.

AIRLINER CHASED BY UFOS, 1963

On an unspecified day in October 1963, a Li-2 airliner (a Soviet-built version of the Douglas DC-3) on the Kuangtung to Wuhan air route was chased by three luminous unidentified flying objects for fifteen minutes. The pilots gave a minute-by-minute report by radio to the Chinese Civil Aeronautics Administration, and on landing the crew was debriefed by Air Traffic Control. The passengers were interviewed by the authorities and were ordered not to discuss the incident with anyone.[8]

JET FIGHTERS SCRAMBLED, 1964

On 1 January 1964 many citizens in Shanghai observed a huge cigar-shaped aerial object flying slowly toward the southwest. MIG fighters were scrambled in pursuit but failed to force the UFO down. The official explanation was that the object was an American missile.[9]

"COMBAT STATIONS," 1968

In early 1968 four coast guard artillerymen of the naval garrison at Luda, Liaoning Province, in North China saw a gold, luminous, oval-shaped object which flew alongside, leaving a thin trail in the air. It then climbed steeply at an incredible speed and eventually disappeared.

At the moment when the object began to climb, all communications and radar systems failed, almost causing an accident in the fleet. The naval patrol went on alert, and the fleet commander ordered his men to prepare for combat. Half an hour later communications and radar returned to normal. A two-man coast guard patrol reportedly saw the UFO land on the south coast and fired at it with automatic rifles and machine guns, but soldiers sent to investigate found no trace of the object.[10]

A LANDING IN THE GOBI DESERT, 1968

In mid-April 1968 Gu Ying (later an interpreter for the New China Agency) was sent to a military construction regiment in the North Gobi Desert where he was working on an irrigation project when quite late in the day a comrade drew the battalion's attention to a strange phenomenon. This is the firsthand account:

I saw a great disk of light trailing flames as it slowly descended to the Gobi's sands. It was a luminous red-orange in color and had an apparent diameter of 3 meters before it landed. It passed alongside a slight inclination above the horizon. We could see a separate more luminous point of light flashing in the mass of light. As it was less than a kilometer from us when it passed by we could see the detail clearly. It landed suddenly and the commander of the company telephoned the headquarters of the regiment who dispatched a team of motorcycle troops to approach it.

Without doubt the arrival of the motorcycle troops was detected by the disc, because it suddenly ascended like an arrow and disappeared in the sky above. As the northern frontier [with the USSR] passes through this region, most witnesses felt that this was a new reconnaissance machine from the enemy to the north inspecting the progress of work on the canal. We did not know anything about UFOs at that time.

The object left traces of its landing in the form of a seared cross on the ground. As we knew nothing of these objects we did not study the mark. . . . We only thought in political terms and believed that this signified some kind of preparation for an eventual enemy attack from the north. The soldiers long stationed in the Gobi had seen these things before, and the great fireballs in the sky were not so unusual to them. The landing and takeoff were a new twist.[11]

ANOTHER LANDING, 1970

On an unspecified date at 2200 hours in the early part of 1970, a peasant of the Traing District of Fujian Province saw a metallic pan-shaped flying object descend and land behind a hill. The object radiated a brilliant green light and a strange musical tone could be heard emanating from it. The peasant duly reported this to the village head man, and the local Army Commander mobilized hundreds of soldiers who attempted to surround the object.

After about an hour the UFO emitted a bright white light, forcing the soldiers to retreat as it rapidly took off vertically. A member of the militia present (who insisted on anonymity) said that although they could see the brilliant light they were unable to hear any sound while they observed the object.[12]

MILITARY UFO STUDY GROUP FORMED, 1970

While in the foregoing account no names are mentioned, another undated military report from 1970 names Liu Zhangzhou of the People's Liberation Army, who was on sentry duty in the remote Gansu Province when he claims to have seen an entire village enveloped in a strange blue light one night. "I looked toward the source of the light and saw a flattened oval-shaped luminous object in the sky," reported the soldier. "Its center was a golden yellow and it was surrounded by a deep orange-colored cloud. After two minutes it picked up speed and flew to the east." Owing to his fear of the authorities at the time Liu Zhangzhou withheld his story for ten years before coming forward and publicly relating the details.

Apparently many such sightings have been made throughout Gansu and Xingkiang provinces, especially in the Gobi Desert near the Soviet border, and a special military UFO study group was formed to keep track of sightings in the border area.[13]

THE MILITARY CHASE A UFO, 1971

Another witness who claims to have seen a UFO which was immediately investigated by the military is Chen Chu, of a People's Liberation Army unit stationed in Dingxian City, Hubei Province. The event occurred sometime during the last ten days of September 1971 while the Army unit was carrying out an assignment in a small valley north of the city:

> At about half-past-seven, when the sky had just begun to grow dark, we suddenly discovered a circular ball-like object, like the moon, rising slowly to the north of our quarters. The ball gave out a lot of misty gas from its edges. . . . After remaining in the sky for several seconds, it spurted out a strong jet of mist or smoke and rose to a certain height. Then it remained stationary for some seconds, and then rose again to a new height. Then it stopped for some more seconds, and began to drop down until it gradually disappeared in the night sky.
>
> As our Army units were in a state of combat readiness due to the Lin Biao incident[14], we reported our discovery instantly to our superior authorities and dispatched a motor car to pursue the flying object. Because of the ruggedness of the mountain road, the motor car turned back after chasing the object for more than 10 li. . . .
>
> For many years I have tried to explain it as a plane, a balloon or some other flying thing, but have always felt that there is a very great [difference] between such things and the object observed.[15]

MULTIPLE-WITNESS SIGHTINGS, 1976–77

Multiple-witness UFO sightings have been reported in China just as in other countries. The following case is notable for the fact that it occurred on the day that Mao Tse-Tung's obituary was broadcast, on 9 September 1976.

In an area south of Qilou, Longwangmiao, Shan County, Shandong Province, a worker at the Liangshan Cotton Mill observed a spherical flying object at 45° elevation and 3–4,000 meters distance. The upper part of the object was bright silver in color while the lower part was dark gray. It hovered motionless and then moved in the direction of the sun at 3:00 p.m., after Mao's obituary was broadcast. The object was not seen again that night, but it reappeared the following day, when it seemed larger. Then it shrank in size toward noon and finally appeared like a twinkling star in the full daylight sky. It reverted to its former size in the afternoon and then—in full view of more than 1,000 witnesses— flew away abruptly and disappeared at 5:00 p.m. The report was not circulated in China at the time and neither did it appear in the Western press.[16]

The most spectacular multiple-witness sighting ever to have been reported in China took place at 8:30 p.m. on 7 July 1977, at Zhangpo County in Fujian Province. Nearly 3,000 people were watching an open-air showing of the Rumanian film *Alert on the Danube Delta* when a section of the audience suddenly saw two oblate orange-colored luminous objects descending toward the crowd. The objects passed so low over the spectators that they almost touched the ground, emitting a vivid glow and flying only a few meters apart. Heat could be felt and a low humming sound was heard.

Panic spread and people threw themselves to the ground. In the ensuing stampede, two children were trampled to death and 200 more were injured. The UFOs ascended rapidly and disappeared in seconds. Lin Bing-Xiang, a doctor at the county hospital, and Chen Caife, an officer of the County Public Security Bureau, and another official have corroborated this sensational incident. The authorities, suspecting an optical illusion related to the film, reran it, but nothing unusual showed up.[17]

ASTRONOMER'S SIGHTING, 1977

On 26 July 1977 there were many sightings of UFOs reported from Chengdu City, Sichuan Province, and the most detailed account was made by the astronomer Zhang Zhousheng of the Yunnan Observatory:

At 9 to 14 minutes past the 22nd hour, Beijing time, on 26 July 1977, I observed a very astonishing and unexplainable aerial phenomenon . . . in the northern suburb of the Chengdu Municipality. . . . My eyes were suddenly drawn to a strange spiral object in the air. Because of the peculiarity of its appearance, I at once called some other persons to observe it. . . . At the same time, those people who were cooling themselves in places tens of meters away from me had also noticed this strange phenomenon. . . . In appearance, the core of the object was a yellowish bright star; its luminosity was second magnitude, with the core as a starting point, a big Archimedes spiral line (of light) was developed, whose brightness was very evident even under moon light and whose color was blue and somewhat green. . . .

As the spiral line was drawn out from the core, the core could not have been a star, but a comparatively small object. . . . The line wound about the center 3 or 4 rounds. The whole spiral was actually an ellipse (from my point of view), of not very great ellipticity. The diameter of the major axis was about 5 degrees. Its elevation angle with the horizon was about 60 degrees. This strange object was not only big, but it moved in the air in a straight line. . . . It moved with a constant speed, about 10 degrees per minute. Simultaneously with the motion of the core, the spiral line also moved horizontally. No change occurred to the luminosity, size, shape or the various angular measurements, that is to say, the spiral line did not make any rotating displacement and did not leave any traces in the sky. Until 14 minutes past the hour, when the spiral object was covered up by clouds 10 degrees above the horizon, my observation lasted 5 minutes altogether. . . .

From the material supplied by Beijing Planetarium and other agencies, I learned that there were many reports about this phenomenon from various places. The localities were distributed over a north to south belt at least 180 kilometers wide. Our record showed that an earlier position observed was to the east of the Pole Star, 40 degrees above the horizon and with a space displacement of 90 degrees. The duration of the observation was 10 minutes. What was especially important was that, at a distance of 180 kilometers apart, the records about the direction of movement of the strange aerial body in space, made independently by at least two different observers, were basically the same. . . . To the present time this strange phenomenon has not been satisfactorily explained, *yet there were thousands of good observers who had seen it.* We can only let time decide what it really was.[18] [Emphasis added]

FLYING INSTRUCTOR'S SIGHTINGS, 1978–79

At 9:40 p.m. on 26 July 1978 at Shanxi Airport, Shanxi Province, flying instructor Sha Yongkao was piloting a plane with a pupil at 3,000 meters altitude when they saw two glowing objects circle the airport twice before moving off. Yongkao tried unsuccessfully to pursue the objects before radioing his report, and was told that no other aircraft were in the vicinity and that nothing was tracked on radar.[19]

At about 9.10 p.m. in February 1979 Sha Yongkao was flying a night fighter over Hou-Ma in Shanxi Province when he saw an extremely bright luminous object shoot across the sky from south to north, apparently flying supersonic at an altitude of 1,000 meters.[20]

AIR FORCE MULTIPLE-WITNESS SIGHTING, 1978

Not the least extraordinary fact to emerge from the Chinese UFO reports is the number of multiple-witness military cases which rival and occasionally surpass those so far made available in the West. Whether this trend continues remains to be seen, but the following report is an outstanding example of a UFO *witnessed by several hundred personnel*.

On 23 October 1978 a large luminous unidentified object appeared in the sky directly above Lintiao Air Base in Gansu Province. This is Air Force pilot Zhou Qingtong's eyewitness account:

The pilots of our brigade and several hundred other persons in the airfield district were watching a cinema film in an open-air theater. Several minutes after the show had begun, that is at 4 minutes past the 20th hour, there was a flurry of disturbance in the audience and we all looked up at the sky which was cloudless and full of stars. . . .

I saw a huge object flying from east to west. It first appeared in the eastern sky at an angle of 60 degrees above the horizon, then flew over our heads and was cut off from our view by the row of buildings 60 meters to the west. The object had a very peculiar appearance. It was an immense oblong object but was not clearly visible. It had two large lamps, like searchlights, in front, shooting out white light forward, and a luminous trail issued from the rear. Both the front and rear light beams were changing in length and brightness at times, illuminating the space around the object like a mass of smoke or mist.

The speed . . . was not very great, and it progressed in a straight line. It was of a huge size, occupying about 20 to 35 degrees of arc of vision. It was in sight for 2 or 3 minutes. It was clearly not a meteor, nor a swarm of locusts or birds, nor an airplane. *As we are all fighter pilots we could say this with some certainty*. It was not very high above the ground.

After many days we were still talking about it. Someone said, alas! if we only had a camera and had taken a photograph, the question could be solved.[21] [Emphasis added]

Chinese UFO researchers speculate that since there are some similarities in the description of objects, there may be a connection with the sighting by pilot Frederick Valentich over the Bass Strait, Australia, two days earlier, who disappeared together with his plane immediately afterward (see Chapter 7).

POWER FAILURE AND A CLOSE ENCOUNTER, 1979

The wave of sightings continued into 1979, and produced one of the few reports of a power failure associated with UFO activity to come out of China. It is felt that more reports exist, but that the authorities have possibly clamped down on them to avoid public unrest. The incident took place at 2045 hours on 12 September 1979 when witnesses in Xuginglong and Huaihua City in Hunan Province noted a complete power failure in their area. Fifteen minutes later a bright flying object appeared overhead, emitting a vertical stream of white rays. The object flew upward at an angle and vanished soundlessly a minute later, leaving two masses of semi spherical luminous clouds about 100 meters across.[22]

Perhaps because of their controversial (and anti-Marxist?) nature, alleged close encounters with UFO occupants have also not been widely reported so far in China. Yet a few cases have now come to light since the easing of restrictions in 1980. On 13 December 1979 at 4:00 a.m. near Longwangmiao on the Lanxi-Xin'angiang Highway, two truck drivers in separate vehicles observed an extraordinary sight. Wang Dingyuan (of the Weihus Steel Construction Plant) was driving in the front truck when he noticed a powerful vertical beam of light and two "unusual human beings" standing beneath it on the highway. Both drivers came to an abrupt halt and the apparition vanished.

The men discussed the incident, although the second driver, Wang Jianming (of the Jinhus Chemical Works), had seen nothing, so it was decided that they should swap positions, with Wang Jianming driving in front. After five or six kilometers the front driver noticed a beam of light and figures standing beside the highway about 200 meters ahead. The figures were 1.5 meters tall, wore helmets on their heads and "space apparel," with something like a thermos bottle slung across their shoulders and a square pack on their backs. Each was apparently holding what looked like a "short cudgel" in his left hand, and a red light emitted from the top of the helmets.

Wang Jianming stopped his truck, turned off the headlights, and then turned them back on. The figures were still there, even when he repeated the procedure. Wang then dismounted with a crowbar in his hand, and at that moment both the light beam and figures vanished.[23]

TIENTSIN AIRPORT TRACKS UFO, 1980

1980 produced a bumper harvest of UFO sightings in China, when altogether ninety-eight reports were reported to the China UFO Research Organization, although it is believed that many more went unreported. The editor of *Aerospace Knowledge,* Hsieh Chu, was prompted to write: "We can no longer ignore the existence of UFOs because of the great number of sightings reported in our country."[24]

In early August 1980 hundreds of thousands of witnesses saw UFOs for several days running in the skies over Tientsin and the Gulf of Zhili (now called Bo Hai). On the evening of 16 October 1980 at Tientsin Airport, radar officers and technicians of the Tientsin Civil Aviation Bureau were observing the movements of Flight 402 on their radar screens when suddenly an unexplained echo showed up. When the airliner was about two kilometers from the runway, the plane's bright dot of light on the screen veered out of contact for seven seconds or so.

The radar operators had presumed they were watching Flight 402, but when the controller contacted the aircraft and asked for its position they realized that the echo on the screen did not relate to the plane. Flight 402 had taken off from Peking and its flight path would have taken it across Tientsin, crossing the airfield from east to west. Another anomaly was that the radar azimuth was 20°, but at the time the unexplained blip showed up on the radarscope, Flight 402 was bearing about 80°, north of the runway and out of range of the directional radar.

At 2153 hours, when Flight 402 had crossed the airfield to a point thirteen kilometers from the runway, on its final approach, the unexplained echo showed up again in the same position on the radarscope, moving from west to east. It was simultaneously visible on the screen together with the aircraft. A few seconds later it vanished.

Three minutes later the strange echo reappeared. A second aircraft, Flight 404, was also over Tientsin at an altitude of 1,500 meters, but its position was at variance with the echo, and moving in the opposite direction. As Flight 404 was on its final approach, two echoes—instead of one—again appeared on the radarscope. The UFO, from its original position north of the runway, was doing about 250 kilometers per hour. According to the captain of Flight 404, the Automatic Direction Finder (ADF) on his instrument panel registered an anomaly: the indicator needle appeared to lock on to a transmitting source not known on the chart. The captain assumed his instrument was faulty, and asked the radio officer to use his earphones to pick up the radio beacon's audio signal. This was in order, and two minutes later the ADF returned to normal.

Just before touchdown, when Flight 404 was a few hundred meters from the runway, the assistant controller in the tower heard some interference on the radio and assumed it was either the aircraft or the radio room tuning in. "Who's tuning in to the tower?" he asked. "We're working flat out—don't call us!" The aircraft crew and radar personnel also heard the radio interference, but its source could not be identified.[25]

SOME EXTRAORDINARY PARALLELS WITH EVENTS IN

BRITAIN, DECEMBER 1980

In Chapter 4 I referred to the sighting on 15 December 1980 of a UFO over southeast London and northwest Kent, seen by many witnesses for over an hour and by myself for a few minutes. According to those who watched it through binoculars, the object was cone-shaped, with a red nose, silvery center, and sparkling diamond-blue rear section. While studying the Chinese UFO Research Organization's reports I came across some extraordinary parallels with this case. An identical object was seen in Beijing four months later, for instance, when at 7:00 a.m. on 25 April 1981 Du Shengyuan observed a curious object circling in the sky. He immediately tried to telephone the *Beijing Evening News* as well as the Beijing and Central Television stations but was unable to get through as it was too early in the morning. He went back outside and continued to observe the strange object, which by this time was directly overhead at more than 2,000 meters altitude.

> With the aid of binoculars I made it out to be ellipsoid in shape, but more like a bullet [he said in his report]. Its middle part was white, like the moon in daytime but brighter. The bottom was luminous green, like the rays from the launch of a rocket such as we see on television. The whole thing was strangely luminous. I continued my observation until it went out of sight at 0725. It flew in a changeable way, now fast, now very slowly, now stopping altogether before speeding forward. It was watched by all the 20-odd residents in the courtyard.[26]

This is precisely the same description given by Peter McSherry of the December 1980 sighting, with the insignificant exception of that of the rear section of the object, which he described as being "sparkling diamond-blue" rather than "luminous green."

A similar object may also have been seen in China *within thirty hours* of the British sighting. On 14 December 1980, at 1735 hours, four witnesses saw an object "like a cone, smaller at the top and larger at the base" which "jumped up" from the top of a mountain west of Xiangshan and gave out "light blue rays." The object alternately disappeared and reappeared, just as the UFO in London had done.[27]

Peter McSherry and other witnesses said that the UFO they saw occasionally split up into two, three and even more sections which shot away and then regrouped. On 5 June 1981, at 2200 hours, Ding Shiliang and other students at Xi'an University, Shanxi Province, observed a luminous flying object which "split from the middle into two parts, then three, then even four. In another moment two of the units on either side vanished, leaving the two other segments still in position, one above the other." After performing further astonishing separations and disappearances, "another appeared and the two objects approached each other and merged into one. . . . Later it split into two again, diminished in size and finally vanished at 2220, not to return."[28]

Since details of the British sighting in December 1980 are published in this book for the first time, it is impossible for the Chinese to have been aware of these facts. Neither could they have known about the events at Rendlesham Forest, outside US Air Force bases Woodbridge and Bentwaters, between 27 and 29 December 1980, when a landed UFO was seen by a number of military personnel (see Chapter 4) and the Deputy Commander at Woodbridge, Lieutenant Colonel Charles Halt, described another sighting (which he personally witnessed) in his official memorandum to the British Ministry of Defense: "At one point it appeared to throw off glowing particles and *then broke into five separate white objects and then disappeared.*" [Emphasis added]

AIR FORCE JETS AFFECTED BY UFOS, 1982

In the middle of June 1982 UFO activity increased suddenly in northern China, and on 18 June in particular there were many sightings reported from Heilongjiang Province, between 2110 hours and 2253 hours. One of the most interesting cases is that reported by five Chinese Air Force pilots on patrol over North China's military frontier.

At about 2157 hours the jet fighters' electrical power systems began to malfunction and communications and navigation systems failed. Suddenly the pilots encountered an unidentified flying object of a milky yellowish-green luminous color, about the size of the full moon. The object grew larger and picked up speed, at which point it looked "as big as a mountain of mist." Then black spots were seen in the interior of the phenomenon. One pilot stated in his report: "When I first saw the object, it flew toward me at a high rate of speed as it whirled rapidly. While it was rotating it generated rings of light. In the center of the light ring was fire. In 10 seconds the center of the ring exploded, then the body of the object expanded rapidly."

The planes were forced to return to base because of the equipment failures. The other four pilots also prepared reports, which were subsequently published in the first issue of the *Journal of UFO Research,* together with their sketches (see Appendix, p. 471).[29] It is not known if gun-camera film was taken.

UFO PACES AIRLINER, 1985

The selected examples cited above from the 600-plus reports gathered by the China UFO Research Organization illustrate the point that China has experienced the same phenomena as the rest of the world, even if the Chinese have taken longer than any other country to acknowledge the fact. But there is one further case that must be mentioned here because it was reported officially and attracted worldwide attention.

On 11 June 1985 a Chinese Civil Aviation Administration Boeing 747 encountered a UFO on the Peking to Paris flight that almost forced the captain to make an emergency landing. Flight CA 933 was over Lanzhou, the capital of Gansu Province, when the object was observed by Captain Wang Shuting and his crew at 2240 hours. The UFO, located at 39°, 30 minutes north, and 103°, 30 minutes east, flew across the path of the airliner at its altitude of 33,000 feet at a very high speed. The object reportedly illuminated an area of twenty-five to thirty miles and had an apparent diameter of six miles. It was elliptical in shape and had an extremely bright spot in the center, with three horizontal rows of bluish-white lights on the perimeter. The official news release stated that no passengers reported the sighting, which lasted for two minutes.[30]

One is reminded of a similar but much longer sighting that was witnessed by the crew and passengers of a Soviet Aeroflot airliner flying from Tbilisi to Tallin in 1984, when the object (or rather "cloud") was said to be massive in diameter (see Chapter 10). And in August 1985 the pilot of an Olympic Airways flight from Zurich to Athens reported that he had a near collision with a mystery object near the Italian/Swiss border. More UFOs were seen that same month by the crew and forty-five journalists aboard a Boeing 737 en route to Buenos Aires.[31] So the crew of the Chinese jumbo jet were not alone in reporting a dramatic aerial encounter with the ubiquitous UFOs in 1985.

WHAT IS THE OFFICIAL VIEW?

I have tried for several years to ascertain the official Chinese government attitude to the UFO question, and finally succeeded in 1986 when Mr. Zhang Laigui, Air Attaché at the Chinese Embassy in London, sent me an interesting article on the subject that had appeared in the *China Daily* in 1985, together with a translation. The Air Attaché stated in his accompanying letter that he regarded the article as "an official statement and viewpoint of the Chinese government."[32]

The article is headed "UFO Conference Held in Darlian" and reports that several dozen Chinese scientists had gathered in that city in August 1985 to exchange views on UFO research for the first time. Some forty papers were presented and seventeen of these were selected to be published in collected works. The subjects included: viewpoints and methods of the Chinese regarding UFO research; theoretical works on the UFO phenomenon; and the relationship between UFOs and human body sciences.

The article states that there is an enormous degree of interest in the UFO subject in China, and refers to the establishment of the China UFO Research Organization (identified as the China Society of UFO Research, or CSUR), with a total membership of 20,000. Chairman of the CSUR, Professor Liang Renglin of Guangzhou Jinan University, said that more than 600 UFO reports had been made during the past five years in China.

"UFOs are an unresolved mystery with profound influence in the world," the article concludes. "Some people believe in their existence, while the opponents think it's a matter of fiction or illusion. Both views are taken into serious consideration in the world. Various kinds of organizations have been established in the world, including USA, USSR, UK, Japan, and Central and South American nations to try to unveil the UFO mystery."[33]

10

USSR

In 1967 the late Dr. Allen Hynek, America's leading UFO researcher until his untimely death in 1986, confessed that one of his greatest fears was of waking up one morning and reading in his newspaper that the Russians had solved the UFO mystery. Would they perhaps come up with some hitherto overlooked hypothesis that pointed to a natural explanation or, more disturbingly, would the Soviets announce the first contact with an extraterrestrial civilization? "Either story," said Hynek, "would shake America so hard that the launching of Sputnik in 1957 would appear in retrospect as important as a Russian announcement of a particularly large wheat crop."[1]

Earlier in 1967 an extraordinary article appeared in the Russian magazine *Smena,* of which I have an original copy. Dr. Felix Yurevich Zigel, Doctor of Science and Assistant Professor of Cosmology at the Moscow Aviation Institute, a respected scientist who had been in charge of cosmonaut training, announced that UFOs were worthy of scientific study. He referred to the research done in the United States by Dr. Hynek, Dr. Jacques Vallée, and Professor Frank Salisbury, commenting that Dr. Donald Menzel's debunking theories, propounded in his book *Flying Saucers* (which had been translated into Russian in 1962), could no longer be considered valid. Zigel also gave an interesting résumé of sightings by Soviet scientists since 1960, including that of Assistant Professor V. Zaitsev, who during a flight between Leningrad and Moscow on 12 July 1964 "saw what he described as a huge disk which suddenly appeared below the airliner's fuselage, flew a parallel course for a while and then turned aside with a burst of speed."[2] The article caused something of a sensation in a country where hitherto only debunking statements and articles (as well as Menzel's book) had appeared on the subject. But in fact the Soviets had been as deeply concerned as other governments by sightings dating back to 1948 at least.

220

THE CLOSE ENCOUNTERS OF A SOVIET TEST PILOT,

1948–49

Arkadii Ivanovich Apraksin is (or was) a highly decorated Soviet Air Force pilot, having gained in World War II the Red Star, Red Banner, Patriotic War First Class, as well as medals for the defense of Stalingrad and the capture of Berlin. Apraksin was interviewed in September 1951 by I. Y. Furmin, Docent [lecturer] of Voronezh University, who later passed the story to Dr. Zigel. The latter incorporated the following account (which I have abridged) in one of his unpublished manuscripts, which has been translated by the researcher Joe Brill.

On 16 June 1948, while Apraksin was testing one of the latest Soviet jet aircraft, he encountered a "cucumber-shaped" aerial phenomenon flying on a cross course to his. Cones of light beams radiated from the object, which appeared to be descending. Apraksin reported the sighting to his base at Kapustin Yar, Basunchak, and received confirmation that the object had been tracked on radar and had not acknowledged instructions to land. The test pilot was ordered to close with the UFO, and if it refused to land he was to open fire.

When Apraksin closed to within about ten kilometers the light beams "opened up in a fan" and allegedly struck his aircraft, temporarily blinding him. He discovered simultaneously that the entire electrical control systems as well as the engine were inoperable. He managed to glide the plane to a safe landing, however, the UFO having disappeared into a cloud layer.

A detailed statement was prepared and an expert arrived from Moscow who examined the aircraft in detail, cross-examined Apraksin, and checked the completed testimony for contradictions. The pilot was given a forty-five day leave, but ten days before its expiry he was summoned to the Air Force Directorate of the Defense Ministry in Moscow. Apraksin was then sent to an airfield in the European sector of the Arctic, where he was subjected to another interrogation. After spending three months at this airfield, where he test-flew another type of aircraft, Apraksin was recalled to the air base at Kapustin Yar.

On 6 May 1949 Apraksin is said to have taken a new plane for a test flight, and at its maximum ceiling of 15,000 meters he encountered another unidentified object, similar to the previous one. The "flying cucumber" once again directed cones of light at his aircraft from a distance of about ten to twelve kilometers, causing effects as before, but also damaging part of the perspex cockpit canopy, resulting in loss of air pressure. Unable to communicate with base, Apraksin managed to land the plane on the banks of the Volga, forty-nine kilometers from Saratov. He then passed out.

On regaining consciousness Apraksin found himself in a hospital at Saratov. A detailed statement was taken from him again, and after two and a half months he was apparently ordered to appear before a special medical board in Moscow, which then sent him to a psychoneurological institute. During his six months' stay at this "institute" Apraksin was allegedly subjected to psychotherapy and shock therapy. Taped interviews were compared with recordings of his previous report in an effort to uncover inconsistencies. In January 1950 Apraksin appeared before a medical board which judged him "Group One Disabled," effectively barring him from active service. Later that year, and in 1951, he went to the Defense Ministry in Moscow and was received by a deputy minister, but his application for return to duty was refused.

"He assures me that he is in perfect health," wrote Furmin in 1951, and "that everything which he saw occurred in fact; that they do not want to consider him normal for reasons he cannot understand, and that the failure to believe his story will bring harm to the Motherland."[3]

I have so far been unable to trace a reference to Apraksin in recognized books on Soviet aviation. He is not mentioned in Bill Gunston's definitive book, *Aircraft of the Soviet Union*, and the author told me that he has not come across the name. I then wrote to the Director of the M.V. Frunze Central House of Aviation and Space, Moscow, and eventually received the following reply: "The Central House of Aviation and Space . . . has no information about test flight activities of A. I. Apraksin. He is not a Hero of the Soviet Union."[4]

I began to suspect that the story had been concocted, but my confidence in the case was restored when I discovered a reference to it in an official statistical analysis of sightings in the Soviet Union published by the USSR Academy of Sciences.[5] The name of the pilot was not given, so I wrote to Dr. L. M. Gindilis of the Sternberg Astronomical Institute in Moscow, one of the authors of the report, requesting further details, and received the following helpful and interesting reply:

> . . . I must regretfully note that, as it frequently occurs in the studies of anomalous phenomena, the most interesting cases turn out to be not reliable enough in one or another item. In this case . . . the eye witness . . . is Arkadii Ivanovich Apraksin, former pilot. This case (as well as all the

others forming the base for the statistical analysis in the work you cite) is taken from F. Yu. Zigel's card collection. It was written down, from A. I. Apraksin's words, by the assistant professor of the Voronezh University I. Ya. Furman [sic] who was A. I. Apraksin's chance co-traveler in a train on 25 September 1951.

I found I. Ya. Furman's address and sent him a copy of the card from F. Yu. Zigel's collection, asking him to write me whether he agreed with the quoted version and whether he had any additional information about Apraksin. I quote a phrase extracted from his letter of 24 May 1980:

"My one-time acquaintance with Arkadii Ivanovich Apraksin is still exciting me, although during all these long years I was never imbued by a conviction that we have an evidence for existence in reality of the 'brothers in intelligence' . . . By the way, at present I have no information about Arkadii Ivanovich Apraksin, though till early 1970s I did make some [attempts] to find him."

This is all I can communicate to you on this subject.[6]

The case may not be reliable in the sense that there is so far no official trace of Apraksin, yet Furmin confirms his existence and was evidently impressed with the story. The Soviets are skillful in removing names from history books when occasion demands, and perhaps Apraksin, having committed what at that time must have been considered a blasphemy, fell victim to the system.

THE GRU

The Soviets, then, have apparently been as mystified as other governments by UFO sightings. According to an unconfirmed report, the CIA learned of this in 1952 from the GRU (*Glavnoye Razvedyvatelnoye Upravleniye*, or Chief Intelligence Directorate of the Soviet General Staff) via double agent Lieutenant Yuri Popov. A secret GRU directive, UZ-11/14, ordered an investigation into the UFO problem, and stated:

Section 3 . . . It is urgently ordered to discover whether the unidentified flying objects are:
   (a) Secret vehicles of foreign powers which are penetrating Soviet airspace.
   (b) Misinformative activity by imperialistic secret services.
   (c) Manned or unmanned extraterrestrial probes engaged in the investigation of earth; or
   (d) An unknown natural phenomenon.[7]

THE CIA

Under the Freedom of Information Act a number of documents released
by the CIA clearly indicate concern with the Soviet Union's attitude to
the UFO problem. A hitherto secret memorandum from the Assistant
Director of Operations, George Carey, to the Deputy Director of Intelligence, Allen Dulles, dated 22 August 1952, states that ''a search of
Foreign Documents Division files has so far produced no factual evidence
that the subject has been mentioned in the Soviet satellite press within
the past two years,'' but refers to a broadcast from Moscow on 10 June
1951 in which it was stated that the Chief of Nuclear Physics in the US
Naval Research Bureau had explained UFOs as being ''used for strato-
spheric studies. US Government circles knew all along of the harmless
nature of these objects, but they refrained from denying 'false reports,
the purpose behind such tactics was to fan war hysteria in the country.' ''

On 11 September 1952 the CIA's Assistant Director of Scientific Intelligence, H. Marshall Chadwell, sent a secret memorandum to the CIA
Director, General Walter Bedell Smith, in which the former stated:

> Intelligence problems include:
> (1) The present level of Russian knowledge regarding these phenomena.
> (2) Possible Soviet intentions and capabilities to utilize these phenom-
>   ena to the detriment of US security interests.
> (3) The reasons for silence in the Soviet press regarding flying saucers.

US OFFICIALS WITNESS FLYING DISKS IN THE USSR

A fascinating Air Intelligence report by three US officials traveling by
train in Russia in 1955 was declassified thirty years later under provisions
of the Freedom of Information Act. Originally classified Top Secret, it
was downgraded to secret in 1959. The witnesses were Senator Richard
Russell (Republican, Georgia), Lieutenant Colonel E. U. Hathaway, US
Army staff officer assigned to the Senate Armed Forces Committee, and
Ruben Efron, committee consultant. I quote from part of the top secret
cable cited in the report, which was sent to US Air Force Headquarters
on 13 October 1955 by the US Air Attaché at the American Embassy in
Prague, Lieutenant Colonel Thomas Ryan, who had debriefed the witnesses:

> On 4 Oct. 55 at 1910 hours between Atjaty and Adzhijabul in Trans-
> Caucasus region, two round and circular unconventional aircraft resembling

flying disks or flying saucers were seen taking off almost vertically one minute apart. Disk aircraft ascended near dusk with outer surface revolving slowly to right and with two lights stationary on top near middle part. Sparks or flame seen coming from aircraft. No protrusions seen on aircraft which passed over observers' train. Both flying disk aircraft ascended relatively slowly to about 6000 feet, then speed increased sharply in horizontal flight both on northerly heading. Flying attitude of disk remained same during ascent as in cruise, like a discus in flight. Two operating searchlights pointing almost vertical seen near takeoff area located about 1-2 miles south RR line. After sighting Soviet trainmen became excited and lowered curtains and refused permission to look out windows. US observers firmly believe these unconventional aircraft were genuine saucer or disk aircraft.

"We've been told for years that there isn't such a thing," commented Lieutenant Colonel Hathaway to the Air Attaché, "but all of us saw it."[8] A full report was also sent to the CIA.

The searchlight beams suggest that the disks were observed in the vicinity of a military base, and consideration must be given to the possibility that the Russians were testing a secret disk-shaped aircraft—possibly designed with the aid of German scientists who are known to have been working on such an aircraft during World War II.[9] Rumors abound that both the Americans and Russians, as well as the British and Canadians, have successfully developed such disks, but with the exception of a few circular craft such as John Frost's Avro-Car, which despite the extravagant claims made for it was only capable of limited hovering, there seems little evidence for this.[10] The unlikelihood of Soviet-built disks was emphasized in a CIA memorandum from W. E. Lexow, Chief of the Applied Science Division, Office of Scientific Intelligence, dated 19 October 1955:

The objects reportedly sighted by [deleted] are described to be similar to Project "Y" which is in the research stage at Avro Aircraft Ltd., Canada, under contract to the US Air Force . . . The present study calls for a circular wing 30 ft in diameter and about 1.1 ft thick. Its performance is to be as follows:

Speed M [Mach] — 3
Rate of climb   — 120,000 ft min.
Ceiling   — 102,000 ft
Range   — 700 n.m.

The present effort consists of wind tunnel testing sponsored to the extent of $800,000 by the US Air Force. . . . Project "Y" is being directed by

John Frost. Mr. Frost is reported to have obtained his original idea for the flying machine from a group of Germans just after World War II. The Soviets may also have obtained information from this German group.

Since two objects were reportedly seen in operation at one time in an area where it is most unlikely that experimental flying would be conducted, it is likely that these objects were in service. This would indicate very rapid progress in this development for the Soviets. *It does, however, seem inconsistent that the Soviets, if they have such an object in service, would continue their large development and production programs on conventional type aircraft.*

Since our first information on Project "Y" in early 1953, ASD has been on the alert for information which might indicate that the Soviets were working on such a project. Prior to the sighting by [deleted] no such information has been available. [Emphasis added]

SOVIET AIR FORCE ENCOUNTER, 1956

The well-known Soviet pilot, chief navigator of Soviet polar aviation, Valentin Akkuratov, described an encounter with an unidentified aerial object as follows:

In 1956, engaged in strategic ice reconnaissance in a TU [Tupolev] 4 plane in the area of Cape Jesup (Greenland), we dropped down from the clouds to fair weather and suddenly noticed an unknown flying craft moving on our portside parallel to our course. It looked very much like a large pearl-colored lens with wavy, pulsating edges. At first we thought it was an American aircraft of an unknown design, and since we did not want to encounter it we went into the clouds again.

After we had flown for 40 minutes toward Bear Island, the cloud cover ended abruptly; it cleared ahead and on our portside we saw once again that same unknown craft. Making up our minds to see it at close quarters, we changed our course abruptly and began the approach movement, informing our base at Amderma of the maneuver. When we changed our course, the unknown flying machine followed suit and moved parallel at our speed.

After 15 to 18 minutes of flight the unknown craft sharply altered its course, sped ahead of us and rose quickly until it disappeared in the blue sky. We spotted no aerials, superstructure, wings or portholes on that disk. Nor did we see any exhaust gases or condensation trail. It flew at what seemed to us an impossible speed.

Skeptics argue that sightings of this sort, where no solid superstructure is evident, are merely optical phenomena of the mirage, rainbow or halo type. But Dr. Felix Zigel, who cited this report, discounts such inter-

pretations in most cases. He also counters the explanation that ball lightning is the cause of many UFO reports:

> The appearance of UFOs is almost always accompanied by a luminescence
> of air and the formation of an atmospheric plasma. This fact is the basis
> for the "plasma" hypothesis of UFOs as accumulations of atmospheric
> plasma of the ball-lightning type. But this explanation does not hold up
> either. Ball-lightning is always a thunderstorm product, and the appearance
> of UFOs has no relation to weather. Ball-lightning diameters as a rule run
> four to five inches, no larger; the diameter of flying disks are tens and
> even hundreds of times that size.[11]

SENSATIONAL SOVIET ENCOUNTERS, 1959–61

By the 1960s some extraordinary stories—largely unsubstantiated—had
reached the Western media. According to science writer Alberto Fenoglio,
for example, in an article in an Italian journal devoted to missile and
space research,[12] which was subsequently condensed and translated by
Robert Pinotti, Soviet radar and Air Force personnel observed UFOs
circling and hovering for over twenty-four hours above Sverdlovsk, headquarters of Tactical Missile Command, in spring 1959. Fighter aircraft
sent to intercept reported that the UFOs easily outmaneuvered them and
zigzagged to avoid their machine-gun fire.[13]

Fenoglio, who claims to have obtained his information from Soviet
sources in the West, including a well-known diplomat, also described
other sensational sightings during this period. In the summer of 1961
near Rybinsk, 150 kilometers from Moscow, new missile batteries were
being set up as part of Moscow's defense network. A huge disk-shaped
object allegedly appeared at an estimated altitude of 20,000 meters, surrounded by a number of smaller objects. "A nervous battery commander
panicked and gave—unauthorized—the order to fire a salvo at the giant
disk," reported Fenoglio. "The missiles were fired. All exploded when
at an estimated distance of some two kilometers from the target, creating
a fantastic spectacle in the sky. The third salvo was never fired, for at
this point the smaller 'saucers' went into action and stalled the electrical
apparatus of the whole missile base. When the smaller discoidal UFOs
had withdrawn and joined the larger craft, the electrical apparatus was
again found to be in working order."[14]

What are we to make of these sensational stories? In translating Fenoglio's original article, Robert Pinotti noted that skeptics would point to
the anonymity of Fenoglio's informants and conclude that the reports are

a pack of lies. Yet the stories are no more sensational than those reported in the West, and it seems unlikely that a respected journal would have published Fenoglio's material unless there was *some* substance to it.

One report in 1961 seems to have been given some credence by the prestigious USSR Academy of Sciences Institute of Space Research Report. On 31 August several cars were stalled on a highway thirty miles from Moscow when a UFO hovered on top of an overpass for a few minutes. The cars were unable to start their engines until the UFO left the area.[15]

PASSENGERS AND CREW DISAPPEAR FROM AIRCRAFT,

1961

The following story was obtained directly from the Soviet Embassy in London by the British researcher Derek Mansell in January 1965. The report originated with the Moscow Aviation Institute, and a brief account was first published in the West by Alberto Fenoglio in 1962,[16] but Mansell's version contains some additional details. The incident is said to have taken place on an unknown date in 1961.

According to the report, an Antonov An-2P mail-plane took off from an airfield at or near Sverdlovsk, bound for Kurgan, with seven people on board. About 80 to 100 miles from Sverdlovsk, just after the pilot had communicated with ground control, the aircraft disappeared from the radar screen. Ground control tried unsuccessfully to regain communications, so a search was launched involving several helicopters and a large detachment of troops. Since the captain had radioed a position during his last communication it did not take too long to recover the plane.

The aircraft was found in a small clearing in dense forest, completely intact. There was no way it could possibly have landed there, and the authorities stated that it looked as if the plane had been put down gently from above. But most puzzling of all was the fact that *there was no sign of anyone on board*. All the mail was intact, and when the engine was tested it started first time.

The Moscow Aviation Institute report claims that an unidentified object was tracked on radar at the control tower and that strange radio signals were heard at the time of the disappearance. No marks or footprints were found at the site, but according to Fenoglio's version of events, a thirty-meter-wide clearly defined circle of scorched grass and depressed earth was found at a distance of 100 meters from the aircraft.

VOSKHOD I AND II, 1964–65

On 13 October 1964 the crew of *Voskhod I*, Komarov, Feoktistov and Yegorov, were allegedly ordered to make a premature return to earth after having completed only sixteen orbits. The cosmonauts are quoted as saying that they regretted being ordered back so soon, as they had seen many interesting things and wanted to investigate them more fully. Reporting for a German newspaper, S. R. Oilinger claimed that Moscow sources had told him that *Voskhod I* "was repeatedly overtaken by extremely fast flying disks which struck the craft violent shattering blows with their powerful magnetic fields."[17]

There is no hint of any of this in the cosmonauts' account of the space flight, although they did report some "phenomena," for example, the Aurora Australis: "Columns of yellow light hundreds of kilometers tall, rising at right angles to the black horizon. . . . They fringed the entire visible horizon for about two thousand kilometers. We were so entranced, we did not at once realize the nature of the phenomenon we were observing."

There is also no indication that the cosmonauts were ordered to return "prematurely." They report: "When the time was approaching for the descent, we applied by radio requesting that the flight be prolonged for at least another day. We wanted to repeat the whole program, to check and double check our observations, but permission was refused."[18]

Yet the rumors persisted. Researchers Ion Hobana and Julien Weverbergh were told by a Western journalist who attended the *Voskhod* press conference on 21 October at the Grand Hall of Moscow University that Vladimir Komarov was very brief in his delivery, although he was chief spokesman, and answered more evasively than usual. During a question put by a journalist about the possibility of meeting unexpected objects in space, Komarov walked out of the hall without further comment.[19]

On 19 March 1965 the crew of *Voskhod II* are said to have lost all contact with ground control and were forced to make an emergency landing 873 miles from the scheduled landing site. Stories circulated in the media that the spacecraft had come down enveloped in flames, its outside radio antenna burned off, the two-man crew having barely escaped with their lives. At the press conference on 27 March the cosmonauts avoided questions asking them to confirm reports that they had been harassed by an unidentified object, although they did admit to seeing an "unmanned satellite" about half a mile from their capsule at 5:12 a.m. on 19 March, which they had been unable to identify, and said that it had appeared shortly before they lost contact with ground control.[20]

In 1966 the well-known astrophysicist and UFO researcher Dr. Jacques Vallée attended the International Congress of Mathematicians in Moscow and managed to broach the subject of UFOs with a few scientists, he told me in 1986. This may have encouraged them to take a more open stance on the controversy, possibly contributing to the inauguration on 17 May 1967 of a semi-official group, headed by Major General Stolyarov, to conduct an investigation into the subject. According to Dr. Vallée, the Soviet Air Force had 15,000 reports on file at the time. One 1967 report, included in the USSR Academy of Sciences Institute of Space Research Report, states that on 19 September a UFO hovered and maneuvered around an airliner (Flight 404) over Volgograd, witnessed by frightened crewmen and passengers.[21]

FURTHER CIA INTEREST, 1967

An unevaluated CIA report dated 18 August 1967, with the subject heading "Report on Conversations with Soviet Scientists on Subject of Unidentified Flying Objects in the USSR," yields valuable information on the conflicting attitudes of the Soviet scientific community to the problem at the time. The name of the CIA (or CIA-sponsored) scientist who conducted the interviews, as well as the names of the Soviet scientists involved, are deleted, together with the date(s) of the interviews. It is worth recording that from 22 to 31 August 1967, a week after the CIA report was written, Dr. Robert J. Low, co-ordinator of the University of Colorado UFO Project at the time, attended the International Astronomy Union conference in Prague in order to represent the project and to report back on the UFO situation in Iron Curtain countries. Also in attendance was Franklin D. Roach, principal investigator of the Colorado University project. Both men's expenses were paid by the US government, but not through the UFO project.[22] It is quite likely that either Low or Roach could have interviewed the Soviet scientists in Russia prior to the Prague visit: Low visited a number of European countries on project business during the month of August that year.

The first scientist referred to in the CIA report, a radio astronomer, "emphatically stated that he knew of no sightings of UFOs in the USSR and added with a laugh that if they were only seen in the US, they must be of Soviet origin.'' Another unnamed Soviet scientist, who was ''very interested in the problem . . . had read Menzel's book (which has been translated into Russian)[23] but did not accept his conclusions. [He] knew of some sightings in the northern part of the USSR, but said that reports of such sightings are not printed in Soviet newspapers because they are not regarded as scientific observations.'' The CIA report commented: ''This is interesting in view of the readiness of Soviet newspapers to print rather fantastic reports of hypotheses and 'observations' suggested by the more imaginative members of the scientific community. Apparently some official sanction is needed.'' The CIA commentator adds that the anonymous scientist ''has been interested in US reports of UFOs and readily accepts their reality. In fact, it is his personal opinion that the UFOs may originate on Venus.''

The report refers to a stellar spectroscopist who was ''also dissatisfied with Menzel's book and felt that there was definitely an opportunity for additional research.'' The CIA report concluded:

The general feeling one gets is that no official treatment of the UFO problem has been given in the USSR. . . . At the same time, there is almost universal awareness of the history and characteristics of the phenomenon often associated with considerable interest. The result is that a demonstration of the inadequacy of US Official explanations coupled with some proof of the reality of the observations might excite enthusiasm more rapidly among Soviet Astronomers than among their US counterparts who are more strongly influenced by the official ridicule associated with UFOs in the US.

Although the CIA report (which has several paragraphs blacked out) states that there seems to have been ''no official treatment of the UFO problem'' in the USSR, a research committee was established in the Defense Ministry as early as 1955.[24] And during that year, an alleged CIA source told me, leaders of the secret services of the USSR, USA, France and Britain, met in Geneva, where they unanimously agreed to a policy of secrecy on the UFO problem as far as the public was concerned. I have been unable to substantiate this story, however, other than the reliable American journalist Dorothy Kilgallen's comment in her syndicated column on 15 February 1954: ''Flying saucers are regarded as of such vital importance that they will be the subject of a special hush-hush meeting of the world military heads next summer.'' As far as Britain's involvement is concerned, a former Director of MI6 has convinced me that it is pure fabrication. Yet in 1965 George Langelaan, an ex-officer of the French secret service (known at that time as the SDECE—*Service de Documentation Extérieur et de Contre-Espionage*), stated publicly that the Russian and American secret services (if not the British and French) *have* collaborated on the problem, and furthermore had arrived at the conclusion: "The flying saucers exist, their source is extraterrestrial, and the future—relatively quite soon—should permit confirmation of this statement."[25]

Needless to say, no such official confirmation has been forthcoming. But certainly a degree of collaboration between American and Russian scientists was definitely established in the mid-1960s, as I have shown. It is also worth mentioning the comments of Victor Marchetti, former Executive Assistant to the Deputy Director of the CIA, in this connection:

> If it were concluded that UFOs were not of terrestrial origin but, rather, vehicles from outer space . . . the CIA and US Government, aware that the phenomenon was of a worldwide nature, would seek cooperation in the investigation from the earth's other technically advanced nations, such as the United Kingdom, France, Germany, and even the USSR. The CIA would function as the US Government's agent, just as the KGB would be the USSR's, MI6 would be the UK's, and so on. These agencies . . . are quite accustomed to cooperating with each other on matters of mutual interest. Cooperation in the intelligence business is not restricted to allies. There are times when the CIA and KGB have found it advantageous to work together.[26]

THE STOLYAROV COMMITTEE, 1967

On 18 October 1967 the first meeting of the UFO Section of the All-Union Committee on Cosmonautics of the DOSAAF (the Soviet equivalent of the US Department of Defense) took place, attended by 400 people. Retired Soviet Air Force Major General Porfiri Stolyarov was elected Chairman, and Dr. Felix Zigel agreed to be deputy chairman of the semi-official group. Members included a cosmonaut, eighteen scientists and astronomers, as well as 200 qualified observers stationed throughout the country.[27]

Stolyarov, on learning of the existence of a mass of top secret official reports, asked the Soviet Air Ministry whether his group could have access to them. "Yes," he was told. "First set up your group, and then you can have the UFO reports." But Stolyarov was denied access to the reports and when he asked the reason for this was reportedly told, "Because this is too big a matter and you are too small."[28]

On 10 November 1967 both Major General Stolyarov and Dr. Felix Zigel appeared on Moscow Central Television to announce the formation of the committee, at the conclusion of which Dr. Zigel made an extraordinarily outspoken appeal to his fellow countrymen: "Unidentified Flying Objects are a very serious subject which we must study fully. We appeal to all viewers to send us details of any observations of strange flying craft seen over the territories of the Soviet Union. This is a serious challenge to science, and we need the help of all Soviet citizens. Please write to us at the following address in Moscow. . . ."

There is no way this statement would have been broadcast unless it had been officially sanctioned, considering the degree of media censorship in the Soviet Union. The committee was inundated with letters from the public. Within a few days Stolyarov and the committee had over 200 good reports, and the press was not slow in publishing viewers' sightings.[29]

Cover-up

Perhaps the authorities had not anticipated such an enthusiastic response from the public. By the end of November 1967 the DOSAAF Central Section of the All-Union Committee of Cosmonautics, chaired by Army General A. L. Getman, adopted and passed a resolution on the dissolution of the UFO section. None of the members of the UFO section was invited to the meeting, nor were they ever informed as to the reason for this decision.[30]

John Miller, a correspondent of the *Daily Telegraph,* relates an interesting account of his attempt to secure an interview with Stolyarov at the time. Miller managed to track down the UFO section headquarters to an office in the Central House of Aviation and Cosmonautics [Krasnoarmeiskaya Street, Moscow A-167], near the Soviet Air Force Academy, but a secretary said the general was out. An appointment was made for the following day but when Miller returned there was no general, no secretary, *and the office was completely bare.* He questioned a Soviet official working in the building about the Stolyarov Committee and asked what had happened to it. The man shrugged and replied, "You are imagining things, comrade. Everybody knows that UFOs do not exist."[31]

A Defense Intelligence Agency document released in 1985 adds that a Reuters correspondent went to see Major-General Stolyarov a few days after the TV program. "The general was very polite," the report states, and "confirmed the information about the commission, the 18 astronomers and SAF [Soviet Air Force] officers and the 200 observers. In addition, he said five positive sightings had been made. Approximately a week later the Reuters correspondent went back to see General Stolyarov. However, this time the correspondent could not get past the general's secretary; was politely but firmly told the general was no longer available for interview."[32]

Further Reactions to the Stolyarov Committee

Reactions to the formation of the Stolyarov Committee, and all it implied, were worldwide. The *New York Times,* for example, referred to it as an "official" study group, on a parallel with the Colorado University UFO Project commissioned by the US Air Force, and this, according to researchers Hobana and Weverbergh, particularly incensed some of Russia's more conservative scientists. The USSR Academy of Sciences held an Extraordinary General Meeting during which Dr. L. A. Artsimovitch severely reprimanded all UFO protagonists, invoking the honor of Soviet scientists, "who were making themselves look ridiculous in the eyes of their Western colleagues. . . . Even before the Academy had officially pronounced upon the matter Vladimir Lechkoutsov, Secretary of the National Committee of Russian Physicists, had granted an interview to a Canadian newspaper in which he denied the existence of any Russian organization for the solving of the UFO problem."[33]

In the *New York Times* article already cited, Dr. Felix Zigel appealed for international scientific cooperation on the matter:

> Unfortunately, certain scientists both in the Soviet Union and the United States deny the very existence of the problem instead of trying to solve it.
>
> International scientific cooperation as the solution of this problem would long have become a reality had not sensationalism and irresponsible anti-scientific assertions as regards "flying saucers" interfered. . . .
>
> The UFO problem is a challenge to mankind. It is the duty of scientists to take up this challenge, to disclose the nature of the UFO and to establish the scientific truth.[34]

The British government was apparently the first to take up the challenge. According to the Defense Intelligence Agency, on 12 December 1967 (two days after Zigel's appeal was published) the British Embassy was directed by London to investigate the possibility of collaborating with the Soviets:

> The Scientific Counselor of the British Embassy went to the State Committee for Science and Technology and inquired about the UFO Commission and the possibility of British–Russian cooperation in observation of UFOs. The British Counselor was politely received and the commission was freely discussed. The British were told they would receive a reply to their request for cooperation.
>
> The British did not receive an answer and did not pursue the subject. However, on [   ] January 1968 . . . the British Scientific Counselor was told the following: The commission for investigating UFOs had been set up in response to public demand. The commission had met twice, but since there was insufficient information to sustain it the commission would be disbanded after the next meeting.
>
> The British Scientific Counselor believes the original announcement of the commission on TV *was an oversight on the part of the censors* because the commission has not been referred to anywhere else. Mr. [   ] believes *the commission has not been disbanded, but will continue under cover.* . . .
> The preceding information was given to RO by source. RO *also read confidential British files on the subject.*[35] [Emphasis added]

On 20 February 1968 the US Embassy in Moscow sent an unclassified airgram to the US Department of State in Washington, DC, drawing attention to the February issue of *Soviet Life,* in which an article by Zigel referred in detail to the Stolyarov Committee and concluded that international cooperation in studying UFOs was vital. The hypothesis that UFOs originate on other worlds, and that they are flying craft from planets other than earth, Zigel was quoted as having said, "merits the most serious examination."

The existence or nonexistence of the Stolyarov Committee continued to plague Soviet academicians. Even Arkadii Tykhonov, Secretary of the committee, wrote a letter to the editor of the French journal *Phénomènes Spacieux* stating that the information published therein about the establishment of a UFO committee in the USSR was incorrect. "As far as I am concerned," Tykhonov concluded, "being old and ill, I ask that you take this letter into account."[36]

What seems particularly farcical is how anyone could deny the existence of the Stolyarov Committee after its establishment had been officially announced on Moscow Central Television. The authorities were determined to stamp out serious interest in the subject, and in February 1968 *Pravda* (Truth) published the official view in an article signed by

E. Mustel, Chairman of the Soviet Astronomical Services, D. Marynov, President of the All-Union Astronomical and Geodetic Society, and V. Leshkovtsev, Secretary of the National Committee of Soviet Physicists. Not a single object had been sighted over Russian soil which could not be explained, the article said, and people who reported such things were either deceitful or lacking in scientific training. UFOs were "anti-Soviet products of decadent capitalistic warmongering . . . They are not seen by astronomers who attentively study the skies day and night. They are not encountered by scientists who study the state and conditions of earth's atmosphere. They have not been observed by the Air Defense Service of this country."[37] These statements are patently absurd in view of the relatively high incidence of reports by scientists, astronomers, and pilots in the Soviet Union, as officially published eleven years later in a statistical analysis by the Institute of Space Research of the USSR Academy of Sciences.[38]

Dr. Zigel was ordered to terminate his research and was expressly forbidden to have any contact with Western journalists.[39] This is corroborated by the fact that Dr. Edward Condon, head of the Colorado University UFO Project, never received a reply to a letter he sent Zigel, and Dr. Robert Low, Project Co-ordinator, made one attempt at seeking collaboration with the Stolyarov Committee via the Soviet Embassy in Washington, but no further contacts were initiated in view of the lack of a response from Dr. Zigel.[40]

Zigel, although forbidden from carrying out his "dissident" research, nevertheless began privately to compile a manuscript of the mass of about 250 reports that had accumulated as a result of the television broadcast,[41] and was to reemerge at the forefront of Soviet UFO research eleven years later.

BRITISH AIRWAYS SIGHTING, LITHUANIA, 1976

The CIA continued to monitor the UFO phenomenon in the USSR as well as other countries, and a declassified Foreign Intelligence Information Report, with the source deleted, refers to a sighting by the crew of a British European Airways (now British Airways) plane, Flight 831 from Moscow to London, on 10 September 1976:

> Between 1800 and 1900 hours, the aircraft was cruising at an altitude of approximately 33 thousand feet (9,900 meters), apparently inside the border of Lithuania, when a blinding, single source, constant intensity, and sta-

tionary light was observed off the starboard flight path of the aircraft. The light's distance was estimated to be approximately 10 to 15 miles (16 to 24 kilometers) off of the aircraft's path and approximately five to six thousand feet (1,500 to 1,800 meters) below the aircraft, somewhat above a lower cloud layer. The light, which resembled a sodium vapor lamp (yellowish in color), and which was too intense to view directly for any period of time, completely lit the top of the lower cloud layer, giving it a glowing cast.

The light was of such interest that the BEA pilot came onto the aircraft's intercom network, stated that he was somewhat concerned over its presence, and said he had asked the Soviet authorities for an identification of its source. The Soviet authorities came back with a negative identification response, suggesting that he should not ask questions. The light was observed for approximately 10 to 15 minutes, until the aircraft had flown past and left the light source behind.

RIVAL FACTIONS

It was not until 1979 that the subject of UFOs became respectable once more in the Soviet Union. A group within the USSR Academy of Sciences Institute for the Study of Terrestrial Magnetism and Radioactivity was established that year to study "anomalous atmospheric phenomena"— clearly a scientifically more acceptable term. In *Nedelya* (The Week), scientists Migulin and Platov, leaders of the new group, stated that UFOs were unquestionably "natural phenomena" but conceded that "there are a number of phenomena that are resistant to a trivial explanation." The article contained severe criticisms of UFO enthusiasts, who by their inept investigations and popularization of the UFO problem had only served to hinder the new group from arriving at a complete solution to the phenomena "within a few months"! The scientists urged witnesses to send reports of their sightings to the Academy of Sciences.[42]

In late 1978 another group was established by leading UFO researchers Vladimir Azhazha, Deputy Director of the Underwater Research Section of the USSR Academy of Sciences, and Nikita Schnee. The group was to be an official civilian UFO study section under the auspices of the A. S. Popov Scientific and Technical Society for Radio, Electronics and Communications, and called itself BPVTS, short for *Blizhniy Poisk Vnezemnykh Tsivilizatsy s Pomoshch'yu Sredstva Radioelektronika* (Search for Extraterrestrial Civilizations in the Neighourhood of Earth by Means of Radio-electronics).

Members of the section included prominent figures such as Vice Admiral M. M. Krylov, Chief of Communications in the Soviet Navy,

Y. G. Nazarov, deputy head of the Soviet Control Center for Space Flights, and E. V. Khrunov, pilot and cosmonaut. In an interview published in *Tekhnika Molodezhi* (Technical Youth), Khrunov stated: "The UFO problem exists, and it is extremely serious. Thousands of people have seen UFOs, and up till now it is still not clear what they are. We are going to have to make a thorough investigation of this question. It is entirely possible that, concealed behind this question, there lies the problem of communication with extraterrestrial civilizations."[43]

Nikita Schnee, Scientific Secretary of the new section, claimed that attempts to establish similar groups in other cities of the USSR had been thwarted by officialdom, although a group was successfully set up in Estonia. At its inaugural seminar in November 1978 at Moscow University some unknown individuals stormed into the auditorium and disrupted the meeting. Later, the vice-principal of the university appeared and ordered the section to leave the hall because, he said, it had already been booked for another meeting. To emphasize the point he had brought along a number of rather bewildered-looking students, evidently gathered hastily from a nearby auditorium.

According to Schnee, none other than Dr. Felix Zigel was responsible for the interruption, who confirmed as much in a telephone conversation afterward. Learning of the impending seminar, Zigel had tipped off the Moscow City Committee of the Soviet Communist Party, as well as the KGB, and asked them to break up the meeting. Rather than a deliberate attempt by the authorities to discourage UFO research, this interference with the BPVTS group is interpreted by Schnee as a ploy by the jealous Zigel to thwart the activities of other ufologists in the USSR. Schnee's article in *Flying Saucer Review* degenerates into polemics at this point, accusing Zigel of fabricating reports, plagiarism, and self-aggrandizement.

In November 1979 the Moscow headquarters of the A. S. Popov Society ordered the UFO section to change its title to the more innocuous "Section for the Investigation of Anomalous Atmospheric Phenomena." But in December 1979 the Moscow City Committee of the Soviet Communist Party forbade all operations of the section, although the group seems to have continued functioning on an unofficial basis.[44]

GIANT UFO OVER MOSCOW?

On the night of 14 June 1980 one of the most spectacular sightings ever to have taken place in the USSR is said to have occurred. A huge reddish orange horseshoe- or crescent-shaped object (owing to belts of swirling luminous gases flowing around it) appeared over the city of Kalinin, observed by hundreds of witnesses, including the distinguished geophysicist Aleksei Zolotov. As a member of Dr. Zigel's team of scientific UFO investigators, Zolotov immediately phoned Zigel in Moscow, who alerted other members. The object appeared over Moscow eight minutes later and was seen by thousands, including another well-known Soviet ufologist, astrophysicist Sergei Bozhich, who allegedly went down to the streets to calm some of the more hysterical witnesses, who were convinced that the Americans had launched a nuclear attack.[45]

There are good reasons for believing that the "UFO" was nothing more sinister than a Russian satellite launch. Bozhich himself states that he saw at least two fragments of the object detach themselves from the larger object—probably some of the booster rockets—and photographs show a remarkable resemblance to a rocket launch. Indeed, Pekka Teerikorpi, an astronomer from the Turku Observatory in Finland, has shown that the sighting coincided precisely with the launch of *Cosmos 1188,* a military reconnaissance satellite, from the officially non-existent cosmodrome at Plesetsk, north of Moscow. Until recently the very existence of this cosmodrome was a secret, and even many top Soviet scientists and military officers knew nothing about what went on there.

Could it be that Zigel and other aligned ufologists in the USSR are deliberately cultivating some UFO rumors in order to cover up tests of secret new "Star Wars" weapons, as well as more conventional but nevertheless secret military reconnaissance satellites? James Oberg, formerly a senior mission controller with NASA as well as a noted UFO skeptic, certainly thinks so, and believes that the Soviets have an official policy of disinformation with regard to UFOs for precisely this reason. He is equally convinced that the USSR Academy of Sciences' report on UFO statistics in the Soviet Union[46] is based mainly on experiments with the Fractional Orbital Bombardment System (FOBS) which the Russians had been secretly building in violation of the 1963 Outer Space Treaty.[47]

It is certainly true that the Soviet space program is shrouded in secrecy. Rocket launches are seldom announced in advance, and it would suit the Kremlin to spread disinformation about UFO sightings in order to throw a cloak over their real activities. Dr. Zigel, after all, has worked (and I believe still is working) for the Soviet space program, and one would think that he would be able to recognize a rocket launch such as that which occurred on 14 June 1980, even if he had not been informed as to the precise launch time.

In 1979 there were reports of intensive UFO activity over the mountainous areas of Kazakhstan, north of Tashkent, and stories of mysterious lights in the sky were carried by the Soviet press. According to the former head of US Air Force Intelligence, Major General George Keegan, the Russians were testing a "Star Wars" laser or particle-beam weapon at the missile range at Sarychogan, Kazakhstan.[48] Sarychogan is one of the most secret military installations in the USSR, and is completely isolated from the outside world. There, within a giant complex that includes twelve high-energy particle generators, the Soviets are engaged in what the CIA code-named "Project Tora"—the race to produce laser beam weapons capable of knocking out enemy satellites or the warheads of incoming missiles. The Soviets have only recently admitted to having conducted extensive research into strategic defense initiative weapons.

Debunkers such as James Oberg and Philip Klass argue that *all* such reports can be explained in terms of rocket launches, weapons testing, barium cloud experiments, and so on, but one should bear in mind that many reports—especially those involving occupants—cannot be so easily explained, however tempting it may be to do so. It must also be pointed out that Zigel's findings seem to be well researched, and conform to Western findings.

MORE STATEMENTS FROM DR. FELIX ZIGEL

We have seen these UFOs over the USSR; craft of every possible shape: small, big, flattened, spherical. They are able to remain stationary in the atmosphere or to shoot along at 100,000 kilometers per hour. They move without producing the slightest sound, by creating around themselves a pneumatic vacuum that protects them from the hazard of burning up in our stratosphere. Their craft also have the mysterious capacity to vanish and reappear at will. They are also able to affect our power resources, halting our electricity-generating plants, our radio stations, and our engines, without however leaving any permanent damage. So refined a technology can only be the fruit of an intelligence that is indeed far superior to man.

This significant statement was made to the American journalist Henry Gris in an interview for the Italian weekly magazine *Gente* in 1981. Zigel further claimed that he had 50,000 UFO reports on file in the computer of the Moscow Aviation Institute, and added that from the material in his own archives he had compiled eight volumes. Only one had been published, he said, because the others, *if released to the Soviet public, would trigger off an enormous wave of fear and unrest throughout the entire country.*

Zigel went on to state that at least seven landings of extraterrestrial spacecraft had occurred in the vicinity of Moscow between June 1977 and September 1979. He believes that there are three basic categories of UFO occupant: *spacemen,* the least frequently observed, who are very tall beings, three meters or so in height; *humanoids,* who are in general so similar to us in height and in many other respects that they could most probably mingle here undetected, many of whom may already have infiltrated; and what Zigel calls *aliens,* who are around one meter in height and although resembling us in some respects possess relatively large heads with no trace of hair, protruding eyes set far apart, wrinkled faces, and a pair of large nostrils by way of a nose.

In addition to these categories of what he terms "flesh-and-blood extraterrestrials" Zigel states that the spacecraft carry crews of robots or androids which possess the ability to disappear and reappear at will and, not being subject to the physical laws of our planet, seem to be "deliberately constructed in order to confound all our notions of space, matter, time, and dimensions."[49] I have come to similar conclusions after more than thirty years' research, so I find it difficult to equate Zigel's statements with official disinformation.

There seems little doubt, though, that the sighting over Moscow and other areas on 14 June 1980 was *not* of a UFO, and unless Zigel was genuinely mistaken his endorsement of it is puzzling. Even more puzzling is the fact that on the night in question he claims to have received at least two reports of landed UFOs in Moscow. One report allegedly came from a Lieutenant-Colonel Oleg Karyakin, who supposedly saw a "round, flattened object, a classic 'flying saucer,' just like a big bowl reversed on top of a slightly smaller plate, and hanging stationary at a distance of about 30 meters from my house." Karyakin is said to have tried getting closer to the object, but was repelled by an invisible and insurmountable barrier. Several neighbors also observed the object (one reported a humanoid occupant), which took off after a few minutes.[50]

An unlikely but intriguing possibility is that the UFOs were using the launch of *Cosmos 1188* as a cover for their own operations! If the Moscow landing reports were fabricated, however, it is more than likely that the notorious KGB was responsible.

THE KGB

The KGB or *Komitet Gosudarstvennoi Bezopastnosti* (Committee for State Security) is undoubtedly the world's largest secret service, whose estimated personnel is said to number a staggering 1,750,000 in the Soviet

Union alone, and 400,000 abroad (including members of USSR satellite countries' secret services).[51] By 1959 the KGB had a fully fledged disinformation department, known as Department D (for *Dezinformatsiya*) of the First Chief Directorate, which under the late Yuri Andropov was renamed Department A. Disinformation entails the fabrication and dissemination of forged documents, tapes, letters, manuscripts and photographs, as well as the propagation of misleading or malicious rumors and intelligence.[52] The CIA estimates that the Russians spend about $4 billion a year on disinformation—a sobering thought indeed.

If the Soviets are seeking to spread false UFO stories as a means of covering up their space launches and strategic defense initiative ("Star Wars") tests, they may be fooling their own people but they are unlikely to fool Western intelligence. America's National Reconnaissance Office, for example, has sophisticated methods for detecting and tracking any Soviet rocket launch or SDI tests, mostly via satellite.

BAIKONUR, 1982

Some UFO reports that emanate from the Soviet Union read like science fiction, yet they *seem* to come from reliable sources. According to the Latvian-born US journalist Henry Gris, for instance, scientists Dr. Alexei Zolotov and Dr. Vladimir Azhazha (who are both involved in UFO research) told him that two UFOs hovered over the cosmodrome at Baikonur for fourteen seconds on 1 June 1982, one directly above launch pad No. 1. The following day bolts and rivets were found which had allegedly been "sucked out" of the support towers, and welded sections had come apart. The other UFO reportedly hovered over the nearby housing complex, knocking out thousands of panes of glass, or making fine holes in them. As a consequence, the entire cosmodrome was said to have been put out of action for at least two weeks. This story was confirmed to Gordon Creighton by Henry Gris, who added that even James Oberg had admitted to him that the base had indeed been out of commission during the period in question, and could apparently find no explanation for it.[53]

COMMISSION FOR THE INVESTIGATION OF

ANOMALOUS ATMOSPHERIC PHENOMENA

By the beginning of 1983 the Russians were once again admitting that UFOs were a serious subject. An article in *Sovietskaya Kultura* of 6 January stated that the existence of UFOs should not be ruled out, and revealed that a Soviet Air Force pilot had had an encounter with one in 1981. The article said that there were still many unexplained phenomena behind the reports, and urged scientists to collate as much information as possible.[54]

In February 1984 the Commission for the Investigation of Anomalous Atmospheric Phenomena was established in Moscow, although its official announcement in the West was delayed until May. Affiliated to the Committee for the Protection of Natural Environment of the All-Union Council of Scientific Technical Societies, the new commission was comprised of high level scientists and academicians, and was headed by the distinguished former cosmonaut, Pavel Popovitch. Popovitch told the trade union newspaper *Trud* (Labor) that there had been hundreds of reports each year in the Soviet Union, and that most could be explained away. But scientists had been disturbed by events in Gorky, 250 miles from Moscow, the previous year, which defied rational analysis.

On the evening of 27 March 1983 air traffic controllers at Gorky Airport had observed a steel-gray cigar-shaped object flying toward them which failed to respond to radio contact. It was about the size of a conventional aircraft but lacked wings, tail or fin, and was flying at an altitude of 3,000 feet at a speed of up to 125 mph. The object behaved erratically, flying forty-five miles to the southeast of Gorky before turning to head back to the airport, finally vanishing twenty-five miles to the north of the city. Popovitch added that the new commission was taking this report very seriously, since the sighting had been made by reliable and well trained aviation experts who had given precise and scientific observations, and who had tracked the UFO on radar for forty minutes.

The *Trud* article stated that other sightings witnessed by less well-trained observers would not be accepted by the commission,[55] but in July 1984 *Sovietskaya Rossiya* gave a box number at Moscow's main post office where citizens could send their UFO reports.[56]

AEROFLOT FLIGHT 8352 ESCORTED BY UFO, 1984

On 30 January 1985 *Tass,* the official Soviet news agency, gave world-wide circulation to a dramatic UFO report, which first appeared in an article by V. Vostrukhin in *Trud* on that date. According to the report a Tupolev Tu-134a, Flight 8352, flying from Tbilisi to Tallin via Rostov, encountered an unidentified object at 4:10 a.m. on an unspecified date, 120 kilometers from Minsk. The aircraft was operated by an aircrew from the Estonian Administration of the USSR Ministry of Civil Aviation: Igor

Cherkashin (flight captain); Gennadi Lazurin (second pilot); Igor Ognev (navigation officer), and Gennadi Kozlov (air mechanic).

The second pilot first noticed a yellow star-like object above and to starboard which he dismissed as a light refraction in the atmosphere. Suddenly a thin shaft of light shot down from the object toward the ground. Lazurin nudged the air mechanic who, having confirmed the sighting, asked the captain to report it. The shaft of light then suddenly vanished and changed into a vivid cone of light, wider but paler than the first, followed by a third cone, wide and intensely bright. Although it is difficult to estimate distances when dealing with UFOs, all four airmen got the impression that the unknown object was at a height of forty to fifty kilometers above the earth.

The second pilot began to make a quick sketch of this remarkable sight. On the area of ground illuminated by the cone-shaped beam of light, everything—houses and road included—was totally and distinctly visible. The searchlight beam then rose from the ground and centered on the aircraft, and the crew observed a blinding white point of light surrounded by concentric colored circles.

The captain was hesitant about reporting the sighting, but then something happened that dispelled his doubts. The white point of light flared up and changed into a "green cloud," and it seemed to him that the object was now approaching the airliner at an immense speed and was on the point of crossing their course at an acute angle. "Transmit report!" Captain Cherkashin shouted to the navigation officer, but just as the latter began to radio details to Air Traffic Control in Minsk, the object came to a halt. The Minsk controller received and acknowledged the crew's report, remarking politely that unfortunately he could see nothing, either on the radar screen or in the sky.

The "green cloud" then suddenly dropped down to the altitude of the airliner, went straight up vertically, and began to swing from left to right, then down and up once again. Finally, it took up a position beside the airliner and flew alongside at their altitude of 10,000 meters and speed of 800 kilometers per hour. Inside the "cloud" the crew could see a "play of lights" flashing on and off, and then performing fiery zigzag maneuvers.

The navigation officer continued to transmit details of the sighting to Air Traffic Control, who responded: "I see flashes on the horizon. Where do you see your 'cloud'?" The navigation officer reported its position in relation to the airliner. "That fits," said the controller.

The "cloud" continued to change shape, developing a "tail" shaped like a waterspout, wide at the top and narrow at the bottom. Then the "tail" started to rise and from its elliptical shape changed to a "square," then a sharp-nosed wingless "cloud-aircraft." The object shone with a yellow and green glow, giving the crew the impression that it was "mimicking" their plane.

At this point the stewardess came on to the flight deck and said that the passengers wanted to know what the strange object was flying beside them. "Tell them it's a cloud!" replied the captain. "Yellow clouds—lights of cities reflecting from below. Green clouds—tell them it's the Aurora Borealis!"

At that time another Tupolev 134 was passing through the Minsk Air Traffic Control Zone, flying the opposite route. The two aircraft were 100 kilometers apart. Captain Cherkashin asked the other Tu-134 crew if they could see anything, but the reply came back in the negative. The Minsk controller gave the other airliner the coordinates and direction in which they should be able to observe the phenomenon, but they saw absolutely nothing. Only when the two aircraft were fifteen kilometers apart did they begin to see it, and gave a precise description of the "cloud aircraft."

Captain Cherkashin's crew contacted the air traffic controllers at Riga and Vilna, who picked up both the Tu-134 and the UFO. As they passed over Lake Chud and Lake Pskov, the crew were able to make an estimate of the size of the cloud. The two lakes, oblong in shape, are separated by a small sand bar. The Tu-134 was flying at a distance of 120 kilometers to the left of the lakes, and the object was flying to the right of them, in the vicinity of Tartu. From the nose of the object, where it seemed there was what looked like a "solid ball," a beam of light shot out again. The patch of light struck a cloud and then moved down toward the ground. Thus, by mere chance, the "cloud-aircraft" revealed its dimensions and it was possible to assess its length as being equal to that of Lake Pskov, which is about twenty-five miles.

The object continued following the airliner to Tallin in Estonia. After landing there the crew were given some curious details by the air traffic controller: on the Tallin radarscope the Tu-134 was not the only object seen. Although there was only the one aircraft, behind it could be seen two other moving "blips" the whole time, yet the blip of the airliner kept vanishing and reappearing. "I would have understood it all right had you been 'blinking' on the landing radarscope," said the controller. "But on the sky-scanning radar, that never happens—simply *can't* happen."

The *Trud* article concluded with a statement by Dr. Nikolai Zheltukhin, Vice-Chairman of the Commission for Anomalous Phenomena:

> The commission is making a systematic study of sightings of unidentified flying objects observed over the territory of the USSR. The material we have is already quite considerable, so we have something to work on. But one is obliged to note with regret that all the accounts at our disposal suffer to some degree or other from bias or incompleteness. This sighting by the Tallin aircrew has been investigated by the Estonian Section of our commission. . . .
>
> The case is a genuinely interesting one, though we know of others like it. The fact that the object instantaneously reversed its line of flight and shot down an unusually powerful beam of light from a great altitude is unquestionably anomalous. But, in judging the nature of the phenomenon, the commission is guided by the indications of the locality. That is to say, if the phenomenon is local, and limited in space, it can be claimed of it that it is anomalous. But the dimensions of the object in this case, as seen by the airmen, were unintentionally enlarged. It was already very big. It was natural to suppose that, somewhere far away, many thousands of miles distant, some global or atmospheric or geophysical process of a type already known to Science might have been taking place. But to the pilots the things seemed to be quite close. Yet this explanation proved in the end to be unsound, for the pilots were able to establish its distance from them.
>
> Consequently, the only conclusion that can be drawn is that the Tallin aircrew encountered what we call a *UFO*. It is particularly valuable that we now possess a consistent and detailed picture of the transformation in the appearance of unidentified flying objects.[57]

Dr. Zheltukhin concluded his statement by requesting *Trud* readers to report all such sightings to the Commission for Anomalous Phenomena, giving an address in Moscow.[58]

Skeptics will dismiss this extraordinary sighting as a barium cloud experiment or strategic defense initiative test, yet there seem to me to be no intelligent grounds for accepting any hypothesis other than that the Aeroflot crews observed a genuine unidentified flying object which was also tracked on radar. According to Gordon Creighton's sources in the USSR, the date of the incident has now been established as 7 September 1984.

It should be pointed out that *Trud,* a trade union newspaper, normally purveys news strictly dictated by "Communist realism," and the report therefore came as something of a surprise to readers. Possibly to set the record straight, the Soviet military daily paper *Krasnaya Zvezda* (Red Star) debunked the sighting as science fiction three months later. Flying saucers and UFOs observed through the ages are not the transport of extraterrestrial beings, it said, but are more likely apparitions caused by temperature inversions, refracted light or radio waves. Also, the number of artificial objects—discarded booster rockets, decaying satellites and so on—has increased the likelihood of freak appearances in the night-time sky, the article added. The mystery surrounding the Aeroflot sighting could thus be explained as "refracted light beams striking floating space garbage, or as bits of discarded rockets showering down through the atmosphere."

The article contained a rare admission that one sighting in particular had been caused by Soviet space activity. In September 1977 *Tass* had reported that a huge mass of light flared up in the skies over Petrozavodsk in Soviet Karelia near the Finnish border. The strange brilliance "hovered over the city in the form of a jellyfish sending down a multitude of fine beams. . . . The impression was of a torrential rain of light." The sighting was merely caused by a booster rocket falling away during the launch of the *Cosmos 955* satellite, explained *Krasnaya Zvezda*.[59]

The Commission for Anomalous Phenomena is apparently now firmly under the aegis of the prestigious USSR Academy of Sciences, in spite of earlier reports emphasizing the rift between the commission and the academy over treatment of UFO sightings. In March 1985 it was announced that the "special commission of the Soviet Academy of Sciences" had officially acknowledged that the Aeroflot crew of Flight 8352 had encountered "something we call UFOs."[60]

UFO enthusiasts in the Soviet Union, seemingly undeterred by periodic rebuttals from the official press, continue to give lectures and to circulate underground *samizdat* bulletins on sightings and, as we have seen, even the official press occasionally carries positive statements on the subject. The fact that opposing viewpoints are published may be seen as a healthy development in a country where the media is state-controlled. Yet the authorities continue to intercept letters from foreign enthusiasts, as well as to confiscate books and magazines, or remove offending pages from them. The well-known Russian ufologist Valerii Sanarov of Novosibirsk, for example, commented on this state of affairs to the French researcher Jean-François Boadec: "I must say that a great deal of UFO publications are confiscated here by the postal authorities as prohibited items."[61] Later he was more specific: "Please find here enclosed the reply of our postal authorities stating that your parcel has been confiscated as [a] prohibited item. . . . You can see from the postal regulations that the item mentioned

(Article 36—4'f') specifies that prohibited items are those causing political or economic prejudice to the USSR. It follows that your book is capable of such prejudice . . . as many other books.''[62]

There is nothing remarkable about this, however. Letters, articles, magazines and books on *any* subject deemed of political or economic prejudice to the USSR are frequently intercepted or confiscated. I well remember an occasion when I had just arrived at Leningrad by boat in 1969 and had to wait for ten minutes while the customs authorities combed through my copies of *Time* and *Newsweek* magazines, searching for ''anti-Soviet propaganda.'' Apparently nothing could be found and the copies were grudgingly returned to me, with a warning not to leave them in the USSR. Perhaps it was no coincidence that a few days later a (presumed) KGB agent took a photograph of me as I was in line to change money at a bank, afterward disappearing rapidly up some stairs.

During my two visits to the Soviet Union I have detected an undercurrent of enthusiasm for UFOs. Although the subject was taboo at the time and I was advised against meeting other researchers, a young party official told me that sightings in the USSR were widespread and that the subject was followed with a great deal of interest. And at the Moscow Space Museum in 1971, during a concert tour with the London Symphony Orchestra, I saw a number of futuristic paintings depicting flying saucers—with one showing humanoid occupants. Fantasy? Or signposts to the future?

The latest official announcements in the Soviet Union lend credence to the possibility that the late Dr. Hynek's fear may be realized: that the Russians will be the first to break the worldwide cover-up on UFOs. This is indeed an intriguing possibility, and the political and social consequences will, I am certain, have been given careful consideration by CIA analysts. I am equally certain that the Kremlin will have considered what political advantages are to be gained by making such an announcement.

In 1920 a fascinating conversation took place between Lenin and H. G. Wells, which the latter related as follows:

> I said to Lenin that the development of human technology might some day change the world situation. The Marxist conception itself would then become meaningless. Lenin looked at me and he said:
> "You are right. I understood this myself when I read your novel *The Time Machine*. All human conceptions are on a scale of our planet. They are based on the pretension that the technical potential, although it will develop, will never exceed the 'terrestrial limit.' If we succeed in establishing interplanetary communication, all our philosophical, moral and

social views will have to be revised. In this case, the technical potential, become limitless, would impose the end of the role of violence as a means and method of progress."[63]

There is no denying the possibility that once it is established beyond doubt that extraterrestrials are visiting our earth, the social, philosophical, scientific, and economic repercussions would have a profound effect on us all—irrespective of nationality. And should the visitors pose any kind of threat to humanity, the likelihood is that this will lead to an unprecedented degree of unity among nations.

During the Geneva summit conference in November 1985 President Reagan made just this point to Soviet leader Mikhail Gorbachev when he told him "how much easier his task and mine might be in these meetings that we held if suddenly there was a threat to this world from another species from another planet outside in the universe. We'd forget all the little local differences that we have between our countries, and we would find out once and for all that we really are all human beings here on this earth together."[64]

PART THREE

USA

11

1947–54

In 1947 "flying saucers"—a description coined by the press following pilot Kenneth Arnold's famous sighting of nine disk-shaped objects over the Cascade Mountains, Washington, on 24 June—began to be seen in ever-increasing numbers all over the United States. Reports were being made by qualified observers such as military and civilian pilots, air traffic controllers, and others whose jobs depended on their ability to identify objects in the sky. The authorities were alarmed.

Arnold's first sighting had been the subject of an investigation by the FBI and Army Air Forces.[1] The story is so well known that I have not included it here, but an FBI agent's comments on the reliability of the report are worth quoting:

> It is the personal opinion of the interviewer that [Arnold] actually saw what he states he saw in the attached report. It is also the opinion of the interviewer that [Arnold] would have much more to lose than gain and would have to be very strongly convinced that he actually saw something before he would report such an incident and open himself up for the ridicule that would accompany such a report.[2]

The FBI denied any involvement in UFO investigations until 1976, when US Navy physicist Dr. Bruce Maccabee filed a Freedom of Information Act request and obtained about 1,100 pages of documentation on the subject. Only three years earlier, on 25 October 1973, FBI Director Clarence M. Kelley had explained to an inquirer that "the investigation of Unidentified Flying Objects is not and never has been a matter that is within the investigative jurisdiction of the FBI" (see Appendix, p. 475).

Another early sighting which led to a full-scale official investigation was that of Captain Edward J. Smith and his co-pilot Ralph Stevens, flying a United Airlines DC-3, Flight 105, in the vicinity of Emmet, Idaho, on 4 July 1947. The following abbreviated account is extracted from an interview with Captain Smith by a US Navy intelligence officer a few days later. The report was immediately forwarded to the Chief of Naval Intelligence:

> At approximately 2015, the co-pilot called my attention to the first object seen . . . our altitude was approximately 6500, and we were climbing to

our proposed cruising altitude of 8000 . . . the object . . . was sighted at
approximately 290 degrees, or ten degrees to our left. Then an additional
four objects appeared to the left of the main, or first, object. These four
objects appeared slightly smaller than the first object sighted, but all of
the objects appeared on the same plane. . . . They were within our sight
for approximately two minutes, then they disappeared . . . one or two
minutes later, the second group appeared . . . to the right of the plane
. . . [and] stayed within our sight twelve to fifteen minutes, then disappeared. . . .

The objects were flat on the base, the top slightly rough in contour.
The dimensions appeared the same as a DC-3 approximately five miles
from us. . . . Actually we have no idea just how large it was since we
could not determine its distance from us . . . when first sighted, they were
going slow and stayed within sight for quite some time. However, when
we lost sight of them, they seemed to disappear practically immediately.
I think they either put on a tremendous burst of speed and disappeared
from sight, or else they dissipated. Also, it appeared that only one object,
the large one, was controlled, and it in turn controlled the other objects.[3]

THE ROSWELL INCIDENT, 1947

One of the most contentious aspects of the UFO enigma is the allegation
that a number of flying saucers have actually crash-landed and been
recovered by the military in great secrecy. The claim has been generally
dismissed for lack of proof, yet the evidence is compelling. Former US
Air Force intelligence officer Leonard Stringfield, for example, has now
collected at least forty such accounts, some of them from firsthand witnesses.[4] One incident that now seems indisputable—in the sense that
anomalous wreckage was recovered—occurred within a few days of the
United Airlines sighting, and has been the subject of one of the most
thoroughly documented investigations on record.

On the evening of 2 July 1947 a bright, disk-shaped object was seen
flying over Roswell, New Mexico, heading northwest. The following day
widely scattered wreckage was discovered about seventy-five miles northwest of Roswell by a local ranch manager, William Brazel, together with
his son and daughter. The authorities were eventually alerted and a quantity of wreckage was recovered by Major Jesse Marcel, a staff intelligence
officer of the 509th Bomb Group Intelligence Office at the Army Air
Forces base at Roswell Field, together with a Counter-Intelligence Corps
officer. Once the officers had returned to the Roswell base, an official
press statement was released, authorized by Colonel William Blanchard,
confirming that wreckage of a flying disk had been recovered. Marcel

was ordered to load the debris on a B-29 and fly it to Wright Field (now Wright-Patterson AFB) at Dayton, Ohio, for examination.

On arrival at an intermediate stop at Carswell Army Air Forces Base, Fort Worth, Texas (headquarters of the Eighth Air Force), General Roger Ramey took charge and ordered Marcel and others on the plane not to talk to reporters. A second press statement was issued which stated that the wreckage was nothing more than the remains of a weather balloon and its attached tinfoil radar target, and this was prominently displayed at the press conference. Meanwhile, the *real* wreckage arrived at Wright Field under armed guard; Marcel returned to Roswell, and Brazel was held incommunicado for nearly a week while the crash site was stripped of every scrap of debris.

A news leak via press wire from Albuquerque describing this fantastic story was interrupted and the radio station in question, and another, were warned not to continue the broadcast: ''ATTENTION ALBUQUERQUE: CEASE TRANSMISSION. REPEAT. CEASE TRANSMISSION. NATIONAL SECURITY ITEM. DO NOT TRANSMIT. STAND BY. . . .''[5]

The Wreckage

The unidentified wreckage, scattered over an area three-quarters of a mile long by several hundred feet wide, consisted of various types of material, which according to Major Marcel was like nothing he had seen before or since:

> There was all kinds of stuff—small beams about three eighths or a half inch square with some sort of hieroglyphics on them that nobody could decipher. These looked something like balsa wood, and were of about the same weight, except that they were not wood at all. They were very hard, although flexible, and would not burn. There was a great deal of unusual parchment-like substance which was brown in color and extremely strong, and a great number of small pieces of a metal like tinfoil, except that it wasn't tinfoil.

Marcel added that one piece of metal foil, two feet long and a foot wide, was so durable that it could not be dented with a sledgehammer, despite its being incredibly light. Marcel was absolutely convinced that the material had nothing to do with a weather balloon or radar target. His testimony cannot be dismissed, owing to his background in aviation: he had served as bombardier, waist-gunner and pilot, had logged 468 hours of combat flying in B-24 aircraft, and was awarded five air medals for shooting down enemy aircraft in World War II. Toward the end of

the war he was attached to the 509th Bomb Wing, an elite military group
for which all those involved required high-security clearances. Following
the Roswell incident he was promoted to Lieutenant Colonel and assigned
to a Special Weapons Program that specialized in analyzing air samples
to discover if the Russians had detonated their first nuclear bomb.[6]

Were Bodies Recovered?

Marcel was quite certain that no bodies were among the debris, and that
whatever the object was it must have exploded above ground level. But
the evidence suggests that there was *another* crash site, in an area west
of Socorro, New Mexico, known as the Plains of San Agustin, where
witnesses discovered not only a damaged metallic "aircraft" resting on
the flat desert ground, but also dead bodies.

The first witness on the scene was Grady L. "Barney" Barnett, a civil
engineer with the US Soil Conservation Service who was on a military
assignment at the time. He told some friends that in early July 1947 he
had encountered a metallic, disk-shaped "aircraft" about twenty-five or
thirty feet in diameter. While he was examining it, a small group of
people arrived who said they were part of an archaeological research team
from the University of Pennsylvania. Barnett recalled:

> I noticed that they were standing around looking at some dead bodies that
> had fallen to the ground. I think there were others in the machine, which
> was a kind of metallic . . . disk. It was not all that big. It seemed to be
> made of a metal that looked like dirty stainless steel. The machine had
> been split open by explosion or impact.
>
> I tried to get close to see what the bodies were like. They were all dead
> as far as I could see and there were bodies inside and outside the vehicle.
> The ones outside had been tossed out by the impact. They were like humans
> but they were not humans. The heads were round, the eyes were small,
> and they had no hair. The eyes were oddly spaced. They were quite small
> by our standards and their heads were larger in proportion to their bodies
> than ours. Their clothing seemed to be one-piece and gray in color. You
> couldn't see any zippers, belts or buttons. They seemed to me to be all
> males and there were a number of them. I was close enough to touch them
> but I didn't—I was escorted away before I could [do so].
>
> While we were looking at them a military officer drove up in a truck
> with a driver and took control. He told everybody that the Army was taking
> over and to get out of the way. Other military personnel came up and
> cordoned off the area. We were told to leave the area and not to talk to
> anyone whatever about what we had seen . . . that it was our patriotic
> duty to remain silent.[7]

Regrettably this account cannot be regarded as reliable since it was related to friends of the witness in 1950: Barnett died in 1969 and the authors of *The Roswell Incident,* a book which examines the evidence then available, were therefore unable to interview him. But those who knew "Barney" Barnett described him as the very model of a respectable and honest citizen—hardly likely to invent such a fantastic tale. Members of the University of Pennsylvania team have yet to come forward or be located, although William Moore has established that the university *was* involved in archaeological digs in the area at that time.

It is not known for certain if the craft and occupants allegedly witnessed by Barnett were connected with the Roswell wreckage. The Plains of San Agustin, near Magdalena, New Mexico, are about 150 miles west of Brazel's ranch site. Was the wreckage recovered there part of the same craft that had somehow managed to remain airborne for that distance before crashing on the Plains, or was it another craft that had also come to grief? We may never know the full story, but Bill Moore, in one of his updated research papers on the Roswell incident, concludes that while there is insufficient evidence to substantiate Barnett's story or to justify linking it with the *proven* recovery of anomalous wreckage at Brazel's ranch site, this is no reason to dismiss the account out of hand. There is also the intriguing hypothesis that the first press release, announcing the recovery of a crashed disk, was a counterintelligence ploy to deflect attention from the craft and bodies near Magdalena. If so, it worked.

Leading researchers Bill Moore and Stanton Friedman (the latter a nuclear physicist as well as a UFO researcher) have interviewed no less than ninety-two witnesses who provided information about this sensational incident, of whom thirty were involved with the discovery, recovery or subsequent official cover-up, and ten of the original witnesses have identified the object as nonterrestrial in origin.[8]

MAJESTIC 12

According to a document acquired by TV producer Jaime Shandera in 1984, a highly secret panel, code-named "Majestic 12" or "MJ-12," was formed by President Truman in 1947 to investigate UFOs and report on its findings to the President. The document, dated 18 November 1952 and classified TOP SECRET/MAJIC/EYES ONLY, was allegedly prepared for President-elect Dwight Eisenhower, and includes the astonishing statement that *the remains of four alien bodies were recovered two miles from the Roswell wreckage site* (see Appendix, pp. 544–51). The doc-

ument names the twelve high-ranking members of the panel. They were:
Lloyd Berkner, Detlev Bronk, Vannevar Bush, James Forrestal, Gordon
Gray, Roscoe Hillenkoetter, Jerome Hunsaker, Donald Menzel, Robert
Montague, Sidney Souers, Nathan Twining and Hoyt Vandenberg.[9]

Dr. Lloyd Berkner, a scientist who was executive Secretary of the
Joint Research and Development Board in 1946 (under Dr. Vannevar
Bush), also headed a special committee to direct a study that led to the
establishment of the Weapons Systems Evaluation Group. He was also
a member of the CIA's "Robertson Panel," a scientific advisory panel
on UFOs requested by the White House and sponsored by the CIA in
1953 (see Chapter 14).

Dr. Detlev Bronk was an internationally known physiologist and biophysicist who was Chairman of the National Research Council and a
member of the Medical Advisory Board of the Atomic Energy Commission. With Dr. Edward Condon, Director of the National Bureau of
Standards (who later headed the Air Force-sponsored UFO project at the
University of Colorado), Bronk became a member of the Scientific Advisory Committee of the Brookhaven National Laboratory.

Dr. Vannevar Bush, recognized as one of America's leading scientists,
organized the National Defense Research Council in 1941 and the Office
of Scientific Research and Development in 1943, which led to the establishment of the Manhattan Project to develop the first atomic bomb. After
the war Dr. Bush became head of the Joint Research and Development
Board. As the Canadian government scientist Wilbert Smith noted in his
top secret memorandum (see Chapter 8), Dr. Bush headed a "small
group" set up to investigate UFOs, which matter "is the most highly
classified subject in the United States government, rating higher even
than the H-bomb." Could this "small group" have been "Majestic 12"?
If so, Bush's background in co-ordinating top secret intelligence research
projects would have made him the ideal choice to head the group. In
1949, for instance, the US Intelligence Board, the co-ordinating body of
all US government intelligence agencies, commissioned Bush to recommend methods of linking all the intelligence bureaucracies, a move
initiated by James Forrestal—coincidentally another member of MJ-12.

James Forrestal served as Secretary of the Navy before becoming
Secretary of Defense in July 1947 (the time of the Roswell incident), a
position he held until a mental breakdown led to his resignation in March
1949. He committed suicide at Bethesda Naval Hospital in May 1949.

Gordon Gray was Assistant Secretary of the Army at the time when
MJ-12 was established, and became Secretary of the Army in 1949. In

1950 he was appointed as Special Assistant to President Truman on National Security Affairs, and in 1951, according to William Steinman, directed the Psychological Strategy Board[10], referred to in a 1952 CIA memorandum from Director Walter Bedell Smith discussing the psychological warfare implications of UFOs.

Vice Admiral Roscoe Hillenkoetter was the third Director of Central Intelligence (DCI) from 1947 to 1950, and the first Director of the CIA, which was established in the same month as MJ-12— September 1947. Hillenkoetter was one of the first intelligence chiefs to make public his conviction that UFOs were real, and that "through official secrecy and ridicule, many citizens are led to believe the unknown flying objects are nonsense." Hillenkoetter was also on the board of Directors of the National Investigations Committee on Aerial Phenomena, and was therefore in an excellent position to monitor the activities of this influential civilian group.

Dr. Jerome Hunsaker was a brilliant aircraft designer who headed the Departments of Mechanical and Aeronautical Engineering at the Massachusetts Institute of Technology, and was Chairman of the National Advisory Committee for Aeronautics. His opinion on the materials recovered at Roswell would have been invaluable.

Dr. Donald Menzel was Director of the Harvard College Observatory, and is chiefly remembered for his dismissive statements and books on UFOs, *all* of which, he said, could be explained in mundane terms. Menzel would have been helpful as an astronomical consultant to MJ-12, and later as the world's most widely read UFO debunker. He was also involved with the National Security Agency, and held a Top Secret Ultra security clearance.

General Robert Montague was Base Commander at the Atomic Energy Commission installation at Sandia Base, Albuquerque, New Mexico, from July 1947 to February 1951.

Rear Admiral Sidney Souers was the first Director of Central Intelligence (January–June 1946) and in September 1947 (when MJ-12 was set up) became Executive Secretary of the National Security Council. Following his resignation in 1950 Souers was retained as a special consultant to the Executive on security matters.

General Nathan Twining was an outstanding commander of bombing operations in both the European and Pacific theaters during World War II. In 1945 he was appointed Commanding General of Air Matériel Command, based at Wright Field (Wright-Patterson Air Force Base). A declassified secret document reveals that in September 1947 Twining presented the conclusions of AMC that "the phenomenon reported is something real," further details of which will be discussed later. Significantly, Twining suddenly canceled a planned trip to the West Coast on 8 July 1947, the day of the first press release announcing the recovery of a crashed disk near Roswell, "due to a very important and sudden matter." William Moore has learned that while reporters were told that Twining was out of the office, "probably in Washington, DC" he had in fact made a sudden trip to New Mexico, where he remained until 10 July.[11]

The remaining member of the alleged MJ-12 panel was *General Hoyt Vandenberg*. Following a distinguished career in the Army Air Forces he became the second Director of Central Intelligence in 1946, a position he held until May 1947. In August 1948, when a top secret "Estimate of the Situation" by the Air Technical Intelligence Center offered its opinion that UFOs were interplanetary, Vandenberg, Air Force Chief of Staff at the time, ordered the document to be burned.

My inquiries into the authenticity of the Majestic 12 story during a research trip to the United States in 1986 have led me to believe that the group did indeed exist, and the document seems authentic enough. Unfortunately, all the members are now deceased, and my questions addressed to a former Director of the CIA, as well as two ex-Presidents, remain unanswered, which is hardly surprising. But it is interesting that "MJ-12" crops up in an alleged Air Force Office of Special Investigations (AFOSI) document, dated 17 November 1980. Paragraph 2 states: ". . . OFFICIAL US GOVERNMENT POLICY AND RESULTS OF PROJECT AQUARIUS IS STILL CLASSIFIED TOP SECRET WITH NO DISSEMINATION OUTSIDE OFFICIAL INTELLIGENCE CHANNELS AND WITH RESTRICTED ACCESS TO 'MJ TWELVE.' "

AFOSI have informed me that the retyped document is a fabrication,[12] yet the existence of Project Aquarius has now been confirmed by the National Security Agency. It is still classified Top Secret, and details therefore remain exempt from disclosure (see Chapter 17).

There is as yet no official confirmation of the existence of MJ-12, however.

AIR MATÉRIEL COMMAND, 1947

On 23 September 1947 General Twining (then a lieutenant general), Commanding General of Air Matériel Command, sent a secret memorandum to Brigadier General George Schulgen, Chief of the Air Intelligence Requirements Division at the Pentagon, in response to a request from Air Intelligence concerning the "flying disks." In the opinion of AMC, arrived at in a conference with personnel from the Air Institute of Technology, Intelligence T-2; the Office, Chief Engineering Division; and the Aircraft, Power Plant, and Propeller Laboratories of Engineering Division T-3, Twining stated:

> The phenomenon reported is something real and not visionary or fictitious. . . . There are objects probably approximating the shape of a disk, of such appreciable size as to appear to be as large as man-made aircraft. . . . The reported operating characteristics such as extreme rates of climb, maneuverability (particularly in roll), and action which must be considered *evasive* when sighted or contacted by friendly aircraft and radar, lend belief to the possibility that some of the objects are controlled either manually, automatically or remotely.

Twining's report went on to list the apparent common descriptions of the objects (see Appendix, p. 476–78):

(1) Metallic or light reflecting surface
(2) Absence of trail, except in a few instances when the object apparently was operating under high performance conditions
(3) Circular or elliptical in shape, flat on bottom and domed on top
(4) Several reports of well-kept formation flights varying from three to nine objects
(5) Normally no associated sound, except in three instances a substantial rumbling roar was noted
(6) Level flight speeds normally above 300 knots are estimated

The AMC recommended that Army Air Force Headquarters issue a directive assigning a priority security classification and code-name for a detailed study of the disks, including the preparation of complete sets of all available and pertinent data, to be made available to the Army, Navy, Atomic Energy Commission, Joint Research and Development Board (set up by Dr. Vannevar Bush), National Advisory Committee on Aeronautics, Air Force Scientific Advisory Group, RAND (a West Coast think tank), and NEPA (Nuclear Energy for Propulsion Applications).

Twining's report stated that there was a "lack of physical evidence in the shape of crash recovered exhibits which would undeniably prove the existence of these objects," a statement that has been used by debunkers such as Philip J. Klass to dismiss the claim that Twining had examined the Roswell debris. But Twining must surely have been aware of the wreckage since it had been flown to Wright Field (AMC Headquarters) for examination, so why did he cite the lack of physical evidence? As

William Moore explains, if a disk had crashed at Roswell, Twining would have needed to set up a project to gather as much information as possible from all over the world. Assuming that access to crashed disk data would have been on a very high "need-to-know" basis, it would hardly have been appropriate to let those on the other end of the data collection line know why such data was needed. "Indeed," argues Moore, "it might have been best to maintain that there was no crashed disk in order to allay suspicion."[13]

There is strong evidence that the Air Intelligence Requirements Division, headed by Brigadier General Schulgen, to whom Twining had sent the AMC report, *was* aware of the crashed disk material, and that this information could only have come from Twining's office. A secret AIRD five page "Draft of Collection Memorandum" dated 28 October 1947, listing the "current intelligence requirements in the field of Flying Saucer type aircraft" gives much of Twining's AMC data on the phenomenon, and adds some significant and revealing comments: "While there remains a possibility of Russian manufacture, based upon the perspective thinking and actual accomplishments of the Germans, *it is the considered opinion of some elements that the object may in fact represent an interplanetary craft of some kind.*"

Listed under "Requirements . . . 3" are: "Items of construction (a) Type of material, whether metal, ferrous, nonferrous, or nonmetallic. (b) *Composite or sandwich construction utilizing various combinations of metals, metallic foils, plastics, and perhaps balsa wood or similar material. (c) Unusual fabrication methods to achieve extreme light weight and structural stability.*" [Emphasis added] Under "Power plant" the draft memorandum states: "Information is needed regarding the propulsion system of the aircraft. . . . The presence of an unconventional or unusual type of propulsion system cannot be ruled out and should be considered of great interest."

Some of this information simply *must* have come from Twining's office. The reference to "various combinations of metals, metallic foils, plastics, and perhaps balsa wood or similar material" is of course particularly significant in that it closely matches Major Jesse Marcel's description of the Roswell wreckage.[14]

THE DEATH OF CAPTAIN MANTELL, 1948

On 7 January 1948 a flight of four National Guard P-51 Mustang aircraft, led by Captain Thomas Mantell, flying from Marietta, Georgia, to Standiford Field, Kentucky, was requested by the control tower at Godman AFB, Kentucky, to investigate an unidentified flying object in the vicinity of Godman. The official summary describes the incident as follows:

> Three of the ships started to climb toward the object. Pilot Hendricks in NG336 continued on and landed at 1501C [Central Time] at Standiford Field. . . . Pilots Hammond, NG737 & Clements NG800, climbed to 22,000 feet with Mantell in NG3869 then continued on to their original destination because of lack of oxygen arriving there at 1540C. Mantell continued climbing toward object. Standiford operations advised Wright Field Service Center at 1750E [Eastern Time] that NG3869 pilot Mantell crashed 2 miles southwest of Franklin, Kentucky at approximately 1645C. Accident fatal to pilot, major damage to aircraft.[15]

While the official explanation was that Mantell had simply been chasing Venus (later changed to a balloon) and had lost consciousness as a result of oxygen starvation, a 1948 top secret joint Air Force and Naval Intelligence analysis of UFO incidents (declassified in 1985), states: "While it is presumed that this pilot suffered anoxia, resulting in his crash, his last message to the tower was, *'It appears to be metallic object . . . tremendous in size . . . directly ahead and slightly above. . . . I am trying to close for a better look.'* "[16] [Emphasis added]

REQUEST FOR INTERCEPTOR AIRCRAFT

In February 1948 Brigadier General Cabell, Chief of the Air Intelligence Requirements Division (AIRD), sent a secret memo to the Director of Plans and Operations stating that the Commanding General of AMC felt that the responsibility assigned to him for collecting and developing information and intelligence on the "flying disks" should be complemented by a requirement that all Air Force installations in the United States and Alaska "provide a minimum of one each fighter or interceptor type aircraft, with necessary crews, on a continuous alert basis. These aircraft should be equipped with gun camera, and such armament as deemed advisable, in order to secure photographs necessary to the obtainment of all possible data on any reported and sighted unusual phenomena, of the 'flying disk' type, in the atmosphere."[17]

In his reply to the proposal, the Director of Plans and Operations said that stationing fighter planes at all bases on a continuous alert status was not considered feasible on the grounds that the outlay of aircraft and personnel would be too great; "proper interception is not possible, except by accident, without complete radar coverage which the Air Force is not capable of providing. . . . It is doubtful if fighter aircraft would be able to follow up reports emanating, for the most part, from civilian sources."[18]

THE EASTERN AIRLINES SIGHTING, 1948

In the early hours of 25 July 1948 Captain Clarence S. Chiles and co-pilot John B. Whitted, flying an Eastern Airlines DC-3, were approached by an object that seemed to be on a collision course. "Whatever it was, it flashed down toward us and we veered to the left," Chiles told investigators. "It veered to its left and passed us about 700 feet to our right and above us. Then, as if the pilot had seen us and wanted to avoid us, it pulled up with a tremendous burst of flame from the rear and zoomed into the clouds, its prop wash or jet wash rocking our DC-3."

The pilots reported that the object was "a wingless aircraft, 100 feet long, cigar-shaped and about twice the diameter of a B-29 with no protruding surfaces." Captain Chiles said the cabin appeared "like a pilot compartment, except brighter. . . . From the side of the object came an intense, fairly dark blue glow that ran the entire length of the fuselage. . . . The exhaust was a red-orange flame, with a lighter color predominant around the edges."

The sketches drawn by the pilots (see Appendix, p. 479) show that the object had "windows or openings" in its side. To eliminate the possibility that the pilots had merely seen another plane, Air Force Intelligence personnel screened 225 civilian and military flight schedules and found that the only other aircraft in the vicinity was an Air Force C 47—which hardly matches the description given.[19]

TOP SECRET USAF ANALYSES, 1948

Less than two weeks after the Eastern Airlines sighting, Air Technical Intelligence Center (ATIC) decided the time had come to make what intelligence jargon refers to as an "Estimate of the Situation." Captain Edward Ruppelt, former head of the Air Force Project Blue Book, who was one of the few to see the lengthy top secret document, dated 5 August 1948, has confirmed that ATIC concluded that the *UFOs were interplanetary in origin*. General Hoyt Vandenberg, then Chief of Staff, rejected it for lack of proof, even after a group from ATIC visited his office at the Pentagon in an attempt to persuade him to change his mind. Some months later, on Vandenberg's instructions, the document was ordered to be burned.[20]

As a member of the MJ-12 panel, Vandenberg would have had all the proof he needed to establish the extraterrestrial origin of the flying disks. So why then did he reject the ATIC estimate? "The general said it would cause a stampede," Ruppelt told Major Keyhoe. "How could we convince the public the aliens weren't hostile when we didn't know it ourselves?"[21]

In 1985 the hitherto top secret *Analysis of Flying Object Incidents in the U.S.* was declassified and released. Dated 10 December 1948, the nineteen-page document carefully avoids any suggestion that the UFOs could be extraterrestrial, but nevertheless concludes that "some type of flying objects have been observed, although their identification and origin are not discernable."[22]

INTRUSIONS OVER "SENSITIVE INSTALLATIONS,"

1948–50

Official concern over sightings in the vicinity of some of the United States' most sensitive installations, such as the Los Alamos Atomic Energy Commission (AEC) project, led to a deluge of unanswerable questions. In January 1949 Colonel Poland of US Army Intelligence (G-2) sent a memo on behalf of the Commanding General of the 4th Army at Houston, Texas, to the Director of Army Intelligence at the Pentagon:

> Agencies in New Mexico are greatly concerned over these phenomena. They are of the opinion that some foreign power is making "sensing shots" with some superstratosphere device designed to be self disintegrating. . . . Another theory advanced as possibly acceptable lies in the belief that the phenomena are the result of radiological warfare experiments by a foreign power, further, that the rays may be lethal or might be attributed to the cause of the plane crashes that have occurred recently.
>
> Still another belief . . . is that it is highly probable that the United States may be carrying on some top secret experiments. . . . *It is felt that these incidents are of such great importance, especially as they are occurring in the vicinity of sensitive installations,* that a scientific board be sent to this locality to study the situation with a view of arriving at a solution of this extraordinary phenomena with the least practicable delay.[23]
> [Emphasis added]

On 16 February 1949 a secret conference was held at Los Alamos to discuss the UFO phenomena, in particular the so-called "green fireballs" which were then being reported in the area. Among the scientists and military officials present were the nuclear physicist Dr. Edward Teller and Dr. Lincoln LaPaz, an astronomer from the University of New Mexico whose expert opinion was called on throughout the conference. LaPaz was absolutely convinced that the green fireballs were not conventional fireballs or meteorites, and described his own sighting on 12 December 1948: "This fireball appeared in full intensity instantly—there was no increase in light. . . . Its color, estimated to be somewhere around wave length 5200 angstroms, was a hue green, such as I had never observed in meteor falls before. The path was as nearly horizontal as one could determine by visual observation. . . . Just before the end . . . the green fireball broke into fragments, still bright green." LaPaz also ruled out other unconventional types of meteors and fireballs, and left the conference in no doubt that the phenomena were unexplainable.[24]

On 27 and 28 April 1948, Dr. Joseph Kaplan, a member of the Air Force Scientific Advisory Board, visited Kirtland Air Force Base Office of Special Investigations, as well as the AEC's Sandia Base and Los Alamos, under orders from Dr. Theodore von Karman, Secretary of the Scientific Advisory Board. The purpose of the visits, a hitherto secret Air Force memorandum states, was to review the reports of investigations and the circumstances surrounding the "unidentified aerial phenomena" that had been observed in the area, and to make recommendations as to the advisability of a scientific investigation into the occurrences. Drs. Kaplan and LaPaz met with several security personnel at Los Alamos on 28 April, so that Kaplan could try to ascertain the nature of the UFO sightings that had been made there by members of the AEC project and AEC Security Service inspectors. He seems to have been impressed, and stated that he would immediately submit his report to Dr. von Karman: "Dr. Kaplan expressed a great concern, *as these occurrences relate to the National Defense of the United States.* He advised that he felt that this was of extreme importance and should be investigated scientifically."[25] [Emphasis added]

Yet another meeting was convened on 14 October 1949 to discuss the green fireball sightings, and along with the earlier delegates was attended by representatives of the 4th Army, Armed Forces Special Weapons Project, FBI, AEC, Geophysical Research Division of Air Matériel Command and the Air Force Office of Special Investigations. "A logical explanation was not proffered with respect to the origin of the green fireballs," an AFOSI confidential memo stated. "It was, however, generally concluded that the phenomena existed and that they should be studied scientifically until these occurrences have been satisfactorily explained. *Further, that the continued occurrence of unexplained phenom-*

ena of this nature in the vicinity of sensitive installations is cause for concern."[26] [Emphasis added]

Of the US Army Intelligence (G-2) representatives present, it is possible that some included members of the Interplanetary Phenomenon Unit (IPU) of the Scientific and Technical Branch, Counterintelligence Directorate, an elite UFO investigation group allegedly set up by General Marshall in 1947 and disbanded in the 1950s. According to Colonel William Guild, Director of Counterintelligence, "All records pertaining to this unit were surrendered to the US Air Force Office of Special Investigations in conjunction with operation 'BLUEBOOK.' "[27] AFOSI have not released these records to date. Did the Interplanetary Phenomenon Unit learn some disturbing facts that still cannot be revealed? In 1955 General Douglas MacArthur—also rumored to have been involved in establishing the IPU—made an astonishing statement that lends weight to this possibility. "The nations of the world will have to unite," he said, "for the next war will be an interplanetary war. The nations of the earth must someday make a common front against attack by people from other planets."[28]

At weekly conferences of the Army, Air Force, FBI and Naval Intelligence in early 1949, the maximum security attached to the UFO problem was reaffirmed, as a contemporary FBI document reveals: ". . . the matter of 'Unidentified Aircraft' or 'Unidentified Aerial Phenomena,' otherwise known as 'Flying Disks,' 'Flying Saucers,' and 'Balls of Fire' . . . *is considered top secret by Intelligence Officers of both the Army and the Air Forces.*"[29]

Intrusions continued to be reported over nuclear installations and on some occasions led to interception by Air Force jets, as this Army memorandum from Major U. G. Carlan, based on information provided him by Lieutenant Colonel Mildren, confirms:

Since 30 July 1950 objects, round in form, have been sighted over the Hanford AEC Plant. These objects reportedly were above 15,000 feet in altitude. Air Force jets attempted interception with negative results. All units including the antiaircraft battalion, radar units, Air Force fighter squadrons, and the Federal Bureau of Investigation have been alerted for further observation. The Atomic Energy Commission states that the investigation is continuing and complete details will be forwarded later.

The CIA was equally concerned. A secret 1952 report, referring to "Sightings of UFOs reported at Los Alamos and Oak Ridge, at a time when the background radiation count had risen inexplicably," concluded with the following admission: "Here we run out of even 'blue yonder' explanations that might be tenable, and, we are still left with numbers of incredible reports from credible observers."[30]

In February 1949 Professor George E. Valley, a consulting member of the Air Force Scientific Advisory Board, in offering some possible explanations for the sightings which he proposed in a secret report for Project Sign (or Project Saucer), probably came close to the truth:

> If there is an extraterrestrial civilization which can make such objects as are reported then it is most probable that its development is far in advance of ours. This argument can be supported on probability arguments alone without recourse to astronomical hypotheses.
>
> Such a civilization might observe that on earth we now have atomic bombs and are fast developing rockets. In view of the past history of mankind, they should be alarmed. *We should, therefore, expect at this time above all to behold such visitations.*[31] [Emphasis added]

UFOS ENCOUNTERED BY MILITARY AIRCRAFT, 1951

One of a number of reports relating to near collisions with unidentified flying objects was made by US Naval Reserve Lieutenant Graham Bethune, co-pilot on Flight 125 from Keflavik, Iceland, on 10 February 1951. "While flying in the left seat on a true course of 230 degrees at a position of 49–50 North 50–03 West, I observed a glow of light below the horizon about 1,000 to 1,500 feet above the water," Bethune stated in the official report. He continued:

> We both observed its course and motion for about 4 or 5 minutes before calling it to the attention of the other crew members. . . . Suddenly its angle of attack changed, its altitude and size increased as though its speed was in excess of 1,000 miles per hour. It closed in so fast that the first feeling was we would collide in midair. At this time its angle changed and the color changed. It then [appeared] definitely circular and reddish orange on its perimeter. It reversed its course and tripled its speed until it was last seen disappearing over the horizon. Because of our altitude and misleading distance over water it is almost impossible to estimate its size, distance and speed. A rough estimate would be at least 300 feet in diameter, over 1,000 miles per hour in speed and approached to within 5 miles of the aircraft.[32]

In 1956 the US Navy reportedly issued orders to its pilots to engage UFOs in combat if the objects appeared hostile. Operational procedures for a "UFO scramble," given by a briefing officer to pilots at the Los

Alamitos Naval Air Station in California, were highly classified, and most officers there refused to discuss the matter when pressed by journalists.[33]

One of the many US Air Force Intelligence reports now released (currently totaling about 1,800 pages) describes an encounter by Major Ballard and Lieutenant Rogers, of the 148th Fighter Interceptor Squadron, on a training flight in a Lockheed T-33 from Dover Air Force Base, Delaware, on 10 September 1951. Having observed an unidentified object over Sandy Hook, New Jersey, the pilots immediately made a diving turn and followed the object until it disappeared two minutes later:

> Both pilots observed the strange object, which appeared to be the size of an F-86 [Sabre] but much faster (900+ mph), disk-shaped, steady in flight with no visible means of propulsion, and shining silver in color.
>
> At 1100 EDT a radar station at Ft. Monmouth plotted an unidentified, high speed (above 700 mph) object in approximately the same location.
>
> This headquarters has no information regarding natural phenomena, experimental aircraft or guided missiles that could have caused the observations.[34]

THE JULY 1952 FLAP

A massive build-up of sightings over the United States in 1952, culminating in July, caused considerable alarm in military intelligence circles. One such sighting was reported by First Officer William Nash and Second Officer W. H. Fortenberry, flying in a DC-4 of Pan American Airways en route from New York to San Juan on 14 July.

At 9:12 p.m. six glowing disks approached at fantastic speed a mile below the airliner, in the vicinity of Langley AFB, Virginia. The objects appeared to be about 100 feet in diameter and were flying in echelon formation. The leading disk, apparently having sighted the DC-4, slowed down abruptly, then the next two disks "wobbled" momentarily, after which all six UFOs "flipped up on edge," enabling the pilots to estimate their thickness at about fifteen feet. The objects then accelerated away but once again lined up in their original position in echelon formation, and a strange glow around them increased as they performed this maneuver. Two other disks then appeared under the DC-4, glowing brightly as they joined the six ahead. All the disks suddenly darkened, but glowed again when eight objects appeared in line. Finally, the disks climbed to high altitude and disappeared, at a speed computed by the pilots to be 200 miles per minute.[35]

On landing at Miami the crew was interviewed by the Air Force Office of Special Investigations. A declassified Air Force cable, briefly describing these events, was distributed to Army and Navy intelligence, as well as the Armed Forces Security Agency (a forerunner of the National Security Agency), the Joint Chiefs of Staff, and the CIA.[36]

On the night of 19/20 July UFOs were seen all over Washington, DC, by the crews of several airliners, and were tracked on radar at Andrews AFB as well as Air Traffic Control Center at Washington National Airport. Sometimes the unidentified targets would hover, cruise along at 100–130 mph, then accelerate to fantastic speeds. But, as Captain Ruppelt drily commented, no one bothered to inform Air Force Intelligence about the sightings, even though jets had been sent aloft to investigate, and the first they got to hear about it was when a headline story appeared the following morning![37]

A week later, on the night of 26 July, UFOs again hovered and described a series of maneuvers over the nation's capital, and were tracked on radar at Washington National Airport and Andrews AFB. The following USAF Intelligence report (released in 1985) describes these extraordinary events:

Varying numbers (up to 12 simultaneously) of u/i [unidentified] targets on ARTC [Air Route Traffic Control Center, Washington National Airport] radarscope. Termed by CAA personnel as "generally, solid returns," similar to a/c [aircraft] return except slower. No definable pattern of maneuver except at very beginning about 2150 EDT, 4 targets in rough line abreast with 1½ mile spacing moved slowly together (giving about a 1″ trace persisting at an estimated speed of less than 100 mph) on heading of 110. At the same time 8 other targets were scattered throughout scope.

ARTC checked Andrews Approach Control by telephone at 2200 EDT and ascertained that they were also picking up u/i targets. U/i returns were picked up intermittently until about 27/0100 EDT, following which weak and sporadic (unsteady) returns were picked up intermittently for another 3¼ hours. Washington National Tower radar crew reports only one target positively u/i. This return was termed a "very good target" which moved across the scope from West to East at about 30 to 40 mph. However, the radar operators stated that there could have been other u/i targets on their scopes, particularly outside their area of a/c control, which they would not have noticed or would have assumed to be a/c under ARTC Center Control. However, they noticed no other unusual (i.e. very slow or erratic) returns.

ARTC Center controllers also report that a CAA flight inspector, Mr. Bill Schreve, flying a/c # NC-12 reported at 2246 EDT that he had visually spotted 5 objects giving off a light glow ranging from orange to white; his altitude at times was 2200′. Some commercial pilots reported visuals from

"cigarette glow" (red-yellow) to "a light" (as recorded from their conversations with ARTC controllers).

At 2238 EDT the USAF Command Post was notified of ARTC targets.
Command Post notified ADC and KADF at 2245, and 2 F-94's were
scrambled from Newcastle at 2300 EDT. ARTC controlled F-94's after
arrival in area and vectored them to targets with generally negative results
(flew through "a batch of radar returns" without spotting anything). However, one pilot mentioned seeing 4 lights at one time and a second time
as seeing a single light ahead but unable to close whereupon "went out"
(these comments from ARTC controller). One ARTC controller worked a
USAF B-25 . . . for about 1 hr 20 mins about 2230 EDT. B-25 was vectored
in on numerous targets and commented that each vector took him over a
busy highway or intersection.

Maj. Fournet (AFOIN-2A2) and Lt. Holcomb (USN, AFOIN-2C5) arrived at ARTC Center about 27/0015 EDT. Lt. Holcomb observed scopes
and reported "7 good, solid targets." He made a quick check with airport
Weather Station and determined that there was a slight temperature inversion (about 1°) from the surface to about 1000'. *However, he felt that
the scope targets at that time were not the results of this inversion* and so
advised the Command Post with the suggestion that a second intercept
flight be requested. (2nd intercept flight controlled by ARTC, but no strong
targets remained when they arrived. They were vectored on dim targets
with negative results.) Maj. Fournet and Lt. Holcomb remained in ARTC
Center until 0415, but no additional strong targets were picked up: many
dim and unstable targets (assumed due to temperature inversion) were
observed throughout the remainder of the period. . . .

All ARTC crew members emphatic that most u/i returns were "solid."
Finally, it was mentioned that u/i returns have been picked up from time
to time over the past few months *but never before had they appeared in
such quantities over such a prolonged period and with such definition as
was experienced on the night of 26/27 July 52.* [Emphasis added]

The sightings made headline news throughout the world, but were
promptly explained by the Air Force as having been caused by the temperature inversion.[38] Behind the scenes, however, a number of intelligence analysts felt that the UFOs might not be of terrestrial origin. An
FBI memorandum written a few days later, relating to a briefing from
Commander Boyd of the Current Intelligence Branch, Estimates Division,
Air Intelligence, regarding the status of research into the matter, confirms
that Boyd

advised that the objects sighted may possibly be from another planet . . .
[but] that at the present time there is nothing to substantiate this theory
but the possibility is not being overlooked. He stated that Air Intelligence
is fairly certain that these objects are not ships or missiles from another
nation in this world. Commander Boyd advised that intense research is

being carried out by Air Intelligence, and at the present time when credible reportings of sightings are received, the Air Force is attempting in each instance to send up jet interceptor planes in order to obtain a better view of these objects.[39]

AIR FORCE JET ATTEMPTS TO SHOOT DOWN A UFO

It was not just a case of sending Air Force planes aloft to get a closer look, and film UFOs when possible. Captain Edward Ruppelt, Chief of the Aerial Phenomena Branch at Air Technical Intelligence Center, and former head of the Air Force's Project Blue Book, reported that in one instance in the summer of 1952 an Air Force jet attempted to shoot down one of the flying saucers.

On a certain morning (no date is given) a radarscope near a certain Air Force base picked up an unknown target that approached at 700 mph, then slowed down to a point northeast of the airfield. Two F-86 Sabre jets were scrambled but at first were unable to locate the target. The second pilot suddenly spotted what at first he took to be a balloon, but a closer view showed that it was definitely saucer-shaped, "like a doughnut without a hole." He began chasing the object and got as close as 500 yards away when it began to accelerate. When it was at a range of 1,000 yards (the machine gun bullets converge at 1,300 yards) he began firing at the target, but it pulled up into a climb and disappeared in seconds.

Ruppelt was given this report by an intelligence officer at the base, who said that he had been ordered to burn all copies, but had saved one.[40]

It is fortunate that the pilot lived to tell the story. Others have not been so lucky. General Benjamin Chidlaw, former Commanding General of Air Defense Command, told researcher Robert Gardner in 1953: "We have stacks of reports of flying saucers. We take them seriously when you consider *we have lost many men and planes trying to intercept them.*"[41] If there is any truth to this statement, then the authorities have perfectly understandable reasons for withholding the facts about UFOs from the public.

There are few hints of such disturbing facts in the released Air Force Intelligence reports. Many such reports, especially those classified as top secret or higher, remain classified on the grounds that their release would compromise national security. But I do have a document that relates to a possible collision with an unidentified object—an emergency cable sent to the Director of Intelligence at Air Force HQ, dated 26 June 1953:

FLYING OBJECTS WERE SIGHTED BY PILOTS AT APPROX 2130E 24 JUNE PD
TWO JET OUT OF QUONSET POINT HAS [HAD] A MID AIR COLLISION AT 2130E

24 JUNE 53 AIRCRAFT FELL IN FLAMES 15 MILES WEST OF QUONSET POINT
MAS PD AMERICAN AND EASTERN AIRLINES PILOTS WHO REPORTED FLYING
OBJECT WILL SUBMIT ON SIGHTING TO DIR INTELLIGENCE HQ USAF AND
TECH INTELLIGENCE CENTER WRIGHT PATTERSON AFB.

Whether the collision *was* due to an interception of a UFO may never
be known, but it is evident that the incident caused considerable consternation, and the distribution list for the emergency cable included the
CIA, Joint Chiefs of Staff, and the National Security Agency (established
in 1952).

AIR FORCE JET DISAPPEARS WHILE INTERCEPTING A

UFO, 1953

One of the Air Force's most frightening cases that *did* involve an apparent
collision with an unidentified object took place later in 1953. On the
evening of 23 November an Air Defense Command Ground Control
Intercept controller was alerted by the presence of an unidentified and
unscheduled target on his radarscope in the vicinity of Soo Locks, Michigan. An F-89C Scorpion jet was immediately scrambled from Kinross
AFB, piloted by Lieutenant Felix Moncla, Jr., and his observer, Lieutenant R. R. Wilson, in the rear seat.

The GCI controller vectored the F-89 to the target, and noted that the
UFO changed course as the plane approached at over 500 mph. Nine
minutes went by. Gradually the F-89 closed the gap and the controller
advised the men that the target should now be in sight. Suddenly the two
blips on the GCI radarscope merged into one, as if they had collided.
For a moment a single blip remained on the scope but then disappeared.
Marking the position, the controller flashed an emergency message to
Search and Rescue. Possibly Moncla and Wilson had managed to bail
out in time—possibly not.

After an all-night air/sea rescue search, not a trace of wreckage or the
missing men was found. An Air Force press release stated tersely:
". . . The plane was followed by radar until it merged with an object
seventy miles off Keweenaw Point in upper Michigan." The incident has
never been satisfactorily explained.[42]

AIR FORCE JET PILOTS FILM UFOS, 1953–54

During a research trip to the United States in 1976 I had the good fortune
to interview a former Air Force lieutenant who together with other pilots

succeeded in obtaining movie films of UFOs in 1953 and 1954. "Mel Noel" (pseudonym) was twenty years old when he was assigned to a reserve squadron at Lowry AFB, Colorado, and selected for special photo reconnaissance missions to film UFOs.

Prior to the missions Mel Noel and the other pilots were given briefings by Colonel Peterson, who had been assigned to the operation unit from Washington, DC, and acted as flight leader for the missions, of which there were seventy-three in all. The pilots were instructed in the specific aerial maneuvers, weave patterns, and formation flying that would be required in the event UFOs were encountered. They were also warned of certain effects that might influence their F-86A Sabre jets: these included the loss of silicon-damping instruments—airspeed indicator, altimeter, rate-of-climb indicator, and to some extent the gyrocompass—as well as malfunction of the magnetic compass. They were told that there would be no adverse effect on the engine or hydraulic control systems. A high level of radio static could also be expected, they were warned.

The briefings also included the showing of several hours of movie films that had been taken by military pilots, and hundreds of still photographs, *many of which had been confiscated from civilians*, Mel told me.

The pilots were skeptical about the whole business and were convinced they would see nothing. The first few missions were "orientation runs" during which the pilots tightened up their formation flying in different conditions. The initial sighting, in December 1953, was announced by one of the pilots as they were flying at 38,000 feet and 680 knots over the Rocky Mountains in Idaho: "BOGIES AT 9 O'CLOCK LEVEL!"

From Mel's position in the echelon formation he was at first unable to see anything. On sighting a target the formation had been instructed to close in—sixty feet from wing tip to wing tip. "I was not allowed to move from my position until Lee called the move, and from my position that I would go from would be from right wing into the slot, and form a diamond, which means moving in between number two and three aircraft and behind and below number one's position, at which times when I dropped back I could see them out there."

Sixteen saucer-shaped objects, in a vertical "V" formation—seven aloft and nine aft—were flying parallel to the F-86s, at roughly the same speed. Then the formation broke into four groups of four. I asked Mel to describe the objects for me. "There was a form of—an extension on top. I wouldn't call it a cupola, but there was some extension," he said. "We didn't have a crystal-clear image: the only time we had the best outline was when they stopped. There is no deceleration to stop," he explained. "It's just that you're looking, and then you look back, and it's obvious that they have ceased forward motion. And at that time the outline was sharpest, but there was still some haze around them—a silver-gray haze." They were 150–180 feet in diameter and 30–40 feet thick. When the objects accelerated, the haze, or "corona" effect changed color. "It was just like it was going through the colors of the spectrum," Mel said. "You could see it going through the yellows, the oranges, the reds and so forth."

The objects were in sight for a total of eight minutes. Despite the briefing on the effects that should be expected, there was only slight compass malfunction. The pilots had also been warned not to cross the path of the objects, because this had sometimes resulted in damage to *or loss of aircraft*.

Each of the F-86s' six 50-caliber machine guns had been replaced with gun cameras, some with standard film and others with infra-red film. But on the first encounter the pilots assumed that they were unsuccessful in obtaining any film as the cameras were automatically calibrated to trigger at 1,300 yards ahead of the aircraft. "It was our opinion that we never *did* have them at 1,300 yards," Mel told me. "They were everywhere but!"

The cameras, magazines, and all instrumentation were replaced on landing, and the aircraft were given a complete check. "They talked about scanning them for radioactivity—none being found—and this type of thing," Mel said. All four aircraft were always replaced with another four jets following the missions.

"*The second time we got a lot of film*," Mel said. Two weeks later five objects, similar in type to the first group, were seen. The pilots had asked for the gun-cameras to be triggered manually.

We said, "Take it off the sights. There's no way we can get those things at 1,300 yards and lock them there for any length of time." So, on manual, we could of course run the film any time we wanted to. And the cameras fired 1,100 frames a minute, and that's six cameras per airplane, so you're talking about 6,600 frames per minute capability per airplane, so you've got pretty good movement definition. You can tell exactly the size: they can triangulate pretty well with that many cameras. You're talking about—hopefully—a minimum of 12 cameras bearing on a target simultaneously, and that's going to give you some triangulation, depending on the separation of the aircraft.

What happened to the film? I asked. *"We never saw the film. All we knew was that it was always taken to Wright-Pat [Wright-Patterson AFB] or some place else for evaluation."*

Mel and the other pilots began worrying about the possibility of harmful effects on their bodies. If the UFOs could influence the aircraft's instruments, why not the pilots too? "There's something affecting those instruments, and there's something that's pretty strong," Mel said. "What are the physiological effects of this? Are we going to come out of this thing being some babbling idiots, or are we going to start getting the shakes after a few months and so forth, you know?"

Following the third encounter, in 1954, when another five objects were sighted and filmed, the pilots returned to Mountain Home AFB, Idaho, suffering from effects similar to combat fatigue:

This was a matter of maybe thirty minutes after the experience, and we were on the ground coming apart, which is a reaction trigger saying, "Hey, the next time we may come apart *in* the airplane: we may not be able to get on the ground and do it!"

We said, "Give us an Article 15, give us a Section 8 [psychiatric unit], we don't care what it is, but we're not psychologically ready—we're not prepared for this thing, and you're going to be interrogating some dead pilots pretty soon, so get us off this thing!" And they listened, and they let us off. Four days later we got the papers. And that was the end of it.

The pilots were warned at each debriefing following the encounters not to discuss the matter with anyone. This point was driven home more emphatically after the third encounter. "They repeatedly enforced the penalties—JANAP 146 [Joint Army Navy Air Force Publication] Section III—the 10 years in jail, $10,000 fine, and all this kind of stuff," Mel said. "They let us know that was real; that they wouldn't hesitate to enforce that."

Eight years later Mel Noel was encouraged to talk about the experiences publicly, using his pseudonym, having taken legal advice on the matter. The Statute of Limitations normally prohibits those in the military from revealing certain information for ten years, but Mel and his lawyer decided to take the risk and go ahead. Just before his going on one radio show in Washington, DC, Mel told me, a couple of men came up to him:

They showed these credentials—they were CIA—and they said, "This is a Cease and Desist directive . . . because what you're saying is disconcerting to the public's ears." And I said, "Well, I'm not saying anything but fact.'' ''That isn't the point. To continue could be detrimental to your health.'' They had intimidated me, but I didn't want to give them the satisfaction of knowing that they'd done that. But I did do the broadcast, wondering if they'd be there afterward, which they weren't. And then I didn't say anything for quite a while.

There is a great deal more that I learned from Mel Noel during my lengthy interview with him on 22 August 1976, but most of the information is outside the scope of this book.[43] Suffice to say that there is no doubt in my mind that Mel was describing genuine encounters with UFOs, and his knowledge of aircraft and flying is beyond dispute. Since leaving the Air Force, Mel has continued to fly different types of aircraft in his capacity as a commercial pilot. He has also done a great deal of research into UFOs, sometimes in association with his friend Gordon Cooper, the ex-astronaut and Air Force pilot.

In a statement read at the United Nations on 27 November 1978, Cooper revealed that he had encountered UFOs over Germany in 1951: ''Several days in a row we sighted groups of metallic, saucer-shaped vehicles at great altitudes over the base and we tried to get close to them, but they were able to change direction faster than our fighters. I do believe UFOs exist and that the truly unexplained ones are from some other technically advanced civilization.''[44]

As with Mel Noel, Gordon Cooper's testimony will be dismissed by the skeptics and debunkers, who maintain that *all* such incidents can be explained in terms of misperceptions or hoaxes. But the fact remains that literally *hundreds* of reports of close encounters have now been made by American military and civilian pilots which simply cannot be dismissed so easily. I do not insist that *every* UFO reported is an extraterrestrial spacecraft: some can probably be explained in terms of meteorological and astronomical phenomena, balloons, rockets, guided missiles, aircraft, remotely piloted vehicles (RPVs), satellite and rocket re-entries into the atmosphere, and so on. Pilots are not infallible, but their responsible and qualified status places them in the highest category of witness reliability. Furthermore, pilots have absolutely nothing to gain from filing a UFO report. On the contrary, they have much to lose.

12

COLLISION COURSE
1950s Onward

The United States continued to be plagued by sightings of unidentified aerial intruders, and many intelligence reports were forwarded immediately to the Joint Chiefs of Staff, the CIA, and the National Security Agency, which gives some indication of the degree of official concern, despite statements to the contrary. One such report was made from the ground by a GOC (Ground Observer Corps) observer in San Rafael, California, on 28 August 1953:

> FOURTEEN CIGAR SHAPED OBJECTS WITHOUT WINGS WITH . . . LIGHTS ON THEM IN LOOSE V FORMATION. ABOUT THE SIZE OF A BI-MOTOR . . . ACFT. NO SOUND OR MEANS OF PROPULSION OBSERVED. ONE OBJECT APPEARED TO BE LEADING THE FORMATION AT AN ESTIMATED SPEED OF 200 MPH. . . . OBJECTS WERE FIRST OBSERVED HEADING WEST . . . THROUGH BREAKS IN THE CLOUDS. THEN OBJECTS APPEARED TO TURN AND HEAD NORTH DISAPPEARING BEHIND CLOUDS. . . . OBSERVER APPEARED TO BE RELIABLE AND HAS BEEN AN OBSERVER ON DUTY WITH GOC FOR SEV YEARS DURING WWII AND DURING POST WAR YEARS.[1]

Debunkers such as Dr. Donald Menzel went to great lengths to explain away all UFO reports in terms of hallucinations, misidentifications, and hoaxes. I have alluded to the involvement of Menzel with the Majestic-12 group, set up in 1947, and in a letter to Major General Samford, Air Force Director of Intelligence and later Director of the NSA (1956–60), Menzel stated: "I am planning to be in Washington on government business . . . October 22 and 23 [1953] . . . From various reports I judge that some of my explanations of flying saucers have been misinterpreted or misunderstood. . . . I should be delighted to meet with as many members of ATIC [Air Technical Intelligence Center] as find it convenient to come."[2] What was the astronomer's "government business"? Had Menzel's debunking statements gone too far for those in Air Force Intelligence circles who were convinced that genuinely anomalous reports existed for which rational explanations were redundant?

A meeting was arranged for Menzel at the Pentagon on 22 October with representatives of Air Force Headquarters and ATIC. Two months later, the Air Force HQ representative Colonel George Perry of the Directorate of Intelligence, in a letter to Brigadier General W. M. Burgess, Deputy for Intelligence, Air Defense Command (ADC), made some interesting comments regarding the new responsibilities of ADC as they related to the reporting of sightings:

> In your new function in the Unidentified Flying Object Program, it is our understanding that your 4602nd people will do the "leg work" so to speak, and furnish ATIC with its findings. For those types that cannot be identified by your Squadron, ATIC will handle an exploratory point of view.
>
> Many times the publicity connected with this program has been somewhat embarrassing, in that we are dealing with a subject, parts of which are not explainable, and the public feeling is that we are holding back information they should know about. . . .
>
> As you realize, there is a 10–20% area of unexplained objects in this program . . . we would like to offer you guidance in the publicity angle as it pertains to your activity.
>
> We think it would be well for your 4602nd people in the ZI [Interior Zone], to discuss a particular sighting with the public or press, anytime the object can be identified. Meaning, if they can verify the object as a balloon, aircraft, helicopter, etc., go ahead and inform interested parties. However, for those times where the object is *not explainable*, it would be well to advise your people to say something on this order, "The information on this sighting will be analyzed by the Air Technical Intelligence Center at Dayton, Ohio," and leave it go at that. If your people get into analyzing the 10–20% area to the public, every news media across the country will pick up the story.[3] [Emphasis in original]

Here is further proof that the Air Force hierarchy, embarrassed by the UFO phenomenon, sought to play down the unexplainable sightings. Colonel Perry's recommendations were approved and adopted as official Air Force policy, as we shall see.

AIR FORCE REGULATIONS FOR REPORTING UFOS, 1954

In his letter to Brigadier General Burgess, Colonel Perry alluded to the functions of the 4602nd Air Intelligence Service Squadron, which, according to Air Force Regulation 200-2, comprised specialists trained for field collection and investigation of matters of air intelligence interest within the Interior Zone. The squadron's headquarters were at Peterson Field, Colorado, adjacent to Air Defense Command HQ. The 4602nd

AISS was highly mobile: flights were attached to air defense divisions and detachments were attached to each of the defense forces.

All information on UFO sightings was to be reported promptly, the method (electrical in most cases) and priority of dispatch to be selected in accordance with the apparent intelligence value of the report. Electrical reports were to be multiple-addressed to the Commander, Air Defense Command; the nearest Air Defense Division; the Commander, Air Technical Intelligence Center; and the Director of Intelligence at Air Force HQ. In some cases, such reports were forwarded to the CIA and NSA, although there is no mention of this in Air Force Regulation 200-2; not surprisingly, since these agencies took care not to publicize their interest in the phenomenon except to those with a "need to know." Furthermore, the very existence of the National Security Agency was a closely guarded secret, and remained so for many years.

AFR 200-2, dated 12 August 1954 and signed by General Nathan Twining, Chief of Staff and a member of the MJ-12 panel, as well as Colonel K. E. Thiebaud, Air Adjutant General, concluded with the following statement, under the heading "Release of Facts":

> Headquarters USAF will release summaries of evaluated data which will inform the public on this subject. In response to local inquiries, it is permissible to inform news media representatives on UFOB's when the object is positively identified as a familiar object. . . . *For those objects which are not explainable, only the fact that ATIC will analyze the data is worthy of release, due to the many unknowns involved.* [Emphasis added]

SIGHTINGS ABOVE FORT MEADE, 1953–54

On 7 December 1953, according to Army Intelligence records, Private First Class Alfred de Bonise and Sergeant First Class James Conley sighted an unidentified object directly above the Headquarters Battery, 89th AAA Battalion, at Fort George C. Meade, Maryland, where the National Security Agency (established in 1952) was later sited.

At 2130 hours the witnesses' attention was drawn to an object which made a noise that "resembled the sound of an artillery shell in flight. The sound was not like that of an airplane or a truck. There were no further sounds after the initial whirring noise," the report states, and adds: "The object was white and shining 'like a star.' It appeared to be large, very high, and shaped like a round ashtray. It moved with an erratic motion, eventually fading out of sight in a northeasterly direction. De Bonise and Conley observed the object for about twenty minutes."[4]

At 2211 hours on 29 April 1954, an unidentified illuminated object was observed above the Second Army Radio Station, Fort Meade, by the Supervisor Radio Operator and two co-workers, Corporal Flath and Private First Class Hough. Described as round in shape, the color of the sun, and three or four times the size of a large star, the object appeared out of the sky from the southwest at an undetermined speed. "The light emitted by the object was blinking on and off as the object moved across the sky in a straight path," the report states. "When it got above the Second Army Radio Station it stopped blinking and started to disappear by going straight up and becoming smaller in size." The entire sighting lasted for seven minutes. Eastern Air Defense Command as well as Army Intelligence were notified.[5]

Army personnel had strict orders not to discuss their sightings with unauthorized parties, as the following order, signed by Colonel Charles L. Odin, Chief of Staff, shows: "Persons involved in sightings will not discuss or disseminate such information to persons or agencies other than their superior officer(s) and other personnel authorized by the Acting Chief of Staff, G-2, this headquarters."[6]

MYSTERY AIRCRAFT, 1954

In the Prologue I refer to the many reports of mysterious unidentified aircraft—as opposed to disks, cigars, and so on—seen over Scandinavia and, to a lesser extent, the US and Britain in the 1930s. These bizarre sightings have continued to be reported over the years, and I am convinced that the intelligences responsible for UFOs are able either to construct facsimiles of our own aircraft or to manifest themselves in such a way that we are duped into believing they are conventional aircraft, presumably for purposes of subterfuge.

One Air Force Intelligence report that describes an exceptionally well documented sighting of a strange aircraft occurred directly over Carswell AFB, Texas, at approximately 2300 hours on 4 February 1954, in full view of the control tower personnel. The object was first detected by Carswell Ground Control Approach (GCA) Station at a distance of thirteen to fifteen miles, and showed up as a one-inch return on the radarscope at a distance of ten miles. Because the object was approaching the airfield, the GCA operator notified the Airdrome Officer of the Day as well as the control tower.

The object passed directly over the Carswell tower at 3–4,000 feet, observed by all the tower personnel, and was described as having a long fuselage, elliptical wings, and a stabilizer, but with no visible means of propulsion. No sound could be detected. The aircraft had a very bright light in the nose and tail, and two yellowish lights on the bottom of the fuselage. One observer thought he could see a light on each wing tip. The tower operator kept the object under surveillance with standard Air Force binoculars throughout the observation.

Subsequent investigations revealed that no local aircraft were responsible, and that there was "no unusual activity, meteorological, astronomical, or otherwise, that could contribute to [the] sighting." The witnesses (all named) were described as "completely reliable," and as to the content of the report, "probably true." The Joint Chiefs of Staff, the CIA and the NSA were included in the distribution list.[7]

NEAR COLLISIONS WITH AIRLINERS, 1953–57

At midnight on 19 October 1953 an American Airlines DC-6 en route to Washington, DC, was buzzed by a UFO over Conowingo Dam, Maryland. The object appeared to be heading toward the airliner on a collision course, so Captain J. L. Kidd threw the plane into a dive as the UFO streaked overhead and disappeared. Several passengers were thrown into the aisle and Captain Kidd radioed to Washington Airport for ambulances and doctors. The UFO was as large as the DC-6, the crew affirmed. Checks by civil aviation authorities showed that no other aircraft within a 100-mile radius were near the airliner.[8]

An even more serious incident took place on the night of 14 April 1954 when Captain J. M. Schidel of United Airlines Flight 193 was forced to make a sharp climbing turn in order to avoid colliding with an unknown object over Long Beach, California. One passenger was thrown to the floor, breaking a leg, and a stewardess fractured her ankle. "It was in sight just two seconds and made no movement to avoid me," said Schidel. No other known aircraft were in the vicinity at the time.[9]

On 9 March 1957 the Civil Aeronautics Board received a "Flash" message from Miami Air Traffic Control:

DOUGLAS 6A PAA FLIGHT 257. TO AVOID UNIDENTIFIED FLYING OBJECT TRAVELING EAST TO WEST, PILOT TOOK VIOLENT EVASIVE ACTION. OBJECT APPEARED TO HAVE A BRILLIANT GREENISH-WHITE CENTER WITH AN OUTER RING WHICH REFLECTED THE GLOW FROM THE CENTER. . . . ABOVE DESCRIPTION FITS WHAT SEVEN OTHER FLIGHTS SAW. . . . MIAMI REPORTS NO MISSILE ACTIVITY. . . . ORIGINAL REPORTS OF JET ACTIVITY DISCOUNTED.[10]

The airliner was piloted by Captain Matthew Van Winkle, and the sighting took place at 0330 hours, 150 miles east of Jacksonville, Florida. Several passengers were injured and the plane was met by ambulances at San Juan.[11]

On 17 July 1957, Flight 655 en route from Dallas to Los Angeles with Captain E. Bachner at the controls had a near miss with an object "at least the size of a B-47," 100 miles east of El Paso, Texas. Two passengers suffered slight injuries and had to be taken to hospital on landing. No known aircraft were in the vicinity at the time.[12]

AIRLINE PILOTS AFFECTED BY MILITARY

REGULATIONS

Because of reports like these—and there were many others—airline pilots became subject to military restrictions contained in a Joint Army–Navy–Air Force Publication (JANAP), drawn up by the Joint Communications-Electronics Committee and promulgated by the Joint Chiefs of Staff, and could thus find themselves liable to a prison term of up to ten years and/or a fine of $10,000 if they discussed their sightings with the media or public. These restrictions were first imposed during a conference between airline representatives and intelligence officers of the Military Air Transport Service (MATS) in Los Angeles on 17 February 1954.[13]

JANAP 146 relates to Communication Instructions for Reporting Vital Intelligence Sightings (CIRVIS), and unidentified flying objects are listed separately from aircraft and missiles. Under Section III (Security—Military and Civilian), is the following warning:

> All persons aware of the contents of a CIRVIS report are governed by the Communications Act of 1934 and amendments thereto, and Espionage Laws. CIRVIS reports contain information affecting the National Defense of the United States within the meaning of the Espionage Laws, 18 U.S. Code, 793 and 794. The unauthorized transmission or revelation of the contents of CIRVIS reports in any manner is prohibited.[14]

Few pilots were affected by this regulation, however, although the airline companies discouraged public disclosure of sightings, sometimes threatening pilots with their jobs if they did so.

A CIRVIS report headed "Operational Immediate," dated 29 March

1954, gave brief details of a sighting by a United Airlines plane, confirmed by another airliner:

UNIDENTIFIED OBJECT GLOWING BRIGHT GREEN SIGHTED BY UAL-600 FLYING EASTBOUND AT 19 THOUSAND FEET MEAN SEA LEVEL OVER A POINT 12 MILES EAST OF CHEROKEE WYOMING. OBJECT FIRST AP-PEARED 12 TO 15 DEGREES ABOVE HORIZON AND 100 DEGREES TRUE FROM OBSERVATION POINT AND DISAPPEARED BEHIND CLOUD BANK SLANTING DOWNWARD 30 DEGREES TO LEFT OF VERTICAL. TIME OF OBSERVATION 280125M. DURATION 5 SECONDS . . . CAPTAIN SPERRY, UAL-600, CONFIRMED BY CO-PILOT, CONFIRMED BY PILOT N28392 DC3 5 MILES WEST OF SINCLAIR WYOMING AT 13 THOUSAND FEET . . . SAME TIME OF OBSERVATION . . . THIS MESSAGE HAS BEEN RELAYED TO CIA BY ELECTRICAL MEANS.

As with many intelligence reports dating from 1953, the NSA (in this case the Director—or DIRNSA) was on the distribution list, thus proving this Agency's long-denied involvement with the UFO phenomenon.

In December 1958, 450 airline pilots signed a petition protesting at the official policy of debunking sightings, which one pilot described as "a lesson in lying, intrigue, and the 'Big Brother' attitude carried to the ultimate extreme." No less than fifty of the pilots had reported sightings, only to be told by the Air Force that they had been mistaken. At the same time the pilots had been warned that they faced up to ten years in prison (under JANAP 146) if they revealed details of their sightings to the media![15]

Following a sighting by Captain Peter Killian and his crew, as well as thirty-five passengers aboard an American Airlines DC-6 over Penn-sylvania on 24 February 1959, the Air Force issued three separate and contradictory explanations for the incident, without having interviewed any of the witnesses. After Killian exposed these contradictions in news-paper interviews, American Airlines, succumbing to Air Force pressure, told Killian not to publicize the story any further. A senator asked Killian if he would be prepared to testify at a hearing in Washington. "Yes, I would," replied Killian, "*but you would have to subpoena me. Then I could talk.*"[16]

SIGHTING BY HELICOPTER PILOTS, 1954

Another CIRVIS report that was sent to the NSA Director is the following, headed "Emergency" and dated 12 August 1954, from the Flight Service Center, Maxwell AFB, Alabama, to the Commander of Air Defense

Command at Ent AFB, Colorado Springs (since 1953 the main receiving point for UFO reports by the military):

AT 120154Z TOWER OBSERVED AND REPORTED TO BASE OPERATIONS STRANGE STATIONARY OBJECT VARIABLE IN BRILLIANCE LOCATED WEST OF TOWER. AFTER INITIAL SIGHTING . . . IT UNEXPECTEDLY GAINED APPARENT VELOCITY AND SPEEDED ACROSS THE SKY IN NNW HEADING WHICH WAS FOLLOWED BY ITS RETURN TO ITS ORIGINAL POSITION IN RELATION TO THE TOWER AND A NOTICEABLE DESCENT AND MOTIONLESS. TOWER IMMEDIATELY NOTIFIED OPERATIONS AND DISPATCHED A LOCAL HELICOPTER NBR ARMY 267 TO OBSERVE THE PHENOMENA. HELICOPTER STATED THAT OBJECT WAS DEFINITELY NOT A STAR. . . .

AT 0156Z AIRDROME OFFICER AND DRIVER OBSERVED MYSTERY OB-JECT. . . . AT 0205Z TWO MEMBERS OF ALERT CREW OBSERVED OBJECT FROM TOWER. COLUMBUS CAA RADIO ALSO HAS OBJECT IN SIGHT. THE OBJECT THEN BECAME DIMMER AND SHOWING A SLIGHT RED GLOW. AT 0226Z OBJECT STILL STATIONARY. SEVERAL REOCCURRENCE OF VARIABLE BRILLIANCY SHOWN AND NOW BECOMING EXTREMELY DIMMER. 0227Z HELICOPTER 294 RETURNING FROM MISSION SIGHTED OBJECT AND PROCEEDED TOWARD IT. AT 0229Z OBJECT COMPLETELY DISAPPEARED AND . . . 294 LOST SIGHT OF IT. AT 0240Z ARMY OPERA-TIONS CALLED AND ADVISED THAT PILOT OF HELICOPTERS WISHED TO STRESS FACT THAT OBJECT WAS OF A SAUCER LIKE NATURE, WAS STATIONARY AND AT 2000 FT. AND WOULD BE GLAD TO BE CALLED UPON TO VERIFY ANY STATEMENTS AND ACT AS WITNESSES.

AIR FORCE SPECIAL SECURITY SERVICE, 1955

The Air Force Special Security Service (later the Air Force Electronic Security Command), the National Security Agency's air arm, reported some interesting incidents in June 1955 when UFOs were tracked by RB-47 aircraft. The second incident occurred on 4 June when visual and electronic contact with an unknown aircraft was made in the area of Melville Sound, Northwest Territories, Canada.

The crew were first alerted to the object when the aircraft's gun warning light flashed intermittently and the No. 5 radar registered a contact at 7,000 yards range. Visual contact was then made by the crew chief, who described the unknown aircraft as "glistening silver metallic." The object broke off contact to the north with an increase of speed. Although gun camera films were taken, the report states, they were of such poor quality that no useful information could be gleaned. The radar and visual contacts were maintained for a total of nine minutes.

On 7 June an RB-47 en route to Eilson AFB, Alaska, registered electronic contact southeast of Banks Island at 3,500 yards. "The [radar] scope return was small and rectangular [which] the pilot interpreted to be a form of jamming. The target warning light went on and off 3 times in as many minutes."[17]

The Boeing RB-47 was a medium-range reconnaissance aircraft that gathered photographic intelligence (PHOTINT) and electronic intelligence (ELINT) for analysis by the intelligence community, particularly the NSA. It had seven cameras that automatically photographed the ground track, and for ELINT several crews on board operated equipment that intercepted radio and radar signals.

This aircraft, like its successors, also engaged in quick-penetration sorties near potentially hostile borders (in the aforementioned case, the USSR) in order to deliberately trigger radar and radio alerts so that the operating frequencies could be determined and, in time of war, invading bombers could use this information to program their electronic countermeasures equipment (ECM) to jam or confuse enemy radar.[18] That UFOs are reported to have jammed and/or confused our radar systems in these cases, and radio/communications in others, is sufficient grounds, in my opinion, to warrant the close attention of the National Security Agency. World War III could be triggered by confusing UFOs with hostile aircraft or missiles, so it is small wonder that the NSA has been involved in monitoring UFO reports since 1953 (or even 1952).

TV CENSORSHIP, 1958

On 22 January 1958, CBS Television presented a program devoted to UFOs on its "Armstrong Circle Theater Show," and one of those invited to appear was Major Donald Keyhoe, Director of the National Investigations Committee on Aerial Phenomena (NICAP). Keyhoe had cultivated some excellent sources of information within military circles, and had frequently stated on the air—and in his books—that the US government was withholding the facts in order to avoid panic.

Several Air Force spokesmen were also scheduled to appear, but insisted on seeing Keyhoe's script in advance and asked for assurances that no "ad libs" would be permitted. Keyhoe was also told that he would be allotted seven minutes on the program, whereas the Air Force had been given twenty-five minutes air time. When Keyhoe's material was returned, all the salient points had been deleted on the grounds that the script was too long, despite the fact that he had carefully timed it. But Keyhoe had retained one statement, which he planned using:

> There is an official policy, believed in the best interests of the people, not to confirm the existence of UFOs until all the answers are known. Captain Edward J. Ruppelt, former chief of Project Blue Book, has confirmed the existence of four important documents that should be noted. In 1948, in a "Top Secret" estimate, the ATIC [Air Technical Intelligence Center] concluded that UFOs were interplanetary spaceships. In 1952, an Air Force Intelligence analysis of UFO maneuvers brought the same conclusion . . . interplanetary. In January 1953 a report by a panel of top scientists at the Pentagon reached this conclusion: There is strong circumstantial evidence, but no concrete proof that UFOs are spaceships.

Keyhoe was told that he could not use this statement. The final show was a farce, bearing little relation to the program as originally conceived, with the Air Force spokesmen concentrating on some of the sillier stories of contacts with spacemen. By the time Keyhoe appeared with his heavily edited script, little could be done to salvage the situation. But in desperation he suddenly veered from his script on the teleprompter: "And now I'm going to reveal something that has never been disclosed before . . . for the last six months we have been working with a congressional committee investigating official secrecy about UFOs. . . ." But by now the producer had cut the audio off the air and the public never heard Keyhoe's concluding statement: ". . . If all the evidence we have given this committee is made public in open hearings it will absolutely prove that the UFOs are real machines under intelligent control."

NICAP later obtained a statement from the CBS Director of editing, Herbert A. Carlborg, which proves that Major Keyhoe was cut off the air in the interests of security. "This program had been carefully screened for security reasons," he said. "Therefore, it was the responsibility of this network to ensure performance that was in accordance with predetermined security standards. Any indication that there would be a deviation from the script might lead to a statement that neither this network nor the individuals on the program were authorized to release."[19]

CONGRESSIONAL STATEMENTS

In the late 1950s NICAP revealed some significant statements they had received from prominent members of Congress, of which the following give a clear indication of how seriously the aspect of official secrecy about the subject was treated.

Senator Leverett B. Saltonstall (Massachusetts): "We must consider the genuine security necessities . . . but I think there are many cases in which more information should be made available to the public."

Representative Thomas L. Ashley (Ohio): "I share your concern over the secrecy that continues to shroud our intelligence activities on this subject."

Representative William H. Ayres (Ohio): "Congressional investigations have been held and are still being held on the problems of unidentified flying objects. . . . *Since most of the material presented is classified, the hearings are never printed.*"

Representative Walter H. Moeller (Ohio): "[I have] every confidence that the American public would be able to take such information without hysteria. The fear of the unknown is always greater than fear of the known."

Representative Ralph J. Scott (North Carolina): "If this information could be presented in such a way as to appeal to reason, and not to emotion, I think it would be a good thing."[20]

Senator Richard B. Russell, former Chairman of the Senate Armed Services Committee, who had a sighting in the Soviet Union in 1955 (see Chapter 10), was subsequently asked about official secrecy by the aviation columnist Tom Towers. "I have discussed this with the affected agencies of the government," the senator replied, "and they are of the opinion that it is unwise to publicize the matter at this time."[21]

Senator Barry Goldwater, former Air Force Reserve Colonel and Chairman of the Senate Intelligence Committee, has made several attempts to extract the suppressed material on UFOs (see Chapter 16), only to be told that *it is classified above top secret.*

"SERIOUS USAF BUSINESS"

On 24 December 1959 the Air Force issued the following warning to every air base commander in the continental United States:

Unidentified flying objects—sometimes treated lightly by the press and referred to as "flying saucers"—must be rapidly and accurately identified as serious USAF business in the ZI [Interior Zone]. . . .

The phenomena or actual objects comprising UFOs will tend to increase, with the public more aware of goings on in space but still inclined to some apprehension. Technical and defense considerations will continue to exist in this era.

Vice Admiral Roscoe Hillenkoetter, former Director of the CIA (1947–50) as well as a NICAP committee member (see Chapter 14), said that a copy of the warning, issued by the Inspector General, had been sent to the Senate Science and Astronautics Committee. "It is time for the truth to be brought out in open congressional hearings," he said. "Behind the scenes, high-ranking Air Force officers are soberly concerned about the UFOs. But through official secrecy and ridicule, many citizens are led to believe the unknown flying objects are nonsense," and he charged that "to hide the facts, the Air Force has silenced its personnel" through the issuance of a regulation.[22]

In April 1959 Major General Donald J. Keirn, Chief of the USAF nuclear engine program, stated that although the Air Force had no proof that intelligent beings existed elsewhere, the UFO reports had "emphasized our innate curiosity. . . . It is entirely possible that some of them may have passed through our stage of evolution, and may have already achieved a higher level of social and technological culture than our own."[23]

In 1962 an order affecting all Air Force statements on UFOs was disclosed via NICAP by Major William T. Coleman, former Project Blue Book officer and Air Force Headquarters spokesman. The directive covered books, articles and scripts for talks and broadcasts, and Chapter 4, Section B.2.g (AFM 190-4), is particularly apposite:

> When the manuscript concerns military subjects it will be submitted to the Office of Information, which will review it for accuracy, propriety, and conformance with policy, security, and for the deletion of classified matter. The policy applies to active duty personnel, retired personnel, civilian employees, and members of civilian components.
>
> By this order, the Secretary of Air Force Office of Information *must delete all evidence of UFO reality and intelligent control, which would, of course, contradict the Air Force stand that UFOs do not exist. The same rule applies to A.F. press releases and UFO information given to Congress and the public.*[24] [Emphasis added]

Another Air Force spokesman at the Pentagon, Major C. R. Hart, revealed in 1962 that UFO investigations and evaluations involved hundreds of Air Force intelligence officers, as well as *"the best scientific brains available in the laboratories of all government agencies, also scientific investigators in commercial laboratories, whenever needed."* Major Hart also disclosed that the chief Air Force scientific consultant, Dr. J. Allen Hynek, had conferred with the world's leading scientists regarding the

UFO problem. That same year, Lieutenant Colonal Spencer Whedon of the USAF Air Technical Intelligence Center revealed that the Air Force spent an estimated $10,000 on *each* major sighting investigation.[25]

On 29 October 1962, Defense Department Assistant Secretary Arthur Sylvester admitted that withholding information on UFOs from the public was necessary if the ends justified it, and cited Air Force Regulation 11-7, in which it is stated that sometimes information requested by Congress may not be furnished "even in confidence."[26]

But a number of Air Force officers opposed official secrecy on UFOs at this time. "In concealing the evidence of UFO operations the Air Force is making a serious mistake," said Lieutenant Colonel James McAshan. "The public should be informed as to the facts." Major Edwin A. Jerome went further in criticizing "this inane veil of security classification. I suggest we are several centuries behind the intellects of other planets. . . . The national policy should be to educate the public." Colonel Howard Strand, who had three encounters with UFOs while flying F-94 jets, stressed that "too many intelligent, competent observers have reported UFOs and added: "My conclusion is that this is a reconnaissance by an advanced civilization. I urge a congressional investigation of UFOs and the military secrecy surrounding them."[27]

But supposing that some UFOs are dangerous, and have been responsible for the deaths of a number of Air Force pilots, as General Benjamin Chidlaw has confirmed, are the authorities not fully justified in their policy of withholding the facts from the public in the interests of national security? This policy may also have been predicated on a suspicion by intelligence analysts that our planet might be viewed acquisitively by beings from elsewhere, a possibility discussed in Chapter 14.

Fanciful though this scenario seems, it was accorded a measure of credence by Air Force Intelligence Colonel William C. Odell in 1954, when in a script cleared by AF security but never published, entitled *Planet Earth—Host to Extraterrestrial Life*, he stated: "Granted that superintelligents in another solar system are looking for a suitable planet for a second home, why would earth be singled out?" Although Colonel Odell's manuscript had been cleared, potential publishers had been put off by Air Force stipulations that Odell was not to be identified as an AF officer, nor could the clearance by AF Security and Review be mentioned.[28]

RADIATION EFFECTS

UFOs have on many occasions been reported to have emitted radiation of varying types and strengths, and such cases have led to an official clamp-down, almost certainly to avoid public alarm. On 6 November 1957 Olden Moore watched a landed UFO for twenty minutes, thirty miles east of Cleveland, Ohio. The following day Moore was questioned by Army representatives as well as scientists from the Case Institute of Technology. Geiger counter readings taken from the center of a fifty-feet area registered ten times the normal amount, and about fifty percent more at the perimeter. Moore claimed that he had spoken to unspecifed "high officials" in Washington and said that he had been sworn to secrecy.[29]

An ex-Navy pilot who saw three oval-shaped UFOs while flying from Hobbs to Albuquerque, New Mexico, on 13 August 1959, was allegedly warned by an Air Force major at Kirtland AFB that he might become ill after the incident. The UFOs had caused the pilot's Magnesyn compass to revolve, following the bearing of the eight-foot-diameter objects as they circled his Cessna 170. The pilot said that he had been ordered not to discuss the case with anyone (hence anonymity), except for his wife, who had to be prepared in the event he became ill. The Air Force said they would look after him if this happened within six months, but since nothing further was reported about this case as far as I am aware, presumably the pilot was unaffected.[30]

On 21 December 1964 Horace Burns encountered a UFO resembling an inverted spinning-top about 125 feet in diameter near Staunton, Virginia. The object caused the engine of his car to cut out as it remained on the ground for sixty to ninety seconds. Radiation readings taken by Professor Ernest Gehman registered 60,000 counts per minute, confirmed by two other engineers present. It was concluded that the radiation was of the alpha type and not the more dangerous gamma type. On 12 January 1965 two Air Force sergeants from Wright-Patterson AFB went to the site and checked it with a Model 2586 Beta-Gamma Survey Meter. Checks were made at over eight spots, and although rain and snow had fallen in the area since the landing, a high reading was picked up by one of the men, which fact he immediately attempted to suppress. Two weeks later the official report was released, denying that there had been a landing of a UFO or traces of radioactivity.[31]

UFO DESTROYS ATLAS MISSILE, 1964

An astonishing case was revealed in 1982 by a former first lieutenant in
the Air Force, Dr. Robert Jacobs, now Assistant Professor of Radio-Film-
TV at the University of Wisconsin. Dr. Jacobs claims that on 15 September 1964, when he was in charge of the filming of missile tests at
Vandenberg AFB, California, a UFO was responsible for the destruction
of an Atlas missile. "In order to have clear film records of all missile
test firings over the Pacific, we had installed a TV camera, affixed to a
high-powered telescope up on a mountain," Dr. Jacobs reported.

> We kept the telescope locked on to the moving missile by radar, and it
> was while we were tracking one of the Atlas F missiles in this way that
> we registered the UFO on our film.
>   We had a crew of 120 men, and I was in charge. As we watched the
> Atlas F in flight we were delighted with our camera, which was doing
> fine, in fact we were jumping around with excitement, with the result that,
> because we were doing this, we actually missed seeing the most important
> bit of all—our missile's close encounter, at an altitude of 60 miles, with
> a UFO!
>   I only heard about it, in fact, a couple of days later, when I was ordered
> to go and see my superior, Major Florenz J. Mansmann, Chief Science
> Officer of the Unit. With him there in his office there were a couple of
> men. in plain clothes. He introduced them to me only by their first names
> and said they had come from Washington, DC.
>   Then Major Mansmann had the film of the test run through. And, just
> at that point where my men and I had been busy congratulating ourselves
> and each other, Major Mansmann pointed to the screen and said: "Watch
> this bit closely." Suddenly we saw a UFO swim into the picture. It was
> very distinct and clear, a round object. It flew right up to our missile and
> emitted a vivid flash of light. Then it altered course, and hovered briefly
> over our missile . . . and then there came a second vivid flash of light.
> Then the UFO flew around the missile twice and set off two more flashes
> from different angles, and then it vanished. A few seconds later, our missile
> was malfunctioning and tumbling out of control into the Pacific Ocean,
> hundreds of miles short of its scheduled target.
>   They switched on the office lights again, and I found myself confronted
> by three very intense faces. Speaking very quietly, Major Mansmann then
> said: "Lieutenant, just what the hell *was* that?" I replied that I had no
> idea. Then we ran the film through several more times, and I was permitted
> to examine it with a magnifying glass. Then Mansmann again asked me
> what I thought, and I answered that in my opinion it was a UFO. Major
> Mansmann smiled and said: "You are to say nothing about this footage.
> As far as you and I are concerned, it never happened! Right . . . ?"
>   Here then was the confirmation of what the UFO experts had been

saying for years past—that the U.S. government was covering up on what it knew about UFOs.

The film was turned over to the two men in plain clothes from Washington, who I believe were CIA agents. The film hasn't been heard of since. Major Mansmann added: "I don't have to remind you, of course, of the seriousness of a security breach. . . ."

It's been 17 years since that incident, and I've told nobody about it until now. I have been afraid of what might happen to me. But the truth is too important for it to be concealed any longer. The UFOs are real. I know they're real. The Air Force knows they're real. And the U.S. government knows they're real. I reckon it's high time that the American public knows it too.[32]

This incredible case, of true "Star Wars" proportions, alone justifies the reluctance of authorities to disclose the true facts about UFOs, even if outright hostility is not proven by the destruction of one missile. Yet how can we be certain that the incident was an isolated one? Indeed, I have cited one disturbing case reported from the Soviet Union when UFOs were allegedly responsible for the destruction of guided missiles (see Chapter 10), although in that incident the missiles had been launched offensively.

CALIFORNIAN CONTACT, 1965

Stories of encounters with the occupants of UFOs are invariably greeted with a barrage of ridicule, particularly if the witnesses claim to have met beings similar to ourselves in appearance. But having made an intensive study of such cases over a period of several decades, I am absolutely convinced that some of the claimants have had a real, objective experience. The case of Sid Padrick, which took place in California four months after the Atlas missile incident, deserves our attention, not least because the witness was asked by the Air Force not to discuss certain details.

At 2:00 a.m. on 30 January 1965, radio/TV technician Padrick, forty-five years old at the time, encountered a landed UFO near his home at Manresa Beach, near Watsonville, seventy-five miles south of San Francisco. He saw the shadowy outline of an unlit craft some seventy feet in diameter and thirty feet high "like two real thick saucers inverted" approach him and come to rest just above the ground. He panicked, began to run, then heard a voice coming from the craft: *"Do not be frightened, we are not hostile,"* it said. Padrick ran further. The voice repeated the phrase, then added: *"We mean you no harm,"* and invited him on board.

As he cautiously approached the craft, a door opened and he went inside, finding himself in a small compartment about six by seven feet. Another door slid open and he entered, to be met by a man.

The Aliens

"He was no different than me in basic appearance, had clean-cut features, and wore a type of flying suit that covered the body fully," said Padrick. On board were another seven men, similar in appearance, and one woman, described as extremely pretty. They were all about five feet eight inches to five feet nine inches tall.

By our own standards I would say they all looked between 20 and 25 years old, very young, pert, energetic, and intelligent looking. Their features were similar to ours. There was only one feature I noticed that would differ from us greatly, and that was that their faces came to a point, much more than ours. They had sharp chins and noses. Their skin was somewhat of an "Armenian" color. Their eyes were all very dark . . . there was nothing unusual about them—their brightness, depth or luminescence.

All the men appeared to have very short auburn hair, but it looked as though it had never been cut—it looked like a natural growth. The lady had long hair and it was pushed down inside her clothing. . . . Their fingers were a little longer than mine. The hands were very clean—the fingernails looked as if somebody had just given them a manicure.

All of them were wearing two-piece suits—slip-on type—light bluish-white in color. They had no buttons or zippers that I could see. The bottom section actually included the shoes—it looked like boots which continued on up to the waistline, without any break around the ankles, just like a child's snow suit. . . . There was a large band in the middle, and large cuffs, and a large collar that came down with a "V" neck. The collar had a very pretty design on it . . . and the neck piece—right around the neck—had a braid of some kind on it. . . . They had soles and heels. . . . I could hear them walking on the rubbery-like floor.

The first man Padrick saw acted as spokesman, explaining that he was the only one on board who spoke English.

He had no accent whatsoever. It was just as plain and just as perfectly spoken English as anyone has ever spoken on this earth. I believe they can adapt themselves to whatever condition they are working under.

Every question I asked him, he would pause for about 25 or 30 seconds before he would answer, regardless of how minor it was. Perhaps he was getting instructions mentally—in what response to give. I think if the crew communicated with each other, it was through mental telepathy, because I could see nothing that would indicate communication otherwise.

Inside the Craft

Each of the rooms that was occupied had instrument panels on the walls, with the crew members concentrating on the instruments. "They merely glanced around at me when I entered their room, then turned back to their work, as if they were unconcerned," said Padrick.

> Some rooms had four or five instruments, others had 15 or 20, but they were of a similar type in each room. They were nothing like ours. I didn't get close to any of the walls that had the movable instruments on them, because when I started to advance in that first room he held out his hand for me not to advance and I didn't, either. He didn't say why and I didn't ask. I saw markings on some of the instruments; something like a tape moving along, with little tiny dots and dashes on it—like our teletype tapes, except they were going from left to right. . . . I wouldn't classify it as a code, like our CW [Continuous Wave]. There were no screens, such as our oscilloscopes. They had meters, but I could not see dials on them. He said they lit up only when in use.

Padrick was shown an oblong lens, which he took to be part of a viewing system, with a magnified three-dimensional effect. On it he saw an object which he was told was a "navigation craft" that looked like a "blimp."

> This was 2:45 or 3:00 in the morning, and the object was in sunlight, so it had to be pretty far out—I imagine 1,000 miles out, or better. I didn't see any markings or portholes in it . . . he told me that the power source [of the craft he was in] was transferred to them from the other craft, and that it did all the navigation and manipulation through space.
>
> He told me they don't measure time and distance as we know it but rather in terms of light. When I asked him how fast they traveled through space, he answered that their speed was limited only by the speed at which they could transfer their energy source.

Outside the Craft

After a while the spaceman told Padrick that they had traveled some distance and were now parked in a deserted area, which on subsequent investigation turned out to be near Leggett, California, 175 miles north-west of Watsonville.

After we had landed on the hillside, he told me to step out so that I could come back to the place later—to know this was real and not dreamed. I stepped out alone and walked around the outside of the ship.

I felt the hull. It seemed very hard but not metallic: I never felt anything like it before. The closest thing to it I ever felt on this earth would be a windshield—plexiglass. It had a very fine finish, a highly polished finish. He didn't tell me that touching this craft would do me harm, and I had no bad effects from it—none whatever. I was outside for not more than three minutes. I got down and looked at the legs it was on and I tried to find markings on it: I didn't find a mark on it anyplace.

Origin and Purpose

Padrick asked where the craft and its people came from, and received a somewhat cryptic reply. "He told me they were from a planet in back of a planet which we observe—but we do not observe them. He did not say we couldn't observe them—he merely said we didn't observe them. . . . I think their planet is in our solar system."

Padrick was shown a photo of a city on the visitors' planet. "Every building in that picture was rounded off, half-moon shaped. I saw windows in the buildings. I cannot say the picture looked like anything I had ever seen before, because the buildings were spaced differently—offset from each other. It looked like they put one about 50 feet from another and the next one 150 feet. There appeared to be roads in the distance and there was foliage in the foreground—trees and bush too."

The spaceman described his Utopian society to Padrick. *"As you know it, we have no sickness, we have no crimes, we have no police force. We have no schools—our young are taught at an early age to do a job, which they do very well. Because of our long life expectancy we have a very strict birth control. We have no money. We live as one."*

Padrick asked what the purpose of the visit was. The man replied: *"Observation only."* Padrick explained:

I don't think it meant for them to observe us, I think it was for *me* to observe *them* . . . because he did not ask me at any time my name, my age, how many teeth I had, how many members of my family: he didn't ask me one thing about myself, and this leads me to believe that they know about us already, and he came for us to observe them. . . . They did say they would come for further observations. . . . I think they are observing people, mostly. There was no mention of earthquakes, fault-lines, or of anything government-wise, or political-wise, or anything that would affect our future [except that] they gave me the impression that they will pick up more people in future.

A Spiritual Experience

Sid Padrick was taken into what was referred to by the visitors as a "consultation room." The color effect in this room defied description. *"Would you like to pay your respects to the Supreme Deity?"* he was asked.

> When he said that I almost fainted. I didn't even know how to accept it. I said to him, "We have one, but we call it God, Are we talking about the same thing?" He replied, *"There is only one."* . . . So I knelt and did my usual prayer. . . . Until that night I had never felt the presence of the Supreme Being—but I did feel Him that night.
>
> It's obvious that they are on a very high scientific level, but their relation with the Supreme Being means a lot more to them than their technical and scientific ability and knowledge. I would say that their religion and their science are all in one.

Padrick was taken back to where he had been picked up two hours earlier, then stepped out of the craft and walked home.

The Air Force Investigation

Sid Padrick reported his experience to the Air Force, and was grilled for three hours by a team headed by Major D. B. Reeder of Hamilton AFB. ". . . they tried to frighten me. They said, 'Mr. Padrick, you are a real lucky person . . . these craft that come down here are real hostile, and you had no business even approaching them.' I disagreed with them, because when this craft came down, they did not want to frighten me . . . they did not *tell* me to go aboard their craft, they *invited* me aboard."

The Air Force told Padrick that there had been two instances where hostility had been involved—one the Mantell case, and the other an incident when an aircraft completely vanished from a radar screen. But the Air Force did tell Padrick that there was more than one group of UFOs visiting earth, and that there were friendly as well as hostile craft, from more than one source.

> There were certain details they [the Air Force] asked me not to talk about publicly, but I think in telling it that everything should be disclosed. I can see no reason for anything being held back. They didn't want me to say that the space people had no money. They didn't want me to disclose the type and shape of the craft because that would indicate that the Air Force is not doing its duty. I told them I could see no reason for that, either. . . .

They didn't want me to divulge their means of communication and where they got their power from. Also, the man's name—they told me I should never repeat that because it didn't mean anything. The spaceman had said *"You may call me Xeno."* He didn't say it *was* his name. [Xeno means "stranger" or "foreigner."][33]

Many will wonder if I have taken leave of my senses in including this story. But there are hundreds of such encounters reported by men and women all over the world and in order to understand all the possible reasons behind the official cover-up it is essential to examine a few that may be relevant, which I believe Sid Padrick's to be. Unfortunately I never met the man: he disappeared from the scene in the late 1960s, having become tired of being harassed. But I have studied every inflection of his voice in the recorded interview on which this account is based, and am perfectly satisfied that he is speaking the truth. Under a barrage of cross questioning by civilian investigators at the time, his answers were always clear, precise, and without guile, and he was always quick to appreciate the humorous aspects of the incredible situation he found himself in.

THE SILENCERS

Mysterious men dressed in Air Force uniform or bearing impressive credentials from government agencies, who intimidate witnesses and sometimes confiscate evidence from them, have now become inextricably enmeshed in UFO lore, as I have shown. In 1967 even the Air Force was obliged to acknowledge that such incidents took place, but denied any involvement. "These men are not connected with the Air Force," said Colonel George Freeman, Pentagon spokesman for Project Blue Book.

After highway inspector Rex Heflin took four Polaroid photographs of a low flying UFO near Santa Ana, California, on 3 August 1965, he was visited at his home by a man claiming to represent "North American Air Defense Command G-2" (possibly the USAF Aerospace Intelligence Division) who demanded the prints. They were never returned. Heflin had previously loaned the photos to the El Toro Marine Station and had received them back safely, so he assumed that NORAD (or whoever) would do likewise.

Major General M. Magee, NORAD's Chief of Staff, later told Representative James B. Utt (Republican, California): "For your information NORAD does not have the responsibility for the evaluation of UFOs and therefore would not knowingly be in the business of collecting UFO pictures for evaluation," he claimed.

Police officers and other witnesses to a UFO sighting at Wanaque, New Jersey, in 1966, were assembled by a man wearing an Air Force uniform who told them they hadn't seen anything and should not discuss the matter any further. "We checked with the local Air Force base," said Colonel Freeman, "and discovered that no one connected with the Air Force had visited Wanaque on the date in question. Whoever he was, he wasn't from the Air Force."

In April 1966 a man claiming to represent "a government agency so secret that he couldn't give its name" grilled two twelve-year-old boys for two hours about a disk-shaped object that had pursued them at ground level.

"We haven't been able to find out anything about these men," said Colonel Freeman. "By posing as Air Force officers and government agents they are committing a federal offense."[34]

Perhaps Colonel Freeman was telling the truth, and was genuinely unaware of government involvement in these incidents. Owing to compartmentation of intelligence he may not have had a "need to know" about the investigations, nor would he necessarily have known which agency was involved. And if he did, it would hardly have been in the government's best interests to admit as much. The Air Force Office of Special Investigations (AFOSI), with a long history of involvement in clandestine UFO investigations, might have been responsible, as could NORAD itself. There are other factors to be taken into consideration. The CIA, for example, is not above using agents posing as Air Force officers when the occasion demands—they don't go around wearing CIA badges!

There is another agency, hidden in Air Force Intelligence but run by the CIA, whose very existence was denied by the US government until comparatively recently. I refer to the most secret intelligence agency in the United States: the National Reconnaissance Office. The NRO was established in 1960, and although its primary function is the operation of spy satellites, its estimated annual budget of $3 billion and staff of 50,000[35] could easily allow for secret UFO investigations. There is no evidence of this so far, however, and my Freedom of Information request for documents in 1986 not surprisingly drew a blank, although the Air

Force did send me "the only record we have responsive to your request," this being the memorandum from Colonel Charles Halt to the British Ministry of Defense relating to the landing of a UFO outside RAF/USAF Woodbridge in December 1980 (see Chapter 4).

My point is that many, *if not all,* of the mysterious agents who intimidate witnesses could well originate with the government, rather than with—as some have suggested—the so-called "men in black." But there have been a number of disturbing reports of encounters with the nefarious MIB which simply cannot be dismissed, stories so incredible that witnesses seldom report them for fear of ridicule. And if the paraphysical abilities of the MIB are factual, then it is obvious that we are not dealing with government intimidators.

NORAD

The North American Aerospace Defense Command is responsible for protecting the North American continent from attack by enemy missiles or aircraft. While the vast majority of the 25,000 observations each day that are recorded by NORAD's Space Detection and Tracking System (SPADATS) and the Naval Space Surveillance System (NAVSPASUR) turn out to be readily identifiable, a certain percentage relate to "uncorrelated observations," of which there have been approximately 10 million since the early 1960s. Assuming that the majority of these, too, can be explained, we are still left with possibly thousands of bona fide UFO reports. NORAD has released a number of documents under provisions of the Freedom of Information Act which detail some incidents, such as the intrusions over Strategic Air Command (SAC) bases—including nuclear missile bases—in Maine, Michigan, Montana, North Dakota and Canada, in 1975 (see Chapter 8), but many more are being withheld. When Citizens Against UFO Secrecy (CAUS) filed an FOIA request for this data in NORAD files, they were quoted a search fee of over $155,000![36]

The much respected researcher Raymond Fowler, who once served with the USAF Security Service, has revealed details of a NORAD-related incident that occurred on 5 March 1967. NORAD radar tracked an uncorrelated target descending over the Minuteman missile site at Minot AFB (91st Strategic Missile Wing), North Dakota. Strike teams were notified immediately and sighted a metallic disk-shaped UFO with bright flashing lights moving slowly over the site. Three armed trucks chased the intruder until it stopped and hovered at 500 feet. The teams had orders to capture the UFO undamaged if it landed, but it then began circling over a launch control facility. F-106 jets were about to be scrambled when the UFO climbed vertically and disappeared at high speed.[37] Fowler has received confirmation from undisclosed sources that there have been other instances when UFOs have hovered directly over nuclear missile sites.

In the spring of 1966 the command and status consoles at a launch control center in Great Falls, Montana, indicated that a fault existed in each of the ten missiles simultaneously. The missile crew checked the faults electronically and discovered that a "no-go fault condition" existed in the guidance and control systems, which meant in effect that none of the missiles could have been launched. Above-ground personnel had reported seeing UFOs at the precise moment the failures were detected. An identical incident occurred during the week of 20 March 1967, Fowler reports, when radar at Malstrom AFB, Montana, confirmed the presence of a UFO at the same time that ten missiles became inoperative.[38]

If these events actually took place—and I see no reason to doubt that they did, given the documented cases of intrusions by UFOs over missile sites in 1975—then we must give due consideration to the possibility that in the event of a full-scale nuclear alert all our intercontinental ballistic missiles will be rendered impotent. This is indeed a comforting thought, with profound implications for the survival of humanity. But there is an additional possibility that the UFO intelligences are merely demonstrating that we have no adequate defense against *them*.

POLICE CHIEF PHOTOGRAPHS "SPACEMAN"

In October 1973 the United States was inundated with sightings, leading to a revival of public and media interest in the subject. One of the most impressive reports for me is the encounter of Police Chief Jeff Greenhaw (in fact the only policeman) in the small town of Falkville, Alabama, on 17 October. Shortly before 10:00 p.m. Greenhaw was at home when a woman telephoned him to report that an object with flashing lights appeared to be landing in a field west of the town. Since there had been a spate of UFO sightings in south Morgan County, Greenhaw grabbed his Polaroid camera and drove to the remote area.

Two miles from town he encountered a six-foot-tall, metallic-suited creature standing in the middle of the road. "I got out of my car and said, 'Howdy, stranger,' reported Greenhaw. "He didn't say a word. I reached back, picked up my Polaroid camera, and started taking pictures of him." The policeman took four photographs, then got back into his car and turned on the revolving blue light(s), at which point the creature turned and started running down the road.

"I jumped into my car and took after him," said Greenhaw, "but couldn't catch up with him in a patrol car. He was running faster than any human I ever saw." The car was doing 30–40 mph before going into a spin on the gravel road. The creature had vanished. The "spaceman" moved like a robot and ran in huge paces, Greenhaw said.

A hoax? After Jeff Greenhaw had related his experience on NBC-TV news he began receiving threatening phone calls. Within two weeks of the incident his car engine blew up, his wife left him, and an arsonist set fire to his house trailer, destroying the original prints. To add insult to injury, Greenhaw was forced to resign as police chief. "So now I've lost my car, my wife, my home, and my job. And I guess I'll just have to go wherever I can to find another job," he said.[39] Hoaxers seldom go that far.

ARMY HELICOPTER IN NEAR COLLISION WITH UFO

A day after Greenhaw's experience, on 18 October 1973, four Army Reserve crewmen in a Bell Huey helicopter had an alarming close encounter with a UFO in the vicinity of Mansfield, Ohio. The pilot in command was Captain Lawrence J. Coyne, and the other airmen were Crew Chief Robert Yanacsek, Co-pilot Arrigo Jezzi and Staff Sergeant John Healey. The Army Disposition Form, signed by the four witnesses, records the incident as follows:

> Army helicopter 68-15444 was returning from Columbus, Ohio, to Cleveland, Ohio, and at 2305 hours east, southeast of Mansfield Airport in the vicinity of Mansfield, Ohio, while flying at an altitude of 2500 feet and on a heading of 030 degrees, SSG Yanacsek observed a red light on the east horizon, 90 degrees to the flight path of the helicopter.
>
> Approximately 30 seconds later, SSG Yanacsek indicated the object was converging on the helicopter at the same altitude at an airspeed in excess of 600 knots and on a midair collision heading. CPT Coyne observed the converging object, took over the controls of the aircraft and initiated a power descent from 2,500 feet to 1,700 feet to avoid impact with the object.
>
> A radio call was initiated to Mansfield Tower who acknowledged the helicopter and was asked by CPT Coyne if there were any high performance aircraft flying in the vicinity of Mansfield Airport, however there was no response received from the tower. The crew expected impact from the object; instead, the object was observed to hesitate momentarily over the helicopter and then slowly continued on a westerly course accelerating at

a high rate of speed, clear west of Mansfield Airport then turn 45 degree heading to the northwest.

CPT Coyne indicated the altimeter read a 100 fpm [feet per minute] climb and read 3500 feet with the collective in the full down position. The aircraft was returned to 2500 feet by CPT Coyne and flown back to Cleveland, Ohio. The Flight plan was closed and the FAA Flight Service Station notified of the incident.[40]

"From a speed of 600 miles an hour, it abruptly slowed down to our exact speed of 100 miles an hour and hovered above us," reported Captain Coyne. Co-pilot Jezzi described the object as "cigar-shaped, metallic gray, with a dome on top" and Staff Sergeant Healey added that it was "about 60 feet long, without any portholes or intake openings that we could see. At first it was just showing a red light in the nose. Then a green spotlight at the back swept around and shone into our cabin."[41]

The radio returned to normal ten minutes after the incident, having gone completely dead on both UHF and VHF frequencies just after Coyne had established contact with Mansfield control tower. Some witnesses on the ground reported seeing the helicopter as well as an object "like a blimp" and "as big as a school bus" hovering above the helicopter. When the UFO's green light appeared it was described by the witnesses as "like rays coming down. . . . The helicopter, the trees, the road . . . everything turned green."[42]

WITNESSES SEVERELY HARMED BY UFO—BUT WAS IT

ONE OF OURS?

The further our technology advances, the harder it will be to differentiate between true UFOs and new types of aircraft, spacecraft, and remotely piloted vehicles (RPVs). Researchers are still debating the origin of an unknown aerial device that was seen by three witnesses on the night of 29 December 1980 near Huffman, a suburb of Houston, Texas.

The witnesses, Betty Cash, her friend Vickie Landrum and her seven-year-old grandson Colby were driving toward Dayton, Texas, when at about 9:00 p.m. a fiery object was seen high in the sky which quickly descended to treetop level above the road and hovered in front of them no more than about 135 feet away. Flames were shooting down from the object. The witnesses stopped the car, got out, and watched, although they were all very frightened, particularly Colby who pleaded with the others to get back inside the car. This they did, though Betty Cash spent more time outside than the others. Mrs. Landrum—convinced that the end of the world had arrived—began praying.

The object was described by Betty as an extremely bright light with no distinct shape, but Vickie thought it was oblong with a rounded top and a pointed lower half. Colby is certain that it was diamond-shaped. The bursts of flame coincided with sounds "like a flame thrower" and a "roaring" as well as a "beeping" noise lasted throughout the encounter. The car was so hot that Betty was unable to touch the door with her bare hand.

The witnesses followed the object in the car and noticed that about twenty three twin-rotor helicopters (later identified as Chinooks) appeared to be escorting the fiery object, but never getting closer than about three quarters of a mile. After stopping three more times to watch the spectacle, Betty drove the others home and arrived at her own house at 9:50 p.m. Then horrific physical symptoms became apparent.

Betty reported a blinding headache, pains in her neck, and nodules on her head and scalp that burst, seeping clear fluid. Her eyes swelled shut, she was unable to see properly, and suffered from nausea, vomiting and diarrhea. Four days later she was admitted as a burn victim to Parkway General Hospital, Houston. Various specialists were called in but none was able to properly diagnose her complaints. A week after leaving hospital Betty had to return, still suffering from headaches, nausea, swelling and loss of appetite. Even more alarming, her hair began falling out, leaving a temporary bald patch. By the end of February 1981 Betty's medical bill had risen to $10,000. Finally, Betty developed breast cancer and had to have a mastectomy, although this may be coincidental.

The other witnesses, who spent less time outside the car, were irradiated to a lesser degree. Vickie suffered from inflammation of the eyes, temporary loss of some hair, and developed line-like indentations across her fingernails. Colby suffered from "sunburn" on his face as well as eye inflammation.[43]

There is no question that the three witnesses were subjected to varying degrees of radiation emitting from a vehicle of unknown origin. But whose was it? The presence of helicopters escorting the object suggests that it was an experimental device that had malfunctioned, the main purpose of the helicopters being to ensure that in the event of a forced landing the area could be sealed off immediately by troops. I have heard several rumors from normally reliable sources that the device was either a nuclear-powered experimental space shuttle or "lighting device" that had got into difficulties. The device apparently has an auxiliary conventional rocket propulsion unit. Intriguing but less reliable rumors suggest that the object was a nuclear-powered device on a test flight as part of "Project Snowbird"—allegedly established in 1972 to test fly a recovered alien vehicle.

Betty Cash and Vickie Landrum are in no doubt that the craft was American, and sued the US government for $20 million damages. I kept in touch with Peter Gersten (their lawyer) as the case dragged on in the US District Court, Houston. In August 1986 the case was dismissed on the grounds that no such object was owned, operated or in the inventory of either the Air Force, the Army, the Navy or NASA (experts from each were represented in court). But as the principal investigator of the case, John Schuessler, emphasizes, hardly any attention was paid to the evidence regarding the twenty-three helicopters (there were additional witnesses). "Judge Ross Sterling considered the expert testimony to be sufficient reason to dismiss the case," he says. "That means he will not meet Betty Cash, Vickie and Colby Landrum, and he will not hear the evidence they wanted their attorneys to present."[44]

CLOSE ENCOUNTERS OF THE THIRD KIND—A

REALITY?

During a talk given to the Tulsa, Oklahoma, Astronomy Club in 1982, former Air Force intelligence officer Steve Lewis revealed that the twelve years he spent investigating UFOs for the military both in the US *and* abroad convinced him that intelligent extraterrestrial beings are visiting earth. Apologizing for being unable to be more specific owing to strict orders from the Air Force not to divulge specific details about his UFO research from 1965 to 1977 (including a period with Project Blue Book), Lewis stated that only a fraction of information accumulated by the military has been released. He admitted that although the majority of sightings have a mundane explanation, the bona fide reports are often associated with a common feature of very bright, blinding lights. The Air Force believes that the light may be related to an advanced propulsion system, enabling UFOs to travel at the speed of light, Lewis said.

"That movie *Close Encounters of the Third Kind* is more realistic than you'd believe," he told the audience. "You can believe that or not."

Pressed to reveal what had convinced him that UFOs are extraterrestrial spacecraft rather than top secret military devices, Lewis commented: "The records, the information I saw while in my job. *I no longer rule out what the possibilities might be.*"[45]

13

THE DEFENSE
INTELLIGENCE AGENCY

When a Korean Airlines Boeing 747 was shot down after wandering inadvertently into Russian airspace in 1983, resulting in the deaths of 269 people, the agency responsible for monitoring and recording radio communications between the Soviet Air Force pilot and his headquarters—thus proving that orders to shoot down the airliner had in fact been given—was America's highly secret Defense Intelligence Agency. Established in 1961 by Robert McNamara, President Kennedy's Defense Secretary at the time, the DIA's mandate was to coordinate all US military intelligence services (i.e. those of the Air Force, Army and Navy). This upset not only these individual services but also the CIA, who perceived the DIA as a serious rival, since the strength of the military services' intelligence branches combined exceeded that of the CIA.[1] "There is, of course, always the possibility," remarked former CIA Director Allen Dulles in 1963, "that two such powerful and well financed agencies as CIA and DIA will become rivals and competitors."[2] He was right. By 1964 the DIA's control over military intelligence had increased to such an extent that the services were reduced to providing technical intelligence on enemy weapons, running the attaché system and collecting but not analyzing raw intelligence data.[3]

The DIA works for the Secretary of Defense, the Joint Chiefs of Staff, and the Director of Central Intelligence, and is staffed by both military officers and civilians.[4] Its employees are said to number 7,000[5] and its budget in the 1970s was estimated at $100 million per annum. In addition to processing and analyzing intelligence gathered from military sources, which is then turned into finished intelligence reports that are circulated within the Pentagon and the intelligence community, the DIA prepares daily and weekly intelligence digests as well as its own estimates of enemy capabilities.[6]

In 1980 I spoke with Peter Gersten, the New York lawyer representing Citizens Against UFO Secrecy (CAUS). He told me that in 1979 the DIA had submitted a motion to the US Attorney indicating that they had searched their complete record systems and had no documents on UFOs other than three that they had found and released. One involved a Peruvian incident in June 1980, while another related to some sightings in the Soviet Union that they were in the process of translating. The DIA had released the other document in 1977 to Charles Huffer, a teacher at the Berlin American High School in Germany. It deals with the now well-known case of UFOs sighted by an Imperial Iranian Air Force pilot in September 1976 (see pages 318–321).[7]

In view of the DIA's denials that they had any further material on UFOs, it is interesting that in December 1985 the Agency released a total of thirty seven UFO-related documents—amounting to 139 pages—to researcher Ray Boeche, who generously forwarded copies to me. In their covering letter to Boeche the DIA explained that "it has been determined that there are 53 documents responsive to your [FOIA] request. Of these 53 documents, portions of 15 are properly classified and are not releasable."

Some of the released documents, stamped "Best Copy Available," are barely legible. The earliest dates back to 1957, which is curious since the DIA was founded in 1961. Most probably the earlier reports were later forwarded to the DIA by the relevant service intelligence agencies. Illegibility on some of the documents is due either to the fact that the DIA considered them so insignificant that they were not worth preserving in legible form, or that they have been made deliberately illegible. It is evident from some of the documents that the primary concern of the DIA (or submitting agencies) was sightings related to Soviet activity.

FINLAND, 1957

The earliest legible reports refer to sightings in Finland in December 1957, one of which states that:

a brilliant, elongated object, resembling a cigar—a long cigar—was sighted by two farmers in the terrain east of [illegible]. The object came into sight from the western sky. Its flight was horizontal, i.e. parallel to the earth, and its altitude was considerable. The line of flight was almost due east. Its speed was [illegible] that of a meteor or a Sputnik. The mysterious object was visible for a [illegible].

The report on Finnish sightings concludes: "It is significant that the majority of the sightings here reported, as well as the majority of those reported in earlier months, were [bordering] the Soviet frontier. The possibility has been suggested that the Russians are conducting some of their tests from a vessel or vessels in far Northern waters.''

AFGHANISTAN, 1959

The DIA's primary concern with UFO reports continued to focus on the possibility of Russian missile tests. An unclassified report dated 3 December 1959, supplied to the DIA by the Army, refers to sightings in Afghanistan in November of that year: ''On 8 November a huge luminous object was seen moving at great speed over the sky in Kandahar. The object which was flying in a North Westerly direction had a downward movement and soon after it was seen it blew up with a loud roar on Shurad mountains, causing slight earth tremors in the area. No losses have been reported so far.''

Although the Army was unable to secure any further information about the incident, and another on 29 November (both of which had been reported in news bulletins), the most probable explanation is that Soviet missile tests were being conducted near the Afghanistan border. Lieutenant Colonel Sandiland, who prepared the Army intelligence report, comments scathingly on the likelihood of UFOs being responsible: ''Afghanistan, with grim determination, has decided to advance from the 13th to the 20th century as quickly as possible. If more advanced countries have sighted UFO—Well—So has Afghanistan.''

On 2 December 1959 a bright, circular object was observed in the sky over Ghazni, heading south-west, which disappeared after two minutes. This drew another caustic comment from Lieutenant Colonel Sandiland: ''Afghanistan, having sighted three UFOs within a period of two months, is rapidly catching up with other progressive nations—in this respect at least.''

ANTARCTICA, 1965

A wave of sightings in South America in 1965 was reported to the DIA by US Air and Naval Attachés, and although many of the reports were taken from newspapers, some originated with official sources, such as the following accounts of sightings in Antarctica which were obtained from the Chief of the Argentine Navy Hydrographic Service by the US Naval Attaché in Buenos Aires. The accounts summarize reports by Argentine, Chilean and British base personnel at Deception Island, part of the British-owned South Shetland Islands.

On 2 June 1965 an unusual object was sighted by a meteorologist and four other witnesses at the British Bravo Base. The sighting lasted for fifteen to twenty minutes. The object moved rapidly and was of a brilliant color, solid-appearing, and noiseless. On 20 June the Commander of the Chilean Aquirre Cerda Base, Juan Barrera, together with Chilean Air Force pilot Lieutenant Benavidez, a meteorologist, and seven other witnesses, observed a UFO which maneuvered rapidly on an oscillating course for twenty-five minutes. But the most interesting sightings took place on 3 July at the Chilean base, as the following official summary shows:

ON THREE JULY AT ONE NINE TWO ZERO HOURS THE METEOROLOGIST AND EIGHT OTHER PERSONS AT THE CHILEAN BASE AQUIRRE CERDA OBSERVED DURING TWO ZERO MIN (CLEAR NIGHT, TWO EIGHTHS STRATOCUMULUS AND STARRY SKY, MOON FOURTH QUARTER) AN OBJECT APPEARING AS A STATIONARY LIGHT AT TIMES AND OF SOLID APPEARANCE LIKE A CELESTIAL BODY, NOISELESS, WHITE COLOR WITH BORDERS LIKE A BRILLIANT STAR, MOVING EAST TO WEST TRAJECTORY WITH OSCILLATIONS, DISAPPEARING IN THE CLOUDS, ELEVATION FOUR DASH FOUR FIVE DEGREES OVER THE HORIZON. ON THREE JULY AT ONE NINE FOUR TWO HOURS METEOROLOGIST AND SIX PERSONS FROM THIS BASE OBSERVED BY NAKED EYE, BINOCULARS, AND THEODOLITE FOR A PERIOD OF ONE HOUR AND TWO MINUTES (CLEAR NIGHT, TWO EIGHTHS STRATUS, ONE EIGHTH CIRRUS, STARRY SKY, MOON FOURTH QUARTER) AN OBJECT DESCRIBED AS MORE BRILLIANT THAN A STAR OF THE FIRST MAGNITUDE WHICH WAS STATIONARY AT TIMES WITH FLASHING BRILLIANCE (APPEARING AND DISAPPEARING), MOVING ABOVE THE STRATUS AND BELOW THE CIRRUS AT TIMES, OF A SOLID APPEARANCE AND NOISELESS, ITS CENTER COLORED RED, BORDERS CHANGING FROM YELLOW TO GREEN TO ORANGE TO BLUE TO WHITE, AND LIKE A BRILLIANT IRIDESCENT STAR, SMALL TRAJECTORY VARIATION, SIZE COMPARABLE TO THE HEAD OF HALF INCH NAIL HEAD, FINALLY DISAPPEARING IN ALTITUDE AND DISTANCE. FORM WAS ROUND AND OVAL SHAPED. DIRECTION OBSERVED NORTH NORTHWEST APPROXIMATELY THREE THREE FIVE DEGREES FROM TRUE NORTH AND THREE ZERO DEGREES ABOVE THE HORIZON, APPROXIMATELY AT A DISTANCE OF ONE ZERO TO ONE FIVE KILOMETERS. SOME PHOTOGRAPHY TAKEN OF THIS SIGHTING. . . . TWO VARIOMETERS WORKING AFFECTED BY MAGNETIC FIELD DISTURBANCE DURING THE TIME OBJECT SIGHTED.

Newspaper articles, forwarded to the DIA by the US Air Attaché in Santiago, Chile, contained additional information. The photographs—about ten in all—were taken by Corporal U. D. Martinez, but proved to be of little value owing to the distance of the object. The magnetic traces, however, recorded on a magnetovariometer, were considered highly evidential. The Air Attaché, while hypothesizing that a satellite may have been responsible for some of the sightings, nevertheless concluded in his report: "Some credence must be given to the existence or the occurrence of some type of phenomenon in as much as reports emanated from such widely reported locations as to rule out mass hysteria or collusion."

The Argentine Navy published an official communiqué on the sighting, based on the statements of the Argentine, Chilean, and British witnesses. The Secretariat of the Argentine Navy also confirmed that the occurrence had been witnessed by scientists of the three naval bases and that the facts described by these people were in complete agreement.[8] The Commandant of the Chilean Air Force Antarctic Base, Don Mario Juan Barrera, commented:

It is rash to say that we all saw a flying saucer, like those in science fiction. But nevertheless it was something real, an object traveling at a staggering speed, that performed evolutions and . . . caused interference in the instruments of the Argentinian base lying on an island that is near to and right opposite our base . . . what we observed was no hallucination or collective psychosis. . . . As far as I am concerned it is a celestial object that I am unable to identify. That it could be an aircraft constructed on this earth, I do not believe possible.

Commandant Daniel Perisse of the Argentine base backed up this statement by declaring that the appearance of the object was no hallucination or mirage, and his description of the object's performance tallied precisely with Barrera's.[9]

The sightings of UFOs on 3 July 1965 were not the first in Antarctica. In 1950 Commander Augusto Vars Ortega of the Chilean Navy reported that UFOs had circled his base. "During the bright Antarctic night," he said, "we saw flying saucers, one above the other, turning at tremendous speeds. We have photographs to prove what we saw." The pictures were 1,200 feet of color movie film, but when Major Donald Keyhoe attempted to obtain a copy from the Chilean Embassy in Washington in 1956 he was informed that the film was classified and could not therefore be made available.[10] In May 1972 officers of the Chilean Air Force and Army had two sightings of UFOs which caused a weakening of radio signals in the 3,200 kilocycle waveband.[11]

CHILE, 1965

In September 1965 the US Air Attaché in Santiago forwarded a news report to the DIA of a sighting by the crew of Chilean National Airlines Flight LAN 904 on the 6th of that month. The captain of the DC-6b was Marcelo Cisternas, Chief of Flight Operations for the airline, who described the sighting as follows:

It was something mechanical—zigzagging—its movements were not precise—suddenly it changed direction and came directly toward us—it gave me the impression that it had suddenly located us with radar. . . . During the 13 to 14 minutes this strange object followed us, it gave me the impression that when it located us it tried to identify us. At once we requested information from the Flight Control Tower in Arica and Iquque. We were informed that no other flights had been scheduled in that zone. . . .

I have never had a similar experience. I didn't believe in "them." It was not an optical vision due to atmospherical reflections. I am sure it was a mechanical apparatus. [Our] plane was flying at an altitude of 8,500 feet . . . the night was cloudy and without stars . . . the co-pilot, the engineer, hostess and steward also saw it. It emitted a light of an intense color, then changed and turned to radiant white. It was suspended at a distance of about 3 kms from us, in a straight line. It was more or less 2130 hours. Suddenly the same way it appeared it withdrew at an incredible speed.

BRAZIL, 1967

An interesting Brazilian Air Force report was obtained from official sources by the US Air Attaché in Rio de Janeiro in March 1967:

On 27 March 1967 the crew of a Brazilian Air Force C-47 and the crew of a Cruzeiro do Sul photo mapping aircraft reported having seen a flying saucer in the vicinity of Porto Alegre, Rio Grande do Sul. The object was initially sighted by the BAF crew who described it as a reddish colored full moon that appeared to be flying in circles. The BAF C-47 advised Salgado Filho Tower of the sighting, and the tower asked the Cruzeiro do Sul aircraft to intercept and identify the object. The Cruzeiro do Sul aircraft made contact with the object and pursued it for 15 minutes before it finally disappeared. No pictures were taken. . . .

In addition to the reported sightings by the aircraft crews, the object was also reportedly seen by ground observers in the Porto Alegre area. A more recent reported sighting occurred on 30 March 1967 in Rio [illegible]. However, this one was reported only by ground observers. The object was

described as completely white, silent, flying at low altitude, and would
disappear and reappear at regular intervals. This particular sighting received
very little publicity in [the news] media. As yet the Air Ministry has not
issued any official comment on these sightings and is presently studying
the statements of the aircraft crews and ground observers.

Official UFO research in Brazil was conducted at this time (and still
is, as far as I am aware) by the Brazilian Air Force UFO Study Division,
based in São Paulo. Although Brazil is one of the few countries in the
world where sightings (especially the more sensational ones) are publicized regularly, official censorship has been imposed since the 1960s. In
1969 a Brazilian Air Force directive issued to local officials stated: "You
will not under any circumstances give any information on UFO activity
to any press, radio, or television reporter or representative. *This is a
matter of National Security,* and all press releases will be made by the
Brazilian Air Force Public Relations Department."[12] A 1973 São Paulo
State directive, entitled *Institutional Act No. 5 (State Security),* warns:
"It is forbidden for TV, radio, newspapers, and other news media to
divulge UFO reports without the prior censorship of the Brazilian Air
Force."[13]

PROJECT MOON DUST

Of the 139 pages of DIA documents now released, four contain intriguing
references to "Project Moon Dust." This project was, and possibly still
is, a foreign space debris program of the US Air Force System Command's
Foreign Technology Division at Wright-Patterson Air Force Base, Dayton, Ohio, and while its primary function would seem to be the recovery
of missile and satellite debris, there are indications that it has also been
involved in the recovery of more exotic artifacts.

A UFO sighting over Agadir, Morocco, on 11/12 January 1967, for
example, led to translations of two articles being sent to the DIA by the
US Defense Attaché in Rabat, who commented: ". . . the page one
coverage afforded this sighting demonstrates a high level of local interest
in the subject of UFOs and presages future reporting which could be
valuable in pursuit of Project MOON DUST." Another UFO report from
Morocco a couple of months later gave "Project MOON DUST" as its
reference.

Ray Boeche has subsequently uncovered further information about the
project, having filed a number of Freedom of Information requests with
the CIA, DIA, Department of Defense, National Security Council and

Air Force. Ray informed me that Project Moon Dust was "definitely UFO-related,"[14] but no really significant documents have been released to him so far.

NEW ZEALAND, 1965–68

The DIA apparently showed great interest in the controversial theories of Captain Bruce Cathie, the New Zealand airline pilot who claims to have discovered evidence for a worldwide grid system used by UFOs. Cathie's meetings with US Defense Attachés in Wellington are documented, as well as his correspondence with them, in the released DIA documents.

Cathie first approached the US Embassy in Washington in the mid-1960s, since which time the DIA kept a file on him. The earliest documented memo is from Colonel John Burnett, Air Attaché, to the Foreign Technology Division at Wright-Patterson AFB, dated 26 August 1965, from which I quote the following extract:

> Captain Cathie visited with me for about one half hour. I observed this New Zealander to be not only rational but intelligent and convinced that certain UFOs he and others have seen are from outer space—probably Venus. He hesitated in expressing his beliefs re the Venus origin, explaining that it usually tended to convince people that he was a bit of a crackpot.

The Foreign Technology Division responded by sending Colonel Burnett a brochure outlining the findings of the Air Force on UFOs, adding: "Since no evidence exists that these objects represent interstellar travel there is no basis for Captain Cathie's beliefs." Despite the FTD's apparent skepticism, Colonel Burnett continued to send them details of Cathie's findings and calculations for at least another year.

Bruce Cathie told me that it was Colonel Burnett who revealed that intensive UFO research was carried out at Wright-Patterson AFB[15], referred to in Cathie's second book:

> The scientific laboratory there, set up for the purpose, was described as a complex of buildings covering a large area and staffed by many of the world's top scientists. Experimental work was carried out twenty-four hours a day, 365 days a year. At one stage the official [Colonel Burnett] asked me if I would consider a trip to America to visit the base. Naturally I said I would—any time they cared to put out an invitation. Perhaps the idea was vetoed in the States, for I heard no more of this.

It is difficult to prove such a sensational allegation, but I have no reason to doubt Captain Cathie's integrity. Naturally, there is no reference to this in any of the DIA documents on him.

By 1967 Colonel Burnett had been replaced by Colonel Lewis Walker, who seems to have been less impressed with Cathie's ideas than his predecessor. But this did not prevent Walker from forwarding Cathie's material to the DIA at the Pentagon. An Intelligence Information Report dated 8 February 1968 states:

Captain Cathie is still employed as an aircraft F-27 Friendship pilot by National Airways Corporation. . . . His superiors know of his interest and activity in UFO's and his forthcoming book "Harmonic 33." He has been checked for security reasons and no adverse reports are known. . . . He admits that many people consider him some kind of nut but he persists in his theory. On [ ] January 1968 he came to my office and reported that four UFO's had been detected by the Auckland Air Traffic Control radarscope on [ ] January 1968 at 2335 hours local time. . . . Three objects were 15 miles apart in line, with the fourth object in line 30 miles behind the three. Relative speed was extremely high. In addition, two UFO's— disc-shaped—appeared east of Auckland Airport on the same track as first four. Captain Cathie was asked if official reports were submitted on these sightings, and he said no, that Civil Aviation personnel had been warned not to report any more of these observations. Captain Cathie was advised to submit any additional information he might have. . . .

Captain Cathie is a lean, wiry New Zealander, with an apparently above average knowledge of mathematics. . . . He is intensely sincere in his efforts . . . he is spending an enormous amount of time and effort trying to prove his theory that an overall master plan exists by an alien race— purpose not defined.

By May 1968, however, Colonel Walker seems to have become fed up with Cathie. A report to the DIA dated 1 May indicates that although Cathie was not considered a "nut," on the last three occasions that he called at the Defense Attaché's office to discuss his latest findings, "These conversations were ignored." Cathie had complained that he had been put under surveillance and that in April he had been accosted by three Americans in Invercargill, who had asked him to accompany them, which he refused to do. Cathie believed that these men came from a US Navy vessel, but according to Colonel Walker the only US ship that was south of Auckland at the time was the USS *Eltanin,* which was in the Antarctic, however. The report concludes:

Capt. Cathie said that he had been cleared by the NZ government to pursue his research and that he had a letter to this effect signed by the Prime Minister. He stated that the Member of Parliament from his area, Dr. Findley, had interceded for him and obtained government approval for his work. He then asked the DATT [Defense Attaché] to "call your agents off. I have official approval to continue my work. I don't want them tailing me."

The DATT made no reply to this request. This man is obsessed with his theory and no amount of argument can convince him that he has not stumbled on a highly complicated system which he says leads directly to the existence of UFOs.

I sent copies of these documents to Captain Cathie in 1986, and asked him for a comment. "He [Colonel Walker] is only saying that in his opinion I am obsessed with my research," he replied, "and that there is no way they can talk me out of it. Which is fairly correct, except for the word obsessed. My research is my hobby and I find it most interesting. The evidence which I now have on hand will prove without doubt that my unified equations are correct."[16]

ARGENTINA, 1968

The extent of the DIA's interest in UFO reports can be demonstrated by its efficiency in collecting newscuttings on the subject, and a wave of sightings in Argentina from June to August 1968 led to the Defense Attaché in Buenos Aires, Colonel Charles Greffet, forwarding no less than twenty-three newsclippings to the Pentagon. It could be argued that the DIA is merely the world's most expensive newsclipping agency, or that its *only* concern is with UFO reports that relate to hostile foreign aircraft or missiles. While it is obvious that mundane intelligence-gathering is the DIA's primary function, many reports, such as the following summaries, reflect a concern with more exotic UFOs:

1. La Razon (Buenos Aires) 8 Jun 68—Describes how two experienced pilots, 22 and 13 years with Aerolineas Argentinas, saw a UFO while flying over Punta Arenas. . . .
3. Los Principlos (Cordoba) 5 July 68—Outlines details on the invention of a geomagnetic and light detector to warn of the presence of UFOs. Second article, same source, quotes Argentine Commander-in-Chief of Navy as suggesting that Argentine armed forces are participating in an investigation of UFOs. . . .

5. Diario del Pueblo (Tandil) 13 July 68—Describes landing of a UFO at the Air Force Base at Tandil. . . .

13. La Razon (Buenos Aires) 26 July 68—Describes attempt by five policemen in Olavarria to capture and later shoot three crew members of UFO. . . .

16. La Razon (Buenos Aires) 27 July 68—Relates new sighting near La Pastora, Alvear, and Tapalque. The latter describes the crew and inability of machine-gun bullets to affect them. . . .

22. La Razon 3 Aug 68—Relates argument by a Professor Alexander Eru supporting theory of flying saucers. . . .

Colonel Greffet comments: "It is significant to note that a state of concern exists [among] the population in many parts of Argentina."

Reference No. 3 mentions the suggestion that the Argentine armed forces were participating in an investigation of UFOs. Back in 1964, in fact, the volume of sightings had grown so huge that the Argentine Air Force set up its own UFO department, known as Division OVNI.[17] And in 1978 the gendarmeria of Argentina released official police reports of sightings (many having occurred in 1968) to the lawyer Antonio Baragiola.[18]

KOREA, 1970

The following report was received by the DIA from an official of the Republic of Korea (ROK) Intelligence Agency:

On 10 and 11 February 1970 a meeting of all commanding officers (CO) of ROK Air Force (ROKAF) Security Units (SU) throughout the ROK was held at ROKAF Headquarters in SEOUL. . . . At that meeting the ROKAF Chief of Staff gave those in attendance a highly-classified briefing concerning recent sightings of UFOs in KANGWON-do, ROK.

Since the beginning of 1970 ROKAF radar stations along the eastern coast of the ROK in KANGWON-do have been sighting (detecting) maneuvers of large balloon-shaped objects at high altitude just north of the extreme Eastern Sector of the Korean DMZ [Demilitarized Zone]. On several occasions these UFOs, which the ROKAF officials are assuming to be dirigibles because of their shape and speed, have penetrated ROK air space, traveled in a southeasterly direction over KANGWON-do and then exploded. ROK efforts to recover debris subsequent to the explosions have been unsuccessful.

The ROKAF Chief of Staff speculated that if current maneuvers of the UFOs prove to be successful, then NK [North Korea] may use the self-propelled balloons for dropping agents, propaganda, or even epidemic germs into the ROK. His briefing and speculation caused consternation among the ROKAF SU [Security Units] CO's because this was the first report they had had of such penetrations.

The most likely explanation for these "UFOs" is that they were North Korean reconnaissance balloons, as the report suggests, yet there were some puzzling factors, such as the lack of recovered debris. An evaluation of the report was requested, but this has not been included in the released DIA documents. I recall that antiaircraft guns opened fire on the UFOs when they made an appearance over the Blue House, the Korean President's official residence, but no hits were scored.

SPAIN, 1973–74

A wave of sightings in Spain in 1973–74 attracted DIA attention, and Captain Richard Fox, Acting Defense Attaché in Madrid, forwarded summaries of twenty-nine sightings which had been translated from local newspaper reports. Fox pointed out that the reports had not been checked for their validity but that the data was being forwarded "strictly for information of those parties interested."

One of the sightings was witnessed on 23 March 1974 by the chauffeur of the President of the Cadiz Provincial Commission on a highway near Sanlucar do Barrameda. A luminous, metallic object "moved up with great brilliancy. As observer approached object, he felt a strange sensation. His car finally came practically to a stop, wavering back and forth like a feather."

Another interesting report was made by a truck driver at Valdehijaderos on the night of 27 March 1974 who allegedly saw:

> . . . three silver ships parked on the highway with light similar to floodlight. Observer stopped motor of his car and some figures approached him. He ran, frightened, and they followed him. He threw himself into a gutter. His pursuers passed within 2 meters and he saw them. They were about 2 meters tall, had arms and legs but he did not see their faces. After they passed he returned to the truck. The beings returned to observe him again, then they entered their ships and left. Next day the Guardia Civil made an investigation. They found a hole in the ground, which the truck driver said he had not made.

Captain Fox commented: "It is of interest to note that in April of this year teams of extrasensory perception specialists held a meeting in Malaga for the purpose of scientifically studying the UFOs seen in that vicinity. Results of this meeting unknown.''

In 1976 the Spanish government opened its files on UFOs to Juan Jose Benitez, a reporter on *La Gaceta del Norte,* who had been invited to Madrid by the Air Ministry. On 20 October, in an office of an Air Force lieutenant general who was Chief of Staff, Benitez was handed a file of seventy-eight folio pages containing documentation on twelve of their best cases, as well as photographic material including film taken by Spanish Air Force pilots, which had hitherto been secret.[19]

PAKISTAN/AFGHANISTAN/USSR, 1974

A DIA Intelligence Information Report, with the delightful subject heading "Balls of Fire," contains a report translated from an Urdu language newspaper describing a sighting in December 1974:

> According to a statement by Mr. Mohammad Riaz, Executive Engineer Pakistan PWD, Warsak, who was in Patan area at about 7 p.m. on Dec. 18, a circular light appeared above the V shaped mountain overlooking the approach to Patan. The circle around the light went on expanding. As the circle expanded the light emanating from it became less and less. At first he thought it was a reflection from the moon but the moon was in a different position. He said that the circular light went on expanding for about 15 to 25 minutes. Eight days after the appearance of this light, the area was shaken by the earthquake. At the time he saw the light, those present along with him were: Rasul Khan, Executive Engineer, Captain Tariq, a doctor, Mr. Farooq Khan, an officer of the Frontier Constabulary.

The General Staff Army Attaché who prepared the report comments that "ARMA has discussed these reports with DATT/ARMA Afghanistan who says that he has not heard of any such reports in Kabul. However, he has jokingly suggested that the phenomenon may simply have been sightings of Santa Claus preparing for Christmas. Despite DAO Kabul's skepticism we would appreciate an evaluation from DIA." The DIA's evaluation has not been made available, but the sighting, in my opinion, almost certainly relates to a barium cloud experiment, released into the upper atmosphere by rocket.

IRAN, 1976

One of the most important DIA documents is that describing the sensational sighting by the crew of Imperial Iranian Air Force Phantom jets who encountered a UFO over Tehran in September 1976, when one of the jets attempted to fire a guided missile at it. The report was sent by the Defense Attaché at the US Embassy in Tehran to the DIA. The distribution list included the White House, Secretary of State, National Security Agency, and of course the CIA:

A. AT ABOUT 1230 A.M. ON 19 SEP 76 THE IMPERIAL IRANIAN AIR FORCE (IIAF) COMMAND POST RECEIVED FOUR TELEPHONE CALLS FROM CITIZENS LIVING IN THE SHEMIRAN AREA OF TEHRAN SAYING THAT THEY HAD SEEN STRANGE OBJECTS IN THE SKY. SOME REPORTED A KIND OF BIRD-LIKE OBJECT WHILE OTHERS REPORTED A HELICOPTER WITH A LIGHT ON. THERE WERE NO HELICOPTERS AIRBORNE AT THAT TIME. THE COMMAND POST CALLED BG YOUSEFI, ASSISTANT DEPUTY COMMANDER OF OPERATIONS. AFTER HE TOLD THE CITIZEN IT WAS ONLY STARS AND HAD TALKED TO MEHRABAD TOWER HE DECIDED TO LOOK FOR HIMSELF. HE NOTICED AN OBJECT IN THE SKY SIMILAR TO A STAR BIGGER AND BRIGHTER. HE DECIDED TO SCRAMBLE AN F-4 FROM SHAHROKHI AFB TO INVESTIGATE.

B. AT 0130 HRS ON THE 19TH THE F-4 TOOK OFF AND PROCEEDED TO A POINT ABOUT 40 NM NORTH OF TEHRAN. DUE TO ITS BRILLIANCE THE OBJECT WAS EASILY VISIBLE FROM 70 MILES AWAY. AS THE F-4 APPROACHED A RANGE OF 25 NM HE LOST ALL INSTRUMENTATION AND COMMUNICATIONS (UHF AND INTERCOM). HE BROKE OFF THE INTERCEPT AND HEADED BACK TO SHAHROKHI. WHEN THE F-4 TURNED AWAY FROM THE OBJECT AND APPARENTLY WAS NO LONGER A THREAT TO IT THE AIRCRAFT REGAINED ALL INSTRUMENTATION AND COMMUNICATIONS. AT 0140 HRS A SECOND F-4 WAS LAUNCHED. THE BACKSEATER ACQUIRED A RADAR LOCK ON AT 27 NM, 12 O'CLOCK HIGH POSITION WITH THE VC (RATE OF CLOSURE) AT 150 NMPH. AS THE RANGE DECREASED TO 25 NM THE OBJECT MOVED AWAY AT A SPEED THAT WAS VISIBLE ON THE RADARSCOPE AND STAYED AT 25 NM.

C. THE SIZE OF THE RADAR RETURN WAS COMPARABLE TO THAT OF A 707 TANKER. THE VISUAL SIZE OF THE OBJECT WAS DIFFICULT TO DISCERN BECAUSE OF ITS INTENSE BRILLIANCE. THE LIGHT THAT IT GAVE OFF WAS THAT OF FLASHING STROBE LIGHTS ARRANGED IN A RECTANGULAR PATTERN AND ALTERNATING BLUE, GREEN, RED AND ORANGE IN COLOR. THE SEQUENCE OF THE LIGHTS WAS SO FAST THAT ALL THE COLORS COULD BE SEEN AT ONCE. THE OBJECT AND THE PURSUING F-4 CONTINUED ON A COURSE TO THE SOUTH OF TEHRAN WHEN ANOTHER BRIGHTLY LIGHTED OBJECT, ESTIMATED TO BE ONE HALF TO ONE THIRD THE APPARENT SIZE OF THE MOON, CAME OUT OF THE ORIGINAL OBJECT. THIS SECOND OBJECT HEADED STRAIGHT TOWARD THE F-4 AT A VERY FAST RATE OF SPEED. THE PILOT ATTEMPTED TO FIRE AN AIM-9 MISSILE AT THE OBJECT BUT AT THAT INSTANT HIS WEAPONS CONTROL PANEL WENT OFF AND HE LOST ALL COMMUNICATIONS (UHF AND INTERPHONE). AT THIS POINT

THE PILOT INITIATED A TURN AND NEGATIVE G DIVE TO GET AWAY. AS HE TURNED THE OBJECT FELL IN TRAIL AT WHAT APPEARED TO BE ABOUT 3–4 NM. AS HE CONTINUED IN HIS TURN AWAY FROM THE PRIMARY OBJECT THE SECOND OBJECT WENT TO THE INSIDE OF HIS TURN THEN RETURNED TO THE PRIMARY OBJECT FOR A PERFECT REJOIN.

D. SHORTLY AFTER THE SECOND OBJECT JOINED UP WITH THE PRIMARY OBJECT ANOTHER OBJECT APPEARED TO COME OUT OF THE OTHER SIDE OF THE PRIMARY OBJECT GOING STRAIGHT DOWN, AT A GREAT RATE OF SPEED. THE F-4 CREW HAD REGAINED COMMUNICATIONS AND THE WEAPONS CONTROL PANEL AND WATCHED THE OBJECT APPROACH THE GROUND ANTICIPATING A LARGE EXPLOSION. THIS OBJECT APPEARED TO COME TO REST GENTLY ON THE EARTH AND CAST A VERY BRIGHT LIGHT OVER AN AREA OF ABOUT 2–3 KILOMETERS. THE CREW DESCENDED FROM THEIR ALTITUDE OF 26M TO 15M AND CONTINUED TO OBSERVE AND MARK THE OBJECT'S POSITION. THEY HAD SOME DIFFICULTY IN ADJUSTING THEIR NIGHT VISIBILITY FOR LANDING SO AFTER ORBITING MEHRABAD A FEW TIMES THEY WENT OUT FOR A STRAIGHT IN LANDING. THERE WAS A LOT OF INTERFERENCE ON THE UHF AND EACH TIME THEY PASSED THROUGH A MAG. BEARING OF 150 DEGREE FROM MEHRABAD THEY LOST THEIR COMMUNICATIONS (UHF AND INTERPHONE) AND THE INS FLUCTUATED FROM 30 DEGREES–50 DEGREES. THE ONE CIVIL AIRLINER THAT WAS APPROACHING MEHRABAD DURING THIS SAME TIME EXPERIENCED COMMUNICATIONS FAILURE IN THE SAME VICINITY (KILO ZULU) BUT DID NOT REPORT SEEING ANYTHING. WHILE THE F-4 WAS ON A LONG FINAL APPROACH THE CREW NOTICED ANOTHER CYLINDER SHAPED OBJECT (ABOUT THE SIZE OF A T-BIRD AT 10M) WITH BRIGHT STEADY LIGHTS ON EACH END AND A FLASHER IN THE MIDDLE. WHEN QUERIED THE TOWER STATED THERE WAS NO OTHER KNOWN TRAFFIC IN THE AREA. DURING THE TIME THE OBJECT PASSED OVER THE F-4 THE TOWER DID NOT HAVE A VISUAL ON IT BUT PICKED IT UP AFTER THE PILOT TOLD THEM TO LOOK BETWEEN THE MOUNTAINS AND THE REFINERY.

E. DURING DAYLIGHT THE F-4 CREW WAS TAKEN OUT TO THE AREA IN A HELICOPTER WHERE THE OBJECT APPARENTLY HAD LANDED. NOTHING WAS NOTICED AT THE SPOT WHERE THEY THOUGHT THE OBJECT LANDED (A DRY LAKE BED) BUT AS THEY CIRCLED OFF TO THE WEST OF THE AREA THEY PICKED UP A VERY NOTICEABLE BEEPER SIGNAL. AT THE POINT WHERE THE RETURN WAS THE LOUDEST WAS A SMALL HOUSE WITH A GARDEN. THEY LANDED AND ASKED THE PEOPLE WITHIN IF THEY HAD NOTICED ANYTHING STRANGE LAST NIGHT. THE PEOPLE TALKED ABOUT A LOUD NOISE AND A VERY BRIGHT LIGHT LIKE LIGHTNING. THE AIRCRAFT AND AREA WHERE THE OBJECT IS BELIEVED TO HAVE LANDED ARE BEING CHECKED FOR POSSIBLE RADIATION. RO COMMENTS: (C) ACTUAL INFORMATION CON-

TAINED IN THIS REPORT WAS OBTAINED FROM SOURCE IN CONVER-
SATION WITH A SUB-SOURCE, AND IIAF PILOT OF ONE OF THE F-4S.
MORE INFORMATION WILL BE FORWARDED WHEN IT BECOMES
AVAILABLE.

This exceptional report was originally released to Charles Huffer in
1977, although he had initially been denied the document. Attached to
it was a DIA Defense Information Report Evaluation, a rarity among
documents released by the Agency. The concluding comments are remarkable:

> An outstanding report. This case is a classic which meets all the criteria
> necessary for a valid study of the UFO phenomenon:
>
> a) The object was seen by multiple witnesses from different locations
> (i.e. Shamiran, Mehrabad, and the dry lake bed) and viewpoints (both
> airborne and from the ground).
> b) The credibility of many of the witnesses was high (an Air Force
> general, qualified aircrews, and experienced tower operators).
> c) Visual sightings were confirmed by radar.
> d) Similar electromagnetic effects (EME) were reported by three sep-
> arate aircraft.
> e) There were physiological effects on some crew members (i.e. loss
> of night vision due to the brightness of the object).
> f) An inordinate amount of maneuverability was displayed by the UFOs.[20]

It is perhaps not without significance that the DIA chose to exclude this
evaluation in the set of documents released to Ray Boeche, although they
included the actual intelligence report. One wonders just how many other
positive evaluations remain classified in the DIA files at the Pentagon.

TEHRAN, 1978

Further sightings in Iran interested the DIA in 1978. The following case,
though not acquired through official sources, merits inclusion here. The
report was sent by the local Defense Attaché's office to the Joint Chiefs
of Staff at the Department of Defense, Pentagon, this being the normal
routing for foreign intelligence reports. As with the previous case, the
distribution list included the Secretary of State, National Security Agency,
and the CIA. The report was quoted from the Iranian English language
newspaper, *Tehran Journal*, dated 18 July 1978:

> An unidentified flying object was seen by a number of people in the northern
> part of the city on Sunday night. Officials from the control tower at Mehra-

bad Airport and a Lufthansa aircrew also reported unusual readings on their instruments.

Residents in northern Tehran were the first to spot the strange glowing object floating toward Saveh. They had been sleeping on the terraces of their houses, and immediately informed the control tower at Mehrabad Airport and the National Radio Network. The control tower confirmed the existence of the object but would give no further details. Soon afterward, the Lufthansa plane sent in its report.

A similar flying object was seen last April by a local airline pilot, who claimed that he had photographed the object, but could not release photographs until the security division of the civil aviation authorities gave their permission. He claimed that while flying between Ahvaz and Tehran at 24,000 feet, he and his co-pilot had sighted a glittering object and had managed to photograph it. A Mehrabad radar control official said that on that occasion they had detected an object some 20 times the size of a jumbo jet on their screens.

Civil Aviation Organization chief has . . . called for an investigation but the results of this inquiry have not yet been made public.

An eye witness said yesterday that he was alone on his balcony on Sunday night when suddenly he saw the object emerge in the sky and hover directly above him. ''I was so upset that I wanted to scream, but could not do so,'' he said. He added that he felt better once he realized that his neighbors had also seen it.

BOLIVIA, 1979

An unevaluated DIA intelligence report, titled ''Moon Dust—Object Found Near Santa Cruz,'' describes an intriguing story of an unidentified object which was recovered on a farm near Santa Cruz, Bolivia, in August 1979. The object was ''possibly a fuel tank or part of a satellite,'' according to the Defense Attaché at the US Embassy in La Paz, yet seems to have remained unidentified. Furthermore, there had been a similar occurrence in Bolivia in May 1978 which led to an interesting exchange of cables between the Embassy and the State Department. In this earlier case, Secretary of State Cyrus Vance replied in a secret cable that, having checked with the appropriate government agencies, ''No direct correlation with known space objects that may have entered the earth's atmosphere near May 6 can be made.''[21]

According to the DIA report, a strange object was found on a farm near Santa Cruz on 16 August 1979, which was about seventy centimeters in diameter and two meters in circumference with a hole in one side and a metal skin covering of about a half-inch thickness. The *El Deber* newspaper of 17 August quoted Colonel Ariel Coca, Director of the Bolivian Air Force Academy, as saying that the sphere was made of a special light alloy, but very resistant, and had no signs or marks that could identify its origin. Colonel Coca said that he would inform his superiors about "the phenomenon" so that a study could be made to determine its origin, and an analysis made in case it was radioactive. An accompanying photograph showed the colonel examining the sphere, which had a hole in it measuring about nine inches in diameter. The DIA report added that a movie film and color prints of the object would be forwarded to the Agency's DT-3 division (Technical Data and Foreign Material Branch, Directorate of Scientific and Technical Intelligence).

Another such object was discovered on the same day, according to *El Diario* of 19 August. This second one was found 200 kilometers north of Santa Cruz by Gonzalo Menacho Viveras, who heard a whistling sound and saw a "fireball," followed by an explosion. After dawn on the Friday morning the witness started looking around the area of impact and found a sphere. Since it was not heavy he took it home and kept it there until his friend Nataniel Hurtado learned of the other sphere in Cotoca and passed on information about the second object. He said that the following evening a "silent aircraft" with three lights was seen flying over the explosion site.

Although the witnesses in both cases reported the objects as "fireballs," no signs of impact could be seen in the areas where they were discovered, and the spheres appeared to have landed smoothly. The witness who discovered the second sphere said that there were some burned plants in the immediate area but no sign of impact on the soft ground. The object weighed about six kilograms and had a diameter of eighty centimeters. The outside metal was similar to copper, and had apparently been exposed to very high temperatures. It was made of two pieces joined without any signs of rivets and had a hole of irregular shape in the top and next to it another small round hole. In both these the material had melted and at the end of the sphere there was a round area that looked like "a cork in a bottle held in place by three semi-melted screws." An explosion had apparently destroyed the interior of the spheres.

The DIA has not released any evaluation of these cases, although it is doubtful if the objects were anything other than terrestrial in origin, despite a few puzzling factors.

PERU, 1980

Last but certainly not least of the DIA documents relates to two sightings by Peruvian Air Force personnel in May 1980, including the interception and attempted destruction of a UFO. The source of information was a Peruvian Air Force officer who, according to the US Air Attaché in Lima, "observed the event and is in a position to be party to conversation concerning the event. Source has reported reliably in the past." The details of this extraordinary case are as follows:

> SOURCE TOLD RO ABOUT THE SPOTTING OF AN UNIDENTIFIED FLYING OBJECT IN THE VICINITY OF MARIANO MELGAR AIR BASE, LA JOYA, (PERU 16805S, 0715306W). SOURCE STATED THAT THE VEHICLE WAS SPOT-TED ON TWO DIFFERENT OCCASIONS. THE FIRST WAS DURING THE MORNING HOURS OF 9 MAY 80, AND THE SECOND DURING THE EARLY EVENING HOURS OF 10 MAY 80.
>
> SOURCE STATED THAT ON 9 MAY, WHILE A GROUP OF FAP [PERU-VIAN AIR FORCE] OFFICERS WERE IN FORMATION AT MARIANO MAL-GAR [sic], THEY SPOTTED A UFO THAT WAS ROUND IN SHAPE, HOVERING NEAR THE AIRFIELD. THE AIR COMMANDER SCRAMBLED AN SU-22 [Sukhoi] AIRCRAFT TO MAKE AN INTERCEPT. THE PILOT, ACCORDING TO A THIRD PARTY, INTERCEPTED THE VEHICLE AND FIRED UPON IT AT VERY CLOSE RANGE WITHOUT CAUSING ANY APPARENT DAMAGE. THE PILOT TRIED TO MAKE A SECOND PASS ON THE VEHICLE, BUT THE UFO OUT-RAN THE SU-22.
>
> THE SECOND SIGHTING WAS DURING THE HOURS OF DARKNESS. THE VEHICLE WAS LIGHTED. AGAIN AN SU-22 WAS SCRAMBLED, BUT THE VEHICLE OUT-RAN THE AIRCRAFT. . . .
>
> RO HAS HEARD DISCUSSION ABOUT THE SIGHTING FROM OTHER SOURCES. APPARENTLY SOME VEHICLE WAS SPOTTED, BUT ITS ORIGIN REMAINS UNKNOWN.

The Defense Attaché did not request an evaluation from the DIA, presumably because it was obvious that a genuine UFO was involved and there would have been little point in further commentary. The distribution list for the report included, again, the National Security Agency, Secretary of State and the CIA. In view of the CIA's statement to me that "there is no organized Central Intelligence Agency effort to do research in connection with the UFO phenomena, nor has there been an organized effort to collect intelligence on UFOs since the 1950s," one wonders why the CIA remained on the DIA distribution list from the period 1976–80, unless the CIA's qualifying rider that they have received "various kinds of reports of UFO sightings" since the 1950s would account for this inconsistency.[22]

Another puzzling factor is the complete absence of British and Australian reports among the declassified DIA documents. Britain and Australia have had an enormous number of sightings over the years, as we have seen. Are we to conclude that some of these reports—especially the military ones—are of no interest to the Agency? I do not believe this for one moment, and am convinced that there is an agreement between the DIA and British as well as Australian defense intelligence chiefs not to include such documentation in the released Freedom of Information cases. There is a very close liaison, for example, between the DIA and the Ministry of Defense, via the Defense Intelligence Agency Liaison in London (DIALL), which has its office in the MoD's main building in Whitehall.[23] In view of Britain's "special relationship" with the DIA, CIA, and NSA, it seems logical to me that UFO reports of significance would be passed on to the DIA by the MoD, just as reports would also be forwarded to the NSA by Government Communications Headquarters (GCHQ), Britain's equivalent of the NSA which works hand in glove with that Agency. The British government—having as yet no Freedom of Information Act—is anxious not to compromise its official position vis-à-vis the UFO controversy, but I am reliably informed that there is a close interchange of information on the subject by the relevant agencies.

Despite some obviously significant reports, the DIA has not released any worthwhile analyses, with the exception of the 1976 Tehran case. This is probably at the request of the Director of Central Intelligence, who in addition to being head of the CIA manages the entire community of intelligence agencies throughout the US government. Admiral Stansfield Turner, Director of Central Intelligence (DCI) during the Carter administration, is scathing about the DIA's analytic product, however, which he describes as "well below the caliber of the rest of the Intelligence Community."[24] Admiral Turner also points out that the CIA's analytic work competes with that of the DIA and other intelligence agencies, and leaves us in no doubt that the CIA is superior in this respect.[25] Unlike the CIA, the DIA cannot present its analyses directly to the National Security Council, although the Secretary of Defense can, if he chooses, present DIA estimates that differ from those of the CIA.[26] Of course, neither agency is prepared to release its analyses of the UFO phenomenon, so we are forced to draw our own conclusions from the released documents. Perhaps we should be grateful for these. At the same time, the DIA denied for years that they possessed any documents on UFOs other than those few they released in the late 1970s; further evidence that governments worldwide are reluctant to acknowledge their serious concern with the ubiquitous UFO phenomenon.

14

THE CENTRAL INTELLIGENCE AGENCY

The Central Intelligence Agency is America's equivalent of the British Secret Intelligence Service (SIS or MI6) and was formed, with Britain's help, out of the Office of Strategic Services (OSS) and the Central Intelligence Group in 1947. The CIA officially employs a staff of about 16,000, but this figure does not take into account its foreign agents or the thousands of contracted personnel, neither does it include subsidiary staff from other branches of the US government. It has an estimated annual budget of $1 billion.

The CIA is divided into four Directorates, each Directorate containing many different offices and services. The *Directorate of Operations* oversees foreign intelligence (espionage) as well as counterintelligence, and includes the Covert Action Staff (disinformation and propaganda). The *Directorate of Science and Technology* monitors scientific and technical developments in foreign countries, and includes the Office of SIGINT (Signals Intelligence) operations, the Foreign Broadcast Information Service and the National Photographic Interpretation Center. The *Directorate of Intelligence* is largely responsible for the analysis of intelligence, with offices of analysis for the Soviet Union, Europe, Near East and South Asia, Africa and Latin America. It also includes the Office of Scientific and Weapons Research, the Office of Imagery Analysis, and the Office of Global Issues. The *Directorate of Administration* is responsible for personnel, training, finance, medical services, security, logistics and communications.[1]

Above these four Directorates is the *National Intelligence Council* (formerly the Intelligence Resources Advisory Committee) which coordinates the various methods of intelligence-gathering according to the priorities assigned to the requests that are presented to it. At the same level of authority are the national intelligence officers who prepare the national intelligence estimates which go to the National Security Council and sometimes to the President.[2]

According to Todd Zechel, a former employee of the National Security Agency, all four directorates of the CIA have been engaged in collecting, analyzing and suppressing UFO data since 1948. Zechel claims that the National Photographic Interpretation Center, established within the Directorate of Science and Technology in 1953, has been analyzing all UFO photographic data, and the Office of Scientific Intelligence (as it was then called) has been analyzing worldwide UFO data since its inception, including nonphotographic cases, physical evidence and secondary analysis of photographic cases.

Zechel further claims that domestic reports were collected by the CIA from the Air Force, via the Pentagon's Office of Current Intelligence, and from other intelligence agencies such as the NSA and Defense Intelligence Agency, via links with their communications networks. Domestic reports have been collected from the CIA's Domestic Operations Division (Domestic Collection Division) offices in cities throughout the United States, Zechel maintains. Foreign reports were collected by the National Foreign Assessment Center via the Foreign Broadcast Information Service, the Office of Current Intelligence and the Office of Operations, as these departments were called until the 1970s.

Zechel also makes the disturbing claim that agents of the CIA's Directorate of Operations have interrogated UFO witnesses and that agents of the Domestic Operations Division have been involved in harassing, intimidating and even silencing witnesses.[3] Is there any evidence for these claims, which were made by Zechel in 1977?

THE CIA AND THE FREEDOM OF INFORMATION ACT

It is largely due to the efforts of Todd Zechel, together with William Spaulding of Ground Saucer Watch (GSW), an Arizona-based UFO research organization[4], that almost 1,000 pages of CIA UFO-related documents were released under provisions of the Freedom of Information Act (FOIA) in 1978, following months of legal battles. Henry Rothblatt and Peter Gersten, two New York lawyers who acted on GSW's behalf, had sued the CIA in 1977 under the FOIA in a successful attempt to force the Agency to release its files on UFOs. On 20 December 1978 a press release announcing "CIA Releases UFO Documents" was distributed to the news media in Washington, DC. It had been prepared by Citizens Against UFO Secrecy (CAUS), an organization founded a few months previously by Todd Zechel.[5]

There are believed to be over 10,000 pages of classified UFO documents at the CIA's headquarters in Langley, Virginia, yet the Agency has admitted to withholding only fifty-seven documents. Peter Gersten told me in 1980 that the CIA failed to disclose the existence of 200 or more documents, based on references in the released documents. Perhaps this can be explained by the fact that in 1980 the House of Representatives passed the Foreign Affairs Committee Bill, which effectively exempted the CIA from the majority of requirements flooding into it under the FOIA.[6] And yet, out of nine exemptions to the FOIA, *not one pertains to UFO records*. When researchers such as myself request certain UFO records from the CIA, NSA, DIA, and other agencies, we are often told that they are exempt from release due to national security or that "records cannot be released because they have been destroyed" or that "the information is properly classified and cannot be released." How curious, then, that the official US Air Force position is that "no UFO reported, investigated, and evaluated by the Air Force has ever given any indication of a threat to our national security."[7]

THE RELEASED CIA DOCUMENTS

The CIA's public position on UFOs—prior to the release of the documents—is best summed up in a letter to Bill Spaulding, dated 26 March 1976:

> In order that you may be aware of the true facts concerning the involvement of the CIA in the investigation of the UFO phenomena, let me give you the following brief history. Late in 1952, the National Security Council levied upon the CIA the requirement to determine if the existence of UFOs would create a danger to the security of the United States. The Office of Scientific Intelligence established the Intelligence Advisory Committee to study the matter. That committee made the recommendations [in] the Robertson Panel Report. At no time prior to the formation of the Robertson Panel and subsequent to this issuance of the panel's report [January 1953], has the CIA engaged in the study of UFO phenomena. The Robertson Panel Report is the summation of the Agency's interest and involvement in this matter.

The released documents, most of which are in my possession, categorically show that the CIA's interest in UFOs predates the National Security Council directive to set up the Robertson Panel. It was in fact the CIA that urged the NSC to conduct the investigation, as is evident from the following extracts taken from a four-page memorandum to the Director of the CIA (DCI), General Walter Bedell Smith, from H. Marshall Chadwell, Assistant Director of Scientific Intelligence, dated 24 September 1952:

1. Recently an inquiry was conducted by the Office of Scientific Intelligence to determine whether there are national security implications in the problem of "unidentified flying objects," i.e. flying saucers; whether adequate study and research is currently being directed to this problem in its relation to such national security implications; and what further investigation and research should be instituted, by whom, and under what aegis.

2. It was found that the only unit of government currently studying the problem is the Directorate of Intelligence, USAF, which has charged the Air Technical Intelligence Center (ATIC) with the responsibility for investigating the reports of sightings. . . . A worldwide reporting system has been instituted and major Air Force bases have been ordered to make interceptions of unidentified flying objects. . . .

3. Since 1947, ATIC has received approximately 1500 *official* reports of sightings. . . . During 1952 alone, *official* reports totaled 250. Of the 1500 reports, Air Force carries 20 percent as *unexplained* and of those received from January through July 1952 it carries 28 percent *unexplained*. . . .

4. . . . public concern with the phenomena . . . indicates that a fair proportion of our population is mentally conditioned to the acceptance of the incredible. In this fact lies the potential for the touching-off of mass hysteria and panic. . . .

8. . . . In order to minimize risk of panic, a national policy should be established as to what should be told the public regarding the phenomena. . . .

11. I consider this problem to be of such importance that it should be brought to the attention of the National Security Council in order that a community-wide coordinated effort toward its solution may be initiated.

Although Marshall Chadwell states in paragraph 2 that "the only unit of government currently studying the problem is the Directorate of Intelligence, USAF," the CIA had been closely monitoring the phenomenon since 1947, as the released documents show. According to investigative journalist Warren Smith the CIA first became interested in UFO reports prior to its establishment in 1947, when it was known as the Office of Strategic Services (OSS), headed by Major General William ("Wild Bill") Donovan. The "foo-fighters" were being sighted in increasing numbers during the latter stages of World War II, and the OSS was at first convinced that they were German pilotless probes. Investigation by OSS agents in Europe proved otherwise, and Donovan and his staff decided that the foo-fighters were unusual but harmless phenomena.

Shortly after pilot Kenneth Arnold's famous sighting on 24 June 1947,

Smith was told, the OSS met at the prestigious Brooks Club in New York and organized a funded effort to establish the truth about the flying disks. At first it was believed that the Russians were responsible, assisted by captured German scientists, but certain characteristics of the reports negated this theory. The OSS was concerned that such sightings could cause panic, and that phone lines and military communication channels would be swamped. The flying saucers had to be debunked. Psychological warfare and propaganda were brought to bear, using hoaxes, false sightings and wild reports. Articles ridiculing flying saucers were planted in national newspapers and magazines.[8]

A CIA memorandum dated 31 March 1949 from H. L. Bowers to Dr. Machle, with the subject heading ''Notes and Comments on 'Unidentified Flying Objects'—Project Sign'' (an early US Air Force study), concluded:

> Studies on the various possibilities have been made by Dr. Langmuir of GE, Dr. Valley of MIT, Dr. Lipp of Project Rand, Dr. Hynek of Ohio State and the Aero Medical Lab.
>
> That the objects are from outer space or are an advanced aircraft of a foreign power is a possibility, but the above group have concluded that it is highly improbable.
>
> In discussion of this subject with Mr. Deyarmond at Wright Patterson Air Force Base, he seemed to think, and I agree, that the ''flying disks'' will turn out to be another ''sea-serpent.'' However, since there is even a remote possibility that they may be interplanetary or foreign aircraft, it is necessary to investigate each sighting.

Proof that the CIA was monitoring the UFO phenomenon for several years prior to the Robertson Panel in 1953 is contained in several documents. One, classified Eyes Only, is a memorandum from Ralph L. Clark, Acting Assistant Director for the Office of Scientific Intelligence, to the Deputy Director of Intelligence, dated 29 July 1952:

> In the past several weeks a number of radar and visual sightings of unidentified aerial objects have been reported. *Although this office has maintained a continuing review of such reported sightings during the past three years*, a special study group has been formed to review this subject to date. O/CI [Office of Central Intelligence] will participate in this study with O/SI [Office of Scientific Intelligence] and a report should be ready about 15 August. [Emphasis added]

Another document, an informal memorandum written only a few days later, was from Edward Tauss, then Acting Chief of the Weapons and

Equipment Division of the Office of Scientific Intelligence, to the Deputy Assitant Director of the OSI. Although expressing skepticism about the reliability of even the unexplained reports, Tauss nevertheless adds:

> . . . so long as a series of reports remains "unexplainable" (interplanetary aspects and alien origin not being thoroughly excluded from consideration) caution requires that intelligence continue coverage of the subject. . . . It is recommended that CIA surveillance of subject matter, in coordination with proper authorities of primarily operational concern at ATIC, be continued. *It is strongly urged, however, that no indication of CIA interest or concern reach the press or public,* in view of their probable alarmist tendencies to accept such interest as "confirmatory" of the soundness of "unpublished facts" in the hands of the U.S. government. [Emphasis added]

The CIA special study group was established in August 1952, and the documents relating to the briefing make interesting reading, and were classified secret at the time. The first is dated 14 August:

> During the past weeks, with the phenomenal increase in the number of Flying Saucer reports there has been a tremendous stimulation of both public and official interest in the subject. Requests for information have poured in on the Air Force, including an official query from the White House. . . .
>
> At this point, OSI felt that it would be timely to make an evaluation of the Air Force study, its methodology and coverage, the relation of its conclusions to various theories which have been propounded, and to try to reach some conclusion as to the intelligence implications of the problem—if any. In view of the wide interest within the Agency, this briefing has been arranged so that we could report on the survey. It must be mentioned that *outside knowledge of Agency interest in Flying Saucers carries the risk of making the problem even more serious in the public mind than it already is, which we and the Air Force agree must be avoided.* [Emphasis added]

The report adds that "we have reviewed our own intelligence, going back to the Swedish sightings of 1946," and lists the various types of UFO reported to the Air Force:

> Grouped broadly as visual, radar, and combined visual and radar, ATIC has two major visual classes—first, spherical or elliptical objects, usually of bright metallic luster, some small (2 or 3 feet across), most estimated at 100 foot diameter and a few 1000 feet wide. There are variants in this group, such as torpedos, triangulars, pencils, even mattress-shapes. These are all daylight reportings.

The second visual group, all night reporting, consists of lights and various luminosities, such as green, flaming-red or blue-white fire balls, moving points of light, and luminous streamers.

Both categories are reported as single objects, in non-symmetrical groups and in formations of various numbers.

Reported characteristics include three general levels of speed: hovering; moderate, as with a conventional aircraft; and stupendous, up to 18,000 miles per hour in the White Sands Incident. Violent maneuvering was reported in somewhat less than 10%. Accelerations have been given as high as 20 g's. With few exceptions, there has been a complete absence of sound or vapor trail. Evasion upon approach is common.

Radars have shown many unidentified "blips" but there is no reported instance of complete tracking in and out of the maximum drum, and no report of a track from station to station. The blip, in almost every case, passed through the center of the scope.

Various instances of radar/visual sightings are cited, including one that "occurred a few days ago at Wright Field and has not yet been fully analyzed. Two F-94's with cameras were vectored in on a blip. Both pilots sighted an object and one locked on with his AI equipment. Reaching his maximum allowable altitude, he triggered his camera and the negative shows 'an object.' "

The CIA reviewed the likelihood that the UFOs were US weapons, and concluded that this hypothesis was untenable:

This has been denied officially at the highest level of government and to make certain we queried Dr. Whitman, Chairman of the Research and Development Board. On a Top Secret basis, he, too, denies it. However, in view of the Manhattan District early super security, [relating to the first US atom bomb] two factors might be mentioned which tend to confirm his denials—first, the official action of alerting all Air Force commands to intercept, and second, the unbelievable risk aspect of such flights in established airlanes.

The CIA also ruled out the possibility that UFOs were Soviet secret weapons. "Though we know that the Russians have done work on elliptical and delta wing principles," the report states, "we have absolutely no intelligence of such a technological advance as would be indicated here in either design or energy source. Further, there seems to be no logical reason for the security risk which would be involved and there has been no indication of a reconnaissance pattern."

The extraterrestrial hypothesis was then reviewed by the CIA/OSI special study group:

> Even though we might admit that intelligent life may exist elsewhere and that space travel is possible, there is no shred of evidence to support this theory at present. There have been no astronomical observations in confirmation—no slightest indication of the orbitting which would probably be necessary—and no tracking. However, it might be noted that Comdr. McLaughlin (of the White Sands report), a number of General Mills balloon people and many others are reported to be convinced of this theory.

Although the CIA special study group stated that there was not a shred of evidence to support the extraterrestrial hypothesis, a crashed disk was in fact recovered at Roswell, New Mexico, in July 1947, which was believed by those involved in the investigations to be of nonterrestrial origin. However absurd this may seem, there is now massive documentation on the case, which I have reviewed in Chapter 11. But if a disk was recovered, why was the CIA not informed about it? Since there is evidence that the FBI was familiar with the stories of recovered flying disks at the time, this seems rather puzzling. In my view, the explanation is that the true facts about the Roswell disk (and possibly others) were restricted to the small and highly secret group, Majestic 12, formed to investigate and report its findings to the President. One of the members was Vice Admiral Roscoe Hillenkoetter, the CIA's first Director (1947–50), whose statements attesting to the reality and nonterrestrial origin of UFOs appear later in this chapter. Owing to strict compartmentation of intelligence, I very much doubt if the 1952 CIA special study group was aware of all the evidence in favor of the extraterrestrial hypothesis. I am sure that documentation for the reports of recovered disks exists within the CIA, but it is highly unlikely that it will be released for a long time to come.

As to the CIA special study group's statement that there had been no astronomical observations or evidence of orbiting that would tend to support the extraterrestrial hypothesis, there is an interesting story related by Warren Smith in this connection. Smith was allegedly told by a CIA informant that in 1953 the US Air Force developed a sophisticated radar tracking system which detected huge unidentified objects orbiting at 100 to 500 miles above the earth on thirteen different occasions that year. This alarming information was relayed to the Department of Defense and the CIA, and a tracking station was set up at the White Sands Proving Grounds, New Mexico, under the direction of the distinguished astronomer Dr. Clyde Tombaugh (who discovered Pluto in 1930 and who had himself had several unexplainable sightings of UFOs in the late 1940s).

Tombaugh confirmed that such a tracking system existed in an article published in February 1954 for the Astronomical Society of the Pacific, but stated that the project was sponsored by the Army Ordnance Research Department to keep an accurate check on "natural phenomena" in space.[9]

Finally, there is the 1952 CIA group comment on the fourth major theory, then held by the Air Force, that the sightings, given adequate data, could be explained on the basis of either misinterpretation of known objects, or of as yet poorly understood natural phenomena. This theory was endorsed in a lengthy briefing by a Mr. Eng, who nevertheless concluded: ". . . sightings of UFOs reported at Los Alamos and Oak Ridge, at a time when the background radiation count had risen inexplicably. Here we run out of even 'blue yonder' explanations that might be tenable, and we still are left with numbers of incredible reports from credible observers."

Another review of the CIA/OSI study group's findings is to be found in a sanitized copy of a six-page document dated 19 August 1952, originally classified secret. The CIA was puzzled not to have found "one report or comment, even satirical, in the Russian press. This could result only from an official policy decision and of course raises the question of *why* and of whether or not these sightings could be used from a psychological warfare point of view either offensively or defensively," and continues:

Air Force is aware of this and had investigated a number of the civilian groups that have sprung up to follow the subject. One—the Civilian Saucer Committee in California has substantial funds, strongly influences the editorial policy of a number of newspapers and has leaders whose connections may be questionable. Air Force is watching this organization because of its power to touch off mass hysteria and panic. Perhaps we, from an intelligence point of view, should watch for any indication of Russian efforts to capitalize upon this present American credulity.

Of even greater moment is the second danger. Our air warning system will undoubtedly always depend upon a combination of radar scanning and visual observation. We give Russia the capability of delivering an air attack against us, yet at any given moment now, there may be current a dozen *official* unidentified sightings plus many unofficial. At the moment of attack, how will we, on an instant basis, distinguish hardware from phantom? The answer of course [deleted in original] is that until far greater knowledge is achieved of the causes back of the sightings—the little understood phenomena [deleted] has described—we will run the increasing risk of false alerts and the even greater danger of tabbing the real as false.

All this is perfectly understandable, and the CIA continued to be haunted by the specter of World War III being triggered by UFOs mistaken as Soviet missiles or aircraft. The Office of Scientific Intelligence would continue to monitor Russian research and development in the scientific fields involved, the report concluded.

A few days later evidence of Russia's first mention of the subject was cited in a secret memorandum from George G. Carey, Assistant Director for Operations to the Deputy Director of Intelligence, dated 22 August 1952. The second paragraph states:

FBID [Foreign Broadcasts Information Division] has one broadcast on this subject, dated 10 June 1951, which is quoted below:
    Summary—In what appears to be Moscow's first mention of Flying Saucers "Listener's Mailbag" answers questions on the subject to the effect that "The Chief of Nuclear Physics in the US Naval Research Bureau" explained them recently as used for stratospheric studies. US government circles knew all along of the harmless nature of these objects, but if they refrained from denying "false reports, the purpose behind such tactics was to fan war hysteria in the country."

On 2 December 1952 H. Marshall Chadwell, Assistant Director of Scientific Intelligence, sent a secret memorandum to the CIA Director, discussing the preparation of the National Security Council Directive referred to earlier. Paragraph 4 makes particularly interesting reading:

Recent reports reaching CIA indicated that further action was desirable and another briefing by the cognizant A-2 [Air Force Intelligence] and ATIC [Air Technical Intelligence Center] personnel was held on 25 November. At this time, *the reports of incidents convince us that there is something going on that must have immediate attention. . . . Sightings of unexplained objects at great altitudes and traveling at high speeds in the vicinity of major U.S. defense installations are of such nature that they are not attributable to natural phenomena or known types of aerial vehicles.* [Emphasis added]

THE ROBERTSON PANEL REPORT

The situation had evidently become so worrying for the CIA by the end of 1952 that a panel of scientists was convened by the Office of Scientific Intelligence, and the secret meetings were held at the Pentagon from 14–17 January 1953. Although sanitized copies had been available to certain officials outside the CIA for a number of years, the Robertson Panel Report (sometimes referred to as the Durant Report) was not completely declassified until 1975, and even to this day there are those who believe that the report has not been released in its entirety. I wrote to the CIA in 1975 requesting a copy (under the FOIA), and it arrived a few months later.

Members of the Scientific Advisory Panel were Dr. H. P. Robertson (Chairman), whose specialty was physics and weapons systems; Dr. Luis Alvarez (physics and radar); Dr. Lloyd V. Berkner (geophysics); Dr. Samuel Goudsmit (atomic structure and statistical problems); Dr. Thornton Page (astronomy and astrophysics). The associate members were Dr. J. Allen Hynek (astronomy) and Frederick C. Durant (missiles and rockets).

The interviewees were Brigadier William H. Garland, Commanding General of Air Technical Intelligence Center; Dr. H. Marshall Chadwell, Assistant Director of the OSI/CIA; Ralph L. Clark, Deputy Assistant Director OSI/CIA; Lieutenant Colonel F. C. Oder and D. B. Stevenson, OSI staff members; Philip G. Strong, Chief, Operations Staff, OSI; Stephen T. Possony, Acting Chief, Special Study Group, Directorate of Air Force Intelligence; Colonels William A. Adams and Wesley S. Smith, also of Air Force Intelligence; Major Dewey Fournet, Headquarters, Air Force Intelligence Monitor of the UFO Project; Captain Edward J. Ruppelt, Chief, Aerial Phenomena Branch, ATIC; Lieutenant R. S. Neasham and Henry Woo of the US Navy Photo Interpretation Laboratory; and Albert M. Chop, the Air Force press officer handling UFO inquiries.

After twelve hours of meetings, during which the panel was shown movie films of UFOs, case histories of sightings prepared by the ATIC, intelligence reports relating to the Soviet Union's interest in US sightings, as well as numerous charts depicting, for example, frequency and geographic location of sightings, the panel came up with a largely skeptical view of the UFO situation, and in Part IV of the report, headed "Comments and Suggestions of Panel," concluded that "reasonable explanations could be suggested for most sightings . . . by deduction and scientific method it could be induced (given additional data) that other cases might be explained in a similar manner."

The panel also concluded unanimously that "there was no evidence of a direct threat to national security in the objects sighted" and that "the absence of any 'hardware' resulting from unexplained UFO sightings lends a 'will-of-the-wisp' nature to the ATIC problem. The results of their investigation, to date, strongly indicate that no evidence of hostile act or danger exists.'' The panel did not find any evidence either that any of the unexplained objects sighted could be extraterrestrial in origin, but nevertheless noted that:

> Mr. Fournet, in his presentation, showed how he had eliminated each of the known and probable causes of sightings leaving him ''extraterrestrial'' as the only one remaining in many cases. Fournet's background as an aeronautical engineer and technical intelligence officer (Project Officer, BLUEBOOK, for 15 months) could not be slighted. However, the Panel could not accept any of the cases sighted [sic] by him because they were raw, unevaluated reports. . . . Dr. Page noted that present astronomical knowledge of the solar system makes the existence of intelligent beings . . . elsewhere than on the earth extremely unlikely, and the concentration of their attention by any controllable means confined to any one continent of the earth quite preposterous.

The panel members were in agreement with the opinion of OSI that, although there was no evidence of direct threat from the sightings, related dangers might result from the following: ''(a) Misidentification of actual enemy artifacts by defense personnel. (b) Overloading of emergency reporting channels with 'false' information . . . (c) Subjectivity of public to mass hysteria and greater vulnerability to possible enemy psychological warfare.''

One of the panel's recommendations was that a policy of debunking UFO reports should be instigated:

> The ''debunking'' aim would result in reduction in public interest in ''flying saucers'' which today evokes a strong psychological reaction. This education could be accomplished by mass media such [as] television, motion pictures, and popular articles. Basis of such education would be actual case histories which had been puzzling at first but later explained. As is the case of conjuring tricks, there is much less stimulation if the ''secret'' is known. Such a program should tend to reduce the current gullibility of the public and consequently their susceptibility to clever hostile propaganda. The panel noted that the general absence of Russian propaganda based on a subject with so many obvious possibilities for exploitation might indicate a possible Russian official policy.

The panel discussed the various insidious methods that could be implemented to execute such a program: ''It was felt strongly that psychologists familiar with mass psychology should advise on the nature and extent of the program,'' the report states, and three specific psychologists were suggested as consultants. Documentary films and cartoons (Walt

Disney Inc. being recommended for the latter) were proposed, and "It was believed that business clubs, high schools, colleges, and television stations would all be pleased to cooperate in the showing of documentary type motion pictures if prepared in an interesting manner. The use of true cases showing first the 'mystery' and then the 'explanation' would be forceful." Dr. Allen Hynek suggested that amateur astronomers in the US might be a potential source of enthusiastic talent to "spread the gospel."

Another sinister recommendation of the panel was that civilian UFO groups should be watched "because of their potentially great influence on mass thinking if widespread sightings should occur. The apparent irresponsibility and the possible use of such groups for subversive purposes should be kept in mind."

The panel concluded that "the continued emphasis on the reporting of these phenomena does, in these parlous times, result in a threat to the orderly functioning of the protective organs of the body politic," and recommended:

> a. That the national security agencies take immediate steps to strip the Unidentified Flying Objects of the special status they have been given and the aura of mystery they have unfortunately acquired;
> b. That the national security agencies institute policies on intelligence, training, and public education designed to prepare the material defenses and the morale of the country to recognize most promptly and to react most effectively to true indications of hostile intent or action.
>
> We suggest that these aims may be achieved by an integrated program designed to reassure the public of the total lack of evidence of inimical forces behind the phenomena, to train personnel to recognize and reject false indications quickly and effectively, and to strengthen regular channels for the evaluation of and prompt reaction to true indications of hostile measures.

An Air Force Intelligence colonel present at the meetings complained afterward that the CIA merely wanted to bury the subject. "We had over a hundred of the strongest verified reports," he told Major Donald Keyhoe. "The agents bypassed the best ones. The scientists saw just fifteen cases, and the CIA men tried to pick holes in them. Fournet had sightings by top military and airline pilots—even scientists. The agents made it seem as if the witnesses were dopes, so the scientists brushed off the whole Fournet report. . . . I know those CIA agents were only following orders, but once or twice I nearly blew up."[10]

Dr. Allen Hynek, who had been the Air Force's astronomical consultant on UFOs for Project Blue Book both before and after the Robertson

Panel, and until his death in 1986 was considered to be one of the world's leading UFO researchers, has also expressed criticism. "I was an associate member of that panel," he stated, "but was not invited to participate in all the sessions. I was dissatisfied even then with what seemed to me a most cursory examination of the data and the set minds implied by the Panel's lack of curiosity and desire to delve deeper into the subject."[11] Dissatisfied he may have been, but Hynek apparently offered his cooperation with the CIA in the debunking program, as the report shows.

Captain Edward J. Ruppelt, Chief of the Aerial Phenomena Branch, Air Technical Intelligence Center, said that *the CIA ordered the Air Force to debunk sightings and discredit witnesses.* "We're ordered to hide sightings when possible," he told Major Keyhoe, "but if a strong report does get out we have to publish a fast explanation—make up something to kill the report in a hurry, and also ridicule the witness, especially if we can't figure a plausible answer. We even have to discredit our own pilots."[12]

Dr. David R. Saunders, who was on the University of Colorado UFO Committee (see later in this chapter) before resigning in disgust at its bias against the subject, believes that the Robertson Panel Report—as released—is no more than a cover story, "conceived and executed for the dual purposes of confusing foreign intelligence and reassuring the cadre of our own establishment. There is ample precedent for the use of such double and triple layers of security in connection with really important projects. For example, the mere existence of the Manhattan Project was a secret, but the nature and importance of that project was an even bigger secret."[13]

FURTHER DOCUMENTS

Many of the declassified CIA UFO documents relate to sighting reports throughout the world, obtained mostly from foreign newspapers, periodicals, and broadcasts. Since many of these reports have now been published in *Clear Intent*[14], I will not include them here, except in a few instances. It may come as a surprise to those unfamiliar with the workings of intelligence agencies that approximately fifty percent of intelligence gathering originates with open sources, such as newspapers, films, and speeches. Another forty percent comes from reconnaissance satellites and spy planes, eavesdropping devices and other gadgets, while only ten percent is dependent on human intelligence (HUMINT).[15]

A puzzling omission in the released CIA (and other intelligence agency) reports from foreign countries is Great Britain and Australia. Since these countries have had many significant sightings I can only conclude that there has been an official arrangement to preclude such information. Could Britain's Ministry of Defense intelligence chiefs have vetoed any reference in the FOIA declassified documents? Fanciful though the suggestion seems, liaison between the Secret Intelligence Service (SIS or MI6) and the CIA, for example, is almost as close as that of Government Communications Headquarters (GCHQ) and the National Security Agency. Ex-intelligence officer Gordon Creighton has confirmed to me that there was liaison on UFO matters between the CIA and Ministry of Defense in the 1950s, and it would seem logical that such liaison continues in Britain, perhaps with the CIA's Joint Reports and Research Unit at the US Embassy in London, which exchanges intelligence assessments with the Joint Intelligence Staff in the Cabinet Office.[16] I have no evidence for this, however.

CANADA, 1950 AND 1955

Although the majority of UFO reports were obtained by the CIA from open sources, a few were collected directly, such as the following case involving a sighting on board a ship in the North Atlantic, en route from Nova Scotia to an eastern US port, on 4 August 1950. The source for the report is deleted, as are the names of the witnesses, all of whom were interviewed by intelligence officers. This is the third mate's account:

> At 10:00 am on 4 Aug 50 as I was checking the compass at mid-bridge through a bridge port hole, I observed a flying object off the starboard bow. I immediately shouted to the Captain, who was in the chart room, and the Chief Mate, who was below on the port deck, of my observation and went out on the flying bridge myself. The object was approximately 70' above the horizon at a distance of 12 miles. It came toward us, then ran on a course reciprocal to ours and turned off into the horizon in the northeast. I clearly saw its shadow on the water. My impression of the object was that it was elliptical, not unlike a Japanese diamond box kite in shape. I have no idea of its size but the length was about six times the breadth and it had a depth of from two to five feet. It made no noise and was traveling at a tremendous rate of speed. As it traveled through the air, it made a spinning or wobbly motion. After it disappeared in the horizon, I saw it reappear several seconds later, ascending at an even faster speed than when I first observed it. I have no idea what this object was, I never saw anything comparable to it before, and it was one of the most frightening experiences I have ever had. I roughly estimate that the object traveled 28 miles during the 15 seconds I had it under observation.

The collector's note commented that there was a "tremendous discrepancy between the Captain's estimate of the speed and the estimate of the two officers which could not be explained as they were very careful in making their statements and asserted that their observations had been correct," but concluded: "All three men were quite evidently upset by the sighting. Aside from the discrepancies, it was quite evident to the intelligence officers who interviewed these men that they had certainly seen some very unusual object which they could not identify but was just as certainly not any conventional type of aircraft."

A memorandum dated 12 July 1955 from the CIA Office of Scientific Intelligence Chief, Physics and Electronics Division, T. M. Odarenko, to the Acting Assistant Director for Scientific Intelligence, cites an important radar/visual UFO report sent to the Agency by Pepperell Air Force Base, Newfoundland:

> Essentially, the "object" was apparently simultaneously observed by a tanker aircraft (KC 97) pilot (visually) and by a ground radar (type unknown) site (electronically). While such dual (visual and electronic) sightings of UFOBs are reported from time to time, this particular report is somewhat unique in that:
>
> a. The pilot of Archie 29 maintained visual contacts with object calling direction changes of object to (radar) site by radio. Direction changes correlated exactly with those painted on scope by controller.
> b. In previous cases the dual (visual and electronic) sightings are mostly of a few minutes duration at most. This one was observed by radar, at least, for 49 minutes.

UFOS—"MAXIMUM SECURITY"

In 1954 researcher Thomas Eickhoff made an attempt to bring UFO contactee George Adamski to federal court so that the latter could prove by use of the testimony of the two scientists who Adamski claimed had witnessed one of his alleged trips into space[17] that he really had been on board a space ship. This would also have given the government their opportunity to press the case, Eickhoff reasoned, and thereby, when Adamski was (presumably) unable to produce the scientists, they could prosecute him for "an act of fraud committed by illegal use of the U.S. mail system."

> My lawyer [said Eickhoff] suggested a letter of inquiry to be sent to a certain agency in Washington [the CIA] . . . and called me to his office.

He had received the answer which also included instructions for all parties concerned to deny any connections with the statement [which] came from a Mr. [Allen Dulles] of a certain top agency in Washington. Said [Dulles]: "Yes, I did have a case for Federal Court." However [he said], by use of the injunction if necessary he would prevent anyone from testifying in court concerning this book [*Inside the Space Ships*] because *maximum security exists concerning the subject of UFOs*.[18] [Emphasis added]

Allen Welsh Dulles was Director of the CIA (DCI) from 1953 to 1961, and following a FOIA request to the Agency in 1984, I was sent a copy of a letter from Dulles to the Honorable Gordon H. Scherer, House of Representatives, Washington, DC, dated 4 October 1955:

The questions which Mr. Eickhoff has raised in his letter to you are largely outside of the jurisdiction of this Agency. Section 102(d) of the National Security Act of 1947 provides that the CIA shall have no police, subpoena, law-enforcement powers, or internal security functions. Insofar as Mr. Eickhoff appears interested in pursuing the problem of mail fraud in connection with George Adamski's book entitled "Inside The Space Ships," it would appear to be a problem of law enforcement, from which we are specifically barred by statute.

CIA, as a matter of policy, does not comment on the truth or falsity of material contained in books or other published statements, and therefore it is not in a position to comment on Mr. Adamski's book or the authenticity of the pictures which it contains.

The subject matter of Mr. Adamski's book would appear to be more in the jurisdiction of the Department of Defense and the National Science Foundation.

The CIA was unable to locate any further documents pertaining to Adamski. Possibly more exist, possibly not, but certainly the FBI had an extensive file on him, and these documents have now been released under the FOIA.

In 1956 a "Memorandum for the Record" was written by the Chief of the CIA Office of Scientific Intelligence (OSI) Applied Science Division, W. E. Lexow, confirming that the ASD had now assumed responsibility within OSI for "Non-Conventional Types of Air Vehicles." Files would be maintained in ASD on "incoming raw reports where, *in our judgment*, the subject matter may provide information bearing on *foreign* weapons' system research or development." Reports in this category were to be forwarded to the "Fundamental Science Area" for review, and those which did not fit would be forwarded to the FSA for retention or destruction, and reports "which fit under none of the above will be destroyed." The memorandum continued (Reference 2):

e. A chronological file of all OSI correspondence and action taken in connection with the United States U.F.O. program will be maintained by ASD.
f. A file of unfinished intelligence reports published by members of the United States intelligence community on U.F.O. will be maintained in ASD.

The Applied Science Division was anxious to avoid the accumulation of reports "which experience and Reference 2 have shown cannot be analyzed in a manner useful to OSI in carrying out its mission. . . . It has been recommended that the raw intelligence and the obsolete finished reports on UFO now filed in Electronics Division will be destroyed."

In early November 1957, according to researcher Brad Sparks, Congress secretly pressed the CIA for an evaluation of a nationwide UFO "flap" then in progress. The OSI issued instructions to the Office of Operations' Contact Division to have its field offices collect UFO data for the ensuing one-week period. The results of this investigation are yet to be declassifed.[19]

SOCORRO, 1964

The CIA continued to monitor the UFO phenomenon from 1956 onward, and of the many intriguing reports cited by Fawcett and Greenwood in *Clear Intent* is that involving the sighting of a landed UFO complete with two small occupants, reported by Sergeant Lonnie Zamora on 24 April 1964. The case was investigated at the time by the Air Force and FBI, and Dr. Allen Hynek also had a hand in the investigations, as did other investigators such as Ray Stanford.

Sergeant Zamora of the Socorro, New Mexico, Police Department, was chasing a speeding car on US Highway 85 when he heard a roar and saw flames in an area where a dynamite shack was known to be located. Abandoning the car chase, he headed to the area in search of the cause of the noise and flames. Eventually he came across what he thought was an upturned car and two occupants, both dressed in coveralls. Zamora radioed police headquarters and reported that he was going to investigate what he believed to be an automobile accident. Proceeding up the road to a point where he could observe the object, which was in a gully,

Zamora stopped the car, got out, and headed toward the object. The undated CIA report continues:

> The object was on girderlike legs, white . . . and egg-shaped or oval. As he approached the object there were some noises and flame and smoke began to come from the bottom of the vehicle. The noise increased from low pitch to high pitch, was different from that of a jet or helo [helicopter] and not like anything Sgt. Zamora had ever heard. The flame was blue like a welders torch, turning to orange or yellow at the ends. Thinking that the object was going to explode he became frightened. . . . He turned, ran back to get behind the police car, bumping his leg and losing his glasses on the way. He crouched down, shielding his eyes with his arm while the noise continued for another 10 seconds. At this time the noise stopped and he looked up. The object had risen to a point about 15–20 ft. above the ground and the flame had ceased to come from the object. The object had a red marking about 1 ft. or maybe 18 inches in height, shaped like a crescent with a vertical arrow and horizontal line underneath. The object hovered in this spot for several seconds and then flew off in a SW direction following the center of the gully. It cleared the dynamite shack by not more than 3 ft. He watched the object disappear in the distance over a point on Highway 85 about 6 miles from where he was standing. The object took about 3 minutes to travel that far. Disappearance was by fading in the distance and at no time did he observe the object rise more than 20 ft. off the ground.

Zamora had kept in radio contact with police headquarters while proceeding to the location, and since the State Police use the same frequency his call was monitored by Sergeant Chavez of the New Mexico State Police. Zamora had attempted to direct Chavez to the location but the latter took the wrong road and missed the sighting. When he did eventually reach Zamora, three minutes after the object had disappeared, he found that "Sgt. Zamora was pale and upset at what he had witnessed." Sergeant Chavez was skeptical of the situation and proceeded to where Zamora had seen the UFO. "Here he found the marks and burns," the CIA report states. "Smoke appeared to be coming from a bush which was burned but no flames or coals were visible. . . . The marks were fresh and no other marks were in the area. Diagonals of the four impressions intersect in a perpendicular and the major distance seems to be approximately 13 ft. Sgt. Chavez secured the area and contacted local military authorities."

For a full report on this important case it is essential to read Ray Stanford's excellent book, *Socorro "Saucer" in a Pentagon Pantry*.[20] Stanford discovered metal samples at the landing site, for example, and I shall relate the story of what happened to those samples in the following chapter. While there is no official confirmation for the incident, an article subsequently appeared in a CIA publication in which Hector Quintanella, head of the Air Force Project Blue Book at the time, referred to the Socorro case. In a paragraph headed "Diagnosis: Unsolved," Quintanella stated: "There is no doubt that Lonnie Zamora saw an object which left quite an impression on him. There is also no question about Zamora's reliability. He is a serious officer, a pillar of his church, and a man well versed in recognizing airborne vehicles in this area. He is puzzled by what he saw, and frankly, so are we. This is the best documented case on record."[21]

Skeptic Philip Klass believes that the Socorro report was fabricated in order to stimulate the local tourist industry, and cites a number of arguments in support of his hypothesis. He points out, for example, that the alleged landing took place on property owned by Holm Bursum, Mayor of Socorro at the time, and a prominent banker.[22] Interviewed in 1983, Bursum laughed at this suggestion. "The man is silly," he said. "Sure, it was my land where that took place . . . and I was as excited as everybody else. But I sure didn't plan it." Bursum also discounts the idea that Zamora could have fabricated the story. "To my knowledge, Lonnie is not a daydreamer. He's not a practical joker. He's a very serious person and always has been."[23]

THE UNIVERSITY OF COLORADO UFO PROJECT

In 1966 the US Air Force commissioned the University of Colorado to make a scientific study of UFOs, headed by Dr. Edward Condon. On 20 February 1967 Dr. Condon, together with Dr. Richard Low, Dr. David Saunders, Dr. William Price, and Dr. Rachford, visited the CIA's National Photographic Center in order to familiarize themselves with "selected photographic analysis capabilities of NPIC." The following brief extract from a CIA memo dated 23 February 1967 shows how wary the Agency was of allowing Condon's team to reveal the CIA's "unofficial" interest in the controversial UFO problem:

Any work performed by NPIC to assist Dr. Condon in his investigation will not be identified as work accomplished by the CIA. Dr. Condon was advised by Mr. Lundahl to make no reference to CIA in regard to this work effort. Dr. Condon stated that if he felt it necessary to obtain an official CIA comment he would make a separate distinct entry into CIA not related to contacts he has with NPIC.[24]

Rumors that the CIA was responsible for the biased negative conclusions of Dr. Condon have abounded since his committee's *Scientific Study of Unidentified Flying Objects* was published in 1969.[25] There can be no denying the fact that Condon and some key members of his committee deliberately set out to convey to the public an image of scientific impartiality, while systematically debunking the subject, as has been shown in a leaked memorandum from Low to Condon, and in Dr. David Saunders' book on the inside story of the Colorado University UFO study.[26]

When the Colorado University investigation was in the process of making its conclusions, Dr. Condon asked UFO researcher Dr. James Harder what he would do if he were responsible for a project report that might reflect a conclusion that UFOs were a manifestation of extraterrestrial intelligence.

> I said that I thought there would be other issues than the scientific ones [said Dr. Harder], notably international repercussions and national security. He smiled the smile of a man who sees his own opinions reflected in the opinions of others and said that he had given the matter much thought, and had decided that if the answer was to be a positive finding of ETH [Extraterrestrial Hypothesis], he would not make the finding public, but would take the report, in his briefcase, to the President's Science Advisor, and have the decision made in Washington.[27]

THE CIA AND NICAP

The most vociferous civilian UFO research organization opposing government secrecy in the fifties and sixties was the National Investigations Committee on Aerial Phenomena (NICAP), founded by a former Navy physicist, Thomas Townsend Brown, in 1956, and headed for many years by Major Donald Keyhoe, US Marine Corps (retired). NICAP's Board of Governors at one time included former Director of the CIA Vice Admiral Roscoe Hillenkoetter, who had been Pacific Commander of Intelligence during World War II. While on the NICAP board, he made a number of extraordinary statements attesting to the reality and seriousness of the UFO phenomenon. He was convinced that UFOs were unknown objects operating under intelligent control and that "the Air Force is still censoring UFO sightings. Hundreds of authentic reports by veteran pilots and other technically trained observers have been ridiculed or explained away as mistakes, delusions or hoaxes. . . . It is imperative that we learn where the UFOs come from and what their purpose is. The public has a right to know.''

In a signed statement dated 22 August 1960, sent to Congress, Hillenkoetter said:

It is time for the truth to be brought out. . . . Behind the scenes high-ranking Air Force officers are soberly concerned about the UFOs. But through official secrecy and ridicule, many citizens are led to believe the unknown flying objects are nonsense. . . . I urge immediate Congressional action to reduce the dangers from secrecy about Unidentified Flying Objects. . . . Two dangers are steadily increasing:
1. The risk of accidental war from mistaking UFO formations for a Soviet surprise attack.
2. The danger that the Soviet government may, in a critical moment, *falsely* claim the UFOs as secret Russian weapons against which our defenses are helpless.[28]

But in 1962 Hillenkoetter suddenly resigned from NICAP. ''In my opinion, NICAP's investigation has gone as far as possible,'' he wrote in his letter of resignation. ''I know the UFOs are not U.S. or Soviet devices. All we can do now is wait for some action by the UFOs. The Air Force cannot do any more under the circumstances. It has been a difficult assignment for them, and I believe we should not continue to criticize their investigations.''[29] Keyhoe was convinced that Hillenkoetter had been pressurized ''at a very high level'' to resign. Whatever the truth, it was a severe blow to NICAP's prestige, and Keyhoe was bitterly disappointed.

Another former CIA official on the board of NICAP was Colonel Joseph J. Bryan III, founder and original Chief of the CIA's Psychological Warfare Staff, and former Special Assistant to the Secretary of the Air Force as well as aviation adviser to NATO. In a letter to Keyhoe, Colonel Bryan made the following positive statement on the UFO problem:

I am aware that hundreds of military and airline pilots, airport personnel, astronomers, missile trackers and other competent observers have reported sightings of UFOs. I am also aware that many of these UFOs have been reported maneuvering in formation, and that many were simultaneously tracked by radar. It is my opinion that:
The UFOs reported by competent observers are devices under intelligent control. Their speeds, maneuvers and other technical evidence prove them superior to any known aircraft or space devices now produced on earth.

These UFOs are interplanetary devices systematically observing the earth,
either manned or under remote control, or both.

Information on UFOs, including sighting reports, has been and is still
being officially withheld. This policy is dangerous, especially since mistaken identification of UFOs as a secret Russian attack might accidentally
set off war. Unless this policy is changed, a Congressional investigation
should be held to reduce or eliminate this and other dangers.[30]

This statement was made in 1960, shortly after Bryan joined NICAP.
Keyhoe was unaware of Bryan's involvement with the CIA, a fact which
did not emerge until 1977 when Bryan admitted to having been a former
covert official for the Agency, and asked that this not be made public
since "it might embarrass CIA." He denied any association with the CIA
during the period he served on the board of NICAP.[31]

Infiltration

Todd Zechel has uncovered a great deal of evidence for the infiltration
of NICAP by the CIA. Although debunker Philip Klass has tried to
discredit Zechel's background in the intelligence field[32], my own inquiries
have established that Zechel was indeed employed by the Army Security
Service, the forerunner of the National Security Agency, as well as the
NSA itself. Also, his published articles reflect a broad knowledge about
the intelligence community, and I therefore have no hesitation in including
his controversial material here. (For the record, Zechel charges that Klass
is a CIA "asset.")

According to Zechel, a number of CIA covert agents worked themselves into key positions in NICAP. One was Count Nicolas de Rochefort,
now deceased, who had been a member of the CIA's Psychological
Warfare Staff, and who became vice-Chairman of NICAP in the year of
its foundation (1956). Another was Bernard J. Carvalho, who had been
a go-between for such secretly owned companies as Fairway Corporation,
a charter airline used by CIA executives. Carvalho was appointed Chairman of NICAP's membership subcommittee at one time. During the 1960s
former CIA briefing officer Karl Pflock became Chairman of NICAP's
Washington, DC, subcommittee. He is said to have denied that the CIA
ever asked him for information on either UFOs or NICAP.

Zechel further claims that an undated CIA document, anonymously
written, indicates familiarity with G. Stuart Nixon, former assistant to
NICAP's president, John L. Acuff, and states that in the late 1960s and
early 1970s the NICAP daily logs show that Nixon met with several past

and present CIA employees on a frequent basis. The CIA officials allegedly included Art Lundahl, then Director of the CIA's National Photographic Interpretation Center, Frederick Durant, former CIA Office of Scientific Intelligence missile expert and author of the Robertson Panel Report, and Dr. Charles Sheldon, a CIA consultant.

According to Zechel, Major Keyhoe was deliberately ousted by the CIA infiltrators in 1969, after which a former head of the Society of Photographic Scientists and Engineers (allegedly with CIA affiliations), John Acuff, took over as president. Concluded Zechel:

> Maybe it's a coincidence that the founder of the CIA's Psychological Warfare Staff has been on the board [of NICAP] for nearly twenty years. Maybe it's another coincidence that Charles Lombard, a former CIA covert employee (according to himself) would seek out a retired CIA executive to run the organization (i.e. after Jack Acuff was replaced by *retired* CIA agent, Alan N. Hall in 1979!). . . . Or maybe we're all paranoid. . . . Perhaps Keyhoe deserved to be fired from the organization he built with his own sweat, blood, and sacrifice. The timing couldn't have been better, in any case. Keyhoe, after all, was beginning to focus on the CIA in 1969, instead of his tunnel-visioned attacks on the Air Force . . . *if they wanted to destroy the leading anti-secrecy organization of the 1960s, they couldn't have done a better job if they'd tried.*[33]

One documented link between NICAP and the CIA is a letter dated 19 September 1973 to researcher Larry Bryant from John Maury of the CIA's Legislative Council, which refers to the Agency's contact with Richard H. Hall in 1965:

> In January 1965, the Agency made an inquiry into the research being conducted on UFO sightings and contacted Mr. Hall, then Acting Director of the National Investigations Committee on Aerial Phenomena. Mr. Hall explained how his organization operated and loaned the Agency several of its publications which were reviewed and returned. No excerpts were made from the publications, nor did the Agency come to any conclusions on the substance therein. There was no further contact with Mr. Hall or any other representative of his organization, and the Agency had no further interest in the subject of UFOs.

This letter would seem to argue against CIA infiltration of NICAP, although it shows the Agency's interest in the organization in 1965. Why would Hall need to explain "how his organization operated" if the CIA had infiltrated it since 1956? If John Maury was telling the truth, we have to assume that either (a) the lengthy list of NICAP officials with established CIA connections was entirely coincidental—that they joined NICAP for solely personal reasons, or (b) that Maury was unaware of the true purpose of the meeting with Hall, and knew nothing of the CIA/NICAP background. It is also possible, of course, that Maury was dissembling: the CIA, after all, is of necessity not in the habit of revealing its actions and motives!

A memorandum dated 25 January 1965, with the names of the writer and recipient blacked out ("To Chief, Contact Division, Attention [deleted], from Chief [deleted]") throws further light on the meeting with Hall. It begins: "This confirms [deleted] conversation 19 January 1965, at which time various samples and reports on UFO sightings procured from NICAP were given to [deleted] for transmittal to OSI. The information was desired by OSI to assist them in the preparation of a paper for [deleted] on UFOs." There follows a description of NICAP's investigative procedures, with particular reference to Air Force reports:

A printed form, prepared by the Air Force for NICAP's use, is utilized during the interview. . . . It was our understanding that copies of these reports go directly to various Air Force bases. There apparently is a strong feeling on the part of NICAP officials, i.e. Kehoe [sic] and Hall, that the Air Force tends to downgrade the importance of UFO sightings because they (the Air Force) do not care to have too much made of the sightings by the US press. We were told by Mr. Hall that there have been instances where the Air Force has attempted to intimidate witnesses and get them to sign false statements relative to UFO sightings.

A detailed description of NICAP's investigation into radar trackings of UFOs at Patuxent Naval Air Station in December 1964 follows, as well as a sighting "within the last week or 10 days" at Constitution Avenue, Washington, DC. The memo concludes: "[deleted] informed us that she is requesting a security clearance on Mr. Hall predicated upon biographic information provided by [deleted]."

According to researcher Brad Sparks, who has specialized in a study of the CIA's involvement in the subject, former CIA Director John A. McCone asked the Office of Scientific Intelligence for an evaluation of the Washington area's wave of UFO sightings at that time, probably, says Sparks, as a result of the privately expressed concerns of congressmen. The OSI instructed the CIA's local Contact Division office to approach NICAP for a brief résumé of those sightings. After consultation with the Air Force, the OSI informed McCone of its negative conclusions about the wave.[34]

It is self-evident that the CIA had become interested in NICAP's activities by 1965—if not earlier—and an undated CIA memorandum, claimed by the authors of *Clear Intent* to have been written in the early 1970s, gives a highly detailed rundown on NICAP's organization and the impressive credentials of its advisory group, and furthermore confirms that ex-CIA personnel were included therein:

This board relies heavily on both a loosely structured advisory group and a fairly well placed network of investigators. The advisory group is made up of experts in many disciplines including physics, astronomy, anthropology, medicine and psychology. *This group also includes some ex-CIA and Defense Intelligence types who advise on investigative techniques and NICAP/government relations. . . .*

The system of investigators is a good one. . . . As of a few months ago some 35 investigators were located throughout the country, with NICAP in the process of establishing even more. A breakdown of their backgrounds looked like the following: 7 Ph.D.s, 2 MAs or MS, 23 BAs or BS, 1 AA, and 2 with college training but no degrees. Occupationally they included 4 physical scientists, 13 engineers, 3 college profs, 13 specialists, including doctor, technician, computer programmer and businessman. Five of the 35 are pilots.[35] [Emphasis added]

It is my assumption—shared by some other researchers—that the CIA had become concerned by the enormous influence over public opinion that NICAP undoubtedly wielded at the time. No other UFO organization before or since has so consistently and effectively challenged official attempts to debunk the subject. The CIA needed to turn NICAP's skills and energy to suit its own ends. It is hardly surprising that NICAP's influence dwindled significantly from 1970 onward, although other factors may have contributed to this, such as the negative findings of the Condon Report in 1969. But as Lawrence Fawcett and Barry Greenwood point out, Keyhoe was ousted as NICAP's Director in December 1969 by a faction led by the Chairman of the Board, Colonel Joseph Bryan III, former Chief of the CIA's Psychological Warfare Staff. John Acuff, with tenuous links to the CIA, replaced Keyhoe, and he in turn was succeeded by Alan Hall, a retired CIA employee, who apparently accepted the position after a number of other ex-CIA personnel were offered the job. NICAP board member Charles Lombard, a former CIA covert employee, is said to have given his full support to Hall. Serious problems with management ensued and NICAP eventually became so ineffective that it was dissolved; its files were taken over in 1973 by Dr. Allen Hynek's newly formed Center for UFO Studies (CUFOS) in Evanston, Illinois.

The authors of *Clear Intent* offer their opinion—which I share—that the CIA needed to infiltrate NICAP for the following reasons: "(1) To gather intelligence through NICAP's investigators network. (2) To identify and plug leaks from government sources . . . (3) To monitor other hostile intelligence agencies (NICAP received several overtures from the Soviet KGB)." Fawcett and Greenwood further speculate that after NICAP's mismanagement, its effectiveness as a CIA front was diminished, and the Agency allowed it to be taken over by CUFOS. They stop short of suggesting that CUFOS itself may have been infiltrated or influenced by the CIA, but nevertheless theorize that this could happen to any prominent UFO group if it became too effective.[36] It must be remembered that one of the recommendations of the CIA Robertson Panel Report was that civilian UFO groups should be watched "because of their potentially great influence on mass thinking if widespread sightings should occur." With his worldwide knowledge of UFO groups, Dr. Hynek would have been invaluable to the CIA as a consultant, and may have acted in this capacity ever since he sat on the Robertson Panel in 1953.

SURVEILLANCE

Another group which may well have come in for CIA surveillance is the Aerial Phenomena Research Organization (APRO), the world's longest-running UFO group, founded in 1952 by Jim and Coral Lorenzen. APRO was one of two civilian groups to be singled out for monitoring by the CIA's Robertson Panel Report, so the assumption is far from fanciful.

One of APRO's earliest supporters was a man who helped with donations and suggestions for the organization. He also claimed to have a background in intelligence work. A letter from him to the Lorenzens in February 1953 had apparently been used as a platen for what looked like an intelligence report on Coral, inadvertently impressed into the paper. The report listed her previous residences and followed with impressions of her personal character.

On other occasions various salesmen turned up at the Lorenzens' home yet showed little interest in promoting their business, preferring instead to engage the couple in conversation. But, as the Lorenzens are quick to point out, these incidents provide only circumstantial evidence. There is no proof that the CIA was involved. Yet the Lorenzens did establish that at one time they were being monitored by the local Air Force Office of Special Investigations (AFOSI), according to an associate of Coral's, but apparently the dossier was favorable in that neither she nor her husband were prevented from obtaining the high-level security clearances that their work in the Air Force entailed at the time.[37]

In 1974 Dr. Allen Hynek visited APRO's headquarters in Tucson, Arizona, and tried to persuade the Board of Directors to give him a list of APRO's field investigators, together with their addresses and telephone numbers.[38] Hynek's motives may well have been innocent, and perhaps we should give him the benefit of the doubt, particularly since he died in April 1986. Yet certain questions remain unanswered.

Dr. Robert Creegan, one of APRO's consultants in Social Sciences, has also voiced suspicions about Hynek's involvement in the UFO scene. "Professor Hynek was never asked to be a member of either the Robertson Panel in 1953, nor the Condon Commission, 1966–1969. Yet he was able to sit in on at least some of the meetings of both," he wrote in 1985. "He made no evident criticism of the evasiveness of the conclusions in either case. As a matter of fact, the astronomer has been able to attend many or most UFO conferences in the US and abroad, and has gone to the locales of major flaps. Obviously funds were adequate."[39]

I do not know if Dr. Hynek was actually employed as a CIA consultant subsequent to the Robertson Panel, but it seems evident that he was in the best position to perform such a function, with worldwide contacts at official and unofficial levels. Many fellow researchers in a number of countries agree with me that while Hynek was always interested in gathering information, he seemed reluctant to give out much in return. At the same time, it has to be said that his contribution in putting over this controversial subject to the skeptical scientific fraternity has been enormous, for which we owe him a debt of gratitude.

My own experiences of possible surveillance by the CIA have also been circumstantial. In March 1976, for example, I wrote to the CIA Freedom of Information and Privacy Coordinator, Gene F. Wilson, thanking him for sending me a copy of the Robertson Panel Report, and adding that I was on the point of embarking on a tour of the United States with the London Symphony Orchestra, with a scheduled visit to Washington, DC, between 19 and 23 March. On arrival at the Statler Hilton Hotel on the afternoon of 19 March, my photograph was taken in the lobby by a man with a large-format camera and flashgun. Before I had a chance to approach him he made a hasty exit. It may have been coincidental, of course, but it led to a suspicion that the CIA was responsible, since I had deliberately informed them of my impending visit to see what would happen.

In 1985 I filed a request under the Privacy Act to review a copy of my possible file with the Agency, and later provided them with a notarized statement attesting to my identity, in accordance with CIA Privacy Regulations.[40] Under the Privacy Act an individual is supposed to be able to see a copy of his or her file (if one exists) so that amendments can be made to any inaccuracies contained therein. The Agency's main file index in the Directorate of Operations allegedly contains about 7.5 million names and about 750,000 individual personality files. For collection of intelligence from domestic sources the CIA reputedly has another index, containing about 150,000 names as well as about 50,000 files on "active" sources, while the Office of Security is said to have about 900,000 files mostly relating to individuals, including 75 members of Congress in the mid-1970s, as well as records of about 500,000 people who have visited CIA installations.[41] It was not altogether out of the question, I surmised, that in view of my correspondence with the Agency over a ten-year period, and more than a passing interest in its involvement in UFO research, a file on me would exist. I was wrong—apparently. Nearly a year after my initial FOIA request was filed I received a letter from Lee Strickland, Information and Privacy Coordinator, dated 29 July 1986, which stated in part: "Our processing included a search for records in existence as of and through the date of our acceptance letter dated 25 February 1986. No records responsive to your request were located. . . . We appreciate the patience and understanding during the period required to process this request." The search costs, consisting of two on-line computer searches, a quarter-hour's professional time, and an hour of clerical search time fortunately amounted to a relatively modest fee.

MISSING EVIDENCE

Cases involving missing films, photographs and hardware associated with UFO sightings are plentiful, but it is hard to prove that the CIA is responsible. Nevertheless, federal and military intelligence agencies have definitely "borrowed" or taken material which has never been returned, as I have mentioned elsewhere in this book.

Todd Zechel claims that photographic evidence found missing from the Air Force Project Blue Book files eventually found its way to the CIA's Office of Scientific Intelligence in the 1950s, and specifies a number of movie films taken at White Sands Proving Grounds, New Mexico: a cinetheodolite film taken by a camera tracking station on 27 April 1950; a cinetheodolite film taken by two camera stations on 29 May 1950, allegedly showing two huge UFOs traveling at 2,000 mph; and a 35mm film taken by a military pilot on 14 July 1951. Zechel also specifies a 16mm gun-camera film taken by a military pilot at Rapid City, South Carolina, on 12 August 1953, an 8mm film taken at Port Moresby, New Guinea, on 31 August 1953 (see Chapter 7), and a reconnaissance photograph taken by the pilot of an RB-29 aircraft on 24 May 1954 near Dayton, Ohio.[42]

Yet another case cited by Zechel relates to a 16mm film taken by Ralph C. Mayher, a Marine Corps photographer, on 29 July 1952 at Miami, Florida. Mayher had the film processed immediately and submitted it to the Marine Air Station. Some frames were released to the local press and published, but within days Mayher was visited by Air Force and CIA investigators, who allegedly told him to keep quiet about the incident. On 31 July the film was given to the Air Force for analysis and has never been seen since. The few frames given to the press were returned. In June 1975 William Spaulding, Director of Ground Saucer Watch, wrote to the CIA asking for information about the film, and a lengthy correspondence ensued. Spaulding was unsuccessful in obtaining the data he wanted but did manage to discover from the CIA memoranda released to him that some of the information on the Mayher film is still classified.[43]

The CIA memoranda in my possession contain no reference to the Agency's having examined the film, but it is evident that five stills were studied, and a memo dated 7 November 1957 states that "the original negatives are in Air Force hands." Another memo, dated 12 December 1957, adds that the "five photographs of flying saucers which were obtained from [deleted]" were returned, and that "[deleted] asked if it would be possible for us to submit to him any evaluations which might have been made on these photographs and I replied that it was very doubtful but that I would pass on the request to headquarters." Back came the reply on 20 December 1957:

We did not receive evaluations of photography which source submitted. For your information only, the material was reviewed at a "high level" and returned to us without comments . . . The subject of UFO was under the review of CIA for a limited time only. This was caused by a request from "the hill" which stemmed from all of the publicity given to recent UFO sightings. We assume that the request has been satisfied because the case has been closed and the subject dropped by CIA. . . . We would suggest to source that any correspondence on the subject be directed to the Air Force. . . . It appears that source is trying to set himself up as the local clearing house for UFO sightings. If source desires to show his photographs on TV this is the prerogative, naturally without any CIA disclosures, and we could have no objection.

No evidence of the actual film having been reviewed or confiscated is contained in the released documents. Probably the writers were unaware of the complete picture—their comments on the CIA's involvement in UFO research betray considerable ignorance—or else the Air Force retained the film. The evidence is arbitrary, but the film has not been returned.

Freelance journalist Warren Smith relates a rather sinister encounter with alleged CIA agents in the 1970s when he was coerced into handing over a piece of metal that he had acquired from a farmer who had discovered some fragments after witnessing a UFO hovering over his orchard in Wisconsin. Word got around about the incident and the farmer reported being subsequently visited by a "fertilizer salesman" who seemed more interested in learning about the samples than selling fertilizer. The farmer informed the "salesman" that he had given one of the pieces to Smith. The salesman told the farmer that he was staying in a motel and suggested that it might be the same one as Smith. When the latter learned of this he tied the piece of metal to the inside of his motel room's television set at the Holiday Inn, Madison, as a precaution.

"Within one day, I was the most popular person in Madison, particularly when I was out," said Smith. "I asked the maids and motel maintenance man to watch my room during my absence. Two men with a room key were moving in as soon as I left. One maid had the courage to enter the room on the pretense of checking it for cleanliness. She excused herself when she saw the two men going through my suitcase."

When Smith visited the farmer again he learned that two men in Air Force uniforms had persuaded him to part with his metal fragment, citing "national security, a danger to the world, and the government's desire to have that fragment of metal" as the reasons. On Smith's return to the motel the two men were waiting—one stretched out on the bed and the other sitting at the desk. After an exchange of false pleasantries one of the men said, "You have something we want. A farmer gave you a piece of metal the other day. Our job is to pick it up."

Smith prevaricated for as long as possible, pretending that he had sent the fragment to someone else, but the men began to threaten him, warning that he should think of his wife, children, and career. Smith asked for identification. "Name the agency and we'll produce it," they replied. "Would you like Air Force, FBI or maybe NORAD [North American Aerospace Defense Command]?" Smith finally agreed to give them the piece of metal on condition that they answered a few questions, and the conversation was continued over coffee at the motel restaurant. The men refused to answer questions, of course, but before leaving revealed that "UFOs involve more than you or any civilian can realize. They're the most important thing and perhaps the greatest hazard that mankind has ever faced."

As the men drove off Smith memorized the license number and eventually discovered—with the aid of friends who had access to law enforcement channels—that the unissued license plate had been given to a Chicago man with close links to the CIA. Or so Smith claims.[44] It is difficult to know how much credence should be given to the story. Smith neglects to mention the date or the name of the farmer he spoke to, so it is difficult to check the facts. My letter to Smith sent care of his publishers in New York was returned "Unknown," and I have yet to receive a reply to a copy sent to his British publisher. However, I did discuss the alleged incident with the researcher and author Brad Steiger in 1986, whom Smith called on the phone immediately following the incident. (Steiger had previously tried contacting Smith at the motel, only to be told that he was not registered there.) Brad told me that whereas Smith was inclined to exaggerate his stories on occasions and indulge in practical jokes, in this particular instance he sounded genuinely frightened by the experience he had just undergone.

DISINFORMATION

Miles Copeland, former CIA organizer and intelligence officer, related an interesting story to me involving the Agency's attempt on one occasion to use fictional UFO sightings to spread disinformation. The purpose, in this case, was to "dazzle" and "intoxicate" the Chinese, who had themselves on several occasions fooled the CIA into sending teams to a desert in Sinkiang Province, West China, to search for nonexistent underground "atomic energies."

The exercise took place in the early 1960s, Copeland told me, and involved launching fictional UFO sighting reports from many different areas. The project was headed by Desmond Fitzgerald of the Special Affairs Staff (who made a name for himself by inventing harebrained schemes for assassinating Fidel Castro). The UFO exercise was "just to keep the Chinese off-balance and make them think we were doing things we weren't," Copeland said. "The project got the desired results, as I remember, except that it somehow got picked up by a lot of religious nuts in Iowa and Nebraska or somewhere who took it seriously enough to add an extra chapter to their version of the New Testament!"

"I wouldn't attribute too much Machiavellian thinking behind it," Copeland advised me, "because in those days the CIA was just doing all sorts of things . . . characterized by a lot of rich guys who read too many John Buchan books and were just horsing around!"[45]

Miles Copeland said that he couldn't recall anything else about the CIA's involvement with UFOs, but this is hardly surprising since, as he himself acknowledges:

> Regardless of the trust placed in any employee, he is allowed to know only what he needs to know in order to carry out his job. Moreover, these agencies are so organized that their secrets are tightly compartmentalized. Even the Director of the Central Intelligence Agency is "protected" by need-to-know regulations which keep from him all information that is not essential to his job—and this would be almost all of the detailed information held in his organization.[46]

Warren Smith claims to have acquired a great deal of knowledge about the CIA's involvement in UFO research from an Agency source, although he freely admits that he might have been fed false information. According to Smith's informant, the CIA maintains a worldwide surveillance on the UFO situation. Foreign journals, for example, are sent to the Agency's foreign translation departments and, when translated, are fed into computers. "The data is cross-indexed and can easily be retrieved," says Smith. "If someone wants to know how many sightings of low level flying saucers have been reported in a specific nation, or worldwide, the computer will provide a summary. . . . I have obtained data from the computer on several different occasions. It is always quite precise. I'm still a little dubious about the 'help' given by my informant. But it has always proven to be factual."

Smith was allegedly given a great deal of information about the CIA's conclusions regarding the phenomenon. It reads like something straight out of *The Invaders,* but I feel it should be included here nevertheless. According to Smith's informant, UFOs represent an advanced technology from another planet, which in many respects is similar to earth. The problem is that their sun is dying and their planet has begun to cool. "The aliens have decided their only way to survive is to migrate to another world that would have an environment similar to their own planet," Smith was supposedly told. "Our planet represents the one opportunity for their civilization to endure. The problem for mankind is that we're living here." Smith's source went on to explain that—not surprisingly—it would be impossible for our civilization to absorb immigrants from another planet.

"The social turmoil would be beyond comprehension. The economic chaos that would come about would destroy the foundations of our lives," Smith was told.

The CIA has ostensibly obtained data showing that the UFOs have conducted a systematic plan of surveillance, beginning with collecting plant and animal specimens, then establishing contact at random with humans. "Currently, they are embarked on a biological study of people to determine how we differ," the informant volunteered. "They're determining whether our two races can interbreed and, if so, what the mutant will look like, its genetic composition, and so forth. . . . We also know they've tested our defenses to see if we can withstand an invasion. Therefore, at some time in the future, we expect UFOs to become increasingly hostile."

Smith wanted to know if the world's governments know about this alarming situation. "Some do," he was told. "Others are on a need to know basis. We've maintained secrecy because the truth might destroy us." Why then was Smith given this information? "It doesn't have the official stamp," was the reply. "You're not the only person who is receiving information. A slow, gradual release of the facts will prevent panic."

Smith asked about the wilder tales of encounters with UFOs. "Some of those come from our government attempting to confuse the facts," the informant said. "Many of the reports are being created by the aliens to achieve the same ends. The past several years has produced some incredibly wild contactee reports. We believe the extraterrestrials are testing our ability to withstand psychological warfare. To date, the people selected haven't done too well in that respect."

The official added that he expected an increase in bizarre contactee cases such as those where witnesses have been approached by UFOs and then had their memories erased. (Since this conversation took place in the early 1970s there has indeed been an increase in such cases.) "We know there's a purpose behind their actions and the end result may not be for the betterment of humanity," he said.

"Can we believe the CIA story?" asks Warren Smith. "Or is this another of the agency's efforts to confuse the facts in ufology?"[47]

DECLINING CIA INTEREST?

A series of released CIA Domestic Collection Division memos written in 1976 give the impression that the Agency was no longer actively engaged in UFO research at this time, although one memo, dated 14 April, confirms that the Agency still retained experts on the subject: "Source seeks guidance from CIA UFO experts as to material in his report that should remain classified." A 26 April memo confirms that the CIA was continuing to monitor the phenomena, but not on an official basis:

> It does not seem that the government has any formal program in progress for the identification/solution of the UFO phenomena. Dr. [deleted] feels that the efforts of independent researchers, [deleted], are vital for further progress in this area. *At the present time, there are offices and personnel within the agency who are monitoring the UFO phenomena*, but again, this is not currently on an official basis. Dr. [   ] feels that the best approach would be to keep in touch with and in fact develop reporting channels in this area to keep the agency/community informed of any new developments. In particular, any information which might indicate a threat potential would be of interest, as would specific indications of foreign developments or applications of UFO research. . . . We wish to stress again, that there does not now appear to be any special program on UFOs within the intelligence community. [Emphasis added]

Another CIA/DCD memo written a month later (27 May 1976) states:

> Our source felt that [deleted] work might be of interest to the US government and that it should be evaluated by the Agency. The source also felt that it could be analyzed outside the context of its UFO connection if necessary to remove it from a controversial subject.
>
> As before we are faced with the problem of having UFO related data which is deemed potentially important for the US by our S&T [Science and Technology] sources, evaluated. As you are aware, at this time there is no channel or working group to which we can turn for this type of analysis and dissemination. Thus, if it is acceptable to you we will continue to periodically advise you or your designee of any new or potentially important FI [Foreign Intelligence] developments which might arise from current independent scientific research on the UFO phenomena.

Finally, a CIA/DCD memo dated 14 July 1976 sheds further light on the CIA's apparent attitude to the subject at the time:

> At a recent meeting to evaluate some material from [deleted], you mentioned a personal interest in the UFO phenomena. As you may recall, I mentioned my own interest in the subject as well as the fact that DCD had been receiving UFO related material from many of our S&T sources who are presently conducting related research. These scientists include some

who have been associated with the Agency for years and whose credentials remove them from the "nut" variety.

The attached material came to my attention through these sources and it appears to have some legitimate FI or community interest potential.

The [deleted] work being carried out by Dr. [deleted] should, in the view of our S&T sources, be evaluated by the Agency or community.

In view of the expertise associated with your office, as well as your own interest in the subject, I felt you might like to see the material.

These Domestic Collection Division memoranda appear to indicate the CIA's declining involvement in UFO research, although it is evident that the Agency continued to monitor the subject. Since intelligence is highly compartmentalized, the probability exists that the writers of the DCD memos did not have access to all the information on the subject obtained by the Science and Technology Division, nor other divisions of the Agency. It is also probable that the DCD officers were unaware of any hypothetical above top secret research still being conducted within the CIA and other intelligence agencies.

One of the last CIA documents to be released under the Freedom of Information Act is an unevaluated Foreign Intelligence Information Report relating to a sighting by the crew of a British Airways plane on 10 September 1976, which I have included in Chapter 10. It is therefore obvious that the Agency continued to maintain a close watch on UFO reports, and from more recent documents released by other agencies, such as the Defense Intelligence Agency, it is evident that the CIA continues to monitor all UFO reports, since these other agencies apparently have orders to forward details to the Agency immediately.

In 1983 I wrote to the CIA's Information and Privacy Coordinator, Larry R. Strawderman, asking the following questions: Is the CIA still involved in the study of UFO reports? How many—or what percentage—of those reports remain unexplained? Of those unexplained reports, has the Agency found any evidence of extraterrestrial activity, in the sense that intelligently controlled vehicles are operating in our atmosphere? I received the following reply:

There is no organized Central Intelligence Agency effort to do research in connection with the UFO phenomena, nor has there been an organized effort to collect intelligence on UFOs since the 1950s. Since then there have been sporadic instances of correspondence dealing with the subject and the receipt of various kinds of reports of UFO sightings.

The Agency interest lies in its forewarning responsibility. This interest is principally in the possibility of a hostile power developing new weapon

systems which might exhibit phenomena that some might categorize as
an UFO.

Under the Freedom of Information Act the only role of my office is to
provide Agency records that can be described so that they can be located
and reviewed for declassification and release to the public. In view of this,
and in view of the fact that this Agency terminated active participation in
any investigation into the UFO phenomena many years ago, I regret that
I am unable to address the other questions posed in your letter[48].

Brian Freemantle, author of *CIA*, has confirmed to me that according
to his information the Agency's involvement in the UFO question was
mainly in the early 1950s, and that it has substantially diminished since
then. Freemantle considered including a chapter in his book on the Agency's interest in UFOs, but he was unable to obtain enough information.
"The problem was that the CIA's inquiries were conducted largely by
their Scientific and Technical Division, with whom I had no contacts,"
he explained to me.

As you will be aware, intelligence agencies are strictly compartmented
and people who assisted me did not have access to divisions other than
their own. I was told at one stage, however, that the Agency contracted
out some of their research through Stanford University, in Palo Alto,
California. And that the concentration of inquiries, both in the early 1950's
and subsequently, has come under the umbrella of Air Force intelligence
and the National Security Agency—through its electronic expertise—rather
than the CIA itself.[49]

Todd Zechel, a former employee of the National Security Agency,
maintains that the NSA has always played a subordinate role to the CIA
in this respect, and whatever UFO data it gathered was passed on to the
CIA, where it was analyzed by the Office of Scientific Intelligence, with
the NSA kept in ignorance of the conclusions. Admiral Stansfield Turner,
former Director of Central Intelligence, confirms that the NSA is essentially subservient to the Director of Central Intelligence, but that there
have been occasions when it has performed its own analysis and failed
to turn over the material to the CIA. States Turner:

The NSA is mandated to collect intelligence, not to analyze it. It must do
enough analysis about what it has collected to decide what it should collect
next . . . this level of analysis is termed "processing." Processing is
regularly stretched by the NSA into full-scale analysis. . . . Although the
NSA has excellent analysts to do its processing, it does not have the range
of analytic talent needed for responsible analysis, nor all of the relevant

data from the other collecting agencies needed for a comprehensive job
. . . and is less likely to take account of photographic or human intelligence.

Professional rivalry seems to have caused considerable problems between the two agencies, Turner reports.[50]

To what extent this rivalry has caused problems with regard to analysis
of the UFO question I do not know, and my comments to Admiral Turner
on the matter were not touched on in his answering letters. I also asked
the admiral: (a) if he was briefed on the subject following his appointment
as DCI; (b) whether it was possible that some highly secret information
had been withheld from him during his tenure; and (c) if he was aware
of the highly-classified group Majestic 12. In his friendly and helpful
replies, the former DCI pointed out that he was not specially briefed on
the subject, but in due course he did look at what information the Agency
had. He believes that I am drawing unwarranted conclusions from the
available data. Anytime there is a UFO sighting, he explained, the intelligence agencies must take an interest. Regarding information still being
withheld, the admiral emphasized that it is only comparatively recently,
under the Freedom of Information Act, that hitherto secret information
has been declassified and released to the public. There was also not the
slightest evidence to support the theory that sensitive information had
been withheld from him.

The admiral emphasized an important and perfectly understandable
point: that there is a genuine concern that anything written in intelligence
channels that gives any credence whatsoever to UFOs, when released to
the public, may be highly distorted.[51] He refrained from commenting in
any way on Majestic 12.

WHY NO LEAKS?

One of skeptic Philip Klass's main objections to the cover-up hypothesis
is that there have been no leaks of information from intelligence sources
regarding the subject of UFOs, and that it is next to impossible to keep
anything secret for long in Washington. Aside from the fact that there
have been a number of positive statements made by ex-intelligence chiefs,
there have also been occasional leaks by those claiming association with
or employment by intelligence agencies, which I have referred to in this
and other chapters.

Todd Zechel believes that former intelligence personnel such as Victor
Marchetti, John Marks, and Philip Agee, who leaked a great deal of

information on practically everything about the CIA *except* its involvement in UFO research, never had access to UFO data. "Perhaps the dissemination was so restricted they were not privy to it," he says. "Those who could inform us about UFOs are not talking—at least, not publicly. This is perhaps due—besides all the other considerations—to the fact that most of the world's population may not be psychologically prepared to deal with the implications of extraterrestrial life, and these men theorize that now is not the time for such an announcement."[52]

In a letter published in 1985, Zechel argues persuasively that secrets *can* be kept by citing an instance during his service with the Army Security Agency when a Soviet rocket and space capsule were recovered, partially intact.

> All told, several hundred persons were involved in the operation. Most were intelligence personnel with very high security clearances. Over a period of time, one supposes, as many as 1000 persons have had access to the secret. Yet to this day not one word about the operation has leaked out anywhere—except for what is revealed here. Obviously, the event did not have the same transcendental impact as the recovery of a crashed flying saucer, but it does provide a model of a similar big secret that was kept. And it does demonstrate that properly motivated and cleared personnel can keep a lid on something of sensational value.[53]

AN EX-CIA OFFICIAL GIVES REASONS FOR THE COVER-UP

In 1979 Victor Marchetti, former Executive Assistant to the Deputy Director and Special Assistant to the Executive Director of the CIA, stated that during his time in the Agency UFOs were not normally discussed *because the subject came under the area of "very sensitive activities."* Marchetti said that although he had heard rumors from "high levels" in the Agency of "little gray men" whose craft had crashed being kept by the Air Force at the Foreign Technology Division, Wright-Patterson Air Force Base, he had not seen any conclusive evidence for the reality of UFOs. But he concedes that the CIA's attempts to debunk the phenomenon have all the classic hallmarks of a cover-up.

Marchetti believes that the released CIA/UFO information tells us perhaps more than the government thinks. From the very beginning in 1947 the CIA has closely monitored UFO reports on a worldwide basis. Although most of the FOIA documents indicate only a routine interest in the problem, which was handled largely by the Foreign Broadcast Information Service, Foreign Documents Division, and the Domestic

Contact Service—all innocuous, nonclandestine units—they also disclose, by inference, a standing requirement of the Directorate of Science and Technology for gathering UFO data. This, in turn, indicates other collection units, says Marchetti, such as the Clandestine Services, the CIA's directorate which was given the task of providing information from all over the world on the UFO phenomenon. "However," he adds, "few such reports were released—and that implies a cover-up!" His theory is that:

we have, indeed, been contacted—perhaps even visited—by extraterrestrial beings, and the U.S. government, in collusion with the other national powers of the earth, is determined to keep this information from the general public. The purpose of the international conspiracy is to maintain a workable stability among the nations of the world and for them, in turn, to retain institutional control over their respective populations. Thus, for these governments to admit that there are beings from outer space . . . with mentalities and technological capabilities obviously far superior to ours, could, once fully perceived by the average person, erode the foundations of the earth's traditional power structure. Political and legal systems, religions, economic and social institutions could all soon become meaningless in the mind of the public. The national oligarchical establishments, even civilization as we now know it, could collapse into anarchy. Such extreme conclusions are not necessarily valid, but they probably accurately reflect the fears of the "ruling classes" of the major nations, whose leaders (particularly those in the intelligence business) have always advocated excessive governmental secrecy as being necessary to preserve "national security."[54]

15

NASA

The National Aeronautics and Space Administration, established in 1958, coordinates and directs the aeronautical and space research program in the United States. Its budget for space activities alone is larger than the general budgets of a number of the world's important countries.

Although officially a civilian agency, NASA collaborates with the CIA, Department of Defense, National Reconnaissance Office, National Security Agency and other agencies, and many of its personnel have high security clearances owing to the sensitive intelligence aspects of many of its programs. Research into UFOs is one such program.

On 11 May 1962 NASA pilot Joseph A. Walker admitted that it was one of his appointed tasks to detect unidentified objects during his flights in the rocket-powered X-15 aircraft, and referred to five or six cylindrical or disk-shaped objects that he had filmed during his record-breaking fifty-mile-high flight in April that year. He also admitted that it was the second occasion on which he had filmed UFOs in flight. "I don't feel like speculating about them," he said during a lecture at the Second National Conference on the Peaceful Uses of Space Research in Seattle, Washington. "All I know is what appeared on the film which was developed after the flight."[1]

Britain's *FSR* magazine cabled NASA headquarters requesting further information and copies of stills from the film taken by Walker. "Objects recently reported by NASA pilot Joe Walker have now been identified as ice flaking off the X-15 aircraft," NASA replied. "Analysis of additional film cameras mounted on top the X-15 led to identification of the previously unidentifiable objects. . . . *No still photos are available.*"[2] [Emphasis added]

On 17 July 1962 Major Robert White piloted an X-15 to a height of fifty-eight miles, and on his return reported having seen a strange object at the top of his climb. "I have no idea what it could be," he said. "It was grayish in color and about thirty to forty feet away." Then, according to *Time* magazine, Major White is reported to have said excitedly over his radio: "There *are* things out there. There absolutely is!"[3]

"Two years ago," a NASA scientist said in 1967, "most of us regarded UFOs as a branch of witchcraft, one of the foibles of modern man. But so many reputable people have expressed interest in confidence to NASA, that I would not be in the least surprised to see the space agency begin work on a UFO study contract within the next twelve months.''

One of those who expressed interest was Dr. Allen Hynek, who wanted NASA to use its superlative space-tracking network to monitor and document the entry of unidentified objects into the earth's atmosphere. The problem then—as now—is that UFO sightings tracked by NASA remain exempt from public disclosure since they are classified top secret. But there have been leaks.

In April 1964 two radar technicians at Cape Kennedy revealed that they had observed UFOs in pursuit of an unmanned Gemini space capsule. And in January 1961 it was reliably reported that the Cape's automatic tracking gear locked on to a mysterious object which was apparently following a Polaris missile over the South Atlantic.[4]

A 1967 NASA Management Instruction established procedures for handling reports of sightings of objects such as ''fragments or component parts of space vehicles known or alleged by an observer to have impacted upon the earth's surface as a result of safety destruct action, failure in flight, or reentry into the earth's atmosphere,'' and also includes ''reports of sightings of objects not related to space vehicles.'' A rather euphemistic way of putting it, to be sure, but the internal instruction continues: ''It is KSC [Kennedy Space Center] policy to respond to reported sightings of space vehicle fragments and *unidentified flying objects* as promptly as possible. . . . *Under no circumstances will the origin of the object be discussed with the observer or person making the call.*''[5] [Emphasis added]

A 1978 NASA information sheet gives the Agency's official policy on the subject:

NASA is the focal point for answering public inquiries to the White House relating to UFOs. *NASA is not engaged in a research program involving these phenomena, nor is any other government agency.* Reports of unidentified objects entering United States air space are of interest to the military as a regular part of defense surveillance. Beyond that, the U.S. Air Force no longer investigates reports of UFO sightings.[6]

In 1978 CAUS (Citizens Against UFO Secrecy) filed a request for information relating to a NASA report entitled *UFO Study Considerations,* which had previously been prepared in association with the CIA. In his response, Miles Waggoner of NASA's Public Information Services

Branch denied this. "There were no formal meetings or any correspondence with the CIA," he stated. Following another inquiry by CAUS, NASA's Associate Administrator for External Relations, Kenneth Chapman, explained that the NASA report had been prepared solely by NASA employees but that the CIA had been consulted by telephone to determine "whether they were aware of any tangible or physical UFO evidence that could be analyzed; the CIA responded that they were aware of no such evidence, either classified or unclassified."[7]

NASA's statement in the 1978 information sheet that it was not engaged in a research program involving UFOs, "nor is any other government agency," is demonstrably false, as is its denial of Air Force investigations.

PRESIDENT CARTER SEEKS TO RE-OPEN

INVESTIGATIONS

During his election campaign in 1976, Jimmy Carter revealed that he had seen a UFO at Leary, Georgia, in 1969, together with witnesses, prior to giving a speech at the local Lions Club. "It was the darndest thing I've ever seen," he told reporters. "It was big, it was very bright, it changed colors and it was about the size of the moon. We watched it for ten minutes, but none of us could figure out what it was. One thing's for sure; I'll never make fun of people who say they've seen unidentified objects in the sky."[8]

Carter's sighting has been ridiculed by skeptics such as Philip Klass and Robert Sheaffer. While there appear to be legitimate grounds for disputing the date of the incident, Sheaffer's verdict that the UFO was nothing more exotic than the planet Venus is not tenable.[9] As a graduate in nuclear physics who served as a line officer on US Navy nuclear submarines, Carter would not have been fooled by anything so prosaic as Venus, and in any case he described the UFO as being about the same size as the moon.

"If I become President," Carter vowed, "I'll make every piece of information this country has about UFO sightings available to the public and the scientists."[10] Although President Carter did all he could to fulfill his election pledge, he was thwarted, and it is clear that NASA had a hand in blocking his attempts to reopen investigations. When Carter's science adviser, Dr. Frank Press, wrote to NASA Administrator Dr. Robert Frosch in February 1977 suggesting that NASA should become the "focal point for the UFO question,"[11] Dr. Frosch replied that although he was prepared to continue responding to public inquiries, he proposed that "NASA take no steps to establish a research activity in this area or to convene a symposium on this subject."

In a letter from Colonel Charles Senn, Chief of the Air Force Community Relations Division, to Lieutenant General Duward Crow of NASA, dated 1 September 1977, Colonel Senn made the following astonishing statement: *"I sincerely hope that you are successful in preventing a reopening of UFO investigations."* So it is clear that NASA (as well as the Air Force and almost certainly the CIA and National Security Agency) was anxious to ensure that the President's election pledge remained unfulfilled.

DR. JAMES MCDONALD

Dr. James McDonald, senior physicist at the Institute of Atmospheric Physics and Professor in the Department of Meteorology at the University of Arizona, who committed suicide in unusual circumstances in 1971, tried unsuccessfully to persuade NASA to take on primary responsibility for UFO investigations. He reported in 1967:

> Curiously, I have said this both in NASA and fairly widely reported public discussions before scientific colleagues, yet the response from NASA has been nil. . . . Even attempting to get a small group within NASA to undertake a study group approach to the available published effort seems to have generated no response. I realize, of course, that there may be semi-political considerations that make it awkward for NASA to fish in these waters at present, but if this is what is holding up serious scientific attention to the UFO problem at NASA this is all the more reason Congress had better take a good hard look at the problem and reshuffle the deck. . . . I have learned from a number of unquotable sources that the Air Force has long wished to get rid of the burden of the troublesome UFO problem and has twice tried to "peddle" it to NASA—without success.[12]

While McDonald recognized that there were "semi-political considerations" affecting NASA's reluctance to become publicly involved in UFO investigations, he failed to perceive that UFOs are more an intelligence problem than a scientific one. He was simply unaware of the true extent of NASA's secret involvement.

THE PIONEERS

One of the great pioneers in astronautics is Dr. Hermann Oberth, whom I had the honor of meeting in 1972. In 1955 Oberth was invited by Dr. Wernher von Braun to go to the United States where he worked on rockets with the Army Ballistic Missile Agency, and later NASA at the George C. Marshall Space Flight Center. Oberth's statements on the UFO question have always been unequivocal, and he told me that he is convinced UFOs are extraterrestrial in origin. In the following he elaborated on his hypothesis for UFO propulsion:

> . . . today we cannot produce machines that fly as UFOs do. They are flying by means of artificial fields of gravity. This would explain the sudden changes of directions. . . . This hypothesis would also explain the piling up of these disks into a cylindrical or cigar-shaped mothership upon leaving the earth, because in this fashion only one field of gravity would be required for all disks.
>
> They produce high-tension electric charges in order to push the air out of their path . . . and strong magnetic fields to influence the ionised air at higher altitudes. . . . This would explain their luminosity. . . . Secondly, it would explain the noiselessness of UFO flight. Finally, this assumption also explains the strong electrical and magnetic effects sometimes, but not always, observed in the vicinity of UFOs.[13]

Earlier, Dr. Oberth hinted that there had been actual contact with the UFOs at a scientific level. "We cannot take the credit for our record advancement in certain scientific fields alone; we have been helped," he is quoted as having said. When asked by whom, he replied: "*The people of other worlds.*"[14] There are persistent rumors that the US has even test-flown a few advanced vehicles, based on information allegedly acquired as a result of contact with extraterrestrials and the study of grounded UFOs.

In 1959 Dr. Wernher von Braun, another great space pioneer, made an intriguing statement, reported in Germany. Referring to the deflection from orbit of the US *Juno 2* rocket, he stated: "We find ourselves faced by powers which are far stronger than we had hitherto assumed, and whose base is at present unknown to us. More I cannot say at present. *We are now engaged in entering into closer contact with those powers*, and in six or nine months' time it may be possible to speak with more precision on the matter."[15] [Emphasis added]

There has been nothing further published on the matter. As Dr. Robert Sarbacher has commented (see Chapter 16), von Braun was probably involved in the recoveries of crashed UFOs in the late 1940s, and it is my opinion that he was constrained from elaborating on the subject owing to the security oath that he must have been subject to. I cannot prove this, of course, any more than I can substantiate information I have received from a reliable source that top secret contacts have been made by extraterrestrials with selected scientists in the space program.[16] It must be admitted, though, that von Braun's statement comes close to corroborating this. What else could he have meant when he said, "We are now engaged in entering into closer contact with those powers"? The Soviets?

NASA WITHHOLDS PHYSICAL EVIDENCE

That NASA has been engaged in UFO research behind the scenes is alone proven, to my satisfaction at least, by its shady involvement in the analysis of metal samples discovered at the site where Sergeant Lonnie Zamora encountered a landed UFO and occupants at Socorro, New Mexico, in April 1964 (see Chapter 14). On 31 July 1964 Ray Stanford and some members of NICAP visited NASA's Goddard Space Flight Center at Greenbelt, Maryland, in order to have a rock with particles of metal on it analyzed by NASA scientists. Dr. Henry Frankel, head of the Spacecraft Systems Branch, directed the analysis. The particles had apparently been scraped on to the rock by one of the UFO's landing legs. On first inspection of the rock through a microscope, Dr. Frankel declared that some of the particles "look like they may have been in a molten state when scraped onto the rock," and expressed the desire to remove them from the rock for further analysis. Stanford agreed to this, but said that he wanted to retain half of the particles for his own use.

The researchers were invited to go to lunch while NASA engineers conducted their analysis. After lunch, Stanford and the others (Richard Hall, Robert McGarey, and Walter Webb), returned to the laboratory building. A NASA technician brought the rock over to the group. "As he handed it to me," said Stanford, "I was able to carefully observe it in the bright light inside the room. *The whole thing had been scraped clean.* Someone had gone over that rock with the equivalent of a fine-toothed comb. There was nothing, *not a speck* of the metal left . . . even the very few tiny particles that I had known were rather well hidden had been removed."

When Stanford complained, the technician insisted that half of the samples were still on the rock, as promised, but seeing Stanford's disbelief hastily left the room. Dr. Frankel then returned, and after Stanford had remonstrated with him, explained what had happened. "Well, we tried to leave you some," he said, "but we also had to get enough to make an accurate analysis. The sample will be placed under radiation this afternoon, where it will remain the entire weekend. Monday, we will remove it for X-ray diffraction tests. That should tell us the elements it contains . . . if you will call me, say on Wednesday, I should be able to tell you something very definite."

Before contacting Dr. Frankel again, Stanford and McGarey had a meeting with a US Navy captain in Washington who was interested in the Socorro case. The captain told the researchers that they would never get their metal samples back from Frankel. "If that metal is in any way unusual," he said, "he will never give you any documentation to prove it . . . Those boys at Goddard know that they must report any findings as important as a strange UFO alloy to the highest authority in NASA. Once that authority receives the news, the President will be informed, for the matter is pertinent to national security and stability. A *security* directive will instruct those self-appointed authorities at Goddard as to just whose hands the matter is really in. . . ."

On 5 August 1964 Ray Stanford phoned Dr. Frankel at the Goddard Space Flight Center. "I'm glad you called," the scientist said. "I have some news that I think will make you happy." He went on:

> The particles are comprised of a material that *could not occur naturally.* Specifically, it consists predominantly of *two metallic elements,* and *there is something that is rather exciting about the zinc-iron alloy of which we find the particles to consist: Our charts of all alloys known to be manufactured on earth, the U.S.S.R. included, do not show any alloy of the specific combination or ratio of the two main elements involved here. This finding definitely strengthens the case that might be made for an extraterrestrial origin of the Socorro object.*

Dr. Frankel added that the alloy would make "an excellent, highly malleable, and corrosive-resistant coating for a spacecraft landing gear, or for about anything where those qualities are needed." He also said that he was prepared to make a statement before a congressional hearing to this effect, if necessary.

Frankel went on to say that further analysis would be carried out, and that Stanford should call him again the following week. On 12 August Stanford placed a call to Frankel, but was told by his secretary that he was "not available" and suggested he try contacting him the following day. On 13 August Stanford phoned again. "Dr. Frankel simply is not available today," the secretary announced. "He wonders if you might try him the first part of next week?"

On 17 August Stanford rang Frankel's office, only to be told yet again that he was not available. Ominously, the secretary added: *"Dr. Frankel is unprepared, at this time, to discuss the information you are calling about."* On 18 August Stanford tried again. "I'm sorry," the secretary said, "but *Dr. Frankel is in a top-level security conference.* I doubt that he will be able to talk with you until tomorrow or the next day."

Failing to get hold of Frankel the following day, Stanford left a telephone number with the secretary. On 20 August Thomas P. Sciacca, Jr., of NASA's Spacecraft Systems Branch phoned Stanford. "I have been appointed to call you and report the *official* conclusion of the Socorro sample analysis," he said. "Dr. Frankel is no longer involved with the matter, so in response to your repeated inquiries, I want to tell you the results of the analysis. *Everything you were told earlier by Dr. Frankel was a mistake.* The sample was determined to be silica, SiO_2."

In 1967 Dr. Allen Hynek invited Ray Stanford to a lecture he was giving in Phoenix, and afterward Hynek asked: "Whatever happened with the analysis at Goddard of that metallic sample from the rock you took from the Socorro site?" Both Hynek and Stanford had been closely involved in investigations at the landing site, but Stanford was puzzled as to how Hynek knew about the NASA analysis. "I was not sure where Hynek had learned of the fact that I had taken the rock which Lonnie Zamora had pointed out to both of us, and which the astronomer had ignored," he said. "I was interested to note that he specifically knew it was analyzed at Goddard. That fact had never been published."

Stanford told Hynek that NASA's "official" analysis had revealed it to be common silica. "That cannot be true!" exclaimed Hynek. "I am familiar with the analysis techniques involved. Silica could not be mistaken for a zinc-iron alloy. They haven't given you the truth! I would accept Frankel's original report and forget the later disclaimer."[17]

Given that the original analysis was accurate, it is worth recording NASA Administrator Dr. Robert Frosch's statement in the letter he wrote to President Carter's science adviser, Dr. Frank Press, in 1977: "There is an absence of tangible or physical evidence available for thorough laboratory analysis. . . . To proceed [therefore] on a research task without a disciplinary framework and an exploratory technique in mind would be wasteful and probably unproductive."[18]

THE SILVER SPRING FILM

In my first book I devoted a chapter to the controversial 8mm color movie film taken by George Adamski in the presence of Madeleine Rodeffer and other unnamed witnesses outside Madeleine's home at Silver Spring, Maryland, in February 1965. I have been taken to task for endorsing the authenticity of this "obviously fake" film taken by a "proven charlatan," but I have yet to see any conclusive evidence that it was actually faked. Both my co-author Lou Zinsstag and I exposed as many of the inconsistencies in Adamski's claims that were available to us at the time of writing, but that short piece of film, taken a few months before Adamski's death, remains authentic in my opinion at least.

Sometime between 3 and 4 p.m. on 26 February 1965 an unidentified craft of the famous type photographed by Adamski in 1952 (and others subsequently) described a series of maneuvers over Madeleine's front yard, retracting and lowering one of its three pods and making a gentle humming and swishing sound as it did so. Adamski began filming the craft with Madeleine's 8mm camera. "It looked blackish-brown or gray-ish-brown at times," Madeleine told me, "but when it came in close it looked greenish and blueish, and it looked aluminum: it depended on which way it was tilting. Then at one point it actually stood absolutely still between the bottom of the steps and the driveway." The craft then disappeared from view, but reappeared above the roof and described maneuvers once more before finally disappearing vertically. Madeleine told me that she could make out human figures at the portholes, but details were obscured.

When the film was developed the following week something was obviously wrong with many of the frames and it was apparent that it had been interfered with. Obviously faked frames had been substituted by person or persons unknown. "They took the original film," Madeleine believes, "and what I think they did was rephotograph portions of the original . . . and then fake some stuff. The film I got back is not the original film at all."

Fortunately enough frames showing the craft as they had remembered it survived out of the twenty-five feet that had been taken, and these were analyzed by William T. Sherwood, an optical physicist who was formerly a senior project development engineer for the Eastman-Kodak Company in Rochester, NY. I spent many hours discussing the film with Bill, and in 1968 he provided me with a brief technical summary of his evaluations as they related to the prints he made from the "original" film.

It's hard to capture the nuances of the original film. None of the movie duplicates are good: too much contrast. The outlines look "peculiar" due to distortions, I believe, caused by the "forcefield." The glow beneath the flange is, I think, significant. Incidentally, the tree [near the top of which the craft maneuvered] is very high (90 ft?). Roughly, the geometry of imagery is this:

$$\frac{\text{object size}}{\text{image size}} \simeq \frac{\text{distance}}{\text{focal length}} \quad \text{or} \quad \frac{27\text{ft}}{2\text{mm}} \simeq \frac{90\text{ft}}{9\text{mm}}$$

In 1977 Bill Sherwood sent me further details of his evaluations:

The camera was a Bell & Howell Animation Autoload Standard 8, Model 315, with a f1.8 lens, 9–29 mm, used in the 9mm position. . . . As you can measure, the image on the film (original) is about 2.7mm maximum. So for a 90ft distant object, [the diameter] would be about 27 feet. . . . It was a large tree, and the limb that the saucer seems to "touch" could have been about that distance from the camera . . . but unfortunately I could not find a single frame where the saucer could clearly be said to be *behind* the limb. So it is not conclusive as for distance, and therefore for size. . . . In some of the frames of the original, portholes are seen.

In reply to my query as to whether it was possible to authenticate the film unequivocally, Bill said that there is no absolutely foolproof way of assessing whether a photo is "real" or not. One must just take everything into account, including as much as one can learn about the person involved, and then make an educated guess. In the final analysis, he said, it comes down to this question: "Is this the kind of person whom I can imagine going to all the trouble and expense of simulating what only a well-equipped studio with a large budget could begin to approximate, and defending it through the years with no apparent gain and much inconvenience?"

One of the peculiarities of the film is that the outlines of the craft look peculiarly distorted at times. Bill Sherwood believes this is due to a powerful gravitational field that produces optical distortions, an opinion that is shared by Leonard Cramp, an aeronautical engineer and designer who has worked for De Havilland, Napier, Saunders-Roe and Westland Aircraft companies (at Napier he patented the invention of an Induction Mixed-Fluid Ramjet). In his pioneering book, *Piece for a Jig-Saw*, Cramp proposed a theory to account for this peculiar effect:

Earlier, when discussing light in terms of the G [gravitational field] theory, we saw how we might expect such a field to form an atmospheric lens, producing optical effects which might be further augmented by other field effects as well as the gravitational bending of light. . . .

Now it follows that if there would be a local *increase* in atmospheric pressure due to a powerful G field, then similarly we could expect a *decrease* in atmospheric pressure to accompany a powerful R [repulsion] field, and again we would not be surprised to find optical effects . . . we can now say, while a G field might produce optical magnifying properties, an R field could produce optical *reducing* properties.[19]

Leonard Cramp had not seen the Silver Spring film prior to publishing his book, and was delighted that it seemed to confirm his hypothesis. Like Bill Sherwood and myself, he is in no doubt that the film is authentic.

On 27 February 1967 (two years after it had been taken) the film was shown to twenty-two NASA officials at the Goddard Space Flight Center. Discussion afterward lasted for an hour and a half, and just before Madeleine left, one of the two friends with her was allegedly told that it was "a very important piece of film" and that the craft was 27 feet in diameter (the figure calculated independently by Bill Sherwood).[20] Unfortunately, I have been unable to confirm this.

In reply to my queries, NASA scientist Paul D. Lowman Jr., of the Geophysics Branch at Goddard, stated that according to one of those present, Herbert A. Tiedemann, everyone considered the Silver Spring film to be fake. Dr. Lowman, who had helped set up the meeting but was unable to attend, offered the following comments on the color photos from the film that I sent him:

First, it is not possible to make any precise determination of the object's size from the relationship (which is basically correct) quoted by Mr. Sherwood. Given any three of these quantities, one can calculate the fourth. The focal length and image size are obviously known, but not the distance, which can only be roughly estimated. The equation can be no better than its most inexact quantity, and one might as well just estimate the size of the object directly. My own strong impression is that these frames show a small object, perhaps up to 2 or 3 feet across, a short distance from the camera. Judging from the photo of Mrs. Rodeffer's house, a 27 foot UFO would have occupied most of the cleared area in the front yard, and from such a short distance would have been a very large photographic object.[21]

Although Bill Sherwood readily concedes that his estimate of the precise distance from the camera is arbitrary, he is sure that it is reasonably accurate, and my own tests at the site show that, with the camera lens set on wide angle (as it was at the time), an object of this approximate size and distance would appear exactly as it does on the film. That either Adamski or Madeleine (or both) could have faked the film using a small model, and then have the audacity to show it at NASA, seems far-fetched in the extreme. Moreover, to produce the distortion effects as well as the lowering and retracting of one of the pods with a small model, is out of the question as far as I am concerned. As a semi-professional photographer I can speak with some authority on the matter myself.

Following the death of Adamski, Madeleine Rodeffer experienced a great deal of ridicule and harassment, and nearly all copies of the "faked" film have been stolen—in the United States and elsewhere.

Two photographs of an identical craft were taken by young Stephen Darbishire in the presence of his cousin Adrian Myers in Coniston, England, in February 1954. For the benefit of those who contend that Darbishire had faked the pictures and recanted later, the following statement from a letter he wrote to me in 1986 is illuminating:

> . . . when I said that I had seen a UFO I was laughed at, attacked, and surrounded by strange people . . . In desperation I remember I refuted the statement and said it was a fake. I was counter-attacked, accused of working with the "Dark Powers" . . . or patronizingly "understood" for following orders from some secret government department.
>
> There was something. It happened a long time ago, and I do not wish to be drawn into the labyrinth again. Unfortunately the negatives were stolen and all the prints gone . . .[22]

THE ASTRONAUTS

In the early 1970s I had the pleasure of several meetings in Britain and the US with the former US Navy test pilot, intelligence officer, and pioneer astronaut Scott Carpenter, who had reputedly seen UFOs and photographed one of them during his flight in the *Mercury 7* capsule on 24 May 1962. Scott vehemently denied this, and poured scorn on other reports of sightings by fellow astronauts. I noticed that he appeared to be ill at ease when discussing the subject, and whenever I produced documentary evidence for official concern in this area he became visibly nervous. But in November 1972 Scott kindly wrote on my behalf to astronauts Gordon Cooper, Dick Gordon, James Lovell and James McDivitt, asking about reports attributed to them. James Lovell replied as follows:

> I have to honestly say that during my four flights into space, I have not seen or heard any phenomena that I could not explain. . . . *I don't believe*

any of us in the space program believe that there are such things as
UFOs. . . . However, most of us believe that there must be a star like our
sun that also has a planetary system [which] must support intelligent life
as we know it. . . . I hope this is sufficient information for Tim Good,
and I hope he isn't too disappointed in my answer.[23] [Emphasis added]

But according to the transcript of Lovell's flight on *Gemini 7*, an
anomalous object was encountered:

SPACECRAFT: Bogey at 10 o'clock high.
CAPCOM: This is Houston. Say again 7.
SPACECRAFT: Said we have a bogey at 10 o'clock high.
CAPCOM: Gemini 7, is that the booster or is that an actual sighting?
SPACECRAFT: We have several, looks like debris up here. Actual sighting.
CAPCOM: . . . Estimate distance or size?
SPACECRAFT: We also have the booster in sight . . .

Franklin Roach, of the University of Colorado UFO study set up by the
Air Force in 1966, concluded that in addition to the booster traveling in
an orbit similar to that of the spacecraft, "there was another bright object
[the 'bogey'] together with many illuminated particles. It might be con-
jectured," he said, "that the bogey and particles were fragments from
the launching of Gemini 7, but this is impossible if they were traveling
in a polar orbit as they appeared to be doing."[24]

James McDivitt confirmed that although he did see an unidentified
object during the *Gemini 4* flight on 4 June 1965, he does not believe it
was anomalous:

During Gemini 4, while we were in drifting flight, I noticed an object out
the front window of the spacecraft. It appeared to be cylindrical in shape
with a high fineness ratio. From one end protruded a long, cylindrical pole
with the approximate fineness of pencil. I had no idea what the size was
or what the distance to the object was. It could have been very small and
very near or very large and very far away.

I attempted to take a photograph of this object with each of the two
cameras we had on board. Since this object was only in my view for a
short time, I did not have time to properly adjust the cameras and I just
took the picture with whatever settings the camera had at that time. The
object appeared to be relatively close and I went through the trouble of
turning on the control system in case I needed to take any evasive actions.

The spacecraft was in drifting flight and when the sun shone on the
duty window, the object disappeared from view. I was unable to relocate
it, since the attitude reference in the spacecraft was also disabled, and I
did not know which way to maneuver to find it.

After landing, the film from Gemini 4 was flown back to Houston immediately, whereas Ed White and I stayed on the aircraft carrier for three days. During this period of time a film technician at NASA evaluated the photographs and selected what he thought was the photograph of this particular object. Unfortunately, what he selected was a photograph of sunspots [flares] on the window and had nothing whatsoever to do with the object that I had seen. The photograph was released before I returned and had a chance to point out the error in the selection. I, subsequently, went through the photographs myself and was unable to find any photograph like the object I had seen. Apparently, the camera settings were not appropriate for the pictures.

I do not feel that there was anything strange or exotic about this particular object. Rather, only that I could not identify it. In a combination of both Gemini 4 and Apollo 9 I saw numerous satellites, some of which we identified and some of which we didn't. . . . I have seen a lot of objects that I could not identify, but I have yet to see one that could be identified as a spaceship from some other planet. I do not say that there aren't any, only that I haven't seen any. I hope this helps Tim.[25]

Although the NORAD computer facility was unable to trace a satellite near enough to account for the sighting, I am inclined to believe that what McDivitt *might* have seen was a secret American reconnaissance satellite, which naturally NORAD could not disclose.

Neither Gordon Cooper nor Dick Gordon replied to Scott's letter, it seems, and I have never been able to receive a reply from Cooper, although he has spoken publicly of his interest in the subject. In fact, Cooper's interest in UFOs was one of the reasons that inspired him to become an astronaut. "I . . . had the idea that there might be some interesting forms of life out in space for us to discover and get acquainted with," he wrote in 1962. "As far as I am concerned there have been far too many unexplained examples of unidentified objects sighted around this earth . . . the fact that many experienced pilots had reported strange sights . . . did heighten my curiosity about space . . . This was one of several reasons, then, why I wanted to become an Astronaut."[26]

In 1978 Cooper attended a meeting of the Special Political Committee of the United Nations General Assembly in order to discuss UFOs. Later that year a letter from Cooper was read at another UN meeting:

. . . *I believe that these extraterrestrial vehicles and their crews are visiting this planet from other planets, which are obviously a little more advanced than we are here on earth.*

I feel that we need to have a top-level, coordinated program to scientifically collect and analyze data from all over the earth concerning any type of encounter, and to determine how best to interface with these visitors in a friendly fashion.

    . . . Also, *I did have occasion in 1951 to have two days of observation of many flights of them, of different sizes, flying in fighter formation,* generally from east to west over Europe. [Emphasis added]

Cooper said that most astronauts were reluctant to discuss UFOs "due to the great numbers of people who have indiscriminately sold fake stories and forged documents abusing their names and reputations without hesitation." But he added that there were "several of us who do believe in UFOs" and who have had occasion to *see a UFO on the ground*, or from an aircraft. "There was only one occasion from space which may have been a UFO," Cooper's letter revealed, without elaborating.[27]

A UFO seen on the ground by an astronaut? The only reference I have to such an incident is contained in an article which the late Lou Zinsstag translated from the French for me in 1973. Unfortunately, I have neither the name of the paper nor the date, but the article was written by J. L. Ferrando, based on an interview with an astronaut at a congress in New York in mid-1973, tape-recorded by Benny Manocchia. The name of the astronaut? None other than Gordon Cooper! The following extracts are highly significant—if true:

> For many years I have lived with a secret, in a secrecy imposed on all specialists in astronautics. I can now reveal that every day, in the USA, our radar instruments capture objects of form and composition unknown to us. And there are thousands of witness reports and a quantity of documents to prove this, but nobody wants to make them public. Why? Because authority is afraid that people may think of God knows what kind of horrible invaders. So the password still is: we have to avoid panic by all means.
>
> I was furthermore a witness to an extraordinary phenomenon, here on this planet earth. It happened a few months ago in Florida. There I saw with my own eyes a defined area of ground being consumed by flames, with four indentations left by a flying object which had descended in the middle of a field. Beings had left the craft (there were other traces to prove this). They seemed to have studied topography, they had collected soil samples and, eventually, they returned to where they had come from, disappearing at enormous speed. . . . I happen to know that authority did just about everything to keep this incident from the press and TV, in fear of a panicky reaction from the public.

I immediately wrote to Cooper at Aerofoil Systems Inc., Cape Canaveral, Florida, asking if there was any truth to these statements. "If the whole story is a hoax," I said, "somebody ought to be sued." But there was no reply from him, even when I sent reminders and a stamped addressed envelope. I then wrote to Scott Carpenter, asking if he would forward it to Cooper, and this he promised to do. To this day, I have heard nothing.

In the same letter to Scott I asked for the complete story of the photograph he took during his flight in *Mercury 7* on 24 May 1962. According to a commentator on BBC TV in 1973, Carpenter had been withdrawn from duties as an astronaut for wasting time taking pictures of "sunrise." I thought this rather unlikely, especially since Scott's friend André Previn told me that Scott had not been allowed in space again owing to a slight heart murmur. The released photograph shows what some have interpreted as a UFO; others as a lens flare, ice crystals, or the fabric and aluminum balloon that was deployed at one stage. I wanted the facts.

When I reminded Scott of my request a year later, he replied that he resented "your continuing implication that I am lying and/or withholding truths from you. Your blindly stubborn belief in Flying Saucers makes interesting talk for a while, but your inability to rationally consider any thought that runs counter to yours makes further discussion of no interest—indeed unpleasant in prospect—to me. I have sent your letter to Gordon Cooper without comment other than a copy of this letter to you. Let's do be friends, Tim, but let's talk about such things as music and SCUBA diving, where maybe both of us can learn something."[28]

I have never insisted that Scott Carpenter photographed a UFO, but because of the rumors surrounding the incident I wanted to know the truth. To me, that seems reasonable. In any event, my friendship toward and respect for Scott remain undiminished.

An anonymous source with secret clearance claims that Carpenter told him that at no time when the astronauts were in space were they alone: there was constant surveillance by UFOs.[29] And Dr. Garry Henderson, a senior research scientist for General Dynamics, has confirmed that the astronauts are under strict orders not to discuss their sightings with anyone. Dr. Henderson says that NASA "has many actual photos of these crafts, taken at close range by hand and movie camera."[30]

In November 1979 Lou Zinsstag and I received an unofficial invitation to visit the Lyndon B. Johnson Space Center in Houston. The invitation came from Alan Holt, a physicist and aerospace engineer whose main work at that time centered on the development of the astronaut and flight controller training programs associated with the Spacelab. He is also engaged in theoretical research into advanced types of propulsion for spacecraft, and has long been involved in an unofficial NASA UFO study group called Project VISIT (Vehicle Internal Systems Investigative Team). I asked about photographs and films of UFOs allegedly taken by astronauts and was simply told that the National Security Agency screens *all* films prior to releasing them to NASA.

It may be coincidental that a former Director of the National Security Agency and Deputy Director of the CIA, Lew Allen, was appointed head of NASA's Jet Propulsion Laboratory in June 1982. JPL runs NASA's unmanned planetary space program, whose phenomenal achievements include the landing on Mars by the Viking probes and, more recently, the Voyagers which transmitted such spectacular pictures of Jupiter, Saturn and Uranus. Allen had also been the USAF Chief of Staff, and as one of the pioneers of aerial espionage served as Deputy Director for Advanced Plans in the Directorate of Special Projects of the National Reconnaissance Office, and later Director of the NRO's Office of Space Systems.[31] NRO—America's most secret intelligence agency—liaises closely with the CIA, NSA—and of course NASA.

In an interview in 1986 Lew Allen stated that up to a third of JPL's work was funded by the Department of Defense, but gave details of various fascinating civilian projects. "One of the most exciting of these future programs, called Cassini," he said, "is an investigation of Saturn's moon Titan. Its atmosphere was too dense for the Voyagers to give us any clues about what lies beneath. The Cassini mission . . . would probe this atmosphere . . . we've concluded that it is very similar to what the earth's must have been at the earliest stages of its evolution."[32]

Maurice Chatelain, former chief of NASA communications specialists, claims that all the Apollo and Gemini flights were followed at a distance and sometimes quite closely by space vehicles of extraterrestrial origin, but Mission Control ordered absolute secrecy. Chatelain believes that some UFOs may come from our own solar system—specifically Titan.[33]

During a BBC radio interview in December 1972, astronaut Edgar Mitchell, lunar module pilot on *Apollo 14*, was asked by a listener if NASA had made any provisions for encountering extraterrestrials on the moon or nearby planets. He replied in the affirmative. When the interviewer intervened and suggested that, if and when we ultimately come into contact with other civilizations, it would only be via radioastronomy, Mitchell emphatically disagreed, making a point of recommending Allen Hynek's book, *The UFO Experience*, which contradicted official policy on the subject.[34]

I wrote to Dr. Mitchell and asked him to elaborate on this and another statement he made on the program, to the effect that there had been no concealment of UFO sightings either in transit to or on the moon, and that such information was open to all. Mitchell's assistant, Harry Jones, replied: "Dr. Mitchell asked me to write and tell you that to his knowledge there have been no unexplained UFO sightings. *All unexplained sightings have subsequently been explained.* Dr. Mitchell personally attests that there has never been any lid of secrecy placed on any NASA astronaut that he is aware of."[35] [Emphasis added]

Although puzzled by this contradictory reply I did not pursue the matter further, since the publicity from UFO reports in 1973 led to a number of positive statements by some other astronauts. "I'm one of those guys who has never seen a UFO," said Eugene Cernan, Commander of *Apollo 17*, at a press conference. "But I've been asked, and I've said publicly I thought they were somebody else, some other civilization."[36]

In 1979 former Mercury astronaut Donald Slayton revealed in an interview with Paul Levy that he had seen a UFO while test-flying an aircraft in 1951:

> I was testing a P-51 fighter in Minneapolis when I spotted this object. I was at about 10,000 feet on a nice, bright, sunny afternoon. I thought the object was a kite, then realized that no kite is gonna [sic] fly that high.
>
> As I got closer it looked like a weather balloon, gray and about three feet in diameter. But as soon as I got behind the darn thing it didn't look like a balloon anymore. It looked like a saucer, a disk.
>
> About that same time, I realized that it was suddenly going away from me—and there I was, running at about 300 miles an hour. I tracked it for a little way, and then all of a sudden the damn thing just took off. It pulled about a 45-degree climbing turn and accelerated and just flat disappeared.
>
> A couple of days later I was having a beer with my commanding officer, and I thought, "What the hell, I'd better mention something to him about it." I did, and he told me to get on down to intelligence and give them a report. I did, and I never heard anything more on it.[37]

DID APOLLO 11 ENCOUNTER UFOS ON THE MOON?

According to hitherto unconfirmed reports, both Neil Armstrong and Edwin "Buzz" Aldrin saw UFOs shortly after that historic landing on the moon in *Apollo 11* on 21 July 1969. I remember hearing one of the astronauts refer to a "light" in or on a crater during the televised transmission, followed by a request from mission control for further information. Nothing more was heard.

According to former NASA employee Otto Binder, unnamed radio hams with their own VHF receiving facilities that bypassed NASA's broadcasting outlets picked up the following exchange:

MISSION CONTROL: What's there? Mission control calling Apollo 11.
APOLLO 11:   These babies are huge, sir . . . enormous. . . . Oh, God, you wouldn't believe it! I'm telling you there are other spacecraft out there . . . lined up on the far side of the crater edge . . . they're on the moon watching us. . . .[38]

The story has been relegated to the world of science fiction since it first appeared, but in 1979 Maurice Chatelain, former chief of NASA communications specialists and one of the scientists who conceived and designed the Apollo spacecraft, confirmed that Armstrong had indeed reported seeing two UFOs on the rim of a crater. "The encounter was common knowledge in NASA," he revealed, "but nobody has talked about it until now."

Soviet scientists were allegedly the first to confirm the incident. "According to our information, the encounter was reported immediately after the landing of the module," said Dr. Vladimir Azhazha, a physicist and Professor of Mathematics at Moscow University. "Neil Armstrong relayed the message to Mission Control that two large, mysterious objects were watching them after having landed near the moon module. But his message was never heard by the public—because NASA censored it." According to another Soviet scientist, Dr. Aleksandr Kazantsev, Buzz Aldrin took color movie film of the UFOs from inside the module, and continued filming them after he and Armstrong went outside. Dr. Azhazha claims that the UFOs departed just minutes after the astronauts came out on to the lunar surface.

Maurice Chatelain also confirmed that *Apollo 11*'s radio transmissions were interrupted on several occasions in order to hide the news from the public. NASA chief spokesman John McLeaish denied that the agency censored any voice transmissions from *Apollo 11*, but admitted that a slight delay in transmission took place, due simply to processing through electronic equipment.[39]

Before dismissing Chatelain's sensational claims, it is worth noting his impressive background in the aerospace industry and space program. His first job after moving from France was as an electronics engineer with Convair, specializing in telecommunications, telemetry and radar. In 1959 he was in charge of an electromagnetic research group, developing new radar and telecommunications systems for Ryan. One of his eleven patents was an automatic radar landing system that ignited retro rockets at a given altitude, used in the Ranger and Surveyor flights to the moon. Later, at North American Aviation, Chatelain was offered the job of designing and building the Apollo communication and data-processing system.

In his book, Chatelain claims that "all Apollo and Gemini flights were followed, both at a distance and sometimes also quite closely, by space vehicles of extraterrestrial origin—flying saucers, or UFOs . . . if you want to call them by that name. Every time it occurred, the astronauts informed Mission Control, who then ordered absolute silence." He goes on to say:

> I think that Walter Schirra aboard Mercury 8 was the first of the astronauts to use the code name "Santa Claus" to indicate the presence of flying saucers next to space capsules. However, his announcements were barely noticed by the general public. It was a little different when James Lovell on board the Apollo 8 command module came out from behind the moon and said for everybody to hear: "Please be informed that there is a Santa Claus." Even though this happened on Christmas Day 1968, many people sensed a hidden meaning in those words.[40]

I asked Dr. Paul Lowman of NASA's Goddard Space Flight Center what he thought about the *Apollo 11* story. He replied:

> Most of the radio communications from the Apollo crew on the surface were relayed in real time to earth. I am continually amazed by people who claim that we have concealed the discovery of extraterrestrial activity on the moon. The confirmed detection of extraterrestrial life, even if only by radio, will be the greatest scientific discovery of all time, and I speak without exaggeration. The idea that a civilian agency such as NASA, operating in the glare of publicity, could hide such a discovery is absurd, even if it wanted to. One would have to swear to secrecy not only the dozen astronauts who landed on the moon but also the hundreds of engineers, technicians, and secretaries directly involved in the missions and the communication links.[41]

Yet the rumors persist. NASA may well be a civilian agency, but many of its programs are funded by the defense budget, as I have pointed out, and most of the astronauts are subject to military security regulations. Apart from the fact that the National Security Agency screens all films (and probably radio communications as well), we have the statements by Otto Binder, Dr. Garry Henderson and Maurice Chatelain that the astronauts were under strict orders not to discuss their sightings. And Gordon

Cooper has testified to a UN committee that one of the astronauts actually witnessed a UFO on the ground. If there is no secrecy, why has this sighting not been made public?

Not all communications between the astronauts and ground control are public, as NASA itself admits. John McLeaish, Chief of Public Information at the Manned Spacecraft Center (now Lyndon B. Johnson Space Center) in Houston, explained to me in 1970 that although there is no separate radio frequency used by the astronauts for private conversations with mission control, private conversations, "usually to discuss medical problems," are rerouted: "When the astronauts request a private conversation, or when a private conversation is deemed necessary by officials on the ground, it is transmitted on the same S-band radio frequencies as are normally used but it is routed through different audio circuits on the ground; and unlike other air-to-ground conversations with the spacecraft, it is not released to the general public."[42]

But is there any truth to the *Apollo 11* story? A friend of mine who formerly served in a branch of British military intelligence has provided me with unexpected corroboration. I am not permitted to reveal the name of my source, nor the location and date of the following conversation that was overheard and subsequently confirmed by my friend, which will inevitably lay me open to charges of fabricating the story or being the victim of a hoax. Yet the story must be told, however apocryphal.

A certain professor (whose name is known to me) was engaged in an earnest discussion with Neil Armstrong during a NASA symposium, and according to my friend's recollection, part of the conversation went as follows:

PROFESSOR: What really happened out there with Apollo 11?
ARMSTRONG: It was incredible . . . of course, we had always known there was a possibility . . . the fact is, we were warned off. There was never any question then of a space station or a moon city.
PROFESSOR: How do you mean "warned off"?
ARMSTRONG: I can't go into details, except to say that their ships were far superior to ours both in size and technology—Boy, were they big! . . . and menacing. . . . No, there is no question of a space station.
PROFESSOR: But NASA had other missions after Apollo 11?
ARMSTRONG: Naturally—NASA was committed at that time, and couldn't risk a panic on earth. . . . But it really was a quick scoop and back again . . .

Later, when my friend confronted Armstrong, the latter confirmed that the story was true but refused to go into further detail, beyond admitting that the CIA was behind the cover-up.

What does Neil Armstrong have to say about the matter officially? In reply to my inquiry he simply stated: "Your 'reliable sources' are unreliable. There were no objects reported, found, or seen on Apollo 11 or any other Apollo flight other than of natural origin. All observations on all Apollo flights were fully reported to the public."[43]

16

DOWN TO EARTH

THE AZTEC RECOVERY, 1948

It was the columnist Frank Scully who first alerted the world to sensational stories of recovered flying saucers and little men in his best-selling book, *Behind the Flying Saucers*, published in 1950. Scully claimed that up to that time there had been four such recoveries, one of which was alleged to have taken place near Aztec, New Mexico, when sixteen humanoid bodies were recovered together with their undamaged craft. The story sounds ridiculous and is widely dismissed (with the others) as a hoax perpetrated on Scully, and has been the butt of endless jokes ever since. But there is a great deal more to this particular story than has been hitherto supposed.

One point that is invariably overlooked is that the mysterious "Dr. Gee," Scully's principal source of information, was in fact a composite character of *eight* scientists, each of whom supplied him with various details, "Dr. Gee" being merely a convenient literary device as well as a means of protecting his sources.[1] Here then is the story.

According to Scully's informants, the disk that landed near Aztec was 99.99 feet in diameter, its exterior made of a light metal resembling aluminum but so durable that no amount of heat (up to 10,000° was applied) or diamond-tipped drilling had the slightest effect. The disk apparently incorporated large rings of metal which revolved around a central, stabilized cabin, using an unfamiliar gear ratio. There were no rivets, bolts, screws or signs of welding. Investigators were eventually able to gain entry, Scully was told, because of a fracture in one of the portholes, which they enlarged, revealing a knob inside the cabin which when pushed (with a pole) caused a hidden door to open.

Sixteen small humanoids, ranging in height from thirty-six to forty-two inches, were supposedly found dead inside the cabin, their bodies charred to a dark brown color. Scully was told that the craft was undamaged, having landed under its own guidance. The craft was eventually dismantled, the investigators having discovered that it was manufactured in segments which fitted in grooves and were pinned together around the base. The complete cabin section, measuring eighteen feet in diameter, was lifted out of the base of the saucer, around which was a gear that fitted a gear on the cabin. These segments, together with the bodies, were then transported to Wright Field (Wright-Patterson AFB). Some of the bodies were later dissected and examined by the Air Force, and were found to be similar in all respects to human beings, with the exception of their teeth, which were perfect.

Scully actually examined some of the objects recovered from the disk, including a "tubeless radio, some gears" and other items, and said that even after more than 150 tests, the metal of the gears could not be identified.[2]

This then is one of the incredible stories of recovered disks related to Scully, who stood by its authenticity for the rest of his life and never revealed the names of his sources, despite large cash inducements. But is there any truth to it?

New Supportive Evidence?

According to important information published by William Steinman in 1987[3] there is a large grain of truth in the Aztec story, and he has managed to acquire some quite astonishing supportive evidence. Like Scully, however, he is unwilling to divulge his sources, which inevitably lays him open to charges of fabrication.

Steinman has discovered that the Aztec disk came to earth on 25 March 1948, having been detected by three separate radar units in the southwest, one of which is said to have disrupted the craft's control mechanism (see Appendix p.527). The area of impact was calculated by triangulation, and this information was immediately relayed to Air Defense Command (ADC) and General George C. Marshall, then Secretary of State, who allegedly contacted the MJ-12 group as well as the Interplanetary Phenomenon Unit (IPU) of the Army's Counterintelligence Directorate. The IPU operated out of Camp Hale, Colorado, at this time, Steinman claims, and its main function was to collect and deliver disabled or crashed disks to certain specified secret locations.

The craft was recovered within hours by the IPU scout team about twelve miles northeast of Aztec. General Marshall ordered Air Defense Command to go off alert status, and the radar stations were advised that there had been a false alarm. Marshall then gave orders to the commander of the IPU to organize a recovery team, and contacted Dr. Vannevar Bush—the head of MJ-12—to gather together a team of scientists to accompany the IPU to the crash site. Steinman has named these scientists as follows: Dr. Lloyd Berkner, Dr. Detlev Bronk, Dr. Carl A. Heiland, Dr. Jerome Hunsaker, Dr. John von Neumann, Dr. Robert J. Oppenheimer, Dr. Merle A. Tuve, and Dr. Horace B. van Valkenberg.

Four scientists in this group, it will be noted, were members of the original MJ-12 panel set up in September 1947. *Dr. Carl Heiland* was a geophysicist and magnetic sciences expert who was head of the Colorado School of Mines, and according to Steinman leaked details of the recovery to one of Scully's sources, Leo GeBauer. *Dr. Horace van Valkenberg* was an inorganic chemist associated with the University of Colorado. *Dr. Merle Antony Tuve* worked for the Office of Scientific Research and Development during World War II, and is chiefly remembered as a geophysicist for his techniques of radio-wave propagation of the upper atmosphere. *Dr. Robert Oppenheimer* distinguished himself primarily as leader of the Los Alamos atomic-bomb project, commanding the allegiance of the world's top physicists. He was Director of the Institute for Advanced Studies at Princeton from 1947 and became Chairman of the General Advisory Committee of the Atomic Energy Commission. *Dr. John von Neumann*, the famous Hungarian-born mathematician, became a consultant on the atom bomb (Manhattan Project) in 1943. His main area of expertise lay in the design and development of computers. The scientists, according to Steinman, were told by Dr. Bush to assemble at Durango Airfield, Colorado, thirty-five miles to the north of Aztec, with the minimum delay. All those involved in the recovery were sworn to an above top secret oath.

The IPU convoy used a route to the site that avoided main roads, and on arrival road blocks were set up at strategic points within two miles of the recovery area. The owner of a ranch and his family were allegedly held incommunicado and told never to discuss the matter (cf the Roswell incident). Equipment hauling trucks were camouflaged to look like oil-drilling rigs during the operation.

Inside the Craft

The team of scientists arrived at the site a little later than the IPU team and began inspecting the disk. According to Steinman, they entered the craft one by one, entry having been gained via a fractured porthole as described in Scully's account. The portholes themselves looked metallic and only appeared translucent on close inspection. Inside the cabin they found two humanoids, about four feet in height, slumped over an instrument panel, charred deep brown. Another twelve bodies lay sprawled on the floor in a chamber within the cabin, making a total of fourteen bodies (not sixteen as Scully had been told).

An instrument panel supposedly had several pushbuttons and levers with hieroglyphic-type symbols, as well as symbols illuminated on small display screens. Bush and von Neumann discovered that the control panel had drawers which rolled out, but no wiring could be detected. A "book" composed of parchment-like leaves with the texture of plastic (cf Roswell) also contained the strange hieroglyphs—similar to Sanskrit, Oppenheimer thought. This was given to General Marshall, who then passed it on to two leading cryptological experts for analysis, William F. Friedman and Lambros C. Callihamos (who both later led distinguished careers in the National Security Agency).[4]

Dr. Bronk, a physiologist and biophysicist, examined the bodies and asked Bush to get hold of cryogenic equipment with which to preserve them. Cryogenics specialist Dr. Paul A. Scherer, a colleague of Bush's, was contacted and advised Bush to obtain some dry ice. Meanwhile, another small group of scientists and military personnel examined the craft and were eventually able to dismantle it when several interlocking key devices were found which opened up seams at specific points.

Three days later the segments were loaded onto three trucks, together with the bodies, and were covered with a tarpaulin marked "Explosives." The convoy headed at night by the least conspicuous and often most laborious route to the restricted Navy Auxiliary Airfield complex at Los Alamos, arriving one week later. Here they remained for over a year, Steinman claims, before being transported to another base.

The Bodies

Dr. Paul Scherer eventually obtained special preservation containers for the least damaged bodies, Steinman relates. One of the companies that supplied equipment was the Air Research Corporation, of which Scherer was Director of Research and Development; it supplied the liquid nitrogen pump, circulation system, and refrigeration units. Other specimens were given a complete autopsy, by a team headed by Dr. Bronk, of biophysicists, histochemists and pathologists. The results were put in a report, part of which, Steinman claims, appeared in the *Air Force Project Sign Report No. 13*, which has never been released.

According to the report, the bodies were described as averaging forty-two inches in length. The facial features strongly resembled "mongoloid orientals" in appearance, with disproportionately large heads, large "slant" eyes, small noses and mouths. The average weight was around forty pounds. Their torsos were very small and thin, with very thin necks. The arms were long and slender, reaching the knees, with hands containing long and slender fingers with webbing between them. There was no digestive system or gastrointestinal tract, no alimentary or intestinal canal, and no rectal point. No reproductive organs were apparent. Instead of blood, there was a colorless liquid with no red cells which smelled similar to ozone.

This description is at variance with that provided by Scully's informants, who stated that the humanoids were similar in all respects to human beings except in size. This discrepancy could be explained by the fact that Scully—or his informants—confused the case with one of his others. Of course, *both* stories could be a complete fabrication from beginning to end. William Moore is certain that the Aztec story, as related to Scully, is a hoax. He was unable, for example, to find any local residents to back it up. George Bowra, owner of the local Aztec newspaper for many years, spoke to over 100 cowboys, Indians, ranchers and lawmen about the story and never found a single person who could recall either the saucer recovery or subsequent military movements. Moore states furthermore that Steinman has on several occasions made serious misrepresentations on the case to other researchers.[5] While I have a great deal of respect for Bill Moore as a researcher, I am not persuaded by the counterevidence in this instance; at least, for the time being.

Further Evidence

Veteran researcher Leonard Stringfield, a former Air Force intelligence officer who is the world's leading specialist on what he calls "Retrievals of the Third Kind," shares my misgivings about some of the material in Steinman's book, but we are both impressed with his extensive research into the Aztec case. Stringfield has uncovered further evidence himself.

Captain V. A. Postlethwait, who was on detached service with Army G-2 (Intelligence) in 1948, told Stringfield that he was cleared to see a top secret cable describing the crash of a saucer-shaped craft 100 feet in diameter and 30 feet high, with one porthole broken, causing suffocation to the five occupants—who had turned blue as a result. The bodies were about four feet tall with relatively large heads, Postlethwait recollects. The metallic skin of the saucer was too tough to penetrate, although as thin as newspaper. The incident was said to have occurred near White Sands, New Mexico. Aside from a few discrepancies there are some

significant parallels with the Aztec case. Postlethwait revealed to Stringfield, for example, that private property was purchased to facilitate trans-
porting the craft.[6]

Leonard Stringfield has also spoken with Dr. Robert Spencer Carr, a
retired University of South Florida professor who claims to have testimonial evidence from five sources, including a nurse and a high-ranking
Air Force officer who participated in the recovery of a crashed UFO and
occupants in 1948—presumed to be the one at Aztec (although there was
another alleged recovery that year, just across the Mexican border near
Laredo, Texas). In 1982 Stringfield asked Carr to disclose the name of
his principal source, ''on the premise that our ages give us little time
tolerance in our search for truth.''

''When Professor Carr named his source,'' says Stringfield, ''I sat
back dumbfounded. I knew his name well in research, and recalled some
of his comments on UFOs while he served as an Air Force officer. . . .
'Please, Len,' pleaded Carr, 'keep the name to yourself; please spare me
any trouble as long as I live . . . My key witness participated in the 1948
retrieval and saw alien bodies on location.' ''[7]

According to Bill Steinman, two of Carr's sources were aeronautical
engineers who provided important information regarding the saucer's
construction and propulsion. A source now named is Arthur Bray (not
to be confused with the Canadian researcher), a security guard involved
with the recovery project. Carr also interviewed a woman whose father
was present during the recovery. Information pertaining to the flying
saucers must be suppressed, he told his daughter. ''If news of this vehicle's water driven engine got out to the whole scientific community,
that would be the end of the oil industry.''[8] The comment is of course
pure hearsay, but if there is any truth in it a further possible reason for
the cover-up is brought to light.

At the still fenced-off crash site on a plateau twelve miles northeast
of Aztec, Bill Steinman has uncovered charred and scraped-off rocks of
various sizes as well as some metal bracing struts that might possibly
have been used for supporting the craft. On one of his visits to the area
he was shadowed by two unmarked helicopters.

As for George Bowra's claim that no one in Aztec could recall the
incident, Steinman has traced at least four people who knew where the
crash site was located, one of whom, ''V.A.,'' recalls that sometime
between 1948 and 1950 a huge disk-shaped flying object with a dome
on top skimmed about 100 feet above the ground not far from him. The
witness pointed out to Steinman a cliff jutting above the Animas River.

"That thing, or flying saucer, tried hard to clear that cliff, but it hit the very corner up there, shooting sparks and rocks in every direction," he claims. "Finally, it made a right-angle turn in midair and headed straight north [in the direction of the alleged crash site at Hart Canyon]. That's the last I saw of it. I ran into the house and called the military in Albuquerque. I never heard from them about it."

Steinman first became interested in UFOs in 1981 when he read Frank Scully's book, and has since devoted much of his time and resources on the Aztec case and the other recoveries associated with Scully's claims, often in the face of discouraging odds. Steinman's job in quality assurance and analysis in the aerospace industry has aided him in probing the complex and intricate leads that he has pursued.

Writing in the foreword to Steinman's book, *UFO Crash at Aztec,* Leonard Stringfield explains how, like many others, he was led to believe the Scully story was a hoax, his disbelief long being conditioned by a succession of ufologists who for years claimed that Scully "was duped by a scheming Silas Newton and his cohort, Leo Gebauer." But now, thanks to Bill Steinman's painstaking research (as well as some of his own leads), he has been obliged to reevaluate the evidence.[9]

PARADISE VALLEY, 1947

Another of Scully's stories relates to the recovery of a crashed disk in Paradise Valley, north of Phoenix, Arizona, in 1947. According to Scully's informants the craft was thirty-six feet in diameter, and two humanoid bodies were retrieved—one sitting inside and the other halfway out of the "hatch."

In January 1987 I spoke to former businessman and private pilot Selman E. Graves, who witnessed part of the recovery operation with two friends during a rabbit hunting trip on a Saturday morning in early October 1947. The incident took place at Cave Creek, Graves told me, in the northwest section of Paradise Valley, on property owned by his friend Walt Salyer, whose son was Graves' brother-in-law.

Graves arrived at the house with four others, expecting to be met by Salyer who was to join them on the hunting trip. "When we arrived that morning," Graves told me, "Salyer and his wife were away. He'd been living in the basement and had just completed an upstairs section, so we made ourselves at home. He came back about twenty minutes later and was kind of distressed to find us there, which was unlike him. . . . He told us that we couldn't go due west of there, that it wasn't a good time to hunt there, and that the Air Force had restricted the area; that if we fired our guns in that direction we could hit someone, and so forth.

"We told him we were interested in going to the Go John Mine, at right angles to what was the Cave Creek Road. This place today is called Carefree—it didn't exist then—and Cave Creek was just a couple of small shacky homes."

Graves and two others from the hunting party went ahead on horseback, leaving Salyer and two other men at the house. "We said we'd meet them at the River Road, which was just at right angles . . . and his property sat on the corner there," Graves recalled.

"There were some mine shafts—what you might call an outcropping—and a small hill, and we went up there and the three of us could look back and see everything that was taking place. From this vantage point you could see Salyer's house and I could see the corral very clearly . . . and his water tank, and so you had perspective there as to size. And there was a large—I can best describe it as a large aluminum dome-shaped thing there, which was roughly the size of the house—it was measured to be thirty-six feet in diameter.

"We could see that there were pitched buildings—tents—and men moving about. We at that time didn't have any idea what we were looking at. We thought it might have been an observatory dome, except why would they have it down there on that piece of ground?

"We didn't leave there until probably about 10–10:30 at night, so we were actually around there a good twelve hours," Graves said. The three men later met up with the others at Salyer's house. "The others had bypassed us on the road and went on up to the Go John Mine. We never went to the mine at all," he explained.

Selman Graves told me that he thought little about the incident until he read Scully's book years later, and was astonished to learn of the Paradise Valley recovery. Later he met Silas Newton, one of Scully's informants, who provided further information. "Supposedly there were a couple of small humanoids—about four and a half feet tall—that were reported to have been there," said Graves. "What I tied that in with was Salyer's great anxiety about our going near the deep freeze! It was abnormal. . . . I expect that probably what happened was that Salyer—(an ex-military man)—was the first one to see this object and notify the authorities. If you want to make a conjecture, perhaps they thought, 'Jeepers! What are we going to do with these bodies? How are we going to keep them?' "

"My brother-in-law said that he saw afterward a 'vehicle' and won-

dered if it was part of what we had viewed—not knowing what it was—
and this military flatbed truck going from the Cave Creek Road south, which
at that time would have been the most logical way for them to get out of
there. It seems to me that it would have had to have been something to do
with the military or Air Force. . . . There wasn't anything else so I presume
that that was actually sections [of the object] being trucked out. . . .''

Cover-up

The lengths to which the authorities went to literally cover-up the landing
site are quite remarkable. "Right after the war," Selman Graves told
me, "they made a topographical of that area in little quarter quadrangles,
and they showed the site on it because . . . the marks in the desert stay
quite well: it takes a long time for them to erode. . . . *In that short span
of time they made another quadrangle and you couldn't get hold any
more of the original one.* They changed the location of Cave Creek Road:
they moved the thing east and you wouldn't even know there had ever
been another road there now unless you were really familiar and had
really studied around. Also, there were some changes to the new River
Road and the grading of it. . . .''

"The federal government sponsored a project through the state . . .
subsequently the state came in and told the county area of what was going
to be Carefree that they had to locate some satisfactory spot for refuse
disposal . . . *and what they did was take the site of the landing and dig
it up with a bulldozer.*"

Selman Graves, who strikes me as being totally genuine, told me that
he personally witnessed the bulldozing operations years later. "I went in
to observe what was taking place," he said. "The ditches were somewhat
helter-skelter. They were not doing a methodical digging, burning,
burying—in other words digging a new excavation. . . . It was kind of
helter-skelter, or just mucking up everything, destroying, and so on. . . .
While I was watching it a fellow, rather well groomed for a bulldozer
operator, stopped the machine, got off and came over and asked if he
could help me. I said, 'Well, I'm just interested in what you're doing. I
find it rather interesting because for what you're supposed to be doing
you're not really using a system that would go with it.' 'Oh, of course
we are,' he said. 'No you're not,' I said. 'Look at what you're doing
here. How long has this been going on anyway?' 'Oh,' he said, 'something
like eight years.' 'That's a long time,' I said. 'It doesn't look like that
sort of an operation.' 'Oh yes,' he said. 'It's the way we're doing it.'

"I said, 'You're sure about that time? It can't have been that long.' 'Oh no,' he said, 'I'm quite sure.' I said, 'Isn't that odd. I was here about a year ago and there was nothing going on here. I guess you're mistaken.' He laughed and said, 'That's right. I guess you're right. I'm mistaken.'

"Then he became more talkative, *and told me that he'd done this operation for them in a place over on the Arizona/California border between Kingman and Barstow. . . .*" This site was the scene of a recovery operation in May 1953, as we shall shortly learn.

The most convincing evidence that Scully's claims are fundamentally sound has been provided by the Canadian government scientist Wilbert Smith, who stated in a 1950 top secret document that the subject of flying saucers was classified higher than the H-bomb, and that "their modus operandi is unknown but concentrated effort is being made by a small group headed by Doctor Vannevar Bush." Smith's informant was Dr. Robert Sarbacher, a consultant to the Research and Development Board, and in his handwritten notes made after the interview (see Appendix, pp.519–21), Smith recorded the following, dated 15 September 1950:

SMITH:	. . . I have read Scully's book on the saucers and would like to know how much of it is true.
SARBACHER:	*The facts reported in the book are substantially correct.*
SMITH:	Then the saucers do exist?
SARBACHER:	Yes: they exist.
SMITH:	Do they operate as Scully suggests on magnetic principles?
SARBACHER:	We have not been able to duplicate their performance.
SMITH:	Do they come from some other planet?
SARBACHER:	All we know is, we didn't make them, and it's pretty certain they didn't originate on earth.
SMITH:	I understand the whole subject is classified.
SARBACHER:	*Yes, it is classified two points higher even than the H-bomb. In fact it is the most highly classified subject in the US government at the present time.*
SMITH:	May I ask the reason for the classification?
SARBACHER	*You may ask, but I can't tell you.*[10] [Emphasis added]

ANOTHER RECOVERY IN 1948?

Todd Zechel has interviewed a retired provost marshal [Colonel John W. Bowen] at Carswell AFB, Texas, who is alleged to have participated in the recovery of a ninety-foot-diameter disk thirty miles inside the Mexican border, near Laredo, Texas, in 1948 (or possibly 1950). Apparently one dead alien, four and a half feet tall, had been recovered. Zechel also traced another Air Force colonel who was flying an F-94 Lockheed Starfire over Albuquerque, New Mexico, when reports came in that a UFO had been clocked at 2,000 mph. The colonel saw the object himself before it disappeared from radar screens at his base (Dyess AFB, Texas). The object was believed to have come to ground in Mexico, thirty miles from Laredo. After landing, the colonel and another pilot took off in a light aircraft and headed for the crash site, where they managed to land. Troops surrounded the disk, which had been covered with a canopy. The pilots were refused permission to view it and were summoned to Washington where they were sworn to secrecy.[11]

Leonard Stringfield interviewed a man who claims to have seen a television news item about the event (on WDEL-N, Wilmington, Delaware). "It was about 1948, maybe later, when my wife and I were watching the news," Leon Crice told Stringfield in 1980. "A disk-shaped object was shown stuck, slightly tilted, in a sand dune. It had a dome at the top and no windows." The object had allegedly crashed on the Mexican border, near the Rio Grande. Soldiers were seen moving around the object, with jeeps and a low boy rig, as well as Mexican civilians in the background.

At the moment when the narrator referred to bodies being recovered and the craft transported to a base in California, Crice claims, his voice was cut off and the screen went dead, without explanation or apology.[12] Pending further corroboration it is difficult to place much credence in the story. Why have the television newsreel crew not come forward, for example? Or were they, too, sworn to secrecy?

RECOVERY IN ARIZONA, 1953

Raymond Fowler, formerly with the USAF Security Service and one of America's leading researchers, is convinced by one particular UFO recovery story which was related to him in person by a highly reputable witness with impeccable credentials who claims to have participated in the analysis of a recovered disk in May 1953. The witness, given the pseudonym "Fritz Werner" by Fowler, held a number of engineering and management positions at Wright-Patterson AFB from 1949 to 1960, during which period he worked in the Office of Special Studies. As a designer of aircraft landing gear, he headed a branch of the Aircraft Laboratory at Wright Air Development Center. During a special assignment for the Air Force on contract to the Atomic Energy Commission's

"Operation Upshot-Knothole" in Nevada in May 1953, Werner, whose job at the time involved measuring the effects of blast on various types of building following nuclear tests, received a phone call one evening from Dr. Ed Doll, the test Director, informing him that he would be required for a special job the following day.

Werner reported for duty and was driven to Indian Springs AFB, near the proving ground, where he was joined by about fifteen other specialists. "We were told to leave all valuables in the custody of the military police," Werner recalled. "We were then put on a military plane and flown to Phoenix, Arizona. We were not allowed to fraternize. There, we were put on a bus with other personnel, who were already there. The bus windows were blacked out so that we couldn't see where we were going. We rode for an estimated four hours. I think we were in the area of Kingman, Arizona, which is northwest of Phoenix and not too far from the atomic proving ground in Nevada."

During the bus trip Werner and the others were told that a highly secret Air Force vehicle had crashed, and were instructed to investigate the accident in terms of their own special expertise. On arrival at the site the personnel were escorted to an area where two floodlights illuminated the "aircraft." In his sworn statement, Werner describes the scene on 21 May 1953:

> The object was constructed of an unfamiliar metal which resembled aluminum. It had impacted 20 inches into the sand without any sign of structural damage. It was oval and about 30 feet in diameter. An entranceway hatch had been vertically lowered and opened. It was about 3½ feet high and 1½ feet wide. I was able to talk briefly with someone on the team who did look inside only briefly. He saw two swivel seats, an oval cabin, and a lot of instruments and displays.
>
> A tent pitched near the object sheltered the remains of the only occupant of the craft. It was about 4 feet tall, with dark brown complexion and it had 2 eyes, 2 nostrils, 2 ears, and a small round mouth. It was clothed in a silvery, metallic suit and wore a skull cap of the same type of material.

Werner's job was to find out how fast the vehicle's forward and vertical velocities had been by determining the angle and depth of impact into the sand.

As soon as each of the specialists had completed their jobs he was interviewed on tape then escorted back to the bus. "After we all returned to the bus," Werner stated, "the Air Force colonel who was in charge had us raise our right hands and take an oath not to reveal what we had experienced. I was instructed to write my report in longhand and not to type or reproduce it.'' Werner told Fowler that he sympathized with the cover-up. The Air Force believed that UFOs were interplanetary, he said, but did not know where they came from, and were anxious to avoid panic.[13]

Leonard Stringfield has learned a few more details about the incident from Fritz Werner. Regarding the alien body, for instance, he said it was very slender, with disproportionately long arms. "Since it's been 27 years, details like this are pretty foggy and I may even be influenced by other descriptions I've seen or heard in the interim," he wrote to Stringfield in 1980. "In short, I don't really remember any earlobes; eyes; I didn't see; head shape was oval; don't recall that there was a nose, per se. . . ." Werner said that he and the other specialists were checked for radiation and other possibly harmful effects, but none had been found.[14]

If there were only a few of these incredible stories it would be easy to dismiss them as straightforward hoaxes, delusions or disinformation by the intelligence community in order to discredit the subject. But there are *dozens* of cases, and Leonard Stringfield and others are convinced that a fair proportion are absolutely authentic. Stringfield has been the most outspoken champion of the retrieval cases and even though he has steadfastly refused to disclose the names of his sources—a prerequisite to being given the information—he has on occasion received death threats warning him not to discuss the matter publicly.

ALIEN BODIES AT WRIGHT-PATTERSON AFB, 1959

In his book *Preuves Scientifiques OVNI* (Monaco 1981), Jean-Charles Fumoux relates how Leon B. Visse, an alleged expert on histons (elements connected with cellular genetic material), was invited in 1959 to a military compound at Wright-Patterson AFB, where he was asked to perform an experiment on the histonic weight of particular cells. In the first experiment Visse found an inordinately low histonic weight, far lower than human cells. Either he was mistaken or there had to be a complete revision of genetic theories, he reasoned. But Visse obtained the same results when he repeated the experiment, so he asked if he could look at the organism from which the cells came. To his astonishment, Visse was taken into a special room where the corpses of two humanoids lay.

The bodies were very tall—a little over seven feet—and from their terrible injuries appeared to have been in an accident, although the heads were intact, Fumoux relates, and continues: "the forehead high and broad.

Very long blond hair. The eyes were stretched toward the temples which gave them an Asiatic look. The nose and mouth were small. The lips were thin, perfectly delineated. The chin was small and slightly pointed. The two faces were beardless. Despite slight differences in their facial appearances, the two humanoids looked like twins.'' The bodies had been preserved in formalin but remained perfectly white, apparently lacking the keratin granules which cause normal human beings to tan in strong sunlight. The eyes were very light blue and looked no different from normal, Visse reported. The hands were human-like but slender, while their feet were absolutely flat, with small toes.

Dr. Jean Gilles of the French Center for Scientific Research (CNRS) eventually tracked down Leon Visse, who promptly denied that he had been personally involved in the case. Nevertheless, he admitted there was some truth to the story. Only a highly qualified biologist could have come up with such a story, he told Dr. Gilles. It had been alleged, for example, that the aliens' bodies exhibited a far more developed lymphatic system than normal, and Visse explained that, hypothetically, hyperdevelopment of the lymphatic system might be a normal attribute of extraterrestrial beings.

Another of the alleged witnesses, Professor André Lwoff, also denied involvement and said he had never heard of Visse. So what are we to make of this extraordinary story? A straightforward hoax? Dr. Gilles summarized his feelings about Visse in a letter to Leonard Stringfield in 1982:

> I have no definite opinion if he was the right man or not; for me it's 50% yes—50% no. Visse had indeed knowledge about covert operations. . . . It seemed to me—but it could have been my imagination—that he was accustomed to military ways of thinking and behavior. . . . Visse was absolutely unmoved by the Fumoux story when I told him . . . he didn't show any surprise, he was not shocked at all by the odd subject. . . . In short, I believe Fumoux knew *something* about alien/retrieval affairs. But what he knew was certainly distorted.

Dr. Gilles concluded that either Dr. Visse or Fumoux, or both, knew the truth about the Wright-Patterson incident but had subsequently covered it up with disinformation. Two further points are worth noting. Visse had allegedly been sworn to secrecy for ten years by the Americans, and it was precisely ten years later (in 1969) that he revealed the story for the first time, according to Fumoux. Fumoux himself had been in the French Air Force and had ties with the intelligence community.[15] Was the story a way of bringing out the truth—albeit in a distorted form—or simply a hoax from beginning to end? Like so many apocryphal accounts of alien retrievals, we shall simply have to suspend judgment until the day arrives when the authorities decide to reveal the facts.

GUARDED UFO SEEN BY SEVERAL US NAVY PILOTS AT WRIGHT-PATTERSON AFB, 1962

Thanks to researcher Tommy Blann, Leonard Stringfield was able to contact a former US Navy test pilot (now a commercial pilot)—identified as "P.J."—who together with other Navy pilots inadvertently came across a saucer-shaped "aircraft" guarded at Wright-Patterson AFB in 1962. In April of that year, while temporarily attached to the 354th TAC Fighter Wing as an exchange pilot, the 352nd Tactical Fighter Squadron was sent to Wright-Patterson AFB on a hurricane evacuation from Myrtle Beach, South Carolina. As Flight Commander of the "B" Flight Bluebirds, it was P.J.'s custom to keep his men physically and mentally fit by organizing a program of running, touch football or handball.

On the first day, as P.J. led his flight crew of five on a running exercise through the base, the group came across an extraordinary sight, P.J. related to Stringfield:

As we crossed two baseball fields we approached the first hangar which, without hesitating, we guessed was the Special Services Hangar. We busted through both doors on a full sprint to look for the equipment room [to] check out for gear. Once inside, we were stunned by dead silence and [were] approached by an air police sentry with a sub-machine gun.

Standing about eight feet away was a strange-looking object. It was about 12–15 feet long and eight feet deep and resembled two plates stuck together. . . . It was suspended off the ground by two engine test stands. There were no markings or insignia, but most noticeable; it was without rivets. The object was roped off and eight guards stood parade rest around it.

The guard challenged by saying: "I don't think you're supposed to be here, Sir." I replied in the affirmative and we turned about face. . . . Once outside, we had reassured each other that the good old U.S. had developed, or had all along, flying saucers in service.

On our return to Myrtle Beach AFB . . . a week later, I was requested to report to the Brigadier General of the Combat Wing. . . . He informed me that I had broken security. He only asked one question—"What did you see?" My reply was "Nothing!" His answer was "You have the right answer to the question," and I was dismissed. . . .

Having a Top Secret clearance enabled me to gain valuable information

that otherwise would be impossible to obtain . . . for a brief 30 seconds
[we saw] a disk-shaped object of metallic color. . . . I cannot confirm
anything other than it was there.

P.J. was puzzled by the relative lack of security. "It wasn't even
located in the test facility of Wright-Patterson AFB," he said. "It was
near the flight line having just arrived or awaiting deployment. That is
just my guess."[16]

RECOVERY IN NEW MEXICO, 1962

Tommy Blann has interviewed an Air Force colonel who claims to have
been present during the recovery of a crashed disk and humanoid occupants in northern New Mexico in the summer of 1962. According to
Colonel "X," the craft looked like two saucers end-on-end, was of a
dull aluminum color, had a dark section around the center, and was about
thirty feet in diameter and twelve feet high. Blann was told that there
was no noticeable landing gear and that the craft had apparently skidded
on impact, digging up a small trench. Colonel "X" said that a team of
eight men was at the site, wearing jump suits and gas masks, and that
each had a specific task to perform. Only preliminary analysis is conducted
at retrieval sites, the colonel stated, and went on to describe the scene
further:

> There were two bodies recovered from the craft and they were put in a
> large unmarked silver van and whisked off. I did not get a good look at
> the bodies; however, they looked small and were dressed in silver, skin-
> tight flight suits. They were taken to Holloman AFB as well as the craft,
> and then sections of the craft were sent to various research labs, including
> Los Alamos Laboratories. I believe the bodies were also taken to Los
> Alamos and samples sent to other locations.

Colonel "X" revealed that underground installations, as well as isolated areas of military reservations, have squadrons of unmarked helicopters with sophisticated instrumentation which are dispatched to monitor
areas of UFO activity or airlift them out of the vicinity in the event of a
malfunction.

Tommy Blann asked the colonel about the many rumors that crashed
disks and bodies were sent to Wright-Patterson AFB. "In the earlier
years," he replied, "they had taken some bodies to this base, but later
it depended on where they were found. They had a hell of a time setting

up procedures for this operation, as well as getting craft out of the area
without it being observed. Usually this was done at nighttime." Colonel
"X" told Blann he believed that in more recent years the bodies were
flown outside the US to a secret naval installation on an island in the
Pacific.[17]

The reference to special squadrons of unmarked helicopters is intriguing and has been substantiated on numerous occasions, most significantly perhaps in the case of Betty Cash and Vickie and Colby Landrum,
who saw about twenty-three helicopters "escorting" an unidentified flying
object near Huffman, Texas, on 29 December 1980 (see Chapter 12).
Leonard Stringfield has learned from several sources that this unit is (or
was) called the "Blue Berets," and has personally spoken with one of
the former members of this elite group who confirmed that one of its
tasks was to assist in UFO retrieval operations.[18]

SENATOR GOLDWATER CONFIRMS WITHHELD

UFO DATA

In Chapter 13 I referred to Captain Bruce Cathie's claim that a secret
UFO research center is permanently manned at Wright-Patterson AFB.
Leonard Stringfield has uncovered some additional evidence to support
this claim, having spoken with an intelligence officer (J.K.) who stated:
"Since 1948, secret information concerning UFO activity involving the
U.S. military has been contained in a computer center at Wright-Patterson
AFB. At this base, a master computer file is maintained with duplicate
support backup files secreted at other military installations. . . . Get the
complete 'Dump File,' both the master and the support backup files, and
you've got all the hidden UFO data."

J.K. also claims to have seen on one occasion nine deceased alien
bodies at the base, preserved in deep freeze conditions under a thick glass
enclosure. The area was under heavy guard and J.K. was told at the time
(1966) that thirty bodies in total were held there. He did not see any alien
craft but was told that some were stored at the base and elsewhere,
including Langley AFB, Virginia, and McDill AFB, Florida.[19]

From another source Stringfield has learned that the bodies at Wright-
Patterson were stored in 1953 in Building 18-F, third floor, and then at
Langley AFB, Hampton Roads, Virginia.[20] Senator Barry Goldwater,
former Chairman of the Senate Intelligence Committee, visited Wright-
Patterson hoping to get permission from General Curtis LeMay to examine

the UFO evidence stored there, but was refused. Copies of letters from Goldwater to various researchers (in my files) are worth quoting here. In a letter to Shlomo Arnon on 28th March 1975, he wrote:

The subject of UFOs is one that has interested me for some long time. About ten or twelve years ago I made an effort to find out what was in the building at Wright-Patterson Air Force Base where the information is stored that has been collected by the Air Force, and I was understandably denied this request. *It is still classified above Top Secret.* I have, however, heard that there is a plan under way to release some, if not all, of this material in the near future. I'm just as anxious to see this material as you are, and I hope we will not have to wait much longer. [Emphasis added]

On 11 April 1979 Goldwater wrote to Lee Graham. "It is true I was denied access to a facility at Wright-Patterson," he confirmed. "Because I never got in, I can't tell you what was inside. *We both know about the rumors.*" The room that the Senator tried to visit is called the Blue Room, and according to my information it contains UFO artifacts, but *not* craft or bodies. In another letter to Lee Graham, dated 19 October 1981, Goldwater wrote:

First, let me tell you that I have long ago given up acquiring access to the so-called blue room at Wright-Patterson, as I have had one long string of denials from chief after chief, so I have given up.

In answer to your questions, one is essentially correct. I don't know of anyone who has access to the blue room, nor am I aware of its contents and I am not aware of anything having been relocated. . . .

To tell you the truth, Mr. Graham, this thing has gotten so highly classified, even though I will admit there is a lot of it that has been released, *it is just impossible to get anything on it.* [Emphasis added]

KIRTLAND AFB, NEW MEXICO, 1980

According to official documents released under the Freedom of Information Act, there were a number of low-level intrusions by unidentified flying objects in the vicinity of nuclear weapons storage areas at Kirtland AFB, New Mexico, in August 1980. The sightings were associated with radar jamming and blackout, as these Air Force Office of Special Investigations (AFOSI) complaint forms reveal:

On 13 August 80, 1960 COMMSq Maintenance Officer reported Radar Approach Control equipment and scanner radar inoperative due to high frequency jamming from an unknown cause. Total blackout of entire radar approach system to include Albuquerque Airport was in effect between 1630–2215 hrs. Radar Approach Control backup systems also were inoperative. . . . Defense Nuclear Agency Radio Frequency Monitors determined, by vector analysis, the interference was being sent from an area . . . located NW of Coyote Canyon Test area. It was first thought that Sandia Laboratory, which utilizes the test range was responsible. However . . . no tests were being conducted in the canyon area.[21]

On 2 Sept 80, SOURCE related on 8 Aug 80, three Security Policemen assigned to 1608 SPS, KAFB, NM, on duty inside the Manzano Weapons Storage Area sighted an unidentified light in the air that traveled from North to South over the Coyote Canyon area of the Department of Defense Restricted Test Range. . . . The Security Policemen identified as: SSGT STEPHEN FERENZ, Area Supervisor, AIC MARTIN I. RIST and AMN ANTHONY D. FRAZIER, were later interviewed separately by SOURCE. . . .

At approximately 2350 hrs., while on duty in Charlie Sector, East Side of Manzano, the three observed a very bright light traveled with great speed and stopped suddenly in the sky over Coyote Canyon. The three first thought the object was a helicopter, however, after observing the strange aerial maneuvers (stop and go), they felt a helicopter couldn't have performed such skills. The light landed in the Coyote Canyon area. Sometime later, [the] three witnessed the light take off and leave proceeding straight up at a high speed and disappear. . . .

On 11 Aug 80, RUSS CURTIS, Sandia Security, advised that on 9 Aug 80, a Sandia Security Guard (who wishes his name not to be divulged for fear of harassment), related the following: At approximately 0020 hrs., he was driving East on the Coyote Canyon access road on a routine building check of an alarmed structure. As he approached the structure he observed a bright light near the ground behind the structure. He also observed an object he first thought was a helicopter. But after driving closer, he observed a round disk shaped object. He attempted to radio for a backup patrol but his radio would not work. As he approached the object on foot armed with a shotgun, the object took off in a vertical direction at a high rate of speed. . . .

On 22 Aug 80, three other security policemen observed the same aerial phenomena described by the first three. Again the object landed in Coyote Canyon . . . Coyote Canyon is part of a large restricted test range used by the Air Force Weapons Laboratory, Sandia Laboratories, Defense Nuclear Agency and the Department of Energy. . . .

. . . another Security Guard observed an object land near an alarmed structure sometime during the first week of August, but did not report it until just recently for fear of harassment.[22]

Paul Bennewitz, who runs a scientific firm in Albuquerque, has succeeded in taking photographs and over 2,600 feet of 8mm movie film of

UFOs flying in the vicinity of the Manzano Weapons Storage area and Coyote test area, according to other AFOSI documents. Bennewitz, with whom I have been in communication, has also recorded periods of high magnetic activity emanating from the Manzano/Coyote Canyon area on his electronic surveillance equipment, and believes that UFOs cause this by emitting high frequency pulses.

In late 1980 the Aerial Phenomena Research Organization (APRO) received the following anonymous letter which may provide some clues regarding the mysterious events at Kirtland AFB:

On July 16, 1980, at between 10:30 and 10:45 AM, Craig R. Weitzel, [address given] a Civil Air Patrol Cadet from Dobbins AFB . . . visiting Kirtland AFB, NM, observed a dull metallic colored UFO flying . . . near Pecos, New Mexico . . . a secret training site for the 1550th Aircrew Training and Testing Wing, Kirtland AFB. . . . WEITZEL was with ten other individuals, including USAF active duty airmen, and all witnessed the sightings. WEITZEL took some pictures of the object. WEITZEL went closer to the UFO and observed the UFO land in a clearing approximately 250 yds. NNW of the training area. *WEITZEL observed an individual dressed in a metallic suit depart the craft and walk a few feet away.* The individual was outside the craft for just a few minutes. When the individual returned the craft took off toward the NW.

The following evening Weitzel was visited at his temporary billet on Kirtland AFB by a man dressed in a dark suit, the letter continues. The man was described as six foot three inches tall, of slender build, with dark black hair and wearing sunglasses. ''The individual identified himself as a Mr. Huck from Sandia Laboratories, a secret Department of Energy contractor on Kirtland AFB. Mr. Weitzel, not being from the Albuquerque area, did not know what Sandia was.'' After obtaining an explanation from the man, Weitzel let him in.

''The individual told Weitzel that he saw something yesterday near Pecos that he shouldn't have seen. The individual stated that the craft was a secret craft from Los Alamos, NM [and] demanded all the photographs. Mr. Weitzel explained that he didn't have any photographs as [they] were with a USAF airman and Weitzel didn't know the individual's name.'' Weitzel was warned not to mention the sighting to anyone or he would be in serious trouble.

How the man had known about the sighting puzzled Weitzel, who had told no one about the incident. He called Kirtland AFB Security Police and reported the matter to them, and they in turn referred it to the Air

Force Office of Special Investigations. An AFOSI special agent, referred to in the letter as "Mr. Dody," but more probably Richard C. Doty (cited in official AFOSI documents at the time), took a statement from Weitzel and obtained all the photographs of the UFO.

The anonymous letter concluded:

> I am a USAF Airman assigned to the 1550th Aircrew Training and Testing Wing at Kirtland AFB. . . . I was with Weitzel during the sighting: however, I did not see the craft land. . . .
>
> I have every reason to believe the USAF is covering up something. I have spent a lot of time looking into this matter and I know there is more to it than the USAF will say. I have heard rumors, but serious rumors, that the USAF has a crashed UFO stored in the Manzano Storage area. . . . This area is heavily guarded by USAF Security. I have spoken with two employees of Sandia Laboratories, who also store classified objects in Manzano, and they told me that Sandia has examined several UFOs during the last 20 years. Parts of one that crashed near Roswell, NM . . . was examined by Sandia scientists. That is still being stored in Manzano.
>
> I have reason to believe OSI is conducting a very secret investigation into UFO sightings. OSI took over when Project Blue Book closed. I was told this by my commander, Col. Bruce Purvine. Col. Purvine also told me that the investigation was so secret that most employees of OSI don't even know it. But Col. Purvine told me that Kirtland AFB, AFOSI District 17 has a special secret detachment that investigates sightings around this area. They have also investigated the cattle mutilations in New Mexico. . . .
>
> I must remain anonymous because I am a career airman with time remaining on active duty. I feel I would be threatened if I disclosed my name.

MILITARY INTELLIGENCE OFFICER EXAMINES

RECOVERED UFOS AND ALIEN BODIES AT SECRET

BASE IN ARIZONA

One of the most fascinating stories relating to recovered UFOs and humanoid occupants was related by a former military intelligence officer to the psychiatrist and researcher Dr. Berthold Schwarz in the early 1980s. Dr. Schwarz graduated from Dartmouth College and Dartmouth Medical School and received his M.D. from the College of Medicine, New York University; he is a Diplomate of the American Board of Psychiatry and Neurology, as well as a Fellow of the American Board of Psychiatry and Neurology. Because I know him to be totally objective in his analyses of UFO cases and witnesses I am including the following story, which was first published in his book *UFO Dynamics*.[23]

The intelligence officer is now a successful private citizen, who has received many commendations for his courage under fire during the Vietnam War, and has written a number of authoritative monographs on security matters as well as being fluent in several Oriental languages. "The officer's credentials seem as impeccable as his need for anonymity," Schwarz reports. "Interviews of some people who know him well and who are known to myself vouchsafe for his honesty and excellent work record. . . . The officer spoke in a clear, direct manner, but it was obvious that he did not enjoy discussing his experiences. It was as if he was relieved to tell me what happened, and then he wanted to have nothing further to do with the subject."

The witness claims that while serving with a military intelligence unit in the 1970s he met a fellow intelligence officer who invited him to see some recovered alien bodies at a secret base in Arizona. He said to Schwarz:

> I doubt if I could ever find that place again. There was a highway above ground that went over the base, and after a turn at the entrance, we went underground. We violated every security code in the book. Because of this and the fact that I had a top secret clearance at the time I wondered if this was a set-up—that they wanted to put a man with combat experience in this spot and see what he does—to sow the seeds of doubt. It was too obvious. We used a staff car and not a private one. We entered a vaulted area. Now, this was on a weekend, and the security amazed me because it was so lax.

The Humanoids

> When we got in I observed five humanoid figures. . . . Remember, I doubted what I saw. They were very, very white. There were no ears; no nostrils. There were only openings: a very small mouth and their eyes were large. There was no facial hair, no head hair, no pubic hair. They were nude. I think the tallest one could have been about 3½ feet—maybe a little bit taller. As I recall there were three males and two females. The heads were large—not totally out of proportion—but large . . . it wasn't exaggerated, in other words. Slender fingers: slender legs. There was a small bone structure.

"Did you see any genitals?" asked Dr. Schwarz. "I don't remember seeing that in the men or the female organs in the women. . . . I don't remember seeing breasts on the women,'' the officer responded. So how could he tell that some of them were women? He replied that his friend had told him so (the sex presumably having been determined during autopsy). ''When I saw the smallest female in the group I could see clear suture marks. My friend said there had been an autopsy and that from a study of her brain it was estimated that she was 200 years old. The smallest woman had a complete autopsy, opened with a Y incision. . . . There was no bruising on the body. There were no signs of injuries to any of the bodies. . . . He told me that they were vegetarians. The teeth were smooth, flat and very small.''

Dr. Schwarz then questioned the witness more closely about the physical details of the alien bodies:

SCHWARZ: How about the eyes . . . ?

OFFICER: Oh, that was interesting. They were tear-shaped with the slant going to the outside.

SCHWARZ: Wrap around?

OFFICER: No, no. They were not. They were large, open.

SCHWARZ: Did they have lids? Could you tell?

OFFICER: No, I could not tell.

SCHWARZ: Eyebrows? Or anything like that?

OFFICER: No brows. Two openings for the nostrils and the same for the ears. They were delicate. They looked as if you touched them they would break. No signs of wrinkling on them either.

SCHWARZ: How could you make the guess that the lady was more than 200 years old?

OFFICER: This is what I asked him. He said from the count of the ridges on the brain. I never heard of that before.

SCHWARZ: Approximately when did this happen?

OFFICER: In the middle '70s. But they had this [craft and entities] from several years before. . . .

The officer claimed that the craft had been tracked on radar as it came to earth, the location pinpointed by triangulation. ''When they [the military] got out there they found a small hole. Evidently a meteorite had hit this craft, causing rapid decompression, and the people died from that.'' The officer saw parts of this craft at the secret base in Arizona, including the seats. ''The seats were a dull bronze metal—not cold to touch. I left my fingerprints all over. I still doubt everything. They still have the craft but where, I don't know.''

A Craft Stored at the Base

The intelligence officer claims to have seen a complete recovered craft at the base which came to grief in Nevada and was found half-buried in sand, yet completely undamaged.

From the bottom it was almost flat. It was almost 20 feet across—almost—because I walked it. There was a slight dome, but with a gradual rise. It was dull silver, but it was not paint. Inside the craft no cloth, but dull brown material like a coating over it. . . . There was a chair in front of a screen. It looked like a screen. It might have been for some navigational purpose. He wouldn't tell me about it.

There were instruments off to the side. Anyway, there were other slots to the side, and a big piece of metal moved—a computer-like appearance. There were switches and lights. I saw symbols. The screen looked like a TV—circular, no grid marks. You could put your hand in it. It was more than seven feet high, as I judged it when I walked in and therefore I would guess about four feet round. I didn't ask about the symbols, triangles, circles, rectangles, odd shapes. . . .

The cabin wasn't dull, it was bright. Everything was flush, nothing standing out. There were levers by the seats—stuff I can't describe. There were no holes or rivets. A [container] came out of the wall and part of the food was there. They must have been vegetarians. The aisle was very narrow with thick black cloth over it. There were no screws, weld marks or rivets—smooth as if it were painted, but it wasn't painted. It was not metal, yet it was firm, not cloth or plastic or fibreglass. . . . They knew how to open and close the doors. This guy had been handling it for some time.

Was It a Hoax?

It is tempting to dismiss the intelligence officer's story as a hoax, yet Dr. Schwarz is convinced that nothing would be gained by this. The witness himself constantly expressed doubts, as indeed would anyone who found themselves in a similar situation. "Now that I look back on it, I doubt what I saw," he said. "I find it difficult to believe. . . . I figure that the deal in Arizona was a 'sow-and-seed' to sow the disbeliever among the crowds. It is really a damn good maneuver when you think about it, because it comes from a man with good credentials, who was spewing forth madness. So, if you look at it in that light, yes, it does make sense now."

Dr. Schwarz is equally convinced that the intelligence officer's story is not the product of a deranged mind:

> As far as I am aware he has experienced no previous emotional instability, use of psychoactive or psychedelic drugs, or contact with noxious chemicals in line of duty. . . . My cursory psychiatric examination of this person revealed no evidence for overt psychopathology, and if what he is saying is apocryphal or untrue, one would have to ask what his motive would be in view of his failure to receive any monetary gain or prestige from his story. If his account is part of a ruse on his part, or if he is consciously or surreptitiously being used by organizations for purposes not clear at this time, this would be an extraordinarily expensive operation, and many would have been fooled for no ostensible reason.

Harassment

Following these extraordinary experiences at the secret Arizona base, the officer's family was visited by fellow intelligence personnel. "I get the feeling that some of my brother spooks did the usual follow-up," he related to Schwarz:

> Although I had the rank, I did not have the "need to know." They never said a thing, but they just sort of asked—my family was getting used to this. My Dad is a good officer. Although he has seen and taken a lot in his career, he was effectively shook. He was visited by three nondescript individuals in a nondescript car with credentials that were not authenticated . . . not FBI. . . . They wouldn't attract open attention by their clothing or conversation. Dad never saw their eyes . . . they wore sunglasses. . . . They asked questions about my career. . . . They would come and ask questions in my neighborhood and then get out, leaving everybody upset. My family would get calls from Washington. Now that I am married and because my wife's relatives are in Eastern Europe, I lost my Top Secret clearance, and I don't have the access that I used to have.

There was further harassment, Bert Schwarz related to me in 1983:

> . . . shortly after he told me his story with much sweat, he was visited by two Mutt and Jeff characters in dark suits who said they were from the government, flashed appropriate credentials and then proceeded to tell him everything that he had told me, plus that which he didn't tell me for obvious reasons. Shortly afterward, his double-locked, steel door apartment was broken into and various war medals, snapshots, negatives and other memorabilia were taken. . . . It is a rather involved and sticky situation, as you might surmise.[24]

In 1984 I corresponded with the anthropologist and psychic researcher Dr. Eric Dingwall about this case. Since Dr. Dingwall (who died in 1986) had a background in military intelligence (MI6) and was keen to learn about the stories of recovered UFOs and their occupants, I thought his opinion would be valuable. He was, however, skeptical. "I know a good deal about Schwarz," he told me. "He is, I am told, a very warm hearted person with a touching faith in the fundamental goodness of human nature, and thus a massive credulity in matters 'supernatural.' Did it not strike you as possible that the tale of the retrieved UFOs and their occupants might not have been a 'try-on' by his informant just to see how much he would believe?"[25]

I put this to Dr. Schwarz. "Of course, I must come across as a charming, simple minded fool who believes in the fundamental goodness of human nature," he responded. "To be a therapist you have to have this approach, that is true. On the other hand, you're not born yesterday and you see every slimy, rotten thing that human beings are capable of also. Believe me, that is even more incredible than the claims of some of the paranormal phenomena."

Schwarz remains convinced by the officer's sincerity and integrity, and has kept in touch with him from time to time, "but, as you might imagine, he is tight-lipped about what he had told me. Once he did say, however, that he probably should have said nothing."[26]

FURTHER CONFIRMATION FOR THE RECOVERIES

However unbelievable the stories of recovered UFOs and their occupants may seem, there has been confirmation from reliable sources that a number of such incidents *did* actually take place. The late Dr. Robert Sarbacher, former consultant to the Research and Development Board and President and Chairman of the Board of the Washington Institute of Technology, sent a letter to William Steinman in 1983 which clearly acknowledges this fact:

> Relating to my own experience regarding recovered flying saucers, I had no association with any of the people involved in the recovery and have no knowledge regarding the dates of the recoveries. . . .
>
> Regarding verification that persons you list were involved, I can only say this: *John von Neumann was definitely involved. Dr. Vannevar Bush was definitely involved, and I think Dr. Robert Oppenheimer also.*
>
> My association with the Research and Development Board under Doctor Compton during the Eisenhower administration was rather limited so that

although I had been invited to participate in several discussions associated with the reported recoveries, I could not personally attend the meetings. I am sure that they would have asked Dr. von Braun, and the others that you listed were probably asked and may or may not have attended. This is all I know for sure. . . .

About the only thing I remember at this time is that *certain materials reported to have come from flying saucer crashes were extremely light and very tough*. I am sure our laboratories analyzed them very carefully.

There were reports that instruments or people operating these machines were also of very light weight, sufficient to withstand the tremendous deceleration and acceleration associated with their machinery. I remember in talking with some of the people at the office that I got the impression these "aliens" were constructed like certain insects we have observed on earth, wherein because of the low mass the inertial forces involved would be quite low.

I still do not know why the high order of classification has been given and why the denial of the existence of these devices.[27] [Emphasis added]

So, although Dr. Sarbacher was not directly involved in the recoveries, his comments leave no doubt that there was more than one recovery, and that some of the scientists cited by Steinman in his report on the Aztec case were definitely involved.

General George C. Marshall, US Army Chief of Staff in World War II, and Secretary of State for Foreign Affairs (1947–49), has also confirmed that the authorities have recovered UFOs and their occupants. In 1951 General Marshall spoke with Dr. Rolf Alexander, following sightings at Mexico City Airport when many films and photographs were taken while newsmen awaited the arrival of the general.

Marshall later revealed to Dr. Alexander that the UFOs were from another planet and that they were friendly; their hovering over defense establishments and airports was taken to mean that they could blow us all to bits if they had any evil intent. Marshall stated that they were undoubtedly trying to work out a method of remaining alive in our atmosphere before landing and establishing friendly communications, and that the US authorities were convinced that earth had nothing to fear from them.

Questioned about landings, *Marshall admitted that there had actually been contact with the men in the UFOs, and that on three occasions there had been landings which had proved disastrous for the occupants*. On each of these occasions, he said, breathing the heavily oxygenated atmosphere of earth had literally incinerated the visitors from within and burned them to a crisp. This last piece of information does not completely tally with the contemporary reports I have cited, in which it is claimed that some of the alien bodies survived in a good state of preservation. But what are we to make of the comment that there had been "actual contact"? Regrettably, Marshall did not elaborate on this tantalizing revelation.

Asked by Dr. Alexander why such emphasis had been put on denying the existence of UFOs and censoring reports, Marshall replied that the US wanted her people to concentrate on the real menace—Communism—and not be distracted by the visitors from space. He went on to say that the famous Orson Welles prewar broadcast of H. G. Wells' science fiction story *The War of the Worlds* had demonstrated what reaction might be expected were the true facts generally known: a welter of hysterical nonsense and a complete disorientation from the tasks in hand. Rumors and speculation would create an atmosphere that the propagandists of the Kremlin would be certain to exploit, he said.[28]

I do not know how accurately Dr. Alexander reported his meeting with General Marshall, but I do know that he was trusted and respected by some contemporary researchers, and therefore unlikely to have made up the story. Furthermore, he refused to allow Marshall's name to be associated with the news release at the time, and it was not published until his own death as well as Marshall's.

In a letter to Derek Dempster, the first editor of *FSR*, Dr. Alexander made a comment that is as relevant today as it was then. "The trouble is," he wrote, "UFOs, alas, are no longer news unless we can manage to land one and have it photographed, and its crew interviewed by the press. This may not be impossible, but no one has managed it yet."[29]

17

ABOVE TOP SECRET

THE NATIONAL SECURITY AGENCY

Founded in 1952 under President Truman, America's vast National Security Agency has grown into the world's largest eavesdropping empire, with an estimated annual budget in 1985 of $2 billion. Based in 1,000 acres at Fort George Meade, Maryland, the NSA has its own college (18,000 students at the last count), its own power station, television station and studio, and a total of 50,000 personnel. It is divided into ten main departments, including four operational divisions, five staff and support sections, and one training unit, whose basic functions are: Signals Intelligence (SIGINT), Electronics Intelligence (ELINT), Radar Intelligence (RADINT), Communications Security (COMSEC), and Human Intelligence (HUMINT).

In 1982 a sensational book by James Bamford, *The Puzzle Palace,* revealed a wealth of hitherto secret information about the NSA—an agency so secret that it was sometimes referred to as "No Such Agency."[1] There is not one single reference to the subject of UFOs, however. Until recently, few outside the intelligence community had the slightest hint of NSA involvement with UFOs. When Robert Todd wrote to the NSA in 1976 requesting information on its role in UFO research, he received a blunt reply: ". . . please be advised that NSA does not have *any* interest in UFOs in *any* manner."[2]

Thanks to Citizens Against UFO Secrecy (CAUS), eighteen documents on UFOs originating with the NSA were admitted during litigation against the CIA. Lawyer Peter Gersten filed a request under the Freedom of Information Act for their release, but was informed that the documents were exempt from disclosure—under 5 US Code, Section 552 (b)(1)— in the interests of national security. After another unsuccessful attempt under the FOIA to obtain the documents, Gersten eventually succeeded in securing the release of two documents in January 1980. The NSA admitted that other documents on UFOs were being withheld, in addition to the original eighteen, and that a further seventy-nine documents were being referred to other originating agencies for review.[3] Later that year

Above left: Frederick Valentich, the young Australian pilot who disappeared together with his Cessna aircraft immediately after reporting a UFO hovering above him on 21 October 1978. (*Guido Valentich*)

Above right: 'Unidentified flying objects are a very serious subject which we must study fully. We appeal to all viewers to send us details of strange flying craft seen over the territories of the Soviet Union. This is a serious challenge to science and we need the help of all Soviet citizens. . . .' Professor Felix Zigel of the Moscow Aviation Institute, Moscow Central Television, 10 November 1967. (*Henry Gris*)

Below: In 1984 the Commission for the Investigation of Anomalous Atmospheric Phenomena was established in Moscow under the aegis of the Soviet Academy of Sciences. The commission was headed by Pavel Popovitch, who said that there were hundreds of UFO reports in the USSR each year and that although most could be explained, others could not. *(Popperfoto)*

Above left: Dr. Vannevar Bush, who headed the Research and Development Board after the war, was mentioned by Wilbert Smith in 1950 as being the head of a small group investigating UFOs. That group was Majestic 12, secretly established in 1947. *(Popperfoto)*

Above right: General Nathan Twining, who as Commanding General of Air Materiel Command in 1947 signed a document testifying to the reality of UFOs. General Twining was also a member of Majestic 12. *(Popperfoto)*

Below: President Truman (*right*) awarding the Distinguished Service Medal to Defense Secretary James Forrestal in March 1949. Two months later Forrestal committed suicide. He was another member of the Majestic 12 group, established under Truman. *(Popperfoto)*

Above left: General Hoyt Vandenberg, Director of Central Intelligence (1946-47) and another Majestic 12 member. In 1948, as US Air Force Chief of Staff, he ordered a Top Secret 'Estimate of the Situation' by Air Technical Intelligence Center – which suggested that UFOs were interplanetary – to be destroyed. *(Imperial War Museum)*

Above right: 'It is time for the truth to be brought out. . . . Behind the scenes high-·ranking Air Force officers are soberly concerned about the UFOs. But through official secrecy and ridicule, many citizens are led to believe the unknown flying objects are nonsense. . . .' Admiral Roscoe Hillenkoetter, Director of the CIA (1947–50), and a member of Majestic 12, in a letter to Congress, 1960. *(CIA)*

Below left: 'The Central Intelligence Agency has reviewed the current situation. . . . Since 1947, approximately 2,000 official reports of sightings have been received and, of these, about 20% are as yet unexplained. It is my view that this situation has possible implications for our national security which transcend the interests of a single service. . . .' General Walter Bedell Smith, Director of the CIA (1950–53), in a 1952 memorandum to the National Security Council. *(Imperial War Museum)*

Below right: '. . . The matter is the most highly classified subject in the United States Government, rating higher even than the H-bomb. Flying saucers exist. Their *modus operandi* is unknown but concentrated effort is being made by a small group headed by Doctor Vannevar Bush. . . .' Wilbert Smith, in a Top Secret Canadian Government memorandum, 21 November 1950. *(Van's Studio Ltd)*

Above left: A UFO photographed by a US Marine Air Group pilot over the North East China Sea during the Korean War. The object came relatively close to the aircraft then flew off at over 1,000 mph, increased acceleration and disappeared. (*W. Gordon Allen*)

Above right: Mel Noel, a USAF pilot who took gun-camera movie film of UFOs in 1953 and 1954 while flying special reconnaissance missions to search for UFOs. (*Author*)

Below: An F-86 Sabre jet of the type flown by Noel.

Above left: Major Donald Keyhoe on CBS TV in January 1958 when he was cut off the air in the middle of making a statement testifying to the reality of UFOs, as confirmed for him by Pentagon sources. (*CBS*)

Above right: ' . . . several days in a row we sighted groups of metallic, saucer-shaped vehicles at great altitudes over the base [Germany, 1951] and we tried to get close to them, but they were able to change direction faster than our fighters. I do believe UFOs exist and that the truly unexplained ones are from some other technically advanced civilization.' Gordon Cooper, former USAF pilot and NASA astronaut, United Nations UFO Debate, 27 November 1978. (*Popperfoto*)

Below left: X-15 pilot Joe Walker after attaining a new speed record of 3,370 mph in the rocket-powered plane on 25 May 1961. A year later Walker admitted that it was one of his tasks to look for UFOs during his flights in the X-15, and he filmed some objects during another record-breaking flight in April 1962. (*Popperfoto*)

Below right: Astronaut Scott Carpenter at the press conference following his problematic orbital flight in Mercury 7 on 24 May 1962. It is rumoured that Carpenter encountered a UFO on the flight but he denies this. (*Popperfoto*)

Above left: Neil Armstrong, who, together with 'Buzz' Aldrin, is reported by reliable sources to have encountered UFOs during the Apollo 11 landing on the moon in July 1969. Armstrong emphatically denies this. (*NASA*)

Above right: 'I'm one of those guys who has never seen a UFO. But I've been asked, and I've said publicly I thought they were somebody else; some other civilization. . . .' Eugene Cernan, Apollo 17 Commander, 1973. (*NASA*)

Below left: In 1974 Professor Hermann Oberth, the great pioneer of space travel, wrote in *UFO News,* 'It is my conclusion that UFOs do exist, are very real, and are spaceships from another or more than one solar system. They are possibly manned by intelligent observers who are members of a race carrying out long-range scientific investigations of our earth for centuries. . . .' (*Author*)

Below right: One of four polaroid photos taken by Police Chief Jeff Greenhaw near Falkville, Alabama, on 17 October 1973. The 'spaceman' then ran off, taking huge paces, and the policeman was unable to catch up in his patrol car. Greenhaw suffered a spate of bad luck following the incident: someone burned down his mobile home; his car engine blew up; he was asked to resign from his job, and his wife left him. (*Jeff Greenhaw*)

Above: 'A purely psychological explanation is ruled out . . . the discs show signs of intelligent guidance, by quasi-human pilots . . . the authorities in possession of important information should not hesitate to enlighten the public as soon and as completely as possible.' Dr Carl Gustav Jung, 1954. (*Douglas Glass/Popperfoto*)

Below: A British Aerospace Hawk of the Air Force of Zimbabwe. On 22 July 1985 two Hawks were scrambled from Thornhill AFB to investigate a UFO that had been tracked on radar and seen by many. When the Hawks arrived above Bulawayo the UFO accelerated vertically from 7,000 to 70,000 feet in less than a minute. The Hawks returned to base where the object was still visible for a few minutes before disappearing at high speed. (*Air Force of Zimbabwe*)

Above left: ' . . . In the firm belief that the American public deserves a better explanation than that thus far given by the Air Force, I strongly recommend that there be a committee investigation of the UFO phenomena. I think we owe it to the people to establish credibility regarding UFOs and to produce the greatest possible enlightenment on this subject.' Former President Gerald Ford, in a letter he sent as a Congressman to L. Mendel Rivers, Chairman of the Armed Services Committee, 28 March 1966. (*Popperfoto*)

Above right: 'If I become President, I'll make every piece of information this country has about UFO sightings available to the public, and the scientists. I am convinced that UFOs exist because I have seen one. . . .' Former President Jimmy Carter during his election campaign in May 1976. (*Popperfoto*)

Below: Meeting at the United Nations on 14 July 1978 to discuss the need for UN support for UFO studies. *Left to right:* Gordon Cooper, Jacques Vallée, Claude Poher, J. Allen Hynek, Prime Minister of Grenada Sir Eric Gairy, UN Secretary General Kurt Waldheim and (*near right*) David Saunders. In 1967 former UN Secretary General U Thant confided to friends that he considered UFOs to be the most important problem facing the UN next to the war in Vietnam. (*United Nations/Saw Lwin*)

NSA representative Eugene Yeates admitted in a court hearing that the NSA had found a total of 239 documents on UFOs that were relevant to the FOIA request.

Following another refusal to release more documents, Peter Gersten filed suit against the NSA on behalf of CAUS in the District Court, Washington, DC, in the spring of 1980 to obtain the 135 documents then admitted to being withheld by the agency. Judge Gesell studied a twenty-one-page NSA affidavit in camera and ruled that the agency was fully justified in withholding the documents in their entirety:

> The bulk of the material withheld consists of communications intelligence reports, which defendant asserts are protected by Exemptions 1 and 3 of the Freedom of Information Act. . . . The Court first carefully reviewed the public affidavit of National Security Agency official Eugene Yeates and then, after receiving plaintiff's opposition, examined personally a top secret affidavit from Yeates, submitted by defendant *in camera*. . . . On the basis of these affidavits, the Court finds that the claimed exemptions have been properly and conscientiously applied.
>
> *The communications intelligence reports clearly relate to the most sensitive activities of the defendant.* . . .
>
> Throughout the Court's review of this material, the Court has been aware of the public interest in the issue of UFOs and the need to balance that interest against the agency's need for secrecy. The *in camera* affidavit presents factual considerations which aided the Court in determining that *the public interest in disclosure is far outweighed by the sensitive nature of the materials and the obvious effect on national security their release may well entail.* . . . The case is dismissed.[4] [Emphasis added]

The in-camera affidavit (see Appendix, pp.535–39) was itself classified at a level *above* top secret—Top Secret Umbra, the highest classification for SIGINT documents at the time. "Top Secret" refers to intelligence material which if revealed is considered gravely damaging to the interests of the state. The additional stamp (such as ROYAL, COSMIC, or, in the case of MJ-12—MAJIC) restricts access still further to those with a "ticket" to the "compartment"—a need to know about that particular intelligence matter. It may therefore be safely inferred that the subject matter of the NSA affidavit is of the utmost intelligence sensitivity. While not denying its involvement in UFO research, the NSA states that the main reason for nondisclosure is that the documents would reveal the means whereby it obtained the COMINT and SIGINT information in the first place. According to its affidavit (which the NSA sent me, in censored form, in 1983):

> In processing the plaintiff's FOIA request, a total of two hundred and thirty-nine documents were located in NSA files. Seventy-nine of these documents originated with other government agencies and have been referred by NSA to those agencies for their direct response to the plaintiff. . . . One document . . . is an account by a person assigned to NSA of his attendance at a UFO symposium and it cannot fairly be said to be a record of the kind sought by the plaintiff. Another document . . . was recently declassified and released to plaintiff. Two additional non-COMINT records have been released . . . with the exempted material deleted. . . .
>
> The remaining one hundred and fifty-six records being withheld are communications intelligence (COMINT) reports which were produced between 1958 and 1979. For purposes of my discussion here, these records are organized into three groups based upon the source of the report.

The following thirteen pages of the affidavit are almost totally blacked out. The only information we are given by the NSA's Chief of Policy, Eugene Yeates, is as follows:

> As I have stated in my open affidavit, when alerted to the extent of NSA's capability, and if given information from which inferences could be drawn as to the processing methods used, foreign intelligence services would be able to evade or defeat portions of NSA's present foreign intelligence efforts. . . . The disclosure of other records at issue here, would result in the loss of the intelligence information. . . . The value of the intelligence data collected from these sources is obvious.

In the final two pages of the affidavit we are told that:

> . . . the one hundred and fifty-six [deleted] reports relating to COMINT activities at issue here are based on intercepted communications of foreign governments or SIGINT operations and, thus, remain properly classified. In conducting this review I have weighed the significant need for openness in government against the likelihood of damage to our national security at this time and have determined that each record should continue to be classified. No meaningful portion can be segregated from the records without revealing classified information about the intercepted communications underlying the COMINT reports.[5]

Of 502 lines in the affidavit, 412 are totally or partially deleted. While I am all in favor of the NSA protecting its intelligence-acquiring capability, I find it difficult to accept that the deleted portions relate exclusively to these matters. And why did the NSA not produce any of the documents for the judge to examine, as is customary in a dispute on whether material is properly classified?

An appeal to the US Court of Appeals in October 1981 led nowhere. As William Moore comments:

> In a brief decision issued barely a week after the oral arguments were presented (normal time for such decisions is about two months), the panel . . . upheld the lower court's position virtually without comment. All three judges, along with U.S. defense attorney Cheryl M. Long (but not plaintiff attorney Gersten) had been granted special security clearances to enable them to view the same NSA classified affidavit which had been presented to Judge Gesell a year earlier.[6]

Peter Gersten filed a petition in 1982 to have the US Supreme Court hear the case of *CAUS* v. *NSA*. The eighty-four-page petition argued against the NSA's "sweeping classifications of all UFO data," but in March 1982 the Supreme Court upheld the earlier ruling of the District Court.

The Central Security Service

All my Freedom of Information requests to the NSA have been dealt with by the Central Security Service (CSS), the agency's "inner sanctum." Created in 1972 under President Nixon, the CSS is, according to James Bamford, the "eyes and ears of America's cryptological establishment. They are the soldiers, sailors, Marines and airmen who sit in long rows with earphones, turning dials, activating tape recorders, and tapping out messages on six-ply, multicolored carbon paper."

"Before NSA can attach a code or read a message," Bamford explains, "it first must be able to capture and record the elusive signal. Such is the job of the Central Security Service, an invisible organization virtually unknown beyond Fort Meade."[7]

I have already drawn attention to the fact that the NSA has been receiving UFO reports from the military since 1953. Why? Because the NSA needs to gather as much information as possible on a twenty-four-hour basis for its main client, the CIA. The NSA has now improved its eavesdropping capability to the extent that it can monitor virtually any communication transmitted from anywhere in the world—and beyond. Coded and scrambled messages, broadcasts, Telex, satellite transmissions, and even commercial and private telephone calls are monitored when deemed necessary. Thus the NSA, together with other similar agencies, most particularly Britain's GCHQ (with whom it has a very close relationship), is in a position to know almost anything of intelligence significance that is transmitted electronically. Through the joint NSA/GCHQ agreement, any telephone call entering or leaving Britain, for instance, can be monitored, because the relevant computers are programmed to search every international circuit for particularly sensitive names and numbers.[8] At least, such is its reputed capability. The NSA knows, for example, when a pilot reports a UFO sighting by radio, and can monitor any subsequent news stories about the incident. The CIA stands ready to ensure that a potentially significant story is debunked with the minimum delay: that is, of course, if the media take the story seriously in the first place. (The CIA has at various times owned or subsidized dozens of newspapers, news services and radio stations.)

Examples of NSA's Involvement

While working with the NSA in 1964, Todd Zechel saw messages transmitted from the Air Force Special Security Service (an NSA/USAF subsidiary) to the CIA's Special Security Office—a CIA cover within NSA's communications network. The transmissions were radar plottings of a UFO flying in an erratic manner near the border of a certain country, which had been picked up by a reconnaissance plane during a tracking mission.

Zechel assumes that the CIA had issued instructions to the NSA to report on all UFOs it tracked. "The fact that the messages were being routed to the CIA station certainly indicates a prior arrangement to do so," he believes. "I think it would be safe to assume that the CIA—which worked closely with Air Force Special Security anyway—had instructed the unit to keep them informed of any sightings."

Zechel relates that it did not come as a surprise to any of those with whom he worked at the NSA that UFOs existed or that the CIA had an interest in them. "In fact," he says, "most of the personnel I worked with were convinced of the reality of UFOs, and many had had personal experiences with these puzzling craft during the course of their jobs." He states that although certain personnel in the NSA know a great deal about the UFO phenomenon, and have encountered much in the way of photographic and radar intelligence (PHOTINT and RADINT), the NSA is for the most part kept ignorant of the analysis. "NSA has always been in a subordinate role to the CIA,'' he claims, ''and whatever data it did gather was passed on to the CIA. Therefore, the analysis of the data was performed by CIA personnel; specifically, the CIA's Office of Scientific Intelligence, with NSA being kept ignorant of the conclusions.''[9]

Nuclear physicist Stanton Friedman, one of America's leading UFO researchers, has obtained details of an alarming incident which included a statement by a security specialist attached to a unit of the Air Force Security Service, based with the 6947th Security Squadron whose mission was the monitoring of all Cuban military communications:

In March of 1967 . . . Cuban radar installations reported a bogey approaching the Cuban land mass from the northeast. 2 MiG-21 interceptors were scrambled when the bogey crossed Cuban air space at an altitude of approximately 10,000 meters and at a speed approaching Mach [1]. The interceptors were directed to the bogey by Cuban Ground Control Intercept and were guided to within 5 kilometers of the object.

The wing leader reported the object was a bright metallic sphere with no visible markings or appendages. After a futile attempt to contact the object for identification, Cuban Air Defense headquarters ordered the wing leader to arm his weapons and destroy the object. The wing leader reported his missiles armed and his radar locked-on.

Seconds later the wing man began screaming to the ground controller that the wing leader's aircraft had exploded. After regaining his composure he further reported that there was no smoke or flame; the aircraft had disintegrated. Cuban radar reported the object quickly accelerated and climbed beyond 30,000 meters and at last report was heading south-southeast toward South America.

A spot report was sent to National Security Agency headquarters, which is standard procedure in any case involving aircraft loss by an enemy country. NSA is required to acknowledge receipt of such a report, however they didn't and therefore we sent a follow-up report. *Within hours we received orders to ship all tapes and pertinent intelligence to the Agency and were told to list the incident in the squadron files as aircraft loss due to equipment malfunction.*[10] [Emphasis added]

Brad Sparks, an expert on intelligence matters as they pertain to the UFO question, points out that the data sent to the NSA would include direction-finding measurements which the agency could later combine with other listening sites' data in order ''to triangulate the location and altitude of the MiG-21 flight paths. If the AFSS equipment in Florida [Key West Naval Air Station] was sensitive enough,'' Sparks believes, ''the UFO could have been tracked by its reflection of the Cuban ground and airborne radars.''

As a result of filing FOIA requests on the incident to NSA, CIA, Air Force, and Navy, researcher Robert Todd was interrogated by the FBI —partly because he was on the point of taking up the CIA's suggestion of checking with the Cuban government for further details! One of the FBI agents explained to Todd that the Bureau had been asked to investigate the matter by the NSA owing to the fact that NSA has no law-enforcement responsibilities. The agents began intimidating Todd by reading the espionage laws, reminding him that these carried a penalty of life imprisonment or even death in some cases. No charges were brought against him, however.[11]

This incident serves to highlight a number of reasons, some of them perfectly straightforward and reasonable, why the intelligence community would need to cover up the results of its investigations into UFO reports. But an alarming report of a UFO causing the destruction of a jet— regardless of which air force it belonged to—is surely cause for the gravest concern in high places of office and does not fall into any conventional category of classification. We should bear in mind that some other withheld NSA documents may well relate to similar incidents. I have already documented disturbing cases of aircraft having disappeared in the immediate vicinity of UFOs, although the association is not always proven.

Perhaps one of the NSA's withheld documents relates to the following report, which I obtained via a defense source during a visit to South Africa in 1981. On 18 June 1977 two South African Air Force pilots, both with fifteen years and 7,000 hours flying experience, disappeared forty miles northwest of Ludoritz, together with their French-built Mirage F1CZ jets. The last radio contact was at 1048 hours, and at about 1115 hours the planes simply vanished from the radar screen. It was evident that the pilots were frantically trying to communicate with base: the radio call button was being pressed but no transmission could be heard.

A simple accident—perhaps a collision? Both planes were equipped with life gear. A Navy ship was in the area within an hour and a helicopter within two hours. Weather conditions were good: 3/8ths altocumulus at 25,000 feet and high cirrus at 45–50,000 feet—the altitude the planes were flying. No trace was ever found of either the pilots or planes.

No UFOs were reported in the area as far as I know, although it was made clear to me that the Air Force believed that no conventional explanation could account for the disappearance. The SAAF takes UFOs extremely seriously, in company with air forces throughout the world. As early as 1953 a Defense Headquarters spokesman in Pretoria revealed that there had been some reliable sightings by SAAF officers and added:

"There is now a regular exchange of information between our Air Force and the Royal Air Force. Reports have also been referred to military intelligence."[12] In 1955 the Air Chief of Staff, Brigadier Melville, admitted that the South African Department of Defense classified official information on the subject as "Top Secret—Not to be Divulged."[13]

UFO Hypothesis and Survival Questions

In late 1983 I wrote to NSA's Director of Policy, James Devine, asking if he was prepared to admit that NSA still monitored the UFO situation and what conclusions had been arrived at. On the one hand, I said, we are told that the vast majority of sightings can be explained and that there is no evidence that any of the unexplained reports constitute a defense threat, while on the other hand documents released under the FOIA show that many sightings relate to high-performance, structured vehicles, reports of which are treated extremely seriously at high level.

"I appreciate your frustration in attempting to obtain information on such a complex topic," Mr. Devine replied. "Unfortunately, however, I have nothing further to add to the information in Mr. Yeates' affidavit."[14]

I had not expected, of course, that the NSA would let me know its conclusions on the matter, since it seems evident from the twenty-one-page affidavit that these are classified above top secret. But one of the handful of documents released by the NSA on the subject addresses the problem of "human survival implications" relating to UFO phenomena. The document, entitled *UFO Hypothesis and Survival Questions*, was sent to me by the NSA in 1984. It was originally classified, the NSA's Deputy Director of Policy, Frederick Berghoff, explained, "because certain portions tangentially discussed protected activities pertaining to the NSA/CSS. Most of the remaining portions of the document reflected open-source information on UFOs. The text of this document is being released to you in its entirety. The deletions reflect classification markings which are no longer applicable as well as the name of an NSA/CSS employee."

The 1968 seven-page NSA article discusses the various hypotheses for UFOs, which I summarize below:

HOAXES   . . . Rarely have men of science, while acting within
                          their own professional capacities, perpetrated hoaxes.
                          The fact that UFO phenomenon [sic] have been wit-

nessed all over the world from ancient times, and by considerable numbers of reputable scientists in recent times, indicates rather strongly that UFOs are not all hoaxes. . . .

HALLUCINATIONS   . . . a considerable number of instances exist in which there are groups of people and a radar or radars seeing the same thing at the same time; sometimes a person and a guncamera confirm each other's testimony. . . . The sum of such evidence seems to argue strongly against all UFOs being hallucinations. . . .

NATURAL PHENOMENA   If this hypothesis is correct the capability of air warning systems to correctly diagnose an attack situation is open to serious question. . . . Many UFOs have been reported by trained observers to behave like high speed, high performance, high altitude rockets or aircraft. The apparent solidity and craft-like shape of the objects have often been subject to radar confirmation. . . .

Sometimes the phenomena appear to defy radar detection and to cause massive electromagnetic interference. . . .

SECRET EARTH PROJECTS   . . . Undoubtedly, *all UFOs* should be carefully scrutinized to ferret-out such enemy (or "friendly") projects. Otherwise a nation faces the very strong possibility of being intimidated by a new secret "doomsday" weapon.

EXTRA-TERRESTRIAL INTELLIGENCE   If "they" discover you it is an old but hardly invalid rule of thumb, "they" are your technological superiors. . . . Human history has shown us time and again the tragic results of a confrontation between a technologically superior civilization and a technologically inferior people. . . .

Although the well-informed NSA author delves deeply into the problems associated with confrontation between a technologically advanced society and an inferior one on earth, there is no conclusion as to whether or not UFOs could be extraterrestrial in origin.

NSA also sent me a heavily censored three-page monograph and appendix on UFOs by the same writer. "We wish to emphasize," Mr. Berghoff wrote, "that these draft documents were never published, formally issued, acted upon, or responded to by any government official or agency. Moreover, they are not NSA/CSS reports and in no way reflect an official NSA/CSS position concerning UFOs. They are subject to the provisions of the FOIA only because they have been retained by this Agency for historical reference purposes."[15]

Projects Aquarius, Sigma, and Snowbird

In a leaked document purporting to originate with the US Air Force Office of Special Investigations (AFOSI)—its authenticity denied to me by both AFOSI and NASA—there is an intriguing reference to "Project Aquarius." Another leaked memo mentions "Project Sigma," allegedly initiated in 1954 to establish communication with aliens. "This Project met with positive success," the spurious-looking document states, and goes on to describe how a USAF intelligence officer "met two aliens at a pre-arranged location in the desert of New Mexico . . . this project is continuing at an Air Force base in New Mexico." The same document lists "Project Snowbird" (referred to in Chapter 12), allegedly established in 1972; its mission was to test fly a recovered alien aircraft. The project is said to be continuing in Nevada.

The second document looked decidedly bogus to me, and yet there is evidence that the projects exist (or existed). An FOIA request to NSA by a researcher asking for details on the projects brought the reply: "Please be advised that Project Aquarius does not deal with unidentified aerial objects. We, therefore, have no information to provide to you on the matter." The reply, from NSA's Chief of Information Policy Dennis Chadwick, continues:

> In your letter you also ask for information on Projects Sigma and Snowbird. The FOIA provides that a person has a right of access to federal agency records, except to the extent that such records are protected from disclosure by one of nine exemptions. It does not require that an agency answer questions. As I mentioned in my letter of 29 February, Sigma and Snowbird are not NSA projects; therefore, we have no information to give you on these topics.
>
> Since you indicate in your letter that you will not be paying the $15,000.00 fee to search for records pertaining to Aquarius, this response completes our action on your request.[16]

A fee of $15,000 is outlandish by any standards. The researcher accordingly narrowed down his FOIA request relating to Project Aquarius, and in April 1986 Julia Wetzel, NSA Director of Policy, responded:

> The document located in response to your request as stated in your 7 March letter has been reviewed by this Agency as required by the FOIA and has been found to be currently and properly classified . . . and remains TOP SECRET. . . . The document is classified because its disclosure could reasonably be expected to cause exceptionally grave damage to the national security . . . no portion of the information is reasonably segregable.[17]

So, while there is no proof that Project Aquarius is related to UFOs, there is at least some evidence now to suggest that it is. I remain impressed with the leaked AFOSI document, part of which states: "THE OFFICIAL GOVERNMENT POLICY AND RESULTS OF PROJECT AQUARIUS IS STILL CLASSIFIED TOP SECRET WITH NO DISSEMINATION OUTSIDE OFFICIAL INTELLIGENCE CHANNELS AND WITH RESTRICTED ACCESS TO 'MJ TWELVE.' "

NSA has now confirmed the existence of Project Aquarius and that it is still classified top secret. Will the existence of the top secret Majestic 12 panel be similarly confirmed in due course?

THE ATTITUDE IN SOME OTHER COUNTRIES

The superpowers may have a monopoly on top secret information about UFOs, but the attitude of officialdom in less powerful nations is of no less significance. Over the years some very revealing statements have been made by defense chiefs, although there has been a marked reluctance more recently to admit to serious investigations. In 1986 I wrote to the embassies of forty countries requesting a statement on the official position with regard to the subject. I received only a dozen or so replies, the majority indicating that no official policy was pursued.

Brazil

In Chapter 13 I cite two official directives that prove just how seriously UFOs are taken in Brazil. *"This is a matter of National Security*, and all press releases will be made by the Brazilian Air Force Public Relations Department" says one, issued in 1969, while a 1973 São Paulo State directive forbids the media "to divulge UFO reports without the prior censorship of the Brazilian Air Force."

Dr. Olavo T. Fontes was one of Brazil's pioneer investigators back in the 1950s, and had contacts with Naval Intelligence sources who left him in no doubt about the high priority attached to the subject. In a letter sent to the Aerial Phenomena Research Organization (APRO) on 27 February 1958, Dr. Fontes provided some revealing information:

> . . . The Brazilian Navy, for example, receives monthly classified reports from the U.S. Navy and sends back to them any information available here. . . . In Brazil only the persons who work on the problem know the real situation: intelligence officers in the Army, Navy and Air Force; some high-ranking officers in the High Command; the National Security Council and a few scientists whose activities are connected with it; and a few members of certain civilian organizations doing research for military projects.

All information about the UFO subject from the r
classified or reserved for official uses, it is *top secret.*
and military officers in general are not entitled to know
is not informed of the whole truth.

Military authorities throughout the world agree th
entitled to know anything about the problem. Some m
that such a knowledge would be a tremendous shock—enough to par y
the life in our country for many years in the future.

Dr. Fontes believed that people have a right to know what is being
concealed from them. "Secrecy is something which does not breed security but fear," he wrote. "Can the military take decisions that may
affect the future of the whole of mankind?" In this connection I am
reminded of a comment by Groucho Marx. "Military intelligence," he
once remarked, "is a contradiction in terms. . . ."

There have been some encouraging new developments in Brazil, however, which indicate that the military authorities are now inclined to be
more open with the populace. When UFOs saturated radar screens and
were seen by the pilots of seven aircraft on the night of 19 May 1986,
the incidents were publicly confirmed by the Air Minister and reported
worldwide.

The first incident occurred at 2110 hours when Colonel Ozires Silva,
formerly president of the Embraer aircraft firm and currently head of the
Petrobras oil company, together with Commander Alcir Pereira da Silva,
were alerted by São Paulo radar to the presence of unidentified traffic in
their vicinity. The pilots—flying an Embraer Xingu—saw a "dancing"
point of light in the sky which, when they flew closer, appeared as a
bright red-orange light which came on for 10–15 seconds, then off,
reappearing in a different location. This went on for about 30 minutes.

Brazilian Defense Center (CINDACTA) went on full alert as radar
screens in the area became saturated with unknown targets, causing disruption to air traffic. Three F-5E Tiger jets were scrambled from Santa
Cruz AFB near São Paulo, followed by three Mirage III jets from Anápolis AFB.

One of the F-5 pilots, Lieutenant Kleber Caldas Marinho, was vectored
to a target but saw nothing at first. Ground and airborne radar confirmed
that an object was thirty-five miles away, and when Marinho caught sight
of it he reported an intense reddish light that changed colors to white,
green, and back to red. Marinho's attempts to close on the target were
futile. It was, he said, "like attempting to reach a point at infinity."

Captain Marcio Jordão, another F-5 pilot, managed to reduce the distance from the target to 12 miles but it then moved out to sea beyond the 200-mile limit from Santa Cruz.

One of the Mirage pilots, Captain Armindo Souza Viriato de Freitas, provided some more details:

> . . . I was warned by ground control that there were several targets ahead of me, at a distance of 20 miles and ranging in number from 10 to 13. I was also advised that the targets were approaching my plane, and finally that they were following me at a distance of 2 miles [sic]. I had to lower my plane, as the lights had descended, but from then on they climbed vertically. This was my only visual contact, but I could see them in my radar at a distance of 12 miles.

The Anápolis AFB radar controller advised Captain Viriato that he had thirteen targets behind his plane at one stage—seven to one side and six to the other. The objects made incredible 180° turns on the pilot's radar set, although he was unable to spot them in the air. "No plane I know can make turns like that at 1,000 kilometers an hour," he said. The speed of the objects at other times varied from 150 to 800 kph. Lieutenant Valdecir Fernando Coelho, one of the air traffic controllers, was equally at a loss to explain the incidents, which lasted for over three hours. "In my 14 years of experience as a radar operator, I never saw anything like this," he said.

Air Minister Brigadier Otávio Júlio Moreira Lima later informed the President of Brazil, José Sarney, about the intrusions. At the press conference the Air Minister declared that "radar is not subject to optical illusions. Radar echoes are due to solid objects, or to massive clouds, which were not present that night" (the weather was clear).

According to one report, the President of Brazil personally authorized the decision to release the story publicly.[18]

There have now been millions of sightings reported worldwide, and by all accounts Brazil is one of the most inundated. This brings me to a question often raised: Why don't more people see UFOs? "I'd give anything to see one. Why don't I?" I am frequently asked. I know the feeling. During a wave of sightings in South America in 1965 I happened to be touring in Argentina, Brazil, Chile, Columbia, Peru, Uruguay and Venezuela, spending a lot of time in the air. I saw absolutely nothing that could be construed as an anomalous UFO. A tour of Australia in 1966 during a flurry of sightings was equally frustrating in this respect. I have also spent a total of several years traveling throughout the United

States (1963–86) and only once did I see a UFO (together with Madeleine Rodeffer at her home in Silver Spring, Maryland, in 1967). I can only offer my opinion that it seems to be a question of being in the right place at the right time. Although I have seen three aerial objects in my life that I am unable to explain, it looks as if I have been in rather a lot of the wrong places at the wrong time. . . .

Indonesia

"UFOs sighted in Indonesia are identical with those sighted in other countries," stated Air Marshal Roesmin Nurjadin, Commander-in-Chief of the Indonesian Air Force, in 1967. "Sometimes they pose a problem for our air defense and once we were obliged to open fire on them."[19]

The most active periods for UFO reports in Indonesia were 1953–54 and 1964–65, according to Air Commodore J. Salutun, Member of Parliament and Secretary of the National Aerospace Council of the Republic of Indonesia. Salutun has confirmed the incident referred to by Air Marshal Nurjadin: "The most spectacular UFO incident in Indonesia occurred when, during the height of President Sukarno's confrontation against Malaysia, *UFOs penetrated a well-defended area in Java for two weeks at a stretch, and each time were welcomed with perhaps the heaviest antiaircraft barrage in history*." [Emphasis added]

"I am convinced that we must study the UFO problem seriously for reasons of sociology, technology and security," Salutun says. "The study of UFOs may lead to new and revolutionary concepts in propulsion and space technology in general, from which our present state-of-the-art may benefit." He continues: "The study of UFOs is a necessity for the sake of world security in the event we have to prepare for the worst in the space age, irrespective of whether we become the Columbus or the Indians."[20]

Japan

I shall never forget the overwhelming hospitality accorded me by Japanese ufologists during my first visit to that country in 1964. While discussions focused on more general aspects of the subject, I was unable to acquire any information regarding the official line at that time, and my recent response from the Embassy of Japan in London shed no further light on the matter. "Although there is a considerable interest in UFOs in the private sector," I was told, "the Japanese government has not yet set up

any research institute or department for them.''[21] Yet there *is* evidence
for official concern in Japan.

In 1967 General Kanshi Ishikawa, Chief of Air Staff of Japan's Air
Self-Defense Force, made the following important statement:

> If UFOs are flying objects hovering in the sky, they should be caught by
> radar. Much evidence tells us they have been tracked by radar; so, UFOs
> are real and they may come from outer space. . . . I can imagine that there
> are two types of UFOs; small ones for scouting and large ships for inter-
> stellar travel, utilizing electro-magnetic fields.
>
> The dream of our pilots is to acquire the technique of gravity-control,
> capable of perfectly free maneuverability. I believe the saucer-shape is the
> best design from the point of view of hydrodynamics. . . . UFO photo-
> graphs and various materials show scientifically that there are more ad-
> vanced people piloting the saucers and motherships.[22]

''UFOs are impossible to deny,'' said Colonel Fujio Hayashi, Commander of the Air Transport Wing, Irima Air Squadron, in the late 1960s.
''When we pilots scramble we have to identify the object clearly, whether
it is an enemy or not. . . . Though it is said that these unknown objects
might be the secret weapons of some powers, it is very strange that we
have never been able to find out the source for over two decades.''[23]

In September 1977 Lieutenant General Akira Hirano, Chief of Staff
of the JASDF, admitted: ''We frequently see unidentified objects in the
skies. We are quietly investigating them.'' The following day, however,
it was explained that the general had made a mistake: Hirano's staff
denied that he had mentioned official investigations. ''If they're hostile,
we want to have a full explanation before we upset the general populace,''
an official admitted later, on condition that his name was not published.

Major Shiro Kubota claims to have had an alarming encounter with a
UFO which led to the death of Lieutenant Colonel Toshio Nakamura,
who was flying with him in an F-4EJ Phantom on 9 June 1974 when the
incident is alleged to have occurred. Nakamura told a reporter:

> We thought at first we were going up to intercept a Soviet bomber, of the
> type which sometimes tests our northern air defenses. After Toshio got us
> airborne, our Ground Control Intercept (GCI) explained to us that we were
> going upstairs to check out a bright-colored light reported by dozens of
> observers and showing on radar. Several minutes later, we broke out of
> the clouds and leveled off at 30,000 feet on a clear, moonless night. That
> was when we spotted the light a few miles ahead.
>
> Even at first, I felt that this disk-like, red-orange object was a flying

craft, made and flown by intelligent beings. It appeared to be about 10 meters in diameter, with square-shaped marks around its side which may have been windows or propulsion outlets. Toshio aimed us straight toward it and, as it grew larger in our gun sight, it dipped into a shallow turn, as if sensing our presence. . . .

Toshio armed our 20mm cannon and closed in on the UFO. Suddenly, the object reversed direction and shot straight at us. . . . Toshio threw the stick to the left and forced us into a sudden, violent dive. The glowing red UFO shot past—missing us by inches. Then it made a sharp turn and came at us again. . . . The UFO began making rapid, high-speed passes at us, drawing closer and closer. Several times, the strange object narrowly missed us.

And then—if the report is to be believed—the UFO struck the Phantom jet. Both pilots ejected, but Nakamura's parachute caught fire and he fell to his death. The UFO either disappeared or disintegrated.

Japanese Air Defense authorities conducted a lengthy investigation into the incident, but no findings have been released to date, beyond an admission that the Phantom—serial number 17-8307—crashed, killing Nakamura, following a collision with "an aircraft or object unknown." Rather than remain silent about the incident Kubota retired from active service.

Major General Hideki Komura, an adviser to Japan's top intelligence agency, the *Naicho* (Cabinet Research Office), has admitted that investigations into UFOs are carried out at a top level. At first, he explained, the JASDF openly solicited reports from the public. "This was in the late 1950s and we were, frankly, imitating your own Project Blue Book," he told the American reporter. "But we were deluged. Interest was so great, and so many reports poured in, that we were unable to separate the 'good' reports from the *garakuda* [rubbish]. We had to give up. It simply was not working."

General Komura was reluctant to disclose details of investigations then (1977) being conducted by defense and intelligence agencies, but revealed: *"We cooperate very closely with your [U.S.] government.* Remember how we invited your Foreign Technology Division officials here to examine the MiG-25 jet we received from a defecting Soviet pilot? [Britain's MI6 had been instrumental in securing Lt. Belenko's defection.] The Foreign Technology Division is the outfit under which Project Blue Book once operated. We have cooperated many times on other issues, and visitors from another planet would certainly be a legitimate subject for inquiry."[24]

Of the many reports of sightings by Japanese airline pilots, the most recent example is that of the crew of a Japan Air Lines cargo flight on the night of 17 November 1986. Flight JAL 1628 was entering US airspace at 39,000 feet and Captain Kenju Terauchi and his crew were making final preparations before descending to Anchorage Airport. Suddenly they noticed some unusual lights accompanying the Boeing 747. "They were flying parallel and then suddenly approached very close," said Terauchi. He caught a brief glimpse of the main object's walnut-shaped silhouette and judged it to be *"two times bigger than an aircraft carrier."*

The pilot was instructed by air traffic control to descend to 4,000 feet and make turns, but the objects continued to follow the plane for thirty-two minutes before vanishing. US Federal Aviation Administration authorities admitted that the objects were tracked on radar but had not registered on the radar tapes.

The FAA investigated the incident and found the crew to be "normal, professional, and rational." Captain Terauchi, a pilot for twenty-nine years, said that he was unable to explain the phenomenon in conventional terms and speculated that it may have been extraterrestrial in origin since the objects moved and stopped so quickly and suddenly. "We were carrying Beaujolais from France to Japan," he said. "Maybe they wanted to drink it."[25]

New Zealand

"The Ministry of Defense in New Zealand is not specifically charged with any formal responsibility for investigating so-called UFOs," I was informed in 1985, "and neither is any other government department. The Ministry does however take an active interest in all such reports and within the limitations of its resources conducts investigations as necessary."[26] The Ministry kindly sent me the results of their investigation into the famous UFO sightings (tracked on radar and filmed) over East Coast South Island on 20/21 and 30/31 December 1978. But I would prefer to mention an important case that was not acknowledged as having taken place by the MoD, and was related to me personally by a witness.

Derek Mansell, Director of Data Research for Contact UK, served in the Royal Air Force from 1950 to 1955 before spending five years in the Royal New Zealand Air Force as a ground crew airman. Sometime in June of 1956 or 1957 (regrettably he can't recall the exact date), Derek told me that a Bristol 170 Mk 31M Freighter in which he was flying on a weekly freight run from Dunedin to Auckland encountered a UFO over Wellington, although no one on board actually saw the object.

Suddenly the aircraft seemed to have flown into a violent squall with the usual accompanying turbulence. "We were enveloped in a shadow, like a cloud," Derek told me, "the engines started to run badly and the dials didn't function correctly. The compass spun like mad, and all communications to ground and other aircraft failed." After about twenty-five minutes everything returned to normal.

When the Freighter landed at Ohakea the pilot of a Douglas C-47 Dakota, which had also just landed and had been following the Freighter, asked if the latter had seen a huge metallic disk, about 250 feet in diameter, with a blue light on top and a red one on the bottom, which had apparently been just above the Freighter. They replied in the negative, but mentioned the sudden turbulence and interference with instruments and communications. The Dakota pilot reported that he was unable to contact the Freighter at this time, and said that the UFO had shadowed the other plane for twenty-five minutes. According to Derek, photographs were taken of the object by the Dakota crew which have never been released.

The Air Movements Officer asked the Commanding Officer of Ohakea Air Force Base to attend the subsequent debriefing, which lasted two hours. The crews of both the Freighter and Dakota were forbidden to leave the room while the CO asked the adjutant to bring in forms which they were obliged to sign, warning them not to discuss the matter with anyone, and reminding them of their obligations under the Official Secrets Act.

Zimbabwe

At 5:45 p.m. on 22 July 1985 two Hawk jets of the Air Force of Zimbabwe were scrambled from Thornhill Air Base, following sightings of a UFO from Bulawayo and five other urban centers in the western province of Matabeleland South. The object was seen from the control tower at Bulawayo Airport and tracked on radar. "This was no ordinary UFO," said Air Marshal Azim Daudpota. "Scores of people saw it. It was no illusion, no deception, no imagination." The object was described by trained observers at Bulawayo Airport as rounded, with a short cone above it. It shone very brightly in the afternoon sky and was difficult to see distinctly. The Hawks arrived above Bulawayo to find the UFO hovering at about 7,000 feet, but it suddenly accelerated to a height of 70,000 feet in less than a minute. The Hawks leveled off at 31,000 feet then returned to Thornhill, where the object was seen for a few moments before disappearing horizontally at high speed.[27]

Air Commodore David Thorne, Director General of Operations, told me that the UFO appeared to follow the Hawks back to base. Unfortunately no gun-camera footage was taken as the jets were not carrying film at the time, he explained. "This is the first sighting in Zimbabwe where airborne pilots have tried to intercept a UFO," he said. Although the air commodore was unable to comment on behalf of the Zimbabwe government, he nevertheless stated: *"As far as my Air Staff is concerned, we believe implicitly that the unexplained UFOs are from some civilization beyond our planet."*[28]

REASONS FOR SECRECY

Although I have enumerated various reasons for the cover-up of UFO information throughout this book, it might be appropriate in this final chapter to review the opinions of various experts as well as to offer my own personal assessment of the situation.

Protection of Intelligence

While the NSA claims that the deletions in its above top secret affidavit relate solely to the protection of its intelligence-gathering capabilities, I feel certain that is only half the truth. Since 1946 it must have been evident to defense intelligence chiefs studying the "ghost aircraft" wave in Scandinavia and elsewhere that intelligently controlled objects of unknown origin and purpose were operating in our atmosphere. Even as early as 1942, when mysterious objects appeared over Los Angeles, General George Marshall, as Army Chief of Staff, was unable to account for the sighting in conventional terms.

By July 1947, when sightings proliferated throughout the United States, and a disk crashed at Roswell, New Mexico, it must have become obvious that the "flying saucers" were of extraterrestrial origin. Apart from the fact that an admission to this effect would generate public alarm, the military needed to learn as much as possible about the construction and propulsion of the craft, in the event that another nation (particularly the Soviet Union) might acquire this knowledge first; hence another reason for absolute secrecy attached to the investigations. Wilbert Smith learned in 1950 from Dr. Robert Sarbacher that the stories of recovered disks were factual, that the subject was classified two points higher than the H-bomb at the time, and that a small group—probably Majestic 12—was headed by Dr. Vannevar Bush in order to learn as much as possible about the "modus operandi" of the saucers—and only those with a need to know were to be kept informed of the findings. An intelligence matter classified two points higher than the H-bomb is unlikely to be revealed except to those with very high security clearances: even at that level, the degree of dissemination would be strictly compartmented.

Nuclear physicist Stanton Friedman, who has been involved in many highly classified projects in the nuclear industry, is equally certain that a main reason for secrecy about UFOs is defense considerations:

> From a government and military viewpoint, the most significant aspect of visits to planet earth by technologically sophisticated vehicles is the potential for military utilization by earth-based groups of that technology. Surely the first government to be able to duplicate that hyper-maneuverable high speed flights of flying saucers will use that capability for the delivery of nuclear and other weapons . . . for defense and attack purposes. In the real world of the late 20th century these potential information gains from the careful scientific investigation of flying saucers—in the air or captured—greatly overshadow any philosophical, religious or humanitarian concerns of the general public. One need only note that collectively the countries of planet earth spend about 400 billion dollars [1979] on military items each year. Is it really any wonder that governments do not want to reveal whatever sophisticated scientific data they have about flying saucers?[29]

Former Air Force fighter pilot Lieutenant Colonel Donald Ware shares this opinion. He believes that by 1947 (following the Roswell incident) the top military authorities had concluded that some UFOs were extra-terrestrial. They would then have realized, he says, "that if our adversaries acquired the technology represented by these vehicles before we did, our security would be severely threatened. Information on such technology must receive the most extreme protection."[30]

Although there have been at least forty accounts of UFOs alleged to have been recovered throughout the US and elsewhere, the evidence suggests that it took a long time—possibly several decades—before we could even begin to comprehend the alien technology. As Stanton Friedman puts it:

> You might have handed Thomas Edison one of today's pocket calculators forty years ago, and there's no way in the world he could have figured

out how it worked. So if they have significantly advanced technology, it's
going to take a lot of effort for us. Even if we figure out how it works,
that doesn't mean we can duplicate it. It's like knowing about A-bombs;
without the fissionable material, you can't build them, no matter how much
you know about them. So it's a multiprong problem, and one that I don't
expect the people working in secret would talk about in public. Because
*he who is able to duplicate flying saucers in quantity is going to rule this
planet.*[31]

Military and Political Embarrassment

No government is happy to admit that alien vehicles invading our airspace
can come and go as they please, and that our defense against them is
inadequate. That some UFOs have been responsible for the disappearance
and even destruction of our aircraft is not something that could be admitted
openly. I have documented several such alarming incidents, as well as
quoting General Benjamin Chidlaw's privately expressed statement in
1953 that "we have lost many men and planes trying to intercept them."
As a head of US Continental Air Defense at the time, he presumably
knew what he was talking about.

Nobody likes to look silly. Fear of ridicule is a very compelling reason
for politicians to debunk the subject, especially if they do not have access
to all the facts. British Air Minister George Ward expressed this point
perfectly in 1954. While publicly debunking UFO reports as "balloons"
in the House of Commons, he admitted privately: "Until I've got a saucer
on the ground in Hyde Park and can charge the public sixpence a go to
enter, it must be balloons, otherwise the government would fall and I'd
lose my job!"

Ward explained that if he admitted the existence of UFOs without
evidence that the general public could actually touch, they would consider
that the government had gone barmy. This is an honest admission by an
air minister who was fully convinced of the reality of UFOs (see Chapter
2), and it proves to me that Her Majesty's Government at the time had
not been fully apprised of the true situation by those in American intelligence circles who were fully aware that actual alien craft had already
been recovered. The Americans were evidently less than enthusiastic
about allowing the British to exhibit a flying saucer in Hyde Park.

Very few politicians—in Britain, the States, and worldwide—have
the faintest idea about the subject, which is why their repeated pronouncements debunking all the reports are so convincing. And those few
who have troubled to study the matter may be so bewildered and even

alarmed by the awesome complexity of the phenomenon that they would rather say nothing at all.

Politicians furthermore are unlikely to speak out on such a controversial topic without a mandate from the electorate. I have calculated that only about one hundred people in Britain have written to their Members of Parliament about UFOs. So why should MPs make fools of themselves on such a controversial subject when they can so easily make fools of themselves on far less controversial matters?

British pioneer Waveney Girvan wrote in 1955:

> The "Government" and the "Air Force" are only generic terms for a collection of officials. Although I happen to know that photographs of the objects are to be found on Air Force and Admiralty files, I doubt whether believers in the interplanetary theory are likely to form more than fifty percent among those high-ranking officers who have access to more information than has been vouchsafed to the public at large . . . there is likely to be disagreement on the subject in official ranks as there is among the less privileged.[32]

While a great deal more information has come to light since this was written, many of those in high office are still denied access to the above top secret data, owing to compartmentation of intelligence. There are precedents for this. A high-ranking defense official told me that he was once privy to above top secret information (*not* UFO-related) that only about fifty people had access to. The "compartment" list did not include either the Minister of Defense or the Prime Minister. If you want to keep a secret, the fewer people who know about it, the better.

Society in Upheaval?

In Chapter 15 I discussed the case of Ray Stanford and the metal fragments he discovered at the site in Socorro, New Mexico, where Sergeant Lonnie Zamora encountered a landed UFO and occupants in 1964. Stanford and colleagues took the samples to NASA's Goddard Space Flight Center where preliminary analysis determined that the metal shavings were of a highly unusual type: so unusual, in fact, that they were promptly confiscated. Later, Stanford and Robert McGarey had the opportunity of discussing reasons for the cover-up with a US Navy captain, who in rather melodramatic terms offered his opinions on the matter.

"You had no right to that kind of dynamite," he said. "What do you want to do? Blow up the whole economy, the entire social structure, and

every other institution worth keeping?'' The captain continued: ''Those
in a position to know are under no delusion. They know the facts. People
are not ready to know the facts, and they have no *need* to know them.
They could, half of the people maybe, go off the deep end.''

Stanford asked if those in the know cracked up on learning the facts.
''I doubt it,'' he was told. ''But, those men are trained to accept and
meet crisis. They are capable of rational judgment in the face of the
unexpected. . . . Their decisions are based on experience in considering
the welfare of *large* groups of people. That provides experience and
discernment that the average man, even the UFO researcher, never has.''[33]

I very much doubt that the fabric of society would be destroyed if
selected facts were released. Once the initial incredulity had subsided,
there would certainly be widespread concern as to the visitors' motives,
disturbances on the stock market, but also a great deal of excitement and
perhaps a reassessment of our role in the universal scheme of things. If
such an announcement was made, Stanton Friedman believes, ''the stock
market would go down, mental hospital admissions and church attendance
would go up, and there would be an immediate push on the part of the
younger generation—never alive when there wasn't a space program—
for a whole new view of ourselves; instead of as Americans, Chinese,
Canadians, Israelis; as earthlings. There isn't any government on this
planet that wants its citizens to owe their primary allegiance to the planet,
instead of an individual government. Nationalism is the only game in
town.''[34]

Public reaction to an admission by one of the superpowers that some
UFOs are extraterrestrial would be predicated on how much we are told,
and this must present our leaders with an awesome dilemma. Such an
admission would lead to a deluge of questions, some of which simply
cannot be answered without disclosing vital defense interests; alarming
cases of missing aircraft; abductions; genetic experiments; and bizarre
cases that will remain beyond our comprehension for centuries to come.
In this respect I am fully in sympathy with the current official policy.
''From an intelligence point of view,'' says Dr. James Harder, ''the UFO
phenomenon must be truly awesome—the worst of science fiction come
to life. . . . However, over the years, the intelligence agencies must have
come to the realization that the strangers from space are nothing exactly
new—that evidence from the past indicates that we are experiencing only
an intensification of what may have been going on for centuries.''[35]

The effects on the economic and political front are equally deserving
of consideration. ''Every nation is concerned about the effects on world-

wide economies and political power structures if the world were to be in touch with aliens with a different technology,'' Stanton Friedman believes. ''Is the oil in the ground now worthless? . . . Would the big shots of today be deposed tomorrow? The best policy is to hope that the aliens go away or that the contacts and shakings up of earthly society happen during the next administration's reign.''[36]

Perhaps the most comprehensive summary of reasons for official secrecy on UFOs is contained in the Majestic 12 briefing paper, allegedly prepared by Admiral Hillenkoetter for President-Elect Eisenhower in 1952:

> . . . Implications for the National Security are of continuing importance in that the motives and ultimate intentions of these visitors remain completely unknown. . . . It is for these reasons, as well as the obvious international and technological considerations and the ultimate need to avoid a public panic at all costs, that the Majestic-12 Group remains of the unanimous opinion that imposition of the strictest security precautions should continue without interruption into the new administration . . .

The Attitude of C. G. Jung

The great Swiss psychologist Dr. Carl Gustav Jung made a thorough study of UFOs since first becoming interested in 1946, and in addition to being a consultant to the Aerial Phenomena Research Organization (APRO) wrote a book entitled *Flying Saucers: A Modern Myth of Things Seen in the Skies*[37], which has led skeptics to jump to the conclusion that he regarded the phenomenon as entirely psychological in origin. Nothing could be further from the truth.

While it is true that Jung devoted much space in his book to the individual and collective psychological reasons why people need to believe in flying saucers, he was in no doubt regarding their objective reality, a point overlooked in his book and in an article published in 1954:

> A purely psychological explanation is ruled out by the fact that a large number of observations indicate a natural one, even a physical one. . . . The American Air Force (despite its contradictory statements), as well as the Canadian, consider the observations to be real. . . . However, the ''disks'' . . . *do not behave in accordance with physical laws* but as though without weight, *and they show signs of intelligent guidance, by quasi-human pilots.* [Original emphasis]

His position on the cover-up was unequivocal. ''What astonishes me most,'' he wrote, ''is that the American Air Force, despite all the information in its possession and its so-called fear of creating panic, seems to work systematically to do that very thing . . . since it has never yet published an authentic and certain account of the facts, only occasionally allowing information to be dragged out of it by journalists.''[38]

"If it is true that the AAF or the government withholds tale-telling facts,'' he wrote to Major Donald Keyhoe, "then one can only say that this is the most unpsychological and stupid policy one could invent. It is self-evident that the public ought to be told the truth, because ultimately it will nevertheless come to daylight. There can hardly be any greater shock than the H-bomb and yet everybody knows of it without fainting.''[39]

Jung's opinions regarding the effects on society if the extraterrestrial origin of UFOs is officially confirmed are worth quoting in detail:

> If . . . the extraterrestrial origin of the phenomena should be confirmed . . . it would put us, without doubt, in the extremely precarious position of primitive communities today in conflict with the superior culture of the whites: the rudder would be removed from our grasp, and we should lose our pleasant dreams.
>
> Naturally, it would be chiefly our science and our technology which would have to be consigned to the scrap-heap. What such a catastrophe would mean on the moral plane we can in some sort judge by the ruin of primitive cultures of which we are the witnesses. *That the construction of these machines proves a scientific technology, and one immensely superior to ours, admits of no two opinions.* Just as the Pax Britannica put an end to the disputes between the tribes of Africa, so our world could unroll its Iron Curtain and use it as scrap iron, with all the millions of tons of guns, warships and munitions. But we would have been "discovered" and colonised—sufficient reason for universal panic!
>
> If we wish to avoid such a catastrophe, the authorities in possession of important information should not hesitate to enlighten the public as soon and as completely as possible and should, above all, stop these ridiculous antics of mysteries and vague allusions.[40] [Original emphasis]

WHY NO OPEN CONTACT?

Why, journalists ask me, don't flying saucers land in Hyde Park or on the White House lawn, hold a televised press conference, and establish proper diplomatic relations with us instead of carrying on in such an elusive manner? Aside from the fact that long-term observation of our belligerent, disunited and relatively primitive planet—to say nothing of the hostile reception accorded them at times—would have convinced the visitors that landing openly might not be in their best interests, there are some legal ramifications to be considered. For a start, the UFO that first lands openly is in for a heap of trouble from government agencies that regulate air travel, such as flying through controlled airspace without clearance and landing an unlicensed aircraft. Immigration and customs regulations would be similarly daunting, even though in London we do have an Aliens Registration Office. As to establishing diplomatic relations, a man who tried to set up a Martian Embassy in Regents Park some years ago was ordered by a High Court judge to stay away from the property.

Asked in Detroit what reaction the visitors from space would receive if they landed openly, the majority of those polled said that a friendly reception could be expected. "I'd welcome them," said one. "They couldn't be any stranger than what's walking around Detroit." Others were less optimistic. "If they landed in Detroit they'd probably get mugged," said one, while another was positively discouraging. "I'd teach them to stay on their own planet. We've got enough people on welfare without supporting a bunch of Martians."[41]

It is my conviction that we are being visited by several different groups of extraterrestrials, and that while some may not be well disposed toward us, the majority are essentially benevolent. All share a common "foreign" policy of avoiding open contact with earth, which to me seems entirely logical. From my own investigations throughout the world, however, I am convinced that *selective* contacts have been made with hundreds of individuals. The visitors have no need to establish open contact, nor do they want the majority of us to know what they are doing here.

When police patrolman Herbert Schirmer encountered a landed UFO in Ashland, Nebraska, on 3 December 1967, he was told by the occupants that:

> . . . They have been observing us for a long period of time and they think that if they slowly put out reports and have their contacts state the truth it will help them . . . They have no pattern for contacting people. It is by pure chance so the government cannot determine any patterns about them. There will be a lot more contacts . . . to a certain extent they want to puzzle people. They know they are being seen too frequently and they are trying to confuse the public's mind.[42]

WHERE DO THEY COME FROM AND WHY ARE THEY HERE?

There are many hypotheses for the origin of UFOs other than the extra-terrestrial one: secret aircraft and spacecraft; natural phenomena; a secret civilization based on earth; time travelers from our own future (which is good news since it presupposes that we have a future); denizens of other dimensions; or psychological "projections." Regarding the latter, a miasma of psychological and sociological hypotheses has been proposed to ac-count for UFO sightings. None of these theories comes anywhere near explaining *all* the facts. The extraterrestrial hypothesis may not fulfill this requirement, but it is the only one that explains *most* of the facts.

There are about 100,000 million stars in our galaxy alone. To put that figure into perspective, it would take almost 3,000 years to count those stars at the rate of one per second. Many of the stars are likely to have planets around them, on some of which life may have evolved to the extent that space travel and colonization are commonplace.

Since I do not know where the visitors come from I can only speculate as to their origin, although I have been informed by reliable sources that some of them have bases within our solar system—even here on earth. Neither do I know why they are here, although I can think of numerous reasons for their visits. From a tourist's point of view, for example, earth offers some spectacular attractions. A vested interest in earth and its resources—unique in the solar system—is another, more probable reason. "We are not here for entirely philanthropic purposes," my most reliable source of information was told.

I believe that man's progress on planet earth has been monitored by beings whose technological and mental resources make ours look prim-itive and theirs "supernatural" by comparison. The fact that many of the visitors are similar to us physiologically indicates that we share a genetic link. Could it be that some of them have had a hand in our evolution?

Now that our technology has reached the stage where we are endan-gering the planet and expanding our interests in space, surveillance has intensified. Is it mere coincidence that the modern wave of sightings began during World War II as we began developing nuclear weapons and rockets? Is it also coincidental that UFOs have exhibited so much interest in our nuclear missile sites and have demonstrated their ability to paralyze launching systems?

ARE WE ENTITLED TO THE TRUTH?

It is as well at this stage to remind ourselves of the official position on the subject as set out by the US government. From 1947 to 1969 a total of 12,618 sightings was reported to Project Blue Book, the USAF Fact Sheet sent to me in late 1986 states. Of these, 701 remained unidentified. The conclusions of Project Blue Book were as follows:

> (1) No UFO reported, investigated, and evaluated by the Air Force has ever given any indication of threat to our national security; (2) there has been no evidence submitted to or discovered by the Air Force that sightings categorized as "unidentified" represent technological developments or principles beyond the range of present-day scientific knowledge; and (3) there has been no evidence indicating that sightings categorized as "unidentified" are extraterrestrial vehicles. . . . Since Project Blue Book was closed [1969], nothing has happened to indicate that the Air Force ought to resume investigating UFOs.[43]

All of these statements are demonstrably false. For one thing, reports of UFOs affecting national security were not routed to Project Blue Book and are therefore not included in the 75,000 plus pages of Blue Book records now stored at the National Archives Building in Washington, DC. As Brigadier General Bolender confirms in a 1969 Air Force memo: " . . . *reports of unidentified flying objects which could affect the national security* are made in accordance with JANAP 146 or Air Force Manual 55–11, *and are not part of the Blue Book system.*"[44] [Emphasis added]

Although a few UFO reports affecting, but apparently not compromising, national security can be found among the 1,800 pages of USAF Intelligence documents released in 1985/86, many top secret reports remain exempt from disclosure, according to the records.[45] The CIA, DIA, NSA, and other agencies are withholding top secret (and above) information pertaining to UFOs that would compromise national security if released, and it is evident that what *has* been released represents only the tip of the iceberg.

The policy statement that "nothing has happened to indicate that the Air Force ought to resume investigating UFOs" is disproven by the released documents indicating continued investigations by the Air Force Office of Special Investigations. That no sightings "represent technological developments or principles beyond the range of present-day scientific knowledge" is sheer nonsense, given the wealth of documentary evidence from unimpeachable sources testifying to the contrary. Even if the testimonial evidence is arbitrary, what about the many photographs and films showing UFOs as structured objects that have either been confiscated or withheld, to say nothing of the retrieved craft and occupants?

We have learned to live—however uneasily—with the threat of nuclear annihilation hanging over us like the sword of Damocles. Surely nothing that governments are concealing about UFOs can compare with this prospect? The intelligence community should be reminded that they are accountable to the Congress: that even if certain matters affecting national security simply cannot be revealed, we are entitled to know some of the truth at least. "The public has a right to know," declared former CIA Director Admiral Hillenkoetter in 1960. "It is time for the truth to be brought out in open Congressional hearings . . . through official secrecy and ridicule, many citizens are led to believe the unknown flying objects are nonsense."

Nearly thirty years later we are still being misled. Until we wake up to the fact that information of quite unprecedented significance is being withheld from us we shall continue to remain in ignorance for decades to come. Unless, that is, the visitors decide to declare themselves more openly. . . .

APPENDIX

OCS 21347-86

~February 26, 1942.

MEMORANDUM FOR THE PRESIDENT:

The following is the information we have from CHQ at this moment regarding the air alarm over Los Angeles of yesterday morning:

"From details available at this hour:

"1. Unidentified airplanes, other than American Army or Navy planes, were probably over Los Angeles, and were fired on by elements of the 37th CA Brigade (AA) between 3:12 and 4:15 AM. These units expended 1430 rounds of ammunition.

"2. As many as fifteen airplanes may have been involved, flying at various speeds from what is officially reported as being 'very slow' to as much as 200 MPH and at elevations from 9000 to 18000 feet.

"3. No bombs were dropped.

"4. No casualties among our troops.

"5. No planes were shot down.

"6. No American Army or Navy planes were in action.

"Investigation continuing. It seems reasonable to conclude that if unidentified airplanes were involved, they may have been from commercial sources, operated by enemy agents for purposes of spreading alarm, disclosing location of antiaircraft positions, and slowing production through blackout. Such conclusion is supported by varying speed of operation and the fact that no bombs were dropped."

DECLASSIFIED
E.O. 11652, Sec. 5(E) and 5(D) or (E)
OSD letter, May 3, 1972
By ___ NARS Date: 4-9-74

(Sgd) G. C. MARSHALL

Chief of Staff.

21347
86

Orig. dispatched to Pres.
2/12/42

akn

Memo from General George Marshall to President Roosevelt giving details of the Los Angeles air alarm in February 1942

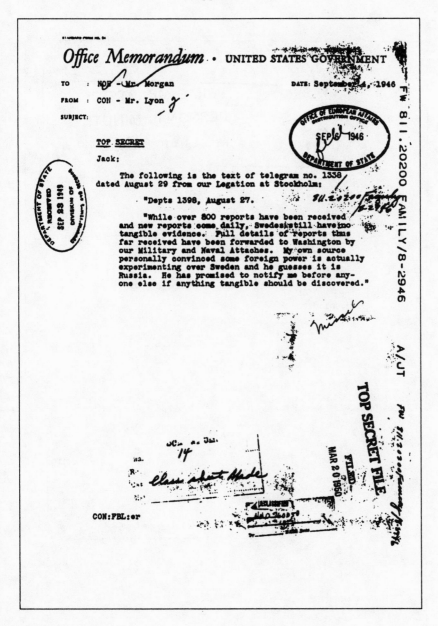

Top Secret Department of State memo referring to the ''ghost rocket''
wave of 1946

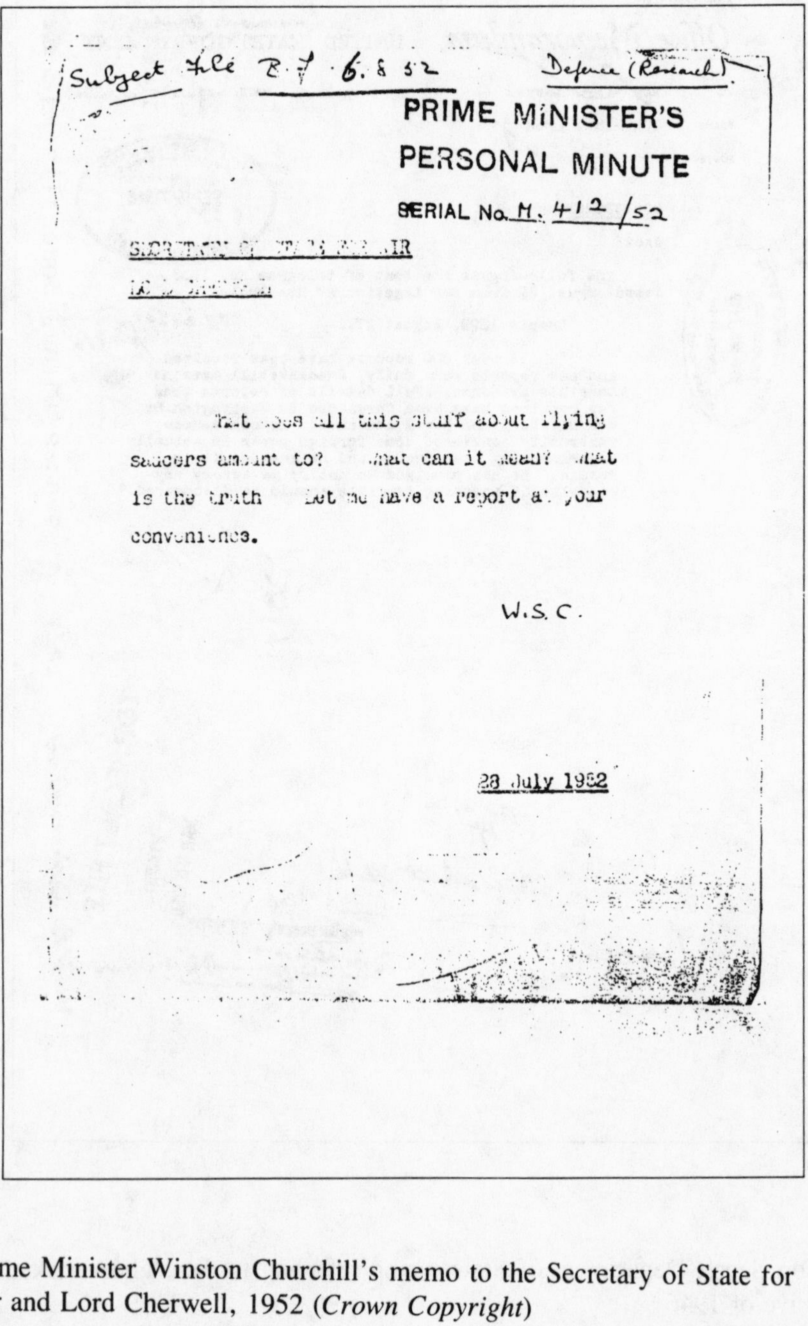

Subject File B.7.6.852   Defence (Research)

**PRIME MINISTER'S
PERSONAL MINUTE**

SERIAL No. M. 412/52

SECRETARY OF STATE FOR AIR

LORD CHERWELL

What does all this stuff about flying saucers amount to?   What can it mean?   What is the truth   Let me have a report at your convenience.

W.S.C.

28 July 1952

Prime Minister Winston Churchill's memo to the Secretary of State for Air and Lord Cherwell, 1952 (*Crown Copyright*)

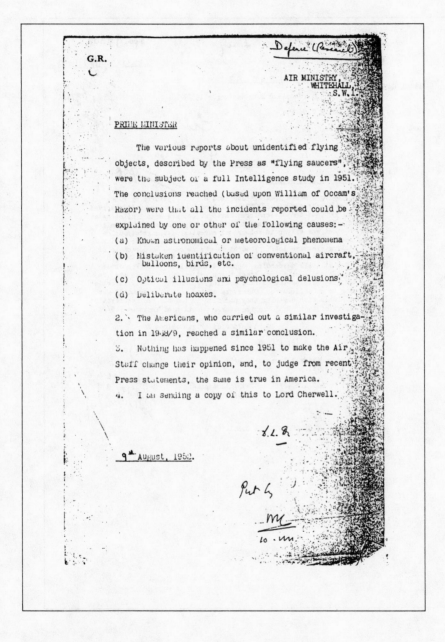

The Air Minister's response, revealing his ignorance of American findings
(*Crown Copyright*)

A|AMS & u|

D. O po. 1| #302.

63430

By.

AM/DD. OPS. (AD) /2/4274/P   M E S S A G E

(Received 20th September, 1952)

From:-   C.T.F. 178.

To:-   C. in C. Aircastlant.

Reptd.to:-   Air Ministry London.

Film on
Folder 58.

DSR
25/9.

UNCLASSIFIED   DEFERRED

A 1/41 Sep. 19

Following unusual incident observed R.A.F. Topcliffe by number
officers and airmen aircrew 191053 local time. Meteor aircraft observed
at approx. 500 feet and descending. White object was seen 5 miles astern
at approx. 15000 feet and moving at comparatively slow speed on similar
course. Object was silver in colour and circular. It maintained slow
forward speed before commencing descent. Swinging in pendular motion
like a falling sycamore leaf. Thought by observers to be parachute or
cowling from Meteor aircraft. Aircraft had turned towards Dishforth and
object. Whilst still descending, appeared to follow suit. Pendulous
motion and descent ceased and object began rotary   about its own
axis. Suddenly accelerated at an incredible speed   terly direction
but turning to a S.E. course. Observers stated that ... movements were
not identifiable with anything they had seen in the air and acceleration
was in excess of that of a shooting star. Duration of incident 1 5/20
seconds.

                         Time of origin 191644 Z

Copies to:-

        A.I.3.(B) (ACTION)

Recirculated Registry Telegrams 22/9/52.
Authority A.I.3.(B).
Copies to:-

        A.C.A.S.(OPS) (ACTION) (2 copies)
        A.C.A.S.(I) (2 copies)
        C.A.S.
        S. OF S.
        D.H.O.
        M. OF DEFENCE FOR D.S.I. (2 c   ).

An Air Ministry report giving details of the sighting by personnel at RAF
Topcliffe, Yorkshire, in September 1952 (*Crown Copyright*)

The attached statement was dictated by Mr. Briggs to Mrs. Travis on the morning of the 23rd February 1955 at my request.

My own electrician, Heath, reported his conversation and I subsequently interviewed Mr. Briggs, with my wife and younger daughter, and as a result of his account, Heath and I accompanied him to the place from which he saw the Flying Saucer.

We followed the marks of his bicycle in the snow very easily, and exactly at the spot which he described the tracks came to an end, and foot marks appeared beside it. Next to the foot marks there were the marks of a body having fallen in the snow, and then the marks of a bicycle having been picked up again, there being a clear gap of 3ft. between where the front wheel marks originally ended and then started again. The rear wheel marks were continuous but blurred. From then on the bicycle tracks led back to the drive.

The bicycle tracks absolutely confirm Mr. Briggs' story, so far as his own movements are concerned.

He, Heath and I searched the area over the spot where the Flying Saucer was estimated to have been, but candidly we could see no unusual signs.

The snow at the bottom of the meadow had melted much more than that at the top, and it would have been difficult to see any marks.

This statement has been dictated in the presence of Heath and Mr. Briggs, and Heath and I have carefully read Mr. Briggs' statement, and we both attest that this is the exact story which he told us.

Mr. Briggs was still dazed when I first saw him, and was worried that no one would believe his story. Indeed, he made a point of saying that he had never believed in Flying Saucer stories before, and had been absolutely amazed at what he had seen.

He did not give me the impression of being the sort of man who would be subject to hallucinations, or would in any way invent such a story. I am sure from the sincere way he gave his account that he, himself, is completely convinced of the truth of his own statement.

He has offered to swear to the truth of this statement on oath on the Bible if needed, but I saw no point in asking him to do this.

Mountbatten of Burma

I confirm that I have read and agree with the above statement.

R K Heath

Statement by Lord Mountbatten relating to the reported landing of a UFO at his estate in 1955 (*Broadlands Archives*)

<u>Statement by Frederick S. Briggs, 8, Chambers Avenue, Romsey, Hants.</u>

I am at present employed at Broadlands as a bricklayer and was cycling to my work from Romsey on the morning of Wednesday, the 23rd February 1955. When I was about half way between the Palmerston or Romsey Lodge and the house, just by where the drive forks off to the Middlebridge Lodge, I suddenly saw an object hovering stationary over the field between the end of the gardens and Middlebridge drive, and just on the house side of the little stream.

The object was shaped like a child's huge humming-top and half way between 20ft. or 30ft. in diameter.

Its colour was like dull aluminium, rather like a kitchen saucepan. It was shaped like the sketch which I have endeavoured to make, and had portholes all round the middle, rather like a steamer has.

The time was just after 8.30 a.m. with an overcast sky and light snow on the ground.

I turned off the drive at the fork and rode over the grass for rather less than 100 yards. I then dismounted, and holding my bicycle in my right hand, watched.

While I was watching a column, about the thickness of a man, descended from the centre of the Saucer and I suddenly noticed on it, what appeared to be a man, presumably standing on a small platform on the end. He did not appear to be holding on to anything. He seemed to be dressed in a dark suit of overalls, and was wearing a close fitting hat or helmet.

At the time the Saucer was certainly less than 100 yards from me, and not more than 60ft. over the level where I was standing, although the meadow has a steep bank at this point, so that the Saucer would have been about 80ft. over the lower level of the meadow.

As I stood there watching, I suddenly saw a curious light come on in one of the portholes. It was a bluish light, rather like a mercury vapour light. Although it was quite bright, it did not appear to be directed straight at me, nor did it dazzle me, but simultaneously with the light coming on I suddenly seemed to be pushed over, and I fell down in the snow with my bicycle on top of me. What is more, I could not get up again. Although the bicycle only weighs a few lbs. it seemed as though an unseen force was holding me down.

Whilst lying on the ground I could see the tube withdrawn quickly into the Saucer, which then rose vertically, quite as fast as the fastest Jet aircraft I have seen, or faster.

There had been no noise whatever until the Saucer started to move, and even then the noise was no louder than that of an ordinary small rocket let off by a child on Guy Fawkes Night.

It disappeared out of sight into the clouds almost instantaneously, and as it went, I found myself able to get up. Although I seemed to be lying a long time on the ground I do not suppose, in reality, it was more than a few seconds.

The statement by Frederick Briggs, who claimed to have witnessed the incident (*Broadlands Archives*)

2.

I felt rather dizzy, as though I had received a near knockout blow on the point of the chin, but of course there was no physical hurt of any sort, merely a feeling of dizziness.

I picked up my bicycle, mounted it and rode straight on to Broadlands where I met Heath standing by the garage.

I was feeling very shaky and felt I must regain my confidence by discussing what I had seen. I said to him: "Look, Ron, have you known me long enough to know that I am sane and sober at this hour of the morning?" He laughed and made some remark like, "Well, of course." Then I told him what I had seen.

Heath and I went back along the road where I showed him the tracks of my bicycle. I then went back to work, where I saw my foreman, Mr. Hudson, and told him what I had seen.

Frederick S. Briggs.

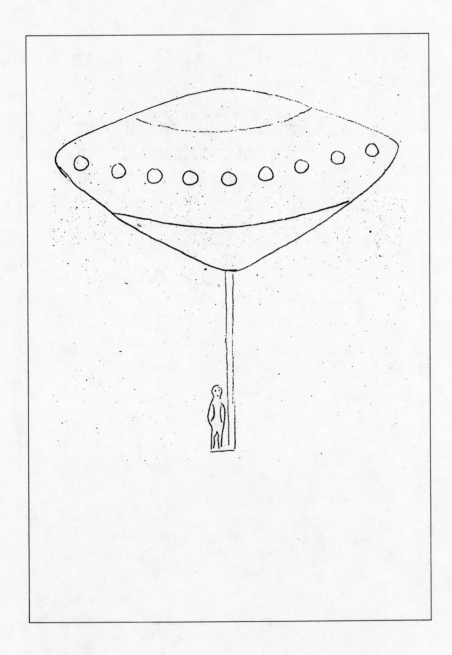

Frederick Briggs' drawing of the UFO and its humanoid occupant (*Broadlands Archives*)

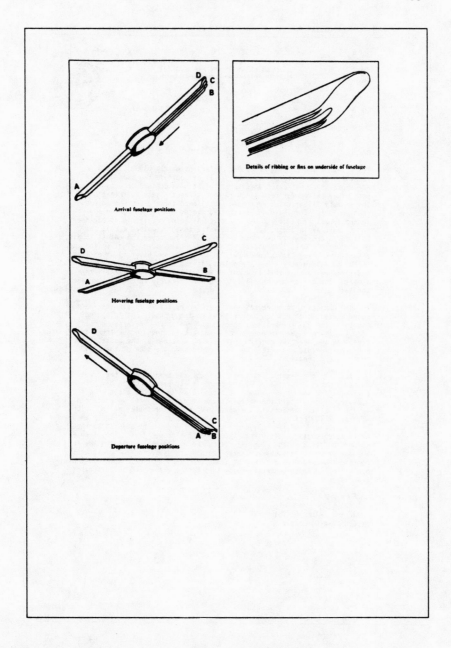

UFO seen by former RAF Intelligence officer and British Airways flight administration officer J.B.W. Brooks at Moigne Downs, Dorset, in October 1967 (*FSR Publications, Ltd.*)

DEPARTMENT OF THE AIR FORCE
HEADQUARTERS 81ST COMBAT SUPPORT GROUP (USAFE)
APO NEW YORK 09755

REPLY TO
ATTN OF.   CD   13 Jan 81

SUBJECT: Unexplained Lights

TO: RAF/CC

1. Early in the morning of 27 Dec 80 (approximately 0300L), two USAF
security police patrolmen saw unusual lights outside the back gate at
RAF Woodbridge. Thinking an aircraft might have crashed or been forced
down, they called for permission to go outside the gate to investigate.
The on-duty flight chief responded and allowed three patrolmen to proceed on foot. The individuals reported seeing a strange glowing object
in the forest. The object was described as being metalic in appearance
and triangular in shape, approximately two to three meters across the
base and approximately two meters high. It illuminated the entire forest
with a white light. The object itself had a pulsing red light on top and
a bank(s) of blue lights underneath. The object was hovering or on legs.
As the patrolmen approached the object, it maneuvered through the trees
and disappeared. At this time the animals on a nearby farm went into a
frenzy. The object was briefly sighted approximately an hour later near
the back gate.

2. The next day, three depressions 1 1/2" deep and 7" in diameter were
found where the object had been sighted on the ground. The following
night (29 Dec 80) the area was checked for radiation. Beta/gamma readings
of 0.1 milliroentgens were recorded with peak readings in the three depressions and near the center of the triangle formed by the depressions.
A nearby tree had moderate (.05-.07) readings on the side of the tree
toward the depressions.

3. Later in the night a red sun-like light was seen through the trees.
It moved about and pulsed. At one point it appeared to throw off glowing
particles and then broke into five separate white objects and then disappeared. Immediately thereafter, three star-like objects were noticed
in the sky, two objects to the north and one to the south, all of which
were about 10° off the horizon. The objects moved rapidly in sharp angular
movements and displayed red, green and blue lights. The objects to the
north appeared to be elliptical through an 8-12 power lens. They then
turned to full circles. The objects to the north remained in the sky for
an hour or more. The object to the south was visible for two or three
hours and beamed down a stream of light from time to time. Numerous individuals, including the undersigned, witnessed the activities in paragraphs
2 and 3.

CHARLES I. HALT, Lt Col, USAF
Deputy Base Commander

Colonel Charles Halt's report to the Ministry of Defense describing the
sensational events at RAF Woodbridge in December 1980

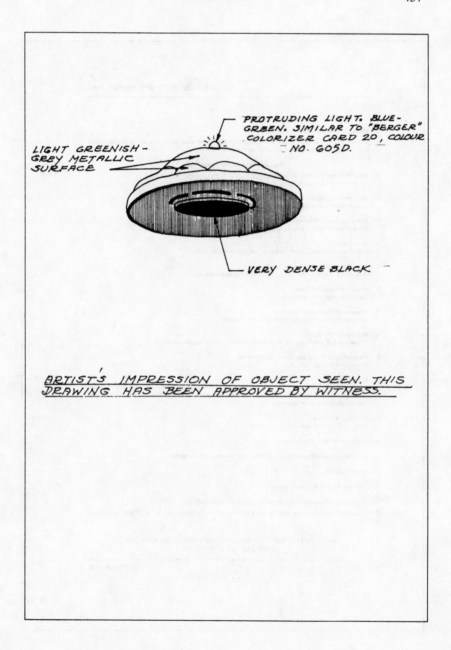

PROTRUDING LIGHT. BLUE-GREEN. SIMILAR TO "BERGER" COLORIZER CARD 20, COLOUR NO. 605D.

LIGHT GREENISH-GREY METALLIC SURFACE

VERY DENSE BLACK

ARTIST'S IMPRESSION OF OBJECT SEEN. THIS DRAWING HAS BEEN APPROVED BY WITNESS.

The UFO seen by a woman police constable near Isfield, Sussex, in 1977 (*Patricia B. Grant*)

Chapter 4

3 UNIDENTIFIED FLYING OBJECTS

A controller receiving a report about an unidentified flying object must obtain as much as possible of the information required to complete a report in the format shown below.

Report of Unidentified Flying Object

A. **Date, Time and Duration of Sighting**
Local times to be quoted.

B. **Description of Object**
Number of objects, size, shape, colours, brightness, sound, smell, etc.

C. **Exact Position of Observer**
Geographical location, indoors or outdoors, stationary or moving.

D. **How Observed**
Naked eye, binoculars, other optical device, still or movie camera.

E. **Direction in which Object was First Seen**
A landmark may be more useful than a badly estimated bearing.

F. **Angular Elevation of Object**
Estimated heights are unreliable.

G. **Distance of Object from Observer**
By reference to a known landmark wherever possible.

H. **Movements of Object**
Changes in E, F and G may be of more use than estimates of course and speed.

J. **Meteorological Conditions During Observations**
Moving clouds, haze, mist, etc.

K. **Nearby Objects**
Telephone or high-voltage lines; reservoir, lake or dam; swamp or marsh; river; high buildings, tall chimneys, steeples, spires, TV or radio masts; airfields, generating plant; factories; pits or other sites with floodlights or other lighting.

L. **To Whom Reported**
Police, military organisations, the press, etc.

M. **Name and Address of Informant**

N. **Any Background Information on the Informant that may be Volunteered**

O. **Other Witnesses**

P. **Date and Time of Receipt of Report**

The details are to be telephoned immediately to AIS (Military), LATCC.

The completed report is to be sent by the originating air traffic service unit to the Ministry of Defence (AFOR).

A LIST OF TELEPHONE NUMBERS AND LOCATIONS IS SHOWN IN THE
DIRECTORY AT APPENDIX H

5.7.84   AMENDMENT 31

Instructions to air traffic controllers for reporting UFO sightings (1984)

CONFIDENCIAL

INFORME QUE FORMULA EL COMANDANTE DEL AREA DE AVIACION (S.V.) SOBRE LA NOTICIA DE APARICION DE OBJETOS VOLADORES NO IDENTIFICADOS EN EL POLIGONO DE TIRO DE LAS BARDENAS REALES EL DIA 2 DE ENERO DE 1.975.

En el Polígono de Tiro de Las Bardenas Reales a 8 de Enero de 1.975.

Testigos presenciales

Soldado	(Mecánico)
Cabo	(Estudiante)
Soldado	(Agricultor)
Soldado	(Agricultor)
Soldado	(Agricultor)
Sargento 1ª	

Se adjunta fotocopia de las declaraciones de estos testigos e Informe del Comandante del Destacamento, así como un croquis de las evoluciones que según dichas declaraciones, efectuaron dos objetos voladores no identificados sobre dicho Polígono.

Circunstancias que concurrieron en la observación.

El Sargento 1ª observó el segundo de los objetos voladores con unos prismáticos.
La observación del Cabo y los Soldados que estaban de guardia en la Torre Principal, fué a simple vista.
Las condiciones meteorológicas en el momento de la observación eran:
Despejado y con claridad suficiente para percibir los perfiles de los montes cercanos, había bruma por el horizonte.
Los medios de apreciación de distancia y alturas se realizaron por medio de referencias sobre el terreno.
Durante todo el tiempo de la observación no se apreció ningún ruido extraño.

CONCLUSIONES

Tomada declaración a todos los testigos presenciales, uno por uno, y por separado, no hubo ninguna contradicción, todos coincidieron exactamente en sus manifestaciones.
De sus informes se desprende, que el día 2 de Enero sobre las 23,00 horas un objeto volador no identificado, sobrevoló el Campo de Tiro de Bardenas Reales, inicialmente a escasa altura sobre el terreno y a poca velocidad hasta el momento en que llegó a la altura de la Torre Principal, lugar de la observación, en el que se elevó rápidamente adquiriendo gran velocidad y desapareció en dirección N.W.

CONFIDENCIAL

Official report of the sighting by military personnel at Las Bardenas Reales near Zaragoza Air Base, January 1975 (*Spanish Air Force*)

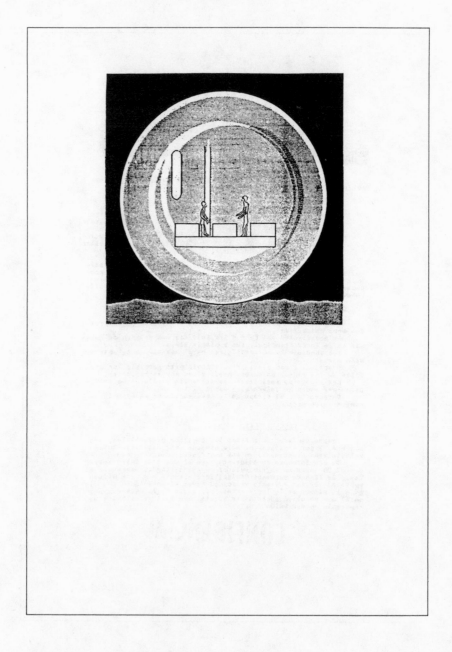

Official drawing of the object and occupants seen by Dr. Padrón León
and witnesses in the Canary Islands on 22 June 1976 (*Spanish Air Force*)

COMMONWEALTH OF AUSTRALIA   DEPARTMENT OF TRANSPORT

AIRCRAFT ACCIDENT INVESTIGATION SUMMARY REPORT

Publication of this report is authorized by the Secretary under the provisions of Air Navigation Regulations 283 (1)

Reference No. **V116/783/1047**

1. LOCATION OF OCCURRENCE

	Height a.m.s.l.	Date	Time (Local)	Zone
Not known	–	21.10.78	Not known	EST

2. THE AIRCRAFT

Make and Model	Registration	Certificate of Airworthiness
Cessna 182L	VH-DSJ	Valid from 14 February 1968

Certificate of Registration issued to	Operator	Degree of damage to aircraft
Cephus Day, 33 Reserve Road, Beaumauris. Victoria	SAS Southern Air Services, Northern Avenue, Moorabbin Airport, Victoria	Not known
		Other property damaged –

Defects discovered

3. THE FLIGHT

Last or intended departure point	Time of departure	Next point of intended landing	Purpose of flight	Class of operation
Moorabbin	1819 hours	King Island	Travel	Private

4. THE CREW

Name	Status	Age	Class of licence	Hours on type	Total hours	Degree of injury
Frederick VALENTICH	Pilot	20	Private	Not known	150 (Approx.)	Presumed Fatal

5. OTHER PERSONS (All passengers and persons injured on ground)

Name	Status	Degree of injury	Name	Status	Degree of injury

6. RELEVANT EVENTS

The pilot obtained a Class Four instrument rating on 11 May 1978 and he was therefore authorised to operate at night in visual meteorological conditions (VMC). On the afternoon of 21 October 1978 he attended the Moorabbin Briefing Office, obtained a meteorological briefing and, at 1723 hours, submitted a flight plan for a night VMC flight from Moorabbin to King Island and return. The cruising altitude nominated in the flight plan was below 5000 feet, with estimated time intervals of 41 minutes to Cape Otway and 28 minutes from Cape Otway to King Island. The total fuel endurance was shown as 300 minutes. The pilot made no arrangements for aerodrome lighting to be illuminated for his arrival at King Island. He advised the briefing officer and the operator's representative that he was uplifting friends at King Island and took four life jackets in the aircraft with him.

The aircraft was refuelled to capacity at 1810 hours and departed Moorabbin at 1819 hours. After departure the pilot established two-way radio communications with Melbourne Flight Service Unit (FSU).

The pilot reported Cape Otway at 1900 hours and the next transmission received from the aircraft was at 1906:14 hours. The following communications between the aircraft and Melbourne FSU were recorded from this time: (Note: The word/words in brackets are open to other interpretations.)

TIME	FROM	TEXT
1906:14	VH-DSJ	MELBOURNE this is DELTA SIERRA JULIET is there any known traffic below five thousand
:23	FSU	DELTA SIERRA JULIET no known traffic
:26	VH-DSJ	DELTA SIERRA JULIET I am seems (to) be a large aircraft below five thousand

The official report on the case of Frederick Valentich, who disappeared with his aircraft immediately after reporting a UFO in October 1978 (*William Chalker*)

RELEVANT EVENTS (cont'd)

TIME	FROM	TEXT
:46	FSU	D D DELTA SIERRA JULIET what type of aircraft is it
:50	VH–DSJ	DELTA SIERRA JULIET I cannot affirm it is four bright it seems to me like landing lights
1907:04	FSU	DELTA SIERRA JULIET
:32	VH–DSJ	MELBOURNE this (is) DELTA SIERRA JULIET the aircraft has just passed over over me at least a thousand feet above
:43	FSU	DELTA SIERRA JULIET roger and it it is a large aircraft confirm
:47	VH–DSJ	er unknown due to the speed it's travelling is there any airforce aircraft in the vicinity
:57	FSU	DELTA SIERRA JULIET no known aircraft in the vicinity
1908:18	VH–DSJ	MELBOURNE it's approaching now from due east towards me
:28	FSU	DELTA SIERRA JULIET
:42		// open microphone for two seconds //
:49	VH–DSJ	DELTA SIERRA JULIET it seems to me that he's playing some sort of game he's flying over me two three times at a time at speeds I could not identify
1909:02	FSU	DELTA SIERRA JULIET roger what is your actual level
:06	VH–DSJ	my level is four and a half thousand four five zero zero
:11	FSU	DELTA SIERRA JULIET and confirm you cannot identify the aircraft
:14	VH–DSJ	affirmative
:18	FSU	DELTA SIERRA JULIET roger standby
:28	VH–DSJ	MELBOURNE DELTA SIERRA JULIET it's not an aircraft it is // open microphone for two seconds //
:46	FSU	DELTA SIERRA JULIET MELBOURNE can you describe the er aircraft
1909:52	VH–DSJ	DELTA SIERRA JULIET as it's flying past it's a long shape // open microphone for three seconds // (cannot) identify more than (that it has such speed) // open microphone for 3 seconds // before me right now Melbourne
1910:07	FSU	DELTA SIERRA JULIET roger and how large would the er object be
:20	VH–DSJ	DELTA SIERRA JULIET MELBOURNE it seems like it's stationary what I'm doing right now is orbiting and the thing is just orbiting on top of me also it's got a green light and sort of metallic (like) it's all shiny (on) the outside
:43	FSU	DELTA SIERRA JULIET

RELEVANT EVENTS (cont'd)

TIME	FROM	TEXT
:48	VH-DSJ	DELTA SIERRA JULIET // open microphone for 5 seconds // it's just vanished
:57	FSU	DELTA SIERRA JULIET
1911:03	VH-DSJ	MELBOURNE would you know what kind of aircraft I've got is it (a type) military aircraft
:08	FSU	DELTA SIERRA JULIET confirm the er aircraft just vanished
:14	VH-DSJ	SAY AGAIN
:17	FSU	DELTA SIERRA JULIET is the aircraft still with you
:23	VH-DSJ	DELTA SIERRA JULIET (it's ah nor) // open microphone 2 seconds // (now) approaching from the southwest
:37	FSU	DELTA SIERRA JULIET
:52	VH-DSJ	DELTA SIERRA JULIET the engine is is rough idling I've got it set at twenty three twenty four and the thing is (coughing)
1912:04	FSU	DELTA SIERRA JULIET roger what are your intentions
:09	VH-DSJ	my intentions are ah to go to King Island ah Melbourne that strange aircraft is hovering on top of me again // two seconds open microphone // it is hovering and it's not an aircraft
:22	FSU	DELTA SIERRA JULIET
:28	VH-DSJ	DELTA SIERRA JULIET MELBOURNE // 17 seconds open microphone //
:49	FSU	DELTA SIERRA JULIET MELBOURNE

There is no record of any further transmissions from the aircraft.

The weather in the Cape Otway area was clear with a trace of stratocumulus cloud at 5000 to 7000 feet, scattered cirrus cloud at 30000 feet, excellent visibility and light winds. The end of daylight at Cape Otway was at 1918 hours.

The Alert Phase of SAR procedures was declared at 1912 hours and, at 1933 hours when the aircraft did not arrive at King Island, the Distress Phase was declared and search action was commenced. An intensive air, sea and land search was continued until 25 October 1978, but no trace of the aircraft was found.

7. OPINION AS TO CAUSE

The reason for the disappearance of the aircraft has not been determined.

Approved for publication		(A.R. Woodward) Delegate of the Secretary	Date 27.4.1982

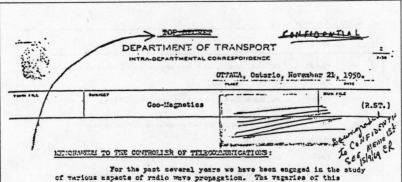

TOP SECRET   CONFIDENTIAL

DEPARTMENT OF TRANSPORT
INTRA-DEPARTMENTAL CORRESPONDENCE

OTTAWA, Ontario, November 21, 1950.

SUBJECT   Geo-Magnetics   (R.ST.)

MEMORANDUM TO THE CONTROLLER OF TELECOMMUNICATIONS:

For the past several years we have been engaged in the study of various aspects of radio wave propagation. The vagaries of this phenomenon have led us into the fields of aurora, cosmic radiation, atmospheric radio-activity and geo-magnetism. In the case of geo-magnetics our investigations have contributed little to our knowledge of radio wave propagation as yet, but nevertheless have indicated several avenues of investigation which may well be explored with profit. For example, we are on the track of a means whereby the potential energy of the earth's magnetic field may be abstracted and used.

On the basis of theoretical considerations a small and very crude experimental unit was constructed approximately a year ago and tested in our Standards Laboratory. The tests were essentially successful in that sufficient energy was abstracted from the earth's field to operate a volt-meter, approximately 50 milliwatts. Although this unit was far from being self-sustaining, it nevertheless demonstrated the soundness of the basic principles in a qualitative manner and provided useful data for the design of a better unit.

The design has now been completed for a unit which should be self-sustaining and in addition provide a small surplus of power. Such a unit, in addition to functioning as a 'pilot power plant' should be large enough to permit the study of the various reaction forces which are expected to develop.

We believe that we are on the track of something which may well prove to be the introduction to a new technology. The existence of a different technology is borne out by the investigations which are being carried on at the present time in relation to flying saucers.

While in Washington attending the NARB Conference, two books were released, one titled "Behind the Flying Saucer" by Frank Scully, and the other "The Flying Saucers are Real" by Donald Keyhoe. Both books dealt mostly with the sightings of unidentified objects and both books claim that flying objects were of extra-terrestrial origin and might well be space ships

...... 2

Top Secret Canadian government memorandum from Wilbert Smith, November 1950 (*Stanton Friedman*)

from another planet. Scully claimed that the preliminary studies of one saucer which fell into the hands of the United States Government indicated that they operated on some hitherto unknown magnetic principles. It appeared to me that our own work in geo-magnetics might well be the linkage between our technology and the technology by which the saucers are designed and operated. If it is assumed that our geo-magnetic investigations are in the right direction, the theory of operation of the saucers becomes quite straightforward, with all observed features explained qualitatively and quantitatively.

I made discreet enquiries through the Canadian Embassy staff in Washington who were able to obtain for me the following information:

a. The matter is the most highly classified subject in the United States Government, rating higher even than the H-bomb.

b. Flying saucers exist.

c. Their modus operandi is unknown but concentrated effort is being made by a small group headed by Doctor Vannevar Bush.

d. The entire matter is considered by the United States authorities to be of tremendous significance.

I was further informed that the United States authorities are investigating along quite a number of lines which might possibly be related to the saucers such as mental phenomena and I gather that they are not doing too well since they indicated that if Canada is doing anything at all in geo-magnetics they would welcome a discussion with suitably accredited Canadians.

While I am not yet in a position to say that we have solved even the first problems in geo-magnetic energy release, I feel that the correlation between our basic theory and the available information on saucers checks too closely to be mere coincidence. It is my honest opinion that we are on the right track and are fairly close to at least some of the answers.

Mr. Wright, Defence Research Board liaison officer at the Canadian Embassy in Washington, was extremely anxious for me to get in touch with Doctor Solandt, Chairman of the Defence Research Board, to discuss with him future investigations along the line of geo-magnetic energy release.

.... 3

The "small group headed by Doctor Vannevar Bush" was the above Top Secret Majestic-12 panel, established in September 1947

- 3 -

I do not feel that we have as yet sufficient data to place before Defence Research Board which would enable a program to be initiated within that organization, but I do feel that further research is necessary and I would prefer to see it done within the frame work of our own organization with, of course, full co-operation and exchange of information with other interested bodies.

I discussed this matter fully with Doctor Solandt, Chairman of Defence Research Board, on November 20th and placed before him as much information as I have been able to gather to date. Doctor Solandt agreed that work on geo-magnetic energy should go forward as rapidly as possible and offered full co-operation of his Board in providing laboratory facilities, acquisition of necessary items of equipment, and specialized personnel for incidental work in the project. I indicated to Doctor Solandt that we would prefer to keep the project within the Department of Transport for the time being until we have obtained sufficient information to permit a complete assessment of the value of the work.

It is therefore recommended that a PROJECT be set up within the frame work of this Section to study this problem and that the work be carried on a part time basis until such time as sufficient tangible results can be seen to warrant more definitive action. Cost of the program in its initial stages are expected to be less than a few hundred dollars and can be carried by our Radio Standards Lab appropriation.

Attached hereto is a draft of terms of reference for such a project which, if authorized, will enable us to proceed with this research work within our own organization.

(W.B. Smith)
Senior Radio Engineer

WBS/cc

DEPARTMENT OF NATIONAL DEFENCE
INFORMATION SERVICES

MINISTÈRE DE LA DÉFENSE NATIONALE
SERVICES D'INFORMATION

D1350-500/A (DIS)
Ottawa, Ontario
K1A 0K2

Ottawa 4, Ontario

October 24, 1972

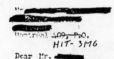

Montreal 409, P.Q.
HIT-3M6

Dear Mr.

Thank you for your letter concerning your request for information regarding UFOs.

We are sending you the information we have on Unidentified Flying Objects. Prior to 1968, all sightings of UFOs reported to Canadian Forces Headquarters were investigated by the Director of Operations. It has not been the practice to allow the general public to study these files.

Since the beginning of 1968, UFO reports received by the Canadian Forces are passed to the National Research Council. The branch examines reports for scientific reasons warranting further investigation. The department of National Defence and other Federal Government agencies may be called upon to carry out these investigations for NRC.

Canadian Forces Headquarters has never made a public statement concerning UFOs, however, we endeavour to carry out our investigations with an open mind. We neither agree with nor deny the existence of UFOs. Investigations to date indicate that there is no evidence to suggest that UFOs present a threat to the world, however, certain reports suggest that they exhibit a unique scientific or advanced technology that could possibly contribute to scientific or technical research.

It is hoped that the information is of interest to you. May we suggest that further enquiries be sent to the National Research Council, Montreal Road, Ottawa 7, Ontario.

Yours sincerely,

L. A. Bourgeois
Brigadier General
Director General Information

Note: We regret our departmental library has no knowledge of the publication in question...

Letter from Canada's Department of National Defense, 1972

AG

CINC-NORAD
conference Msg
Nov. 11, 1975
From A confidential source

C O N F I D E N T I A L
SUBJ: SUSPICIOUS UNKNOWN AIR ACTIVITY
THIS MESSAGE IN FIVE PARTS.
PART I. SINCE 28 OCT 75 NUMEROUS REPORTS OF SUSPICIOUS
OBJECTS HAVE BEEN RECEIVED AT THE NORAD COC. RELIABLE
MILITARY PERSONNEL AT LORING AFB MAINE, WURTSMITH AFB,
MICHIGAN, MALMSTROM AFB MT, MINOT AFB ND, AND CANADIAN
FORCES STATION FALCONBRIDGE ONTARIO, CANADA, HAVE
VISUALLY SIGHTED SUSPICIOUS OBJECTS. PART II. OBJECTS
AT LORING AND WURTSMITH WERE CHARACTERIZED TO BE
HELICOPTERS. MISSILE SITE PERSONNEL, SECURITY ALERT
TEAMS AND AIR DEFENSE PERSONNEL AT MALMSTROM MONTANA
REPORT AN OBJECT WHICH SOUNDED LIKE A JET AIRCRAFT.

PAGE 2 RUWRNLA5289 C O N F I D E N T I A L
FAA ADVISED THERE WERE NO JET AIRCRAFT IN THE
VICINITY. MALMSTROM SEARCH AND HEIGHT FINDER RADARS
CARRIED THE OBJECT BETWEEN 9500 FT AND 15,600 FT AT
SPEED OF SEVEN KNOTS. THERE WAS INTERMITTENT
RADAR CONTACT WITH THE OBJECT FROM 0807530Z THRU 09003Z
NOV 75. F-106S SCRAMBLED FROM MALMSTROM COULD NOT
MAKE CONTACT DUE TO DARKNESS AND LOW ALTITUDE. SITE
PERSONNEL REPORTED THE OBJECT AS LOW AS 200 FT AND
SAID THAT AS THE INTERCEPTORS APPROACHED THE LIGHTS
WENT OUT, AFTER THE INTERCEPTORS HAD PASSED THE
LIGHTS CAME ON AGAIN. ONE HOUR AFTER THE F-106S

PAGE 1   C O N F I D E N T I A L   00001111

North American Aerospace Defense Command document relating to
sightings over nuclear missile bases in 1975

TURNED TO BASE MISSILE SITE PERSONNEL REPORTED
E OBJECT INCREASED TO A HIGH SPEED; RAISED IN
TITUDE AND COULD NOT BE DISCERNED FROM THE STARS.
RT III. MINOT AFB ON 10 NOV REPORTED THAT THE
TE WAS BUZZED BY A BRIGHT OBJECT THE SIZE OF A
R AT AN ALTITUDE OF 1000 TO 2000 FT, THERE WAS
NOISE EMITTED BY THE VEHICLE. PART IV, THIS
RNING, 11 NOV 75, CFS FALCONBRIDGE REPORTED
ARCH AND HEIGHT FINDER RADAR PAINTS ON AN OBJECT

GE 3 RUWRNLB5489 C O N F I D E N T I A L
TO 30 NAUTICAL MILES SOUTH OF THE SITE RANGING
ALTITUDE FROM 25,000 FT TO 72,000 FT. THE SITE
MMANDER AND OTHER PERSONNEL SAY THE OBJECT
PEARED AS A BRIGHT STAR BUT MUCH CLOSER. WITH
NOCULARS THE OBJECT APPEARED AS A 100 FT DIAMETER
HERE AND APPEARED TO HAVE CRATERS AROUND THE
TSIDE. PART V. BE ASSURED THAT THIS COMMAND IS
ING EVERYTHING POSSIBLE TO IDENTIFY AND PROVIDE
LID FACTUAL INFORMATION ON THESE SITINGS. I
VE ALSO EXPRESSED MY CONCERN TO SAFOI THAT WE
ME UP SOONEST WITH A PROPOSED ANSWER TO QUERIES
OM THE PRESS TO PREVENT OVER REACTION BY THE
BLIC TO REPORTS BY THE MEDIA THAT MAY BE BLOWN
T OF PROPORTION. TO DATE EFFORTS BY AIR GUARD
LICOPTERS, SAC HELICOPTERS AND NORAD F106S HAVE
ILED TO PRODUCE POSITIVE ID.
DS-2.
T
5489
NNOTES
J

Drawing of an object seen over Peking in April 1981, identical to a UFO seen over London in December 1980 (UFOs over Modern China *by Paul Dong and Wendelle Stevens*)

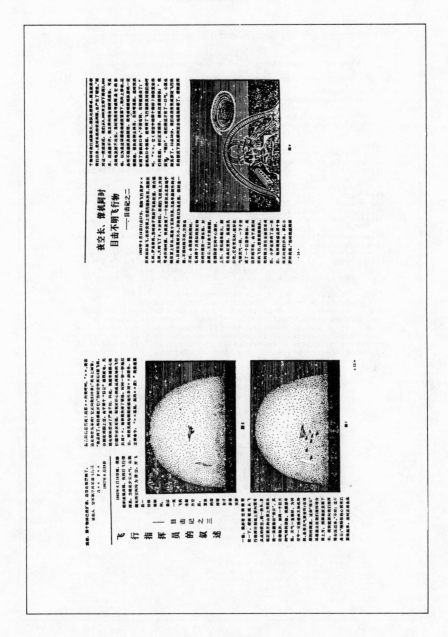

Report of sighting by Chinese Air Force pilots over the North China military frontier in June 1982 (*China UFO Research Organization/Journal of UFO Research*)

(English translation of UFO article written in Chinese)

People have great interest in UFO in China,20,000 people are involved in UFO research.
          --New China News Agency,Darlian,27,August 1985.

          People in China now are having great interest in UFO,the mys-tery of universe.Several dozens of Chinese scientists gathered inDarlian recently to exchange their UFO research for the first time.
          The description on the phenomenon of UFO is seen in historic-al records in China long ago. It was said that the first general-ly recognized UFO photograph in the would is taken in Tianjin, China in 1945.
          In 1981, a China society of UFO Research(CSUR)was establi-shed,with some regional sub-societies,in an attempt to uncover the mystery of UFO.CSUR has more than 2,000 menbers,with the regional societies,all menbers totalling some 20,000. It has tow publications,named "Exploration of UFO"and "Space exploration"
          Chairman of the CSUR,Professor Liang Renglin of Guangzhou Jinan University says that more than 600 UFO phenomena have been observed during the past 5 years in China.
          During the conference in Darlian,some 40 papeers on UFO were provided,17 out of these papers were selected to be publi-shed in collected works. Contents of the works will be:
          --Viewpoits and methods of the Chiness people to study UFO.
          --UFO phenomena found in China.
          --Theoretical works on UFO phenomena
          --Relation between UFO and human body science.
UFO is an undiscovered mystery with profound influence in the world. Some people believe its existence,while the opponents think it's a matter of fiction or illusion.Both views are taken into serious consideration in the world.Various kinds of orga-nizations have been established in the world,including USA,USSR, UK,Japan,and Central and South American Nations to try to unveal the UFO mystery.

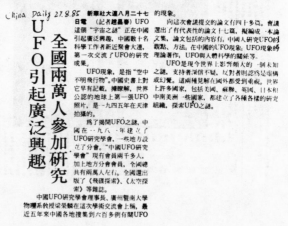

Article (and translation) from *China Daily* sent to the author by the Chinese Embassy in London

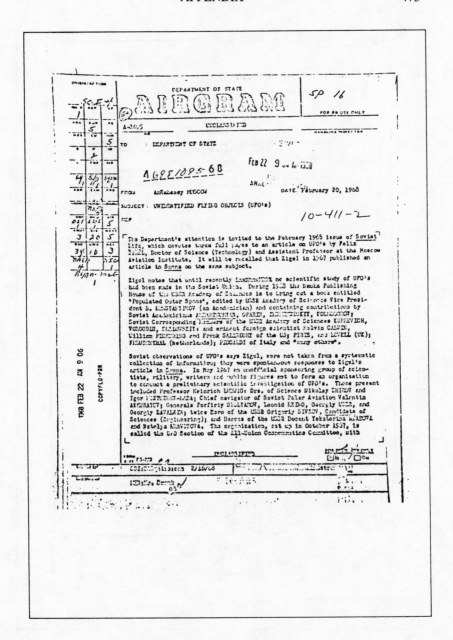

US Department of State airgram relating to UFO research in the USSR,
1967–68

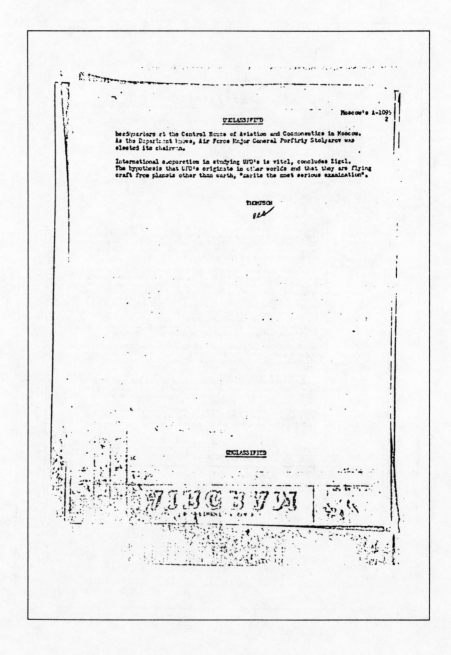

UNCLASSIFIED   Moscow's A-1095
                                                        2

headquarters at the Central House of Aviation and Cosmonautics in Moscow.
As the Department knows, Air Force Major General Porfiriy Stolyarov was
elected its chairman.

International cooperation in studying UFO's is vital, concludes Ziget.
The hypothesis that UFO's originate in other worlds and that they are flying
craft from planets other than earth, "merits the most serious examination".

                        THOMPSON

UNCLASSIFIED

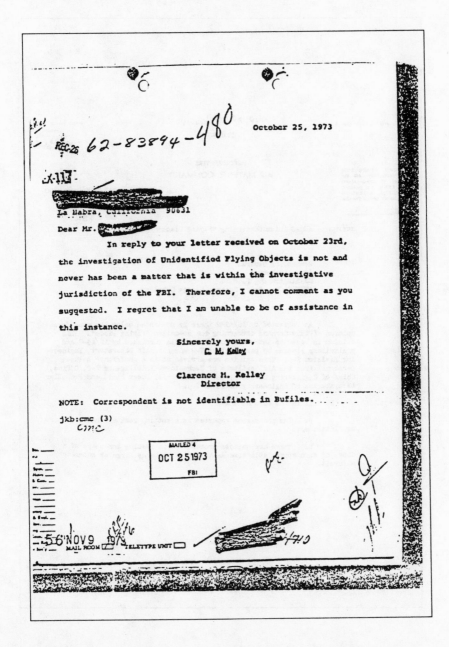

October 25, 1973

REC-26 62-83894-480

X-117

La Habra, California 90631

Dear Mr.

In reply to your letter received on October 23rd, the investigation of Unidentified Flying Objects is not and never has been a matter that is within the investigative jurisdiction of the FBI. Therefore, I cannot comment as you suggested. I regret that I am unable to be of assistance in this instance.

Sincerely yours,
C. M. Kelley

Clarence M. Kelley
Director

NOTE: Correspondent is not identifiable in Bufiles.

jkb:cmc (3)
cmc

MAILED 4
OCT 25 1973
FBI

56 NOV 9 1973
MAIL ROOM ☐   TELETYPE UNIT ☐

Letter from the FBI Director denying the Bureau's involvement in the investigation of UFOs. In 1976 the FBI released 1,100 pages of UFO-related documentation.

Mare'E Form No. 10-514 (Rev 10 Sep 46)   CAS NND 76 0168 5-4-78   WF-L7 JAN 47 20000

SECRET

SAVE

IN REPLY ADDRESS BOTH
COMMUNICATION AND EN-
VELOPS TO COMMANDING
GENERAL, AIR MATERIEL
COMMAND, ATTENTION
FOLLOWING OFFICE SYMBOL:

TSDIN

HEADQUARTERS
AIR MATERIEL COMMAND

TSDIN/HMM/ig/6-4100
WRIGHT FIELD, DAYTON, OHIO

SEP 2 3 1947

SUBJECT: AMC Opinion Concerning "Flying Discs"

TO: Commanding General
       Army Air Forces
       Washington 25, D. C.
       ATTENTION: Brig. General George Schulgen
                   AC/AS-2

    1.   As requested by AC/AS-2 there is presented below the considered
opinion of this Command concerning the so-called "Flying Discs". This
opinion is based on interrogation report data furnished by AC/AS-2 and
preliminary studies by personnel of T-2 and Aircraft Laboratory, Engineering Division T-3. This opinion was arrived at in a conference between
personnel from the Air Institute of Technology, Intelligence T-2, Office,
Chief of Engineering Division, and the Aircraft, Power Plant and Propeller
Laboratories of Engineering Division T-3.

    2.   It is the opinion that:

        a.   The phenomenon reported is something real and not visionary
or fictitious.

        b.   There are objects probably approximating the shape of a
disc, of such appreciable size as to appear to be as large as man-made
aircraft.

The Air Matériel Command report of September 1947 confirming UFO
reality, signed by General Nathan Twining, who had just been assigned
to the Majestic 12 group

    c. There is a possibility that some of the incidents may be caused by natural phenomena, such as meteors.

    d. The reported operating characteristics such as extreme rates of climb, maneuverability (particularly in roll), and action which must be considered evasive when sighted or contacted by friendly aircraft and radar, lend belief to the possibility that some of the objects are controlled either manually, automatically or remotely.

    e. The apparent common description of the objects is as follows:-

    (1) Metallic or light reflecting surface.

SECRET   U-39552

SECRET

Basic Ltr fr CG, AMC, WF to CG, AAF, Wash. D. C. subj "AMC Opinion Concerning "Flying Discs".

    (2) Absence of trail, except in a few instances when the object apparently was operating under high performance conditions.

    (3) Circular or elliptical in shape, flat on bottom and domed on top.

    (4) Several reports of well kept formation flights varying from three to nine objects.

    (5) Normally no associated sound, except in three instances a substantial rumbling roar was noted.

    (6) Level flight speeds normally above 300 knots are estimated.

    f. It is possible within the present U. S. knowledge — provided extensive detailed development is undertaken — to construct a piloted aircraft which has the general description of the object in subparagraph (e) above which would be capable of an approximate range of 7000 miles at subsonic speeds.

    g. Any developments in this country along the lines indicated would be extremely expensive, time consuming and at the considerable expense of current projects and therefore, if directed, should be set up independently of existing projects.

    h. Due consideration must be given the following:-

    (1) The possibility that these objects are of domestic origin - the product of some high security project not known to AC/AS-2 or this Command.

    (2) The lack of physical evidence in the shape of crash recovered exhibits which would undeniably prove the existence of these objects.

As a member of Majestic-12, Twining was well aware that physical evidence *had* actually been recovered, but was obliged to cover up the fact.

> (3) The possibility that some foreign nation has a form
> of propulsion possibly nuclear, which is outside of
> our domestic knowledge.

3.   It is recommended that:

a.   Headquarters, Army Air Forces issue a directive assigning
a priority, security classification and Code Name for a detailed study of
this matter to include the preparation of complete sets of all available
and partinent data which will then be made available to the Army, Navy,
Atomic Energy Commission, JRDB, the Air Force Scientific Advisory Group,
NACA, and the RAND and NEPA projects for comments and recommendations,
with a preliminary report to be forwarded within 15 days of receipt of
the data and a detailed report thereafter every 30 days as the investi-

                         S——
                        -2-   U-39552
                       SECRET

Basic Ltr fr CG, AMC, WF to CG, AAF, Wash. D.C. subj "AMC Opinion Concerning "Flying Discs"

gation develops. A complete interchange of data should be effected.

4.   Awaiting a specific directive AMC will continue the investigation within its current resources in order to more closely define the
nature of the phenomenon. Detailed Essential Elements of Information
will be formulated immediately for transmittal thru channels.

                              N. F. Twining
                              N. F. TWINING
                              Lieutenant General, U.S.A.
                              Commanding

                       SECRET
                        -3-   U-39552

                              AAG 000 GENERAL "C"

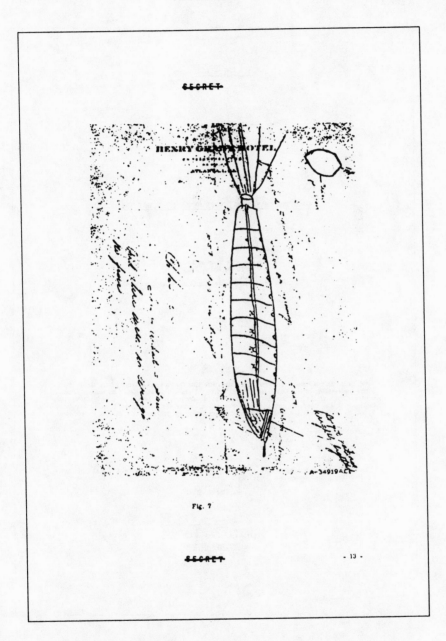

Drawing by Captain Chiles of the object which nearly collided with his airliner over Alabama in July 1948, as included in a Top Secret Air Intelligence report, part of which follows

Air Intelligence Report No. 100-203-79

ANALYSIS OF FLYING OBJECT INCIDENTS IN THE U. S.

Air Intelligence Division Study No. 203
10 December 1948.

Directorate of Intelligence and Office of Naval Intelligence

DISTRIBUTION "C"

WARNING: This document contains information affecting the national defense of the United States within the meaning of the Espionage Act, 50 U.S.C., 31 and 32, as amended. Its transmission or the revelation of its contents in any manner to an unauthorized person is prohibited by law. Reproduction of the intelligence in this publication, under the provisions of Army Regulation 380-5, is authorized for United States military agencies provided the source is indicated.

Directorate of Intelligence   Office of Naval Intelligence
Headquarters United States Air Force   Navy Department

Washington, D. C.

DECLASSIFIED
Authority AF INA MURC 5781 85
By CR.T. NARS Date 3/2/54

k. On 7 January 1948, a National Guard pilot was killed while attempting to chase an unidentified object up to 30,000 feet. While it is presumed that this pilot suffered anoxia, resulting in his crash, his last message to the tower was, "it appears to be metallic object....of tremendous size....directly ahead and slightly above....I am trying to close for a better look."

l. On 5 April 1948, three trained balloon observers from the Geophysics Laboratory Section, Watson Laboratories, N.J. reported seeing a round, indistinct object in the vicinity of Hollman Air Force Base, New Mexico. It was very high and fast, and appeared to execute violent maneuvers at high speed. The object was under observation for approximately 30 seconds and disappeared suddenly.

m. A yellow or light colored sphere, 25 to 40 feet in diameter was reported by Lt. Comdr. Marcus L. Lowe, USN, just south of Anacostia Naval Air Station, D.C., while he was flying on 30 April 1948. It was moving at a speed of approximately 100 miles per hour at an altitude of about 4,500 feet. Although winds aloft were from the north-northwest, its course was to the north.

n. On 1 July 1948, twelve disks were reported over the Rapid City Air Base by Major Hammer. These disks were oval-shaped, about 100 feet long, flying at a speed estimated to be in excess of 500 mph. Descending from 10,000 feet, these disks made a 30-degree to 40-degree climbing turn accelerating very rapidly until out of sight.

o. On 17 July 1948, a report from Kirtland Air Force Base describes a sighting in the vicinity of San Acacia, New Mexico, of seven unidentified objects flying in a "J" formation at an estimated height of 20,000 feet above the terrain. The formation varied from "J" to "L" to circle after passing the zenith. Flashes from the objects were observed after passing 30 degrees beyond the zenith but there was no smoke or vapor trail. If the reported altitude is correct the speed was estimated at 1,500 miles per hour, according to the report.

p. Other sightings of lights and trails, rather than disks, have been reported, viz:

(1) On 12 September 1947, the pilot and co-pilot of a Pan American aircraft, en route from Midway to Honolulu, saw a blue-white light approaching, changing to twin reddish glows upon withdrawal. The pilot estimated the speed of the light at about 1,000 knots.

(2) On 15 June 1948, Mr. Booneville, territory manager for the B.F. Goodrich Company, observed a reddish glow with a jet exhaust in the vicinity of Miles City, Montana. This glowing light made no sound, traveled about twice the speed of a conventional aircraft and flew from noth to south several times in a wide arc, finally disappearing over the horizon.

q. During the early morning of 25 July 1948, two Eastern Airlines pilots reported having seen a huge flying craft similar to a V-2 pass their aircraft in flight. (See Figs. 7 and 8.) The attached drawings made by these two observers very closely resemble a flying object reported to have been seen on 20 July 1948, by A. D. Otter, chief investigator of Court of Damage Inquiry, and his daughter at Arnham, Netherlands. This object appeared to be a wingless aircraft having two decks. The craft, sighted four times through scattered clouds and unlimited visibility, was traveling at high speed at a high altitude. A sound similar to that made by a V-2 was reported.

r. An object, similar in shape to the one in the preceding incident was reported by an experienced American newspaper reporter about 25 kilometers northeast of Moscow on 3 August 1948. A Russian acquaintance identified it as a rigid airship but the reporter disagrees because it flew at a high, but not excessive speed.

s. On 1 October 1948 at approximately 2030 hours the pilot of a F-51 aircraft, 2nd Lt. George F. Gorman (North Dakota Air National Guard), flying near Fargo, North Dakota, sighted an intermittent white light about 3,000 feet below his 4,500 feet cruising altitude. The pilot pursued the light which appeared to then take evasive tactics. The object or light out-turned, out-speeded, and out-climbed the F-51 in every instance during the attempt to intercept. The pilot lost contact 27

A page from the Air Intelligence Report. Note the official confirmation for the last message of Captain Mantell (top of page).

HEADQUARTERS FOURTH ARMY
Fort Sam Houston, Texas

452.1 AKADB   13 January 1949   /dob

SUBJECT: Unconventional Aircraft (Control No. A-1917).

TO   : Director of Intelligence, GSUSA
        Washington 25, D. C.

    1. The inclosed Summary of Information, subject, "Unconventional
Aircraft (Control No. A-1917," dated 13 Jan 49, is forwarded for your
information and any action deemed necessary.

    2. Agencies in New Mexico are greatly concerned over these phe-
nomena. They are of the opinion that some foreign power is making
"sensing shots" with some super-stratosphere devise designed to be self-
disintegrating. They also believe that when the devise is perfected
for accuracy, the disintegrating factor will be eliminated in favor of
a warhead.

    3. Another theory advanced as possibly acceptable lies in the
belief that the phenomena are the result of radiological warfare
experiments by a foreign power, further, that the rays may be lethal
or might be attributed to the cause of some of the plane crashes that
have occurred recently.

    4. Still another belief that is advanced is that, it is highly
probable that the United States may be carrying on some top-secret
experiments.

    5. It is felt that these incidents are of such great importance,
especially as they are occurring in the vicinity of sensitive installations,
that a scientific board be sent to this locality to study the situation
with a view of arriving at a solution of this extraordinary phenomena with
the least practicable delay.

    6. It is further requested that this headquarters be informed of
action taken on this and a previous report in order that reporting
agencies may be advised.

        FOR THE COMMANDING GENERAL:

1 incl: EUSTIS L. POLAND
 as stated   Colonel, GSC
                                         AC of S, G-2

US Army Intelligence report, January 1949

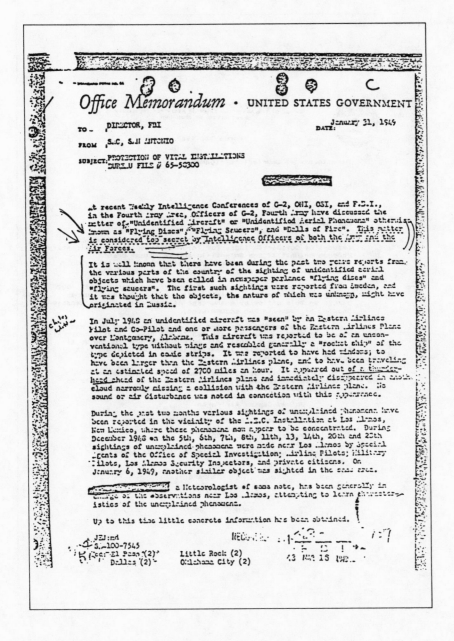

Office Memorandum · UNITED STATES GOVERNMENT

TO - DIRECTOR, FBI   DATE: January 31, 1949

FROM - S.C, S.H LUTCHIO

SUBJECT: PROTECTION OF VITAL INSTALLATIONS
BUREAU FILE # 65-58300

At recent Weekly Intelligence Conferences of G-2, ONI, OSI, and F.B.I., in the Fourth Army Area, Officers of G-2, Fourth Army have discussed the matter of "Unidentified Aircraft" or "Unidentified Aerial Phenomena" otherwise known as "Flying Discs", "Flying Saucers", and "Balls of Fire". This matter is considered top secret by Intelligence Officers of both the Army and the Air Forces.

It is well known that there have been during the past two years reports from the various parts of the country of the sighting of unidentified aerial objects which have been called in newspaper parlance "flying discs" and "flying saucers". The first such sightings were reported from Sweden, and it was thought that the objects, the nature of which was unknown, might have originated in Russia.

In July 1948 an unidentified aircraft was "seen" by an Eastern Airlines Pilot and Co-Pilot and one or more passengers of the Eastern Airlines Plane over Montgomery, Alabama. This aircraft was reported to be of an unconventional type without wings and resembled generally a "rocket ship" of the type depicted in comic strips. It was reported to have had windows; to have been larger than the Eastern Airlines plane, and to have been traveling at an estimated speed of 2700 miles an hour. It appeared out of a thunderhead ahead of the Eastern Airlines plane and immediately disappeared in another cloud narrowly missing a collision with the Eastern Airlines plane. No sound or air disturbance was noted in connection with this appearance.

During the past two months various sightings of unexplained phenomena have been reported in the vicinity of the A.E.C. Installation at Los Alamos, New Mexico, where these phenomena now appear to be concentrated. During December 1948 on the 5th, 6th, 7th, 8th, 11th, 13, 14th, 20th and 25th sightings of unexplained phenomena were made near Los Alamos by Special Agents of the Office of Special Investigation; Airline Pilots; Military Pilots, Los Alamos Security Inspectors, and private citizens. On January 6, 1949, another similar object was sighted in the same area.

~~▬▬▬▬▬▬~~ a Meteorologist of some note, has been generally in charge of the observations near Los Alamos, attempting to learn characteristics of the unexplained phenomena.

Up to this time little concrete information has been obtained.

JEJ:md
S. 100-7545
Reg: El Paso (2)   Little Rock (2)
Dallas (2)   Oklahoma City (2)   43 MAY 15 1949

DEPARTMENT OF THE ARMY
OFFICE OF THE ASSISTANT CHIEF OF STAFF FOR INTELLIGENCE
WASHINGTON, DC 20310-1001

REPLY TO
ATTENTION OF

March 12, 1987

Directorate of Counterintelligence

Mr. Timothy Good

Dear Mr. Good:

This is in response to your Freedom of Information Act request of October 7, 1986, for information on the Interplanetary Phenomenon Unit of the Scientific and Technical Branch, Counterintelligence Directorate, Department of the Army. Your request was received in this office on 15 October 1986.

Please excuse the delay in responding to your request, but due to an extraordinary administrative and operational burden placed on this office by a shortage of personnel, a considerable backlog of requests has accumulated.

Please be advised that the aforementioned Army unit was disestablished during the late 1950's and never reactivated. All records pertaining to this unit were turned over to the US Air Force, Office of Special Investigations in conjunction with operation "BLUEBOOK."

Therefore, we suggest that you initiate a Freedom of Information Act request with the Air Force for the answers to your questions. You should address your request to:

    United States Air Force
    HQ AFOSI/DADF
    Attention: Freedom of Information
    Bolling Air Force Base
    Washington, D.C. 20332

Again my apologies for taking so long to answer your request.

                            Sincerely,

US Army Intelligence letter confirming the existence of the Interplanetary Phenomenon Unit, alleged to have been involved in UFO recovery operations

(CONFIDENTIAL (

MEMORANDUM FOR RECORD:

SUBJECT: Flying Discs   G-3

The following information was furnished Major Carlan by
Lt Colonel Mildren on 4 August 1950:

Since 30 July 1950 objects, round in form, have been
sighted over the Hanford AEC Plant. These objects reportedly were above 15,000 feet in altitude. Air Force
jets attempted interception with negative results. All
units including the anti-aircraft battalion, radar units,
Air Force fighter squadrons, and the Federal Bureau of
Investigation have been alerted for further observation.
The Atomic Energy Commission states that the investigation is continuing and complete details will be forwarded
later.

U. G. C.

U. G. CARLAN
Major, GSC
Survey Section

DECLASSIFIED
5-79-10
By ___ NARS. Date 4/19/79

PERMANENT RECORD UNIT

CONFIDENTIAL

US Army Intelligence report, 1950

CONFIDENTIAL

FLEET LOGISTIC AIR WING, ATLANTIC/CONTINENTAL
AIR TRANSPORT SQUADRON ONE
U. S. NAVAL AIR STATION
PATUXENT RIVER, MARYLAND

10 February 1951

C O N F I D E N T I A L

MEMORANDUM REPORT to Commanding Officer, Air Transport Squadron ONE

Subj: Report of Unusual Sighting on Flight 125/9 February 1951

I, Graham E. BETHUNE, was Co-Pilot on Flight 125 from Keflavik, Iceland
to Naval Air Station, Argentia on the 10th of February 1951. At 0055Z I
signed and observed the following object:

                 While flying in the left seat at 10,000 feet on a true course
of 230 degrees at a position of 49-50 North 50-03 West, I observed a glow of
light below the horizon about 1,000 to 1,500 feet above the water. Its
bearing was about 2 O'Clock. There was no overcast, there was a thin transparent group of scuds at about 2,000 feet altitude. After examing KINGDON
the object for 40 to 50 seconds I called it to the attention of Lieutenant
KINGDON in the right hand seat. It was under the thin scuds at roughly 30
to 40 miles away. I asked "What is it, a ship lighted up or a city, I know
it can't be a city because we are over 250 miles out." We both observed its
course and motion for about 4 or 5 minutes before calling it to the attention
of the othercrew members. Its first glow was a dull yellow. We were on an
intercepting course. Suddenly its angle of attack changed, its altitude and
size increased as though its speed was in excess of 1,000 miles per hour. It
closed in so fast that the first feeling was we would collide in mid air. At
this time its angle changed and the color changed. It then definitely circular
and redish orange on its primiter It reversed its course and tripled its speed
until it was last seen disappearing over the horizon. Because of our altitude
and misleading distance over water it is almost impossible to estimate its
size, distance and speed. A rough estimate would be at least 300 feet in diameter,
over 1,000 miles per hour in speed and approached within 5 miles of the aircraft.

                          /s/Graham E. BETHUNE
                          Lt, U.S. Naval Reserve

                                                    ENCLOSURE (4)

US Navy Intelligence report, 1951

AF FORM 112—PART I
APPROVED

COUNTRY
U.S.A.   TR-1-51E
                    AIR INTELLIGENCE INFORMATION REPORT

SUBJECT
UNIDENTIFIED FLYING OBJECT
AREA ACCOUNTED ON   FROM (Agency)
    USA   HQ EADF
DATE OF REPORT   DATE OF INFORMATION   EVALUATION
21 SEPTEMBER 1951   10 SEPTEMBER 1951   -6
PREPARED BY (Officer)   SOURCE
    LT. COL. BRUCE K. BAUMGARDNER   EADF   870904
REFERENCES (Control number, directive, previous report, etc., as applicable)

SUMMARY.

On 10 September, Major Ballard and Lt. Rogers were participating in a
training flight from Dover AFB, Delaware to Mitchel AFB, New York (Direct),
when they spotted an unidentified object over Sandy Hook, New Jersey.

The time was 1135 EDT, and the weather was CAVU. When spotted, the object
was at an estimated altitude of 8,000 feet. Flying at 20,000 feet, the pilot
immediately made a diving turn in his T-33 and followed and timed the object
until it disappeared two minutes later.

Both pilots observed the strange object, which appeared to be the size of
an F-86 but much faster (900 + mph), disc-shaped, steady in flight with no
visible means of propulsion, and shiny silver in color.

At 1110 EDT a radar station at Ft. Monmouth plotted an unidentified, high
speed (above 700 mph) object in approximately the same location.

This headquarters has no information regarding natural phenomena, experimental aircraft or guided missiles that could have caused the observations.

Request USAF evaluation of incident be furnished this headquarters.

                                        BRUCE K. BAUMGARDNER
                                        Lt. Colonel, USAF
                                        Director of Intelligence

INCLS.
1. Rpt. - 1st Lt. W.S. Rogers
2. Rpt. - Maj. E. Ballard
3. Map
4. Rpt. - Ft. Monmouth

DISTRIBUTION BY ORIGINATOR
2 cy - CO ADC, Ent AFB, Colorado Springs, Colo.
1 cy - CO AMC, Wright-Patterson AFB, Dayton, Ohio, ATTN: MCIS

USAF Intelligence report, 1951

```
SID A16G                    DEPARTMENT OF THE AIR FORCE
                              STAFF MESSAGE DIVISION
HQC168S
                            INCOMING UNCLASSIFIED MESSAGE
        TMB13S                                      REC. STF. MSG. V.
YTA209                                          JUN 26  15 4 2 '53
VEDLS4D023                                           HQ. USAF
EFD002
EMERGENCY JEDUP JEDEN JEPFF JEPHQ JEPRS 555
DE JEDLS 3B
O 261445Z
FM COMDR OLMSTED FLTSV MIDDLETOWN PENN
TO JEPHQ/DIR OF INTEL HQ USAF WASHDC
JEDUP/AIR TECHINTELCEN WRIGHT-PATTERSON AFB OHIO
JEDEN/COMDR ADC ENT AFB COLO
JEPFF/COMDR MATS WASHDC
JEPRS/COMDR HQ FLTSV WASHDC
ATTN ATIAA 2C FLYOBRT SUPPLEMENTAL INFO REF FLYOBRT 24 JUNE
53 PD FLYING OBJECTS WERE SIGHTED BY PILOTS AT APPROX 2130E 24
JUNE PD TWO JET OUT OF QUONSET POINT MAS HAS A MID AIR COLLISION AT
2130E 24 JUN 53 AIRCRAFT FELL IN FLAMES 15 MILES WEST OF QUONSET
POINT MAS PD AMERICAN AND EASTERN AIRLINES PILOTS WHO REPORTED FLYG
OBJECT WILL SUBMITT ON SIGHTING TO DIR INTELLIGENCE HQ USAF AND AIR
TECH INTELLIGENCE CENTER WRIGHT PATTERSON AFB
25 1450Z JUN JEDLS

   ACTION:  OIN

   INFO :  OOP, OOP-CP, OAC, ARMY , NAVY, JCS, CIA, NSA

   AF IN :  11479    (26 Jun 53)                    CWS/feh


HQ FORM 0-309d
JAN 51
PREVIOUS EDITIONS OF THIS FORM MAY BE USED          19-69780-1   U.S. GOVERNMENT PRINTING OFFICE
```

USAF Intelligence report, 1953. Note that the distribution list includes
the National Security Agency, established in 1952.

*AFR 200—2
1—5

AIR FORCE REGULATION }
NO. 200—2 }

DEPARTMENT OF THE AIR FORCE
WASHINGTON, 12 AUGUST 1954

INTELLIGENCE

Unidentified Flying Objects Reporting (Short Title: UFOB)

1. Purpose and Scope. This Regulation establishes procedures for reporting information and evidence pertaining to unidentified flying objects and sets forth the responsibility of Air Force activities in this regard. It applies to all Air Force activities.

2. Definitions:

a. *Unidentified Flying Objects (UFOB)*— Relates to any airborne object which by performance, aerodynamic characteristics, or unusual features does not conform to any presently known aircraft or missile type, or which cannot be positively identified as a familiar object.

b. *Familiar Objects*—Include balloons, astronomical bodies, birds, and so forth.

3. Objectives. Air Force interest in unidentified flying objects is twofold: First as a possible threat to the security of the United States and its forces, and secondly, to determine technical aspects involved.

a. *Air Defense.* To date, the flying objects reported have imposed no threat to the security of the United States and its Possessions. However, the possibility that new air vehicles, hostile aircraft or missiles may first be regarded as flying objects by the initial observer is real. This requires that sightings be reported rapidly and as completely as information permits.

b. *Technical.* Analysis thus far has failed to provide a satisfactory explanation for a number of sightings reported. The Air Force will continue to collect and analyze reports until all sightings can be satisfactorily explained, bearing in mind that:

(1) To measure scientific advances, the Air Force must be informed on experimentation and development of new air vehicles.

(2) The possibility exists that an air vehicle of revolutionary configuration may be developed.

(3) The reporting of all pertinent factors will have a direct bearing on the success of the technical analysis.

4. Responsibility:

a. *Reporting.* Commanders of Air Force activities will report all information and evidence that may come to their attention, including that received from adjacent commands of the other services and from civilians.

b. *Investigation.* Air Defense Command will conduct all field investigations within the ZI, to determine the identity of any UFOB.

c. *Analysis.* The Air Technical Intelligence Center (ATIC), Wright-Patterson Air Force Base, Ohio, will analyze and evaluate: All information and evidence reported within the ZI after the Air Defense Command has exhausted all efforts to identify the UFOB; and all information and evidence collected in overseas areas.

d. *Cooperation.* All activities will cooperate with Air Defense Command representatives to insure the economical and prompt success of an investigation, including the furnishing of air and ground transportation, when feasible.

5. Guidance. The thoroughness and quality of a report or investigation into incidents of unidentified flying objects are limited only by the resourcefulness and imagination of the person responsible for preparing the report. Guidance set forth below is based on experience and has been found helpful in evaluating incidents:

a. Theodolite measurements of changes of azimuth and elevation and angular size.

b. Interception, identification, or air search

*This Regulation supersedes AFR 200—2, 26 August 1953, including Change 200—2A, 2 November 1953.

action. These actions may be taken if appropriate and within the scope of existing air defense regulations.

c. Contact with local aircraft control and warning (AC&W) units, ground observation corps (GOC) posts and filter centers, pilots and crews of aircraft aloft at the time and place of sighting whenever feasible, and any other persons or organizations which may have factual data bearing on the UFOB or may be able to offer corroborating evidence, electronic or otherwise.

d. Consultation with military or civilian weather forecasters to obtain data on: Tracks of weather balloons released in the area, since these often are responsible for sightings; and any unusual meteorological activity which may have a bearing on the UFOB.

e. Consultation with astronomers in the area to determine whether any astronomical body or phenomenon would account for or have a bearing on the observation.

f. Contact with military and civilian tower operators, air operations offices, and so forth, to determine whether the sighting could be the result of misidentification of known aircraft.

g. Contact with persons who might have knowledge of experimental aircraft of unusual configuration, rocket and guided missile firings, and so forth, in the area.

6. ZI Collection. The Air Defense Command has a direct interest in the facts pertaining to UFOB's reported within the ZI and has, in the 4602d Air Intelligence Service Squadron (AISS), the capability to investigate these reports. The 4602d AISS is composed of specialists trained for field collection and investigation of matters of air intelligence interest which occur within the ZI. This squadron is highly mobile and deployed throughout the ZI as follows: Flights are attached to air defense divisions, detachments are attached to each of the defense forces, and the squadron headquarters is located at Peterson Field, Colorado, adjacent to Headquarters, Air Defense Command. Air Force activities, therefore, should establish and maintain liaison with the nearest element of this squadron. This can be accomplished by contacting the appropriate echelon of the Air Defense Command as outlined above.

a. All Air Force activities are authorized to conduct such preliminary investigation as may be required for reporting purposes; however, investigations should not be carried beyond this point, unless such action is requested by the 4602d AISS.

b. On occasions—after initial reports are submitted—additional data is required which can be developed more economically by the nearest Air Force activity, such as: narrative statements, sketches, marked maps, charts, and so forth. Under such circumstances, appropriate commanders will be contacted by the 4602d AISS.

c. Direct communication between echelons of the 4602d AISS and Air Force activities is authorized.

7. Reporting. All information relating to UFOB's will be reported promptly. The method (electrical or written) and priority of dispatch will be selected in accordance with the apparent intelligence value of the information. In most instances, reports will be made by electrical means: Information over 24 hours old will be given a "deferred" precedence. Reports over 3 days old will be made by written report prepared on AF Form 112, Air Intelligence Information Report, and AF Form 112a, Supplement to AF Form 112.

a. *Addressees:*

(1) *Electrical Reports.* All electrical reports will be multiple addressed to:

(a) Commander, Air Defense Command, Ent Air Force Base, Colorado Springs, Colorado.

(b) Nearest Air Division (Defense). (For ZI only.)

(c) Commander, Air Technical Intelligence Center, Wright-Patterson Air Force Base, Ohio.

(d) Director of Intelligence, Headquarters USAF, Washington 25, D. C.

(2) *Written Reports:*

(a) Within the ZI, reports will be submitted direct to the Air Defense Command. Air Defense Command will reproduce the report and distribute it to interested ZI intelligence agencies. The original report together with notation of the distribution effected then will be forwarded to the Director of Intelligence, Headquarters USAF, Washington 25, D. C.

(b) Outside the ZI, reports will be submitted direct to Director of Intelligence, Headquarters USAF, Washington 25, D. C. as prescribed in "Intelligence Collection Instructions" (ICI), June 1954.

b. *Short Title.* "UFOB" will appear at the beginning of the text of electrical messages and in the subject of written reports.

c. *Negative Data.* The word "negative"

2

in reply to any numbered item of the report format will indicate that all logical leads were developed without success. The phrase "not applicable" (N/A) will indicate that the question does not apply to the sighting being investigated.

d. *Report Format.* Reports will include the following numbered items:

(1) Description of the object(s):

(a) Shape.

(b) Size compared to a known object (use one of the following terms: Head of a pin, pea, dime, nickel, quarter, half dollar, silver dollar, baseball, grapefruit, or basketball) held in the hand at about arms length.

(c) Color.

(d) Number.

(e) Formation, if more than one.

(f) Any discernible features or details.

(g) Tail, trail, or exhaust, including size of same compared to size of object(s).

(h) Sound. If heard, describe sound.

(i) Other pertinent or unusual features.

(2) Description of course of object(s):

(a) What first called the attention of observer(s) to the object(s)?

(b) Angle of elevation and azimuth of the object(s) when first observed.

(c) Angle of elevation and azimuth of object(s) upon disappearance.

(d) Description of flight path and maneuvers of object(s).

(e) Manner of disappearance of object(s).

(f) Length of time in sight.

(3) Manner of observation:

(a) Use one or any combination of the following items: Ground-visual, ground-electronic, air-electronic. (If electronic, specify type of radar.)

(b) Statement as to optical aids (telescopes, binoculars, and so forth) used and description thereof.

(c) If the sighting is made while airborne, give type aircraft, identification number, altitude, heading, speed, and home station.

(4) Time and date of sighting:

(a) Zulu time-date group of sighting.

(b) Light conditions (use one of the following terms): Night, day, dawn, dusk.

(5) Locations of observer(s). Exact latitude and longitude of each observer, or Georef position, or position with reference to a known landmark.

(6) Identifying information of all observer(s):

(a) Civilian—Name, age, mailing address, occupation.

(b) Military—Name, grade, organisation, duty, and estimate of reliability.

(7) Weather and winds-aloft conditions at time and place of sightings:

(a) Observer(s) account of weather conditions.

(b) Report from nearest AWS or U. S. Weather Bureau Office of wind direction and velocity in degrees and knots at surface, 6,000', 10,000', 16,000', 20,000', 30,000', 50,000', and 80,000', if available.

(c) Ceiling.

(d) Visibility.

(e) Amount of cloud cover.

(f) Thunderstorms in area and quadrant in which located.

(8) Any other unusual activity or condition, meteorological, astronomical, or otherwise, which might account for the sighting.

(9) Interception or identification action taken (such action may be taken whenever feasible, complying with existing air defense directives).

(10) Location of any air traffic in the area at time of sighting.

(11) Position title and comments of the preparing officer, including his preliminary analysis of the possible cause of the sighting(s).

(12) Existence of physical evidence, such as materials and photographs.

e. *Security.* Reports should be unclassified unless inclusion of data required by d above necessitates a higher classification.

8. Evidence. The existence of physical evidence (photographs or materiel) will be promptly reported.

a. *Photographic:*

(1) *Visual.* The negative and two prints will be forwarded, all original film, including wherever possible both prints and negatives, will be titled or otherwise properly identified as to place, time, and date of the incident

3

AFR 200-2
8-9

(see "Intelligence Collection Instructions" (ICI), June 1954).

(2) *Radar.* Two copies of each print will be forwarded. Prints of radarscope photography will be titled in accordance with AFR 95-7 and forwarded in compliance with AFR 95-6.

b. *Materiel.* Suspected or actual items of materiel which come into possession of any Air Force echelon will be safeguarded in such manner as to prevent any defacing or alteration which might reduce its value for intelligence examination and analysis. .

9. Release of Facts. Headquarters USAF will release summaries of evaluated data which will inform the public on this subject. In response to local inquiries, it is permissible to inform news media representatives on UFOB's when the object is positively identified as a familiar object (see paragraph 2b), except that the following type of data warrants protection and should not be revealed: Names of principles, intercept and investigation procedures, and classified radar data. For those objects which are not explainable, only the fact that ATIC will analyse the data is worthly of release, due to the many unknowns involved.

BY ORDER OF THE SECRETARY OF THE AIR FORCE:

OFFICIAL:

K. E. THIEBAUD
Colonel, USAF
Air Adjutant General

DISTRIBUTON:
S; X:
  ONI, Department of the Navy 200
  G-2, Department of the Army 10

N. F. TWINING
Chief of Staff, United States Air Force

E M E R G E N C Y
12 AUGUST 1954
A64   PAGE ONE OF TWO

1251 G-2

Y 120445Z
FM CMDR FLIGHT SERV CENTER MAXWELL AFB ALA
TO CMDR ADC ENT AFB COLO SPGS COLO
SEC DEF WASHDC

/C I R V I S/

AT 120154Z TOWER OBSERVED AND REPORTED TO BASE OPERATIONS STRANGE
STATIONARY OBJECT VARIABLE IN BRILLANCE LOCATED DUE WEST OF TOWER.

AFTER INITIAL SIGHTING OF STATIONARY OBJECT IT UNEXPECTEDLY GAINED
APPARENT HIGH VELOCITY AND SPEEDED ACROSS THE SKY IN NNW HEADING

WHICH WAS FOLLOWED BY IT,S RETURN TO IT,S ORIGINAL POSITION IN
RELATION TO THE TOWER AND A NOTICABLE DESCENT AND MOTIONLESS.

TOWER IMMEDIATEDLY NOTIFIED OPERATIONS AND DISPATCHED A LOCAL
HELICOPTER NBR ARMY267 TO OBSERVE THE PHENOMENA. HELICOPTER

STATED THAT OBJECT WAS DEFINITELY NOT A STAR WAS APPROX IMATELY
20 MILES WEST AT 2000FT. HIS FUEL WOULD NOT PERMIT FURTHER

OBSERVATION. AT 0156Z AIRDROME OFFICER AND DRIVER OBSERVED MYSTERY
OBJECT. AIRDROME OFFICER PROCEED TO TOWER FOR FURTHER OBSERVATION.

AT0205Z TWO MEMBERS OF ALERT CREW OBSERVED OBJECT FROM TOWER.
COLUMBUS CAA RADIO ALSO HAS OBJECT IN SIGHT. THE OBJECT THEN BECAME

DIMMER AND SHOWING A SLIGHT RED GLOW. AT 0226Z OBJECT STILL STATIONARY
SEVERAL REACURRANCE OF VARIABLE BRILLANCY SHOWN AND NOW BECOMING

EXTREMELY DIMMER. 0227Z HELICOPTER 294 RETURNING FROM MISSION
SIGHTED OBJECT AND PROCEEDED TOWARD IT. AT0229Z OBJECT COMPLETELY

DISAPPEARED AND PILOT OF 294 LOST SIGHT OF IT. AT 0240Z ARMY
OPERATIONS CALLEED AND ADVISED THAT PILOT OF HELICOPTERS WISHED TO

STREE FACT THAT OBJECT WAS OF A SAUCER LITE NATURE, WAS STATIONARY
AND AT 2000 FT. AND WOULD BE GLAD TO BE CALLED UPON TO VERIFY ANY

DIST: 92   AF   ARMY   ACT
       002 302 05 50 ASTSECNAVAIR CG CIA DIRNSA JCS/SITROOM
           OSD   CNO/OOD
DLVY NR 127 CD/AL   BEPN BEPJC BEPS

NOTE:"THIS MSG HAS BEEN RELAYED TO CIA BY ELECTRICAL MEANS"

A 1954 USAF Intelligence report from Maxwell AFB, Alabama. The
distribution list includes the Director of the National Security Agency
(DIRNSA).

PAGE TWO OF A64

STATEMENTS AND ACT AS WITNESSES. THIS REPORT HAS BEEN TAKEN FROM
TOWER AND OPERATIONS REPORT. EYE WITNESSES WHO AGREE WITH ALL

STATEMENTS ARE AS FOLLOWS. A1C CHARLES LEWIS AF12391185 AACS
DETACHMENT 1926-E LAWSON AF, AND A/1C WILLIAM N. WATSON

AF14335250 1926-3 AACS DETACHMENT LAWSON AFB THER WERE TOWER
OPERATIORS ON DUTY.

PILOTS OF ARMY HELICOPTERS WERE, R.T. WADE WOJG W22038773 506TH
ELICOPTER COMPANY FT. GENNING GA. U.S. TARMA WOJG W2153299 506TH

HELICOPTER COMPANY FT. BENNING GA.
JACK SELLERS CAABOX 1025 COLUMBUS, GA. CAA RADIO OPERATIOR
COLUMBUS RADIO. O. A. REGISTER AF13455155 HQS. SQDN AIR BASE. GROUP
LAWSON AF BASE OPERATIONS DISPATCHER ON DUTY.

PAGE TWO OF TWO

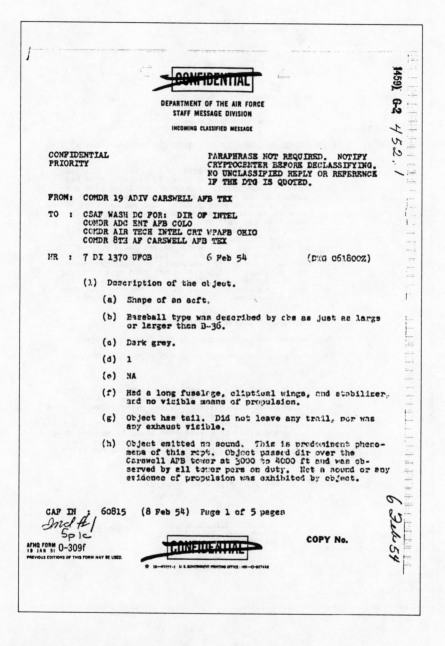

<del>CONFIDENTIAL</del>

DEPARTMENT OF THE AIR FORCE
STAFF MESSAGE DIVISION

INCOMING CLASSIFIED MESSAGE

CONFIDENTIAL   PARAPHRASE NOT REQUIRED. NOTIFY
PRIORITY   CRYPTOCENTER BEFORE DECLASSIFYING.
                               NO UNCLASSIFIED REPLY OR REFERENCE
                               IF THE DTG IS QUOTED.

FROM: COMDR 19 ADIV CARSWELL AFB TEX

TO :   CSAF WASH DC FOR: DIR OF INTEL
        COMDR ADC ENT AFB COLO
        COMDR AIR TECH INTEL CRT WPAFB OHIO
        COMDR 8TH AF CARSWELL AFB TEX

NR :   7 DI 1370 UFOB   6 Feb 54   (DTG 061800Z)

        (1) Description of the object.

             (a) Shape of an acft.

             (b) Baseball type was described by cbs as just as large
                  or larger than B-36.

             (c) Dark grey.

             (d) 1

             (e) NA

             (f) Had a long fuselage, cliptical wings, and stabilizer,
                  and no visible means of propulsion.

             (g) Object has tail. Did not leave any trail, nor was
                  any exhaust visible.

             (h) Object emitted no sound. This is predominent pheno-
                  mena of this rept. Object passed dir over the
                  Carswell AFB tower at 3000 to 4000 ft and was ob-
                  served by all tower pers on duty. Not a sound or any
                  evidence of propulsion was exhibited by object.

CAP IN : 60815   (8 Feb 54) Page 1 of 5 pages

Incl #1
Sp 1c

AFHQ FORM 0-309f
19 JAN 51
PREVIOUS EDITIONS OF THIS FORM MAY BE USED.

<del>CONFIDENTIAL</del>   COPY No.

☆ 16—61727—1 U.S. GOVERNMENT PRINTING OFFICE: 1951—O—927444

Two pages from a USAF Intelligence report describing the sighting of a
mysterious aircraft at Carswell AFB, Texas, in 1954

DEPARTMENT OF THE AIR FORCE
STAFF MESSAGE DIVISION

INCOMING CLASSIFIED MESSAGE

CONFIDENTIAL

MR :: 7 DI 1370 UFOB fr COMDR 19 ADIV CARSWELL AFB TEX (cont'd)

    (1) Object was first detected by the Carswell GCA Sta
at a distance of 13 to 15 mi fr Carswell attn was
drawn to the object because of the large rtrn presented on the scope. Object when viewed on 10 mi
scope gave a rtrn of 1 inch. Obr scanned from 10
degs to 02 degs on search and object retained the
same rtrn dur this opn. Because of the unusual
rtrn, and because object was approaching directly
over the fld the GCA opr notified the Airdrome Off
of the Day and the tower. Object had a very bright
white light in the nose and tail and two yellowish
lights on bottom of fuselage. One observer reported
that he thought object also had some type of light
on each wg tip, but other two did not substantiate
this. One observer kept object under surveillance
with binoculars. No cabin or other lights were observed.

    (2) Description of course of object.

      (a) Unusual radar rtrn recd by GCA site at Carswell.

      (b) Not aval. GCA redar could not furn this info.

      (c) 05 degrees

      (d) Object approached Carswell on a heading of 030 degs
fr the SW. Object did not change crse at anytime
while under observation. Object passed directly over
the Carswell tower and maintained heading of 030 degs
until out of sight. Object was watched for an estimat
5 minutes after it passed over tower by pers on duty.
The bright white light in the tail estimated that
object passed 5 to 6 miles NW of Meacham Fld which is
NW of the city of Fort Worth.

CAF IN : 60815   (8 Feb 54)   Page 2 of 5 pages

AFHQ FORM 0-309f
19 JAN 51
PREVIOUS EDITIONS OF THIS FORM MAY BE USED.

COPY No.

```
                              MESSAGE CENTER

     VZC2QMAY864ILN118
     MULTI                                                    12843
     ACTION
           DIAI
     DISTR
           CJCS(01) DJS(03) J3(14) J5(02) NMCC SECDEF(07) DPSECDEF
           NMIC SECDEFI ASDIISA(10) IDIA(15)
       *   SECSTATE WASH DC
       *   C I A
       *   NSA WASH DC
       *   WHITE HOUSE WASH DC
           CMC
       *   CSAF WASH DC
       *   CNO WASH DC
       *   CSA WASH DC
            FILE(1)
     (053)


     TRANSIT/230630Z/230810Z/001140TOR2670804
     DE RUDMHRA #9573 2670615
     ZNY CCCCC
     P 230630Z SEP 76
     FM USDAO TEHRAN
     TO RUEKJCS/DIA WASHDC
     INFO RUEKJCS/SECDEF DEPSECDEF WASHDC
     RUFRBAA/COMIDEASTFOR
     RUDOECA/CINCUSAFE LINDSEY AS GE/INCF
     RHFRAAB/CINCUSAFE RAMSTEIN AB GE/INOCN
     RUSNAAA/EUDAC VAIHINGEN GER
     RUSNAAA/USCINCEUR VAIHINGEN GER/ECJ=2
     BT
                              1235 SEP76
     THIS IS IR(6 846 0139 76)
     1. (U) IRAN
     2. REPORTED UFO SIGHTING (U)
     3. (U) NA
     4. (U) 19 & 20 SEP 76
     5. (U) TEHRAN, IRANI 20 SEP 76
     6. (U) F-6
     7. (U) 6 846 0008 (NOTE RO COMMENTS)
     8. (U) 6 846 0139 76
     9. (U) 22SEP 76
     10. (U) NA
     11. (U) "INITIATE" IPSP PT=1440

     PAGE  1                                        00110101  53
```

A Defense Intelligence Agency (DIA) report on the encounter by pilots
of the Imperial Iranian Air Force in 1976. Note the distribution list.

MESSAGE STATION

PAGE 2   12343
12. (U) USDAO, TEHRAN, IRAN
13. (U) FRANK B. MCKENZIE, COL, USAF, DATT
14. (U) NA
15. (C) THIS REPORT FORWARDS INFORMATION CONCERNING THE
SIGHTING OF AN UFO IN IRAN ON 19 SEPTEMBER 1976.
     A. AT ABOUT 1230 AM ON 19 SEP 76 THE IMPERIAL IRANIAN
AIR FORCE (IIAF) COMMAND POST RECEIVED FOUR TELEPHONE CALLS
FROM CITIZENS LIVING IN THE SHEMIRAN AREA OF TEHRAN SAYING
THAT THEY HAD SEEN STRANGE OBJECTS IN THE SKY. SOME REPORTED
A KIND OF BIRD-LIKE OBJECT WHILE OTHERS REPORTED A HELICOPTER
WITH A LIGHT ON. THERE WERE NO HELICOPTERS AIRBORNE AT THAT
TIME. THE COMMAND POST CALLED BG YOUSEFI, ASSISTANT DEPUTY
COMMANDER OF OPERATIONS. AFTER HE TOLD THE CITIZEN IT WAS ONLY
STARS AND HAD TALKED TO MEHRABAD TOWER HE DECIDED TO LOOK FOR
HIMSELF. HE NOTICED AN OBJECT IN THE SKY SIMILAR TO A STAR
BIGGER AND BRIGHTER. HE DECIDED TO SCRAMBLE AN F-4 FROM
SHAHROKHI AFB TO INVESTIGATE.
     B. AT 0130 HRS ON THE 19TH THE F-4 TOOK OFF AND PROCEEDED
TO A POINT ABOUT 40 NM NORTH OF TEHRAN. DUE TO ITS BRILLIANCE
THE OBJECT WAS EASILY VISIBLE FROM 70 MILES AWAY.
AS THE F-4 APPROACHED A RANGE OF 25 NM HE LOST ALL INSTRUMENTATION
AND COMMUNICATIONS (UHF AND INTERCOM). HE BROKE OFF THE
INTERCEPT AND HEADED BACK TO SHAHROKHI. WHEN THE F-4 TURNED
AWAY FROM THE OBJECT AND APPARENTLY WAS NO LONGER A THREAT
TO IT THE AIRCRAFT REGAINED ALL INSTRUMENTATION AND COM-
MUNICATIONS. AT 0140 HRS A SECOND F-4 WAS LAUNCHED. THE
BACKSEATER ACQUIRED A RADAR LOCK ON AT 27 NM, 12 O'CLOCK
HIGH POSITION WITH THE VC (RATE OF CLOSURE) AT 150 NMPH.
AS THE RANGE DECREASED TO 25 NM THE OBJECT MOVED AWAY AT A
SPEED THAT WAS VISIBLE ON THE RADAR SCOPE AND STAYED AT 25NM.
     C. THE SIZE OF THE RADAR RETURN WAS COMPARABLE TO THAT OF
A 707 TANKER. THE VISUAL SIZE OF THE OBJECT WAS DIFFICULT
TO DISCERN BECAUSE OF ITS INTENSE BRILLIANCE. THE
LIGHT THAT IT GAVE OFF WAS THAT OF FLASHING STROBE LIGHTS
ARRANGED IN A RECTANGULAR PATTERN AND ALTERNATING BLUE, GREEN,
RED AND ORANGE IN COLOR. THE SEQUENCE OF THE LIGHTS WAS SO
FAST THAT ALL THE COLORS COULD BE SEEN AT ONCE. THE OBJECT
AND THE PURSUING F-4 CONTINUED ON A COURSE TO THE SOUTH OF
TEHRAN WHEN ANOTHER BRIGHTLY LIGHTED OBJECT, ESTIMATED TO BE
ONE HALF TO ONE THIRD THE APPARENT SIZE OF THE MOON, CAME
OUT OF THE ORIGINAL OBJECT. THIS SECOND OBJECT HEADED STRAIGHT
TOWARD THE F-4 AT A VERY FAST RATE OF SPEED. THE PILOT
ATTEMPTED TO FIRE AN AIM-9 MISSILE AT THE OBJECT BUT AT THAT

PAGE 2   00110101

PAGE 3   12343
INSTANT HIS WEAPONS CONTROL PANEL WENT OFF AND HE LOST ALL
COMMUNICATIONS (UHF AND INTERPHONE), AT THIS POINT THE PILOT
INITIATED A TURN AND NEGATIVE G DIVE TO GET AWAY, AS HE
TURNED THE OBJEAZ FELL IN TRAIL AT WHAT APPEARED TO BE ABOUT
3-4 NM, AS HE CONTINUED IN HIS TURN AWAY FROM THE PRIMARY
OBJECT THE SECOND OBJECT WENT TO THE INSIDE OF HIS TURN THEN
RETURNED TO THE PRIMARY OBJECT FOR A PERFECT REJOIN.
    D, SHORTLY AFTER THE SECOND OBJECT JOINED UP WITH THE
PRIMARY OBJECT ANOTHER OBJECT APPEARED TO COME OUT OF THE
OTHER SIDE OF THE PRIMARY OBJECT GOING STRAIGHT DOWN,AT A
GREAT RATE OF SPEED, THE F-4 CREW HAD REGAINED COMMUNICATIONS
AND THE WEAPONS CONTROL PANEL AND WATCHED THE OBJECT APPROACH
THE GROUND ANTICIPATING A LARGE EXPLOSION, THIS OBJECT APPEARED
TO COME TO REST GENTLY ON THE EARTH AND CAST A VERY BRIGHT
LIGHT OVER AN AREA OF ABOUT 2-3 KILOMETERS,
THE CREW DESCENDED FROM THEIR ALTITUDE OF 26M TO 15M AND
CONTINUED TO OBSERVE AND MARK THE OBJECT'S POSITION, THEY
HAD SOME DIFFICULTY IN ADJUSTING THEIR NIGHT VISIBILITY FOR
LANDING SO AFTER ORBITING MEHRABAD A FEW TIMES THEY WENT OUT
FOR A STRAIGHT IN LANDING, THERE WAS A LOT OF INTERFERENCE
ON THE UHF AND EACH TIME THEY PASSED THROUGH A MAG, BEARING
OF 150 DEGREE FROM EHRABAD THEY LOST THEIR COMMUNICATIONS (UHF
AND INTERPHONE) AND THE INS FLUCTUATED FROM 30 DEGREES - 80 DEGREES,
THE ONE CIVIL AIRLINER THAT WAS APPROACHING MEHRABAD DURING THIS
SAME TIME EXPERIENCED COMMUNICATIONS FAILURE IN THE SAME
VICINITY (KILO ZULU) BUT DID NOT REPORT SEEING ANYTHING,
WHILE THE F-4 WAS ON A LONG FINAL APPROACH THE CREW NOTICED
ANOTHER CYLINDER SHAPED OBJECT (ABOUT THE SIZE OF A T-BIRD
AT 10M) WITH BRIGHT STEADY LIGHTS ON EACH END AND A FLASHER
IN THE MIDDLE, WHEN QUERIED THE TOWER STATED THERE WAS NO
OTHER KNOWN TRAFFIC IN THE AREA, DURING THE TIME THAT THE
OBJECT PASSED OVER THE F-4 THE TOWER DID NOT HAVE A VISUAL
ON IT BUT PICKED IT UP AFTER THE PILOT TOLD THEM TO LOOK
BETWEEN THE MOUNTAINS AND THE REFINERY,
    E, DURING DAYLIGHT THE F-4 CREW WAS TAKEN OUT TO THE
AREA IN A HELICOPTER WHERE THE OBJECT APPARENTLY HAD LANDED,
NOTHING WAS NOTICED AT THE SPOT WHERE THEY THOUGHT THE OBJECT
LANDED (A DRY LAKE BED) BUT AS THEY CIRCLED OFF TO THE
WEST OF THE AREA THEY PICKED UP A VERY NOTICEABLE BEEPER
SIGNAL, AT THE POINT WHERE THE RETURN WAS THE LOUDEST WAS
A SMALL HOUSE WITH A GARDEN, THEY LANDED AND ASKED THE PEOPLE
WITHIN IF THEY HAD NOTICED ANYTHING STRANGE LAST NIGHT, THE
PEOPLE TALKED ABOUT A LOUD NOISE AND A VERY BRIGHT LIGHT

PAGE 3   00110101

PAGE 4   12P43
LIKE LIGHTENING. THE AIRCRAFT AND AREA WHERE THE OBJECT IS
BELWEVED TO HAVE LANDED ARE BEING CHECKED FOR POSSIBLE RADIATIO',
RO COMMENTS: (C) ACTUAL INFORMATION CONTAINED IN THIS REPORT
WAS OBTAINED FROM SOURCE IN CONVERSATION WITH A SUB-SOURCE, AND
IIAF PILOT OF ONE OF THE F-4S, MORE INFORMATION WILL BE
FORWARDED WHEN IT BECOMES AVAILABLE.

BT
N9575
ANNOTES
JEP 117

23 SEP 1976 13 II
CIA--DS-3C
OX5-5865

PAGE 4   00110101

NNNN
230810Z

DEPARTMENT OF DEFENSE
JOINT CHIEFS OF STAFF
MESSAGE CENTER

```
VZCZCMLT918                              ZYUW
MULT                                                    17337
ACTION
     DIAI
DISTR
     J3(14) J5(R2) J3INMCC SECDEF(87) SECDEF: ASDIISA(18)
     IDIAI(85) ILDIA(29) NMIC
  -  CMC CC WASHINGTON DC
  -  CSAF WASHINGTON DC
  -  CNO WASHINGTON DC
  -  CSA WASHINGTON DC
  -  C I A
  -  SECSTATE WASHINGTON DC
  -  NSA WASH DC
     FILE
(858)


TRANSIT/238888Z/231181Z/883181TOR2841858
DE RUOMHRA #8934 2841921
ZNR UUUUU
P 238888Z JUL 78
FM USDAO TEHRAN IR
TO RUEKJCS/DIA WASHDC//DB-382//
INFO RUSNAAA/USCINCEUR VAIHINGEN GE
RUSNAAAA/EUDAC VAIHINGEN GE
RUFRBAA/COMIDEASTFOR MANAMA BAHRAIN
RUDOECA/CINCUSAFE/INCP/LINDSEY AB GE
RHFRAAB/CINCUSAFE/INDCN/RAMSTEIN AB GE
BT
UNCLAS JUL 78                    REG'D   26 JUL '78

THIS IS IIR 6 848 8392 78

1. COUNTRY: IRAN
2. REPORT NUMBER: 6 848 8392 78
3. TITLE: UFO SPOTTED OVER NORTH OF TEHRAN IRAN
4. OMITTED.
5. DATE OF INFO: 788718
6. DATE OF REPORT: 788719
7. DATE/PLACE OF ACO: 788718
8. REFERENCE: INITIATIVE
9. ASSESSMENT: SOURCE C, INFO 3
18. ORIGINATOR: USDAO (OPS) TEHRAN, IRAN
11. REQUEST EVALUATION: NO

PAGE  1                                    8P111818  58
```

DIA report on sightings over Tehran in 1978

DEPARTMENT OF DEFENSE
JOINT CHIEFS OF STAFF
MESSAGE CENTER

PAGE 2   17337
12. PREPARING OFFI A.B. GRAZINI, ISC, USN, OPS
13. APPROVING AUTH: THOMAS E. SCHAEFER, COL, USAF, DATT
14. SOURCE: TEHRAN JOURNAL NEWSPAPER
15. SPECIAL INSTRUCTIONS: DIRC, NO,
16. SUMMARY: THIS REPORT FORWARDS INFORMATION WHICH WAS OBTAINED
FROM THE IRANIAN ENGLISH LANGUAGE NEWSPAPER, THE TEHRAN JOURNAL,
DATED 18 JULY 1978 AND PROVIDES INFORMATION CONCERNING THE SIGHTING
OF AN UFO OVER THE NORTHERN SECTOR OF TEHRAN.
17. THRU 21. OMITTED.
22. DETAILS: THE FOLLOWING INFORMATION IS QUOTED FROM THE 18 JULY
1978 EDITION OF THE TEHRAN JOURNAL NEWSPAPER:
"UFO SPOTTED OVER NORTH OF TEHRAN"
"TEHRAN—AN UNIDENTIFIED FLYING OBJECT WAS SEEN BY A NUMBER OF
PEOPLE IN THE NORTHERN PART OF THE CITY ON SUNDAY NIGHT.
OFFICIALS FROM THE CONTROL TOWER AT MEHRABAD AIRPORT AND A LUFTHANZA
AIRCREW ALSO REPORTED UNUSUAL READINGS ON THEIR INSTRUMENTS.
RESIDENTS IN NORTHERN TEHRAN WERE THE FIRST TO SPOT THE STRANGE
GLOWING OBJECT FLOATING TOWARDS SAVEH. THEY HAD BEEN SLEEPING ON THE
TERRACES OF THEIR HOUSES, AND IMMEDIATELY INFORMED THE CONTROL TOWER
AT MEHRABAD AIRPORT AND THE NATIONAL RADIO NETWORK.
THE CONTROL TOWER CONFIRMED THE EXISTANCE OF THE OBJECT BUT WOULD GIVE
NO FURTHER DETAILS. SOON AFTERWARDS, THE LUFTHANZA PLANE SENT IN
ITS REPORT.
A SIMILAR FLYING OBJECT WAS SEEN LAST APRIL BY LOCAL AIRLINE PILOT, WHO
CLAIMED THAT HE HAD PHOTOGRAPHED THE OBJECT, BUT COULD NOT RELEASE
THE PHOTOGRAPHS UNTIL THE SECURITY DIVISION OF THE CIVIL AVIATION
AUTHORITIES GAVE THEIR PERMISSION.
HE CLAIMED THAT WHILE FLYING BETWEEN AHVAZ AND TEHRAN AT
24,000 FEET, HE AND HIS CO-PILOT HAD SIGHTED A GLITTERING OBJECT
AND HAD MANAGED TO PHOTOGRAPH IT.
A MEHRABAD RADAR CONTROL OFFICIAL SAID THAT ON THAT OCCASION THEY HAD
DETECTED AN OBJECT SOME 20 TIMES THE SIZE OF A JUMBO JET ON THEIR
SCREENS.
CIVIL AVIATION ORGANIZATION CHIEF HAS MOHERI CALLED FOR AN INVESTIGATION.
BUT THE RESULTS OF THIS ENQUIRY HAVE NOT YET BEEN MADE PUBLIC.
AN EYE WITNESS SAID YESTERDAY THAT HE WAS ALONE ON HIS BALCONY ON
SUNDAY NIGHT WHEN SUDDENLY HE SAW THE OBJECT EMERGE IN THE SKY AND HOVER
DIRECTLY ABOVE HIM.
I WAS SO UPSET THAT I WANTED TO SCREAM, BUT COULD NOT DO SO, HE SAID,
HE ADDED THAT HE FELT BETTER ONCE HE REALIZED THAT HIS NEIGHBORS HAD
ALSO SEEN IT.
THIS CURRENT REPORT IS THE THIRD UFO SIGHTING IN IRAN IN LESS THAN A YEAR."

PAGE 2   0011101O

DEPARTMENT OF DEFENSE
JOINT CHIEFS OF STAFF   RECEIVED
MESSAGE CENTER
JUN -3 1980

VZCZCMLT565   7YUY DIA 115-26   18134
MULT
ACTION
    DIAI
DISTR
    IADR(R1) J5(R2) J3INMCC NIDS SECDEF(07) SECDEFI USDP(15)
    ATSDIAE(01) ASDIPA&E(R1) IIDIA(20) NMIC
-   CMC CC WASHINGTON DC
-   CSAF WASHINGTON DC
:   CNO WASHINGTON DC
-   CSA WASHINGTON DC
:   CIA WASHINGTON DC
:   SECSTATE WASHINGTON DC
-   NSA WASH DC
    FILE
(047)

TRANSIT/1542115/1542207/R0R152TOR154220A
DE RUESLMA #4888 1542115
7NY CCCCC
R R220527 JUN 80
FM USDAO LIMA PERU
TO RUEKJCS/DIA WASHDC
INFO RULPALJ/USCINCSO QUARRY HTS PN
RULPAFA/USAFSO HOWARD AFB PN
BT
SUBJI IR 6 876 0146 R8 (U)
THIS IS AN INFO REPORT, NOT FINALLY EVAL INTEL
1. (U) CTRYI PERU (PE)
2. TITLE (U) UFO SIGHTED IN PERU (U)
3. (U) DATE OF INFOI 8P051R
4. (U) ORIGI USDAO AIR LIMA PERU
5. (U) REQ REFSI Z-D13-PE030
6. (U) SOURCEI 6 876 0138. OFFICER IN THE PERUVIAN AIR FORCE
WHO OBSERVED THE EVENT AND IS IN A POSITION TO BE PARTY
TO CONVERSATION CONCERNING THE EVENT. SOURCE HAS REPORTED
RELIABLY IN THE PAST.

7.   SUMMARYI SOURCE REPORTED THAT A UFO WAS SPOTTED
ON TWO DIFFERENT OCCASIONS NEAR PERUVIAN AIR FORCE (FAP) BASE
IN SOUTHERN PERU. THE FAP TRIED TO INTERCEPT AND DESTROY THE
UFO, BUT WITHOUT SUCCESS.

PAGE 1   PPI0111I

DIA report on sightings by Peruvian Air Force Officers in 1980

DEPARTMENT OF DEFENSE
JOINT CHIEFS OF STAFF
MESSAGE CENTER

PAGE 2   18134
8A.   DETAILS: SOURCE TOLD RO ABOUT THE SPOTTING OF AN
UNIDENTIFIED FLYING OBJECT IN THE VICINITY OF MARIANO MELGAR AIR
BASE, LA JOYA, PERU (1688S5, 8715396W). SOURCE STATED THAT THE
VEHICLE WAS SPOTTED ON TWO DIFFERENT OCCASIONS. THE FIRST WAS
DURING THE MORNING HOURS OF 9 MAY 88, AND THE SECOND DURING
THE EARLY EVENING HOURS OF 10 MAY 88.
          SOURCE STATED THAT ON 9 MAY, WHILE A GROUP OF FAP
OFFICERS WERE IN FORMATION AT MARIANO MALGAR, THEY SPOTTED A
UFO THAT WAS ROUND IN SHAPE, HOVERING NEAR THE AIRFIELD. THE
AIR COMMANDER SCRAMBLED AN SU-22 AIRCRAFT TO MAKE AN
INTERCEPT. THE PILOT, ACCORDING TO A THIRD PARTY, INTERCEPTED
THE VEHICLE AND FIRED UPON IT AT VERY CLOSE RANGE WITHOUT
CAUSING ANY APPARENT DAMAGE. THE PILOT TRIED TO MAKE A
SECOND PASS ON THE VEHICLE, BUT THE UFO OUT-RAN THE SU-22.
          THE SECOND SIGHTING WAS DURING HOURS OF DARKNESS.
THE VEHICLE WAS LIGHTED. AGAIN AN SU-22 WAS SCRAMBLED, BUT THE
VEHICLE OUT-RAN THE AIRCRAFT.
8B.   ORIG CMTS: RO HAS HEARD DISCUSSION ABOUT THE
SIGHTING FROM OTHER SOURCES. APPARENTLY SOME VEHICLE WAS
SPOTTED, BUT ITS ORIGIN REMAINS UNKNOWN.
9. (U) PROJ NO: N/A
10. (U) COLL MGMT CODES: AB
11. (U) SPEC INST: NONE, DIRC: NO.
12. (U) PREP BY: NORMAN M. RUNGE, COL, AIRA
13. (U) APP BY: VAUGHN E. WILSON, CAPT, DATT, ALUSNA
14. (U) REG EVAL: NO REL TO: NONE
15. (U) ENCL: N/A
16. (U) DIST BY ORIG: N/A

RT
#488A
ANNOTES
JAL 117

PAGE 2   PP181111
NNNN
0222087

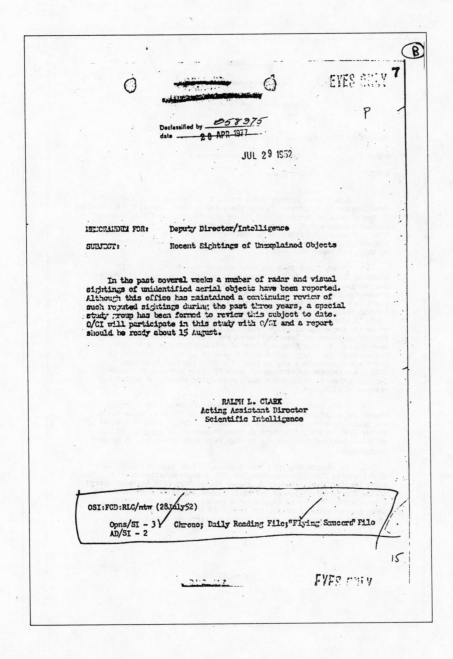

JUL 2 9 1952

MEMORANDUM FOR: Deputy Director/Intelligence

SUBJECT: Recent Sightings of Unexplained Objects

In the past several weeks a number of radar and visual
sightings of unidentified aerial objects have been reported.
Although this office has maintained a continuing review of
such reported sightings during the past three years, a special
study group has been formed to review this subject to date.
O/CI will participate in this study with O/SI and a report
should be ready about 15 August.

RALPH L. CLARK
Acting Assistant Director
Scientific Intelligence

OSI:FCD:RLC/mtw (28July52)

Opns/SI - 3   Chrono; Daily Reading File;"Flying Saucer" File
AD/SI - 2

15

EYES ONLY

MEMORANDUM FOR: Director of Central Intelligence

THROUGH   : Deputy Director (Intelligence)

SUBJECT   : Flying Saucers

1. Recently an inquiry was conducted by the Office of Scientific Intelligence to determine whether there are national security implications in the problem of "unidentified flying objects," i.e., flying saucers; whether adequate study and research is currently being directed to this problem in its relation to such national security implications; and what further investigation and research should be instituted, by whom, and under what aegis.

2. It was found that the only unit of Government currently studying the problem is the Directorate of Intelligence, USAF, which has charged the Air Technical Intelligence Center (ATIC) with responsibility for investigating the reports of sightings. At ATIC there is a group of three officers and two secretaries to which come, through official channels, all reports of sightings. This group conducts investigation of the reports, consulting as required with other Air Force and civilian technical personnel. A world-wide reporting system has been instituted and major Air Force Bases have been ordered to make interceptions of unidentified flying objects. The research is being conducted on a case basis and is designed to provide a satisfactory explanation of each individual sighting. ATIC has concluded an arrangement with Battelle Memorial Institute for the latter to establish a machine indexing system for official reports of sightings.

3. Since 1947, ATIC has received approximately 1500 _official_ reports of sightings plus an enormous volume of letters, phone calls, and press reports. During July 1952 alone, _official_ reports totaled 250. Of the 1500 reports, Air Force carries 20 percent as _unexplained_ and of those received from January through July 1952 it carries 28 percent _unexplained_.

4. In its inquiry into this problem, a team from CIA's Office of Scientific Intelligence consulted with a representative of Air Force Special Studies Group; discussed the problem with those in charge of the Air Force Project at Wright-Patterson Air Force Base; reviewed a considerable volume of intelligence reports; checked the Soviet press and broadcast indices; and conferred with three CIA consultants, who have broad knowledge of the technical areas concerned.

A CIA memo to the Director, 1952

c. The reasons for silence in the Soviet press regarding flying saucers.

10. Additional research, differing in character and emphasis from that presently being performed by Air Force, will be required to meet the specific needs of both operations and intelligence. Intelligence responsibilities in this field as regards both collection and analysis can be discharged with maximum effectiveness only after much more is known regarding the exact nature of these phenomena.

11. I consider this problem to be of such importance that it should be brought to the attention of the National Security Council in order that a community-wide coordinated effort towards its solution may be initiated.

H. MARSHALL CHADWELL
Assistant Director
Scientific Intelligence

- 4 -

other foreign
obtaining

C O N F I D E N T I A L 141445Z APR 76 STAFF

CITE DCD/[   ]

TO: PRIORITY DCD/HEADQUARTERS.

ATTN: [   ]

FROM: DCD/[   ]

SUBJECT: CASE [   ] -   UFO RESEARCH

REF (A): DCD/HEADQUARTERS 14596

    (?): FORM 618 DATED 9 APRIL 1976, UFO STUDY.

    1. SOURCE'S FULL NAME IS [   ]
HE IS EMPLOYED AS [   ]

    2. REFERENT B MATERIAL CLASSIFIED CONFIDENTIAL AT HIS
REQUEST. SOURCE SEEKS GUIDANCE FROM CIA UFO EXPERTS AS TO
MATERIAL IN HIS REPORT THAT SHOULD REMAIN CLASSIFIED. [   ]

That the CIA has its own UFO experts is proven by this 1976 memo.

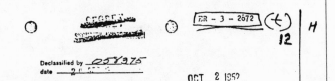

Declassified by _058375_
date _2 ...._

OCT 2 1952

MEMORANDUM TO: Director of Central Intelligence

THROUGH: Deputy Director (Intelligence)

FROM: Assistant Director, Office of Scientific
                      Intelligence

SUBJECT: Flying Saucers

1. PROBLEM—To determine: (a) Whether or not there are national
   security implications in the problem of "unidentified
   flying objects"; (b) whether or not adequate study and
   research is currently being directed to this problem
   in its relation to such national security implications;
   and (c) what further investigation and research should
   be instituted, by whom, and under what aegis.

2. FACTS AND DISCUSSION—OSI has investigated the work currently
   being performed on "flying saucers" and found that the
   Air Technical Intelligence Center, DI, USAF, Wright-
   Patterson Air Force Base, is the only group devoting
   appreciable effort and study to this subject, that ATIC
   is concentrating on a case-by-case explanation of each
   report, and that this effort is not adequate to corre-
   late, evaluate, and resolve the situation on an overall basis. The current problem is discussed in detail
   in TAB A.

3. CONCLUSIONS—"Flying saucers" pose two elements of danger
   which have national security implications. The first
   involves mass psychological considerations and the
   second concerns the vulnerability of the United States
   to air attack. Both factors are amplified in TAB A.

4. ACTION RECOMMENDED—(a) That the Director of Central Intelligence advise the National Security Council of the
   implications of the "flying saucer" problem and request
   that research be initiated. TAB B is a draft memorandum to the NSC, for the DCI's signature. (b) That
   the DCI discuss this subject with the Psychological
   Strategy Board. A memorandum to the Director,
   Psychological Strategy Board, is attached for signature as TAB C. (c) That CIA, with the cooperation
   of PSB and other interested departments and agencies,
   develop and recommend for adoption by the NSC a

A CIA memo to the Director, 1952

H

policy of public information which will minimize concern
and possible panic resulting from the numerous sightings
of unidentified objects.

H. MARSHALL CHADWELL
Assistant Director
Scientific Intelligence

ANNEXES:
    TAB A—Memorandum to DCI, through DDI, Subject: Flying
        Saucers.
    TAB B—Letter to National Security Council with enclosure.
    TAB C—Memo to Director, Psychological Strategy Board with
        enclosure.

CONCURRENCES:

Date: _____

                             LOFTUS E. BECKER
                      Deputy Director/Intelligence

ACTION BY APPROVING AUTHORITY:

                      Date: _____

Approved (disapproved):

                      WALTER B. SMITH
                      Director

- 2 -.

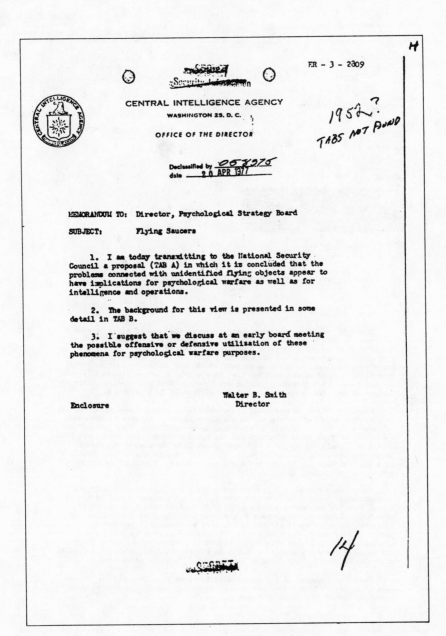

A memo from CIA Director Walter Bedell Smith, who became a member of the Majestic 12 group in 1950

UNTRY	Belgian Congo		
BJECT	Military; Sc..ntific - Air	INFORMATION	1952
W BLISHED	Daily newspaper	DATE DIST. 16 Aug 1952	
HERE BLISHED	Vienna	NO. OF PAGES	2
TE BLISHED	29 Mar 1952	SUPPLE	
NGUAGE	German	REPORT	

THIS IS UNE...

URCE   Die Presse.

FLYING SAUCERS OVER BELGIAN CONGO URANIUM MINES

Fritz Sitte

Recently, two fiery disks were sighted over the uranium mines located in the southern part of the Belgian Congo in the Elisabethville district, east of the Luapula River which connects the Meru and Bangweolo lakes. The disks glided in elegant curves and changed their position many times, so that from below they sometimes appeared as plates, ovals, and simply lines. Suddenly, both disks hovered in one spot and then took off in a unique zigzag flight to the northeast. A penetrating hissing and buzzing sound was audible to the on-lookers below. The whole performance lasted from 10 to 12 minutes.

Commander Pierre of the small Elisabethville airfield immediately set out in pursuit with a fighter plane. On his first approach he came within about 120 meters of one of the disks. According to his estimates, the "saucer" had a diameter of from 12 to 15 meters and was discus-shaped. The inner core remained absolutely still, and a knob coming out from the center and several small openings could plainly be seen. The outer rim was completely veiled in fire and must have had an enormous speed of rotation. The color of the metal was similar to that of aluminum.

The disks traveled in a precise and light manner, both vertically and horizontally. Changes in elevation from 800 to 1,000 meters could be accomplished in a few seconds; the disks often shot down to within 20 meters of the tree tops. Pierre did not regard it possible that the disk could be manned, since the irregular speed as well as the heat would make it impossible for a person to stay inside the stable core. Pierre had to give up pursuit after 15 minutes since both disks, with a loud whistling sound which he heard despite the noise of his own plane, disappeared in a straight line toward Lake Tanganyika. He estimated their speed at about 1,500 kilometers per hour.

Pierre is regarded as a dependable officer and a zealous flyer. He gave a detailed report to his superiors which, strangely enough, in many respects agreed with various results of research.

Two CIA reports from 1952

CENTRAL INTELLIGENCE AGENCY

INFORMATION FROM
FOR__N DOCUMEN_S OR RADIO BROADCASTS

REPORT NO. OO-W-23682

CD NO. --

DATE OF
INFORMATION 1952

DATE DIST. 23 Aug 1952

Daily newspaper

WHERE
PUBLISHED Athens

NO. OF PAGES 2

DATE
PUBLISHED 9 Jul 1952

LANGUAGE Greek

SUPPLEMENT TO
REPORT NO.

THIS IS UNEVALUATED INFORMATION

OURCE I Kathimerini.

"FLYING SAUCERS" IN EAST GERMANY

Berlin, July -- Furnished with the sworn testimony of an eyewitness, Oscar Linke, a 48-year-old German and former mayor of Gleimershausen, West Berlin intelligence officers have begun investigating a most unusual "flying saucer" story. According to this story, an object "resembling a huge flying pan" and having a diameter of about 15 meters landed in a forest clearing in the Soviet Zone of Germany.

Linke recently escaped from the Soviet Zone along with his wife and six children.

Linke and his 11-year-old daughter, Gabriella, made the following sworn statement last week before a judge: "While I was returning to my home with Gabriella, a tire of my motorcycle blew out near the town of Hasselbach. While we were walking along toward Hasselbach, Gabriella pointed out something which lay at a distance of about 140 meters away from us. Since it was twilight, I though that she was pointing at a young deer.

"I left my motorcycle near a tree and walked toward the spot which Gabriella had pointed out. When, however, I reached a spot about 55 meters from the object, I realized that my first impression had been wrong. What I had seen were two men who were now about 40 meters away from me. They seemed to be dressed in some shiny metallic clothing. They were stooped over and were looking at something lying on the ground.

"I approached until I was only about 10 meters from them. I looked over a small fence and then I noticed a large object whose diameter I estimated to be between 13 and 15 meters. It looked like a huge frying pan.

"There were two rows of holes on its periphery, about 30 centimeters in circumference. The space between the two rows was about 0.45 meters. On the top of this metal object was a black conical tower about 3 meters high

"At that moment, my daughter, who had remained a short distance behind me, called me. The two men must have heard my daughter's voice because they immediately jumped on the conical tower and disappeared inside.

"I had previously noted that one of the men had a lamp on the front part of his body which lit up at regular intervals.

"Now, the side of the object on which the holes had been opened began to glitter. Its color seemed green but later turned to red. At the same time I began to hear a slight hum. While the brightness and hum increased, the conical tower began to slide down into the center of the object. The whole object then began to rise slowly from the ground and rotate like a top.

"It seemed to me as if it were supported by the cylindrical plant which had gone down from the top of the object, through the center, and had now appeared from its bottom on the ground.

"The object, surrounded by a ring of flames, was now a certain number of feet above the ground.

"I then noted that the whole object had risen slowly from the ground. The cylinder on which it was supported had now disappeared within its center and had reappeared on the top of the object.

"The rate of climb had now become greater. At the same time my daughter and I heard a whistling sound similar to that heard when a bomb falls.

"The object rose to a horizontal position, turned toward a neighboring town, and then, gaining altitude, it disappeared over the heights and forests in the direction of Stockheim."

Many other persons who live in the same area as Linke later related that they saw an object which they thought to be a comet. A shepherd stated that he thought that he was looking at a comet moving away at a low altitude from the height on which Linke stood.

After submitting his testimony to the judge, Linke made the following statement: "I would have thought that both my daughter and I were dreaming if it were not for the following element involved: When the object had disappeared, I went to the place where it had been. I found a circular opening in the ground and it was quite evident that it was freshly dug. It was exactly the same shape as the conical tower. I was then convinced that I was not dreaming."

Linke continued, "I had never heard of the term 'flying saucer' before I escaped from the Soviet Zone into West Berlin. When I saw this object, I immediately thought that it was a new Soviet military machine.

"I confess that I was seized with fright because the Soviets do not want anyone to know about their work. Many persons have been restricted to their movements for many years in East Germany because they know too much."

- E N D -

EXCERPTS:

NASA

National Aeronautics and
Space Administration

INFORMATION SHEET

Number 78-1

Prepared by:

LFF-3/Public Services Branch
Office of External Relations
NASA Headquarters
Washington, DC 20546

UNIDENTIFIED FLYING OBJECTS

The information contained here has been compiled to respond to queries on Unidentified Flying Objects directed to the White House as well as NASA.

NASA is the focal point for answering public inquiries to the White House relating to UFOs. NASA is not engaged in a research program involving these phenomena, nor is any other government agency.

Reports of unidentified objects entering United States air space are of interest to the military as a regular part of defense surveillance. Beyond that, the U.S. Air Force no longer investigates reports of UFO sightings.

February 1, 1978

NASA Information Sheet perpetuating the myth that no government agency is engaged in UFO research

NATIONAL INVESTIGATIONS COMMITTEE ON AERIAL PHENOMENA (NICAP)©
301-949-1267   3535 University Blvd. West
                            Kensington, Maryland 20795

REPORT ON UNIDENTIFIED FLYING OBJECT(S)

This form includes questions asked by the United States Air Force and by other Armed Forces' investigating agencies, and additional questions to which answers are needed for full evaluation by NICAP.
After all the information has been fully studied, the conclusion of our Evaluation Panel will be published by NICAP in its regularly issued magazine or in another publication. Please try to answer as many questions as possible. Should you need additional room, please use another sheet of paper. Please print or typewrite. Your assistance is of great value and is genuinely appreciated. Thank you.

1. Name **Jimmy Carter**   Place of Employment

   Address **State Capitol Atlanta**   Occupation   **Governor**
                                        Date of birth
                                        Education
                                        Special Training **Graduate**
   Telephone **(404) 656-1776**   Military Service **Nuclear Physics**
                                                          U.S. Navy

2. Date of Observation **October 1969**   Time   AM   PM   Time Zone
                                                        7:15   **EST**

3. Locality of Observation **Leary, Georgia**

4. How long did you see the object?_____ Hours **10-12** Minutes_____ Seconds

5. Please describe weather conditions and the type of sky; i.e., bright daylight, nighttime, dusk, etc. **Shortly after dark.**

6. Position of the Sun or Moon in relation to the object and to you. **Not in sight.**

7. If seen at night, twilight, or dawn, were the stars or moon visible? **Stars.**

8. Were there more than one object? **No.**   If so, please tell how many, and draw a sketch of what you saw, indicating direction of movement, if any.

9. Please describe the object(s) in detail. For instance, did it (they) appear solid, or only as a source of light; was it revolving, etc.? Please use additional sheets of paper, if necessary.

10. Was the object(s) brighter than the background of the sky? **Yes.**

11. If so, compare the brightness with the Sun, Moon, headlights, etc. **At one time, as bright as the moon.**

12. Did the object(s) —   (Please elaborate, if you can give details.)

    a. Appear to stand still at any time? **yes**   f. Drop anything?
    b. Suddenly speed up and rush away at any time? g. Change brightness? **yes**
    c. Break up into parts or explode?   h. Change shape?   **size**
    d. Give off smoke?   i. Change color?   **yes**
    e. Leave any visible trail?

    Seemed to move toward us from a distance, stopped-moved partially away—returned, then departed. Bluish at first, then reddish, luminous, not solid.

13. Did object(s) at any time pass in front of, or behind of, anything? If so, please elaborate giving distance, size, etc, if possible. **no.**

14. Was there any wind? **no.**   If so, please give direction and speed.

15. Did you observe the object(s) through an optical instrument or other aid, windshield, windowpane, storm window, screening, etc? What? **no.**

16. Did the object(s) have any sound? **no**   What kind?   How loud?

17. Please tell if the object(s) was (were) —

    a. Fuzzy or blurred.   b. Like a bright star.   c. Sharply outlined. **X**

President Carter's UFO sighting (*NICAP*)

18. Was the object —   a. Self-luminous? x   b. Dull finish?   c. Reflecting?   d. Transparent?

19. Did the object(s) rise or fall while in motion? came close, moved away—came close then moved away.

20. Tell the apparent size of the object(s) when compared with the following held at arm's length:

     a. Pinhead   c. Dime   e. Half dollar   g. Orange   i. Larger
     b. Pea   d. Nickel   f. Silver dollar   h. Grapefruit

    Or, if easier, give apparent size in inches on a ruler held at arm's length. About the same as moon, maybe a little smaller. Varied from brighter/larger than planet to apparent size of moon.

21. How did you happen to notice the object(s)? 10-12 men all watched it. Brightness attracted us.

22. Where were you and what were you doing at the time? Outdoors waiting for a meeting to begin at 7:30pm

23. How did the object(s) disappear from view? Moved to distance then disappeared

24. Compare the speed of the object(s) with a piston or jet aircraft at the same apparent altitude. Not pertinent

25. Were there any conventional aircraft in the location at the time or immediately afterwards? If so, please elaborate. no.

26. Please estimate the distance of the object(s). Difficult. Maybe 300-1000 yards.

27. What was the elevation of the object(s) in the sky? Please mark on this hemisphere sketch.
About 30° above horizon.

28. Names and addresses of other witnesses, if any.

Ten members of Leary Georgia Lions Club

29. What do you think you saw?

     a. Extraterrestrial device?   e. Satellite?
     b. UFO?   f. Hoax?
     c. Planet or star?   g. Other? (Please specify).
     d. Aircraft?

30. Please describe your feelings and reactions during the sighting. Were you calm, nervous, frightened, apprehensive, awed, etc.? If you wish your answer to this question to remain confidential, please indicate with a check mark. (Use a separate sheet if necessary)

31. Please draw a map of the locality of the observation showing North; your position; the direction from which the object(s) appeared and disappeared from view; the direction of its course over the area; roads, towns, villages, railroads, and other landmarks within a mile.

Appeared from West--About 30° up.

32. Is there an airport, military, governmental, or research installation in the area? No

33. Have you seen other objects of an unidentified nature? If so, please describe these observations, using a separate sheet of paper. No

34. Please enclose photographs, motion pictures, news clippings, notes of radio or television programs (include time, station and date, if possible) regarding this or similar observations, or any other background material. We will return the material to you if requested. None.

35. Were you interrogated by Air Force investigators? By any other federal, state, county, or local officials? If so, please state the name and rank or title of the agent, his office, and details as to where and when the questioning took place.

Were you asked or told not to reveal or discuss the incident? If so, were any reasons or official orders mentioned? Please elaborate carefully. No.

36. We should like permission to quote your name in connection with this report. This action will encourage other responsible citizens to report similar observations to NICAP. However, if you prefer, we will keep your name confidential. Please note your choice by checking the proper statement below. In any case, please fill in all parts of the form, for our own confidential files. Thank you for your cooperation.

You may use my name.   (x)   Please keep my name confidential.   ( )

37. Date of filling out this report   Signature:

9-18-73   Jimmy Carter

DEPARTMENT OF THE AIR FORCE
WASHINGTON D C 20330

OFFICE OF THE SECRETARY   1 SEP 1977

Lieutenant General Duward L. Crow, USAF (Ret)
National Aeronautics and Space Administration
400 Maryland Avenue
Washington, D. C. 20546

Dear General Crow:

Inclosed are the UFO Fact Sheet and standard response
to UFO public inquiries you requested.

I sincerely hope you are successful in preventing a
reopening of UFO investigations.

                                 Sincerely,

                                 CHARLES H. SENN, Colonel, USAF
                                 Chief, Community Relations Division
                                 Office of Information

Attachments

Action Copy to ___AOA___
I lu Cory to   _____
A35481   AB,AC,
                S.F.L, W. C
                DE
r c'd in NASA   9-2-77
                NONE
                _____

Letter from Colonel Senn to Lieutenant General Crow of NASA, 1977

Sept. 15-1950

Notes on interview through L/C. Bremner with Dr. Robert I Sarbacher.

WBS: I am doing some work on the collapse of the earth's magnetic field as a source of energy, and I think our work may have a bearing on the flying saucers.

RIS What do you want to know.

WBS I have read Scully's book on the saucers and would like to know how much of it is true.

RIS The facts reported in the book are substantially correct.

WBS Then the saucers do exist?

RIS. Yes: they exist.

WBS Do they operate as Scully suggests on magnetic principles?

Notes by Canadian government scientist Wilbert Smith, made after his interview with Dr. Robert Sarbacher (via Lt. Col. Bremner) in 1950 (*Arthur Bray*)

PLS. We have not been able to duplicate their performance

PBS Do they come from some other planet?

PLS All we know is, we didn't make them, and it's pretty certain they didn't originate on the earth.

PBS I understand the whole subject of Saucers is classified

PLS. Yes, it is classified two points higher even than the H-bomb. In fact it is the most highly classified subject in the US Government at the present time.

PBS May I ask the reason for the classification?

PLS You may ask, but I can't tell you

WEB   Is there any way in which I can get more information, particularly as it might fit in with our own work.

R.I.S.   I suppose you could be cleared through your own Defense Department and I am pretty sure arrangements could be made to exchange information. If you have anything to contribute, we would be glad to talk it over, but I can't give you any more at the present time.

Note: The above is written out from memory following the interview. I have tried to keep it as nearly verbatim as possible.

COMPLAINT FORM

Hq 1 V o S

I	ADMINISTRATIVE DATA		
TITLE KIRTLAND AFB, NM, 8 Aug – 3 Sep 80, Alleged Sigthings of Unidentified Aerial Lights in Restricted Test Range.	DATE 2 - 9 Sept 80		TIME 1200
	PLACE AFOSI Det 1700, Kirtland AFB, NM		
	HOW RECEIVED		
	X IN PERSON	TELEPHONICALLY	IN WRITING

SOURCE AND EVALUATION

MAJOR ERNEST E. EDWARDS

RESIDENCE OR BUSINESS ADDRESS Commander, 1608 SPS, Manzano Kirtland AFB, NM	PHONE 4-7516

CR __44__ APPLIES

II	SUMMARY OF INFORMATION

REMARKS

1. On 2 Sept 80, SOURCE related on 8 Aug 80, three Security Policemen assigned to 1608 SPS, KAFB, NM, on duty inside the Manzano Weapons Storage Area sighted an unidentified light in the air that traveled from North to South over the Coyote Canyon area of the Department of Defense Restricted Test Range on KAFB, NM. The Security Policemen identified as: SSGT STEPHEN FERENZ, Area Supervisor, AIC MARTIN W. RIST and AMN ANTHONY D. FRAZIER, were later interviewed separately by SOURCE and all three related the same statement; At approximately 2350hrs., while on duty in Charlie Sector, East Side of Manzano, the three observed a very bright light in the sky approximately 3 miles North-North East of their position. The light traveled with great speed and stopped suddenly in the sky over Coyote Canyon. The three first thought the object was a helicopter, however, after observing the strange aerial maneuvers (stop and go), they felt a helicopter couldn't have performed such skills. The light landed in the Coyote Canyon area. Sometime later, three witnessed the light take off and leave proceeding straight up at a high speed and disappear.

2. Central Security Control (CSC) inside Manzano, contacted Sandia Security, who conducts frequent building checks on two alarmed structures in the area. They advised that a patrol was already in the area and would investigate.

3. On 11 Aug 80, RUSS CURTIS, Sandia Security, advised that on 9 Aug 80, a Sandia Security Guard, (who wishes his name not be divulged for fear of harassment), related the following: At approximately 0020hrs., he was driving East on the Coyote Canyon access road on a routine building check of an alarmed structure . As he approached the structure he observed a bright light near the ground behind the structure. He also observed an object he first thought was a helicopter. But after driving closer, he observed a round disk shaped object. He attempted to radio for a back up patrol but his radio would not work. As he approached the object on foot armed with a shotgun, the object took off in a vertical direction at a high rate of speed. The guard was a former helicopter mechanic in the U.S. Army and stated the object he observed was not a helicopter.

4. SOURCE advised on 22 Aug 80, three other security policemen observed the same

DATE FORWARDED HQ AFOSI Hq 1 V o S	10 Sep 80	AFOSI FORM SS ATTACHED ☐ YES ☐ NO
DATE 8 Sept 80	TYPED OR PRINTED NAME OF SPECIAL AGENT RICHARD C. DOTY, SA	SIGNATURE
DISTRICT FILE NO 80178 93-c/22		DCII RESULTS

AFOSI FORM 1 PREVIOUS EDITION WILL BE USED

NEGATIVE ✓   POSITIVE (See attached)

USAF Office of Special Investigations (AFOSI) report describing events at Kirtland AFB, New Mexico, in 1980

CONTINUED FROM COMPLAI FORM 1, DTD 9 Sept 80

aerial phenomena described by the first three. Again the object landed in Coyote
Canyon. They did not see the object take off.

5. Coyote Canyon is part of a large   restricted test range used by
the Air Force Weapons Laboratory, Sandia Laboratories, Defense Nuclear Agency
and the Department of Energy. The range was formerly patrolled by Sandia
Security, however, they only conduct building checks there now.

6. On 10 Aug 80, a New Mexico State Patrolman sighted a aerial object land
in the Manzano's between Belen and Albuquerque, NM. The Patrolman reported
the sighting to the Kirtland AFB Command Post, who later referred the patrolman
to the AFOSI Dist 17. AFOSI Dist 17 advised the patrolman to make a report
through his own agency. On 11 Aug 80, the Kirtland Public Information office
advised the patrolman the USAF no longer investigates such sightings unless
they occurs on an USAF base.

7. WRITER contacted all the agencies who utilized the test range and it was
learned no aerial tests are conducted in the Coyote Canyon area. Only ground
tests are conducted.

8. On 8 Sept 80, WRITER learned from Sandia Security that another Security
Guard observed a object land near an alarmed structure sometime during the first
week of August, but did not report it until just recently for fear of
harassment.

9. The two alarmed structures located within the area contains HQ CR 44
material.

N M C C
THE NATIONAL MILITARY COMMAND CENTER
WASHINGTON, D.C. 20301

21 Janaury 1976
0630 EST

MEMORANDUM FOR RECORD

Subject: Report of UFO - Cannon AFB NM

Reference: AFOC Phonecon 21055 EST Jan 76

The following information was received from the Air Force
Operations Center at 0555 EST:

"Two UFOs are reported near the flight line at Cannon AFB,
New Mexico. Security Police observing them reported the UFOs
to be 25 yards in diameter, gold or silver in color with blue
light on top, hole in the middle and red light on bottom. Air
Force is checking with radar. Additionally, checking weather
inversion data."

J.B. MORIN
Rear Admiral, USN
Deputy Director for
Operations, NMCC

National Military Command Center report of a sighting at Cannon AFB,
New Mexico, in 1976

WASHINGTON INSTITUTE OF TECHNOLOGY
OCEANOGRAPHIC AND PHYSICAL SCIENCES

DR. ROBERT I. SARBACHER
PRESIDENT AND CHAIRMAN OF BOARD

November 29, 1983

*Answer
from Dr. Sarbacher
Received 12-5-83
Wm Steinman*

Mr. William Steinman
15043 Rosalita Drive
La Mirada, California 90638

Dear Mr. Steinman:

I am sorry I have taken so long in answering your letters.
However, I have moved my office and have had to make a
number of extended trips.

To answer your last question in your letter of October 14,
1983, there is no particular reason I feel I shouldn't or
couldn't answer any or all of your questions. I am delighted to answer all of them to the best of my ability.

You listed some of your questions in your letter of
September 12th. I will attempt to answer them as you had
listed them.

        1.   Relating to my own experience regarding re-
covered flying saucers, I had no association with any
of the people involved in the recovery and have no knowledge regarding the dates of the recoveries. If I had I
would send it to you.

        2.   Regarding verification that persons you list
were involved, I can only say this:

        John von Neuman was definitely involved. Dr.
Vannever Bush was definitely involved, and I think Dr.
Robert Oppenheimer also.

        My association with the Research and Develop-
ment Board under Doctor Compton during the Eisenhower
administration was rather limited so that although I had
been invited to participate in several discussions associated withthe reported recoveries, I could not personally
attend the meetings. I am sure thatthey would have asked
Dr. von Braun, and the others that you listed were probably
asked and may or may not have attended. This is all I know
for sure.

333 Dumont Clive

500 BRAZILIAN AVENUE   PALM BEACH, FLORIDA 33480   305-833-1116

Letter from the late Dr. Robert Sarbacher confirming that the US authorities have recovered alien bodies as well as craft (*William Steinman*)

Mr. William Steinman
November 29, 1983 - Page 2

    3.   I did receive some official reports when I was
in my office at the Pentagon but all of these were left
there as at the time we were never supposed to take them
out of the office.

    4.   I do not recall receiving any photographs such
as you request so I am not in a position to answer.

    5.   I have to make the same reply as on No. 4.

I recall the interview with Dr. Brenner of the Canadian
Embassy. I think the answers I gave him were the ones you
listed. Naturally, I was more familiar with the subject
matter under discussion, at that time. Actually, I would
have been able to give more specific answers had I attended the meetings concerning the subject. You must understand
that I took this assignment as a private contribution. We
were called "dollar-a-year men." My first responsibility
was the maintenance of my own business activity so that my
participation was limited.

About the only thing I remember at this time is that certain
materials reported to have come from flying saucer crashes
were extremely light and very tough. I am sure our
laboratories analyzed them very carefully.

There were reports that instruments or people operating
these machines were also of very light weight, sufficient
to withstand the tremendous deceleration and acceleration
associated with their machinery. I remember in talking
with some of the people at the office that I got the
impression these "aliens" were constructed like certain
insects we have observed on earth, wherein because of the
low mass the inertial forces involved in operation of
these instruments would be quite low.

I still do not know why the high order of classification has
been given and why the denial of the existence of these
devices.

I am sorry it has taken me so long to reply but I suggest
you get in touch with the others who may be directly involved
in this program.

                              Sincerely yours,

                              Dr. Robert I. Sarbacher

P. S.   It occurs to me that Dr. Bush's name is inccorrect
         as you have it. Please check the spelling.

              and so I correct it.

Office Memorandum • UNITED STATES GOVERNMENT

TO   DIRECTOR, FBI   DATE: March 22, 1950

FROM   GUY HOTTEL, SAC, WASHINGTON

SUBJECT: FLYING SAUCERS:
INFORMATION CONCERNING

Flying Discs or Flying Saucers

The following information was furnished to SA _____ by
_____

An investigator for the Air Forces stated that three so-called
flying saucers had been recovered in New Mexico. They were
described as being circular in shape with raised centers, approximately 50 feet in diameter. Each one was occupied by three bodies
of human shape but only 3 feet tall, dressed in metallic cloth of
a very fine texture. Each body was bandaged in a manner similar
to the blackout suits used by speed flyers and test pilots.

According to Mr. _____ informant, the saucers were found in New
Mexico due to the fact that the Government has a very high-powered
radar set-up in that area and it is believed the radar interferes
with the controling mechanism of the saucers.

No further evaluation was attempted by SA _____ concerning the
above.

RHK:VIN

A 1950 FBI memo relating to the reports of crashed disks

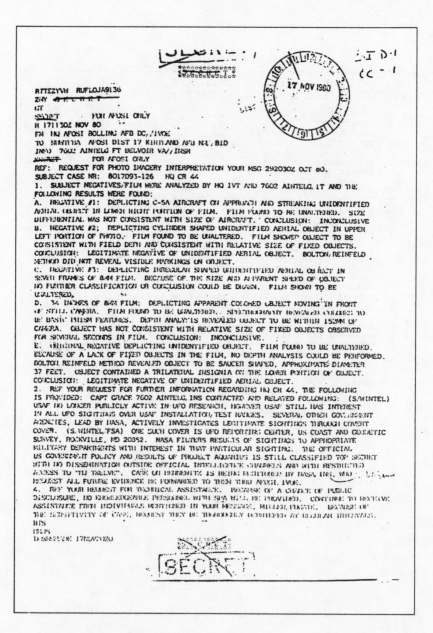

The retyped USAF Office of Special Investigations document describing analysis of film taken near Kirtland AFB in 1980. Note references to NASA (which should be NSA) Project Aquarius, and MJ-12.

NNUOSIUIS
RG #341
Entry #267
Box #206

Tab #13
1/12/T

ACCESS RESTRICTED

The item identified below has been withdrawn from this file:

File Designation   TS5 - 2862
                     Rpt. TR-DE-3A

Date   15 Oct. 55

From   Air Tech. In Tel Ctr.

To

In the review of this file this item was removed because access to it is restricted. Restrictions on records in the National Archives are stated in general and specific record group restriction statements which are available for examination. The item identified above has been withdrawn because it contains:

[X] Security- Classified Information

[ ] Otherwise Restricted Information

WITHDRAWAL NOTICE

USAF
        Authority

28 June '85
        Date
        Bm

NATIONAL ARCHIVES AND RECORDS ADMINISTRATION   NA FORM 1400 (4-85)

Many Top Secret UFO reports are being withheld. This is an example of a USAF Intelligence withdrawal notice (1985).

Please Post in Radio Room and on the Bridge

FOR EARLY WARNING IN DEFENSE OF THE NORTH AMERICAN CONTINENT

MERINT
RADIOTELEGRAPH PROCEDURE

1. WHAT TO REPORT

Report immediately all airborne and waterborne objects which appear to be HOSTILE, SUSPICIOUS or are UNIDENTIFIED.

Guided Missiles

Surface warships positively identified as not U. S. or Canadian

Aircraft or contrails which appear to be directed against the United States, Canada, their Territories or possessions

Submarines

Unidentified Flying Objects

2. SEND TO ANY

United States Naval Radio Station
Canadian Naval Radio Station
United States Coast Guard Radio Station
United States Commercial Radiotelegraph Station
Canadian Department of Transport Coastal Station

Receiving station will relay to military destination

3. HOW TO SEND

* MERINT MERINT MERINT (Coastal Station) DE (Own Signal Letters) K (Own Signal Letters) DE (Coastal Station) K
EMERGENCY (For U. S. or Canadian Naval or Coast Guard Radio Stations) or
RAPID US GOVT COLLECT (For U. S. Commercial Coastal Stations) or
RUSH COLLECT (For Canadian Dept of Transport Coastal Stations)

4. SEND TO ONE DESTINATION

The military makes a clear distinction between UFOs and hostile aircraft. (*US Navy*)

Sketch by aircraft illustrator Denis Crowe of object he saw taking off
from Vaucluse Beach, Sydney, on 19 July 1965 (*Denis Crowe*)

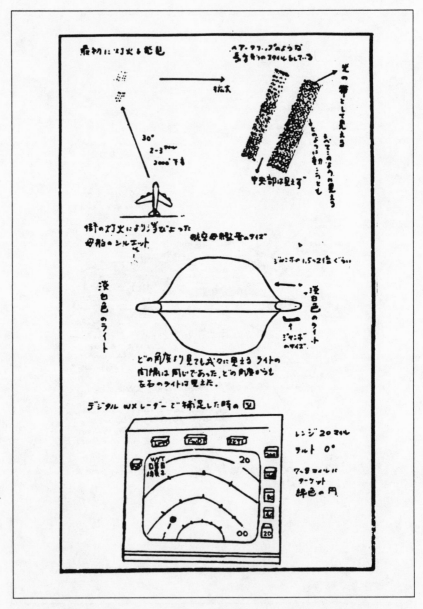

JAL Captain Kenju Terauchi prepared these illustrations of what he saw when his Boeing 747 encountered strange lights over Alaska, Nov. 17, 1986. In the top drawing, Terauchi shows the UFO lights nearly in front of the plane and a close-up of the lights. In the middle, he depicts what the UFO looked like after he glimpsed it in silhouette. The JAL jumbo jet is dwarfed by the huge object. In the bottom drawing, the pilot shows where the UFO first appeared on the plane's radar. *(FAA/MUFON)*

COMPAÑIA DE AVIACION "FAUCETT" S. A.
HOTEL BOLIVAR 926 - CASILLA 1429
LIMA

FLIGHT REPORT   FROM: CAPT. OSWALDO SANVITI
REF: O.V.N.I.

The following report is made to contribute to clarify the long story about Flying Saucers.

I was flying my plane, a Douglas DC-4 of the Compañia de Aviación "Faucett" S.A. of Lima -Perú, from Chiclayo to Lima on Feb.2,1967, altitude: 7,000 feet, and at 24:30 G.M.T.hour, we saw at the W of our plane a very luminous object which we confused initially with a star or a planet,but,after we were very sure that the apparent movement of the object was NOT the effect of our plane,we could see that object was coming fast closer to our plane,we estimated the distance about 8 nautical miles, at this time it was really a spectacle, it had so much light that all the passengers of our plane saw and started to be very nervous and exclaimed,"There is an OVNI." After a while the OVNI passed over my plane and stopped right over us. At this moment we noticed a 15° left oscilation on our Radio Compass and later a 20° right without stopping, all the lights in the main cabin started to reduce the intensity, the same as our fluorescent lights of the cockpit and all radios (reception) out, almost a bit of static noise. (After the flight we were informed that our transmission was 5 x 5 O.K.)

The OVNI from the 9°0 position over our plane moved over to the E of our plane increasing its light about a 50% into a bluish light and disappeared with a fantastic speed (perhaps the speed of light). After 5 minutes the OVNI returned with another one and situated itself on a close distance on our tail section and in this formation we flew till 5 minutes before landing at the Lima International Airfield.

This is all we can say about in honor of truth.

Capt. Oswaldo Sanviti

Note. On another sheet I drew the approximately form and colors the OVNI had.

Report of sighting by Captain Oswaldo Sanviti and his crew and passengers over Peru on 2 February 1967 (*UFO News*)

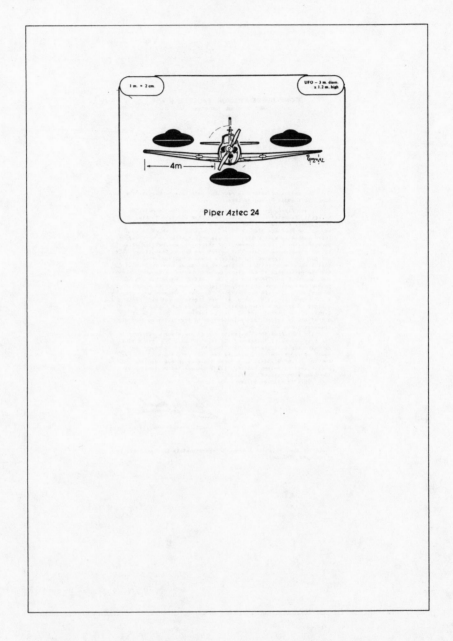

On 3 May 1974 Carlos Montiel was surrounded by three objects that temporarily paralyzed the controls of his aircraft as he was flying over Mexico. (*Robert Gonzales/APRO*)

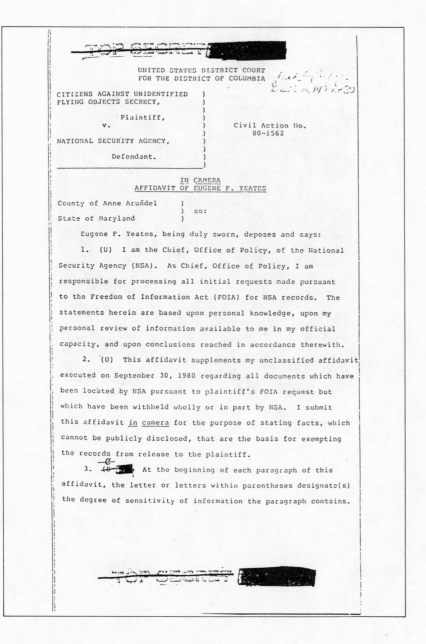

TOP SECRET

UNITED STATES DISTRICT COURT
FOR THE DISTRICT OF COLUMBIA

CITIZENS AGAINST UNIDENTIFIED   )
FLYING OBJECTS SECRECY,   )
)
            Plaintiff,   )
      v.   )   Civil Action No.
)   80-1562
NATIONAL SECURITY AGENCY,   )
)
            Defendant.   )
_____)

IN CAMERA
AFFIDAVIT OF EUGENE F. YEATES

County of Anne Arundel   )
) ss:
State of Maryland   )

      Eugene F. Yeates, being duly sworn, deposes and says:

      1. (U) I am the Chief, Office of Policy, of the National
Security Agency (NSA). As Chief, Office of Policy, I am
responsible for processing all initial requests made pursuant
to the Freedom of Information Act (FOIA) for NSA records. The
statements herein are based upon personal knowledge, upon my
personal review of information available to me in my official
capacity, and upon conclusions reached in accordance therewith.

      2. (U) This affidavit supplements my unclassified affidavit
executed on September 30, 1980 regarding all documents which have
been located by NSA pursuant to plaintiff's FOIA request but
which have been withheld wholly or in part by NSA. I submit
this affidavit in camera for the purpose of stating facts, which
cannot be publicly disclosed, that are the basis for exempting
the records from release to the plaintiff.

      3. (C) At the beginning of each paragraph of this
affidavit, the letter or letters within parentheses designate(s)
the degree of sensitivity of information the paragraph contains.

TOP SECRET

Five pages from the 21-page above Top Secret affidavit giving the National Security Agency's reasons for withholding its documents on UFOs

The letters "U", "C", "S" and "TS" indicate respectively that the information is unclassified or is classified CONFIDENTIAL, SECRET or TOP SECRET.

THE RELEVANT DOCUMENTS

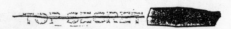

4.   In processing the plaintiff's FOIA request, a total of two hundred and thirty-nine documents were located in NSA files. Seventy-nine of these documents originated with other government agencies and have been referred by NSA to those agencies for their direct response to the plaintiff. One document, which I addressed in paragraph 20c of my public affidavit, was erroneously treated as part of the subject matter of plaintiff's FOIA request. It is an account by a person

2

(1) Two of the records at issue here were produced

(2)

b.

6

EXEMPTION OF THE COMINT REPORTS

10. (S—

13

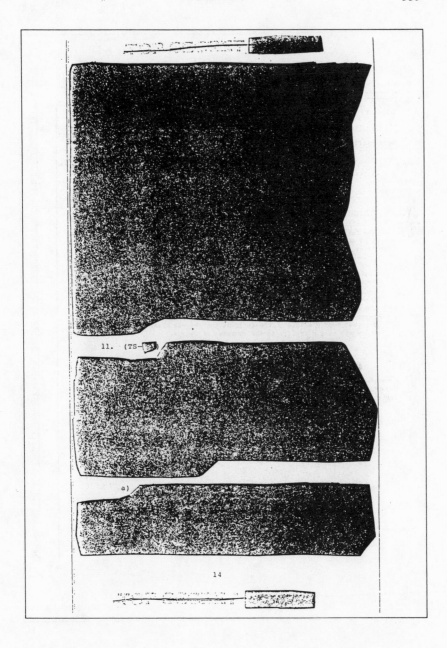

USAF Intelligence report, 1952. Objects seen entering or leaving the sea have been observed for many years.

Memorandum for Mr. Ladd

       Mr. ████████ also discussed this matter with Colonel L. R. Forney of MIS. Colonel Forney indicated that it was his attitude that inasmuch as it has been established that the flying disks are not the result of any Army or Navy experiments, the matter is of interest to the FBI. He stated that he was of the opinion that the Bureau, if at all possible, should accede to General Schulgen's request.

SWR:AJB

ADDENDUM

I would recommend that we advise the Army that the Bureau does not believe it should go into these investigations, it being noted that a great bulk of those alleged discs reported found have been pranks. It is not believed that the Bureau would accomplish anything by going into these investigations.

DML

(Clyde Tolson)

I think we should do this

7-15

(J.Edgar Hoover)

I would do it but before agreeing to it we must insist upon full access to discs recovered. For instance in the Sw. case the Army grabbed it & would not let us have it for cursory examination

- 2 -

H

Handwritten note by FBI Director J. Edgar Hoover referring to a recovered disk which the Bureau was denied access to in 1947

DEPARTMENT OF DEFENSE
OFFICE OF PUBLIC INFORMATION
WASHINGTON 25, D. C.

26 January 1953

Henry Holt & Company
383 Madison Avenue
New York 17, N.Y.

Dear Sirs:

This will acknowledge your letter of recent date regarding
a proposed book on "flying saucers" by Major Donald E. Keyhoe,
U. S. Marine Corps, retired.

We in the Air Force recognize Major Keyhoe as a responsible,
accurate reporter. His long association and cooperation with the
Air Force, in our study of unidentified flying objects, qualifies
him as a leading civilian authority on this investigation.

All the sighting reports and other information he listed have
been cleared and made available to Major Keyhoe from Air Technical
Intelligence records, at his request.

The Air Force, and its investigating agency, "Project Bluebook,"
are aware of Major Keyhoe's conclusion that the "Flying Saucers" are
from another planet. The Air Force has never denied that this
possibility exists. Some of the personnel believe that there may
be some strange natural phenomena completely unknown to us, but that
if the apparently controlled maneuvers reported by many competent
observers are correct, then the only remaining explanation is the
interplanetary answer.

Very Truly Yours
Albert M. Chop
Air Force Press Desk

Letter from Albert Chop to Major Donald Keyhoe's publishers, 1953

1180012790

Country: USSR   XY Reel 1876 Frame
Subject: Unidentified Flying Objects (U)   Rpt: 1 901 0007 68
D.I.: 10 Nov 67 - 10 Jan 68   D.R.: 19 January 1968
Pl & Date Acq: Moscow, USSR   No. Pages: 2
  30 Dec 67 to 11 Jan 68   Ref: DIRS: 1C1
Eval: A-2   Originator: USAIRA MOSCOW USSR
Source: Official Liaison   Prep by:

Info Spec: RDV/fv   Appr Auth: MELVIN J. NIELSEN
Distr: MAP/BTL/EVT(6)   COLONEL, USAF, DEFENSE ATTACHE
                                 Entire Report

SUMMARY:

                Report includes information on Russian commission set
up to study Unidentified Flying Objects. Of particular interest is the fact that at
first the Russians publicized the commission, but now claim the commission has been
disbanded.
REPORT:
     1. (U) In early November 1967 (exact date believed to be 10 Nov) Moscow TV
presented a program on Unidentified Flying Objects. On 12 Nov 67 a Reuters release

2/4

1180012790
USSR   Rpt: 1 901 0007 68
in the U.S. press (believe article was in Daily Telegraph) reported the TV program.
     2. (U) The essence of the TV program, and Reuters report based on the TV
program, was that the Russians had recently set up a commission to study UFOs. The
Chairman of the Commission is retired SAF Major General A. V. STROLYANOV, a former
Technical Services Officer. The group consisted of 18 astronomers and SAF officers
plus 200 observers.
     3.   A day or two after the TV program, the Reuters correspondent went
to see General STROLYANOV. The General was very polite, confirmed the information
about the commission, the 18 astronomers and SAF officers and the 200 observers. In
addition, he said five (5) positive sightings had been made.
     4.   Approximately a week later the Reuters correspondent went back to
see General STROLYANOV. However, this time the correspondent could not get past the
General's secretary, was politely but firmly told the General was no longer available for interview.
     5.   On 13 December 1967, the British Embassy was directed by London to
further investigate the subject with a view to cooperating with the Russians in
observation teams for UFOs.
     6.   The Scientific Counselor of the British Embassy went to the State
Committee for Science and Technology and inquired about the UFO Commission and the
possibility of British-Russian cooperation in observation of UFOs. The British
Counselor was politely received and the commission was freely discussed. The British

2/4

Defense Intelligence Agency report mentioning attempt by British government in 1967 to collaborate with the Soviets in UFO research

Operation Majestic 12

The following seven pages are from the Majestic 12 briefing document allegedly prepared for President-elect Eisenhower by Admiral Roscoe Hillenkoetter in November 1952, and classified TOP SECRET/MAJIC —EYES ONLY. It was made available to me unofficially in early 1987, prior to release in the United States.

At the time of writing, only one of the eight attachments—Attachment "A"—has been released to me, this being the Special Classified Executive Order establishing Operation Majestic 12, signed by President Truman in September 1947.

General Walter Bedell Smith, who replaced James Forrestal (MJ-3) in August 1950, became Director of Central Intelligence in October that year. It is my assumption that successive DCI's—who head the entire intelligence community as well as the CIA—are automatically assigned to MAJIC-12. It also seems logical to assume that each President is briefed about MJ-12 prior to taking office. According to the Air Force Office of Special Investigations document of November 1980, (see Appendix, P.528), MJ-12 was still functioning that year, and I have been informed that it still exists, although probably under a different name.

The confirmation that actual alien bodies were recovered during the first retrieval operation is of course sensational news—if true. Until the information contained in this document was made available, it was by no means certain that bodies were found following the retrieval of UFO wreckage seventy-five miles northwest of Roswell, New Mexico, in July 1947.

The existence of the Majestic 12 group and the authenticity of the document is officially denied at the time of writing. It remains to be seen whether further evidence, including photographs, or—dare I hope?— actual exhibits from the Roswell recovery as well as others alleged to have taken place, will be made available. Or will they remain classified—above Top Secret?

TOP SECRET / MAJIC
EYES ONLY
NATIONAL SECURITY INFORMATION

* * * * * * * * * * * * *
* TOP SECRET *
* * * * * * * * * * * * *

EYES ONLY   COPY <u>ONE</u> OP <u>ONE</u>.

BRIEFING DOCUMENT: OPERATION MAJESTIC 12

PREPARED FOR PRESIDENT-ELECT DWIGHT D. EISENHOWER: (EYES ONLY)

18 NOVEMBER, 1952

<u>WARNING</u>! This is a TOP SECRET - EYES ONLY document containing
compartmentalized information essential to the national security
of the United States. EYES ONLY ACCESS to the material herein
is strictly limited to those possessing Majestic-12 clearance
level. Reproduction in any form or the taking of written or
mechanically transcribed notes is strictly forbidden.

* * * * * * * * * * * * *
* TOP SECRET *
TOP SECRET / MAJIC   T52-EXEMPT (E)
EYES ONLY   EYES ONLY

TOP SECRET / MAJIC

EYES ONLY

* TOP SECRET *

COPY ONE OF ONE.

SUBJECT: OPERATION MAJESTIC-12 PRELIMINARY BRIEFING FOR
PRESIDENT-ELECT EISENHOWER.

DOCUMENT PREPARED 18 NOVEMBER, 1952.

BRIEFING OFFICER: ADM. ROSCOE H. HILLENKOETTER (MJ-1)

NOTE: This document has been prepared as a preliminary briefing
only. It should be regarded as introductory to a full operations
briefing intended to follow.

. . . . . .

OPERATION MAJESTIC-12 is a TOP SECRET Research and Development/
Intelligence operation responsible directly and only to the
President of the United States. Operations of the project are
carried out under control of the Majestic-12 (Majic-12) Group
which was established by special classified executive order of
President Truman on 24 September, 1947, upon recommendation by
Dr. Vannevar Bush and Secretary James Forrestal. (See Attachment
"A".) Members of the Majestic-12 Group were designated as follows:

> Adm. Roscoe H. Hillenkoetter
> Dr. Vannevar Bush
> Secy. James V. Forrestal*
> Gen. Nathan F. Twining
> Gen. Hoyt S. Vandenberg
> Dr. Detlev Bronk
> Dr. Jerome Hunsaker
> Mr. Sidney W. Souers
> Mr. Gordon Gray
> Dr. Donald Menzel
> Gen. Robert M. Montague
> Dr. Lloyd V. Berkner

The death of Secretary Forrestal on 22 May, 1949, created
a vacancy which remained unfilled until 01 August, 1950, upon
which date Gen. Walter B. Smith was designated as permanent
replacement.

* TOP SECRET *

TOP SECRET / MAJIC

EYES ONLY   T52-EXEMPT (E)

TOP SECRET / MAJIC
EYES ONLY
* TOP SECRET *
****

COPY ONE OF ONE.

On 24 June, 1947, a civilian pilot flying over the Cascade
Mountains in the State of Washington observed nine flying
disc-shaped aircraft traveling in formation at a high rate
of speed. Although this was not the first known sighting
of such objects, it was the first to gain widespread attention
in the public media. Hundreds of reports of sightings of
similar objects followed. Many of these came from highly
credible military and civilian sources. These reports resulted in independent efforts by several different elements
of the military to ascertain the nature and purpose of these
objects in the interests of national defense. A number of
witnesses were interviewed and there were several unsuccessful
attempts to utilise aircraft in efforts to pursue reported
discs in flight. Public reaction bordered on near hysteria
at times.

In spite of these efforts, little of substance was learned
about the objects until a local rancher reported that one
had crashed in a remote region of New Mexico located approximately seventy-five miles northwest of Roswell Army Air
Base (now Walker Field).

On 07 July, 1947, a secret operation was begun to assure
recovery of the wreckage of this object for scientific study.
During the course of this operation, aerial reconnaissance
discovered that four small human-like beings had apparently
ejected from the craft at some point before it exploded.
These had fallen to earth about two miles east of the wreckage
site. All four were dead and badly decomposed due to action
by predators and exposure to the elements during the approximately one week time period which had elapsed before their
discovery. A special scientific team took charge of removing
these bodies for study. (See Attachment "C".) The wreckage
of the craft was also removed to several different locations.
(See Attachment "B".) Civilian and military witnesses in
the area were debriefed, and news reporters were given the
effective cover story that the object had been a misguided
weather research balloon.

****
* TOP SECRET *
****
EYES ONLY TOP SECRET / MAJIC   T52-EXEMPT (E)
EYES ONLY

TOP SECRET / MAJIC
EYES ONLY
••••••••••••••
* TOP SECRET *
••••••••••••••

<u>EYES ONLY</u>   COPY <u>ONE</u> OF <u>ONE</u>.

A covert analytical effort organized by Gen. Twining and
Dr. Bush acting on the direct orders of the President, resulted in a preliminary concensus (19 September, 1947) that
the disc was most likely a short range reconnaissance craft.
This conclusion was based for the most part on the craft's
size and the apparent lack of any identifiable provisioning.
(See Attachment "D".) A similar analysis of the four dead
occupants was arranged by Dr. Bronk. It was the tentative
conclusion of this group (30 November, 1947) that although
these creatures are human-like in appearance, the biological
and evolutionary processes responsible for their development
has apparently been quite different from those observed or
postulated in homo-sapiens. Dr. Bronk's team has suggested
the term "Extra-terrestrial Biological Entities", or "EBEs",
be adopted as the standard term of reference for these
creatures until such time as a more definitive designation
can be agreed upon.

Since it is virtually certain that these craft do not originate in any country on earth, considerable speculation has
centered around what their point of origin might be and how
they get here. Mars was and remains a possibility, although
some scientists, mostly notably Dr. Menzel, consider it more
likely that we are dealing with beings from another solar
system entirely.

Numerous examples of what appear to be a form of writing
were found in the wreckage. Efforts to decipher these have
remained largely unsuccessful. (See Attachment "E".)
Equally unsuccessful have been efforts to determine the
method of propulsion or the nature or method of transmission
of the power source involved. Research along these lines
has been complicated by the complete absence of identifiable
wings, propellers, jets, or other conventional methods of
propulsion and guidance, as well as a total lack of metallic
wiring, vacuum tubes, or similar recognizable electronic
components. (See Attachment "F".) It is assumed that the
propulsion unit was completely destroyed by the explosion
which caused the crash.

••••••••••••••
* TOP SECRET *
••••••••••••••

<u>EYES ONLY</u> TOP SECRET / MAJIC   T52-EXEMPT (E)
EYES ONLY

TOP SECRET / MAJIC
EYES ONLY

••••••••••••••
• TOP SECRET •
••••••••••••••••

<u>EYES ONLY</u>   COPY <u>ONE</u> OF <u>ONE</u>.

A need for as much additional information as possible about
these craft, their performance characteristics and their
purpose led to the undertaking known as U.S. Air Force Project
SIGN in December, 1947. In order to preserve security, liason
between SIGN and Majestic-12 was limited to two individuals
within the Intelligence Division of Air Materiel Command whose
role was to pass along certain types of information through
channels. SIGN evolved into Project GRUDGE in December, 1948.
The operation is currently being conducted under the code name
BLUE BOOK, with liason maintained through the Air Force officer
who is head of the project.

On 06 December, 1950, a second object, probably of similar
origin, impacted the earth at high speed in the El Indio -
Guerrero area of the Texas - Mexican boder after following
a long trajectory through the atmosphere. By the time a
search team arrived, what remained of the object had been almost
totally incinerated. Such material as could be recovered was
transported to the A.E.C. facility at Sandia, New Mexico, for
study.

Implications for the National Security are of continuing importance in that the motives and ultimate intentions of these
visitors remain completely unknown. In addition, a significant
upsurge in the surveillance activity of these craft beginning
in May and continuing through the autumn of this year has caused
considerable concern that new developments may be imminent.
It is for these reasons, as well as the obvious international
and technological considerations and the ultimate need to
avoid a public panic at all costs, that the Majestic-12 Group
remains of the unanimous opinion that imposition of the
strictest security precautions should continue without interruption into the new administration. At the same time, contingency plan MJ-1949-04P/78 (Top Secret - Eyes Only) should
be held in continued readiness should the need to make a
public announcement present itself. (See Attachment "G".)

••••••••••••••
TOP SECRET / MAJIC
EYES ONLY

<u>EYES ONLY</u>   T52-EXEMPT (E)

TOP SECRET / MAJIC

EYES ONLY

•••••••••••••
• TOP SECRET •
•••••••••••••

EYES ONLY   COPY <u>ONE</u> OF <u>ONE</u>.

ENUMERATION OF ATTACHMENTS:

•ATTACHMENT "A".......Special Classified Executive
                     Order #092447. (TS/EO)

•ATTACHMENT "B".......Operation Majestic-12 Status
                     Report #1, Part A. 30 NOV '47.
                     (TS-MAJIC/EO)

•ATTACHMENT "C".......Operation Majestic-12 Status
                     Report #1, Part B. 30 NOV '47.
                     (TS-MAJIC/EO)

•ATTACHMENT "D".......Operation Majestic-12 Preliminary
                     Analytical Report. 19 SEP '47.
                     (TS-MAJIC/EO)

•ATTACHMENT "E".......Operation Majestic-12 Blue Team
                     Report #5. 30 JUN '52.
                     (TS-MAJIC/EO)

•ATTACHMENT "F".......Operation Majestic-12 Status
                     Report #2. 31 JAN '48.
                     (TS-MAJIC/EO)

•ATTACHMENT "G".......Operation Majestic-12 Contingency
                     Plan MJ-1949-04P/78: 31 JAN '49.
                     (TS-MAJIC/EO)

•ATTACHMENT "H".......Operation Majestic-12, Maps and
                     Photographs Folio (Extractions).
                     (TS-MAJIC/EO)

•••••••••••••
• TOP SECRET •

TOP SECRET / MAJIC

EYES ONLY   EYES ONLY   T52-EXEMPT (E)

TOP SECRET

EYES ONLY

THE WHITE HOUSE
WASHINGTON

September 24, 1947.

MEMORANDUM FOR THE SECRETARY OF DEFENSE

Dear Secretary Forrestal:

As per our recent conversation on this matter, you are hereby authorized to proceed with all due speed and caution upon your undertaking. Hereafter this matter shall be referred to only as Operation Majestic Twelve.

It continues to be my feeling that any future considerations relative to the ultimate disposition of this matter should rest solely with the Office of the President following appropriate discussions with yourself, Dr. Bush and the Director of Central Intelligence.

Harry Truman

TOP SECRET
EYES ONLY

ACKNOWLEDGMENTS

The author would like to thank the following for their assistance in the preparation of this book:

Walter Andrus and the Mutual UFO Network; Leslie Banks DFC, AFC; John Berry; Mark Birdsall and the Yorkshire UFO Society; Ray Boeche; Bob Boyd and the Plymouth UFO Research Group; Arthur Bray; the Center for UFO Studies; the Central Intelligence Agency; William Chalker and the Australian Center for UFO Studies; Miles Copeland; Dr. Robert Creegan; the Defense Intelligence Agency; Hilary Evans; Lucius Farish and the UFO Newsclipping Service; the Federal Bureau of Investigation; Raymond Fowler; Brian Freemantle; Stanton Friedman; Peter Gersten; Dr. L. M. Gindilis; Barry Greenwood and Citizens Against UFO Secrecy; Dr. Pierre Guérin; Bill Gunston; Colonel Charles Halt; Harry Harris; the Trustees of the Imperial War Museum; Zhang Laigui and the Chinese Embassy, London; Coral Lorenzen and the Aerial Phenomena Research Organization; Andrew Lownie; Donald McCormick; Derek Mansell and Contact International; the Ministry of Defense; William Moore; the National Aeronautics and Space Administration; the National Security Agency; HRH Prince Philip, Duke of Edinburgh; Colin Phillips; Popperfoto; the Public Record Office; Ian Ridpath; the Royal Australian Air Force; Chris Rutkowski; James Salandin; Dr. Berthold Schwarz; Stan Seers; Anne Smith; Ray Stanford; Michael J. Taylor; Air Commodore David Thorne; Mollie Travis and the Trustees of the Broadlands Archives; Admiral Stansfield Turner; the U.S. Air Force, Army, and Navy intelligence branches; Guido Valentich; Todd Zechel.

Special thanks are due to Lord Hill-Norton for his courageous Foreword; Ralph Noyes, for a great deal of help and advice; Paul Dong, William Steinman, and Wendelle Stevens, for the extensive use of material from *UFOs over Modern China* and *UFO Crash at Aztec*; Leonard Stringfield for the use of material from his pioneering publications on UFO retrievals; and Gordon Creighton, editor of *Flying Saucer Review*, for allowing the author to take advantage of the wealth of information contained in this fine journal.*

* FSR Publications Ltd., P.O. Box 12, Snodland, Kent, ME6 5J2, England

NOTES

Introduction

1. Letter to the author from Chapman Pincher, 4 October 1981.
2. *Hansard* (House of Lords), Vol.397, No. 23, 18 January 1979, p.1310.

Prologue

1. Keel, John A.: "Mystery Aeroplanes of the 1930s," Part I, *FSR*, Vol. 16, No.3, 1970, pp.10–13.
2. *New York Times*, 3 February 1934.
3. Keel, John A.: "Mystery Aeroplanes of the 1930s," Part II, *FSR*, Vol.16, No.4, 1970, pp.9–14.
4. Collins, Paul T.: "The UFOs of 1942," *Exploring the Unknown*, No. 48, September 1968.
5. Ibid.
6. Clark, Jerome, and Farish, Lucius: "The Mysterious Foo Fighters of WWII," *UFO Report*, Vol.2, No.3, New York, 1975, pp.44–7, 64–6.
7. Edwards, Frank: *Flying Saucers—Here and Now!*, Lyle Stuart, New York, 1967, p.77.
8. Durrant, Henry: *Le Livre Noir des Soucoupes Volantes*, Laffont, Paris, pp.81–6. (However, Durrant now admits that he invented the story of "Sonder Büro" and "Operation Uranus.")
9. Lore, Gordon, and Deneault, Harold: *Mysteries of the Skies*, Robert Hale, London, 1969, p.127.
10. Gross, Loren E.: "Ghost Rockets of 1946," *The Encyclopedia of UFOs* (edited by Ronald D. Story), New English Library, London, 1980, pp.147–49.
11. Flammonde, Paris: *UFO Exist!*, G. P. Putnam's Sons, New York, 1976, pp.127–34.
12. *New York Times*, 23 August 1946.
13. Jones, Professor R. V.: "The Natural Philosophy of Flying Saucers," *Physics Bulletin*, Vol.19, July 1968, pp.225–30.
14. *New York Times*, 11 October 1946.
15. *Daily Telegraph*, London, 6 September 1946.
16. Fowler Raymond E.: *UFOs.: Interplanetary Visitors*, Exposition Press, New York, 1974, pp.105–6.
17. *Sydney Sun*, 25 February 1967. The "foreign officials" cited by Santorini are here identified as being from the Pentagon.

PART ONE: GREAT BRITAIN

Chapter 1
1943–54

1. Letter from Air Marshal Sir Victor Goddard, *FSR*, Vol.24, No.1, 1978, pp.30–1
2. Edwards, Frank: *Flying Saucers—Here and Now!*, Lyle Stuart, New York, 1967, p.77.
3. Ibid., pp.77–8.
4. Letter to the author from Simon Weeden, Defense Secretariat 8, Ministry of Defense, 28 November 1980.
5. *Analysis of Flying Object Incidents in the U.S.*, Air Intelligence Report No. 100–203–79, Directorate of Intelligence and Office of Naval Intelligence, 10 December 1948.
6. Twining, Lieutenant General N. F.: *A.M.C. Opinion Concerning "Flying Discs,"* HQ Air Matériel Command, to Commanding General, Army Air Forces, 23 September 1947.
7. Memorandum from H. Marshall Chadwell, Assistant Director of Scientific Intelligence, to the Director of Central Intelligence, CIA, September 1952.
8. *Sunday Dispatch*, London, 21 September 1952.
9. Ruppelt, Captain Edward J.: *The Report on Unidentified Flying Objects*, Doubleday, New York, 1956, p.196.
10. Ibid., p.130.
11. *Sunday Dispatch*, London, 28 September 1952.
12. Ibid., 7 December 1952.
13. Pitt, John: "Tell us please, Mr. Birch!," *FSR*, Vol.2, No.5, 1956, pp.10–13.
14. Letter to the author from P. M. Hucker, Secretariat (Air Staff) 2a, Ministry of Defense, 10 July 1985.
15. Letter to Ralph Noyes from Group Captain Harold B. Collins, 26 January 1985.
16. Keyhoe, Major Donald E.: *Aliens from Space*, Panther Books, London, 1975, p.27.
17. Girvan, Waveney: *Flying Saucers and Common Sense*, Frederick Muller, London, 1955, pp.106–14.
18. *The Times*, London, 25 November 1954.
19. Dempster, Derek: "Week-End Pilot in Near Collision with Flying Saucer," *FSR*, Vol.1, No.1, 1955, p.2; reprinted in *FSR*, Vol.30, No.2, 1984, pp.13–15.
20. Interview with the author, 10 October 1985.
21. *FSR*, Vol.30, No.2, 1984, pp.13–15.
22. *Sunday Dispatch*, London (headline story), 7 November 1954.
23. Leslie, Desmond: "Politicians and the UFO," *FSR*, Vol.9, No.3, 1963, pp.8–10.
24. *Sunday Dispatch*, London, 28 March 1954.

25. Letter to the author from Major the Hon. Andrew Wigram, Buckingham Palace, 10 December 1985.
26. Zinsstag, Lou and Good, Timothy: *George Adamski—The Untold Story*, Ceti Publications, Beckenham, England, 1983.
27. Ziegler, Philip: *Mountbatten*, Collins, London, 1985, p.493.
28. Leslie, Desmond: "Did Flying Saucers Land at Broadlands?," *FSR*, Vol.26, No.5, 1980, pp.2–4.
29. Leslie also relates that Briggs told him of a second encounter the following day, when the occupants of the UFO invited him for a trip to Egypt! Briggs was anxious that Mountbatten should not be told about this, but Leslie passed the story on to General Sir Frederick Browning, the Queen's Private Secretary at the time, who in turn passed Leslie's written account to Mountbatten. The latter said that he did not believe a word of it, but his signed statement testifying to Briggs' honesty with regard to the first encounter still stands.
30. Ziegler, Philip: op.cit., p.494.

Chapter 2
Room 801–Top Secret (1955–59)

1. Dempster, Derek: Editorial, *FSR*, Vol.1, No.2, 1955.
2. *Los Angeles Examiner*, 23 May 1955.
3. *FSR*, Vol.1, No.3, 1955, p.6
4. Rehn, Gösta K.: *UFOs Here and Now!*, Abelard-Schuman, London, 1974, pp.38–40.
5. Letter from F.H.C. Wimbledon, *FSR*, Vol.24, No.1, 1978, p.31.
6. *Sunday Times*, 9 April 1978.
7. Thayer, Gordon D.: "Optical and Radar Analyses of Field Cases," *Scientific Study of Unidentified Flying Objects*, Bantam Books, New York, 1969, p.164. See also pp.248–56, and McDonald, Dr. James E.: "UFOs over Lakenheath in 1956," *FSR*, Vol.16, No.2, 1970, pp.9–17, 29. The best synopsis of the case is by Thayer in *The Encyclopedia of UFOs*, New English Library, London, 1980, pp.200–202.
8. Bowen, Charles: "The Hazards of Television," *FSR*. Vol.18, No.2, 1972, pp.18–19.
9. Interview with the author, 21 August 1985.
10. Thornton, Dr. Clifford: "The Wardle Mystery," *FSR*, Vol.3, No.3, 1957, p.4.
11. Norris, Geoffrey: "Something in the Sky," *Royal Air Force Flying Review*, Vol.12, No.12, 1957. pp. 14–16, 46.
12. *Sunday Dispatch*, London, 11 July 1954.
13. Letter from Lord Dowding to Alberto Perego, February 26, 1957.
14. *Sunday Dispatch*, London, 7 April 1957.
15. "RAF Radar picks up UFO over Scotland," *FSR*, Vol.3, No.3, 1957, pp.2–3.
16. *Reynolds News*, 15 June 1957.

17. "UFO Cuts out Radio of an Airliner over Kent," *FSR*, Vol.3, No.6, 1957, p.2.
18. "UFO Over British A-Bomber Base," *FSR*, Vol.4, No.1, 1958, p.6.
19. *FSR*, Vol.4, No.4, 1958, p.5.
20. Letter to the author from Andrew Mathewson, Defense Secretariat 8, Ministry of Defense, 20 September 1984.
21. *FSR*, Vol.4, No.5, 1958, back page.
22. *FSR*, Vol.5, No.1, 1959, p.2.
23. *FSR*, Vol.5, No.2, 1959, p.2.
24. *FSR*, Vol.5, No.3, 1959, p.10.
25. Sanskrit word for "flying chariot," according to Desmond Leslie, described in his book *Flying Saucers Have Landed*, co-authored with George Adamski; Werner Laurie, London, 1953. Revised version published by Neville Spearman, London, 1970.
26. The order forbidding aircrews to discuss their sightings publicly was issued by the Air Ministry on 25 January 1954, according to Harold T. Wilkins in *Flying Saucers Uncensored*, Arco Publishers, London, 1956, p.118.
27. Leslie, Desmond: "Politicians and the UFO," *FSR*, Vol.9, No.3, 1963, pp.8–10.

Chapter 3
A Matter of National Security (1960–79)

1. Muirfield, Roger: "Silence in the Press: A Glimpse behind the Scenes," *FSR*, Vol.6, No.3, 1960, pp. 16–19.
2. Girvan, Waveney: Editorial, *FSR*, Vol.6, No.5, 1960, pp.1–2.
3. "Security Procedures in the Public Service," *First Radcliffe Committee Report*, Her Majesty's Stationery Office, London, April 1962.
4. Letter to the author from Chapman Pincher, 4 October 1981.
5. "The Secret of Room 105," *Time*, 2 September 1985.
6. Girvan, Waveney: "A Landing at Cosford?," *FSR*, Vol.10, No.2, 1964, p.17; "The Cosford UFO: The Mystery Deepens," *FSR*, Vol.10, No.3, 1964, pp.31–2; "The Lessons of Cosford," *FSR*, Vol.10, No.4, 1964, pp.1–2.
7. *Camberley News*, 15 March 1963.
8. *Hansard* (House of Commons), 15 July 1964.
9. *Daily Telegraph*, London, 20 July 1966.
10. Letter to the author from the Rt. Hon. Lord Wilson of Rievaulx, 1 January 1985.
11. Letter to the author from the Rt. Hon. Edward Heath, MP, 12 February 1982.
12. From the official report, sent to Jonathan Caplan.
13. *National Enquirer*, US, September 1967.
14. *UFO Contact*, Vol.2, No.7, Denmark, 1967, p.191.
15. Chapman, Robert: *Unidentified Flying Objects*, Robert Barker, London, 1969, pp.412–4.

16. Letter to the author from Peter Hucker, Secretariat (Air Staff) 2, Ministry of Defense, 22 August 1985.
17. Letter to the author from Peter Hucker, 30 May 1986.
18. Brooks, Angus: "Remarkable Sighting near Dorset Coast," *FSR*, Vol.14, No.1, 1968, pp.3–5.
19. Chapman, Robert: op. cit., pp.25–35.
20. *Daily Express*, London, 7 November 1967; Falla, Geoffrey: *Vehicle Interference Project*, British UFO Research Association, 1979.
21. Evans, Hilary: *The Evidence for UFOs*, Aquarian Press, 1983, pp.74–5.
22. *Hansard* (House of Commons), 8 November 1967.
23. Ibid., 22 November 1967
24. Ibid., 22 January 1968.
25. Ibid., 11 June 1968.
26. "Flying Saucers—and the people who see them," BBC Television, 9 May 1968.
27. Stanway, Roger H. and Pace, Antony R.: *Flying Saucer Report: UFOs Unidentified, Undeniable*, privately published, 1972.
28. Ibid., pp.62–5.
29. Ibid., appendices 1 and 2.
30. Letter to the author, 8 October 1986.
31. Interview with David Ross, Secretariat AS2a, Ministry of Defense, 23 October 1986.
32. Interview with David Ross, 8 December 1986.
33. Wood, Frank: "Alleged CEIII at Winchester," *FSR*, Vol.22, No.5, 1976, pp.13–14.
34. Bowen, Charles: Editorial, *FSR*, Vol.23, No.1, 1977, pp.1–2.
35. Letter to the author from Simon Weeden, Defense Secretariat 8, Ministry of Defense, 18 November 1981.
36. *Daily Mirror*, London, 18 August 1978.
37. *Middlesex Chronicle*, 15 September 1978.
38. Birdsall, Graham and Mark: "Landing and possible traces near Leeds," *Northern Ufology*, No.62, July 1979.
39. BUFORA (Yorkshire Branch) report forms.
40. *Yorkshire Post*, 24 February 1979.
41. Interview with Mr. Tebbs, 27 July 1986.
42. *Hansard* (House of Lords), 18 January 1979, available as *The House of Lords UFO Debate*, with preface by Lord Clancarty, Open Head Press/Pentacle Books, London, 1979.

Chapter 4
December 1980

1. Letter to the author from B.A. Buckingham, for Chief Officer, Civil Aviation Authority, Heathrow Airport, 30 December 1980.
2. Letter to the author from Simon Weeden, Defense Secretariat 8, Ministry of Defense, 25 March 1981.

3. *Pilot*, Vol.20, No.4, April 1986. It is claimed that Lockheed F-19 Stealth aircraft have made nearly 30 visits to Britain, operating in and out of RAF/ USAF Mildenhall. The F-19, according to a *Pilot* source, has almost silent engines as well as a low infra-red signature, which together with its low radar profile *and* "chameleon" skin coating (adapting to the surrounding terrain) make it very difficult to detect. Thirty F-19s have reportedly been based at RAF/USAF Lakenheath since autumn 1986.

4. Letter to Robert Todd from Col. Peter W. Bent, Commander, Headquarters, 513th Combat Support Group (USAFE), APO, New York 09127, 14 June 1983.

5. Butler, Brenda, Street, Dot and Randles, Jenny: *Sky Crash*, Neville Spearman, Sudbury, Suffolk, 1984, p.34. Revised version, Grafton Books, London, 1986.

6. Ibid., p.102.

7. Ibid., pp.104–5.

8. *Omni*, Vol.5 No.6, 1983.

9. *Sky Crash*, op. cit., p.167.

10. Ibid., pp.7–10, 90–1.

11. Ibid., p.27.

12. Ibid., pp.191–3.

13. Ibid., pp.94–8. For details of Warren's regression under hypnosis see pp.232–44.

14. Randles, Jenny: "Military Contact alleged at Air Base," *FSR*, Vol.26, No.6, 1980 (published 1981), p.iii.

15. Randles, Jenny: "The Rendlesham Forest Mystery," *FSR*, Vol.27, No.6, 1981 (published 1982) pp.4–8.

16. *News of the World*, 2 October 1983.

17. *Daily Telegraph*, London, 17 October 1983.

18. *Hansard* (House of Commons), 24 October 1983.

19. Letter to Ralph Noyes from Brian M. Webster, Defense Secretariat 8, Ministry of Defense, 20 March 1984.

20. Letter to Ralph Noyes from Peter M. Hucker, Defense Secretariat 8, Ministry of Defense, 15 May 1985.

21. A copy of the Halt tape is available from the Yorkshire UFO Society (YU-FOS), 12 Miles Hill Street, Leeds LS7 2EQ.

22. *East Anglian Daily Times*, 25 October 1984.

23. The Office of Special Investigations, with headquarters at Bolling Air Force Base, DC, is a separate counterintelligence service of the US Air Force, which investigates security threats to the Air Force, such as UFO sightings over bases that interfere with radar or communications.

24. Noyes, Ralph: *A Secret Property*, Quartet Books, London, 1985, pp.182–3.

25. Letter to Admiral of the Fleet Lord Hill-Norton from Lord Trefgarne, Parliamentary Under-Secretary of State for the Armed Forces, Ministry of Defense, 19 June 1985.

26. Letter from Admiral of the Fleet Lord Hill-Norton to Lord Trefgarne, 24 June 1985.

27. Interview with Colonel Charles A. Halt, 6 October 1986.

Chapter 5
Per Ardua Ad Astra (1981 onward)

1. *Daily Telegraph*, London, 6 August 1981.
2. Fuller, John G.: *Aliens in the Skies*, G.P. Putnam's Sons, New York, 1969, p.87.
3. *Plymouth Evening Herald*, 28 October 1981.
4. Boyd, Bob: *UFOs over Plymouth*, PUFORG, P.O. Box 75, Plymouth PL1 1SQ.
5. *Hansard* (House of Lords), 4 March 1982.
6. "Out of Court," BBC Television, 10 March 1982.
7. *Hansard* (House of Lords), 7 April 1982.
8. First published in *Viewpoint Aquarius* by Rex Dutta in July 1978, the document is reproduced in *The House of Lords UFO Debate*; full transcript with preface by Lord Clancarty and notes by John Michell, Open Head Press, London, 1979, p.36.
9. *Reading Evening Post*, 16 March 1983.
10. Letter to the author from Mrs. P. J. Titchmarsh, Defense Secretariat 8, Ministry of Defense, 25 April 1983.
11. Letter to the author from Captain Paula Hoffman, Chief of Public Affairs, USAF (Europe), Headquarters 20th Tactical Fighter Wing, RAF Upper Heyford, 12 July 1983.
12. George Adamski was the first witness to describe a central column on board a UFO. See his *Inside the Space Ships*, Neville Spearman, London, 1956.
13. *Aldershot News*, 14 October 1983.
14. *National Enquirer*, 17 July 1984.
15. Letter to the author from Peter M. Hucker, Secretariat (Air Staff) 2a, Ministry of Defense, 30 May 1986.
16. Letter to the author from Miss G. J. Jamieson, Defense Secretariat 8, Ministry of Defense, 21 October 1980.
17. Bailey, Martin: "It's official: there *are* UFOs," *Observer*, 4 March 1984.
18. *Hansard* (House of Commons), 9 March 1984.
19. *Hansard* (House of Commons), 14 March 1984.
20. *Lancashire Evening Telegraph*, 1 May 1984.
21. *Focus*, Stanmore, 5 May 1984.
22. Interview with Ruth Novelli, 8 May 1984.
23. *Stanmore & Harrow Observer*, 11 May 1984.
24. Interview, 10 May 1984.
25. *Evening Standard*, London, 3 May 1984.
26. Interview with Tim Mahoney, 10 May 1984.
27. Letter to the author from Peter M. Hucker, Secretariat (Air Staff) 2a, Ministry of Defense, 30 May 1986.
28. Grant, Patricia B.: "A Very Personal Encounter 'Somewhere in Sussex,' " *FSR*, Vol.25, No.2, 1979, pp.18–25; plus Mrs. Grant's voluminous file on the case.
29. Interview with Sergeant Tony Dodd, 13 July 1986.

30. Randles, Jenny: *The Pennine UFO Mystery*, Granada, London 1983, pp.122–35, 147–68.
31. "Central Weekend," Central Television, Birmingham, 5 September 1986.
32. Bunyan, Tony: *The Political Police in Britain*, Quartet Books, London, 1977, pp.187, 191.
33. *Daily Telegraph*, London, 19 January 1983; *The Times*, London, 16 April 1984.
34. Bloch, Jonathan and Fitzgerald, Patrick: *British Intelligence and Covert Action*, Brandon, Dingle, Co. Kerry, Ireland, 1983, pp.22–3.
35. Letter from James Rusbridger, *Daily Telegraph*, London, 13 December 1986.
36. Interview with George Dyer, 18 March 1985.
37. Interview with Peter Hucker, Ministry of Defense, 18 March 1985.
38. *The Air Force List 1985*, Her Majesty's Stationery Office, London, 1985, p.72; *The Civil Service Year Book 1985*, Her Majesty's Stationery Office, London 1985, column 106.
39. DI55 was first mentioned by the MoD to Yorkshire UFO Society investigator Mick Hanson in 1986, and was subsequently confirmed to the author by David Ross of MoD AS2, 23 October and 8 December 1986.
40. Letter to the author from Ralph Noyes, 28 April 1985.
41. "Unidentified Flying Objects," Chapter 4, Section 3, Amendment 31, *Manual of Air Traffic Services* (Part I), 5 July 1984.
42. Letter to the author from Dr. Robert F. Creegan, State University of New York at Albany, 15 August 1985.
43. Creegan, Robert F.: "Signs of Panic," *APRO Bulletin*, Vol.32, No.3, 1984, p.7.

PART TWO: AROUND THE WORLD

Chapter 6
France, Italy, Portugal and Spain

1. *Sunday Dispatch*, London, 3 October 1954.
2. "French Minister Speaks on UFOs," *France-Inter*, 21 February 1974, translated by Gordon Creighton, *FSR*, Vol.20, No.2, 1974, pp.3–4.
3. Michel, Aimé: *Flying Saucers and the Straight-Line Mystery*, Criterion Books, New York, 1958, pp.44–6.
4. *FSR*, Vol.28, No.5, 1982, pp.15–16.
5. *FSR*, Vol.2, No.2, 1956, p.3.
6. Michel, Aimé: op. cit., pp.5–7.
7. See *The Report on Unidentified Aerial Phenomena* by the Institute of Advanced Studies of National Defense (France), available from the Center for UFO Studies.
8. *Sud-Ouest*, Bordeaux, 17 February 1965.
9. Michel, Aimé: "The Valensole Affair," *FSR*, Vol.11, No.6, 1965, pp.7–9; Michel and Bowen, Charles: *The Encyclopedia of UFOs* (edited by Ronald D. Story), New English Library, London, 1980, p.377; Bourret, Jean-Claude:

The Crack in the Universe, Neville Spearman, London, pp.98–106 (original title: *La Nouvelle Vague des Soucoupes Volantes*, France-Empire, Paris, 1974).

10. Gilles, Dr. Jean F.: "The Bankruptcy of the French UFO Research Body, GEPAN," *FSR*, Vol.28, No.5, 1982, p.15.

11. Creighton, Gordon: "The Gendarmerie and UFOs," *FSR*, Vol.17, No.5, 1971, pp.27–8, quoting *La Revue d'Études et d'Information de la Gendarmerie Nationale*, No.87, Premier Trimestre, 1971.

12. Sachs, Margaret: *The UFO Encyclopedia*, Perigee Books, G.P. Putnam's Sons, New York, 1980, pp.132–3.

13. Gilles, Dr. Jean F.: op. cit., p.17.

14. Lagarde, Fernand: "A Warning to All," *FSR*, Vol.28, No.1, 1982, p.2.

15. Guérin, Dr. Pierre: "Are the Reasons for the Cover-Up *Solely* Scientific?" *FSR*, Vol.28, No.6, 1982, pp.2–8.

16. "GEPAN Quietly Delivers the Goods!," *FSR*, Vol.29, No.1, 1983, pp.21–2.

17. Paskov, David: "Flying saucer has the boffins baffled," *Sunday Express*, July 24, 1983.

18. Creighton, Gordon: "Another French Report on GEPAN," *FSR*, Vol.30, No.3, 1984, p.27.

19. Baker, Sherry: "UFO Update," *OMNI*, Vol.8, No.4, 1986, p.83.

20. Letter to the author from Colonel Claude Rossello, Attaché de l'Air, Ambassade de France, London, 30 October 1986.

21. Ibid., 18 November 1986.

22. Chassin, General L.M.: "Success is in Sight," *FSR*, Vol.7, No.6, 1961, pp.3–5.

23. Perego, Dr. Alberto: "The Great Cross above the Vatican," *FSR Case Histories*, No.15, June 1973, pp.3–6.

24. *Veneto Notte*, 19 November 1973, quoted in *FSR*, Vol.20, No.5, 1973, p.iii.

25. Chiumiento, Antonio: "UFO Alert at a NATO Base in Italy," *FSR*, Vol.30, No.2, 1984, pp.2–5.

26. Creighton, Gordon: "A Problem for the Italian Minister of Defense?" *FSR*, Vol.24, No.1, 1978, pp.26–7.

27. Pinotti, Roberto: "The Italian Ministry of Defense and UFOs," *FSR*, Vol.24, No.6, 1978, pp.14–15, 18.

28. Verga, Maurizio: "Two Entity Reports in Italy," *FSR*, Vol.24, No.6, 1978, pp.24–5, quoting *La Sicilia*, 6 July 1978.

29. Ferreira, Captain Jose Lemos: "Air Force Pilots Spend 40 Minutes with Saucers," *FSR*, Vol.4, No.3, 1958, pp.2–3.

30. Ribera, Antonio: "Spanish Jets Chase UFO," *FSR*, Vol.14, No.3, 1968, p.26.

31. Letters to the author from Philip J. Klass, 26 July and 18 September 1985.

32. Letter to the author from Dr. G. Kremser, Max-Planck-Institut für Aeronomie, Katlenburg-Lindau, Germany, 2 August 1977.

33. *Daily Telegraph*, London, 9 September 1968.

34. Creighton, Gordon: "UFO Lands on Spanish Air Force Target Range," *FSR*, Vol.24, No.5, 1978, pp.17–18.

35. *Guardian*, London, 9 January 1975.
36. *ABC*, Seville, 29 June 1976, quoted in *FSR*, Vol.22, No.3, 1976, p.2.
37. Creighton, Gordon: "The Spanish Government Opens its Files," *FSR*, Vol.23, No.3, 1977, p.3.
38. Benitez, Juan Jose: "Release of Further Official Spanish Documents on UFOs," *FSR*, Vol.25, No.2, 1979, pp.24–8.
39. Sanchez, Jesus Maria: "Canary Islands Landing: Occupants Reported," *FSR*, Vol.23, No.3, 1977, pp.4–7.
40. Benitez, Juan Jose: op. cit., p.28.
41. *Yorkshire Post*, 24 September 1976.
42. Benitez, Juan Jose: op. cit., pp.24–8; *Sociedad*, 21 November 1976.
43. Smith, Dr. Willy: "Unknown Intruder over Portugal," *International UFO Reporter*, November–December 1985, pp.6–8, Center for UFO Studies (CUFOS), 2457 W. Peterson Avenue, Chicago, Illinois 60659. The Portuguese Embassy kindly sent me an official report on this and some other Air Force sightings, and commented: ". . . the position of our government is of cautious alert. Pilots of the Portuguese Air Force are instructed to register details of any non-identified objects which they might see while flying." (Letter to the author from the Cultural Counsellor, Portuguese Embassy, London, 14 January 1987).
44. Benitez, Juan Jose: "Jetliner 'Intercepted' by UFO near Valencia," *FSR*, Vol.25, No.5, 1979, pp.13–15.
45. Benitez, Juan Jose: "Anniversary Aerial Encounters," *FSR*, Vol.26, No.6, 1980, pp.12–14; UPI, 15 November 1979.
46. *ABC*, Seville, 29 June 1976.

Chapter 7
Australia

1. Letter to the author from W. A. Smither, Defense Public Relations, Department of Defense (Air Force Office), Canberra, 30 August 1982.
2. Standard Department of Defense pro-forma reply, RAAF Public Relations Office.
3. Norman, Paul B.: "Countdown to Reality," *FSR*, Vol.31, No.2, 1986, pp.13–22.
4. Ibid., p.14.
5. *FSR*, Vol.4, No.3, 1958, p.6.
6. Norman, Paul B.: op. cit., p.14.
7. Chalker, W.: "Australian A.F. UFO Report Files," *APRO Bulletin*, Vol.30, No.10, 1982, pp.5–7.
8. Holledge, James: *Flying Saucers over Australia*, Horwitz Publications, Sydney, 1965, p.31.
9. Chalker, W.: op. cit., p.7.
10. Holledge, James: op. cit., pp.22–4; Seers, Stan and Lasich, William: "North Queensland UFO Saga 1966," *FSR*, Vol.15, No.3, 1969, pp.2–5; Dutton,

T.W.S.: "The Ion Engine and the UFOs," *Australasian Engineer*, Sydney, October 1970.

11. Chalker, W.: "Australian A.F. UFO Report Files" (Part II), *APRO Bulletin*, Vol.30, No.11, 1982, p.6.

12. Zachary, Ted [Todd Zechel]: "The CIA Has Proof that UFOs Exist!," *UFO Report*, New York, August 1977.

13. Seers, Stan, and Lasich, William: op. cit.

14. *FSR*, Vol.29, No.1, 1983, pp.20–21.

15. Chalker, W.: "The North West Cape Incident: UFOs and nuclear alert in Australia," *International UFO Reporter*, Center for UFO Studies (CUFOS), January/February 1986, pp.9–12.

16. Seers, Stan: *UFOs—The Case for Scientific Myopia*, Vantage Press, New York 1983, pp.7–11.

17. Letter to the author from Colin A. Phillips, UFO Research Queensland, 1 September 1985.

18. Chalker, W.: "The UFO Connection: Addendum," *FSR*, Vol.31, No.5, 1986, p.20.

19. Chalker, W.: "Australian A.F. UFO Report Files," *APRO Bulletin*, Vol.30, No.11, 1982. pp.4–5.

20. Holledge, James: op. cit., p.89.

21. Hervey, Michael: *UFOs over the Southern Hemisphere*, Horwitz Publications, Sydney, 1969, pp.18–19.

22. Chalker, W.: op. cit., p.5.

23. Hopkins, Budd, *Missing Time,* Richard Marek, New York, 1981, p.253.

24. Letter to M. L. Roberts, Queensland Flying Saucer Research Bureau, from John Meskell, Criminal Investigation Branch, Townsville, 28 July 1965. A photostat of the original is in the author's possession, kindly supplied by Colin Phillips.

25. Letter to Peter E. Norris, Commonwealth Aerial Phenomena Investigation Organization (CAPIO), from Squadron Leader R. J. Wheeler, Directorate of Air Force Intelligence, 18 August 1965, supplied by Colin Phillips.

26. Letter to Peter Norris from D. S. Graham, for Director-General of Civil Aviation, 3 November 1965.

27. Seers, Stan: op. cit., p.92.

28. Hynek, J. Allen: *The UFO Experience: A Scientific Enquiry*, Abelard-Schuman, London, 1972, p.15.

29. Seers, Stan: op. cit., pp.75–9. The airliner sighting reported by radio station 4KZ was investigated by Keith Basterfield in *A Report of UFOs from Aircraft Crew Members in Australia*, published by the Australian Center for UFO Studies, February 1980. Basterfield reports that in 1978 efforts to trace the pilot were unsuccessful but that a check with staff at Cairns Airport revealed that the incident did apparently occur as several of the Ansett-ANA staff there did recall the event, although only vaguely.

30. Deyo, Stan: *The Cosmic Conspiracy*, West Australian Texas Trading, 1978, pp.28–9.

31. Norman, Paul: "Motherships over Australia," *FSR*, Vol.24, No.5, 1978, pp.9–13.

32. Norman, Paul: "Countdown to Reality," *FSR*, Vol.31, No.2, 1986, p.17.
33. *Newsletter No.26*, UFO Investigation Center of New South Wales, December 1969.
34. Bolotin, Professor H.H.: "UFOs—Do They Come From Outer Space?," 1977; article supplied to the author by the Department of Defense (Air Force Office).
35. Chalker, W.: "The UFO Connection: Startling Implications for Australia's North West Cape, and for Australia's Security," *FSR*, Vol.31, No.5, 1986, pp.13–21.
36. *Aircraft Accident Investigation Summary Report*, Department of Transport, Ref. No. V116/783/1047, 27 April 1982.
37. Chalker, W.: "The Missing Cessna and the UFO," *FSR*, Vol.24, No.5, 1978, pp.3–5.
38. Norman, Paul: op. cit., p.17.
39. *Melbourne Herald*, 9 December 1980.
40. Letter to the author from Guido Valentich, September 1985.
41. Letter to the author from William C. Chalker, 13 September 1985.
42. Chalker, W.: "Vanished?—The Valentich Affair Re-examined," *FSR*, Vol.30, No.2, 1984, pp.6–12. See also the letter from Bill Chalker in *FSR*, Vol.30, No.4, 1984, p.28.
43. Ibid.
44. Ibid.
45. Ibid.
46. Letter to the author from Guido Valentich, September 1985.
47. Chalker, W.: "The Valentich—Bass Strait Affair," *The Encyclopedia of UFOs* (edited by Ronald D. Story), New English Library, London, 1980, pp.379–80.
48. Chalker, W.: "The UFO Connection: Startling Implications for Australia's North West Cape, and for Australia's Security," *FSR*, Vol.31, No.5, 1986, p.18.

Chapter 8
Canada

1. Bray, Arthur: *The UFO Connection*, Jupiter Publishing, 1979, P.O. Box 5528, Station "F," Ottawa, Ontario K2C 3M1, pp.57–66.
2. Letter to Wilfred Daniels, signed on behalf of F. G. Nixon, Director, Telecommunications and Electronics Branch, Department of Transport, 29 April 1964, published in *FSR*, Vol.10, No.4, 1964, p.29.
3. Bray, Arthur: op. cit., p.186.
4. Ibid., p.188.
5. Ibid., pp.147–52.
6. Ibid., pp.153–59.
7. Ibid., pp.62–3.
8. Ibid., pp.63–6.
9. Ibid., pp.66–9.

10. Ibid., pp.70, 191.
11. Edwards, Frank: *Flying Saucers—Serious Business*, Lyle Stuart, New York, 1966, pp.87–8.
12. Ibid., p.86.
13. *The Canadian Magazine/Star Weekly*, 4 January 1969.
14. Howard, James: "The BOAC Labrador Sighting of 1954," *FSR*, Vol.27, No.6, 1981, pp.2–3.
15. Kanon, Gregory M.: "UFOs and the Canadian Government—Part I," *Canadian UFO Report*, Vol.3, No.6, 1975, pp.21–3.
16. Kanon, Gregory M.: "UFOs and the Canadian Government—Part II," *Canadian UFO Report*, Vol.3, No.7, 1976, pp.17–18.
17. *Canadian—United States Communications Instructions for Reporting Vital Intelligence Sightings* (CIRVIS/MERINT) JANAP 146 (E), The Joint Chiefs of Staff, Washington, DC 20301, 31 March 1966.
18. *Sun*, Vancouver, 12 January 1985.
19. Kanon, Gregory M.: op. cit., "UFOs and the Canadian Government—Part II," pp.17–18.
20. *Sun*, Vancouver, 12 January 1985.
21. Kanon, Gregory M.: "UFOs and the Canadian Government—Part II," pp.17–18.
22. Letter to an inquirer (name deleted) from Brigadier General L. A. Bourgeois, Director, General Information, Department of National Defense, Ottawa, 24 October 1962.
23. Bray, Arthur: op. cit., p.56.
24. *Toronto Star*, 10 October 1968.
25. Bray, Arthur: "Government Cover-up Exposed," *Canadian UFO Report*, Vol.3, No.2, 1974, pp.20–22.
26. Magor, John: *Our UFO Visitors*, Hancock House, Saanichton, BC, and Seattle, Washington, 1977, p.74.
27. Letter from John Pushie, *Journal UFO*, Vol.2, No.4, 1981, pp.13–15.
28. *Sun*, Vancouver, 26 April 1976.
29. *Journal UFO*, Vol.2, No.2, 1981, p.11.
30. Rutkowski, Chris: "The Falcon Lake Incident," Parts I–III, *FSR*, Vol.27, Nos. 1,2, and 3, 1981.
31. Cannon, Brian: "Strange Case of Falcon Lake—Part II," *Canadian UFO Report*, Vol.1, No.2, 1969.
32. Lorenzen, Jim and Coral: *UFOs over the Americas*, Signet Books, New York, 1968, p.41.
33. Rutkowski, Chris: op. cit.
34. Letter from Graham Conway, *FSR*, Vol.29, No.2, 1983, p.28, iii.
35. Kanon, Gregory M.: "UFOs and the Canadian Government—Part I," *Canadian UFO Report*, Vol.3, No.6, 1975, p.21.
36. Bray, Arthur: *The UFO Connection*, pp.45–6.
37. Kanon Gregory M.: "Something's Up Here with Us!", *Canadian UFO Report*, Vol.4, No.6, 1978, pp.3–4.
38. Bray, Arthur: *The UFO Connection*, p.45.
39. Kanon, Gregory: "Something's Up Here with Us!"

40. Bray, Arthur: *The UFO Connection*, p.45.
41. Smith, Wilbert B.: "Official Reticence," *FSR*, Vol.6, No.3, 1960, pp.30–31, iv.
42. Smith, Wilbert B.: "Why I Believe in the Reality of the Spacecraft," *FSR*, Vol.4, No.6, 1958, pp.8–11.
43. Letter from Wilbert Smith to Ronald Caswell, 23 February 1959.

Chapter 9
China

1. Heng, Sheng-Yen: "UFOs—An Unsolved World Puzzle," *People's Daily*, 13 November 1978.
2. *Guang Ming Daily*, 12 May 1980.
3. Stevens, Wendelle C., and Dong. Paul: *UFOs over Modern China*, UFO Photo Archives 1983, P.O. Box 17206, Tucson, Arizona 85710, p.22.
4. Bowen, Charles: "The Brightening of the Chinese UFO Scene," *FSR*, Vol.27, No.5, 1981, pp.16–18.
5. Dong, Paul: "UFO Reports from China (1)," *FSR*, Vol.28, No.2, 1982, pp.21–3.
6. Associated Press, 14 July 1947.
7. Stevens and Dong: op. cit., p.33.
8. Ibid., pp.44–5.
9. Ibid., p.45.
10. Ibid., pp.48–9.
11. Ibid., pp.49–50.
12. Ibid., p.56.
13. Ibid., pp.61–3. It should be noted that many sightings of UFOs in the Gobi Desert area can probably be attributed to rocket launches from the Shuang-Chengzi missile test center.
14. On 13 September 1971, the Vice-Chairman of the Chinese Communist Party and Minister of National Defense, Lin Biao, and his rebel followers were killed while escaping in an aircraft which crashed in Mongolia.
15. Stevens and Dong: op. cit., p.72.
16. Ibid., p.88.
17. Ibid., pp.93–4; Lee, Anthony: "UFO Reports from China (2)," *FSR*, Vol.28, No.4, 1982, pp.23–4.
18. Stevens and Dong: op. cit., pp.99–102.
19. Dong, Paul: *Feidie Bai Wen Bai Da* (Questions and Answers on UFOs), Deli Shuju, Hong Kong, 1983, summarized and translated by Gordon Creighton in *FSR*, Vol.28, No.6, 1984, pp.14–20; Stevens and Dong: op. cit., p.119.
20. Dong, Paul: Extracts from "Questions and Answers on UFOs," *FSR*, Vol.28, No.6, 1984, p.14.
21. Stevens and Dong: op. cit., pp.119–120.
22. Ibid., p.132.
23. Ibid., pp.140–1.
24. Ibid., p.146.

25. Dong, Paul: op. cit., p.18 (report edited by Leslie Banks).
26. Stevens and Dong: op. cit., pp.216–18.
27. Ibid., p.202.
28. Ibid., pp.219–20.
29. Ibid., pp.243–5.
30. *People's Daily*, 28 July and 9 August 1985.
31. *Sunday Express*, London, 25 August 1985.
32. Letter to the author from Zhang Laigui, Air Attaché, Embassy of the People's Republic of China, London, 25 January 1986.
33. *China Daily*, 27 August 1985.

Chapter 10
USSR

1. *Playboy*, December 1967.
2. Zigel, Professor F. Y.: "Mysteries of the 20th Century: UFOs—What Are They?", edited by B. P. Konstantinov, Vice-President of the USSR Academy of Sciences, *Smena*, Moscow, 7 April 1967.
3. Brill, Joe: "UFOs Behind the Iron Curtain," *Skylook*, No.87, February 1975, Mutual UFO Network (MUFON Inc.), pp.14–15.
4. Letter to the author from V. Bashkirov, Director of the M.V. Frunze Central House of Aviation and Space, Moscow, 22 January 1986.
5. Gindilis, L. M., Menkov, D.A., and Petrovskaya, I.G.: *Observations of Anomalous Atmospheric Phenomena in the USSR: Statistical Analysis*, USSR Academy of Sciences Institute of Space Research Report, PR 473, 1979, pp.1–74. Translation published as "NASA Technical Memorandum No.75665." available from the Center for UFO Studies (CUFOS), 2457 Peterson Avenue, Chicago, Illinois 60659.
6. Letter to the author from Dr. L. M. Gindilis, Sternberg State Astronomical Institute, Moscow, 20 February 1986.
7. Buttlar, Johannes von: *The UFO Phenomenon*, Sidgwick & Jackson, London, 1979, p.65.
8. Air Intelligence Report No. IR 193-55, 13 October 1955.
9. Harbinson, W. A.: *Genesis*, Corgi Books, London, 1980, pp.593–606.
10. I do not discount the probability that saucer-type aircraft have been successfully flown in more recent years.
11. Zigel. Dr. Felix: "Unidentified Flying Objects," *Soviet Life*, London, March 1968.
12. *Oltre il Cielo: Missili e Razzi*, No.105, 1–15 June 1962.
13. "UFOs over Russia," *Flying Saucers*, No.47, Palmer Publications, Amherst, Wisconsin, May 1966, pp.6–10.
14. Ibid.
15. Gindilis, Menkov, and Petrovskaya: op. cit.
16. *Oltre il Cielo: Missili e Razzi*, op. cit.
17. Steiger, Brad: *Flying Saucers Are Hostile*, Award Books, New York, 1967, pp.85–6.

18. Komarov, Vladimir, Feoktistov, Konstantin, and Yegorov, Boris: "24 Hours in Space," *The Astronauts Book*, Panther Books, London, 1966.
19. Hobana, Ion, and Weverbergh: Julien: *UFOs from Behind the Iron Curtain*, Souvenir Press, London, 1974, pp.31–2.
20. Steiger, Brad: op. cit., p.86.
21. Gindilis, Menkov, and Petrovskaya: op. cit.
22. Saunders, David R., and Harkins, R. Roger: *UFOs? Yes!*, Signet, New York, 1968, p.134.
23. Menzel, Donald H.: *Flying Saucers*, Harvard University Press, 1953.
24. *FSR*, Vol.3, No.3, 1957, p.3.
25. *Sud-Ouest*, Bordeaux, 17 February 1965.
26. Marchetti, Victor: "How the CIA Views the UFO Phenomenon," *Second Look*, Washington, DC, Vol.1, No.7, May 1979, pp.2–5.
27. Hobana and Weverbergh: op. cit., p.25; *FSR*, Vol.13, No.6, 1967, p.2. At the inaugural meeting on 17 May 1967, those present included Professor Heinrich Ludwig; Doctors of Science Nikolai Zhirov and Igor Bestuzhev-Lada: chief navigator of Soviet polar aviation, Valentine Akkuratov; Generals Porfiri Stolyarov, Leonid Reino, Georgi Uger, and Georgi Zevalkin; twice Hero of the Soviet Union Grigori Sivkov, Master of Science (engineering); Heroes of the Soviet Union docent Yekaterina Ryabova and Natalia Kravtsova.
28. Creighton, Gordon: "Dr. Felix Zigel and the Development of Ufology in Russia—Part I," *FSR*, Vol.27, No.3, 1981, p.9.
29. Ibid. Hobana and Weverbergh report that Stolyarov, not Zigel, made the concluding statement.
30. Brill, Joe: "UFOs behind the Iron Curtain," *Skylook*, No.86, MUFON Inc., January 1975.
31. *Daily Telegraph*, London, 1 June 1984.
32. Defense Intelligence Agency report, 19 January 1968.
33. Hobana and Weverbergh: op. cit., p.26.
34. *New York Times*, 10 December 1967.
35. Defense Intelligence Agency report, Op. cit.
36. *Phénomènes Spatiaux*, No.15, January 1968.
37. *Pravda*, Moscow, 29 February 1968.
38. Gindilis, Menkov and Petrovskaya: op. cit.
39. Creighton, Gordon: op. cit., p.10.
40. Hunter, Harriot: "Official UFO Study Programs in Foreign Countries," *Scientific Study of Unidentified Objects* (Dr. Edward Condon), Bantam Books, New York, 1969, p.555.
41. Brill, Joe: op. cit., p.14.
42. *Nedelya*, No.3, 1979.
43. *Tekhnika Molodezhi*, No.3, 1979.
44. Schnee, Nikita: "Ufology in the USSR," *FSR*, Vol.27, No.1, 1981, pp.8–13.
45. Creighton, Gordon: "Dr. Felix Zigel and the Development of Ufology in Russia—Part II," *FSR*, Vol.27, No.4, 1981, pp.13–19.
46. Gindilis, Menkov, and Petrovskaya: op. cit.

47. Letter from James Oberg, *FSR*, Vol.28, No.1, 1982, p.25.
48. *Sunday Times*, London, 17 August 1980.
49. *Gente*, 31 July and 7 August 1981.
50. Ibid.
51. Dobson, Christopher, and Payne, Ronald: *The Dictionary of Espionage*, Harrap, London, 1984, pp.211–13.
52. Barron, John: *KGB: The Secret Work of Soviet Secret Agents*, Corgi Books, London, 1975, p.211. See also Schultz, Richard, and Godson, Roy: *Dezinformatsia: Active Measures in Soviet Strategy*, Pergamon-Brassey's, Washington, DC, 1984.
53. Creighton, Gordon: "Naughty Henry Gris says it again! Soviet Space Center knocked out by UFOs," *FSR*, Vol.28, No.6, 1983, pp.27–8.
54. *Guardian*, London, 7 January 1983.
55. *The Times*, 30 May 1984.
56. *Daily Telegraph*, London, 13 July 1984.
57. Vostrukhin, V.: "At 4:10 precisely . . . We report in detail," *Trud*, 30 January 1985, translated by Gordon Creighton, *FSR*, Vol.30, No.5, 1985, pp.14–16.
58. The Commission for Anomalous Phenomena, Box 764, Glavpochamt (Main Post Office), 101,000 Moscow.
59. *Krasnaya Zvezda*, 13 April 1985, quoted in the *Japan Times*, 16 April 1985.
60. *Sunday Times*, London, 10 March 1985.
61. Letter from Valerii I. Sanarov to Jean-François Boadec, 27 August 1982.
62. Ibid., 10 September 1983.
63. Alexandrov, V.: *L'Ours et la Baleine*, Stock, Paris, 1958, quoted by Jacques Vallee in *Anatomy of a Phenomenon*, Neville Spearman, London 1966, p.114.
64. *International Herald Tribune* and *Daily Telegraph*, 5 December 1985.

PART THREE: USA

Chapter 11
1947–54

1. Few are aware that Kenneth Arnold had a second sighting on 29 July 1947, when he saw twenty to twenty-five small brass-colored objects that came within 400 yards of his plane as he was flying over the La Grande valley, Oregon. The movie film he took revealed only a few of the objects and no detail could be made out. (See *The Coming of the Saucers*.)
2. FBI memorandum to the Officer-in-Charge from Frank M. Brown, special agent, 16 July 1947.
3. Interview with Captain E.J. Smith by the District Intelligence Officer, 13th Naval District, Seattle, Washington, 9 July 1947.
4. Stringfield, Leonard H.: *The UFO Crash/Retrieval Syndrome, Status Report II*, Mutual UFO Network (MUFON), 103 Oldtowne Road, Seguin, Texas 78155 (1980).

5. Moore, William L.: *Crashed Saucers: Evidence in the Search for Proof*, William L. Moore Publications and Research, 4219 W. Olive Street, Suite 247, Burbank, California 91505, June 1985, p.46. I can confirm that the news story about the Roswell disk was suppressed, inasmuch as Hughie Green, the well-known TV broadcaster and former Royal Canadian Air Force pilot, told me himself that he listened to the news broadcasts as he was traveling across New Mexico by car. By the time he reached Philadelphia the story had been killed. (See also *The Roswell Incident*, pp.48–49.)

6. Berlitz, Charles and Moore, William: *The Roswell Incident*, Granada, London, 1980, pp.67–72.

7. Ibid., pp.57–63.

8. Moore, William L.: op. cit.

9. Names of the MJ-12 group were first published in *Just Cause*, No.6, December 1985, P.O. Box 218, Coventry, Connecticut 06238.

10. Steinman, William: *UFO Crash at Aztec: An Investigation Report*, UFO Photo Archives, P.O. Box 17206, Tucson. Arizona 85710 (1987).

11. Letter from Lieutenant General Nathan Twining to J.E. Schaefer of the Boeing Airplane Company, 17 July 1947. Additional quotes supplied by William Moore in *Phil Klass & The Roswell Incident: The Sceptics Deceived*, William L. Moore Publications & Research, Burbank, California, 1986.

12. Letter to the author from Noah D. Lawrence, Jr., Headquarters Air Force Office of Special Investigations, Bolling AFB, DC 20332, 19 February 1985.

13. Moore, William L.: op. cit., p.9.

14. Ibid., pp.9–12.

15. Report of Aircraft Accident, signed by Major Armond E. Matthews, Wright Field Service Center, Wright Field, Dayton, Ohio, 9 January 1948.

16. *Analysis of Flying Object Incidents in the U.S.* (Top Secret), Air Intelligence Division Study No. 203, Directorate of Intelligence and Office of Naval Intelligence, Washington, DC. 10 December 1948.

17. Memorandum from Brigadier General C. P. Cabell, USAF, Chief, Air Intelligence Requirements Division, Directorate of Intelligence, HQ Army Air Forces, 12 February 1948.

18. Memorandum from Major General S. E. Anderson, USAF, Director of Plans and Operations, 3 March 1948.

19. Arnold, Kenneth, and Palmer, Ray: *The Coming of the Saucers*, Amherst Press, Wisconsin, 1952, pp.90–91.

20. Ruppelt. Edward J.: *The Report on Unidentified Flying Objects*, Doubleday, New York, 1956, pp-41, 45.

21. Keyhoe, Major Donald E.: *Aliens from Space*, Panther, London, 1973, p.27.

22. *Analysis of Flying Object Incidents in the U.S.*, op. cit., p.2.

23. Memorandum from Colonel Eustis L. Poland, for the Commanding General, HO 4th Army, Fort Sam Houston Texas, to the Director of Intelligence, GSUSA, Washington 25, DC, 13 January 1949.

24. *Report of Trip to Los Alamos, New Mexico, 16 February 1949*, by Commander Richard S. Mandelkorn, USN, Research & Development Division, Sandia Base, Albuquerque, New Mexico.

25. Secret letter from Lieutenant Colonel Doyle Rees, USAF, District Commander, 17th District Office of Special Investigations, Kirtland AFB, New Mexico, to the Director of Special Investigations, Office of the Inspector General USAF, Washington 25, DC, 12 May 1949.

26. Memorandum from Lieutenant Colonel Doyle Rees to Brigadier General Joseph F. Carroll, Director of Special Investigations, 25 May 1950.

27. Letter from Colonel William B. Guild, Director of Counterintelligence, Department of the Army, Office of the Assistant Chief of Staff for Intelligence, Washington, DC 20310, to Richard Hall, 25 September 1980.

28. *New York Times*, 9 October 1955. (?)

29. FBI memorandum from the Special Agent in Charge, San Antonio, Texas, to FBI Director J. Edgar Hoover, 31 January 1949.

30. CIA draft report, 15 August 1952.

31. Project Sign Report No. F-TR-2274-1A, February 1949.

32. Statement by Lieutenant Graham Bethune, US Naval Reserve Fleet Logistic Air Wing, Atlantic/Continental, Air Transport Squadron One, US Naval Air Station, Patuxent River, Maryland, 10 February 1951.

33. *News Tribune*, Fullerton. California, 26 June 1956.

34. Air Intelligence Information report prepared by Lieutenant Colonel Bruce K. Baumgardner, USAF, Director of Intelligence, HQ EADF, 21 September 1951.

35. Keyhoe, Major Donald E.: *Flying Saucers from Outer Space*, Henry Holt & Company, New York 1953, pp.124–6.

36. Department of the Air Force Staff Message Division, Outgoing Classified Message, HQ USAF, AFOIN-2A3, 16 July 1952.

37. Ruppelt, Edward J.: op. cit., p.158.

38. A temperature inversion is caused when a layer of warm air lies adjacent to a cooler layer, producing optical distortions in the atmosphere.

39. FBI memorandum from V.P. Keay to A. H. Belmont, 29 July 1952.

40. Ruppelt, Edward J.: op. cit., pp.2–5.

41. Stringfield, Leonard H.: *Inside Saucer Post . . . 3–0 Blue*, Civilian Research, Interplanetary Flying Objects (CRIFO), Cincinnati, Ohio, 1957, p.91.

42. Keyhoe, Major Donald E.: *The Flying Saucer Conspiracy*, Hutchinson, London, 1957, pp.11–19; Flammonde, Paris: *UFOs Exist!*, G.P. Putnam's Sons, New York, 1976, pp.279–81.

43. Mel Noel told me, for example, that radio contact with the UFOs was established during the third encounter, and a considerable amount of information was given (in English) to all the pilots. Colonel Peterson, the flight leader, claimed later to have had direct physical contact with the extraterrestrials. In 1959 he disappeared over the Atlantic without any trace of his aircraft being found, having previously informed Mel (who by this time had become a close friend) that he was going to join his extraterrestrial contacts. For further information see *The Mel Noel Story*, Saucerian Publications, available from Susanne Stebbing, 41 Terminus Drive, Beltinge, Herne Bay, Kent CT6 6PR, England.

44. *Omni*, Vol.2, No.6, 1980.

Chapter 12
Collision Course (1950s onward)

1. Classified message from Hamilton AFB, California, to HQ USAF, August 31, 1953.
2. Letter from Dr. Donald H. Menzel, Harvard College Observatory, to Major John A. Samford, Air Technical Intelligence Center, Dayton, Ohio, 16 October 1953.
3. Letter from Colonel George Perry, Directorate of Intelligence, to Brigadier General W. M. Burgess, Deputy for Intelligence, Air Defense Command, Ent AFB, Colorado, 23 December 1953.
4. US Army Intelligence report from Lieutenant Colonel W. Miller, Director, Counterintelligence Division, to the Assistant Chief of Staff, G-2, Washington 25, DC, 10 December 1953.
5. Report filed by Irvin Kabus, 890th CIC Det., 30 April 1954.
6. US Army Order 30–13, 31 January 1957.
7. Classified message from the Commander, Carswell AFB, Texas, to the Directorate of Intelligence; Commander, Air Defense Command, Ent AFB, Colorado; ATIC; 8th Air Force, Carswell AFB.
8. Keyhoe, Major Donald E.: *The Flying Saucer Conspiracy*, Hutchinson, London, 1957, pp.48–9.
9. Keyhoe, Major Donald E.: op. cit., p.103.
10. Keyhoe, Major Donald E.: *Aliens from Space*, Panther, London, 1975, p. 186.
11. Edwards, Frank: *Flying Saucers—Serious Business*, Lyle Stuart, New York, 1966, pp.69–70.
12. Lorenzen, Coral and Jim: *UFOs: The Whole Story*, Signet, New York, 1969, p.79.
13. Fowler, Raymond E.: *Casebook of a UFO Investigator*, Prentice-Hall, New Jersey, 1981, pp.182–3.
14. JANAP 146(c), Joint Chiefs of Staff, Joint Communications, Electronics Committee, Washington, DC, 10 March 1954.
15. *Newark Star Ledger*, 22 December 1958.
16. Maney, Professor Charles A.: "The New UFO Policy of the U.S. Air Force," *FSR*, Vol.6, No.5, 1960, pp.6–9.
17. Memo and reports from the Air Force Special Security Office, Headquarters, Northeast Air Command, APO 862, New York, 18 July 1955.
18. Yost, Graham: *Spy-Tech*, Harrap, London, 1985, p.17.
19. Flammonde, Paris: *The Age of Flying Saucers*, Hawthorn Books, New York, 1971, pp.114–16.
20. *FSR*, Vol.5, No.6, 1959, pp.27–8.
21. Keyhoe, Major Donald E.: *Aliens from Space*, pp.89–90.
22. *New York Sunday Times*, 28 February 1960.
23. UPI, Washington, DC, 14 April 1962.
24. *NICAP Bulletin*, August 1962.
25. Ibid.
26. Keyhoe, Major Donald E.: op. cit., pp.103–4.

27. Ibid., p.288.
28. Ibid., pp.152–3.
29. Maney, Professor Charles A.: op. cit., p.8.
30. *The UFO Investigator*, NICAP, March/April 1965.
31. *FSR*, Vol.11, No.3, 1965, pp.3–4; *Fate*, July 1966.
32. *National Enquirer*, 12 October 1982; *FSR*, Vol.29, No.1, 1983, pp.23–4; Crain, T. Scott: "UFO Intercepts Rocket," *MUFON UFO Journal*, January 1987, pp.5–6.
33. *The Little Listening Post*, Vol.12, No.3, 1965, Washington, DC; Clark, Jerome: "Two New Contact Claims," *FSR*, Vol.11, No.3, 1965, pp.20–22; lecture by Sid Padrick at Reno, Nevada, 10 July 1966.
34. Faulkner, Alex: "Mystery Men in Flying Saucer Probe," *Sunday Telegraph*, 29 January 1967; Rankow, Ralph: "The Heflin Photographs," *FSR*, Vol.14, No.1, 1968, pp.21–4.
35. Yost, Graham: op. cit., pp.142–3.
36. Fawcett, Lawrence and Greenwood, Barry J.: *Clear Intent*, Prentice-Hall, New Jersey, 1984, pp.9–11.
37. Fowler, Raymond: op. cit., p.187.
38. Ibid., pp.186–7.
39. *Birmingham News*, Alabama, 19 October 1973; *Decatur Daily*, Alabama, 16 November 1973; Smith, Warren: "Invasion of the UFO Space Men," *Saga*, Vol.49, No.1, October 1974, pp.35, 48.
40. "Near Collision with UFO Report," Army Disposition Form, Flight Operations Office, USAR Flight Facility, Cleveland Hopkins Airport, Cleveland, Ohio 44135, 23 November 1973.
41. *National Enquirer*, 13 December 1973.
42. Zeidman, Jennie: "Coyne (Mansfield, Ohio) Helicopter Incident," *The Encyclopedia of UFOs* (ed. Ronald D. Story), New English Library, London, 1980, pp.93–5.
43. "Burns Follow UFO Incident," *APRO Bulletin*, Vol.29, No.8, 1981, pp.1–4.
44. Schuessler, John: "Cash-Landrum Case Closed?" *MUFON UFO Journal* No.222, October 1986, pp. 12–17.
45. *APRO Bulletin*, Vol.30, No.7, 1982, p.5.

Chapter 13
The Defense Intelligence Agency

1. Dobson, Christopher, and Payne, Ronald: *The Dictionary of Espionage*, Harrap, London, 1984, p.207.
2. Dulles. Allen W.: *The Craft of Intelligence*, Harper & Row, New York, 1963, p.47.
3. Wise, David, and Ross, Thomas B.: *The Invisible Government*, Bantam Books, New York, 1965, p.230.
4. Turner, Stansfield: *Secrecy and Democracy*, Sidgwick & Jackson, London, 1986, p.247.

5. Kennedy, Colonel William V.: *The Intelligence War*, Salamander Books, London, 1983, p.27.
6. Marchetti, Victor, and Marks, John D.: *The CIA and the Cult of Intelligence*, Coronet Books (Hodder & Stoughton), London, 1976, p.117.
7. Fawcett, Lawrence, and Greenwood, Barry: *Clear Intent*, Prentice-Hall, New Jersey, 1984, p.82.
8. *O Estado de São Paulo*, 8 July 1965.
9. *El Mercurio*, Valparaiso, 7 July 1965. See also Lloyd, Dan: "Things are hotting up in Antarctica," *FSR*, Vol.11, No.5, 1965, pp.4–5.
10. Keyhoe, Major Donald E.: *Flying Saucers from Outer Space*, Henry Holt & Company, New York, 1953, p. 44.
11. *Cronica*, Santiago, 19 May 1972.
12. Bemelmans, Hans: "Reports from Ibiuna," *FSR*, Vol.16, No.1, 1970, pp.15–19.
13. Creighton, Gordon: "Brazil: Censorship of UFO Reports," *FSR*, Vol.19, No.6, 1973, p.29.
14. Letter to the author from Ray Boeche, 29 January 1986.
15. Letter to the author from Bruce Cathie, 19 March 1986.
16. Letter to the author from Bruce Cathie, 17 April 1986.
17. ASI, Buenos Aires, 21 April 1964.
18. Uriondo, Oscar A.: "UFOs over the Andes: Official gendarmeria reports revealed," *FSR*, Vol.28, No.4, 1982, pp.11–13.
19. Creighton, Gordon: "The Spanish Government opens Its Files," *FSR*, Vol.23, No.3, 1977, p.3.
20. Fawcett, Lawrence, and Greenwood, Barry: op. cit., p.84.
21. State Department cable, 18 May 1978.
22. Letter to the author from Larry R. Strawderman, CIA Information and Privacy Coordinator, 29 November 1983.
23. Campbell, Duncan: *The Unsinkable Aircraft Carrier*, Michael Joseph, London, 1984, p.144.
24. Turner, Stansfield: op. cit., p.276.
25. Ibid., p.34.
26. Kennedy, Colonel William V.: op. cit., p.39.

Chapter 14
The Central Intelligence Agency

1. Ranelagh, John: *The Agency*, Weidenfeld & Nicolson, London, 1986.
2. Yost, Graham: *Spy-Tech*, Harrap, London, 1985, pp.6–7; Marchetti, Victor, and Marks, John D.: *The CIA and the Cult of Intelligence*, Coronet, London, 1976, pp.96–7.
3. Zachary, Ted [Todd Zechel]: "The CIA Has Proof that UFOs Exist!," *UFO Report*, New York, August 1977.
4. Ground Saucer Watch, 13238 N. 7th Drive, Phoenix, Arizona 85029.
5. Klass, Philip J.: *UFOs: The Public Deceived*, Prometheus Books, Buffalo, NY, 1983, p.10.

6. Freemantle, Brian: *CIA*, Futura, London, 1983, p.73.

7. US Air Force Fact Sheet, 17 December 1969.

8. Smith, Warren: *UFO Trek*, Zebra Books, New York, 1976, pp.221–3.

9. Ibid., pp.224–5.

10. Keyhoe, Major Donald E.: *Aliens from Space*, Granada, London, 1975, p.86.

11. Slate, B. Ann, and Druffel, Ann: "UFOs and the CIA Cover-Up," *UFO Report*, Vol.2, No.4, New York, 1975, p.20.

12. Keyhoe, Major Donald E.: op. cit., p.87.

13. Saunders, Dr. David R., and Harkins, R. Roger: *UFOs? Yes!*, Signet, New York, 1968, p.105.

14. Fawcett, Lawrence, and Greenwood, Barry J.: *Clear Intent*, Prentice-Hall, New Jersey, 1984.

15. Agee, Philip, and Wolf, Louis (editors): *Dirty Work: The CIA in Western Europe*, Zed Press, London 1978, p.310.

16. Campbell, Duncan: *The Unsinkable Aircraft Carrier*, Michael Joseph, London, 1984, p.143.

17. Adamski, George: *Inside the Space Ships*, Arco/Spearman, London, 1956.

18. Stringfield, Leonard: *Inside Saucer Post . . . 3–0 Blue*, Civilian Research, Interplanetary Flying Objects (CRIFO), Cincinnati, Ohio, 1957, pp.41–2.

19. Sparks, Brad C.: "CIA Involvement," *The Encyclopedia of UFOs* (edited by Ronald D. Story), New English Library, London, 1980, p.73.

20. Stanford, Ray: *Socorro "Saucer" in a Pentagon Pantry*, Blueapple Books, Austin, Texas, 1976.

21. *Studies in Intelligence*, CIA, Vol.10, No.4, Fall 1966.

22. Klass, Philip J.: *UFOs Explained*, Random House, New York, 1974, pp.105–14.

23. *Journal*, Albuquerque, New Mexico, 2 August 1983.

24. Fawcett and Greenwood: op. cit., pp. 141–2.

25. Condon, Dr. Edward J.: *Scientific Study of Unidentified Flying Objects*, Bantam Books, New York, 1969.

26. Saunders and Harkins: op. cit.

27. Harder, Dr. James: *APRO Bulletin*, Vol.32, No.4, pp.6–7.

28. Keyhoe, Major Donald E.: op. cit., p.103.

29. Ibid., p.102.

30. Edwards, Frank: *Flying Saucers—Here and Now!*, Lyle Stuart, New York, 1967, pp.42–3.

31. Fowler, Raymond E.: *Casebook of a UFO Investigator*, Prentice-Hall, New Jersey, 1981, p.60.

32. Klass, Philip J.: *UFOs: The Public Deceived*, Prometheus Books, Buffalo, NY, 1983, pp.291–3.

33. Zechel, W. Todd: "NI-CIA-AP or NICAP?," *Just Cause*, January 1979, pp.5–8.

34. Sparks, Brad C.: loc. cit.

35. Fawcett and Greenwood: op. cit., pp.233–4.

36. Ibid., pp.207–8.

37. Lorenzen, Coral and Jim: *UFOs over the Americas*, Signet, New York, 1968, pp. 187–90.

38. *APRO Bulletin*, Vol.33, No.2.
39. *APRO Bulletin*, Vol.32, No.9.
40. CIA Privacy Regulations, Title 32 C.F.R. Section 1901.13.
41. *Report to the President by the Commission on CIA Activities within the United States* (Rockefeller Commission), US Government Printing Office, Washington, DC, June 1975, p.249.
42. Zachary, Ted [Todd Zechel]: "The CIA Has Proof That UFOs Exist!" *UFO Report*, New York, August 1977.
43. Stringfield, Leonard: *Situation Red, The UFO Siege*, Doubleday, New York, 1977, p.154; Spaulding, William: "UFOs: The Case for a Cover Up," *The Unexplained*, Vol.5, No.53, Orbis, London, 1981, p.1044.
44. Smith, Warren: op. cit., pp.210–19.
45. Interview with the author, 22 January 1986.
46. Copeland, Miles: *The Real Spy World*, Sphere, London, 1978, p.26.
47. Smith, Warren: op. cit., pp.220–28.
48. Letter to the author from Larry R. Strawderman, CIA Information and Privacy Coordinator, 29 November 1983.
49. Letter to the author from Brian Freemantle, 9 September 1985.
50. Turner, Stansfield: *Secrecy & Democracy*, Sidgwick & Jackson, London, 1986, pp.227–8, 235.
51. Letters to the author from Admiral Stansfield Turner, 18 June and 15 July 1986.
52. Zachary, Ted [Todd Zechel]: op. cit.
53. Letter from Todd Zechel, *International UFO Reporter*, Center for UFO Studies, November/December 1985, pp.17–19.
54. Marchetti, Victor: "How the CIA Views the UFO Phenomenon," *Second Look*, Vol.1, No.7, Washington, DC, May 1979, pp.2–7.

Chapter 15
NASA

1. *Le Matin*, Paris, 13 May 1962.
2. Letter to *FSR* from NASA, 22 May 1962.
3. *Time*, 27 July 1962.
4. *Evening Standard*, London, 8 February 1967.
5. NASA Management Instruction from Dr. Kurt Debus, Director, John F. Kennedy Space Center, 28 June 1967.
6. NASA Information Sheet, NASA Headquarters, Washington, DC 20546, 1 February 1978.
7. Fawcett, Lawrence, and Greenwood, Barry J.: *Clear Intent*, Prentice-Hall, New Jersey, 1984, p.193.
8. *Daily Telegraph*, London, 2 June 1976.
9. Sheaffer, Robert: *The UFO Verdict*, Prometheus Books, Buffalo, NY, 1981, pp.4–12.
10. *Daily Telegraph*, London, 2 June 1976.

11. Letter from Dr. Frank Press, Executive Office of the President, Office of Science and Technology Policy, Washington, DC 20500, 21 July 1977.

12. Speech to the American Society of Newspaper Editors, Washington, DC, 22 April 1967.

13. Sigma, Rho: "Dr. Hermann Oberth looks at UFOs," *Fate*, December 1968, pp.45–8.

14. Collyns, Robin: *Did Spacemen Colonise the Earth?*, Pelham Books, London, 1974, p.236.

15. *Neues Europa*, 1 January 1959.

16. Zinsstag, Lou, and Good, Timothy: *George Adamski—The Untold Story*, Ceti Publications, Beckenham, England, 1983, p.164.

17. Stanford, Ray: *Socorro "Saucer" in a Pentagon Pantry*, Blueapple Books, Austin, Texas 78763, 1976, pp.120–49.

18. Letter from Dr. Robert A. Frosch, Administrator, NASA Headquarters, Washington, DC 20546, 21 December 1977.

19. Cramp, Leonard G.: *Piece for a Jig-Saw*, Somerton Publishing Co., Cowes, Isle of Wight, 1966, pp.339–40.

20. Zinsstag and Good: op. cit., pp.165–73, 184–5.

21. Letters to the author from Dr. Paul D. Lowman, Jr., Geophysics Branch, Laboratory for Earth Sciences, NASA. Goddard Space Flight Center, Greenbelt, Maryland 20771, 17 May 1984 and 12 January 1987.

22. Letter to the author from Stephen Darbishire, 9 August 1986.

23. Letter to Scott Carpenter from James A. Lovell, Deputy Director, Science and Applications, NASA, Manned Spacecraft Center. Houston, Texas 77058, 12 December 1972.

24. Roach, Franklin E.: "Visual Observations Made by Astronauts," *Scientific Study of Unidentified Flying Objects*, Bantam Books, New York, 1969, pp.207–8.

25. Letter to Scott Carpenter from James A. McDivitt, Senior Vice-President, Power Consumers Company, Jackson, Michigan 49201, 27 November 1972.

26. *We Seven* (written by the Mercury astronauts), Simon & Schuster, New York, 1962, pp.62–3.

27. *The Gazette*, Montreal, 29 November 1978.

28. Letter to the author from Scott Carpenter, 30 November 1974.

29. *The Mel Noel Story*, Saucerian Publications, Clarksburg, West Virginia, p.25.

30. *Saga UFO Special*, No.3.

31. Bamford, James: *The Puzzle Palace*, Sidgwick & Jackson, London, 1983, pp. 192–3.

32. *Omni*, Vol.8, No.4, 1986.

33. Berlitz, Charles: *Doomsday 1999 A.D.*, Doubleday, New York, 1981, pp. 206–7.

34. "Moondrive Special," BBC Radio 4, 11 December 1972.

35. Letter to the author from Harry Jones, executive assistant to Edgar D. Mitchell & Associates Inc., Houston, Texas 77017, 6 February 1973.

36. Chriss, Nicholas: "Cernan Says Other Earths Exist," *Los Angeles Times*, 6 January 1973.

37. *National Enquirer*, 23 October 1979.
38. *Saga UFO Special*, No.3.
39. Faucher, Eric, Goodstein, Ellen, and Gris, Henry: "Alien UFOs Watched Our First Astronauts on Moon," *National Enquirer*, 11 September 1979.
40. Chatelain, Maurice: *Our Ancestors Came from Outer Space*, Pan Books, London, 1980, p.25.
41. Letter to the author from Dr. Paul D. Lowman, Jr., NASA, Goddard Space Flight Center, 17 May 1984.
42. Letter to the author from John McLeaish, Chief, Public Information, Public Affairs Office, NASA, Manned Spacecraft Center, Houston, Texas 77058, 20 May 1970.
43. Letter to the author from Neil A. Armstrong, 29 December 1986.

Chapter 16
Down to Earth

1. Scully, Frank: *In Armour Bright*, Chilton, 1963, p. 199.
2. Scully, Frank: *Behind the Flying Saucers*, Henry Holt & Company, New York, 1950, pp.128–37.
3. Steinman, William S.: *UFO Crash at Aztec*, UFO Photo Archives, P.O. Box 17206, Tucson, Arizona 85710, 1987.
4. Bamford, James: *The Puzzle Palace*, Sidgwick & Jackson, London, 1983, pp.27–31, 115–16, 295; Friedman headed the Code and Cipher Section during World War I and established the Signals Intelligence School in 1931. It was Friedman who coined the terms "cryptanalysis" and "cryptology" and for his remarkable work in this field was awarded the coveted National Security Medal. Callihamos, besides being one of NSA's legendary members, was also an internationally renowned flutist. He wrote books on cryptanalysis with Friedman. Their involvement in the Aztec case is not yet established.
5. Moore, William L.: *Crashed UFOs: Evidence in the Search for Proof*, William L. Moore Publications & Research, 4219 W. Olive Street, Suite #247, Burbank, California 91505, 1985, pp.23–4.
6. Stringfield, Leonard H.: *UFO Crash/Retrievals: Amassing the Evidence, Status Report III*, p.10. Available from the author at 4412 Grove Avenue, Cincinnati, Ohio 45227, to whom those volunteering further information are invited to write.
7. Ibid., p.33.
8. Steinman, William S.: op. cit.
9. Ibid.
10. Wilbert Smith's handwritten notes were obtained from his widow by Arthur Bray, to whom the author is indebted for allowing publication.
11. Stringfield, Leonard H.: *Retrievals of the Third Kind*, UFO Ohio Yearbook, 1979, p.7; "The UFO Crash/Retrieval Syndrome Status Report II: New Sources, New Data, Part II: New Support Data," *FSR*, Vol.28, No.4, 1982, p.7.

12. Stringfield, Leonard H.: *UFO Crash/Retrievals: Amassing the Evidence, Status Report III*, 1982, p.32.
13. Stringfield, Leonard H.: "Retrievals of the Third Kind—Part I," *FSR*, Vol.25, No.4, 1979, pp.18–19.
14. Stringfield, Leonard H.: *UFO Crash/Retrievals: Amassing the Evidence, Status Report III*, 1982, p.43.
15. Ibid., pp.27–30.
16. Ibid., pp.12–13. Letter from P.J. to Stringfield, 13 April 1982.
17. Ibid., pp.24–5.
18. Stringfield, Leonard H.: "The UFO Crash/Retrieval Syndrome Status Report II: New Sources, New Data, Part I," *FSR*, Vol.28, No.2, 1982, pp.3–8.
19. Ibid., pp.6–7.
20. Stringfield, Leonard H.: "The UFO Crash/Retrieval Syndrome Status Report II," *FSR*, Vol.28, No.4, 1982, p.6.
21. Complaint Form, Air Force Office of Special Investigations (AFOSI) District 17, Kirtland AFB, New Mexico, 14 August 1980.
22. Complaint Form, AFOSI Det 1700, Kirtland AFB, 2–9 September 1980 (source and evaluation by Major Ernest E. Edwards).
23. Schwarz, Berthold Eric: *UFO Dynamics* Book II, Rainbow Books/Betty Wright, P.O. Box 1069, Moore Haven, Florida 33471, 1983, pp.536–45.
24. Letter to the author from Dr. Schwarz, 10 October 1983.
25. Letter to the author from Dr. Eric Dingwall, 2 September 1984.
26. Letter to the author from Dr. Schwarz, 18 August 1985.
27. Letter to William S. Steinman from Dr. Robert I. Sarbacher, Washington Institute of Technology (Oceanographic & Physical Sciences), Palm Beach, Florida 33480, 29 November 1983.
28. *FSR*, Vol.2, No.1, 1956, p.2.
29. *FSR*, Vol.11, No.2, 1965, pp.8–9.

Chapter 17
Above Top Secret

1. Bamford, James: *The Puzzle Palace*, Sidgwick & Jackson, London 1983.
2. Letter to Robert Todd from NSA's Information Officer, 20 February 1976.
3. Fawcett, Lawrence, and Greenwood, Barry J.: *Clear Intent*, Prentice-Hall, New Jersey, 1984, pp.181–2.
4. Memorandum Opinion and Order Granting Motion for Summary Judgment in the US District Court, District of Columbia: *Citizens Against UFO Secrecy* (Plaintiff) v. *National Security Agency* (Defendant), 18 November 1980.
5. In-camera affidavit of Eugene F. Yeates (NSA), US District Court of the District of Columbia, 9 October 1980.
6. Moore, William L.: "CAUS v/s NSA Lawsuit goes to U.S. Supreme Court," *APRO Bulletin*, Vol.30, No.1, 1982, pp.2–3.
7. Bamford, James: op. cit., pp. 155–6.

8. Letter from James Rusbridger, *Daily Telegraph*, London, 13 December 1986.

9. Zachary, Ted [Todd Zechel]: "The CIA Has Proof that UFOs Exist!" *UFO Report*, New York, August 1977.

10. Received by Stanton Friedman, 27 October 1977.

11. Sparks, Brad: "FBI Interrogates UFO Researcher: Government May Confiscate Documents," *APRO Bulletin*, Vol.27, No.1, July 1978.

12. Girvan, Waveney: *Flying Saucers and Common Sense*, Frederick Muller, London, 1955, p.119.

13. *FSR*, Vol.1, No.3, 1955, p.23.

14. Letter to the author from James J. Devine, Director of Policy, National Security Agency, Central Security Service, Fort George G. Meade, Maryland 20755, 4 November 1983.

15. Letter to the author from Frederick J. Berghoff, Deputy Director of Policy, NSA/CSS, 21 June 1984.

16. Letter to a US researcher from Dennis C. Chadwick, Chief, Information Policy, NSA/CSS, 3 March 1986.

17. Letter from Julia Wetzel, Director of Policy, NSA/CSS, 15 April 1986.

18. Smith, Dr. Willy: "UFO Chase in Brazil (May 1986)," *FSR*, Vol.32, No.1, 1987, pp.6–8. Because of conflicting accounts in the Brazilian press, some of the details in this case are likely to be inaccurate. My own copy of the report in *O Globo*, 24 May 1986, for example, states that it was Lieutenant Kleber Caldas Marinho who was followed by 13 radar targets, not Captain Viriato.

19. Letter to Yusuke J. Matsumura from Air Marshal Roesmin Nurjadin, Commander-in-Chief, Indonesian Air Force, Djakarta, 5 May 1967.

20. Letter from Air Commodore J. Salutun, Indonesian Air Force, Member of Parliament, Secretary of the National Aerospace Council of the Republic of Indonesia, published in *UFO News*, Vol.6, No.1, 1974, CBA International, Naka P.O. Box 12, Yokohama, Japan 232.

21. Letter to the author from Mrs. J. Clark, Information Officer, Embassy of Japan, 26 November 1986.

22. Interview with General Kanshi Ishikawa, former Chief of Staff, Air Self-Defense Force, when he was a commander of the 2nd Air Wing, Chitose Air Base, published in *UFO News*, Vol.6, No.1, 1974, p.123.

23. Letter from Colonel Fujio Hayashi, Commander, Air Transport Wing, Irima Air Squadron, JASDF, published in *UFO News*, Vol.6, No.1, 1974, p.123.

24. Draper, Richard: "Japan's Secret UFO Probe," *UFO Report*, Vol.5, No.4, New York, 1978, pp.26–9, 51.

25. *Guardian*, London, 3 January 1987; *The Times*, London, 6 January 1987; *Sunday Mirror*, London, 4 January 1987.

26. Letter to the author from Wing Commander S.D. White for Chief of Staff, Air Staff, Ministry of Defense Headquarters, Wellington, NZ, 6 September 1985.

27. *The Herald*, Zimbabwe, 2 August 1985; *The Times*, London, 3 August 1985.

28. Letter to the author from Air Commodore David R. Thorne, Director General

Operations, Headquarters, Air Force of Zimbabwe, Harare, Zimbabwe, 24 October 1985.

29. Friedman, Stanton T.: "The Case for the Extraterrestrial Origin of Flying Saucers," 1979 MUFON *Proceedings*, p.215.
30. Ware, Donald M.: "Security Policy," *MUFON UFO Journal* No.212, December 1985, pp.7, 18, Mutual UFO Network, 103 Oldtowne Road, Seguin, Texas 78155-4099.
31. Friedman, Stanton T.: "Flying Saucers are Real," *Worlds Beyond*, edited by Larry Geis, Fabrice Florin, with Peter Beren and Aidan Kelly, And/Or Press, P.O. Box 2246, Berkeley, California 94702, p.221.
32. Girvan, Waveney: op. cit., p.122.
33. Stanford, Ray: *Socorro "Saucer" in a Pentagon Pantry*, Blueapple Books, Austin, Texas 78763, 1976, p.136.
34. "Central Weekend," Central Television, 5 September 1986.
35. Harder, Professor James A.: "UFO Secrecy—the International Dimension," *APRO Bulletin*, Vol.32, No.4, 1984, pp.6–7.
36. Friedman, Stanton T.: "A Scientific Approach to Flying Saucer Behavior," Joint Symposium sponsored by the Los Angeles and Orange County sections of the American Institute of Aeronautics and Astronautics and the L.A. section of the World Future Society, held in Los Angeles, 27 September 1975.
37. Jung, C. G.: *Flying Saucers: A Modern Myth of Things Seen in the Sky* (translated by R.F.C. Hull), Routledge & Kegan Paul, London, 1959.
38. "Dr. Carl Jung on Unidentified Flying Objects," *FSR*, Vol.1, No.2, 1955, pp.17–18 (originally appearing in *Courier Interplanetaire*, Switzerland, 1954).
39. Keyhoe, Major Donald E.: *Flying Saucers: Top Secret*, G. P. Putnam's Sons, New York, 1960, pp. 235–6.
40. *FSR*, Vol.1, No.2, 1955, pp.17–18.
41. *Free Press*, Detroit, August 1971.
42. Blum, Ralph and Judy: *Beyond Earth: Man's Contact with UFOs*, Corgi Books, London, 1974, p.117.
43. "UFOs and Project Blue Book," Fact Sheet, United States Air Force, Public Affairs Division, Wright-Patterson AFB, Ohio 45433, January 1985.
44. Memorandum from Brigadier General C. H. Bolender, Deputy Director of Development DCS/Research & Development, USAF, 20 October 1969.
45. National Archives and Records Administration withdrawal notices.

INDEX